JONATHAN SWIFT

JONATHAN SWIFT, AGED ABOUT 43
from the portrait by Charles Jervas in the National Portrait Gallery

JONATHAN SWIFT

A Critical Biography

by

JOHN MIDDLETON MURRY

THE NOONDAY PRESS
A Division of FARRAR, STRAUS AND GIROUX

NEW YORK

CONTENTS

PREFACE

THIS book on Swift makes no claim to be the product of original research into unpublished material. It is based simply on some years of study of Swift's writings in books which others have toiled to make. Chief among these are the late Mr. Elrington Ball, whose edition of Swift's correspondence is the more remarkable, in that it was avowedly not a labour of love; the late Mr. Temple Scott, whose edition of Swift's prose works is now in process of being superseded by that of Mr. Herbert Davis; Sir Harold Williams, whose editions of Swift's Poems and the Journal to Stella are exemplary; and the late Mr. D. Nichol Smith, whose edition of Swift's correspondence with Charles Ford was the most notable addition to the work of Swift which has been made in my time. If I sometimes disagree with any of these great authorities, it is always with a sense of my own temerity.

Almost equally great is my debt to the modern historians of the period: to Mr. G. M. Trevelyan's *The Reign of Queen Anne*; to Sir Winston Churchill's *Marlborough*; to Mr. Keith Feiling's *The History of the Tory Party*; and to Mr. G. N. Clark's *The Later Stuarts*.

These are my principal obligations. After careful consideration I have decided not to add a bibliography of the innumerable other works I have read or consulted, I hope, with profit. It would be portentous, and it would add nothing of value to the excellent bibliographies for Swift which already exist.

My aim has been to write a book which should be at once a life of Swift and a critical study of his works. The combination is not very fashionable nowadays. Criticism is one thing and biography another, we are told by many peremptory voices: and never again, if they can help it, the twain shall meet. I am unabashed in holding to a different view. I believe that where the materials for the biography of a great writer are available, the study of his life and work do fructify each other, and that to hold them rigorously apart is, very often, to refuse illumination.

JONATHAN SWIFT

CHAPTER I

KILKENNY TO MOOR PARK: 1667-1689

JONATHAN SWIFT was born in Dublin on November 30, 1667. His father, also Jonathan, was the youngest of seven (or eight) sons of a staunch Royalist parson of Goodrich in Herefordshire who had been practically ruined in the Civil War. At the Restoration five of them in all, all trained in the law, had gone to seek their fortunes in Ireland. The vast territorial upheaval caused by the Cromwellian conquest had created plenty of work for lawyers. Godwin Swift, the eldest brother, did well for himself — the first of his four wives was a cousin of the great Duke of Ormond, who appointed him Attorney-General of the Palatinate of Tipperary — so did William, his junior; and they established some solid connection with Sir John Temple, the Master of the Irish Rolls, by whose influence the youngest brother was appointed Steward to the King's Inns in Dublin in 1665. He was shortly afterwards admitted a solicitor. He was then twenty-five. But a year before that, in 1664, he had married Abigail Erick, a Leicestershire woman. If she has been correctly identified in the register of Wigston Magna, four miles from Leicester, she was ten years older than her husband; if the entry in the burial register is correct, that she died (in 1710) seventy years old, she was the same age. First, a daughter, Jane, was born to them in 1666. While Abigail Swift was carrying a son, her husband died. The son was Jonathan Swift.*

His childhood was very singular. Long afterwards, Swift blamed the imprudent marriage of his parents for consequences which he had felt all his life. And, though it is impossible to trace the connections, one is convinced that the singularity of his childhood was largely accountable for the singularities of his character. Fatherless, separated from his mother, the boy never knew the security of a home. If one single word may characterize the whole of his life it was that of a homeless man. Domesticity was to be, from birth to death, a *terra incognita* to him.

After his father's death, his mother and sister appear to have lived for a time in his uncle Godwin's house. Within a year of his birth young Jonathan Swift was amicably kidnapped. The odd story is told in his own words:

> When he was a year old an event happened to him that seems very unusual; for his nurse who was a woman of Whitehaven, being

* See Appendix I.

13

under an absolute necessity of seeing one of her relations, who was then extremely sick, and from whom she expected a legacy, and being at the same time extremely fond of the infant, she stole him on shipboard unknown to his mother and uncle, and carried him with her, to Whitehaven, where he continued for almost three years. For when the matter was discovered, his mother sent orders by all means not to hazard a second voyage, till he could be better able to bear it. The nurse was so careful of him, that before he returned he had learnt to spell; and by the time that he was three years old he could read any chapter in the Bible.[1]

Presumably he was returned to his mother in Ireland. At the age of six he was sent to Kilkenny College, where he remained until he was fourteen, from 1674 to 1682. Of his schooldays the only picture is given in a letter he wrote at forty:

I have observed from myself and others (and I think it the wisest observation I ever made in my life) that men are never more mistaken, than when they reflect on past things, and from what they retain in their memory, compare them with the present. Because when we reflect on the past, our memories lead us only to the pleasant side, but in present things our minds are chiefly taken up with reflecting on what we dislike in our present condition. So I formerly used to envy my own happiness when I was a schoolboy, the delicious holidays, the Saturday afternoon, and the charming custards in a blind alley; I never considered the confinement ten hours a day to nouns and verbs, the terror of the rod, the bloody noses, and broken shins.[2]

It shows that there had been a time when his memories of school were pleasant enough. Elsewhere, he tells of a great fish he nearly landed from the Nore; it appeared above the surface only to plunge back again and be lost — a type (he said) of all his future disappointments.[3] And Sheridan tells a story of his spending all the money he had — one and sixpence — on buying a horse on the way to the knackers for the glory of riding his own horse through Kilkenny. It promptly fell down dead.[4]

Swift had some school friends: his own cousin, Thomas Swift, who was also to serve as secretary to Sir William Temple, and Francis Stratford, who was to make a fortune as a Hamburg merchant. Congreve he can hardly have known at school, for he did not go to Kilkenny until 1681 or 1682, seven or eight years later than Swift. They can have overlapped at most for a year. Their real acquaintance was made at Trinity, where Congreve was Swift's junior by only three years and they had the same tutor, St. George Ashe, the future Bishop of Clogher.

Did he go home to his mother for the long holidays? If she still lived in Dublin no doubt he did. But one has the uncomfortable feeling that she was no longer there; and that the deep affection and loyalty he felt towards her was grounded in a brief contact of two years before he was sent off to Kilkenny. All her husband had left her was an annuity of £20 a year. When she knew that his uncle had undertaken to provide for the education of her little boy, rather than herself be a burden on Godwin Swift, she chose to return to her home in Leicestershire. That is a mere guess. But one feels that early in his life his mother sacrificed her own feelings for the sake of her boy's career, and that from the time he entered Kilkenny College he did not see her again for many years.

At fourteen, on April 24, 1682, he entered Trinity College as a pensioner — the equivalent of commoner at Oxford. The cost of maintaining a pensioner at Trinity, forty years later, was reckoned at anything between £40 and £50 a year; it was probably rather less in 1682 when Swift was entered.[5] But his uncle did not spend so much on his nephew. Swift was bitterly humiliated by his poverty. As a pensioner, he was nominally on an equal footing with the average gentleman's son; but in fact his allowance was so meagre that he conceived a passionate resentment against his uncle, which he vented on the academic curriculum. 'He gave me the education of a dog', he declared in after life; and in his fragment of autobiography he wrote:

By the ill-treatment of his nearest relations, he was so discouraged and sunk in his spirits that he too much neglected his academic studies, for some parts of which he had no great relish by nature, and turned himself to reading history and poetry: so that when the time came for taking his degree of bachelor of arts, although he had lived with great regularity and due observance of the statutes, he was stopped of his degree for dulness and insufficiency; and at last hardly admitted in a manner little to his credit, which is called in that college *speciali gratia*, on the 15th February 1685 ... and this discreditable mark, as I am told, stands upon record in their college registry.[6]

'When I was young', he said elsewhere, 'I thought all the world, as well as myself was wholly taken up in discoursing on the last new play.'[7] The records show that in the terminal examination immediately before his bachelor's degree, Swift failed in two of his three subjects. Only his Greek and Latin were 'good'; his 'physics', presumably including mathematics and logic, were 'bad', and his Latin essay 'careless'. Delany, who as a famous tutor of Trinity is much the best authority on the matter, is emphatic that his degree was discreditable. 'Swift', he says forcibly, 'is the only man I ever knew who ever fully recovered the disgrace of taking a degree as he took his.' And he is explicit that the shock of the disgrace was a stimulus to Swift. He began to work really hard, and 'he had often been heard to say that from the time of taking his degree he studied at least eight hours a day, one with another, for seven years'.[8]

Nevertheless, it is doubtful whether Swift turned over his new leaf while he was at Trinity. He stayed on after his bachelor's degree to take his master's, and the College records show that he was then continually in trouble with the authorities. A Swift was punished twenty times between November 1685 and October 1687, for cutting chapels and absenting himself from the College without leave. It was probably Jonathan, for though his cousin Thomas was at Trinity at the same time, nothing in his later career suggests the turbulent collegian. For some disrespect towards the Junior Dean, Owen Lloyd, Swift was sentenced to kneel and beg his pardon in 1688. That humiliation would have been gall and vitriol to him; and he characteristically took his revenge twenty years after in a scurrilous portrait of Lloyd and his wife. Later on he became reconciled to Trinity — though not to Lloyd; and he always remained good friends with his tutor, St. George Ashe. But for some years afterwards he cherished a grudge against his old college. When he took his M.A. at Oxford in 1692, he told his uncle William that 'he was ashamed to have been more obliged in a few weeks to strangers than he ever was in seven years to Dublin College'.

Godwin Swift had lost most of his wealth before he died, in 1688; and he may have been in no condition to help Swift as liberally as Swift thought he should have done. But others of the family appear to have come to his aid — in particular, a cousin, Willoughby Swift, who had made some success as a merchant in Lisbon. Just before Swift had kept terms enough — a full seven years — to qualify for his master's degree, the 'troubles' broke out in Ireland. When the entry of King James into Dublin was imminent, the college authorities (on February 19, 1689) gave permission to all members to withdraw 'for their better security'. Swift left Dublin and went to stay with his mother in Leicestershire. After he had spent some months with her at a loose end, the connection between the Swifts and the Temples was successfully invoked, and Swift took service with Sir William Temple at Moor Park near Farnham in Surrey, as his secretary and companion. This was at the end of 1689, when the Temples, who had vacated Moor Park while King William was advancing on London, returned there from their house at Sheen to which they had retired.

Swift's first employment at Moor Park was very temporary. After six months he returned to Ireland, with a recommendation from Temple to Sir Robert Southwell, who was going as Irish Secretary of State to King William on his expedition of re-conquest. Temple had seized the first opportunity of helping his young client. Swift afterwards said that he returned to Ireland primarily on medical advice in the hope of curing 'a giddiness and coldness of the stomach' which afflicted him in consequence of 'a surfeit of fruit'.* It is doubtful whether this was the cause: for Swift is strangely unreliable in his later accounts of his early life. In the same passage he says that, when he returned to Ireland, he had been with Temple at Moor Park for two years.⁹ That is demonstrably false. His contemporary letters show that he cannot have been with Temple more than six months on the first occasion.†

Temple himself in his recommendation stretched a point in Swift's favour by representing that he had come to him immediately after the dispersion of Trinity. He described Swift as having been 'near seven years in the College of Dublin and ready to take his degree as Master of Arts when he was forced away by the desertion of that college upon the calamities of the country'.

Since that time [Temple continued] he has lived in my house, read to me, writ for me, and kept all accounts so far as my small occasions required. He has Latin and Greek, some French, writes a very good and current hand, is very honest and diligent, and has good friends, though they have for the present lost their fortunes, in Ireland, and his whole family having been long known to me obliged me thus far to take care of him. If you please to accept him into your service, either as a gentleman to wait on you, or as a clerk to write under you, and either to use him so if you like his service, or upon any establishment of the College to recommend him to a fellowship there, which he has just pretence to, I shall acknowledge it as a great obligation to me, as well as to him. (May 29, 1690)

The justice of Swift's claim to a fellowship is not obvious; but Temple was always generously inclined. There is no reason at all to suppose, as Macaulay did, that Swift was treated as a menial servant during his first stay at Moor Park. If Swift had had any grievance of that kind against Temple,

---

* On the nature of Swift's lifelong disease, see Appendix II.

† In his 'penitential letter' (October 6, 1694) Swift, who had left Temple early in May, says that he had been 'almost three years' with Temple. Since he left Temple on the first occasion at the end of May 1690 and did not return until Christmas 1691 — an absence of nineteen months — he cannot have come to Temple originally before November 1689.

he would not have failed to revenge it. His status had been that of 'a gentleman to wait on' Temple.

But he had come to Moor Park at a sombre moment for the family. Six months before, John Temple, Temple's only son and only surviving child, had committed suicide at the age of twenty-five, within a week of his appointment as Secretary for War. On April 14, 1689, he filled his pockets with stones, took a boat from the Temple Stairs to Greenwich, and as the waterman was shooting London Bridge, plunged overboard into the rapids, leaving this note upon the seat: 'My folly in undertaking what I was not able to perform has done the King and Kingdom a great deal of prejudice. I wish him all happiness and abler servants than John Temple.' Macaulay says that John Temple's despair was due to his misplaced trust in Richard Hamilton, who falsely professed to be empowered by Tyrconnel to negotiate a submission of the Catholic 'rebels' in Ireland. A yet more pathetic note of his is in existence, endorsed by Dorothy Temple with the touching words: 'Child's paper he writ before he killed himself.'

'Tis not out of any dissatisfaction with my friends, from whom I have received infinitely more kindness and friendship than I deserve, I say it is not from any such reason that I do myself this violence, but having been long tired with the burden of this life, 'tis now become insupportable. From my father and mother I have had especially of late all the marks of tenderness in the world, and no less from my dear brother and sisters to whom I wish and all my friends health and happiness and forgetfulness of me. I am not conscious to myself of any ill action, I despair not of ease in a futurity, the only regret I leave the world with is, that I shall leave my friends for some time (I hope but for a little time) in affliction.[10]

Temple's sister, Lady Giffard, said the disaster cast a damp on his natural good spirits for the rest of his life. What the tragic end of her darling 'little Creeper' meant for Dorothy Temple we can guess.

When the desolate family returned to Moor Park, they brought with them John Temple's two little daughters, his French widow and her mother. It was an unhappy moment for Swift to join the household. As a young man of twenty-two, he was bound to remind them of their loss; as a very sensitive young man he must have found his position appallingly difficult. He naturally sought friendliness and warmth where it was to be found; and he found it in little Hester Johnson, then known as Hetty, afterwards to be famous as Stella. She was a dark-eyed, black-haired, rather delicate little girl of eight years old, with a more childish manner of speech than one would have expected at her age. She, too, was rather lonely, for her position as household favourite had been temporarily disturbed by the arrival of the two little granddaughters. Swift and she were both, for the time being, rather out of things. They cottoned to each other.

Besides the new addition of John Temple's family, the household at Moor Park consisted of Sir William himself aged sixty, Dorothy his wife aged sixty-one, and Martha, Lady Giffard, his sister, ten years younger. She had been devoted to Temple all her life, and had lived with him and Dorothy practically ever since their marriage in 1654. She had indeed left them in 1661 to be married herself to Sir Thomas Giffard, an Irish landowner in co. Meath; but he had died within two months of the marriage, and she had returned to the Temples, a widow of twenty-three, financially independent, but entirely devoted. These were the heads of the household. There were also three dependents with whom we are concerned. One was a poor cousin of Dorothy Temple, Rebecca Dingley, who was about the same age as Swift. The other two were Bridget Johnson and her daughter Hester. Mother and daughter were both in Lady Giffard's service as 'gentlewomen to wait on' her.

3

There is a certain mystery about Bridget and Hester Johnson. Writing immediately after Hester's death on January 28, 1728, Swift gave the following account of her origin.

> She was born at Richmond, in Surrey, on the 13th day of March, in the year 1681. Her father was a younger brother of a good family in Nottinghamshire, her mother of a lower degree, and indeed she had little to boast of her birth. I knew her from six years old and had some share in her education. . . .[11]

That account of her birth is confirmed, up to a point, by the register of Richmond parish church, which says that Hester, daughter of Edward and Bridget Johnson, was baptized on March 20, 1681. Two other children of theirs were subsequently baptized there: Anne, on August 12, 1683, and Edward, on July 8, 1688. Orrery says that Edward Johnson was Sir William Temple's steward.[12] Orrery is not very reliable; and he may have been confused by the fact that Stella's mother, Bridget Johnson, married as her second husband, a Mr. Mose, who certainly had been Temple's steward. But that is all the information we possess about Stella's father. It is singularly meagre.

One thing is certain. Stella was a highly privileged person in the Temple household. Swift himself tells a story which reveals how unusual was her position.

> Some presents of gold pieces being often made to her while she was a girl, by her mother and other friends, on promise to keep them, she grew into such a spirit of thrift, that, in about three years, they amounted to above two hundred pounds. She used to show them with boasting; but her mother apprehending that she would be cheated of them, prevailed, in some months, and with great importunities, to have them put out to interest; when the girl lost the pleasure of seeing and counting her gold . . . her humour took quite the contrary turn; she grew careless and squandering of every new acquisition, and so continued till about two-and-twenty.[13]

Seventy pounds a year in presents of gold pieces to a young girl is an extraordinary amount. The normal salary of a resident secretary, such as Swift was, was £20 a year. It is highly improbable that Stella's mother, who was waiting-woman to Lady Giffard, Temple's sister, received more than this.* It is quite inconceivable that she could have given her daughter more than a tiny fraction of £70 a year. £5 a year would have been munificent, and even that would have been a strain. The 'other friends' must have been the donors; and chief among them must have been Temple himself.

Besides this, Swift's description of Stella gives one more clue to her position in Temple's household: when he says, 'She spoke French perfectly, but forgot much of it by neglect and sickness.'[15] She cannot have learned this from Swift, who never spoke or wrote French well; she must have learned it from Temple himself. But only in this indirect fashion can we gather from Swift's narrative any notion of Stella's real position at Moor Park. Indeed, the narrative is very peculiar. It entirely suppresses Stella's connection with the Temples. Neither the name of the family nor the house is mentioned. There is the bare statement: 'She lived generally in the country with a family where she contracted an intimate friendship with a lady of more advanced years' — and that is all.[16] This strange suppression may perhaps be explained by the hatred of most of the Temple family that Swift came to conceive, when in 1709 Lady Giffard publicly protested against his publication of the third volume of Temple's *Memoirs*. This hatred had been revived and exasperated only two years before Stella died, by a correspondence with Viscount

---

* We do not know the authority for Macaulay's definite statement that Swift's salary was £20; but it is probably correct. Edmund Gibson, the future Bishop of London, who was almost an exact contemporary of Swift, was appointed resident librarian at Lambeth Palace in 1696. He received £20 a year. Lady Giffard's account-book shows that, later in life anyhow, when Bridget Johnson, after marrying Mr. Mose, went back to her as waiting-woman, she received £20 a year.[14]

Palmerston, then the head of the family, in which Swift behaved with great rudeness, and reduced his obligation to Sir William Temple to an indecent minimum.

> I own myself indebted to Sir William Temple, for recommending me to the late King, although without success, and for his choice of me to take care of his posthumous writings. But I hope you will not charge my living in his family as an obligation, for I was educated to little purpose, if I retired to his house on any other motives than the benefit of his conversation and advice, and the opportunity of pursuing my studies. For, being born to no fortune, I was at his death as far to seek as ever, and perhaps you will allow that I was of some use to him. (January 29, 1726)

The claim to complete disinterestedness was extravagant. Swift hoped, reasonably enough, that Temple would secure him advancement. That he did not get it — owing to Temple's sudden death — was no proof that he had not expected it. We know from his letters that he did.

Just as he was anxious, in 1726, to cancel his own obligations to Temple, so in 1728, when writing about Stella, he was anxious to cancel her obligations to the family. Much of the mystery about her derives from this deliberate concealment of Swift's.

Besides what we can deduce from his own narrative, there is other evidence of Stella's privileged position at Moor Park. There is the very substantial legacy Temple bequeathed her. Swift, of course, does not mention that Temple was the donor. 'I found she was a little uneasy upon the death of a person on whom she had some dependence. Her fortune, at that time, was in all not above fifteen hundred pounds.'[17] It all derived from Temple. He left her a lease of lands at Morristown, co. Wicklow, worth £1000; and the remaining £500 appears to have been made up of gifts in his lifetime, which were duly invested for her by Lady Giffard. £1500 in those days was a respectable marriage portion for a gentlewoman. The contrast, too, between this and Temple's bequest to Stella's mother is striking. Mrs. Bridget Johnson received £20 and a half year's wages. Furthermore, though Stella had a younger sister and a brother, Anne and Edward, neither of them apparently was ever a member of the Temple household. For it is fairly clear from Swift's description of his meeting with Anne in the *Journal* for October 3, 1710, that he had never seen her before. 'Your sister looked very well, and seems a good modest sort of girl.' His ignorance of Anne is hardly conceivable if, like Stella, she had lived at Moor Park.

Finally, there is the first-hand testimony of Lady Giffard herself. Towards the end of 1698 she was trying to get a maidservant. Lady Berkeley of

Stratton, her niece, sent her one. Lady Giffard could not keep her because she had been bred as a waiting-gentlewoman, not a maidservant. Poor Lettice — for that was her name — had never made her own bed, nor scrubbed out a room; but 'the cruel thing of all was dining with common servants, and that she said she had never reckoned upon and doubted she should not be able to bear'. Lady Giffard was very sympathetic — the real Lady Giffard, as distinct from Swift's *bête noire*, appears to have been a kind and thoughtful woman — and apologized to Lettice for the misunderstanding. In sending her back to Lady Berkeley, she said Lettice was entitled to the post of gentle-woman in waiting, but that was not what she needed, and anyhow she could not afford to keep another. 'Three gentlewomen', she explained, 'had been a little too much state. I make use of my cousin Dingley whenever I am in want, Hetty's place being the height of her ambition.'[18]

It is a flash of light on the real position of the women at Moor Park as it was a month before Temple's death. Lady Giffard's gentlewomen are Bridget Johnson and Hetty. Rebecca Dingley is the unattached poor relation, who thinks Hetty's position enviable indeed.

4

It is not surprising, in view of the manners of the time and of the unusual position of Hester Johnson in the Temple household, that it was rumoured in Stella's lifetime that she was Temple's natural daughter. Bishop Evans of Meath in 1723 roundly asserted it for a fact.[19] Orrery, writing in 1752, agrees that this was the common report, but maintains that Swift himself did not believe it, or he would have married Stella publicly. But the malicious Orrery bases this argument on his belief that Swift's only reason for not marrying her was that she was socially beneath him.[20] An anonymous writer in *The Gentleman's Magazine* of November 1757, who claims to have known Stella's mother, says that the relation of Temple to Stella was 'univers-ally recognised', and that Temple told Stella she was his daughter. Recently, one of the most eminent of Swift scholars, M. Emile Pons, has proclaimed his conviction that this was the fact.*

That Stella occupied an exceptional position in the Temple household, and in the affections of Temple himself, is certain. But to deduce from that that she was his natural daughter is unwarrantable. Temple's own character has to be brought into the reckoning. In the case of almost any other man of Temple's eminence at that time, to have had and openly to cherish a natural daughter would have been a peccadillo. But the mutual passion of William

* See Appendix III.

and Dorothy Temple is one of the great romances of the 17th century. To suppose he was unfaithful to her is a gratuitous slur upon him, not to be lightly accepted.

Moreover, there were good human reasons why he should have virtually adopted a little girl at about the time he made Stella his favourite. Lady Giffard repeatedly emphasizes his fondness — a stronger word than it is now — for children, 'whose imperfect language and natural and innocent way of talking' delighted him. He was 'infinitely fond of' Lord Arlington's little daughter, with whom he played on the occasion of a memorable interview. Finally, he was bitterly grieved at 'the loss of his only daughter by the small-pox, a child he was infinitely fond of, and none ever deserved it more from a father'. Little Diana Temple died in 1684. Stella was then three years old. What more natural than that Temple should have half-adopted her?

And may we not find here the real clue to the 'little language' of the *Journal to Stella*? It has been generally supposed that this was a cultivated elaboration of Stella's way of talking when Swift first came to Moor Park. To this it has been pertinently objected that Stella was eight years old when Swift arrived, and little girls of eight no longer talk in that way; which is generally true. But, from Lady Giffard's account, it is very likely that Temple did not encourage Stella to grow out of it. That would explain why Swift afterwards imagined that he had known her from the age of six.

That does not clear up everything. It remains curious that we should know so little of Stella's father. If he was Temple's steward, he must have been steward of Temple's estate at Sheen: for his children were all baptized at Richmond — even the boy born on July 6, 1688. So that Edward Johnson did not move with the Temples to Moor Park when they first went there, in November 1686. He presumably died some time before Swift arrived at Moor Park. Anyhow, he vanishes completely. There is no indication that Swift had ever seen him. He never mentions him in his letters to Stella. There is no mention of him in Lady Giffard's surviving papers.

From this evidence and these conjectures we must construct as best we can. The probability that emerges is this. Stella was the eldest daughter of Edward and Bridget Johnson. Her father was the steward of Temple's estate at Sheen, and stayed at Sheen in that capacity when Temple moved to Moor Park in November 1686. We may suppose that Mr. and Mrs. Johnson and their two daughters lived in a cottage near the house at Sheen. In 1685, after the death of his beloved daughter Diana, Temple turned his affection to little Hester Johnson, then four years old, and virtually adopted her. When the Temples moved to Moor Park in 1686, Stella went with them, and returned with them in November 1688, but her father and mother with her sister Anne, remained at Sheen. In 1688 or 1689, in any case before Swift arrived at Moor Park, Edward Johnson died. On his death, Bridget Johnson entered Lady Giffard's service and parted from her children Anne and Edward, who were cared for by a nurse. From 1689 to 1699 both Stella and Mrs. Johnson were in Lady Giffard's service. In Stella's case the service was largely nominal.

CHAPTER II

HERO-WORSHIP: 1691-1693

D URING his first brief employment with Temple Swift had not much to do, nor much to get. Temple did not think his accounts serious enough to require much of Swift's attention, or Swift himself serious enough to be employed upon his manuscripts. He gave him freedom on occasion to hang hopefully about the Court. He had the run of a good library, and he read hard and variously. He made a beginning with teaching Stella.

It was understood that Temple was offering Swift only a temporary refuge, until the situation in Ireland was restored. Accordingly, as soon as King William's preparations for the reconquest were well advanced and it was known that Sir Robert Southwell was to accompany him as Secretary of State, Temple sent Swift off to him with a letter of recommendation, dated May 29, 1690. Swift probably presented it to Southwell in London. King William set out for Ireland on June 4. Swift hung about till the coast was clear.

When the Battle of Boyne was won, on July 11, 1690, he made his way back to Dublin. He said later that the primary motive for his return was the hope of curing his ill-health; but the synchronism of his departure with King William's is too exact to make this credible. He was, with Temple's full approval, following the example and probably the advice of his uncles. Just as uncle William (and indeed his own father) had hurried off at the Restoration to see what he could pick up in Ireland, so Swift hurried off, after King William, to see what he could get. While his uncles were engaged in re-establishing themselves, something might fall to him.

2

One imagines him quartered on his friendly uncle William, who was a successful lawyer attached to the Court of Common Pleas, while he looked about. To make his court, he set about writing a pindaric ode to King William, as the great Benefactor.*

* This is not the so-called *Ode to King William* which appears in editions of Swift's poems previous to that of Harold Williams. Those quatrains are certainly not an Ode; and they are very doubtfully Swift's.

It is not a bad poem. That his hero is good as well as great and therefore truly great is the theme. To modern eyes it is not so clear that his goodness was manifest in the reconquest of Ireland; but Swift has no doubt about it. The defeat of the Irish rebels is indubitably a victory of the Good. The destroying Angel, whom Swift sees in the spirit — 'the spirit of exalted poetry', and who guards and inspires the King in the battle, pronounces doom on the native Irish. Ireland, says the Angel, boasts in vain that

> No pois'nous beast will in her breed
>   Or no infectious weed,
> When she sends forth such a malignant birth,
> When Man himself's the vermin of her earth. . . .[1]

The detestation of the native Irish felt by the Anglo-Irish Protestant breathes furiously in Swift's verse; but so also does his contempt for the 'giddy British populace' whose factions the King had to compose before he could sail to liberate Ireland. So does hatred of the Scots:

> That discontented brood,
> Who always loudest for religion bawl,
>   (As those still do wh' have none at all)
> Who claim so many titles to be Jews,
> (But, surely such whom God did never for his people choose)
>   Still murmuring in their wilderness for food,
>   Who pine us like a chronical disease;
> And one would think 'twere past omnipotence to please.[2]

But the King has pacified even them. Having lulled the factious English and the hungry and greedy Scots, he has been free to annihilate — largely by his own personal valour — the hopes of King James, and with them those of the restless tyrant Louis. He too is now doomed.

> The pride of France
>   Has finished its short race of chance,
> And all her boasted influences are
> Rapt in the vortex of the British star;
> Her tyrant too an unexpected wound shall feel
>   In the last wretched remnant of his days.
> Our Prince has hit him, like Achilles, in the heel,
>   The poisonous dart has made him reel,
>   Giddy he grows, and down is hurl'd,
> And as a mortal to his vile disease,†
> Falls sick in the posteriors of the world.[3]

†*Fistula in ano* adds the author's characteristic gloss. Indeed, a good many of the elements of the mature Swift are evident in these verses. The leopard

will not greatly change these spots. He will never be unmindful of the world's posteriors; he will never hate the Presbyterian Scots any less, or feel less contempt for English faction; he will not go back on his gratitude to King William, even though he will be disappointed by him; and he will never depart from his conviction that greatness without goodness — whatever goodness may be — is despicable. In a word, his first known poem, even though it was hopefully addressed to royalty, has a basic sincerity, which redeems it from flattery; and it has an odd, almost uncouth, energy of utterance. Swift, when he speaks, will at least say *something*.

He wrote other poems at this time which have not survived. One was 'writ to a young lady in Ireland, called *The Ramble*', which two years later he offered to his cousin Thomas as a proof that 'he could not write anything easy to be understood, though it were but in praise of an old shoe'.[4] There was another ode, entitled *The Poet*, of which he quoted the only remaining lines in his verses *To Congreve*.

> Beat not the paths where vulgar feet have trod,
>   But give the vigorous fancy room,
> For when, like stupid alchymists, you try
>   To fix this nimble god,
>   This volatile Mercury,
> The subtle spirit all flies up in fume.[5]

3

Swift did no good to his fortunes in Ireland. After about a year he was back with his mother in Leicester for some months. Since he did not return directly to Moor Park, presumably a new approach to Temple had to be made. It was successful, and Swift returned to his old post in December 1691, having made a stay with cousin Thomas at Oxford on the way. He found Oxford society congenial, and decided to take his M.A. degree there.

On his return he plunged into writing. He told a parson-cousin in Leicester:

There is something in me which must be employed, and when I am alone, turns all, for want of practice, into speculation and thought; insomuch that in these seven weeks I have been here, I have writ and burnt, and writ again, upon almost all manner of subjects more perhaps than any man in England. And this it is which a person of great honour in Ireland (and who was pleased to stoop so low as to look into my mind), used to tell me, that my mind was like a conjured spirit, that would do mischief if I would not give it employment. (February 11, 1692)

That was written to allay his kinsman's apprehensions that he might be involved in an early marriage which would prejudice his chances of preferment. In the Rev. Mr. Kendall's eyes Swift's post with Temple was a splendid opening, and he had been alarmed by the intensity of Swift's conversations with a girl, while he was at Leicester. Swift explained that there was nothing in it; it was merely an outlet for the energy of his mind. It was his habit to throw all of himself into his conversation with women, simply for the sake of release; and this he did regardless of the opinion of the people in Leicester, who anyhow were 'a parcel of wretched fools'. If he enters the Church, as he now thinks of doing, he will have no difficulty at all in restraining himself. As for marriage, he would not dream of it until his position is secured; anyhow, his demands of woman are pitched so high that he will probably put it off to the next world. There was no danger that imprudence of this kind would stand in the way of his advancement; the real obstacle was his 'cold temper and unconfined humour', by which last he meant not an uncontrolled tongue, but a moodiness which he could not restrain or conceal.

The letter gives a clear picture of Swift's condition. His mind was inordinately active and restless, and he was uncertain of his way, in life and letters. Rather reluctantly, he contemplated entering the Church. To this end he prepared himself for his Oxford M.A. He got up his Latin and Greek, but drew the line at 'causes in Philosophy', which made him a little nervous of his performance in the 'acts'.[6] However, he did well, and took his degree, after a few weeks' residence at Hart Hall, on July 5, 1692. Four months later he told his uncle William that it was agreed between Temple and himself that he was not to take orders until the King gave him a prebend.[7] Temple had promised him this, but was unwilling to press for it, because he needed Swift's services. And, in fact, he was now using him to copy and prepare his manuscripts for eventual publication. At the end of the year he sent him to the King and the Earl of Portland to give them his arguments against their proposed veto of the bill for Triennial Parliaments.

4

Swift now stayed at Moor Park for two and a half years. During two of them — that is, to the end of 1693 — Swift's admiration for Temple mounted higher and higher. Then the relation abruptly changed; and in May 1694, Swift left Moor Park, as he imagined, for good. This time, Temple was very annoyed with him; and it appeared like a final break between them. Swift gives two accounts of the incident. One is contemporary, and addressed to his cousin, Deane Swift.

> I left Sir William Temple a month ago, just as I foretold it to you; and everything happened thereupon exactly as I guessed. He was extreme angry I left him; and yet would not oblige himself any further than upon my good behaviour, nor would promise anything firmly to me at all, so that everybody judged I did best to leave him. I design to be ordained September next, and make what endeavours I can for something in the Church. I wish it may ever lie in my cousin's way or yours to have interest to bring me in chaplain of the factory.* (June 3, 1694)

The other account was written many years later.

> Mr. Swift, having lived with Sir William Temple some time, and resolving to settle himself in some way of living, was inclined to take orders ... However, though his fortune was very small, he had a scruple of entering the Church merely for support, and Sir William, then being Master of the Rolls in Ireland, offered him an employ of about £120 a year in that office: whereupon Mr. Swift told him, that since he now had an opportunity of living without being driven into the Church for a maintenance, he was resolved to go to Ireland and take holy orders.[8]

The discrepancy is manifest. Swift told his cousin, at the time, tha Temple 'would not promise anything firmly to him at all'; long afterwards he wrote that Temple had actually offered him a place in the Irish Rolls. The only way to reconcile the statements is to suppose that Temple's offer of the Irish sinecure (for such it must have been) was upon condition Swift stayed with him, which he meant by 'upon good behaviour'.

If we put all the evidence together, what emerges is this. Swift lived and worked contentedly at Moor Park until the end of 1693. It was understood that Temple would eventually get him an English prebend from the King, and that Swift would not take orders until it was secure. Temple did not hurry, because Swift was now indispensable to him; and Swift for a long while cheerfully acquiesced in a delay which was, after all, complimentary to himself. Then, for some reason, he became impatient, and showed it. On condition he stayed with him Temple then offered Swift a sinecure in the Irish Rolls, whereby Swift would have his independence, and Temple his services. Swift then took the unexpected and disconcerting line of saying that he had a scruple about taking orders for a livelihood, that Temple's

---

* The factory was at Lisbon, where Deane Swift had joined his step-brother Willoughby. Willoughby Swift had sent Swift money at Trinity.

offer had removed it, and that he was resolved to enter the Church in Ireland and carve out a career for himself.

The scruple was invented — there is no trace of it in his previous mention of the prebend — and Swift pretended it partly out of pique. But he was taking a very real risk. He was throwing away his chance of patronage, and electing to make his own unaided way in the Church. He seriously asked his cousin to help him to a chaplaincy at Lisbon; and, a little later, when he had managed to get a small living in Ireland, he was just as serious in contemplating marriage and settling down as a fairly humble clergyman in Ireland.

There had been a real crisis of some kind. At this moment in May 1694, and for nearly two years afterwards, Swift was willing to abandon his ambitions, which were bound up with Temple. Why? Was his heart so set on his English prebend that Temple's offer of an Irish sinecure exasperated him? That does not seem even plausible. A sinecure of £120 a year was a very useful thing for a young man. Temple was not treating him badly. Swift must have been bent on breaking with Temple and on making a demonstration that he could and would do without him.

5

For further illumination we must look to Swift's writings in 1692-3. All that has survived of them is verse, and consists of six longish poems: three pindaric odes: *To Dr. William Sancroft, To Sir William Temple*, and *To the Athenian Society*, and, following these, three poems in rhymed couplets: *A Description of Mother Ludwell's Cave, To Congreve*, and the verses *Occasioned by Sir William Temple's Late Illness and Recovery*. This group of poems stands quite apart in Swift's literary production. Considered purely as poetry, they are by no means negligible; but as self-description they are unique. Only in the *Journal to Stella* does Swift uncover himself so much; and what he uncovers there is a formed personality — even, a deliberately shaped personality. Some part of the shaping may well have been due to the reaction of a sensitive nature to the reported judgment of Dryden (who was his second cousin once removed) upon his odes. 'Cousin Swift, you will never be a poet!' That Swift took it hard, we know. Dryden is visibly a *bête noire* in *A Tale of a Tub* and *The Battle of the Books*. Swift could not and would not leave Dryden alone: he was bent on revenge, and when he bit, he bit like a badger, till his teeth met together.

Why did cousin Dryden's judgment cause such resentment? Not because it was unjust, but because it was harsh, and came at a moment when Swift was craving for sympathy and understanding. The judgment was not unjust, but it was only barely just; and it was ungenerous, unimaginative and undiscerning. Even as a poet, Swift was to do well enough in his own restricted vein. But there was an element even in his rhapsodical *Ode to the Athenian Society* which ought not to have been disregarded — a struggling and baffled energy of mind, which makes these poems fascinating now, and redeemed them from insignificance then. What Dryden should have said was: 'Cousin Swift, you will never be a poet ... but there is something there.' But it is easy to be wise after the event. Dryden is not to be blamed for failing to give Swift the encouragement he longed for; but nothing more is needed to explain Swift's bitterness towards him than a consideration of the natural effect of his humiliating verdict upon a young man with the abilities and in the condition of mind which these poems reveal.

The first three poems — the odes — were written at much the same time. Swift gave an account of his methods of composition to cousin Thomas.

It makes me mad to hear you talk of making a copy of verses next morning, which though indeed they are not so correct as your others are, [is] what I could not do under two or three days, nor does it enter my head to make anything of a sudden but what I find to be exceeding silly stuff except by great chance. I esteem the time of studying poetry to be two hours in a morning ... which I esteem for the flower of the whole day, and truly I make bold to employ them that way, and yet I seldom write above two stanzas in a week — I mean such as are to any Pindaric ode — and yet I have known myself in so good humour as to make two in a day, but it may be no more in a week after, and when all is done I alter them a hundred times, and yet I do not believe myself to be a laborious dry writer, because if the fit comes not immediately I never heed it, but think of something else. And besides, the poem I writ to the Athenian Society was all rough drawn in a week, and finished in two days after, and yet it consists of twelve stanzas and some above thirty lines, all above twenty, and yet it so well thought of that the unknown gentlemen have printed it before one of their books ... so that perhaps I was in a good humour all the week, or at least Sir William Temple speaking to me so much in their praise, made me zealous for their cause, for really I take that to be part of the honesty of poets that they cannot write well except they think the subject deserves it.

But that itself will not always hold, for I have had an ode in hand these five months inscribed to my late Lord of Canterbury, Dr. Sancroft, a gentleman I admire at a degree more than I can express ... but I say I cannot finish it for my life, and I have done nine stanzas and do not like half of them ... but there it lies and I sometimes add to it, and would wish it were done to my desire. (May 3, 1692)

That accounts only for the odes *To Sancroft* and *To the Athenian Society*. The ode *To Temple* may not have been begun until the ode *To Sancroft* was finished. In any case they were both finished by the end of 1692.

6

Swift told his cousin that the ode *To Sancroft* was written at the suggestion of Turner, the non-juring Bishop of Ely; but Sancroft's passive refusal of the oaths was more to his taste than Turner's more active Jacobitism. He admired Sancroft for his conscience, his courage and his unworldliness.

Ultimate truth, he declares in his poem, is inaccessible to man; but its image on earth can be found in the true virtue of a mind resolved to combat fate by submission and humility. Such is Sancroft's: in it greatness and goodness are combined. It is beyond the comprehension of the herd. They gaze at the weathercock of state, which is fixed to the Church, and because the weathercock veers, they think the Church has changed. They think Sancroft's motion irregular, but the irregularity is theirs. It is useless, he tells the Muse, for her to try to instruct the multitude.

> Rather put on thy anger and thy spite,
> And some kind pow'r for once dispense
> Thro' the dark mass the dawn of so much sense
> To make them understand, and feel me when I write;
> The Muse and I no more revenge desire,
> Each line shall stab, shall blast, like daggers and like fire.[9]

Why has Britain become the dwelling-place of fiends? It is because of the very mildness of the King's government.

> Our British soil is over-rank, and breeds
> Among the noblest flow'rs, a thousand pois'nous weeds,
> And ev'ry stinking weed so lofty grows
> As if 'twould overshade the Royal Rose.[10]

He checks himself, begs the 'original mildness' of the heavenly truth to forgive his ill-governed anger, and makes excuse.

> 'Tis all the angry slighted Muse can do
> In the pollution of these days;
> No province now is left her but to rail
> And poetry has lost the art to praise
> Alas, the occasions are so few.[11]

Only Sancroft, and his divine Master, could bear without anger or scorn or fear, the caprice of popular sentiment. England is haunted by the spirit of the Jews of old: in the same breath it glorifies and execrates Sancroft, as the Jews did his master. But Sancroft uncomplaining and unregarded goes his way, pointing. the road to Christ, which the world has wholly missed. Avarice and pride lead men blindly on to seek Him in 'Caesar's Court or in Jerusalem' — but the true faith is as uncourtly now, as it was in the beginning.

Why is the Church made subservient to the State, and ruined to repair it? The world imagines that because we have a good and wise King that his subjects are like him. They are not; they follow more easily bad Kings than good. Faction rules them, and faction oppresses and distracts the Church. Therefore Sancroft, no longer able to bear the weight of a mitre almost as heavy as the crown, withdrew. May his successor weather the storm!

But the virtue of Sancroft, says Swift, shines only the brighter now that the robes of office are taken away. The Church, bereft of his care, can but beg the blessing of his prayers. But for what crimes has the Church been exposed so long to the senseless malice of reformers who would

> Strip her of ev'ry ornament and grace
> In striving to wash off th' imaginary paint?

The physicians crowd round the Church on her death bed. Reformers and physicians are all one

> Cordials are in their talk, while all they mean
> Is but the patient's death, and gain —
> Check in thy satire, angry Muse,
> Or a more worthy subject choose:
> Let not the outcasts of this outcast age
> Provoke the honour of my Muse's rage,
> Nor be thy mighty spirit rais'd,
> Since Heaven and Cato both are pleased.[11]

The rest of the poem is said to be lost; but it is unlikely that Swift meant to write more. The odd turn of the last line seems final enough: *Victrix causa deis placuit; sed victa Catoni.* Presumably Swift means that in Sancroft's case the conquered cause pleased both. That the younger Cato was one of the prophets of heaven remained an article of faith with him.

We may leave aside, for the time being, the political and ecclesiastical convictions which Swift expresses. He will remain faithful to them. Much more curious is the conscious curb he puts on the propensity of his Muse to wrathful denunciation of the stupidity of the *mobile* and the knavery of the factions. This dialogue between Swift and his Muse was the constant machinery of his poems at this time. It appears in one form or another in all of them, except *A Description of Mother Ludwell's Cave*, and that is, very exactly, the exception which proves the rule. The poetic assumption is that the Muse, by nature and inclination, is eager to celebrate virtue and innocence. But the opportunities are rare: and for lack of subjects that deserve her praise she turns, perforce, to her subaltern function of exposing and denouncing the enemies of virtue and innocence. Because of the corruption of the times denunciation has become the Muse's second nature.

The significant point is that in this period of his life, Swift was trying to persuade himself that satire is essentially alien to the spirit of poetry. The authentic inspiration of poetry is enthusiasm for the Good — for virtue and innocence. But the indispensable condition of cultivating that rapture is retirement from the world. That blessing he now enjoys at Moor Park; and there, constantly before his eyes, in Temple himself (who had an aversion to satire), he has an exemplar of the virtue and innocence which inspires poetry, and the deliberate retirement which is the condition of producing it, uninhibited by anger or dismay.

All this may seem very naive; but, if we wish to understand Swift at this moment, we must take it seriously. It is the brief and neglected 'romantic' period of his life. What happens to a young man of genius at twenty-five and twenty-six is important.

7

The ode *To Sir William Temple* is an effort to express his gratitude and appreciation at being admitted to Temple's familiar conversation. Though time has reversed the orders of their magnitude so much that many remember Temple because he harboured and employed and educated Swift, his familiarity with Temple was none the less a tremendous event in Swift's life. It is a mistake in proportion to stress the humiliation he endured at Moor Park: it could not have been much, or Swift, in later years, would have made much more of it; and it could not have been deliberately inflicted, or no power on earth would have prevented Swift from taking his revenge. When we consider Swift's sensitiveness and pride and ambition, and the ferocity of his reaction to a slight, it is remarkable that Temple emerges from Swift's hands with so fair a character. Swift suffered because of Temple's moods: but they were not directed at him. The ageing Temple whom Swift knew had just endured one terrible bereavement, he lived in apprehension of another, and he was the prey to intermittent bouts of great physical pain. His courtesy was affable one day and cold on another; but it was always courtesy. And it does not appear that Swift in after-life ever forgot that it was, or ceased to be grateful. True, he did not like to remember his time at Moor Park; but there was never much in his past life to which his thoughts turned lovingly — his home-thoughts of Laracor are unique — and, in particular, what he did not care to remember about Moor Park was the extent of his veneration for Temple, and his own emotional dependence upon him. When Temple was affable, familiar and confidential to him, it filled him with happiness; when Temple was distant, he was in despair. He did not like to remember (when he was the crony of Harley and St. John) that he once thought Temple so marvellous, or that he himself had been so adoring. The ode *To Sir William Temple* remains as evidence of a Swift whom the world has forgotten, and whom he himself desired to forget.

Whether Temple was really a great man is beside the point. He was certainly not a little one. And if among all his contemporaries who were or had been statesmen we had to choose one whom a young man of genius might serve in the full assurance that his service was honourable, Temple was surely the man. His incorruptibility and integrity in an age when the best of statesmen expected to make a fortune out of their offices were extraordinary. Perhaps he lacked that instinctive determination to remain near the centre of power which is necessary to the effective statesman; and there may have been in him the germ of the self-diffidence which was fatal to his son. But there was a political incompatibility between Temple and the policy and the court of Charles II, which was not to be overcome: in policy, he was early and permanently converted to the necessity of an Anglo-Dutch alliance, if the expansive imperialism of Louis XIV was to be resisted. The personal and secret policy of Charles II made that resistance impossible. And there was a moral incompatibility between the life-long lover of Dorothy Osborne and the temper of Charles's court. Rather than struggle unavailingly against the current of the turbid stream, he chose retirement. When, with the advent of Temple's friend and hero, William III, the new world came, he was sixty and too old: besides he was restrained by a scruple, which Swift would appreciate. He had given his word to James II that he would not work against him. Temple is no longer the hero of the historians that he used to be; there was too much of the idealist and perhaps of the dilettante in his composition to suit the modern taste: but as a specimen of a good man in bad times he wears well. And, last but not least, he wrote well. Even at the very end of his life Swift advised the younger Sheridan to take Temple's earlier works as his sole model of English prose.

The youthful Swift revered him; and it is a real tribute to Temple that the mature Swift did not discover that his former idol had feet of clay. He begins his ode *To Sir William Temple* by declaring him to be the one man in whom virtue dwells complete. But had he not been just engaged in putting Sancroft on an equal pinnacle? Swift's answer to that is in the next stanzas of his poem. Sancroft has the virtue of saintliness; but Temple is both a man of goodness and a man of the world; and this last is necessary to complete virtue. Swift, enchanted by his new experience of a gentleman of fine breeding and deep knowledge of affairs, launches into a diatribe against pedantry and the morality of the schools. He has a good fling at his recent masters at Dublin College: and all those who

> For learning's mighty treasures look
>   In that deep grave, a book;
> Think that she there does all her treasures hide
> And that her troubled ghost still haunts there since she died;
> Confine her walks to colleges and schools;
>   Her priests, her train, and followers show
>   As if they all were spectres too!
>   They purchase knowledge at the expense
>   Of common breeding, common sense,
>   And grow at once scholars and fools;
>   Affect ill-manner'd pedantry,
> Rudeness, ill-nature, incivility,
>   And sick with dregs and knowledge grown,
>   Which greedily they swallow down,
> Still cast it up and nauseate company.[13]

In Sir William, knowledge and humanity are combined; he is at once 'learned, good and great'; Virgil, Epicurus and Caesar are joined in him. The exercise of his statesmanship has been in the making of peace, not in the cruelty and futility of war.

> War! that mad game the world so loves to play
>   And for it does so dearly pay;
> For though with loss or victory awhile
>   Fortune the gamesters does beguile,
> Yet at the last the box sweeps all away.[14]

The seventh stanza describes the effect upon Swift of Temple's talk and writing on the political events in which he had been concerned.

> Methinks, when you expose the scene,
>   Down the ill-organ'd engines fall;
> Off fly the vizards, and discover all:
>   How plain I see thro' the deceit!
>   How shallow and how gross the cheat!
>   Look where the pulley's tied above!
>   Great God! (said I) what have I seen!

> On what poor engines move
> The thoughts of monarchs, and designs of states!
> What petty motives rule their fates![15]

Then the Muse — the spirit of Truth — is asked to tell what is the serpent that lurks in courts and either drives virtue out or kills it dead: the monster against which Temple struggled in vain. 'In pieces cut, the viper did re-unite.' It is a simple image; but it would not be easy to find a better one for the hidden power with which Temple had to contend when he was a member of King Charles II's Council. The Third Part of his *Memoirs* conveys precisely this impression of a lurking energy of duplicity and evil, which nowhere comes into full view. Madame, the secret Treaty of Dover, the royal conspiracy to make England Papist again, and to secure the prerogative at the price of the national liberties — the secret springs are plainly visible today; but then they were still obscure.

From this scene of evil, Temple gladly retired. There was nothing else for an honest man to do. Swift is certain of that. And the beloved Muse is only too eager to expatiate on the congenial theme of the pleasures of rural retreat. In Temple is an agriculturist, or at least a horticulturist, who knows his blessings.

> Here we expect from you
> More than your predecessor, Adam, knew . . .
> You strove to cultivate a barren court, in vain;
> Your garden's better worth your nobler pain,
> Hence mankind fell, and here must rise again.[16]

The last line, at least, was as good as Cowley.

The final movement of the poem follows. 'Shall I believe?' Swift asks,

> A spirit so divine
> Was cast in the same mould with mine?

Why does Nature distribute her gifts so unequally? Why is Temple an elder son and a free spirit, while the 'cadets of heaven' have but the leavings, and are condemned to their various forms of drudgery?

> Me she has to the Muse's galleys tied:
> In vain I strive to cross this spacious main,
>   In vain I tug and pull the oar;
>   And when I almost reach the shore,
> Straight the Muse turns the helm, and I launch out again,
>   And yet, to feed my pride,
> Whene'er I mourn, stops my complaining breath,
> With promise of a mad reversion after death.[17]

37

He begs Temple to accept 'this worthless verse'; it is all he has to give.

> Nature the hidden spark did at my birth infuse
> And kindled first with indolence and ease
> And since too oft debauch'd by praise
> 'Tis now grown an incurable disease.
> In vain to quench this foolish fire I try
> In wisdom and philosophy:
> In vain all wholesome herbs I sow
> Where nought but weeds will grow.
> Whate'er I plant (like corn on barren earth)
> By an equivocal birth
> Seeds and runs up to poetry.[18]

Whatever we may think of all this as poetry, there is no doubt about its value as autobiography; moreover, only one stanza of the poem (the ninth) is at all obscure. And the whole gives a clear and valuable picture of at least one aspect of Swift at twenty-five. His converse with Temple is being a liberal education; it has taught him already that the highest kind of virtue is not cloistered. It moves freely in the great world but resists contamination. And the harmony of learning and good breeding and good taste in Temple has taught him to despise the uncouthness and barbarism of pedantry.* He has been given an insight, too, into the mysterious power and pettiness of evil at a Court; he has been taken behind the scenes, but the machinery of the mystery of iniquity remains inexplicable. To be himself a Temple he cannot aspire; he is only one of the 'cadets of heaven'. But he is conscious of a gift of some sort for writing. He labours away at his poems, but without steady inspiration. Nevertheless, though he is quite uncertain of the quality of his verses, he is consoled by a premonition of posthumous fame. For the time being, at any rate, he cannot help himself. By whatever means he tries to suppress his desire to write verses, it always emerges again.

8

If the ode *To Sancroft* took more than six months, and that to Temple perhaps as long, the twelve stanzas of the ode *To the Athenian Society*,

---

* Manners change. Temple was a model of urbanity. Yet consider this from Temple's *Memoirs*. 'During one day at Monsieur *Hoest's*, and having a great cold, I observ'd, every time I spit, a tight handsome Wench (that stood in the Room with a clean Cloth in her Hand) was presently down to wipe it up, and rub the Board clean: Somebody at Table speaking of my Cold, I said, the most Trouble it gave me was to see the poor Wench, take so much Pains about it: Monsieur *Hoest* told me, 'twas well I escap'd so; and if his Wife had been at Home, though I had been an Ambassador, she would have turned me out of Doors for fouling her House.' Whether a rebuke was implied by M. Hoest, one cannot tell; but Temple evidently saw none.

Swift told his cousin, were written in nine days. They are proportionately obscure. The Athenian Society was a group of anonymous contributors whom an enterprising and eccentric bookseller, John Dunton, had gathered together to answer all sorts of queries propounded to them — mainly on points of moral conduct — in *The Athenian Mercury*: which was thus a kind of anticipatory cross between *The Tatler* and *The Gentleman's Magazine*. Swift had seen some issues of the new periodical at Oxford on his way to Moor Park; when he arrived he found that Sir William Temple was corresponding with the Society. Swift genuinely liked the magazine; the spirit of it was generous and not carping: and his liking turned to positive enthusiasm when he discovered that his master endorsed it. 'Sir William Temple, speaking to me so much in their praise made me zealous for their cause.'[19]

Thus the ode *To the Athenian Society* is a pendant to the ode to Temple. What Temple approves Swift must praise. He is transparently sincere in this. Speaking of his *foiblesse* for his own writings and his cousin's, he says:

> I am just so to all my acquaintance: I mean in proportion to my love of them, and particularly to Sir William Temple. I never read his writings but I prefer him to all others at present in England, which I suppose is all but a piece of self-love, and the likeness of humours makes one fond of them as if they were one's own.[20]

Swift's attachment to Temple amounted almost to identification with him

The *Ode* itself is not worth quoting at any length. Easy writing made hard reading. It opens with a stanza comparing the return of peace in Ireland to the subsidence of the Deluge. 'Learning's little household' had taken refuge in the ark. Now the ark has settled, and a dove has been sent forth (we suppose, *The Athenian Mercury*) which now returns with a laurel wreath (Swift's verses). A more elaborate stanza follows in which Swift appears, very figuratively indeed, to describe his own return to Ireland, his writing of his ode *To the King*, his return from Ireland, and his realization that the flood 'had rather watered it than drowned'. From this 'floating piece of Paradise' he — or the Muse: for it is all one — hears an enchanting music

> With many a heavenly song
> Of nature and of art, of deep philosophy and love[21] —

which proceed from the Athenian Society.

Very properly he asks 'the great unknown and far-exalted men' to pardon 'the wild excursions of a youthful pen'. His impertinence is at least good-natured — an impertinence of praise; it is better than impertinence of censure. But to be censured, in these days, is the mark of the elect. The fashionable, free-thinking wits, however, seeing that their attacks have no effect on the anonymous Society, will now declare it has no real existence. He himself is satisfied that it is the enterprise of high-minded men who scorn the current idea that novelty alone can please, and disregard a trivial popularity. Where is true Fame?

> Look where exalted Virtue and Religion sit
> Enthron'd with heav'nly Wit,
> Look where you see
> The greatest scorn of learned vanity.[22]

These can be found in the Athenian Society. Strong in these powers the noble company answers the doubters in the spirit of true philosophy, from whom they have stripped all the modern pedantry in which she has been disguised. How heavenly is her naked beauty!

But the Muse has played one of her old tricks on him. She has inveigled him into praising Woman, under the name of Philosophy. And the Athenian Society conspires with her. In them woman can boast of 'her great unknown Platonic champions'. (*The Athenian Mercury* anticipated *The Tatler* in a civilized and friendly attitude to women.) But, though she presumes on their opinion, and treats man *de haut en bas*, it is men who have given her this new high place. He himself is content to be of the same sex as her champions.

But he grieves to think that the Society will not be able to maintain its high standards: its members will be succeeded by inferior men. 'Censure, and pedantry, and pride' will resume their empire.

> Yet shall these traces of your wit remain
> Like a just map to show the vast extent
> Of conquest in your short and happy reign;
> And to all future mankind shew
> How strange a paradox is true
> That men who liv'd and dy'd without a name,
> Are the chief heroes in the sacred lists of Fame.[23]

Swift meant it to be a light-hearted poem; but lightness of heart cannot always command lightness of touch, and the verses move heavily in their paraphernalia. If this was the poem he showed to Dryden, as Dr. Johnson says, he chose badly. Probably he was influenced, as young men are, by the fact it was the only one in print. But it has its value as autobiography: not only because it is, in mood and intention, excited and spontaneous, but because it throws a little more light on Swift's convictions at this time. He declares himself the enemy of censure, or censoriousness: it is much better and more congenial to praise than to blame, if only there was more to praise. He is the enemy of the modern cynical wit, with its false philosophy of scepticism:

> The wits, I mean the atheists of the age,
> Who fain would rule the pulpit, as they do the stage.[24]

He is the enemy, equally, of the modern speculative philosophy. True philosophy, for him, is moral philosophy, and that consists in a just sense of values, freed of all pedantry and supersubtlety: the recognition and pursuit of that reasonable and human virtue he finds personified in Temple. Whatever thought is in the poem is in full accord with that of his ode to his master, and with Temple's own views.

CHAPTER III

THE CAVE AND THE CRISIS: 1694

THE ode *To the Athenian Society* is dated February 14, 1692. There are no more poems until November 1693. Even if Swift was working on his other two odes until late in 1692, there was an interval of a full year — a long period in the life of an ardent and restless young man. In that interval his attitude changed remarkably. Hitherto, his poems had been, in spite of their careful following of the Cowley pattern, straightforward and even naive. They tell us, clearly, what Swift is thinking and feeling. But much the most striking quality of the verses *To Congreve* (November 1693) is their emotional contortion. A new element is immediately conspicuous — Swift's pride. In the previous poems he had been unassuming and genuinely humble: now he is the contrary. Part of the change no doubt is because he was no longer addressing a Sancroft or a Temple or a great unknown, but a younger friend, who had achieved instant success in the London theatre in the previous January with his comedy *The Old Bachelor*. In October his second play, *The Double Dealer*, was performed.

Congreve was nearly three years younger than Swift. Swift was still obscure; Congreve a sudden bright star. It was a trying situation, and Swift had a struggle to adjust to it. The effort makes the poem, in parts, very obscure. Swift's Muse makes her appearance, as before: but now she has a local habitation. She dwells in Mother Ludwell's Cave, in the grounds of Moor Park.

Three times, he says, he has summoned the Muse to aid him in the verses he wants to write to Congreve; three times she has come and he has disregarded her; three times she has therefore withheld her inspiration. Now she has come again to reproach him.

'I used to honour you; but now I find your pretensions to truth, retirement and innocence are false. You have brought the vices of the town into the country. I never loved anyone better than you; I have never been so scornfully used. You try to send me to your wicked friend like a cast-off mistress, as the beastly fashion is. Find some other trick: this is stale.'

Thus the Muse frowned on his long-designed tribute to Congreve's fame. First, she condemned the impulse to praise a writer for the stage — as in itself alien to poetry. Nevertheless, Congreve's sheer merit has compelled her to assist: so that he must look upon the verses as the greatest compliment she ever made, because she gave her inspiration in spite of herself. Only a truly divine power could span the gulf which separates Congreve's world from Swift's. And let him not imagine that Swift is praising him in order to display his own talent.

But Congreve's merit is such that it softened the Muse's thunder into praise. Thus it conspires with Swift's inveterate and so far unconquered pride: the scorn which holds him back from giving rein to his satire. Because Congreve has given him cause to hope that he will reform the theatre, Swift for the moment looks with mercy on the age.

Congreve's poetic vein is almost pure gold, so rich that it furnishes a whole host of would-be wits with coin which they deface and obscure with their own stupidity. Because they have stolen from him, they carp at him. The pretenders to poetry raise dark clouds of envy, which conceal themselves, but cannot obscure Congreve's light.

Whence do they come — these enemies of wit? Congreve is afraid of them, and courts their favour in his prologues; but he would blush to learn how insignificant they are. These dreadful foes are all bred in the country. They go straight from tops and grammar to the Inns of Court — dung-heaps where schoolboys sprout into men of fashion quicker than mushrooms. Why, a boy went up to town only last year from Farnham Grammar School; this year he returned a finished spark, chattering the gibberish of the pit. After a withering description of him, Swift checks himself. What an absurd and trivial creature to spend his hate upon!

> My hate, whose lash just heaven has long decreed
> Shall on a day make sin and folly bleed.[1]

But this hobbledehoy's pert talk of Congreve, Wycherley and 'Mr. Bayes' as his familiar friends was quite nauseating. Congreve's name is grown prostitute.

> Troth, I could pity you, but this is it,
> You find, to be the fashionable wit.[2]

If the meanest scribbler were to take Congreve's place, these sham-wits could not tell the difference.

Swift meant to praise Congreve. Instead, his Muse's hour has been wasted in ill-timed satire. But what does she care, since men are fools? Her true happiness lies 'in pleasing all that's good among the great': namely, Temple. To him, Swift's Muse is always welcome with her innocent song. If Congreve had the happiness of knowing him, he would pay no regard to anyone inferior; he would be proud to lay his laurels at the feet of the true Apollo.

Let Congreve but come to the Muse's cave at Moor Park, where Druids once received their inspiration.

> Here by a mountain's side, a reverend cave
> Gives murmuring passage to a lasting wave;
> 'Tis the world's wat'ry hour-glass streaming fast,
> Time is no more when th'utmost drop is past;
> Here on a better day, some druid dwelt,
> And the young Muse's early favour felt . . .
> Far in this primitive cell might we pursue
> Our predecessors' footsteps, still in view;
> Here would we sing — But ah! you think I dream,
> And the bad world may well believe the same;
> Yes; you are all malicious standers-by,
> While two fond lovers prate — the Muse and I.[3]

Swift has not given Congreve the serious advice he meant to give; but he gives him a passage from his ode to a Poet — all indeed that remains of it — in which he bids him:

> Beat not the dirty paths where vulgar feet have trod,
> But give the vigorous fancy room . . .

But now come the critics pronouncing doom on his poem — a fresh country-girl in a group of men about town, who jeer and talk lewdly at her. She stares amazed at the chattering herd; then, nauseated by their sight and smell, she runs away.

It is time to say Farewell. The Muse retires into the depths of the Cave, and his inspiration fades.

> In this descending sheet you'll haply find
> Some short refreshment for your weary mind.
> Naught it contains is common or unclean,
> And once drawn up, is ne'er let down again.[4]

At first sight, it seems mainly a left-handed compliment. The best Congreve gets is that his merit is such that Swift's reluctant Muse is constrained — though not for long — to praise him; and that is partly because it fits with the present bent of his pride, which refuses to give rein to the satire accumulating within him. And most of what Swift gives with one hand, he takes away with the other. He insists that there is a great gulf fixed between his world and Congreve's; he pities Congreve for having to conciliate the favour of a worthless audience, who insolently pretend to his familiarity. Swift has a happier fortune. He lives in the company of a man who represents 'all that's good among the great'. Those whom Congreve has to please, Swift is free to flay: and he gives him a foretaste of what he can do in that way. If Congreve only knew Temple, he would change his occupation. Meanwhile, he gives him his own advice to do so.

Is it sour grapes? One cannot pronounce with absolute conviction; but it seems that the element of envy is small, and that Swift speaks his honest sentiments. He does regard writing for the theatre as a dangerous trade, and does deplore that Congreve should have to conciliate the impertinent pretenders to wit. He hates, for his friend as well as himself, the idea of being dependent upon the favour of the ignorant public, and he believes the better part has fallen to himself. Though he knows Congreve will laugh at him, he is more than half-serious in wishing that he shared the service of Temple and the innocent inspiration of the Muse of the Cave. And, finally, it is not insignificant that the contrast between this innocence and the corrupt world foreshadows the contrast between the Houyhnhnms and the Yahoos.

2

Of the more willing inspiration of the Muse of the Cave we have an example in *A Description of Mother Ludwell's Cave*. That this poem is Swift's is as certain as such things can be; and it is highly probable, too, that the manuscript is of Stella's girlish copying. There was nobody else in the Moor Park household who could have composed it; and it fits, with singular aptness, into the context of his poems at this time. It forms a perfect counterpart to his verses *To Congreve*; and it is obvious that it was written at much the same time. Since the verses are not printed in any edition of Swift's poetry, we give them in full.*

A Description of Mother Ludwell's Cave

Hae latebrae dulces et si mihi credis amoenae

Let others with Parnassus swell their theme,
Drink inspiration from the Æonian stream;
Let them draw Phoebus down to patch a line,
Invoke that hackney fry, the tuneful Nine.
I that of Ludwell sing, to Ludwell run,
Herself my Muse, her spring my Helicon.
The neighbouring park its friendly aid allows,
Perfum'd with thyme, o'erspread with shady boughs.
Its leafy canopies new thoughts instil,
And Crooksbury supplies the cloven hill;

* For the evidence on which these opinions are based, see Appendix IV.

Pomona does Minerva's stores dispense,
And Flora sheds her balmy influence.
All things conspire to press my modest Muse:
The morning herbs adorn'd with pearly dews,
The meadows interlac'd with silver floods,
The frizzled thickets, and the taller woods.
The whispering Zephyrs my more silent tongue
Correct, and Philomela chirps a song.
Is there a bird of all the blooming year
That has not sung his early mattins here?
That has not sipped the Fairy Matron's spring,
Or hover'd o'er her cave with wishful wing?
An awful fabric, built by Nature's hand,
Does raise our wonder, our respects command.
Three lucky trees, to wilder art unknown,
Seem on the front a growing triple crown.
At first the arched room is high and wide,
The naked wall with mossy hangings hid,
The ceiling sandy; as you forward press,
The roof is still declining into less.
Despair to reach the end; a little arch,
Narrow and low, forbids your utmost search.
So to her lover the chaste beauteous lass
Without a blush, vouchsafes to show her face,
Her neck of ivory, her snowy breast —
These shown, she modestly conceals the rest.
A shallow brook that, restless underground,
Struggled with earth, here a moist passage found.
Down through a stony vein the waters roll,
O'erflowing the capacious iron bowl.
O happy bowl! that gladness can infuse,
And yet was never stain'd with heady juice.
Here thirsty souls carouse with innocence,
Nor owe their pleasure to their loss of sense.
Here a smooth floor had many a figure shown
Had virgin footsteps made impression,
That soft and swift, Camilla-like, advance,
While even movements seem to fly a dance.
No quilted couch, the sick man's daily bed,
No seats to lull asleep diseases made,
Are seen, but such as healthy persons please,
Of wood or stone, [offer] the wearied ease.
   O might I still enjoy this peaceful gloom,
The truest entrance to Elysium!

> Who would to the Cumæan den repair?
> A better Sibyl, wiser power is here.
> Methinks I see him from his palace come,
> And with his presence grace the baleful room.
> Consider, Ludwell, what to him you owe,
> Who does for you the noisy court forgo.
> Nay, he a rich and gaudy silence leaves;
> You share the honour sweet Moor Park receives.
> You, with your wrinkles, admiration move;
> That, with its beauty, better merits love.
> Here's careless nature in her ancient dress,
> There she's more modish, and consults the glass.
> Here she's an old, and yet a pleasant dame;
> There she'll a fair, not painted, virgin seem.
> Here the rich metal has through no fire pass'd;
> There tho' refin'd, by no alloy debas'd.
> Thus Nature is preserved in every part,
> Sometimes adorn'd, but ne'er debauch'd by art,
> Where scatter'd locks that dangle on the brow
> Into more decent hairy circles grow.
> After inquiry made, though no man love
> The curling iron, all the comb approve.[5]

The poem is charming in its way, and it has personal touches which delight. Of these the most original and pleasing is in the last four lines, which, we believe, were added to the poem by Swift when he gave it to Stella to copy. The poem comes to its proper end with

> Sometimes adorn'd, but ne'er debauch'd by art.

The last four lines were added for the little copyist's edification. In themselves, they are flat, and rather silly; but if they were meant to be copied and taken to heart by the twelve-year old Stella, they become entirely charming. One can see her, copying laboriously and unsuspectingly, her hair untidy and the tip of her tongue showing: and then it suddenly dawns on her that the message is meant for her. Swift was to play the same trick on her, thirty years afterwards.

One fancies, too, that Pomona dispensing Minerva's stores may be an autumn picture of Swift munching apples on his way to meditate and compose in the Cave. Then there is the sketch of Temple leaving the 'rich and gaudy silence' of Moor Park to visit the Cave where his secretary went to seek inspiration in solitude. And it contains yet another of those tributes to Temple which may have been naive, but are not fulsome. This reverent admiration for the good great man was spontaneous and sincere; and Swift was single-minded in desiring, as the best that could happen to his friend Congreve, that he should share it.

The intimate connection of these verses with those *To Congreve* is manifest. Swift has dropped pindarics and is now working in rhymed couplets. Those on the Cave are a specimen of that 'innocent song' which, he told Congreve, was welcome to Temple; they expatiate on the charms of the Cave, which, he suggested to his friend, would be the ideal retreat for him also to compose in and regain his innocence.

3

A month later, in December 1693, came the last of the six poems: that *Occasioned by Sir William Temple's Illness and Recovery*. It is obscure and fascinating: psychologically the most important of them all. The change in Swift's attitude it reveals is so sudden, so revolutionary, and so nakedly avowed.

The first thirty lines tell how the Muse had appeared to him twice in the same place: once, a year ago, to inspire him to sing Temple's praises; now she has appeared again, again like evening sunshine after a stormy day. She is astonished at the change in him.

> What mortal change does in thy face appear,
> Lost youth, she cry'd, since first I met thee here!
> With how undecent clouds are overcast
> Thy looks, when every cause of grief is past!
> Unworthy the glad tidings which I bring ... [6]

Although Temple has recovered, Swift remains dejected, and out of humour to attempt a poem of thanksgiving. But the Muse herself offers him a theme. She describes what she has seen of the grief and anxiety of Dorothea (Dorothy Temple) and Dorinda (Martha Giffard) during Temple's illness.

> Mild Dorothea, peaceful, wise, and great,
> Trembling beheld the doubtful hand of fate;
> Mild Dorothea, whom we both have long
> Not dared to injure with our lowly song;
> Sprung from a better world, and chosen then
> The best companion for the best of men:
> As some fair pile, yet spar'd by zeal and rage,
> Lives pious witness of a better age;
> So men may see what once was womankind
> In the fair shrine of Dorothea's mind. [7]

The picture of Dorothy Temple is memorable. It requires something of an effort to remember that her exquisite love-letters were then unknown. But Swift responded in his way to her quality. He depicts her as a being apart whom he has not dared to profane by a poem. ('We both', of course, is Swift and his Muse: the relation between them becomes more and more intimate in this curious sequence of poems until the final catastrophe.) The praise of Lady Giffard, too, is interesting; it shows how remote from Swift's mind, while he lived at Moor Park, was his subsequent animus against her.

> Thus when Dorinda wept, joy every face forsook
> And grief flung sables on each menial look;
> The humble tribe mourned for the quickening soul
> That furnish'd spirit and motion through the whole.[8]

Lady Giffard was the life of the house. Dorothy and Martha, says the Muse, are still anxious at heart. Let him write to comfort and encourage them! Here is

> large matter to employ
> The fancy furnish'd by returning joy;
> And to mistaken men these truths rehearse
> Who dare revile the integrity of verse.[9]

But Swift does not answer, or look up. The Muse summons him to explain his discourtesy. Whereupon he bursts into denunciation of her.

> Malignant goddess! bane to my repose!
> Thou universal cause of all my woes!
> Say whence it comes that thou art grown of late
> A poor amusement for my scorn and hate . . .[10]

Let her tell him why he has now begun to vent his accumulated anger on the Muse herself. 'On you [he says] I now wreak the malice you inspire. I now call you the refuge of fools, the last retreat of dullness. You have no independent being, but are a mere illusion.'

> But a wild form dependent on the brain,
> Scatt'ring loose features o'er the optic vein . . .
> Kindled while reason sleeps, but quickly flies
> Like antic shapes in dreams from waking eyes.
> In sum, a glitt'ring voice, a painted name,
> A walking vapour, like thy sister, Fame.[11]

'But if you really are a feminine power, as your votaries say, why stay with me who am "the dregs of youth"?'

Wert thou right woman, thou would'st scorn to look
On an abandon'd wretch by hopes forsook;
Forsook by hopes, ill fortune's last relief,
Assign'd for life to unremitting grief.[12]

Time passes swiftly and lightly over the happy; like Camilla, he leaves the
corn standing for them; but over the wretched he sweeps his scythe, mows
down the corn, and leaves the bare stubbled earth. See the havoc made in
my face by a brief year. Hope, the last enemy of cruel Time, is dead in me;
and Time and Despair will follow me all the days of my life.

To thee I owe that fatal bent of mind,
Still to unhappy restless thoughts inclin'd;
To thee, what oft I vainly strive to hide,
That scorn of fools, by fools mistook for pride;
From thee whatever virtue takes it rise
Grows a misfortune, or becomes a vice;
Such were thy rules to be poetically great,
'Stoop not to int'rest, flattery or deceit;
Nor with hir'd thoughts be thy devotion paid;
Learn to disdain their mercenary aid;
Be this thy sure defence, thy brazen wall,
Know no base action, at no guilt turn pale.
And since unhappy distance thus denies
T'expose thy soul, clad in this poor disguise,
Since thy few ill-presented graces seem
To breed contempt where thou hast hop'd esteem — '[13]

The poet breaks in upon himself. This condition is intolerable: everlasting
self-deception, endless dissatisfaction. The 'integrity of verse' to which the
Muse has tempted him has brought him only 'a false beam of joy'. The
enchantment is broken!

And from this hour
I here renounce thy visionary power;
And since thy essence on my breath depends,
Thus with a puff the whole delusion ends.[14]

In this remarkable poem is gathered more than one strand of feeling. It is
the record, perhaps the actual resolution, of a complex emotional crisis.
First, and most obviously, it is a final break with poetry — at least of the kind
Swift had been trying so hard to write. It is not yet sufficiently realized how
intensely personal are these early poems of Swift's. Their pindaric form,
their outmoded mechanism, the apparent complexity of much of the inward

dialogue in which the figure of the Muse is employed, the very fact that they are so remote from the style and temper of the mature Swift who had built his artistic persona, have conspired to blind criticism to their emotional nakedness. Two simple and fundamental emotions are incessantly bursting out: an intense admiration for moral beauty and an equally, or even more, intense detestation of a world which was incapable of responding to it. And, rightly or wrongly, Swift had persuaded himself that the excellence of poetry derived from the fidelity of its allegiance to the great and good. The 'integrity of verse' depended upon the poet's loyalty to moral beauty. 'Really I take that to be a part of the honesty of poets that they cannot write well except they think the subject deserves it.'[15] In this moral enthusiasm (he believed) was the true poetic inspiration.

These convictions were inextricably mixed with his devotion to the person of Temple. Temple was the embodiment of moral beauty: he had renounced power, when he found that the price of retaining it was corruption, and retired contentedly to domestic affection and rural delights. In no less than five of these six poems Temple is the centre of the emotional field. Only the ode *To Sancroft* is not essentially connected with him; and that celebrates a virtue in the Archbishop which Temple possessed in even greater perfection. And the final poem is obviously quite as much a farewell to Temple as it is a farewell to poetry. Psychologically, it is the confession of the emotional revolution that has occurred in Swift since his first poetic eulogy of Temple. Now he finds in himself neither joy nor inspiration at Temple's recovery. His enthusiasm and his hopes are dead.

And Swift even makes plain the chief cause of the change: the tender of his admiring affection to Temple has met with no response. The distance in rank and age is too great to be spanned, and his sincerity has earned contempt rather than esteem. No doubt Swift exaggerated Temple's coldness towards him. But what counts is what he felt; and he felt that his admiration and affection had been repulsed. The fatherless and emotionally starved young man had sought a father in Temple; and Temple had failed him.

4

In Swift something was really broken. In the kindly ambience of Moor Park, he had come, like Keats, to believe in 'the holiness of the heart's affections'. Now, he felt they were a delusion, like the poetry they inspired. He put them away like childish things. Never again would he wear his heart upon his sleeve. 'Happiness . . . is a perpetual possession of being well deceived.'[16] The deception was over.

Two literary impulses had been contending within him: one of unstinted admiration for the alliance of the great and good, for the moral virtues of humility, resignation and disinterestedness; the other of indignant anger at the egotism, the stupidity and the knavery of mankind. He had made no effort to conceal their struggle within him; but in his poetry he had deliberately submitted his anger to his admiration, and chosen to regard himself as one called to praise rather than to blame, to admire rather than to excoriate. Temple's declared aversion to satire and burlesque had had, no doubt, its influence upon him.

But, by the time of his verses *To Congreve*, his propensity to satire was getting the upper hand, because his emotional frustration had begun; and simultaneously a note of desperation comes into his insistence on the purity of *his* inspiration. He reveals his sense of growing isolation — he is a dreamer of dreams, and Congreve himself turns into one of the cynical mob. And, though Temple is still the object of his conscious devotion, he is remote. Only Swift and his Muse are left in the Cave.

A month later, in the final poem, he faces the bitter reality. He is quite alone. The Muse is a delusion, and her precepts so many false lights to lure him on to madness and ruin. By tempting him to complete sincerity, she has led him to despair. He turns and annihilates her. She is the chimaera of a sick brain.

The literary crisis and the emotional were two aspects of a single happening. As to the first, not merely was the restraint on Swift's satirical impulse now removed, but the scope of the impulse was vastly and ominously extended. The satire was now free to be vented even on the ideal loyalties which had restrained it. From such an attitude sheer nihilism will never be far away. For better or worse, that generous ardour of soul which is apparent in Swift's early poetry, disappears for ever from his work. He will achieve, in *A Tale of a Tub*, an impressive kind of 'negative poetry', if the phrase be allowed, to describe a wild exuberance in demolishing illusions. In it he 'will give the vigorous fancy room' in a sense and with a motive he did not intend when he coined the phrase to describe the effort of the poet: but that is all, and even that he will hardly achieve again. But we shall not forget that the first clear outline of the vision of the Yahoos came to him as a picture of the reception of his innocent and isolated Muse by an uncomprehending and corrupted world.

Swift now prepared to leave Moor Park. Since Temple refused him the sympathy he craved, he would refuse his patronage. The puzzle of his contradictory accounts of his parting from Temple is explained. It would have been unthinkable that the mature and repressed Swift should tell of his

disappointed affection for Temple, which was the real motive of his paradoxical behaviour. He subsequently represented that he had been oppressed
by a scruple at entering the Church for a livelihood, and that by rejecting
Temple's offer of a secular sinecure he satisfied himself of his own disinterestedness in taking orders. That is demonstrably untrue. In reality, he rejected
Temple's offer because it meant that he must stay with him; and he was
determined to leave him, and to shake off all obligation to him.

He was — or he believed he was — prepared for anything. Whereas his
ambition and his affection had gone hand in hand, now he renounced them
both. He would eagerly have accepted the virtual exile of a chaplaincy in
Lisbon; he was even reconciled to life as a country parson in Ireland. Within
the restricted emotional and social pattern of his age, he felt the analogue of
of the Romantic longing: *N'importe où hors du monde*. And that may have
given a fervour to his taking orders of which he had known nothing before.
The collapse of his enthusiasm, the scepticism of the intimate ideal, may have
helped to find a real refuge in the *credo quia impossibile* which was the note of
his Christian faith.

At the beginning of May 1694, Swift went off to Ireland, staying a month
with his mother on the way. The parting scene between him and Temple
must have been strange. Swift would, from pride, resolutely and impassively
conceal his real motive. His behaviour would strike Temple as astonishing,
ungrateful, stubborn and capricious: a rude refusal of a kindness, a wanton
and unmotived desertion. He would not be deceived by Swift's pretence of
a scruple; and he would now be acutely conscious of all that he was to lose
by the withdrawal of his devotion. No wonder he was 'extreme angry'.

CHAPTER IV

VARINA: 1695-1700

I F there was a touch of bravado in Swift's gesture in breaking with Temple, he quickly had to pay for it. He had not been in Dublin long before he discovered, to his dismay, that no bishop would ordain him, unless he produced a certificate of good character and behaviour from Temple himself. His Swift connections, apparently, were able to get him the promise of a living at Kilroot, on Belfast Lough; but to get into orders without a testimonial from his late master was impossible. Swift desperately tried several bishops before submitting to the grim necessity of writing to Temple. He put it off to the last possible moment. Then he gulped down his pride and wrote on October 6, 1694 what one of the Temple family, probably Lady Giffard, endorsed as his 'penitential letter'.

> May it please your Honour,
> That I might not continue by any means the many troubles I have given you, I have all this while avoided one, which I fear proves necessary at last. I have taken all due methods to be ordained, and one time of ordination is already elapsed since my arrival without effecting it. Two or three Bishops, acquaintances of our family, have signified to me and them ... that it being so many years since I left this Kingdom they could not admit me to the ministry without some certificate of my behaviour where I lived ... The sense I am in, how low I am fallen in your Honour's thoughts, has denied me assurance enough to beg this favour, till I find it impossible to avoid ... I entreat that your Honour ... will please to send me some certificate of my behaviour during almost three years in your family; wherein I shall stand in need of all your goodness to excuse my many weaknesses and follies and oversights, much more to say anything to my advantage. The particulars. expected of me are what relate to morals and learning, and the reasons of quitting your Honour's family, that is, whether the last was occasioned by any ill actions. They are all entirely left to your Honour's mercy, though in the first I think I cannot reproach myself any farther than for infirmities.
> This is all I dare beg at present from your Honour, under circumstances of life not worth your regard. What is left for me to wish, next to the health and felicity of your Honour and family, is, that Heaven would one day allow me the opportunity to leave my acknowledgments at

your foot for so many favours I have received, which, whatever effect they have had upon my fortune, shall never fail to have the greatest upon my mind, in approving myself, upon all occasions,
Your Honour's most obedient and most
dutiful servant,
J. Swift.

He added that unless the certificate were sent immediately it would be too late for the next ordination, in early November. In fact, Swift was ordained on October 25. Temple had sent him the testimonial by return.

This generous gesture could not fail of its impression on Swift. He repented of all that seemed unmannerly and ungrateful in the mode of his departure from Temple, though the substance of his decision, being what it was, remained unaltered. His romantic dream was ended; he had asked too much of Temple, and too much of himself. The idolatry was over, but so was the resentment; he could and did think with gratitude of his master again.

2

He was ordained priest on January 28, 1695, and a fortnight later was appointed to the prebend of Kilroot, which lay east of Carrickfergus and was in effect a great parish of 1600 acres, worth between £100 and £150 a year. Nearly all the inhabitants were Presbyterians of Scotch descent. Swift had no love for them. He had no sympathy whatever for any form of Dissent. He agreed with Temple, whose religion, said Lady Giffard, 'was that of the Church of England which he was born and bred in, and he thought nobody ought to change since it must require more time and pains than one's life can furnish to make a true judgment of that which interest and folly were commonly motives to'[1] — namely, the opinions of Nonconformists. And he also agreed with Temple that it was unreasonable of the State to require more than outward conformity in religion. The social crime was to publish and propagate one's incapacity for belief in the formularies of the national Church.

Swift was now enlisted in the national Church as in a regiment. He had his orders, and intended to obey them. The Ulster Presbyterians were doubly distasteful to him, because they also were organized, and indeed, in virtue of their subvention from the Crown, officially recognized. They were recalcitrant to his ministrations at Kilroot, and he had practically no congregation. But he would not break his heart over that. He read and wrote.

What influenced him deeply was the emotional crisis with Temple. The desire for sympathy and affection was increased rather than diminished by his disappointment. Having failed to find a father, he sought the affection of a wife. He fell in love with a young lady named Miss Jane Waring, who was the cousin of a contemporary of his at Trinity, and the daughter of the archdeacon of Dromore.

The episode is unique in Swift's life, as is the experience at Moor Park which preceded it. Because it also does not fit with the pattern of the later Swift, it has also been neglected. Because Swift was subsequently determined against marriage, it has been supposed that his courtship of Varina cannot have been serious. It was very serious. He fell in love with her, and ardently desired to marry her; and if Varina had had the same ardour, his subsequent history might have been strangely different from what it was.

How the affair began, how it grew, is unknown. Our information begins only when it had reached its climax, more than a year after he had settled at Kilroot. Swift's letter to Varina of April 19, 1696, is at once an appeal and an ultimatum. Two years had passed since he left Temple. His place at Moor Park had been inadequately filled by his cousin Thomas; and now Temple had written to him to suggest that he should resume his post, on more confidential and honourable terms. As Swift put it to Varina: 'I am once more offered the advantage to have the same acquaintance with greatness that I formerly enjoyed, and with better prospect of interest. I here solemnly offer to forgo it all for your sake.'

It is plain from the letter that the courtship had been going on for months; it probably began very soon after Swift had arrived at Kilroot. For some considerable time Swift had been pressing her to marry him, and she had delayed to give him a definite answer, such as would justify him in formally asking her family for their consent. He had lately written her a letter urging his suit again, and before she had replied, Temple's offer had reached him.

Swift was faced with an important decision, the counterpart of his previous decision to part from Temple. His courtship of Varina belonged to the pattern of the future he had then chosen for himself, with his renunciation of ambition and patronage, and his determination to make his way unaided in the restricted sphere of Ireland. Marriage to Varina had become an essential part of the pattern. He wanted to stick to it. He was prepared to build his life on his marriage to her. But she must come to a decision. If she put him off any more, he would, because he must, conclude that her love for him was not what she pretended. Temple's new offer, if Swift accepted it, meant breaking up the pattern again. It meant farewell to Ireland, and farewell to Varina.

3

Swift left her in no doubt that what he wanted was herself; and that he was ready and eager to sacrifice the chance of a more brilliant worldly future for her. But he was not prepared to sacrifice his own integrity to her lack of courage, which would only be proof of her lack of love. The words of Keats to Fanny Brawne come to the mind: 'I am no parson-Romeo; no officer in yawning quarters.' That is the temper in which Swift writes to her a manly and admirable love-letter: against the evidence of which the theory that Swift was physically incapable of a real marriage appears the fantasy it surely is.

Madam,
Impatience is the most inseparable quality of a lover, and indeed of every person who is in pursuit of a design whereon he conceives his greatest happiness or misery to depend. It is the same thing in war, in courts, and in common business. Every one who hunts after pleasure, or fame, or fortune, is still restless and uneasy till he has hunted down his game; and all this is not only very natural, but something reasonable too, for violent desire is little better than a distemper, and therefore men are not to blame in looking after a cure. I find myself hugely infected with this malady, and am easily vain enough to believe it has some very good reasons to excuse it. For indeed, in my case, there are some circumstances which will admit pardon for more than ordinary disquiets. That dearest object upon which all my prospect of happiness depends, is in perpetual danger to be removed for ever from my sight. Varina's life is daily wasting, and though one just and honourable action would furnish health to her, and unspeakable happiness to us both, yet some power which repines at human felicity has that influence to hold her continually doating on her cruelty, and me upon the cause of it. This fully convinces me of what we are told, that the miseries of man's life are all beaten out on his own anvil. Why was I so foolish to put my hopes and fears into the power or management of another? Liberty is doubtless the most valuable blessing of life, yet we are fond to fling it away on those who have been these five thousand years using us ill. Philosophy advises us to keep our desires and prospects of happiness as much as we can in our own breasts, and independent of anything without. He that sends them abroad is likely to have as little quiet as a merchant whose stock depends upon winds, and waves, and pirates, or upon the word and faith of creditors, every whit as dangerous and inconstant as the other.
I am a villain if I have not been poring this half hour over the paper merely for want of something to say to you; or is it rather that I have

so much to say to you, that I know not where to begin, though at last it is all very likely to be arrant repetition?

After hinting that his lack of means may be the obstacle to his success, he goes on:

You have now had time enough to consider my last letter, and to form your own resolutions upon it. I wait your answer with a world of impatience, and if you think fit I should attend you before my journey, I am ready to do so . . . It is possible I may take shipping from hence; otherwise I shall set out on Monday fortnight for Dublin, and after one visit of leave to his Excellency, hasten to England; and how far you will stretch the point of your unreasonable scruples to keep me here, will depend on the strength of the love you pretend for me. In short, Madam, I am once more offered to have the same acquaintance with greatness that I formerly enjoyed, and with better prospect of advantage. I here solemnly offer to forgo it all for your sake. I desire nothing of your fortune; you shall live where and with whom you please till my affairs are settled to your desire, and in the meantime I will push my advancement with all the eagerness and courage imaginable, and do not doubt to succeed.

Varina's fortune was modest: £75 a year, the furnishings of a house, and £400, say, £100 a year in all: rather smaller than Stella's.[2] Swift could hardly have been more generous in his offer. What he is insisting upon, as his later letter shows, is that she shall, whether she marries him now or not, break away from her family, whose influence upon her he regards as pernicious — to her health and to her soul. She professes to love him; then let her show it in obeying him in this, which is wholly for her good. Let her show that she is his woman. Having made his offer and his demand, his pulse quickens, and he grows fiery.

Study seven years for objections against all this, and by Heaven they will at last be no more than trifles or put-offs. It is true you have known sickness longer than you have me, and therefore perhaps you are more loath to part with it as an older acquaintance. But listen to what I here solemnly protest, by all that can be witness to an oath, that if I leave this Kingdom before you are mine, I will endure the utmost indignities of fortune rather than ever return again, though the King himself would send me back his Deputy. And if it must be so, preserve yourself in God's name, for the next lover who has those qualities you admire so much beyond any of mine, and who will highly admire you for those advantages which shall never share any esteem from me. Would to Heaven you were but a while sensible of the thoughts into which my present distractions plunge me; they hale me a thousand ways, and I not able to bear them. It is so, by Heaven: the love of Varina is of more tragical consequence than her cruelty. Would to God you had treated and scorned me from the beginning. It was your pity opened the first way to my misfortune; and now your love is finishing my ruin. And it is so then? In one fortnight I must take eternal farewell of Varina, and I wonder will she weep at parting a little to justify her poor pretences of some affection for me? And will my friends continue reproaching me for the want of gallantry, and neglecting a close siege? How comes it they all wish us married together, they knowing my circumstances and yours extremely well, and I am sure love you too much, if it be only for my sake, to wish you anything that might cross your interest or your happiness?

Surely, Varina, you have but a very mean opinion of the joys that accompany a true, honourable, unlimited love; yet either nature or our ancestors have hugely deceived us, or else other sublunary things are dross in comparison. Is it possible you cannot be yet insensible to the prospect of a rapture and delight so innocent and so exalted? Trust me, Varina, Heaven has given us nothing else worth the loss of a thought. Ambition, high appearance, friends, and fortune, are all tasteless and insipid when they come in competition; yet millions of such glorious minutes we are perpetually losing, for ever losing, irrecoverably losing, to gratify empty forms and wrong notions, and affected coldnesses and peevish humour. These are the unhappy encumbrances which we who are distinguished from the vulgar do fondly create to torment ourselves. The only felicity permitted to human life we clog with tedious circumstances and barbarous formality. By Heaven, Varina, you are more experienced and have less virgin innocence than I. Would not your conduct make one think you were hugely skilled in all the little politic methods of intrigue? Love, with the gall of too much discretion, is a thousand times worse than with none at all. It is a peculiar part of nature which art debauches, but cannot improve. We have all of us the seeds of it implanted in ourselves, and they require no help from courts or fortune to cultivate and improve them. To resist the violence of our inclinations at the beginning, is a strain of self-denial that may have some pretences to set up for a virtue; but when they are grounded at first upon reason, when they have taken firm root and grown up to a height, it is folly — folly as well as injustice, to withstand their dictates; for this passion has a property peculiar to itself, to be most commendable in its extremes, and it is as possible to err in the excess of piety as of love.

These are the rules I have long followed with you, Varina, and had you been pleased to imitate them, we should both have been infinitely happy. The little disguises, and affected contradictions of your sex, were all, to say the truth, infinitely beneath persons of your pride and mine; paltry maxims that they are, calculated for the rabble of humanity. O Varina, how imagination leads me beyond myself and all my sorrows! It is sunk, and a thousand graves lie open! No, Madam, I will give you no more of my unhappy temper, though I derive it all from you.

Farewell, Madam, and may love make you awhile forget your temper to do me justice. Only remember, that if you still refuse to be mine, you will quickly lose, for ever lose, him that is resolved to die as he has lived, all yours.

Jon. Swift.

4

We have quoted the letter at length, for it is surely important to an understanding of Swift. It has an accent which will never be heard again in Swift's writing. And it has been undervalued and misinterpreted. Because, four years later, when Swift was, very reluctantly, compelled to return to Ireland, and Varina attempted to renew relations, he wrote her a cold and steely letter, it is supposed that he could not have been in passionate earnest in this one. Because it is unique, in its fervid love-idealism, it is, in effect, dismissed as an aberration. Because Stella and Vanessa are the love-heroines of Swift's later life, Varina has to be discounted. It is a mistake. Stella and Vanessa belong to the time when Swift had deliberately renounced the passion of love, when he could, if he willed — and he did will — without great difficulty be immune from its importunity. But Swift's love for Varina belonged to the heyday of the blood: it was directed, from the beginning, towards marriage as its right and natural consummation. It was the healthy natural love of a naturally passionate, and naturally generous nature. Her rejection of it was probably as important in Swift's life as anything that happened to him. If we want the true answer to the eternal question: Why did he not marry Stella?* we do not have to seek it in fantastic theories, of concealed consanguinity, or physical incapacity, or overweening pride; it is simple enough. It was because of his rejection by Varina.

Swift had broken with Temple because he had suffered a deep emotional humiliation. He had renounced his ambition, and resigned himself to a modest but independent career in Ireland. His need of affection and sympathy was great. Almost as soon as he got to his Irish parish, he thought he had found it in Varina. She pitied him; she had at least imagination enough

* We believe Swift did formally marry Stella: but it was a marriage only in name.

to understand that he was lonely and sick at heart. At the touch, all his prudential resolutions about marriage went by the board; and perhaps some of his exaggerated 'metaphysical' demands for wifely perfection too. Naturally, quickly, and inevitably he fell in love. Varina was not very strong: he did not care; marriage would put that to rights. She was not very rich: he did not care; and anyway he had no intention of touching her money. And he was quite confident that if she became his wife, he would make his way somehow. But one thing, he did ask: that she should love him as he loved her, simply, directly, straightforwardly. He would not stand being coquetted with. That was an insult to his integrity. Love and artifice were incompatible. He had given her time. Now he insisted on a straight answer. If she hedged any more, it was an end between them. It was goodbye to her, goodbye to Ireland, goodbye to the pattern of his life of which his marriage to her had become part.

Probably, Varina was rather scared by this passionate resolute man of twenty-nine. Probably, she could not believe that he really meant his ultimatum, and persuaded herself that if he loved her as he said he did, he could not break with her for temporizing a little longer. Swift did mean what he said. He was generous, but he was fiercely proud. He had offered all himself, and he expected all of her. He did not get it, and he went his way. He said to himself: Never again! Never again would he expose himself to emotional humiliation at the hands of a woman. He never did. And four years later he did what a more happily constituted man perhaps would not have done. He inflicted a deliberate humiliation on Varina, in revenge.

He returned to Moor Park. For nearly two years he kept his Irish prebend, which for so long provided him with an income independent of Temple; in January 1698 he resigned it and managed to pass it on to a neighbouring clergyman, the Rev. John Winder. So long as he kept his prebend, Varina's friends and acquaintances imagined that he was still her suitor. By the conventions of the day he ought to have been. The affair had gone too far for Swift to break it off; only Varina could now do that. But he had told her plainly enough that he despised the conventions. If their acquaintances, if Varina herself chose to believe his ultimatum was not serious, the more fools they. When the news came that Swift had resigned his prebend, there was gossip and indignation at his behaviour. He was unmoved.

Swift returned to Temple as his acknowledged literary executor to be. In his absence his place as secretary had been filled by his cousin, Thomas Swift. It is certain that Thomas Swift was in Temple's service in 1694 and in the spring of 1696, when he witnessed Temple's will,[3] and there is no indication that Jonathan and he were there together. Besides, Temple would have had no use for the two of them. It was probably the experience of Thomas Swift which taught Temple to appreciate Jonathan, and made him eager to get him back again. A rather cryptic passage in a letter of Lady Giffard to Lady Berkeley seems to refer to them both:

> I had an answer today of the question I told you I asked in my last about the secretary's money. He says he has accounts for £25 0. 0. but by accounts of other years signed by his brother's hand he thinks he has pretence for several sums for journeys and other things which when he knows more exactly he will tell me. I have sent him with another compliment from Papa to the King where I fancy he is not displeased with finding occasions of going. (December 30, 1698)[4]

We imagine the 'brother' is Thomas Swift. Perhaps Lady Giffard momentarily forgot that they were only cousins, or called them brothers because they filled the same post. But the situation, as we understand it, was that Swift had put in his own bill for £25, but on comparing his account with his predecessor's found that he was entitled to be paid for various items for which he had not charged. It is a mere sidelight, but sidelights on Swift at this moment are scarce; and the letter shows that Lady Giffard at this time was kindly disposed towards him.

He worked upon Temple's manuscripts, which he copied and corrected under Temple's supervision. He enlarged *A Tale of a Tub*, which he had begun at Kilroot; he composed *The Battle of the Books* as a contribution to Temple's side in the controversy over the Ancient and Moderns, which his essay on *Ancient and Modern Learning* had aroused. He read a great deal: notably Lucretius, three times in one year, but Thucydides only in Hobbes's translation. 'He thought exercise of great necessity,' says Dr. Johnson, 'and used to run half a mile up and down a hill every two hours'; which must have surprised and amused his master. He acted as Temple's emissary to Court, and tried to improve his interest there. He counted on the help of Sunderland who (he says) was Temple's intimate friend until his death; but Sunderland resigned on December 26, 1697. He wrote to Winder:

> Ten days before my resignation (of Kilroot), my Lord Sunderland fell and I with him. Since that there have been other courses, which if

they succeed, I shall be proud to own the methods, or if otherwise, very much ashamed. (April 1, 1698)

They did not succeed; and we know nothing of the methods.

And he became conscious of Hester Johnson as a woman. He had always been close friends with her, since he first came to Moor Park. She was then eight years old, and the favourite of the house. It had been part of his duty to teach her to read and write. We have seen her copying a poem for him when she was twelve. Now, on his return from Kilroot, she was fifteen. To his picture of her at that moment he frequently recurs in after-life. He says that up to that time she had been rather sickly.

But then grew into perfect health, and was looked upon as one of the most beautiful, graceful and agreeable young women in London, only a little too fat. Her hair was blacker than a raven, and every feature in perfection.[5]

6

It was a fatality for Stella that Swift became conscious of her as a woman, and no longer a child, at the moment that he had been humiliated by Varina: when he had discarded the life-pattern of which marriage was a part, and decided for ambition and the larger world. Had his two years' absence from Moor Park been of a different character — neutral, if that can be imagined — he might have grown to regard Stella as his mate, despite the disparity of years. But the scales were now hopelessly weighted against his falling in love with her. His disillusion and determination never to expose himself again, and the armour of cynicism in which he now took up the adventure of ambition, together determined the nature of his response to her. His little pupil must remain his little pupil. She had, indeed, a claim on his affections and a right to his intimacy; but always on the basis of child to man. He had begun to educate her, and he resumed her education. But now it was more serious. It was no longer a matter of reading and writing and sums; it was a matter of values. His values were hers, or becoming hers. Truth, integrity — those 'principles of honour and virtue' which he afterwards took pride in having inculcated in her — these were straightforward enough. But on the value which is of supreme importance to a woman, the value of love, what had he to say? Probably he said nothing wittingly. It was forbidden ground. But he could not stop himself from getting on to the edge of it. That disdain of feminine artifice which he taught her, for example — when that is learned, what does the woman do? Declare her love?

As far as Stella knew, when Swift broke with Temple, in 1694, and she was thirteen, her wayward, moody, humorous tutor, with his alternate exaltations and depressions and his gorgeous jokes, had left her for ever. She would never see him again. Suddenly and unexpectedly he returned, outwardly the same, but inwardly a changed man. Not that she would or could have been conscious of the nature of the change. But she would know there was a difference. Uncertainty had given place to certainty. He was decided, determined — a much more obviously important figure in the household, and a parson in cassock and bands; a man of authority, in the vigour of manhood, while Temple was declining; almost, but not quite a father; and like a father, resolved not to take her seriously as a woman. He treated her new womanhood as a kind of game for which she was dressing up. This is evident in a letter he wrote to her early in 1698: when she was seventeen and he thirty-one, and she had gone with the family to Temple's house in Pall Mall.

> I received your kind letter from Robert by word of mouth, and think it a vast condescension in you to think of us in all your greatness. Now we shall hear nothing of you for five months but 'we courtiers'. Loory [Lady Giffard's bird of paradise] is well and presents his humble duty to my Lady, and love to his fellow-servant. . . .
> Mr. Mose [Temple's steward] and I desire you will remember our love to the King, and let us know how he looks. Robert says the Czar is here, and is fallen in love with you, and designs to carry you to Muscovy; pray provide yourself with muffs and sable tippets &c. . . .
> I desire your absence heartily, for now I live in great state, and the cook comes in to know what I please to have for dinner: I ask very gravely what is in the house, and accordingly give orders for a dish of pigeons, or, &c. . . .

It seems an odd, cruel trick of destiny by which Swift became inevitably the centre of Stella's emotional life, just when he had decided never to give himself again to a woman. One can say he was too proud for refusing to make a second submission; or that it is wrong for a man to fix the pattern of his life in a renunciation — a renunciation which, as time would reveal, his inmost soul regretted. Swift, by an effort of the will, distorted his own deeply affectionate nature. That is his tragedy. Pride and love contended within him to the end. But the evidence is that twice he was willing to throw his pride away, and give himself; and the gift was refused.

Swift was now definitely entrusted with the task of editing and publishing Temple's manuscripts according to his instructions; and Temple added a codicil to his will in February, 1698, leaving him £100 for his pains. It was neither princely nor niggardly — a fair reward. Temple himself was beginning to break up. He suffered badly from gout, and was confined to his room upstairs for weeks on end. We have glimpses of him crawling downstairs with a pain in his knee, discussing his gout like a connoisseur with the local doctor, surprising and gladdening the family by eating a plate of roast beef and enjoying it, and last of all surviving an anxious journey to the Somersets at Petworth and going to bed 'insufferably pert' over winning twelve guineas at cards.[6] That was in September, 1698. No one seems to have suspected that the end was near. Swift, in a letter written a fortnight before he died, shows no apprehension of immediate danger, though he had been sufficiently concerned to keep a record of the variations in Temple's health since June. On January 29, 1699, he suddenly died, 'and with him', Swift wrote on that day, 'all that was good and amiable among men'. 'That great man', he called him in his fragment of autobiography, nearly thirty years later, in spite of his animus against the family.

Temple's death compelled Swift once more to face the problem of a career. The preferment Temple had promised him had not materialized. His anxiety not to lose Swift's services had delayed him from pushing his claims till it was too late. Swift had to leave Moor Park and Stella and get busy. He petitioned the King for his promised prebend, and for some months hung about the Court, hoping that the Earl of Romney — on the strength of the great friendship he professed for Temple — would put in a word for him. But he did nothing; and Swift had to content himself with the offer of a chaplain-secretaryship to Lord Berkeley, on his appointment as a Lord Justice of Ireland. In spite of his solemn vow to Varina that, if she refused him, he would endure 'the utmost indignities of fortune' rather than return to Ireland, he was coming back again. It was, as he confessed, a mortification to his pride.

In this year 1699 Swift set down a number of resolutions to govern his conduct 'when I come to be old'.[7] He was now thirty-two. What did he reckon 'old'? It would be interesting to know. He reckoned himself old when Vanessa succumbed to his attractions. But that was when the inconceivable had happened. For one of his resolutions was: 'Not to hearken to flatteries or conceive I can be beloved by a young woman.' Another was 'Not to marry a young woman.' Whether he had Stella in mind, who can say?

But with his peculiar trick of keeping his women, in imagination, younger then they were, it is not impossible that he thought of himself as grown old when Stella was still a young woman.

But one — perhaps the strangest — of the resolutions must surely refer to her. 'Not to be fond of children, nor let them come near me hardly.' Swift himself had not been old when Stella was a child. But Temple had been, and little Stella had been his darling. Was there something in Temple's 'infinite fondness' for children, and for Stella in particular, that made Swift so determined to avoid it? Was it to him just a sign of dotage? Did the £200 in gold pieces shock him? Or was it simply that he was afraid of his own vulnerability? That his fondness for children might break down his resolution? It is impressive that one of the sweetest relations in human life should have filled him with apprehension and dismay.

Whatever was behind it, he stuck to his resolution, not only in old age but in all the years between. It would be hard in all his writings to find a single tender reference to a child.

8

Swift, in his own account, says he was appointed chaplain and secretary to Lord Berkeley.

He attended his Lordship, who landed near Waterford; and Mr. Swift acted as secretary the whole journey to Dublin. But another person had so far insinuated himself into the earl's favour, by telling him that the post of secretary was not proper for a clergyman, nor would be any advantage to one who aimed only at Church preferments, that his lordship after a poor apology gave that office to the other. In some months the Deanery of Derry fell vacant; and it was the Earl of Berkeley's turn to dispose of it. Yet things were so ordered that the secretary having received a bribe, the Deanery was disposed of to another, and Mr. Swift was put off with some other Church livings not worth above a third part of that rich Deanery; and at this present time, not a sixth: namely, the Rectory of Agher, and the Vicarage of Laracor and Rathbeggan in the Diocese of Meath; for which his letters patent bear date the 24th of February following [i.e. 1700]. The excuse pretended was his being too young, although he were then thirty years old.[8]

In retrospect, he was exaggerating his misfortunes. It is very improbable that Berkeley intended, or promised, that Swift should be his official secretary at Dublin Castle. It was not the office of a clergyman, and Swift's subsequent relations with Berkeley do not suggest that he thought he had been deceived by him. His secretaryship was merely a temporary appointment during the journey. His assertion that Arthur Bushe, the secretary, gave the Deanery of Derry away from him for a bribe is also in conflict with the contemporary evidence. Dr. John Bolton, who was appointed, accepted it with reluctance, and only on condition that he was allowed to retain the vicarage of Ratoath which he had previously held with the adjacent vicarage of Laracor, in which Swift succeeded him.[9] Over this separation of Laracor from Ratoath, Swift probably had a legitimate grievance, which was remedied by his appointment to the prebend of Dunlavin in St. Patrick's Cathedral six months later. Swift's subsequent mortification at losing an English Deanery and being compelled to return to Ireland warped his memory.

9

During his last years at Moor Park, Swift had kept up some correspondence with Varina. From the safety of England he felt he could permit himself to remain friends. But the failure of his English hopes, the collapse of his gesture, and his return to Ireland put him on his guard again, lest Varina should interpret it as a return to her. His pride was again, but differently, involved. She wrote complaining that the style of his letters was altered since his return, and asked the reason why. He replied by recalling his original decision to say goodbye to her.

I have told you the cause abundance of times. I had used a thousand endeavours and arguments, to get you from the company and place you are in; both on the account of your health and humour which I thought were like to suffer very much in such an air, and before such examples. All I had in answer from you was nothing but a great deal of arguing, and sometimes in a style so very imperious as I thought I might have been spared, when I reflected how much you had been in the wrong. The other thing you would know is, whether this change of style be owing to the thoughts of a new mistress. I declare, upon the word of a Christian and a gentleman, it is not; neither had I ever thoughts of being married to any person but yourself. I had ever an opinion that you had a great sweetness of nature and humour, and whatever appeared to the contrary, I looked upon it only as a thing put on as necessary before a lover; but I have since observed in abundance of your letters such marks of a severe indifference, that I began to think it was hardly possible for one of my few good qualities to please you. I never knew any so hard to be worked upon, even in matters where the interest and concern are entirely your own: all which, I say, passed easily while we were in the state of formalities and ceremony; but, since that, there is no other way of accounting for this untractable behaviour in you, but by imputing it to a want of common esteem and friendship for me.

Swift was recounting the past, of four years before, and what he now said was entirely in accord with what he had written then. When his love became serious and urgent, she evaded it; and he had concluded, as he had warned her he would, that she did not reciprocate his love.

Perhaps it would have been better if he had stopped there. But he knew that in the eyes of the world, or their common acquaintance, she had some sort of claim at least to be asked again; and that by the conventions of court-ship she was entitled to regard his ultimatum as not quite seriously meant. Though in himself, as he told her, he despised the conventions, and therefore did not admit the claim, he felt constrained to behave as though it had some substance. And Varina herself was behaving as though it had. She had implied that his inquiry as to her fortune, and his declaration that the amount of it was indifferent to him because he desired none of it, was tantamount to an engagement to her. This he repudiated in his letter. He had inquired, simply to know whether they would have enough to live on together. And, anyhow, her £100 a year was enough to enable her, if she had wanted to, to break away from her family while she waited for him to improve his own position.

> I think at the same time that no young woman in the world of the same income would dwindle away her health and life in such a sink, and among such family conversation: neither have all your letters been once able to persuade me that you had the least value for me, because you so little regarded what I so often said upon that matter.

Swift's demand upon her had been unusual and unconventional. She was timid and it frightened her. 'Marry me now, or later,' he had said, 'but show me that you love me as I love you — and prove it by showing the world that you are my woman and I your man. Show you have chosen me, by breaking free of all this horrible mess of coyness on your part and worldly consideration on your family's.' Instead of saying 'Yes, I will' to this, you have evaded my straight demand and interpreted all my forthrightness in terms of the marriage-bargaining I detest. You say now that my new livings — £200 a year — make marriage possible. In fact, they are barely £50 a year better than my old one. But that is not the point. I loved you and asked you to take a risk. You refused and waited for a certainty. 'I singled you out at first from the rest of women; and I expect not to be used like a common lover.'

'That is exactly how you have used me, though I warned you of the
consequences. Now I will deal with you in your own terms, or the terms
you have learned from your family.'

My uncle Adam asked me one day in private, as by direction, what my
designs were in relation to you, because it might be a hindrance to you
if I did not proceed. The answer I gave him, which I suppose he has
sent you, was to this effect: that I hoped I was no hindrance to you;
because the reason you urged against a union with me was drawn from
your indisposition, which still continued; that you also thought my
fortune not sufficient, which is neither at present in a condition to
offer you; that if your health and my fortune were as they ought, I
would prefer you above all your sex; but that in the present condition
of both, I thought it was against your opinion, and would certainly
make you unhappy; that, had you any other offers which your friends
or yourself thought more to your advantage, I should think I were very
unjust to be an obstacle in your way.

Here, in replying to the inspired soundings of uncle Adam, he is notably
silent about his real demands upon Varina. They were not such as marriage-
broking relatives would understand or appreciate. And Varina, though she
may have understood them, had behaved as though she did not. She had
acquiesced in a declaration of passionate love being degraded into a negotiation. Whether of her own motion, or influenced by her family, she had made
two excuses for refusing him, or two conditions for accepting him. Now she
must put up with the consequences. He will make *his* conditions for accepting *her*, and she will see how she likes that.

He sets them out ruthlessly. Complete subordination is what he now
requires. The conditions were such as any woman with an atom of spirit
left in her must refuse: not so much for their substance as their tone.

I desire, therefore, you will let me know if your health be otherwise
than it was when you told me the doctors advised you against marriage,
as what would certainly hazard your life. Are they or you grown of
another opinion in this particular? Are you in a condition to manage
domestic affairs, with an income of less perhaps than three hundred
pounds a year? Have you such an inclination to my person and humour,
as to comply with my desires and way of living, and endeavour to
make us both as happy as you can? Will you be ready to engage in
those methods I shall direct for the improvement of your mind, so as
to make us entertaining company for each other, without being
miserable when we are neither visiting or being visited? Can you bend
your love and esteem and indifference to others the same way as I do
mine? Shall I have so much power in your heart, or you so much

government of your passions, as to grow in good humour upon my approach, though provoked by a — ? Have you so much good-nature as to endeavour by soft words to smooth any rugged humour occasioned by the cross accidents of life? Shall the place wherever your husband is thrown be more welcome than courts and cities without him? In short, these are some of the necessary methods to please men, who, like me, are deep-read in the world; and to a person thus made, I should be proud in giving all due returns towards making her happy. These are the questions I have always resolved to propose to her with whom I meant to pass my life; and whenever you can heartily answer them in the affirmative, I shall be blessed to have you in my arms, without regarding whether your person be beautiful, or your fortune large. Cleanliness in the first, and competency in the other, is all I look for. I desire, indeed, a plentiful revenue, but would rather it should be of my own.

He had not 'always resolved' to put these questions; he had not dreamed of putting them to Varina four years before, when he was pressing her to marry him. They are meant to show that love is dead in him.

Probably Varina did not attempt to reply. Swift has been blamed for his lack of chivalry and his brutality, rather unfairly, by those who have not allowed for his former passionate sincerity. It is not a simple case of revenge: of returning humiliation for humiliation. It is subtler, and more revealing than that. He replied to her on the level to which she had chosen to demean their relation. 'I gave you the choice [he says in effect] of love on the one hand, or artifice, diplomacy and bargaining on the other. You chose, or let others choose for you, the latter. Here is my answer. It hurts? That will tell you something of how your choice hurt me. You did not believe me serious, when I told you that to refuse my love meant to destroy it. Now you know in what deadly earnest I was. You thought I was one of the common ruck of men: that having cherished a passion, I could not annihilate it. Here is the proof. You little knew how little you knew Jonathan Swift.'

That letter was written on May 4, 1700. He stayed on for a year in Ireland, as Berkeley's chaplain, as Vicar of Laracor, and prebendary of St. Patrick's. On February 16, 1701, he took his D.D. degree at Trinity — it cost him £44 — and shortly afterwards went to England for the remainder of the year. He was now Doctor Swift, and thirty-three years old.

That age is often a spiritual climacteric; and Doctor Swift came to an important decision. He went to see Stella, who was living with Dingley, probably at Farnham, and suggested that she should go to live in Dublin. She needed little persuasion. She knew he was her friend, and that she could trust him. She hoped, surely she hoped, that he would marry her. She was

twenty; and twenty and thirty-three is no bad proportion. He meant nothing
of the kind. All thought of marriage was put now behind him. But he had
conceived an idea at meeting her again. Why not have a passionless friendship with her that would endure? He could control himself: that was certain.
Love, said Iago, is a permission of the will. Doctor Swift agreed. His will
had permitted him to love Varina; that had been part of his pattern of retirement and renounced ambition. It had gone awry, and he had chosen ambition again. With that a lifelong friendship with Stella was compatible. He
liked the idea. But could Stella play her part? Surely, she had not been his
little pupil for nothing. Now she would be his pupil again. He would shape
her into all that he now needed from a woman.

CHAPTER V

'A TALE OF A TUB'

IN 1709 Swift wrote a rather disingenuous *Apology* for the final edition of *A Tale of a Tub*. In it he said that the greater part of the book was finished 'above thirteen years ago, 1696, which is eight years before it was published'. He was not being exact. The only part of the book which can be confidently assigned to 1696 is the allegory of the three brothers — Peter, Martin and Jack. That was, no doubt, in the eyes of hostile contemporaries the most important part of the book, which Swift chiefly set himself to defend in the *Apology*. But it is clear enough from internal evidence that the more distinctive part of the volume: the Digressions of the *Tale*; *The Battle of the Books*, *The Mechanical Operation of Spirit*, were all written in 1697-8. In short, the major part of the volume was written in the two years after his return to Moor Park.

Of the two subordinate pieces, *The Mechanical Operation of Spirit* is, in spirit and in substance, homogeneous with the Digressions of the *Tale*, while the *Battle of the Books* is more independent. But each of them treats in its own fashion what may be called (with reservations) the two main themes of the *Tale*: the suspect origins of all inspiration, and particularly of religious 'enthusiasm', and the asininity of modern criticism. The volume therefore as a whole is a unity, of a sort. There is no more discrepancy between the subordinate pieces and the main one, than there is between the various parts of the *Tale* itself.

What we have called the two themes are rather two threads on which an immense comic embroidery is woven. The distinctive quality of the whole volume is a unique exuberance of comic invention. The injunction Swift had given to the poet —

> Beat not the paths that dirty feet have trod
> But give the vigorous fancy room —

he himself now obeyed with gusto in prose. The total result is a comic masterpiece.

It has been generally supposed that Swift's mind was turned towards making fun of Nonconformist 'enthusiasm' by his experience of the Presbyterians while he was at Kilroot in 1695-6; and it has been objected to this theory that the Scottish Presbyterians were not conspicuous for 'enthusiasm'.

It is a mistake in proportion to press either the theory or the objection. Swift's animus against Presbyterianism was conceived long before he went to Kilroot. In his ode *To the King* he had called the Scots

> That discontented brood
> Who always loudest for Religion bawl
> (As those still do wh'have none at all).

The attitude really springs from his identification of himself with the Cavaliers — and in particular with his grandfather, the sturdy vicar of Goodrich — in their struggle against the Roundheads. The Scottish Presbyterians were the villains of that piece; and Swift never cared to make nice distinctions between Presbyterians and Independents. He knew his *Hudibras* by heart; and that was good enough for him.

But it is unreasonable to conclude that, because Jack in *A Tale of a Tub* is not even a credible caricature of the Presbyterians who irritated him at Kilroot, Swift's experience of them there cannot have set his comic genius in motion against the 'enthusiasts'. It is quite likely that the Presbyterians of Kilroot released the trigger. Anyhow, the story of Peter and Martin and Jack is obviously the first stratum of *A Tale of a Tub*; almost certainly it was written while he was at Kilroot; and, however unlike the typical Scots Presbyterian Jack may be, Scotland is represented in the *Tale* as the original home of religious 'enthusiasm' and the source whence it is constantly replenished. The *sylva Caledonia*, especially when decaying, is the timber most highly esteemed for the manufacture of preaching-tubs; from Σκοτία, the land of darkness, the zealous among the Æolist priesthood have brought their choicest inspiration in every age; and even when they are in their pulpits a continuance of the fundamental inspiration from the North is mechanically assured.

2

The second main thread derives from Swift's championship of Temple in the controversy of Ancients and Moderns. Temple's original *Essay on Ancient and Modern Learning* was published in 1690. Though fanciful and opinionated in parts, it was a serious indictment of the intellectual pride of the Moderns. Their boasted achievements in natural philosophy, or science, had only diverted them from man's primary concern: namely, the discovery of a true moral philosophy, in which the achievement of the Ancients was far superior to theirs. But even here the Ancients were modest: they went humbly to seek wisdom from Egypt and the East. Temple's high praise of the civilization of India and China, for possessing a stability based upon a sound moral philosophy, is remarkable for his time. His main purpose is to refute the complacent assumption that the Moderns have all that the Ancients had, plus their own discoveries. He says, first, that there is no such automatic progress: civilization is, and always has been, exposed to catastrophe and retrogression, and much of what the Ancients themselves had is now lost; second, that there have been periods of manifest decay, for example, of language, on which the power of intellectual conception depends; thirdly, that much of the renewed energy of mind which had certainly followed the revival of learning had been wasted in futile theological disputation; and, fourthly, that even indisputable modern improvements, such as that of navigation by the invention of the compass, have produced only a beggarly increase of real knowledge, owing to commercial avarice. There ought to have been a notable revolution in geographical science; it has been frustrated by the concentration on the profits of trade. Still worse, the barbarous behaviour of Europeans towards the ancient civilizations of the East has destroyed the possibility of beneficent intellectual contact with them.

The influence of Macaulay persists; and it is still customary to dismiss Temple's essay as dilettantism. In fact, it is singularly enlightened, and in some respects, prophetic. Temple, in spite of his occasional extravagance, is to be reckoned one of the earliest and most penetrating critics of the nascent dogma of automatic progress. The only progress that matters, he says again and again, is progress in morality. Are the Moderns really superior to the Ancients in this? The influence of this radical questioning on Swift was great and permanent.

But, in the course of his essay, Temple had made one mistake, and committed one positive blunder. Compared to the main weight of his argument, they were trivial; but they laid him open to attack. He had been rather contemptuous of the modern scientific movement; and he had declared for the antiquity of Æsop and the excellence and the authenticity of the Epistles of Phalaris, against the opinion of 'several learned men (or that usually pass for such, under the name of critics)' that they were not genuine. On the first point, the Rev. William Wotton made a civil and reasoned reply, *Reflections on Ancient & Modern Learning*, in the 18th volume of the *Philosophical Transactions* of the Royal Society, of which Wotton was a fellow. This was in January, 1695. In the meantime, stimulated by Temple's high praise of Phalaris (whom he had bracketed with Æsop as the most ancient of profane authors and the best of their kind) the authorities of Christ Church, Oxford, encouraged one of their younger members, Charles Boyle, to produce a new edition of the *Epistles*. Boyle borrowed a manuscript from the

King's Library, where the famous Bentley was Librarian; and Bentley rudely demanded the return of it before Boyle had finished his collation, on the rather unscholarly ground that when Boyle had done with it, it would be no better than 'a squeezed orange'. Not unjustifiably, in the preface to his new edition, Boyle twitted Bentley for 'his singular humanity'. Bentley in retaliation gave Wotton, who was preparing a second edition of his *Reflections*, a *Dissertation* on the authenticity of Phalaris to be included in his book. In it, Bentley proved decisively enough, from internal evidence, that the *Epistles* were a late production and could not have been written by their supposed author.

3

The second edition of Wotton's *Reflections*, strengthened by Bentley's *Dissertation*, appeared in June, 1697. In the following March the Christ Church men replied in *Dr. Bentley's Dissertation examin'd by the Hon. Charles Boyle Esq.* — a clever attack written mainly by Atterbury. Swift was back at Moor Park, and acting as Temple's confidential and trusted secretary. Now he weighed in, but not as a serious participant in the controversy. In his fecund and irreverent mind Wotton and Bentley were joined together as types of pedantry and criticism; and so they are represented, in *The Battle of the Books*, as spitted together by Boyle's lance, after Bentley had stolen the armour of Phalaris and Æsop from them in their sleep.

> As when a skilful cook has trussed a brace of woodcocks, he, with iron skewer, pierces the tender sides of both, their legs and wings close pinioned to the ribs; so was this pair of friends transfixed, till down they fell, joined in their deaths, so closely joined, that Charon would mistake them both for one, and waft them over Styx for half his fare. Farewell, beloved loving pair! Few equals have you left behind: and happy and immortal shall you be, if all my wit and eloquence can make you.[1]

The Battle of the Books is a delightful fantasia, mainly in the form of a burlesque of Homer. Bentley appears as a sort of Thersites, with Wotton as his young and beloved friend. Wotton is also the son and darling of the hideous goddess, Criticism, who is herself the offspring of Pride and Ignorance. Her function in the battle is limited to helping Bentley and Wotton, in vain. The conception of this goddess is based upon the first page of Temple's essay, where he says the occasion of his writing was his irritation at the complacency of two books praising modern writing at the expense of the classics.

I could not read either of these strains without some indignation, which no quality in men is so apt to raise in me as sufficiency, the worst composition out of the pride and ignorance of mankind.[2]

The hint for the famous episode of the bee and the spider, which actually precipitates the battle of the books, seems also to have come from a passage in Temple's essay *On Poetry*, in which he says that formal critical rules, such as the modern critics attempt to impose, are alien to the genius of poetry.

'Tis as if, to make excellent honey you should cut off the wings of your bees, confine them to their hives or their stands, and lay flowers before them, such as you think the sweetest, and like to yield the finest extraction; you had as good pull out their stings and make arrant drones of them. They must range through fields as well as gardens, choose such flowers as they please, and by proprieties and scents which they only can distinguish . . . [3]

One more step — a big one, no doubt — and the spider comes in as the symbol of criticism, atrabilious and enviously hostile to the free-ranging creativity represented by the bee.

It is manifest that Swift's main purpose in *The Battle of the Books* is not to come to the rescue of Temple (who did not need it), and still less to make a contribution to the controversy (which had now become irrelevant to Temple's real thesis), but to make fun of Wotton and Bentley and Dryden and anybody else who comes into his head — not wholly excluding Homer himself. Swift wants to enjoy himself, to give full rein to the *vis comica* bubbling up within him. Certainly, his sympathies, personal and rational, are with Temple; but his antipathies are much more decisive: against Bentley for his pedantry and bad manners, against Wotton for daring to controvert Temple and to defend science, against Dryden for telling him he would never be a poet. But even these antipathies are not deadly; they are necessary to his creation. No one shoots well without a target.

4

The antipathy to the Dissenters to which he gives vent in *The Mechanical Operation of Spirit* is much more a settled conviction. He not only disliked them for what he considered their presumption, but he considered them a danger to ordered society. But here again the comic spirit takes control, from the beginning. In form it is a parody of a communication to the Royal Society. It is, at the same time, a parody of the fashion of writing essays in the form of letters. It is entirely characteristic of Swift at this moment that he should knock down two, or more, Aunt Sallies at once.

And now, sir, having dispatched what I had to say of forms, or of business, let me entreat you will suffer me to proceed upon my subject; and to pardon me, if I make no further use of the epistolary style till I come to conclude.[4]

From the outset it is clear that he has not the faintest intention of attempting any serious investigation of 'enthusiasm'. His opening is magnificent.

'Tis recorded of Mahomet, that, upon a visit he was going to pay in Paradise, he had an offer of several vehicles to conduct him upwards; as fiery chariots, winged horses, and celestial sedans; but he refused them all, and would be borne to Heaven upon nothing but his ass. Now this inclination of Mahomet, as singular as it seems, hath been since taken up by a great number of devout Christians; and doubtless, with very good reason. For, since that Arabian is known to have borrowed a moiety of his religious system from the Christian faith; it is but just he should pay reprisals to such as would challenge them; wherein the good people of England, to do them all right, have not been backward. For though there is not any other nation in the world so plentifully provided with carriages for that journey, either as to safety or ease, yet there are abundance of us who will not be satisfied with any other machine but this of Mahomet. For my own part, I must confess to bear a very singular respect to this animal, by whom I take human nature to be most admirably held forth in all its qualities, as well as operations: and therefore, whatever in my small reading occurs, concerning this our fellow-creature, I do never fail to set it down by way of commonplace; and when I have occasion to write upon human reason, politics, eloquence, or knowledge; I lay my memorandums before me, and insert them with a wonderful facility of application. However, among all the qualifications ascribed to this distinguished brute, by ancient or modern authors; I cannot remember this talent of bearing his rider to Heaven has been recorded for part of his character, except in the two examples mentioned already; therefore I conceive the methods of this art to be a point of useful knowledge in very few hands, and which the learned world would gladly be better informed in. This is what I have undertaken to perform in the following discourse.[5]

To avoid offending anybody, he continues, he will abandon speaking directly and make use of allegory. For the future, instead of ass he will speak of gifted and enlightened teacher, and for the word rider will be substituted fanatic auditory, or the like.

The effrontery is colossal. It is hardly reasonable even to attempt to take what follows such a prelude seriously. At the critical moment, when Swift pretends he is about to describe the whole process of the mechanical operation of spirit, there is a galaxy of asterisks — a favourite technique of his at this moment; and though he occasionally employs the outward apparatus of logical argument, the substance of it is designedly ridiculous. For example, he elaborately sets out the grounds of 'the dangerous objection' that the spirit cannot possibly enter into a gathering of modern saints. This is based (he says) on the account of the conditions of the descent of the spirit in Acts II. First, the apostles were gathered together with one accord, in one place. No two conventicles, nor any two heads in the same conventicle, were ever in accord. Second, they received the gift of speaking different languages. Modern saints do not understand their own. Third, the modern artists industriously cover their heads, and thus exclude all approaches of the spirit; whereas it is obvious 'that the *Cloven Tongues* never sat on the apostles' heads while their hats were on'. The objection, he concludes, would be valid, if the spirit were a supernatural assistance, approaching from without; but the spirit in the modern saints proceeds entirely from within. Therefore the objection cannot be allowed.

It is all palpably ridiculous, and was meant to be. Moreover, one has the impression that Swift cannot refrain from guying the account of the spirit in the Acts. *C'est le bout de l'oreille qui perce.* And that impression of irresistible irreverence is strengthened as we read on. First, by his discussion of the travellers' story that 'the wild Indians' worship the devil, where we worship God. Some, he says, object to this and believe that all nations whatsoever worship the true God.

> Others, again, inform us that those idolators adore two principles: the principle of good, and that of evil; which indeed I am apt to look upon as the most universal notion that mankind, by the mere light of nature, ever entertained of things invisible. How this idea hath been managed by the Indians and us, and with what advantage to the understandings of either, may deserve well to be examined. To me the difference appears little more than this, that they are put oftener upon their knees by their fears, and we by our desires; that the former set them a-praying, and us a-cursing.[6]

What is wholly estimable is that the Indians keep their deities separate. Not so we who, by our reasoning, extend the dominion of the good power, and contract that of the evil one. We exalt the good, and degrade the evil into a figure of fun. And then we gravely debate whether such and such influences and passions proceed from the evil spirit or the good: as in the case before us. For the past hundred years it has been evenly disputed whether the cant of our English enthusiastic preachers is due to possession or inspiration. The dispute is quite idle.

> For, I think, it is in life as in tragedy, where it is held a conviction of great defect, both in order and invention, to interpose the assistance of præternatural power, without an absolute and last necessity . . . Who that sees a little paltry mortal, droning, and dreaming, and drivelling to a multitude, can think it agreeable to common good sense, that either Heaven or Hell should be put to the trouble of influence or inspection, upon what he is about?[7]

What, if anything, remains of the Christian religion at the end of that disquisition is a question. The residue is not considerable.

Yet again, when Swift comes to his final thesis, which may have a grain of serious intention, that the natural origin of religious enthusiasm is sexual, and that, mere artifice apart, it is the effect of what would now be called a sublimation of physical desire, his language, and presumably his thought, are such as would scandalize the pious Christian.

> I am apt to imagine, that the seed or principle which has ever put men upon visions in things invisible, is of a corporeal nature; for the profounder chemists inform us, that the strongest spirits may be extracted from human flesh. Besides, the spinal marrow being nothing else but a continuation of the brain, must needs create a very free communication between the superior faculties and those below: and thus the *thorn in the flesh* serves for a spur to the spirit.[8]

This cannot be merely a careless fling that strikes St. Paul by accident. Swift must have aimed it.

5

The Mechanical Operation of Spirit is much more closely related to *A Tale of a Tub* than is *The Battle of the Books*, both in substance and in spirit. The *Battle* is a brilliant *jeu d'esprit* on a limited theme, whereas *The Mechanical Operation of Spirit* is homogeneous with *A Tale of a Tub*, and is an expression of the free-ranging comic spirit for which nothing is sacred; and it is also a further elaboration of a theme which is treated in the same fashion in the *Tale* — namely, the sexual origin of religious 'enthusiasm'.

Swift may have taken a hint for the subject, though not for the manner, of his pseudo-scientific investigation from a passing remark in Temple's essay *On Poetry*.

And I am sorry the natural history, or account of fascination, has not employed the pen of some person of such excellent wit, and deep thought and learning, as *Casaubon*, who writ that curious and useful Treatise of *Enthusiasm*, and by it discovered the hidden or mistaken sources of that delusion, so frequent in all regions and religions of the world, and which had so fatally spread over our country in that age in which this treatise was so seasonably published. [Meric Casaubon's *Treatise on Enthusiasm* was published in 1655.] 'Tis much to be lamented that he lived not to complete that work in the second part he promised; or that his friends neglected the publishing of it, if it were left in papers, though loose and unfinished. I think a clear account of enthusiasm and fascination, from their natural causes, would very much deserve from mankind in general, as well as from the commonwealth of learning; might perhaps prevent many publick disorders, and save the lives of many innocent, deluded or deluding people, who suffer so frequently on account of witches and wizards.[9]

But a more potent hint probably came from Andrew Marvell's *The Rehearsal Transprosed*. This witty running attack on Parker, afterwards the time-serving Bishop of Oxford, Swift confessed, in his *Apology*, to having read and admired: a confession greatly to his credit, for not only was *The Rehearsal Transprosed* a defence of the Dissenters against a venomous attack from a High Churchman, but it might have provided Wotton with a little evidence for his criticism that *A Tale of a Tub* was not wholly original. Marvell may have helped Swift to his title, and more.

The title, now dulled by familiarity, is very witty. It was a conflation, into one pungent phrase, of three elements. First, a tale of a tub was an old proverbial expression (used by Sir Thomas More and Ben Jonson) for a cock and bull story; second, a tub was the cavalier slang for a dissenting preacher's pulpit; third, as Swift put it in his Preface, 'seamen have a custom, when they meet a whale, to fling him out an empty tub by way of amusement, to divert him from laying violent hands upon the ship.'

One cannot say, definitely, that Swift got this last notion from Marvell; but it seems likely that he did, and that Marvell himself got it first-hand from the whale-fishers: for he was a native of, and M.P. for Hull, the centre of the Greenland fishery. In *The Rehearsal Transprosed* he writes, against Parker.

From this of the Anabaptists, he falls as severely upon the word 'unhoopable', which I, it seems, used in representing his 'unlimited' etc. But whereas I only threw it out like an empty cask to amuse him, knowing that I had a whale to deal with, and lest he should overset me, he runs away with it as a very serious business, and so moils himself with tumbling and tossing it, that he is in danger of melting his spermaceti.[10]

The figure, as Marvell used it, is vivid and memorable. Further on in the book, Marvell makes the following quotation from Parker.

It were an easy task for a man that understands the anatomy of the brain, the structure of the spleen and hypochondria, the divarications of the nerves, their twisting about the veins and arteries, and the sympathy of the parts, to give as certain and mechanical account of all its fanatic freaks and phrenzies as of any vital or animal function in the body. The philosophy of a fanatic being as intelligible by the laws of mechanism, as the motion of the heart and circulation of the blood, and there are some treatises that give a more exact and consistent hypothesis of enthusiasm than any Descartes has given of the natural results of matter and motion.

On which Marvell comments:

'Tis very well said, and what was to be expected from one as you, of whose philosophy and religion the mechanism is so visible in the *Tentamina*, concerning that sophism of nature, and the *vehemens et effrenata coitus cupiditas et exquisitissima voluptas*.[11]

The *Tentamina* was Parker's treatise. And Marvell was retorting that the origins of Parker's religion were obviously sexual. Swift may have taken both hints and combined them in *The Mechanical Operation*. Marvell might have been surprised to find that the arrows he had shot against the High Churchman had been picked up and shot against the Dissenter.

6

But these, though not without interest, are unessential affiliations. *A Tale of a Tub* is, in every important sense, completely original, as Swift claimed it was. It is an outpouring of the comic spirit, which, when it is in full career, recognizes no *tabus* and makes a joke of everything. Perhaps the greatest masters of this comic spirit are Aristophanes and Rabelais. A German critic has described Aristophanes as inspired by the *Weltvernichtungsidee*: the idea of world-annihilation. For the comic spirit, any cosmos is an illusion to be shattered; but — this is the point — to be shattered gaily, not desperately, with an exuberance of high spirits, and almost with the suggestion that the same force of genius which destroys the existing cosmos might easily create another and a better (as perhaps Shakespeare did). In a real sense this comic spirit is orgiastic; and in its Attic origins it is supposed literally to have been.

It expresses itself in an intellectual Saturnalia; it is ribald and utterly irreverent. But its nature is such that it cannot discredit what it makes fun of, because it works by a suspension, not a negation, of the moral judgment. Euripides and Socrates do not really suffer at the hands of Aristophanes. And, in the particular case of *The Mechanical Operation of Spirit*, it is much to be doubted whether Swift himself, in gaily reducing the faculty of 'visions in things invisible' to an effect of tentigo or pruritus, really imagined he was discrediting it. There is singularly little trace of moral reprobation in his comic accumulation of evidence for his ribald thesis; or, for that matter, in his admired conclusion. He is enjoying himself too much.

> Let that be as it will, thus much is certain, that, however spiritual intrigues begin, they generally conclude like all others; they may branch upwards towards heaven, but the root is in the earth. Too intense a contemplation is not the business of flesh and blood; it must, by the necessary course of things, in a little time let go its hold, and fall into matter. Lovers for the sake of celestial converse are but another sort of Platonics, who pretend to see stars and heaven in ladies' eyes, and to look or think no lower; but the same pit is provided for both; and they seem a perfect moral to the story of that philosopher, who, while his thoughts and eyes were fixed upon the constellations, found himself seduced by his lower parts into a ditch.[12]

When this elemental comic spirit is at work, it is extraordinarily difficult to say how seriously its detailed manifestations are to be taken. It is difficult, because one has the obstinate feeling that it is irrelevant. Seriousness in this sense of the word is always relative to a cosmos, a moral order, a hierarchy of values; which is precisely what the comic spirit repudiates and overturns. Its specific seriousness lies in itself, in its own total significance. It is the evidence of a metaphysical potentiality, a reminder that any order is precarious: perhaps hardly more than the rules of a game.

The excellence of the comic spirit is that it cannot be domesticated. To imagine that it can be manipulated to serve some particular moral order, is to deceive oneself. It undermines all ostensible reservations. Perhaps Shakespeare came as near as anybody who has been possessed by it to controlling it, by means of the technique of the drama. He projected the comic spirit; in Falstaff he put forward a character in whom it was embodied; but the consequence is that Falstaff, as we say, runs away with the play. So it was in his earlier experiment with a truly comic character; Faulconbridge very nearly runs away with *King John*. In both cases for the simple reason that a hierarchy of values cannot be maintained in the presence of the comic spirit.

Hence it is that Swift never wrote anything more patently absurd than when, in 1709, he attempted to excuse *A Tale of a Tub*, as a service done to the Church of England.

> Why should any clergyman of our church be angry to see the follies of fanaticism and superstition exposed, though in the most ridiculous manner; since that is perhaps the most probable way to cure them, or at least to hinder them from further spreading? Besides, though it was not intended for their perusal, it rallies nothing but what they preach against. It contains nothing to provoke them, by the least scurrility upon their persons or their functions. It celebrates the Church of England, as the most perfect of all others, in discipline and doctrine; it advances no opinion they reject, nor condemns any they receive.[13]

Swift must have known that this was futile. The plain fact is that Martin. who represents the Church of England in the story which is the first stratum of the book, is a nonentity even in his own specific context. He has no dramatic reality beyond that he picks out the stitches of the lace on his coat instead of tearing it off; otherwise, he is simply a negation — not-Jack and not-Peter. But that is a minor matter. The more important substance of *A Tale of a Tub* is in the Digressions, where the comic spirit works without even the slight restraint of a story, and they leave precious little room for religion of any kind. If *A Tale of a Tub* was to be of service to the Church of England, it could only be by indirect crooked ways, as Swift had the candour to admit to Stella, at the moment when Harley first received him,

> They may talk of the *you know what*; but, gad, if it had not been for that, I should never have been able to get the access I have had; and if that helps me to succeed, then that same thing will be serviceable to the Church. (October 7, 1710)

Nor could any figure be more apt than that under which Swift represented the royal reception of his book in *Gulliver's Travels*, where the Empress of Lilliput is mortally offended at Gulliver's putting out the fire in her apartments by pissing on it. The offence taken was natural enough; for the stink must have lingered long. And there is an all-pervading odour in the *Tale*, which is certainly not the odour of sanctity.

Presumably, the Digressions of the *Tale* were written either simultaneously with, or immediately after *The Mechanical Operation*, for there are several themes in the lesser work which appear to be taken up and elaborated, in the same vein, in the greater. Since *The Mechanical Operation* can be assigned to 1697 on internal evidence, Swift must have been working on the *Tale* in that year and the next.[14] And the earlier work gives us a glimpse of one of his methods. A passage already quoted shows him diligently and gaily accumulating from a various reading in the classics all the references to asses that he could find. 'And when I have occasion to write on human reason, politics, eloquence, or knowledge; I lay my memorandums before me, and insert them with a wonderful facility of application.' They were not really used for the enthusiastic preacher, but they were turned on to the critics in the first Digression of the *Tale*. The ancients (he says) were so afraid of this terrible tribe, that they did not dare to treat them except figuratively. How he came to discover the secret was that, having been convinced, by Mr. Wotton in particular, of the manifest superiority of the Moderns over the Ancients, he reflected that the Ancients must needs have been conscious of their many imperfections and 'have endeavoured, from some passages in their works, to obviate, soften or divert the censorious reader, by satire, or panegyric upon the critics, in imitation of their masters, the moderns' (which is, of course, the ostensible purpose of his own Digression). Accordingly, he explored the Ancients and found them describing the critic under the constant hieroglyph of the Ass, though eventually they were compelled to abandon it, 'as too nearly approaching the prototype' and to invent even more 'cautious and mystical' terms.

It is all admirable fooling, but serious only in the sense that Swift did seriously believe that most critics were asses; the professionals portentous and pedantic asses, and the amateurs (whom he had anatomized in his verses *To Congreve*) pert and ignorant ones. But if Swift's contempt of critics is to be described as the theme of the first Digression, it must be with the qualification that the variations are, in intention and effect, vastly more important than the theme. And so it is with all the Digressions, which become thicker and thicker as the *Tale* advances, until the story of the three brothers is completely buried under them. By the time he gets to Section VII, a Digression in praise of Digressions, the original story is virtually abandoned. Section VIII, which purports to continue it, does nothing of the kind, and is simply yet another Digression about Æolism, or inspiration by Wind. This is followed by a Digression on Madness, and this by A Farther Digression. The story is not resumed until Section XI, and then only to vanish into a hiatus, a subordinate digression on Ears, and an indication of what the story might have contained if the author had not unfortunately lost his papers. Then comes the serio-comic Conclusion: serious again, in the restricted sense, in that he probably had nothing more to say, and had used up his common-place book.

I am now trying an experiment very frequent among modern authors; which is to write upon nothing; when the subject is utterly exhausted, to let the pen still move on; by some called the ghost of wit, delighting to walk after the death of its body. And to say the truth, there seems to be no part of knowledge in fewer hands, than that of discerning when to have done . . . But now, since, by the liberty and encouragement of the press,[15] I am grown absolute master of the occasions and opportunities to expose the talents I have acquired, I already discover, that the issues of my *observanda* begin to grow too large for the receipts. Therefore, I shall here pause awhile, till I find, by feeling the world's pulse and my own, that it will be of absolute necessity for us both to resume my pen.[16]

CHAPTER VI

THE TROGLODYTE PHILOSOPHER

SUCH being the conception and execution of *A Tale of a Tub*, it is a question whether it is at all legitimate to scrutinize it narrowly for evidences of some fundamental philosophy. Assuredly, any attempt to do so is in danger of losing proportion and turning into pedantry. Thus, for example, critics have discovered and made much of a radical scepticism in the Digression on Madness. If that Digression is to be interpreted literally, radical scepticism is there; but whether this gives any warrant for concluding that this was Swift's considered philosophy at this moment in his life is a very different matter. Radical scepticism, of a sort, is inherent in the comic spirit; it is the condition on which it works. But the comic spirit is, essentially and distinctively, genial; and serious scepticism is not. The distinction is important: the more important because it is not amenable to precise definition. Modern criticism (which may be in need of a modern *Tale of a Tub*) is avid of precise definitions; and this avidity easily leads it to ignore the difference in kind between comic and serious scepticism. In the case of Swift the danger is peculiarly great, because in later life a serious scepticism took increasing hold of him; and one may easily be misled, by taking *A Tale of a Tub* too literally and out of its comic ambience, into supposing that this was his attitude from the beginning.

The *Tale* is, primarily, a manifestation of the comic spirit. Its dominant temper is genial, not savage, exuberant, not destructive. It is a glorious riot of intellectual slapstick. If Swift has his *bêtes noires* — Dissenters, critics, Papists, pedants, virtuosos and Dryden — no one ever thought any the worse of them in consequence of this treatment. There is no hatred, no ferocity; but there is unlimited disrespect. Peter and Jack are comic figures: they would be a roaring success in a puppet-show. Precisely because Martin has to be treated with some respect, to save appearances, he fades into insignificance. But the Church of England itself does not escape. In the Digression on Madness, when Swift invokes four Tory M.P.s — he was at this time a Whig of a sort — to move for a bill to appoint commissioners for the academy of Bedlam who shall choose the appropriate inmates for high employments, no one is at a loss to read his diplomatic asterisks. The commissioners are

> To send for persons, papers and records, to examine into the merits and qualifications of every student and professor, to observe with utmost

exactness their several dispositions and behaviour, by which means, duly distinguishing and adapting their talents, they might produce admirable instruments for the several offices in a state, * * * * *, civil and military.[1]

The missing word is 'religious'. And the Digression ends on the same note. After distinguishing the appropriate Bedlamites for army officers, for lawyers, for city magnates, for ministers of state, and physicians, he concludes:

Another student struts up fiercely to your teeth, puffing with his lips, half squeezing out his eyes, and very graciously holds you out his hand to kiss. The keeper desires you not to be afraid of this professor ... to him alone is allowed the liberty of the ante-chamber, and the orator of the place gives you to understand that this solemn person is a tailor run mad with pride. This considerable student is adorned with many other qualities, upon which at present I shall not farther enlarge . . . . . . Hark in your ear . . . . . . I am strangely mistaken, if all his address, his motions, and his airs would not then be very natural, and in their proper element.[2]

The missing word is 'bishop'. Not that Swift had any particular animus against them yet, or that he was not serious in regarding episcopal government as necessary to a Christian Church. It is simply that the disrespect felt by the comic spirit is universal in its scope.

2

Since the Digression on Madness is the one upon which the philosophical interpreters of the *Tale* most intently focus their microscopes, we may give an account of it.

Swift begins by saying that it is no derogation to Æolism (that is, the cult of inspiration by Wind) that Jack, its chief prophet, had had 'his intellectuals overturned'. For the greatest achievements of individual men in history, namely, the conquest of new empires, the creation of new schemes of philosophy, and the foundation of new religions, have all been performed by persons 'whose natural reason had admitted great revolutions'. The source of the inspiration is indifferent, provided it is substantially Æolic and reaches the brain in the form of vapour.

He will give examples. First of empires: Harry the Great of France made vast preparations for war. The world, not knowing against whom it was intended, was in alarm. A state-surgeon diagnosed the disease, and broke the bag of vapour, and the operation would have been entirely successful if the patient had not died under it.

It was afterwards discovered, that the movement of this whole machine had been directed by an absent female, whose eyes had raised a protuberancy, and, before emission, she was removed into an enemy's country . . . Having to no purpose used all peaceable endeavours, the collected part of the semen, raised and inflamed, became adust, converted to choler, turned head upon the spinal duct and ascended to the brain. The very same principle that influences a bully to break the windows of a whore who has jilted him, naturally stirs up a great prince to raise mighty armies, and dream of nothing but sieges, battles and victories.[3]*

(A note explains that this refers to the assassination of Henri Quatre by Ravaillac.) Conversely, in the case of Louis XIV. He amused himself for thirty years in ravaging Europe. Finally the vapour which animated the hero's brain, in the course of its incessant circulation, settled upon his backside, where it formed a tumour; and the world was left in peace.

Of such mighty consequence it is where those exhalations fix, and of so little from whence they proceed. The same spirits, which, in their superior progress, would conquer a kingdom, descending upon the anus, conclude in a fistula.[5]

Next, the philosophers. Whence arises their disposition to advance new systems 'in things agreed on all hands impossible to be known'? They are generally admitted, except by their immediate disciples, to have been crazed: quite rightly.

For what man, in the natural state or course of thinking, did ever conceive it in his power to reduce the notions of all mankind exactly to the same length, and breadth, and height of his own? Yet this is the first humble and civil design of all innovators in the empire of reason.[6]

It is not possible to account for this phenomenon except by vapours. The reason why the philosophers never fail of disciples is that the strings of human understanding are tuned to different pitches, and those which are of the same pitch as his own respond to the emissions of the philosopher.

* This may be compared with a passage from an early essay of Temple, *The Force of Custome*. 'The same passion which makes me give my servant a box on the ear, makes a *Grand Signior* cause a *Bashaw* to be strangled, or one of his Captains to be impaled. The same lust, spleen, or caprice in pursuit of which I would now lavish away my private fortune, were I a King, would wage wars, make leagues, entertain favourites, profuse my treasures to accomplish: the injustice is, that what is private passion in us, in Princes appears to be public interest, state policy, and grand occasions, nay, where there is no appearance of these, we will rather believe ourselves to be blind than them to be made as other men are.'[4]

And in this one circumstance lies all the skill or luck of the matter; for if you chance to jar the string among those who are either above or below your own height, instead of subscribing to your doctrine, they will tie you fast, call you mad and feed you with bread and water. It is therefore a point of the nicest conduct, to distinguish and adapt this noble talent with respect to the differences of persons and times ... For to speak a bold truth, it is a fatal miscarriage so ill to order affairs, as to pass for a fool in one company, when, in another, you might be treated as a philosopher.[7]

This was Mr. Wotton's fatal mistake.

Lastly, the religious innovators. It is evident on inspection of the history of enthusiasm that without the help of a tincture of this vapour which the world calls madness, 'the world would not only be deprived of those two great blessings, conquests and systems, but even all mankind would unhappily be reduced to the same belief in things invisible'. But the problem is to determine what are the differences in the brain which produce from the same vapour such vastly different effects as Alexander the Great, Monsieur Descartes, and Jack of Leyden.

The present argument is the most abstracted that ever I engaged in; it strains my faculties to their highest pitch; and I desire the reader to attend with the utmost perpensity, for I now proceed to unravel this knotty point.
There in in mankind a certain   *   *   *   *   *
*   *   *   *   *   *   *   *   *
Hic multa desiderantur   *   *   *   *   *   *
*   *   *   *   *   *   *   *   *
*   *   And this I take to be a clear solution of the matter.[8]

Although the greater part of the comic extravagance is necessarily lost in such a summary, the spirit of the whole of this first part of the Digression is manifest. It is not possible to take it seriously, except at our peril. How then can we be justified in regarding the still more famous passage which follows as the expression of a considered philosophy?

3

From his minute investigation (represented by the asterisks) it will now be agreed, he says, that madness is the parent of all mighty revolutions in empire, philosophy, and religion.

For the brain, in its natural position and state of serenity, disposeth its owner to pass his life in the common forms, without any thoughts of subduing multitudes to his own power, his reasons, or his visions; and the more he shapes his understanding by the pattern of human learning, the less he is inclined to form parties, after his particular notions, because that instructs him in his private infirmities, as well as in the stubborn ignorance of the people. But when a man's fancy gets astride on his reason; when imagination is at cuffs with the senses, and common understanding, as well as common sense, is kicked out of doors; the first proselyte he makes is himself; and when that is once compassed, the difficulty is not so great in bringing over others: a strong delusion always operating from without as vigorously as from within.[9]

Granted it sounds a little more serious than what has gone before, must we not remember that the imaginary author of the whole Digression is, avowedly, an ex-member of the honourable society of Bedlam; and that it concludes with a proof positive of his contention that Bedlamites are fitted for the highest offices in society?

Which, I think, is manifest from what I have already shown, and shall enforce by this one plain instance, that even I myself, the author of these momentous truths, am a person whose imaginations are hardmouthed, and exceedingly disposed to run away with his reason, which I have observed, from long experience, to be a very light rider, and easily shook off; upon which account, my friends will never trust me alone, without a solemn promise to vent my speculations in this, or the like manner, for the universal benefit of human kind.[10]

Wheels within wheels, no doubt. Or, if you prefer it, a vicious circle: a madman anatomizing madness. But this is essential to the pattern of the whole Digression: that it is, itself, an example of what happens 'when a man's fancy gets astride on his reason . . . and common understanding as well as common sense is kicked out of doors' — with, of course, one mighty difference, that behind the imaginary ex-Bedlamite is Swift, who created him to be the instrument of his universal irreverence. Swift knows perfectly well what he is doing in using this vehicle of irresponsibility. But to pick and choose among the utterances of the Bedlamite philosopher — to say this is nonsense, and that is the authentic opinion of Swift in person, is an arbitrary and dangerous proceeding. Swift's alibi is impregnable.

With this comprehensive caution we may examine his investigation of happiness. He has said that once a man has converted himself to a delusion it is easy to bring over others: 'for cant and vision are to the ear and eye the same that tickling is to the touch', and the pleasures we most value in life are 'such as dupe and play the wag with the senses'.[11] Happiness, we find, both in relation to the understanding and the senses, consists in 'a perpetual possession of being well deceived'. As for the understanding, 'it is manifest what mighty advantages fiction has over truth'; and man has the right to prefer the former, because things past are no more real than things conceived. As for the senses, the definition of happiness is obviously appropriate. Without delusion all objects would be insipid and faded.

> So that if it were not for the assistance of artificial mediums, false lights, refracted angles, varnish and tinsel, there would be a mighty level in the felicity and enjoyments of mortal men. If this were seriously considered by the world, as I have a certain reason to suspect it hardly will, men would no longer reckon among their high points of wisdom, the art of exposing weak sides, and publishing infirmities. . . .
> In the proportion that credulity is a more peaceful possession of the mind than curiosity; so far preferable is that wisdom, which converses about the surface, to that pretended philosophy, which enters into the depth of things, and then comes gravely back with the informations and discoveries that in the inside they are good for nothing.[12]

Sight and touch are content with outsides; but then comes reason, with tools for cutting and opening, and offers to demonstrate that things are not the same all through. To save all this expensive anatomy, he can assure the reader that reason is in the right.

> In most corporeal beings which have fallen under my cognizance, the outside has been infinitely preferable to the in; whereof I have been farther convinced from some late experiments. Last week I saw a woman flayed, and you will hardly believe how much it altered her person for the worse.[13]

He anatomized a beau with the same result, whence he concluded that the useful philosopher is he who can patch up the flaws in nature rather than he (so fashionable nowadays) who expands and exposes them.

> And he whose fortunes and dispositions have placed him in a convenient station to enjoy the fruits of this noble art; he that can, with Epicurus, content his ideas with the films and images that fly off upon his senses from the superficies of things; such a man, truly wise, creams off nature, leaving the sour and the dregs for philosophy and reason to lap up. This is the sublime and refined point of felicity, called the possession of being well deceived; the serene peaceful state, of being a fool among knaves.[14]

Can we reasonably hold that this is anything more than the fooling of genius? Epicurus has previously been dismissed as a madman; now he reappears as the prototype of true wisdom. And it is only by a comic parody of argument that the felicity of being content with outsides becomes equivalent to the serenity of being a fool amongst knaves. It is essentially a comic extravaganza, admirably yeasted up to a sardonic conclusion.

And so it goes on. All madness proceeds from redundancy of vapours: of which some kinds give strength to the sinews, others vigour to the brain. These latter behave like poltergeists in empty houses, which 'either vanish, and carry away a piece of the house, or else stay at home and fling it all out of the windows', by which is foreshadowed the two main branches of madness. (He has now completely dropped his 'theory' that the vapour is indifferent, but the composition of the brain decisive.) It follows that the true skill lies in finding employment for the redundancy of vapour, and adjusting the season of its action. Curtius jumps into a gulf at the right moment, and is a hero; Empedocles mistimes his jump and becomes a by-word. The elder Brutus is usually held to have personated the madman for the good of the commonwealth.

> But this was nothing else than a redundancy of the same vapour long misapplied, called by the Latins, *ingenium par negotiis*; or (to translate it as nearly as I can) a sort of phrenzy, never in its right element, till you take it up in the business of the state.[15]

That is, the elder Brutus was really mad, but his madness was never at ease till he became a statesman. From that the transition is easy to the suggestion that four raging Tories should back a bill to appoint Commissioners — by implication, themselves — for the proper employment of the talents in Bedlam.

The only thing to do with all this is to enjoy it and laugh. To extract a philosophy out of it, or any part of it, is coining moonshine. If you insist, Swift will only make a fool of you. In exactly the same spirit as he here makes out that madness is the qualification for great actions or great office, earlier on he has maintained that the real beings are the clothes.

> 'Tis true indeed that these animals, which are vulgarly called suits of clothes, or dresses, do according to certain compositions, receive different appellations. If one of them be trimmed up with a gold chain, and a red gown, and a white rod, and a great horse, it is called a Lord-Mayor; if certain ermines and furs be placed in a certain position, we call it a Judge; and so an apt combination of lawn and black satin we entitle a Bishop.[16]

You may take your choice. The eminent are either madmen, or suits of clothes. But it is much simpler, and much saner, to realize that it is irreverent nonsense, and delight in it. How irreverent it is may be gathered from the behaviour of Peter, Martin and Jack (who represent the Roman Catholic, the Anglican and the Dissenting Churches) when, after keeping their coats in good order for seven years, in which 'they travelled through several countries, encountered a reasonable quantity of giants, and slew certain dragons', they came up to town and fell in love with the ladies.

> On their first appearance, our three adventurers met with a very bad reception; and soon with great sagacity guessing out the reason, they quickly began to improve in the good qualities of the town: they writ, and rallied, and rhymed, and sung, and said, and said nothing; they drank, and fought, and whored, and slept, and swore, and took snuff; they went to new plays on the first night, haunted the chocolate houses, beat the watch, lay on bulks, and got claps; they bilked hackney-coach-men, ran in debt with shopkeepers, and lay with their wives; they killed bailiffs, kicked fiddlers downstairs, ate at Locket's, loitered at Will's . . . [17]

Is it any wonder that the poor Queen was shocked, or that a humane and tolerant High Church bishop like Smalridge was horrified when the book was ascribed to him?

4

A Tale of a Tub is a comic masterpiece. It was poured forth out of a cornucopia of invention, which Swift either never commanded or never unloosed again. Dr. Johnson had good excuse for being almost incredulous that it was really Swift's. The copiousness of the images, he truly said, is unique in Swift's writing. 'This wild work', he called it; and said of it, fairly enough: 'Of this book charity may be persuaded to think that it might be written by a man of peculiar character without ill intention; but it certainly is of dangerous example.' Dr. Johnson was perturbed by the thought that the author was a priest, and was to become a dignitary of the Church. He would have agreed with the Queen and her spiritual advisers that he was not a man to be preferred.

That may have been a narrow view; but Dr. Johnson did at least recognize that the *Tale* presents us with some problems. Why was it that Swift never indulged this vein again? We cannot easily believe that·it simply left him. He is reported to have been heard saying, in his old age, when he was reading the *Tale* again: 'Good God, what a genius I had when I wrote that book!' He may then have looked back on it as a kind of visitation. When he was much nearer to it, in 1709, he wrote:

The greatest part of that book was finished above thirteen years since, 1696, which is eight years before it was published. The author was then young, his invention at the height, and his reading fresh in his head. By the assistance of some thinking, and much conversation, he had endeavour'd to strip himself of as many real prejudices as he could; I say real ones, because, under the notion of prejudices, he knew to what dangerous heights some men have proceeded. Thus prepared, he thought the numerous and gross corruptions in Religion and Learning might furnish matter for a satire, that would be useful and diverting. He resolved to proceed in a manner that might be altogether new, the world having been already too long nauseated by endless repetitions upon every subject. The abuses in Religion, he proposed to set forth in the Allegory of the Coats, and the three Brothers, which was to make up the body of the discourse. Those in learning, he chose to introduce by way of digressions. He was then a young gentleman much in the world, and wrote to the taste of those who were like himself; therefore, in order to allure them, he gave a liberty to his pen, which might not suit with maturer years, or graver characters, and which he could easily have corrected with a very few blots, had he been master of his papers, for a year or two before their publication.[18]

The excuse at the end was common form, which he had ridiculed in the *Tale* itself. There is no reason to believe that the MS. was not in his control, or that the first publication in 1704 was not arranged by himself; and it is obvious that the *Tale* could have been made respectable only by total emasculation, not by a 'very few' erasures. The prejudices of which he had stripped himself for the occasion were comprehensive; and it is hard to attach much meaning to his distinction between 'real' ones and — what? Basic and necessary beliefs which he retained and respected? It would be difficult to discover them from the *Tale*. He suggests, of course, that one, and the chief, of these was his belief in the Church of England as by law established; and, no doubt, as far as his conscious intention went, he did mean to spare it. But the 'celebration of it as the most perfect of all others in doctrine and discipline' which he claimed to have performed, was ruled out by his methods. The spirit of irreverence was all-pervasive: indeed, a much more potent 'universal pickle' than Lord Peter's — a universal disintegrator. For the difficulty is to imagine what positive, true, and necessary religion could possibly be when Swift has made a bonfire of its 'corruptions'. Visions in things invisible are sexual sublimations; authority in religion is common fraud; new religions are the productions of madmen. There remains presumably the religion that never was new, which is exempt from authority, and innocent of supernatural experience: in a word, that unknown and infinitesimal quantity of it which would remain when 'all mankind was reduced to the same belief in things invisible', and is probably much the same as the famous religion of all reasonable men. Pending that happy day, since the appetite for religion is universal, and since the important thing is to keep it under control, it is necessary, for the peace of society, that in each separate nation, a minimal religion should be established by law, and its profession made a condition of citizenship.

In this gloss on the conception of religion that emerges from the *Tale*, we are departing from our own maxim not to take it seriously as philosophy. But here is one of the problems with which the *Tale* presents us. For there undoubtedly is some relation between his residual non-religious 'religion', which is all that the fiery furnace of the *Tale* leaves behind, and that of which Swift became so bellicose a champion. The only rational possibility in this field which the *Tale* admits is a religion of outward forms and observances, imposed by the authority of the state, as an essential part of the machinery of an orderly society, accepted as such by rational men, with understanding, and by the herd because they must, and because it meets their need for belief. The acceptance of the rational man is perfectly compatible with inward scepticism. This was, in substance, the attitude of Temple himself. In an early work he wrote:

There is no authority but seeming reason able to range opinion under its laws. Therefore methinks it is too magisterial even in matters of religion to impose anything on man's belief. Faith must surely be an inspiration of heaven or an operation of custom, not a work either of force or reason, it being out of both their spheres. To say: These articles, these miracles you must believe, when perhaps I can no more make myself believe them than I can that 3 and 4 make 8, that water will scorch me, that air will drown me, 'tis e'en as much to say, Sir, you have a wry nose, it does not become you by any means, you must lay it aside, and take one straight and well-shap'd; or, you have a grey, hollow eye, leave it off and put in a full black one. Alas, I can do neither. I can, if that will serve the turn, put in a glass eye, put on a false nose, take up a seeming belief, but not a real one. To say you can believe it signifies nothing to me. So perhaps you can see a mile off, when I am purblind, and cannot see an ell.[19]

Faith, Temple says, is either the inspiration of heaven, or the operation of custom. The inspiration of heaven being ruled out, there remains the operation of custom, by which a man does not change the religion he was born and bred in. Whether it engenders or continues faith is highly doubtful; but reason militates against a change, because it knows it can produce nothing in its place.

This is indistinguishable from what Swift calls the consequence of having 'the brain, in its natural position and state of serenity' which 'disposeth its owner to pass his life in the common forms'. Since most of the 'much conversation' which preceded the writing of the *Tale* was conversation with Temple, one may suppose some influence of the older on the younger man. There is a vast difference between the attitude which Swift had proclaimed in his ode *To Sancroft* and this gentle scepticism of Temple's. Partly under its influence, Swift had shed his 'prejudice' that there existed a realm of eternal truth; but a much deeper influence had been his own emotional disappointment, with which was inextricably combined the disappointment at the failure of his own poetic-moral inspiration.

5

Of this crisis, prolonged and completed by the failure of his courtship of Varina, the *Tale* is the outcome. It is the expression of a great and indubitable poetic energy contorted by a complete rejection of the belief in inspiration on which it had previously fed. The energy pours into a creative orgy of apparent negation. The copiousness of images, which astonished Dr. Johnson, is indeed remarkable. Take the description of wisdom.

But the greatest maim given to that general reception which the writings of our society [of Grub Street] have formerly received (next to the transitory state of all sublunary things) has been a superficial vein among many readers of the present age, who will by no means be persuaded to inspect beyond the surface and the rind of things; whereas, wisdom is a fox, who, after long hunting, will at last cost you the pains to dig out. It is a cheese, which, by how much the richer, has the thicker, the homelier, and the coarser coat; and whereof, to a judicious palate, the maggots are the best. It is a sack-posset, wherein the deeper you go, you will find it the sweeter. Wisdom is a hen, whose cackling we must value and consider, because it is attended with an egg; but then lastly, it is a nut, which, unless you choose with judgment, may cost you a tooth, and pay you with nothing but a worm.[20]

The doctrine of the superiority of outsides to insides had not yet made its appearance. Or take the eulogy of indexes.

For, to enter the palace of learning at the great gate, requires an expense of time and forms; therefore men of much haste and little ceremony, are content to get in by the back door. For the arts are all in a flying march, and therefore more easily subdued by attacking them in the rear. Thus physicians discover the state of the whole body, by consulting only what comes from behind. Thus men catch knowledge, by throwing their wit on the posteriors of a book, as boys do sparrows with flinging salt on their tails. Thus human life is best understood, by the wise man's rule of regarding the end. Thus are the sciences found, like Hercules's oxen, by tracing them backwards. Thus are old sciences unravelled, like old stockings, by beginning at the foot.[21]

Or the passage on fame, 'which we mysterious writers can seldom reach, till we have got into our graves'.

Whether it is, that fame, being a fruit grafted on to the body, can hardly grow, and much less ripen, till the stock is in the earth: or whether she be a bird of prey, and is lured among the rest, to pursue after the scent of a carcass: or whether she conceives her trumpet sounds best and farthest when she stands on a tomb, by the advantage of a rising ground, and the echo of a hollow vault.[22]

Or, to take a last example, which may be reminiscent of Swift's personal experience, his account of the antithetical motion of the imagination.

And whereas the mind of a man, when he gives the spur and bridle to his thoughts, doth never stop, but naturally sallies out into both extremes, of high and low, of good and evil; his first flight of fancy commonly transports him to ideas of what is most perfect, finished, and exalted; till, having soared out of his own reach and sight, not well perceiving how near the frontiers of height and depth border upon each other; with the same course and wing, he falls down plumb into the lowest bottom of things, like one who travels the east into the west, or like a straight line drawn by its own length, into a circle. Whether a tincture of malice in our natures makes us fond of furnishing every bright idea with its reverse; or whether reason, reflecting on the sum of things, can, like the sun, serve only to enlighten one half of the globe, leaving the other half by necessity under shade and darkness; or, whether fancy, flying up to the imagination of what is highest and best, becomes overshot, and spent, and weary, and suddenly falls, like a dead bird of paradise, to the ground; or whether, after all these metaphysical conjectures, I have not entirely missed the true reason; the proposition, however, which has stood me in so much circumstance, is altogether true . . . [23]

There is very much more of this kind of thing; it is the most conspicuous single pattern in the detailed texture of the *Tale*: and it can best be described as poetry *à rebours*, and, with that singular qualification, poetry of a very high order. This concept of negative poetry may be a paradox; but it is not a contradiction in terms. The thing exists. There is plenty of it in Aristophanes; Falstaff's speeches are shot with it. And the reason of its existence is, within limits, plain. A universal derision is just as potent an inspiration as a universal wonder; it is indeed only a peculiar form of wonder. The vision of the comic poet also, 'makes strange things familiar, and familiar things strange'.

6

When we set the *Tale* in its place in Swift's writings, and compare it with what had gone before and what was to come after, we cannot repress the feeling that in it he found his truest and richest vein, the completest expression of his genius. The fumblings and approximations of his previous poetry, the perceptible tension between his impulse to admiration and his impulse to denunciation, are resolved, and his creative energy is free of its frustration. The work is triumphant; it breathes confidence and power. Yet it was followed by a long period of relative silence and comparative impoverishment. *Mrs. Frances Harris's Petition* (1701) is an original and admirable piece of comic poetry; *A Discourse of the Contests and Dissensions between the Nobles and Commons in Athens and Rome* (1701) is a useful and competent pamphlet with a political purpose: but these, and a few unimportant verses, are Swift's total known production until *Baucis and Philemon* (1706). The meagreness of this eight years' sequel to such a work as the *Tale* is amazing. Possibly Swift did some anonymous pamphleteering of which we know nothing, for his subsequent insistence on his services to the Whigs is not justified by his known productions. But that cannot substantially alter the case, for the fact that, if it existed, it is indistinguishable, proves that it was undistinguished: hackwork which Swift preferred to forget.

How can this silence be explained? It seems only by a deliberate act of renunciation or repression of his genius. To get what light on this we can we must return to the breach with Temple in 1694 and the events which followed it. If we have read them rightly, the break with Temple was caused by a combination of emotional disappointment and creative frustration. As part of his gesture of complete independence, Swift took orders and resolved to seek a modest career in Ireland. He might almost have said, with Keats, 'Neither Poetry, nor Ambition, nor Love have any alertness of countenance as they pass by me'; with this difference, that to Swift at this moment, Love appeared as a refuge from Poetry and Ambition, and he sought it ardently.

In the meanwhile, his attitude towards Temple had been softened first by his quick and generous response to his 'penitential' letter, and then by his avowal of his need of Swift's services; so that, when Varina galled his just pride by her hesitation to commit herself to him, he was prepared to break with her, and return to Temple. That is to say, he renounced his new life-pattern and returned to his old one; but to the old one with the difference inevitable from the emotional and intellectual upheaval which had gone between. He now saw Temple in proportion; he was now disenchanted of all idealism — in love, and poetry, and religion. And for the time being he experienced a sense of immense liberation; he felt detached, and happy in his detachment, creatively free to be himself.

A symbolic indication of the change which the events of 1694-1696 produced in Swift may be found in his references to his beloved Cave: Mother Ludwell's Cave, to which he now returned to meditate and compose, as before. The last reference to it had been at the topmost pitch of his self-induced poetic enthusiasm, when in the poem *To Congreve* he had at the same time adjured his friend to 'give the vigorous fancy room', and to retire with him to the Cave.

> Far in this primitive cell might we pursue
> Our predecessors' footsteps still in view;
> Here would we sing — But, ah! you think I dream,
> And the bad world may well believe the same;
> Yes, you are all malicious standers by,
> While two fond lovers prate, the Muse and I.[24]

That is the dizziest flight of what we may call Swift's poetic romanticism. The bird of paradise fell dead to the ground. In quite another spirit Swift referred to the Cave three years afterwards in the *Tale.*

Now, it is not well enough considered, to what accidents and occasions the world is indebted for the greatest part of those noble writings, which hourly start up to entertain it. If it were not for a rainy day, a drunken vigil, a fit of the spleen, a course of physic, a sleepy Sunday, an ill run at dice, a long tailor's bill, a beggar's purse, a factious head, a hot sun, costive diet, want of books, and a just contempt of learning — but for these events, I say, and some others too long to recite (especially a prudent neglect of taking brimstone inwardly) I doubt the number of authors and of writings would dwindle away to a degree most woful to behold. To confirm this opinion, hear the words of the famous Troglodyte philosopher: ' 'Tis certain (said he) some grains of folly are of course annexed, as part of the composition of human nature, only the choice is left us, whether we please to wear them inlaid or embossed, and we need not go very far to seek how that is usually determined, when we remember it is with human faculties as with liquors, the lightest will be ever at the top.'[25]

No one has ever explained who the famous Troglodyte philosopher was. His words have been vaguely felt to be Swift's own, and his designation just an odd and inconsequent invention. But when we remember the importance of the Cave, it becomes meaningful enough. The ardent poetic votary, who sought in the Cave the footsteps of Druids and the inspiration of the innocent Muse, is changed into the cave-dwelling philosopher, who having spoken his cynical wisdom concerning the true occasions of inspiration, then assumes his philosophic gown to deliver his conviction that its cause is the element of folly universal in human nature. The only choice man has, is to give it free vent, or to hold it tight within. Natural instinct, for the most part, determines for the former. He, the famous Troglodyte philosopher, has opted for the latter.

Here, if anywhere in the *Tale*, Swift comes near to showing his hand and avowing its origination. It proceeds from the deliberate repression of inspiration, by the constant reduction of the first impulse of imagination to absurdity. And that, in turn, brings us as close as we can get to the substantial theme of the book. It is many things, but more than anything else it is a laughing and unflagging 'debunking' of inspiration. Literary inspiration is continuously caricatured in the character of the ostensible author of the whole narrative, and in his repeated claim to be an *illuminatus* and to write only for the *illuminati*: from the heretic jargon quoted from Irenaeus on the title-page — *Basima eacabasa eanaa irraurista*, and the rest — to the appeal to the initiate reader to 'beware of Bythus and Sigé and be sure not to forget the qualities of Achamoth'. This ostensible author, who is, of course, not the Troglodyte philosopher but his manikin, unlike the real author, wears his folly embossed.

In my disposure of employments of the brain, I have thought fit to make invention the master, and to give method and reason the office of its lackeys. The cause of this distribution was, from observing it my particular case, to be often under a temptation of being witty upon occasions, where I could be neither wise, nor sound, nor anything to the matter in hand. And I am too much a servant of the modern way, to neglect any such opportunities, whatever pains and improprieties I may be at, to introduce them.[26]

Religious inspiration is 'debunked' in Æolism; and inspiration of every kind in the Digression on Madness. But the whole treatise is ostensibly the production of an inspired Bedlamite. So that the 'debunking' is serious only on the superficial level, and on that in appearance only, for though it has the form of argument, the substance is consistently nonsense. In short, Swift's repressed or discarded inspiration utters itself through the inspiration of a madman to blow the gaff, nonsensically, on all inspiration. A wild work, indeed!

7

It is inconceivable that Swift should have worked precisely this vein again. The *Tale* would anyhow have stood as unique and inimitable. Psychologically considered, it is a prolonged whoop of laughter over a dead self: and a man of genius cannot go on repeating that. But the ensuing silence is another matter. And that can be explained only as the effect of a deliberate and imposed renunciation. If we understand the *Tale* as an intellectual orgy to celebrate his emancipation from idealism, or the flinging away of a false self, which, unfortunately for him, was half a true one, we can appreciate that the adjustment to a new persona was not to be easily accomplished. He had scrapped a lot; and though the immediate sense of release was overwhelming, the denuded life had to be lived. Swift was in the condition of an inverted mystic, who had experienced his negative illumination, and now had to plot his course in the world of existence: a difficult undertaking. Religion was discarded, and he was a clergyman; love was discarded, and he was hungry for intimacy and affection; inspiration was discarded, and he was a genius.

Those motions of the soul which call, or tempt, to self-surrender had betrayed him. Self-surrender ended in humiliation, which was not to be endured. That was the irreducible core of reality in himself. 'I, Jonathan Swift, refuse humiliation.'

The attitude is implicit in the *Tale* itself, which is one prodigious alibi for the author of its universal derision. But thought is one world, and life another; thought is unbounded, life is circumscribed by conditions. To be able to refuse humiliation in life one needs to obtain a position, a situation where this is possible. Poverty forbids it. Money, then. Money enough to enable one truly to feel a contempt of it, not to pretend one. But these are the rudiments. To be able to refuse humiliation depends, finally, upon possessing the power to inflict it — to be felt and recognized and treated as a dangerous adversary, one to be conciliated and not provoked, by the great ones of the earth.

Swift had no resources for this enterprise save his own genius. It would call for all his skill. But the same fundamental impulse that drove him to attempt it relieved him of impediments. His reaction to personal and intimate humiliation, by Temple and Varina, had been the resolve never to expose himself again. He was prepared to travel light, to practise an asceticism of invulnerability in his private relations. He had learned to discipline his body by strict diet and arduous exercise in order to combat his physical weakness; it needed little more to make him master of the thorn in the flesh — a manifest humiliation to be refused. The one problem was to discipline his genius to his purposes. No more 'wild work', excellent though it was, in itself and in the satisfaction it had given him. And he would begin the discipline by keeping it to himself, until the time came when it might be launched with advantage. He must contain his universal derision, and channel his genius, to make it serve the great end.

Here, or hereabouts, is the explanation of Swift's silence after *A Tale of a Tub*, and his suppression of that masterpiece for at least six years. It was the purposeful and deliberate renunciation of the full exercise of his genius, while he sharpened it into a tool for his particular ambition, and while he adjusted himself to the conditions of his peculiar struggle for power.

CHAPTER VII

AMONG THE WHIGS: 1700-1703

LORD BERKELEY was a man of fifty when Swift joined him in 1699. He was a short fat man, who had served for five years after the Revolution as Ambassador to Holland with Matthew Prior for Secretary. Swift described him, many years afterwards, as intolerably lazy and indolent, but he did not quarrel with Macky's description of him as a man of learning and parts. His wife was kindly, good-humoured, genuinely religious, a sensible mother, and a careful manager of the straitened family fortunes. They had two sons, one a distinguished naval officer, and three daughters, of whom one, Penelope, died soon after they reached Ireland, but the eldest, Elizabeth, lived to be nearly ninety.

Lady Betty Berkeley was an unspoiled, vivacious, warm-hearted and witty tom-boy of nineteen when Swift joined the family. She made friends with him, and though she afterwards became, like her father, a stout Whig and teased him on his Toryism, she remained friends with him all his life. She was one of the most visible of the many attractive women who move about the fringes of Swift's life; and one of her most endearing characteristics was that she was a loyal friend. In after life she never hesitated to stand up to Swift in defence of any one she knew whom he maligned. In 1706 she married Sir John Germaine, who was reputed the natural son of William III and was thirty years older than she. Miscarriages and illness robbed her of children; but did not alter the gaiety of her temper. Her husband's death, in 1716, left her a very wealthy woman. She valued her freedom, and did not marry again.

Lady Betty teased Swift by calling him Parson Swift; and went on doing it after he had become Doctor Swift. But the relation between them was cordial; they appreciated each other. She long retained in her memory the brilliant verses he wrote just before the Berkeley family left Ireland. *Mrs. Frances Harris's Petition* is one of the wittiest and one of the most entirely charming pieces Swift ever wrote.

> *To their Excellencies the Lords Justices of Ireland*
> *The humble petition of Frances Harris,*
> *Who must starve and die a maid if it miscarries;*
> *Humbly sheweth,*

That I went to warm myself in Lady Betty's chamber, because I was
    cold;
And I had in a purse, seven pound, four shillings and sixpence, besides
    farthings, in money, and gold. . . .[1]

It ripples with humour: but much of the flavour is lost if it is regarded, as it
often is, as a picture of life below stairs. Mrs. Frances Harris was not a
menial; she was one of Lady Berkeley's gentlewomen. In the verses themselves the maids address her as Madam and Lord Berkeley calls her 'Harry'.
There is a picture of her in *A Ballad on the Game of Traffic*, written a year
later, when Swift was with the Berkeleys in England. She is playing cards
with his Lordship and the other gentlewomen, while her Ladyship looks on.
Much of the peculiar humour of her *Petition* derives from the fact that the
gentlewoman is represented as thinking and talking like a cookmaid. An
even wilder misreading of the verses is that which finds in them a reflection
of the subordinate and invidious position of the chaplain in a noble household, because the lowly Mrs. Harris had counted on marrying him, and he
refuses her because she has lost her fortune of £7 4s. 6d. As though Swift,
of all people, if he had been in such a position, would have laughed about it.

Swift was at his ease in the Berkeley household. He was independent;
he had his livings and his prebend, which, even when he had paid his curate
at Laracor, must have left him £250 a year. (Of this, however, he seems to
have paid Stella and Dingley, 'the ladies', £50 a year, as soon as they came
to Ireland.) This was not wealth, but it was very far from poverty in those
days. He remained with the Berkeleys on the footing of friendship. It is
true he did not refrain from having a dig at the solemn confabulations of his
Lordship and Mr. Secretary Bushe in *The Discovery*, but that piece was
obviously written within a few weeks of Berkeley's arrival in Dublin, when
Swift was smarting under imagined ill-treatment and uneasy from a real
uncertainty. As soon as his independence was secure he became light-
hearted and friendly. *The Petition* was written early in 1701, when Berkeley
had been dismissed by the new Tory government, and was preparing to
depart.

Then my dame Wadgar came, and she, you know, is thick of hearing;
Dame, said I as loud as I could bawl, do you know what a loss I have
    had?
Nay, said she, my lord Colway's folks are all very sad,
For my Lord Dromedary comes a Tuesday without fail;
Pugh! said I, but that's not the business that I ail.[2]

Lord Galway was Berkeley's colleague as Lord Justice; and Lord Drogheda one of their successors. The Berkeleys took their dismissal lightly. Swift seems to have accompanied them to England, in April 1701. On this occasion, probably, he arranged that 'the ladies' should settle in Ireland.

2

During the previous two years Swift had not been idle. He had taken his literary executorship to Temple seriously — or perhaps not quite. In 1700 he had published the first two volumes of Temple's *Letters* with a dedication to the King, and in 1701 he published the third part of Temple's *Miscellanea*. The former volumes are remarkable for a number of concise, vigorous and racy translations by Swift of Temple's letters written in French; the latter for his surprising profession of ignorance (in his preface) concerning the occasion of Temple's writing one of the essays contained in it.

> For the third paper, relating to the controversy about Ancient and Modern Learning, I cannot well inform the reader upon what occasion it was writ, having been at that time in another kingdom; but it appears never to have been finished by the author.

That is a strange statement. In any ordinary sense of the word Swift knew well the general occasion of Temple's posthumous essay: 'Some Thoughts on Reviewing the Essay of Ancient and Modern Learning.' Indeed, he knew the particular occasion, too; for it was the publication of Wotton's *Reflections*. One passage in the essay is virtually a summary of the contents of Wotton's book.

> In the meantime, since the modern advocates yield, though very unwillingly, the pre-eminence of the ancients in poetry, oratory, painting, statuary, and architecture; I shall proceed to examine the account they give of those sciences, wherein they affirm the moderns to excel the Ancients; whereof they make the chief to be, the invention of instruments; Chymistry, anatomy; natural history of minerals, plants, and animals; astronomy and optics; music; physic; natural philosophy; philology; and theology: of all of which I shall make a short survey.[3]

This definitely promises an immediate reply to Wotton point by point. But a *hiatus valde deflendus* follows, and Swift writes:

> *Here, it is supposed, the knowledge of the ancients, and moderns in the sciences was to have been compared; but whether the author designed to have gone through such a book himself, or intended these papers only for hints to somebody else who desired them, is not known.*
> *After which the rest was to follow, written in his own hand, as before.*

It is curious, to say the least, that Temple should unconsciously have used the most distinctive literary technique of *A Tale of a Tub*, also in reply to Wotton. Very naturally, when the *Tale* was actually published three years later, in 1704, Wotton smelt a rat in the editing of Temple's essay, and expressed his suspicions in the third edition of his *Reflections* in 1705. He was uncertain whether Jonathan was the author of the *Tale*; he rather inclined to accept the report that Thomas was; but he was certain that it came from one of them, and from Temple's entourage. He asked how Jonathan Swift (if it was Jonathan) *could* have been ignorant of the occasion of Temple's second essay, and whether it *could* have been mere coincidence that Temple had anticipated the peculiar trick of the *Tale*? His questions were never answered, and have been forgotten.

We suspect the rat Wotton smelt was really there, and that Swift interpolated into Temple's essay not only his own editorial note, but also the whole preceding paragraph, summarizing the contents of Wotton's *Reflections*, which gives rise to his comment. If both are omitted, Temple's essay becomes quite consecutive, and there is left no indication that it was 'unfinished'. That is to say, Swift committed a deliberate hoax. If that was the fact, it was a very good joke, indeed, and a highly characteristic one.

3

Lord Berkeley's supersession was due to the advent of a Tory majority in the general election of February 1701. It was out for blood. The first act of the new Parliament was to impeach Somers, Orford, Halifax and Portland, primarily for conniving at King William's second Partition Treaty. The Lords refused the Bill. Berkeley and Swift, both moderate Whigs, discussed the situation; and Swift propounded the thesis, based on his reading of classical history, that impeachment by the Commons was the beginning of a fatal tyranny of the many. The Whig ministers, now assailed by the furious Tories, had only done their duty as the King's servants: the declaration of war and peace was always the royal prerogative. The House of Commons could criticize, and if it insisted, drive out the King's ministers: but to put them on trial for their lives was the beginning of the quick descent to Hell. Berkeley urged Swift to publish his arguments. Swift took the advice. During the summer months he worked on *A Discourse of the Contests and Dissensions between the Nobles and Commons in Athens and Rome, with the Consequences they had upon both those States*. He finished this rather elaborate treatise by the beginning of August; for the last page expresses the hope that 'during the present lucid interval, the members retired to their homes may suspend a while their acquired complexions, and, taught by the calmness of the scene and the season, reassume the native sedateness of their temper.'⁴ The session had ended, with the Commons still pressing the impeachments, in July.

The political foundation of the *Discourse* is the axiom that, although sovereignty is, historically and rationally, inherent in the whole body of the nation, a well-ordered society is governed by a balance of power between King (or the equivalent) and Nobles and Commons. By this means the sovereignty which belongs to the whole nation is operative. History proves that the greatest danger to this balance lies in the encroachment of the Commons, by which it usurps the power that belongs to the whole. This is tyranny of the Many, and leads inevitably to the tyranny of One. The most specific sign of the approach of this tyranny is the establishment of the process of impeachment. The successive ostracism of Miltiades (Orford), Aristides (Somers), Pericles (Halifax), and Phocion (Portland) were so many steps in the downfall of Athens. Such popular verdicts are invariably wrong. The same evil course of continuous encroachment by the Plebs on the Patricians ended in the overthrow of the Roman Republic and 'the enslavement of the noblest people that ever entered on the stage of the world'.

The danger of this error was extreme, at a moment when there was a powerful and ambitious prince (in France) waiting to take advantage of it. The comfortable belief that owing to their peculiar genius and temper Britons never would be slaves is cant. The genius of a people is incessantly changing. A well-ordered government can be preserved only by the deliberate exercise of the rational will. This cannot prevail in a popular assembly where party rules; for, when listed in a party, its members forsake the commonsense which they use in private life, and, because they agree with the party-leaders in a few points, blindly follow them in all.

The *Discourse* is well argued and well documented, by the standards of the historical knowledge of the time. Swift wisely restrained himself from any patting with the tiger's paw. The nearest he comes to it is in describing the Parliamentary recess as a 'lucid interval'. Moreover, though it suggests that the Tories are behaving furiously and foolishly and is, in effect, a defence of the impeached Whig statesmen, it is not really a party pamphlet. The writer takes his stand above the battle. Whether it had any public effect cannot be known, but it had a private one. It gained for Swift the acquaintance and encouragement of Somers, Halifax and Burnet. It is also said that it gained him an audience with the King; but this is very doubtful.

The introduction to the Whig grandees was delayed till the next year, 1702; for, by a practice which he followed on other occasions, he slipped back to Ireland immediately after the publication of the *Discourse*, to avoid association with it until he knew it was well enough received for him to own it. This practice was due to a peculiar sort of diffidence. Twelve years later he wrote to protest against a proposal that all publications should bear the author's name.

It is certain that all persons of true genius or knowledge have an invincible modesty and suspicion of themselves upon their first sending their thoughts into the world; and that those who are dull and superficial have dispositions directly contrary.[5]

Was this the effect of a real uncertainty about the quality of his writing, or of a pride to which apparent failure was intolerable? Perhaps a mixture of both, but tinged with another consideration; for if his mind was now set on achieving power by his pen, the criterion by which he must judge his own writing was immediate success. Without that, his writing was a failure, whatever its intrinsic qualities might be. Of immediate success his own judgment, in advance, could not possibly be certain. He must await the event.

When he heard in Ireland that the *Discourse* was regarded as impressive enough to be attributed to Somers or Burnet, he felt he could claim it as his own with safety and advantage. It had achieved its purpose; it had brought him almost within the charmed circle of 'the great men': and though we would gladly exchange it now for a companion-piece to *Mrs. Frances Harris's Petition*, a dozen such pieces would not have brought him half so far towards his goal. The *Discourse* was his diploma piece as a political writer: the first milestone along his chosen road.

4

On March 8, 1702, King William died, and with him the hopes of the Whig grandees of a speedy return to power. It was well for England, though rather unfortunate for Swift, that she entered upon the war with France under Tory auspices: it made for unity in the nation. Swift returned to London in April to explore his chances in the 'new world' of Queen Anne, and to take what advantage he could of his success.

I soon grew domestic with Lord Halifax, and was as often with Lord Somers as the formality of his nature (the only unconversable fault he has) made it agreeable to me.
It was then I first began to trouble myself with the difference between the principles of Whig and Tory; having formerly employed myself in other, and I think much better speculations.[6]

This was, perhaps, rather naive of him; but doubtless it was true. The tradition he had imbibed at Moor Park — and Temple's influence upon him was much greater than is generally allowed — was one of detachment from party faction, and personal loyalty to the monarch. That attitude was reinforced by Swift's experience of Ireland, where the English distinction of Whig and Tory was largely irrelevant. There were among the Anglo-Irish hardly any full-blooded Tories, in the sense of men tinged with a practical or sentimental leaning towards Jacobitism. There was no room in Ireland for any deep feud between Protestants. Even in England, now that the Tories, largely under Harley's inspiration, had initiated and passed the Act of Settlement, the real Jacobites were isolated.

In what then could any difference of principle between Whig and Tory be found? It was a real problem. And it was very nearly the correct answer that there was none, and that the party-division was based on the struggle between two groups for power and its emoluments. But it was not quite true; for, speaking roughly, the Whigs had the support of the City of London and the trading and financial interests centred there; they had a tinge of the old Roundhead radicalism, in religion and politics; and, above all, in order to hold their own politically against the Tories, who represented the bulk of the landed interest, from the men of great estates down to the forty-shilling freeholders, and were strong for all the privileges of the established Church, the Whigs needed the support of the Dissenters. As things stood, the Tories had a permanent majority of the citizens of England who possessed full political rights. This situation could only be met by the Whigs if there was a connivance at the practice of Occasional Conformity, whereby the less rigid of the Dissenters, by taking the Anglican sacrament, qualified themselves for office, and in particular for membership of the corporations which elected the borough members. This practice has often been denounced as time-serving; and no doubt it sometimes was. But in the majority of cases, the motives were unexceptionable. It was almost by accident that the Church of England had not been comprehensive enough to include at any rate the majority of English Presbyterians, and it was largely as a result of excluding them that the Church of England after the Restoration elaborated its extravagant theories of divine right, of which the Revolution had made nonsense. Many Presbyterians were simply broad Churchmen. The most eminent of their divines, Baxter, had approved the practice of Occasional Conformity; and it is significant that two of the best-known diarists of the period, whose religious sincerity is apparent, Celia Fiennes and Ralph Thoresby, were both Occasional Conformists. They liked to attend Church sometimes, and Meetings more frequently. They thought they heard better sermons at the Meetings. They were probably right. Generally, the Anglican parson read his sermon dully, with his head bent over his manuscript, while the Dissenting preacher had his by heart, or spoke extempore; and even when the High Church parson was more lively, his sermon was, as often as not, primarily political, like the epoch-making rhodomontade of Dr. Sacheverell, whereas sermons at Meetings were usually devout and edifying.[7]

The primary motive of the High Church party in persistently seeking to legislate against Occasional Conformity was political; they were bent on reducing the political strength of the Whigs. The motive of the Whigs in defending it was equally political. But the majority of the Occasional Conformists themselves were genuinely religious people, averse to extreme sectarianism, who believed that a certain degree of religious uniformity was desirable in the nation, and who held, not unreasonably, that they were entitled to political rights.

5

When Swift began to think seriously about the difference of Tory and Whig, it was on the religious-political issue that he tried to clarify his mind. As an Anglo-Irishman, he had never been in doubt about the necessity of the Revolution, or the validity of a Parliamentary title to the Crown; as an intimate of Temple he had accepted without question King William's policy of resisting the aggrandisement of France by land and sea. Fundamentally, therefore, he was a Whig. In the *Tale*, with all his general derision of Dissent, it is the violent Tories he ridicules by name and nominates commissioners of Bedlam. And on the concrete religious-political issue, according to his account of his conversations with Somers in 1702, he was on the Whig side.

> I knew it was necessary for their party to make their bottom as wide as they could, by taking all denominations of Protestants to be members of their body.[8]

That Swift at least acquiesced in this attitude is shown by his letters to Tisdall eighteen months later. In spite of the fact that he recognized that 'the whole body of the clergy, with a great majority of the House of Commons, were violent for this Bill' (against Occasional Conformity), he confesses that he himself cannot make up his mind, 'though I was mightily urged by some great people to publish my opinion'. Peterborough, Burnet and Somers had assured him that the rejection of the Bill will not harm the Church: 'so that I know not what to think, and therefore shall think no more'.

That was written on December 16, 1703. But in a fortnight he made up his mind, and had written a pamphlet against the Bill.

Pox on the Dissenters and Independents! I would as soon trouble my head to write against a louse or a flea. I tell you what; I wrote against the Bill that was against Occasional Conformity; but it came too late by a day, so I would not print it. But you may answer it if you please; for you know you and I are Whig and Tory. And, to cool your insolence a little, know that the Queen and Court, and House of Lords, and half the Commons almost, are Whigs, and the number daily increases. (February 3, 1704)

It was not so much that the Whigs, in the party sense, were increasing, as that the moderate men among the Tories were detaching themselves from the more violent high-flyers, in the interests of national unity. Prince George himself, who had reluctantly voted for the Bill, at the Queen's request, in 1702, and whispered to Wharton, as he went into the lobby, 'My heart is vid you', absented himself, obviously with the Queen's approval, from the Lords in the debate of December 14, 1703, which was the occasion of Swift's first letter to Tisdall. In that very limited sense Swift was right in saying the Queen and Court had become Whigs. It may have helped to decide his hesitation.

It does not appear that Swift ever changed his position on Occasional Conformity, which was the most violently disputed question of domestic politics throughout Queen Anne's reign. He was resolutely opposed to the removal of the Test; but that was a very different matter, and only the extreme Whigs supported it. Nor was the Test Act repealed until the 19th century. But on grounds of reason and expediency alike Swift remained tolerant of Occasional Conformity. What caused him uneasiness, at the beginning of his acquaintance with the Whig grandees was 'the connivance, or encouragement, given by the Whigs to those writers of pamplets who reflected upon the whole body of clergymen, without exception'. That, he thought, would end by uniting the clergy, as one man, against the Whigs; and, he says, Somers agreed with him.[9]

6

While Swift was in England in 1702, writing the *Discourse*, he spent much time with the Berkeleys. He wrote some amusing verses describing one of their evenings at cards. His Lordship deals cards around for Traffic. The first to get the knave has the deal. Generally it falls to the Doctor.

But then his honour cry'd Godzooks!
And seem'd to knit his brow:
For on a knave he never looks
But h' thinks upon Jack How.[10]

Jack How was the disappointed Whig M.P. for Gloucestershire who turned raging Tory — one of Swift's Commissioners for Bedlam. Then come pictures of the ladies. Her Ladyship, who does not play, but likes looking on, chooses a partner whose stakes she holds, wedged in the corner of her partner's chair, and taking snuff; Dame Floyd — the mother of the beautiful Biddy — cautious of her pence, playing seldom and solemnly; Harris, explaining how she would have won, if — ; Weston hoping to win a crown to pay for the lining of her new gown. At this point he left the verses unfinished on his desk. Lady Betty found them there, and finished them for him.

With these is Parson Swift,
Not knowing how to spend his time,
Does make a wretched shift
To deafen 'em with puns and rhyme.[11]

The joke was good, though the metre was not. Swift replied with a ballad.

Even so Master Doctor had puzzled his brains
In making a ballad but was at a stand;
He had mixt little wit with a great deal of pains,
When he found a new help from invisible hand
Then, good Doctor Swift
Pay thanks for the gift,
For you freely must own you were at a dead lift;
And though some malicious young spirit did do't,
You may know by the hand it had no cloven foot.
Let censuring critics then think what they list on't,
Who would not write verses with such an assistant?[12]

It was Lady Betty who, in after-life, told how Swift, after taking prayers, used to read some religious or moral discourse to her mother. At one time the Countess was very fond of Mr. Boyle's *Meditations*. Swift did not find them so congenial, and shied at plodding through the volume. So he surreptitiously inserted a page of *Meditation on a Broomstick*, and at the next session, gravely read it. Her Ladyship was struck by the title. 'What a strange subject! But there is no knowing what useful lessons of instruction this wonderful man may draw from things apparently the most trivial.' Swift solemnly read on to the end. It is an admirable parody, just a little more portentous and abstruse than its original; and he did not hesitate to risk an equivoque at the end.

> But a broomstick, perhaps, you will say, is an emblem of a tree standing on its head; and pray what is man, but a topsy-turvy creature, his animal faculties perpetually mounted upon his rational, his head where his heels should be, grovelling on the earth! And yet, with all his faults, he sets up to be a universal reformer and corrector of abuses, a remover of grievances, rakes into every slut's corner of nature, bringing hidden corruption to the light, and raises a mighty dust where there was none before; sharing deeply all the while in the very same pollutions he pretends to sweep away: his last days are spent in slavery to women, and generally the least deserving, till, worn out to the stumps, like his brother besom, he is either kicked out of doors, or made use of to kindle flames for others to warm themselves by.[13]

The innuendo of the last sentence, one imagines, must have been outside her Ladyship's range; and anyway it was as easy for Swift to pretend innocence as it was to keep his countenance. When he had finished, some company came and Swift slipped out of the room. Her Ladyship was full of admiration of what she had been hearing — the most surprising of all the wonderful *Meditations*. Which was it? they asked. 'The Meditation on a Broomstick', she replied. They said they had never heard of it. 'Upon my word, there it is. Look into that book, and convince yourselves.' They looked, and found; and, said Lady Betty, when the first surprise was over, her mother enjoyed the joke as much as any of them.

All the evidence is that Swift was happy with the Berkeleys. He was at his ease with them, and they appreciated him. He admired Biddy Floyd, who talked little, but with humour, and who, for all her beauty, never married but became Lady Betty's life-long friend and companion. To her he wrote the charming compliment which conceived the gods as taking due proportions of

> Truth, innocence, good nature, look serene . . .
> Breeding, and wit, and air, and decent pride . . .
> Jove mix'd up all, and his best clay imploy'd
> Then call'd the happy composition, Floyd.[14]

When Lady Betty married, in 1706, and took Biddy with her, Swift continued to pay his welcome visits to Berkeley Castle. We have glimpses of him punning with the Earl about Lady Berkeley's cat. ('And Lady Berkeley talking to her cat, my Lord said she was very impurrtinent; but I defended her and said I thought her Ladyship spoke very much to the poor-puss.')[15]

When the Earl was proposed as Ambassador to Vienna, in 1708, Swift thought of going with him as Queen's Secretary; but, finally, in view of the Earl's declining health, joined in persuading him not to accept the appointment. In 1709 the Earl wrote to him that he would be heartily glad to see as much as possible of him before he went back to Ireland. In another year he was dead, and Swift was grieved to the heart when Lady Berkeley's letter begging him to come to the Castle to entertain her husband in his illness did not reach him until three weeks after his death. It was a genuine tribute to Lady Berkeley that Swift paid to her, and her family, in the dedication of his *Project for the Advancement of Religion.*

My real design is, I confess, the very same I have often detested in most dedications; that of publishing your praises to the world. Not upon the subject of your noble birth, for I know of others as noble; or of the greatness of your fortune, for I know of others far greater; or of that beautiful race (the images of their parents) which call you mother; for even this may perhaps have been equalled in some other age or country. Besides, none of these advantages do derive any accomplishments to the owners, but serve at best only to adorn what they really possess. What I intend is your piety, truth, good sense, and good nature, affability and charity; wherein I wish your Ladyship had many equals, or any superiors; and I wish I could say I knew them, too, for then your Ladyship might have had a chance to escape this address. In the meantime, I think it highly necessary, for the interest of virtue and religion, that the whole kingdom should be informed in some parts of your character: For instance, that the easiest and politest conversation, joined with the truest piety, may be observed in your Ladyship, in as great perfection, as they were ever seen apart in any other persons. That by your prudence and management under several disadvantages, you have preserved the lustre of that most noble family into which you are grafted, and which the unmeasurable profusion of ancestors for many generations had too much eclipsed. Then, how happily you perform every office of life to which Providence has called you: In the education of those two incomparable daughters, whose conduct is so universally admired; in every duty of a prudent, complying, affectionate wife; in that care which descends to the meanest of your domestics; and lastly, in that endless bounty to the poor, and discretion where to distribute it.[16]

It may be a little exaggerated, but the sincerity of Swift's appreciation is indubitable. There were not many people he spoke of in such terms.

Swift was back in Ireland from October 1702 to November 1703. During this time he formed a fairly close friendship with a younger clergyman, the Rev. William Tisdall, whom he seems to have met while at Kilroot. He introduced him to 'the ladies', now settled in Dublin in the newly built William Street; and Tisdall became intimate enough with them for Swift to send Stella messages about her private affairs through him. Two letters written to him by Swift from London, in the winter of 1703, show that the four of them were on very friendly terms indeed. In one he instructs Tisdall how to outwit Stella by the new fashionable trick of 'a bite', and he begins the next:

> I am content you should judge the order of friendship you are in with me by my writing to you, and accordingly you will find yourself the first after the ladies; for I never write to any other, either friend or relation, till long after. (February 3, 1704)

And that is borne out by the rest of the letter.

> I am extremely concerned to find myself unable to persuade you into a true opinion of your own littleness, nor make you treat me with more distance and respect; and the rather because I find all your little pretensions are owing to the credit you pretend with two ladies who came from England. I allow indeed the chamber in William Street to be Little England by their influence, as an ambassador's house, wherever it is, hath all the privileges of his master's dominions: and, therefore, if you wrote the letter in their room, or their company, for in this matter their room is as good as their company, I will indulge you a little. . . .

Tisdall had tried the 'bite' on Stella, and brought it off.

> You seem to talk with great security of your establishment near the ladies, though perhaps if you knew what they say of you in their letters to me, you would change your opinion both of them and yourself. A *bite* — and now you talk of a *bite*, I am ashamed of the ladies' being caught by you, when I had betrayed you and given them warning. I had heard before of the choking, but never of the jest in the church: you may find from thence that women's prayers are things perfectly by rote, as they put on one stocking after another, and no more. But if she be good at blunders, she is as ready at come-offs; and to pretend her senses were gone was a very good argument she had them about her.

Swift twitted his friend for having shown part of his previous letter to Primate Marsh, and assured him that he will guard against any more such indiscretion by making his letter fit to be seen by no one but Tisdall himself. He was as good as his word.

> You seem to be mighty proud [Swift continues] as you have reason if it be true, of the part you have in the ladies' graces, especially of her you call the *party*. I am very much concerned to know it; but since it is an evil I cannot remedy, I will tell you a story. A cast mistress went to her rival, and expostulated with her for robbing her of her lover. After a long quarrel, finding no good to be done; 'Well' says the abdicated lady, 'keep him and [push him up your arse]'* — 'No', says the other, 'that will not be altogether so convenient; however, to oblige you, I will do something that is very near it.' — *Dixi.*

How was an ordinary man in Tisdall's position to interpret that? The bawdy joke has no direct bearing on the situation Swift supposes or pretends between Tisdall, himself and Stella: that he is now the cast lover, and Tisdall his successful rival. But, when it follows 'Since it is an evil I cannot remedy, I will tell you a story,' it could only be read by Tisdall as betokening an extreme of *insouciance* in Swift — as a full, if light-hearted, permission to go in and win. That is not to say that is how Swift meant it. Heaven alone knows how he meant it. But this is how an ordinarily constituted mind — as Swift's was not — would take it.

Swift goes on to suggest that Tisdall should supply his place as Stella's tutor. 'Be always teaching something to Mrs. Johnson, because she is good at comprehending, remembering and retaining.' The rest of his letter is taken up with disinterested practical advice to Tisdall on how to make headway in the Church. Let him not write pamphlets for the public. Anyway, Irish politics are not worth writing about. 'Preach, preach, preach; that is certainly your talent; and you will, some years hence, have time enough to be a writer.'

8

Tisdall, now thinking the coast was clear and that he could count on Swift's good will, wrote shortly after to tell him that he wished to marry Stella, and asking him to help his suit, by putting the proposal to Stella's mother. Swift was now in a quandary. He did not intend to marry Stella, and he did not want to lose her. So he wrote to Tisdall coldly, suggesting that such an early marriage — Tisdall was at least seven years younger than

---

* This phrase is represented by **** *** ** **** **** in Sheridan, who first published the letter. The asterisks are more likely to be Sheridan's than Swift's. There is no doubt about their meaning, and it is important to have it clearly before us.

Swift, and still in his twenties — would hamper his advancement in the Church, and that his income was not sufficient to make Stella and himself happy and easy. He also said that he could not put the proposal formally to Stella's mother at Tisdall's sole request; he must also have Stella's written consent.

Tisdall was mystified and hurt by this change of front. He wrote to Swift to say that his letter was unfriendly, unkind, and unaccountable; that Swift was not treating him frankly; that he felt Swift had designs of his own; and that he was surprised and astonished by them. To all this Swift now replied.

> I might with good pretence enough talk starchly, and affect ignorance of what you would be at; but my conjecture is that you think I obstructed your insinuations, to please my own, and that my intentions were the same with yours; in answer to all which, I will, upon my conscience and honour, tell you the naked truth. First, I think I have said to you before, that, if my fortunes and humour served me to think of that state, I should certainly, among all persons on earth, make your choice; because I never saw that person whose conversation I entirely valued but hers; this was the utmost I ever gave way to. And, secondly, I must assure you sincerely, that this regard of mine never once entered my head to be an impediment to you: but I judged it would, perhaps, be a clog to your rising in the world; and I did not conceive you were then rich enough to make yourself and her happy and easy. But that objection is now quite removed by the assurances of Eaton's livings ... The objection of your fortune being removed, I declare I have no other; nor shall any consideration of my own misfortune in losing so good a friend and companion as her, prevail on me, against her interest and settlement in the world, since it is held so necessary and convenient a thing for ladies to marry; and that time takes off the lustre from virgins in all other eyes but mine.

He goes on to say that his letters to Stella would show that he had acted the part of a friend to Tisdall, though not an active part. He had said to Stella, and to her mother, that the suit had gone so far that it could not be decently broken off without disadvantage to Stella's reputation. He had always stressed her qualities to Tisdall in such a way as to encourage him to make his court to her; and he stresses them again.

> Though it hath come in my way to converse with persons of the first rank, and of that sex, more than is usual to men of my level, and of our function; yet I have nowhere met with a humour, a wit, or conversation so agreeable, a better portion of good sense, or a truer judgment of men and things, I mean here in England; for as to the ladies of Ireland, I am a perfect stranger.

Tisdall, he believes, knows what Stella's fortune amounts to; if he 'resumes his designs', and requires more details, Swift will supply them. He ends:

I give you joy of your good fortunes [namely, the assurance of a good living], and envy very much your prudence and temper, and love of peace and settlement; the reverse of which has been the great uneasiness of my life, and is like to continue so. And what is the result? *En, quis consevimus agros?* I find nothing but the good words and wishes of a decayed ministry, whose lives and mine will probably wear out before they can serve either my little hopes, or their own ambition. Therefore, I am resolved suddenly to retire, like a discontented courtier, and vent myself in study and speculation, till my own humour, or the scene here, shall change. (April 20, 1704)

On the face of it, that is a very frank letter. Neither his fortunes nor his humour suffer him to think of marrying. If they did, he would choose Stella; but since they did not, he had never allowed himself to fall in love with her, but confined himself to valuing her friendship, company and conversation, above that of all other women he knew. He had not permitted his sense of the preciousness of her friendship to induce him to crab Tisdall's courtship. He had simply demurred on prudential grounds, in the interests of both of them.

But his demurrer had been effective. Why should he say to Tisdall 'if you resume your designs', unless Tisdall had abandoned them? And Tisdall himself had written that Swift's letter had had the effect which, he judged, Swift intended. He had been forced to conclude from it that his suit would be unavailing, because Swift did not favour it, as he had been led to expect he would. He had pointed out that Swift's prudential argument was a camouflage, and drawn his own conclusion that the real motive was that Swift wanted Stella for himself. And Stella, who equally knew that the prudential argument was a blind, had come to the same conclusion: which was the one she wanted to come to. Her previous willingness to listen to Tisdall's overtures — an offer of marriage from a *friend* of Swift's was not to be despised — suddenly changed to reluctance, and Tisdall's confidence to the sense of an insuperable obstacle in his way.

And, of course, Swift did want Stella for himself; and the moment she knew it, Tisdall's suit was hopeless. All his seeming frankness, all his apparent encouragement of Tisdall, now that the prudential objection had been removed, was a meaningless gesture — diplomatically correct behaviour and the careful establishment of an alibi. He had effectively queered the pitch of his friend, and he had explicitly avoided any commitment to Stella. Stella, at twenty-three, would hardly have noticed that. It was enough that

Swift wanted her for himself. Marriage would come, in its own good time: when his fortunes, and his humour (which depended on his fortunes) served. She did not understand that Swift wanted her for himself, but on his own terms. The distinction, indeed, was not yet apparent. His terms, for the time being, were also hers.

But not entirely. Swift realized that he could not go on just as he was doing — shooting off to London at his own sweet will, and leaving Stella to her own company, or her own consolations. In his diplomatic way he gave his Dublin friends to understand that he was about to retire from 'court'. Within six weeks of his letter to Tisdall he had returned to Ireland, having stayed in London just long enough to arrange for the publication of *A Tale of a Tub*, with an extremely witty and complimentary dedication to Somers: a perfect example of the 'raillery' which Swift most esteemed and cultivated — a high compliment concealed under apparent detraction.

9

Before the *Tale* was published, in April or May 1704, Swift had made the acquaintance of the leading contemporary wits besides Congreve — Prior, Addison, Steele, and Vanbrugh. His behaviour to Vanbrugh was curious. He made some verses on a house the playwright and architect had built for himself, apparently from material salvaged from the ruins of Whitehall, which had been burned down in 1699. Some of it may pass as legitimate jibing at its smallness; but one passage in particular goes well beyond the limits of fun between friends:

> Just such an insect of the age
> Is he that scribbles for the stage;
> His birth he does from Phoebus raise
> And feeds upon imagin'd bays:
> Throws all his wit and hours away
> In twisting up an ill-spun play:
> This gives him lodging, and provides
> A stock of tawdry stuff besides,
> With the unravell'd threads of which
> The underwits adorn their speech.
> And now he spreads his little fans,
> (For all the Muse's geese are swans)
> And borne on Fancy's pinions, thinks
> He soars sublimest when he sinks:
> But scatt'ring round his fly-blows, dies,
> Whence broods of insect-poets rise.[17]

Vanbrugh, though good-natured, as Swift himself admitted, resented this. Yet Swift persisted in lampooning him. Vanbrugh's vanity may have been the excuse.

With Prior and Addison and Steele his relations were more cordial; and with the first two the friendship was enduring. It was probably through the Berkeleys that he met Prior, for Prior's first diplomatic appointment had been as Secretary to Berkeley's embassy to the Hague, in 1690, and he had served with him there for three years. Anyhow, they were friendly enough for Swift to give Prior proofs, or an advance copy of the *Tale*. Prior showed it to Atterbury, and apparently to Harley as well: for Atterbury wrote to Harley in terms which suggest that Harley also had read it. 'I cannot close this, without expressing the satisfaction I had last night in perusing Mr. Swift's book, which Mr. Prior showed me. 'Tis very well written, and will do good service, but I am afraid by the peculiar manner of writing, he will be too easily discovered.'[18] Evidently, Swift's style was already distinctive to the connoisseurs. This could hardly have happened through his published writings. The only published piece of Swift's at this time was the *Discourse*; and the style of that was not very distinctive. Presumably, *The Battle of the Books* had been circulated in manuscript. If so, Atterbury, as the leader of Christ Church wits in the combat with Bentley, would certainly have seen it.

Addison also knew the secret of the *Tale*: when he published his *Remarks on Several Parts of Italy* in 1705 — likewise dedicated to Somers — he presented Swift with a copy inscribed to him as 'the most agreeable companion, the truest friend, and the greatest genius of his age': an astonishing tribute.* Sheridan tells a story, on the good authority of Ambrose Philips, of Addison's first encounter with Swift.[19] It must have happened in the autumn of 1703. He and his friends, habitués of the St. James's Coffee House, were intrigued by the appearance, day after day, of an unknown clergyman, who put his beaver on the table, and walked rapidly up and down, apparently absorbed in his own thoughts. They came to the conclusion that he was mad, and called him 'the mad parson'. One evening they saw him looking at a country gentleman who had just entered. Suddenly he went up to him, and said aloud: 'Pray, sir, do you remember any good weather in the world?' The countryman was taken aback and stared at him. Then he said: 'Yes, sir, I thank God, I remember a great deal of good weather in my time.' 'That is

* There is no definite evidence that Addison gave Swift his book in 1705; but it seems probable. Addison did not return from his continental travels till the autumn of 1703. By that time Swift was 'domestic with Lord Halifax' and frequently with Somers, with both of whom Addison was familiar. It seems impossible that Addison and he should not have met during his stay in England from November 1703 to May 1704. It is likely too that the famous story, retold in the text, is true; and that Addison had remarked Swift at the Coffee House, before meeting him at the grandees'.

more,' said Swift, 'than I can say: I never remember any weather that was not too hot or too cold — too wet or too dry; but, however God Almighty contrives it, at the end of the year, 'tis all very well.' Whereupon, he picked up his hat and departed. That is too like Swift's peculiar humour not to be true; and it is equally like him to 'produce himself' by such a studied entry upon the stage of the wits.

Within a year of publication the *Tale* had passed into its fourth edition, and the authorship was known outside the inner circle of the wits. Thomas Hearne at Oxford noted it in his *Diary* as a known fact on August 25, 1705. And probably before that Defoe, who was clean outside the wits' circle, had made a striking reference to it in *The Consolidator*.

I had heard of a world in the moon among some of our learned philosophers . . . but none of the fine pretenders — no, not Bishop Wilkins — ever found mechanical engines whose motion was sufficient to attempt the passage. A late happy author, indeed, among his mechanic operations of the spirit, had found out an enthusiasm which, if he could have pursued to its proper extreme, without doubt might, either in the body or out of the body, have landed him somewhere hereabout; but that he formed his system wholly on the mistaken notion of wind, which learned hypothesis being directly contrary to the nature of things in this climate, where the elasticity of the air is quite different, and where the pressure of the atmosphere has, for want of vapour, no force, all his notion dissolved in its native vapour called wind, and flew upward in vivid strakes of a livid flame called blasphemy, which burnt up all the wit and fancy of the author, and left a strange stench behind it that has this unhappy quality in it, that everybody that reads the book smells the author though he be never so far off, nay, though he took shipping to Dublin to secure his friends from the least danger of a conjecture.[20]

Defoe was only partly right in *his* conjecture. If Swift had retired to Ireland merely on account of the *Tale*, he would have returned when he knew its reputation was secure. He did not. He stayed in Ireland longer than he had ever done since he left Trinity in 1689. It was three years and a half before he returned to England, and then as an official envoy of the Church of Ireland, so that his conscience with regard to Stella was clear. Possibly it was with the thought of being eventually entrusted with such a mission that he wrote to King, the Archbishop of Dublin, on December 31, 1704, asking him to press for the extension of Queen Anne's Bounty to the Church of Ireland, by the remission of the First Fruits and Tenths, which, he said, the Queen had promised the Irish clergy.

CHAPTER VIII

FALLOW AND FIRST FRUITS: 1704-1708

SWIFT arrived in Ireland on June 1, 1704, and did not return to England till November 1707. It was a time of fallow in Swift's life, and probably one of the happiest. His gifts and mental energies were at their zenith; but hardly any writing or letters of his have survived from this period. They cannot have been simply submerged, for Swift was a notable figure by now. The knowledgeable ones all knew that he was the author of the *Tale*. One must conclude that he was content to be indolent: busy-idle at Laracor, happy in Stella's company. He wrote very little. But it included the verses on Lord Cutts, nicknamed the Salamander for his intrepidity and good fortune under fire at the siege of Namur; and the first, and on the whole the better version of *Baucis & Philemon*, before Addison had pruned it. The former poem is as unpleasant as the latter is charming.

Swift's grievance against Cutts can hardly have been political. He was certainly not enough of a Tory to have resented Cutts's opposition to the Tack. It must have had something to do with Cutts's behaviour in Ireland, whither he had come in 1705 as Commander-in-Chief at the satisfactory salary of £6000 a year and pickings. Unless we suppose that Swift at this moment was completely unscrupulous in indulging some private vendetta, we must believe that he was genuinely shocked by Cutts's behaviour in Dublin.

The attack is horrid enough, if it was justified. If not, it was an outrage. One is, therefore, impelled to believe it was justified. Even so, we need to seek a motive for letting the poisoned arrow fly.

> So have I seen a batter'd beau
> By age and claps grown cold as snow,
> Whose breath or touch, where'er he came
> Blew out love's torch or chill'd the flame.
> And should some nymph, who ne'er was cruel,
> Like Carleton cheap, or fam'd Duruel,
> Receive the filth that he ejects,
> She soon would find the same effects
> Her tainted carcase to pursue,
> As from the Salamander's spue;
> A dismal shedding of her locks,
> And, if no leprosy, the pox.
> *Then I'll appeal to each bystander*
> *Whether this ben't a Salamander?*[1]

Moral indignation is not a sufficient motive for that. But another can be found. Precisely at this time, Cutts was engaged in repudiating a claim which Steele had made upon him for services rendered while he was Cutts's secretary.[2] Steele had sensibly chosen the moment of Cutts's appointment to a very lucrative post, to ask him to pay his debt. At this time Swift and Steele were good friends. Possibly Steele asked Swift, who would meet Cutts in the Ormond entourage, to give him a reminder; certainly, Steele would have told Swift of Cutts's refusal to pay, and perhaps he commented bitterly on the fact that he had dedicated his *Christian Hero* to him. That would have been more than enough to set Swift throwing vitriol, in *A Description of a Salamander* — or 'The Christian Hero unmasked'.

Baucis & Philemon is wholly delightful. The earlier and longer version is to be preferred. Although Addison improved it in places, he was severe, to the detriment of the poem, on Swift's realism. The description of the hermits' hostile reception by the village:

> They call'd at every door: Good people,
> My comrade's blind, and I'm a creeple . . . [3]

and the rest, is more forceful in the original: so is the account of Baucis's behaviour after being metamorphosed into a parson.

> A shambling awkward gait he took,
> With a demure dejected look,
> Talk'd of his off'rings, tithes and dues,
> Could smoke, and drink, and read the news,
> Or sell a goose at the next town
> Decently hid beneath his gown.[4]

Swift himself may have been the prime agent in modifying this picture, before the poem was published, as smacking too much of the disrespect towards the clergy against which he protested. Swift's poetic veracity and his political principles were a little at odds in this matter. But, on the whole, he succeeds in creating in Philemon a happy medium between Parson Adams and Parson Trulliber, which fits with the picture he was to draw many years later.

An English vicar of £40 a year, lives much more comfortably than one of double the value in Ireland. His farmers, generally speaking, are able and willing to pay him his full dues. He hath a decent church of ancient standing, filled every Lord's Day with a large congregation of plain people, well clad and behaving themselves as if they believed in God and Christ. He hath a house and barn in repair, a field or two to graze his cows, with a garden and orchard. No guest expects more from him than a pot of ale: He lives like an honest plain farmer, as his wife is dressed but little better than Goody. He is sometimes graciously invited by the squire, where he sits at humble distance; if he gets the love of his people, they often make him little useful presents: he is happy by being born to no higher expectations; for he is usually the son of some ordinary tradesman, or middling farmer. His learning is much of a size with his birth and education; no more of either than what a poor hungry servitor can be expected to bring with him from his college.[5]

2

Besides these two poems the only other surviving production of the fallow period are another lampoon on Vanbrugh's house, a few of his thoughts on various subjects, and some verses on the Union with Scotland, of which he was intensely critical. How, he asked, is a Union truly possible between nations which have no unity of religion or law? He had something more than Dr. Johnson's robust prejudice against Scotsmen: he had lived among the Scots Presbyterians of Ulster, and he had found them energetic, determined, disciplined and aggressive. They resented the privileged position of the Church of Ireland, and paid their tithes with reluctance. Swift was persuaded that they 'looked upon Prelacy and Popery as terms convertible'. Moreover these inveterate enemies of Episcopacy were, to some degree, officially recognized. Thus, in Swift's eyes, Ireland, in which it was so difficult to keep the Presbyterians thumbed under, was already a miniature of the new union of England and Scotland.

So tossing faction will o'erwhelm
Our crazy double-bottom'd realm.[6]

Swift's attitude took no account of political realities. He ignored the notorious fact that the Scots themselves had to be dragged to the marriage; and that the only alternative to it was war.

To ask how he reconciled his hostility to the Union with his nominal Whiggism is irrelevant. He did not try to, because he did not need to. All the three years' complicated and precarious negotiations which led to the Union took place while he was in Ireland. And it was a combination of Whigs and moderate Tories which carried them through on the English side to prevent the danger of a Stuart restoration in Scotland. Swift's politics had no such intimate relation to English political realities. His Whig principles — devotion to the Revolution settlement and the Protestant succession — were common to all members of the Church of Ireland, whose position of privilege was untenable on any other basis. His friendly relations with the Whig leaders had arisen from his attack upon impeachment, at a moment when they were being impeached. But objection to impeachment as a political method was certainly not a Whig principle; they were only too eager, when their turn came, to impeach Harley. If Whig, as opposed to Tory, had any positive meaning in Ireland, it meant support of the Presbyterian effort to get the Sacramental Test abolished: to which Swift was violently opposed, as were the great majority of the Irish parliament. Swift's contention, in the only considerable letter that remains from this period, that the English Tory-Whig feud was irrelevant to Irish conditions was perfectly sound — on the assumption that the Test was inviolable.

> Whig and Tory has spoiled all that was tolerable here . . . though it seems to me full as pertinent to quarrel about Copernicus and Ptolemy, as about my Lord Treasurer and Lord Rochester, at least for any private man and especially in our remote scene. (June 15, 1706)

Thus politically disengaged, Swift was able to disregard reality, and to look on the Act of Union merely as the establishment of the High Kirk in Scotland and not at all as a necessary means of securing the Hanover succession. The real English high-flyer, who loathed the idea of the Hanover succession, was consistent in denouncing the Union. Swift was not. From his parochial and irresponsible point of view the establishment of the High Kirk was simply a step towards the political emancipation of the Irish Presbyterians.

3

He may have been encouraged in this attitude by Ormond, who was Lord Lieutenant during most of the three and a half years Swift stayed in Ireland; and who carried through the extension of the Test to that country. Swift was on friendly terms with him; but hardly dreamed that he would turn out to be a Jacobite. When Ormond, the Tory, was superseded by Pembroke, the moderate Whig, in April 1707, Swift was on friendly terms with him also. He entered with gusto into Pembroke's passion for the new vogue of punning, and encouraged him in it. He felt himself to be sufficiently in favour to have a reasonable chance of the bishopric of Waterford, against Pembroke's official chaplain, Dr. Milles of Oxford, who was remarkable for a large Roman nose. Swift did not like Milles. Archbishop King did not like him either. Thomas Hearne, the Jacobite antiquary, considered him to be 'the most meanly fitted for Bishop that was ever preferred from the first

establishment of Episcopacy in these parts'. We may therefore believe that
Swift's prejudice against him was justified. It was violent. Sheridan tells a
story, which sounds true, of Swift's challenging him at Pembroke's table,
to construe

Romanos rerum dominos gentemque togatam.

Milles, who in spite of Hearne, was not a bad scholar, of course construed it
correctly. But Swift insisted he was wrong: it should run thus. ('Rum' was
slang for a country parson) *Romanos* — you've a Roman nose — *rerum* —
you're a rare rum — *dominos* — damn your nose — *gentemque togatam* — and
the whole race of chaplains.' It was the kind of thing in which Pembroke
delighted. But Milles got Waterford.

We have other glimpses of Swift taking his ease in a scholarly and
convivial company of Irish wits and punsters. It chiefly consisted of the
three brothers Ashe, Tom, St. George and Dillon. St. George, the second
brother, had been Swift's tutor at Trinity, then Provost; now he was Bishop
of Clogher. He was a steady and trusted friend. Dillon, or Dilly, Swift's
contemporary at Trinity, was an indolent and easy-going clergyman, fond
of his pipe and fonder of his bottle, with a face so red from potation that
Swift thought it would 'whizz in the water' at the Bath. There was also
Dean Stearne of St. Patrick's, who had just built a new Deanery, at which
the company met; and William Lloyd, the Bishop of Killala. All these had
the great merit in Swift's eyes of being good friends to Stella. To them was
added Sir Andrew Fountaine of Narford, in Norfolk, ten years younger than
Swift, who had come with Pembroke to Ireland as his usher of the Black
Rod. He was much the youngest of the company; but he was already a
famous connoisseur. He became intimate with Swift, whose vein of wild
nonsense he stimulated and appreciated. Pembroke himself sometimes
joined them.

Swift spoke of himself at this time as 'loving Ireland better than he did',
and though he gives as the reason that he had come to share its poverty, the
fact remains. Swift was feeling himself less of an Englishman than he had.
His relations with King, Archbishop of Dublin, who steadily championed
the Anglo-Irish interest, were cordial and confidential. Stella and Dingley
had made Ireland their home. Swift had partly accepted the responsibility
that fell to him when Stella, for his sake, refused Tisdall's offer of marriage.
This was, we believe, the decisive reason for Swift's rather surprising withdrawal from the society of the wits in London, and his apparently contented
acquiescence in a long retirement to Dublin and Laracor. His thoughts of
Moor Park were affectionate. In replying to an invitation by John Temple,

Temple's younger nephew, who now lived there, he tells him that 'no time will make him forget and love it less'. The same letter shows him busy watching over the interests of John Temple and Lady Giffard in their Irish lands.[7]

It is true that the politicians of his acquaintance: Somers, Halifax and Sunderland, were out of play during the time that the Tory ministry of 1702 was gradually being changed to a combination of moderate Tories and moderate Whigs. But Swift was not really committed to the Whigs, and it is difficult to believe that, if ambition had been his dominant motive during this period, he could not have made friends with Harley long before he actually did. Just before he had left for Ireland Harley's influence had succeeded in eliminating the extreme Tories, Nottingham, Seymour and Jersey, from the ministry. His moderate Toryism would have appealed to Swift then as it did later; and it seems that an approach to Harley would have been easy enough. Indeed, Swift hinted later on that Harley had made an approach to him. One feels that, for this time at least, Swift's ambitions were in abeyance, and he was content to lay the foundations of that life in Ireland in companionship with Stella from which, after all, his enduring human satisfactions were derived. To this period belong those experiences of Laracor which tap, like a sprig of spring blossom, at the window of the *Journal.*

> I should be plaguy busy at Laracor if I were there now, cutting down willows, planting others, scouring my canal, and every kind of thing. If Raymond goes over this summer you must submit and make them a visit, that we may have another eel and trout fishing; and that Stella may ride by and see Presto in his morning gown in the garden, and so go up with Joe to the hill of Bree and round by Scurlock's Town. O Lord! how I remember names. Faith, it gives me short sighs: therefore, no more of that if you love me.[8]

This was the time when, largely in spite of himself, his roots were really twisted with Ireland's. Though he hankered after preferment in England, and at one moment seemed on the point of getting it, one has the feeling that Ireland was his destiny, and that in his heart of hearts he was never wholly intent on making his fortune in England. This may be an illusion after the fact. But one entry in the *Journal* bears it out. Ostensibly, Swift had always longed for a prebend of Westminster. He believed that he had been promised one by King William. And yet, when he came in 1710 to visit Prebendary Sartre in the Little Cloisters, he reported to Stella that, though 'he had a delicious house and garden, yet I thought it was a sort of monastic life in those cloisters, and I liked Laracor better'.[9] Swift's head and heart were at odds. His ambition, his sense of what was due to himself, required an English preferment; but his instinct and his desire for happiness in Stella's company pulled him to Ireland.

4

It was as the representative of Ireland — or what he understood by Ireland — that he returned to England at the end of November 1707. He was charged with a mission to solicit the extension of Queen Anne's Bounty to the clergy of the Church of Ireland. Primarily, his business was to keep on prodding the memory of Pembroke, in whose suite he returned as some sort of honorary chaplain; but it was understood between himself and Archbishop King that he was to do what he could to engage any other influential politicians in the cause. It was a delicate affair, because it was imperative not to offend the *amour propre* of Pembroke, whose prestige was involved. Officially, it was through Pembroke and his influence that the grant was being sought. But the pressure of the Junto Whigs on the Ministry was increasing, and an essential part of their scheme was the elimination of Pembroke, who held two offices — Lord Lieutenant and Lord President — which the Junto wanted for Wharton and Somers. So that there was a feeling in the air that Pembroke's credit was declining and that he would not return to Ireland. Another difficulty was the suspicion that as the Junto Whigs gained influence, they would drive a hard bargain, and demand that the concession of the First Fruits and Tenths to the Irish clergy should be requited by their withdrawing their opposition to the repeal of the Test in Ireland.

Swift found the political situation in England extraordinarily tangled, as he edged his way nearer to the centre of affairs. At first, visiting his mother at Leicester, he was enchanted with what he saw and felt. The country was prosperous, the Government was popular.[10] But within six weeks, he discovered in London that 'the people begin to be heartily weary of the war'.[11] In fact, there was already a peace party in the Ministry which, through Harley's adroit manœuvring, had very nearly gained control; and perhaps would have succeeded if the arrest of one of Harley's clerks, named Greg, for treasonable correspondence with France had not smeared Harley himself. It was a lamentable contretemps, for it would have been far better if the peace-party had gained the upper hand at this moment: before the futile carnage of Lille and Malplaquet. Instead, in February 1708, Harley was forced to resign; St. John and his other supporters retired with him; and the Queen was left with nothing to save her from Whig domination. Since the Whigs were bankrupt of any policy for peace, this was a national calamity. Not that the issues were clear. Issues never were clear in those days when no positions or responsibilities were defined, and persons counted for more than policies. But the political uncertainty was only the greater. 'I never in my life saw or heard such divisions and complications of parties . . . You sometimes see the extremes of Whig and Tory driving on the same thing', Swift reported to King, on February 12, 1708. That was to be a frequent and fatal phenomenon in the subsequent history of parliamentary government, in countries in which the subtle conventions and basic decencies of the two-party system could not be established; and it is a reminder that they were far from being established in England yet. At this very moment the Whigs were trying to suborn Harley's clerk into implicating his master in a charge of high treason. The committee of the Lords chosen to examine Greg was packed with Harley's opponents, and the prisoner was offered his life in return for evidence against his master. One scarcely knows which to admire the more: the equanimity of Harley while his life depended on the courage unto death of a minor clerk, or the loyalty and integrity of Greg himself, who stubbornly refused the temptation to save his own life and with his last words proclaimed his master's innocence.

It was hardly the time, when party passions were thus enraged, for Swift to be urging his mission. Pembroke himself was preoccupied. He had helped to turn the scale against Harley in the Council. Now he was feeling uneasy about the consequences to his own position, for the Whigs were pressing Somers for Lord President. Meanwhile, the scare of an invasion by the Pretender was making the Dissenters active in Ireland; they were enlisting in the Militia, and thus able to exert more pressure against the Test. The English parliament was dissolved on April 15, 1708, and the Whigs strengthened their position. At this moment Swift, by the help of Somers and Sunderland, gained an interview with Godolphin. He had not consulted Pembroke about his move, because he knew that at this ticklish juncture Pembroke would resent any implication that his own credit was not enough to secure the grant of the First Fruits. Godolphin, tired and cynical, allowed Swift to present the case; then said he was himself neutral in the matter, but that he supposed that Pembroke would push it, in which case he would tell him what Swift had said. That was not at all what Swift wanted. He had gained nothing whatever from Godolphin, and was in danger of offending Pembroke. So he begged Godolphin not to mention his interview: to which Godolphin agreed.

Then Godolphin let himself go. He said that not a clergyman in England was a shilling the better for the Queen's Bounty, the distribution of which had been disgracefully abused. It was easy enough for the Queen to extend it to Ireland; but he would recommend this to her only on two conditions: that there should be no abuse in distribution, and that proper acknowledgment should be made. In the first condition Godolphin's contempt of the churchmen was manifest. He had long been suspicious of the religious sincerity and galled by the party violence of the High Churchmen, who were for ever raising the alarm that 'The Church was in danger'. He was now a weary and irritable man: in a little while his resentment of Sacheverell's attack upon him would drive him to insist on the impeachment of that empty and noisy clergyman. The second condition Swift understood to mean that the Irish clergy should acquiesce in the repeal of the Test. Immediately after the interview Swift went to Pembroke to ask his permission to approach Godolphin, and received the disconcerting answer that the Lord Treasurer had nothing to do with the matter, which lay entirely between Pembroke and the Queen. Swift did not believe it; he thought, correctly, that Pembroke was bluffing to maintain his prestige: but the reply amounted to a veto on Swift's independent action.

5

Swift's mission had failed completely. There is no sign that he took it to heart. It had been not so much the purpose, as a respectable excuse for coming to London. Stella and Dingley had come at about the same time, and the original plan had been that they and Swift should return to Ireland in the spring. They returned; he stayed behind. London was too expensive for more than a holiday for them; and Ireland was now their home. Stella never visited England again. But the growing ferment of the political situation had both protracted Swift's mission and sharpened his desire to stay. The next turn of the Court kaleidoscope might offer a pattern to suit his mission and himself.

The final shake came with the death of Anne's beloved husband, Prince George, on October 28, 1708. The Whigs had long been pressing for his removal from the Admiralty, of which he was the nominal head, in order that Pembroke might have his place, and so make room for Somers as Lord President and Wharton as Lord Lieutenant of Ireland. By so doing they had mortally offended the Queen. Now that she had lost the Prince, her mingled grief and resentment were pitiful; but she was in no condition to oppose the victory of the Junto. It was 'a new world'.

While it had been preparing, Swift had begun to cherish hopes. He had indeed been offered, presumably by Sunderland, in whose department it lay, the post of Secretary to a proposed embassy of his old friend, Lord Berkeley, to Vienna. Berkeley's health was declining, and the suggestion eventually fell through. But when at the beginning of November, Somers and Wharton entered the ministry, for a moment Swift's hopes rose higher. He believed he had greater credit with Somers than with any other of the grandees, and he had made it clear that though he reckoned himself a Whig on the vital matters of the Revolution and the Protestant succession, he was also a High Churchman, and especially so in reference to Ireland. So that Somers, Swift thought, knew with whom he was dealing. Meanwhile, Archbishop King was pressing Swift to obtain the chaplaincy to the new Lieutenant, even though it was common knowledge he would be Wharton. King said he was sure that Swift was too honest to go on ill terms, and that none would be explicitly offered. To be chaplain to the Viceroy, they were agreed, was the shortest road to high preferment in the Church of Ireland. Had not Milles got Waterford this way at the beginning of the year? Swift smiled a little at the advice: for the good Archbishop had a few enviable preferments at his own disposal, and one was vacant at the moment. The 'golden prebend' of Swords passed from one of the Archbishop's relatives to another.

Swift says positively that he 'made no manner of application' for the chaplaincy to Wharton, but it seems that he let Somers put his name forward, on his own clear terms: that he would not aid or abet any move towards the repeal of the Test in Ireland. Since Wharton and Sunderland were both determined to 'raise the Protestant interest in Ireland', by bringing the Presbyterians into play, Swift's passive candidature was rejected, in favour of a clergyman who at the crucial moment preached a sermon to the Irish Protestants in London, on the need of a rapprochement between the Church and the Nonconformists to make a common front against the Papists. By this timely conversion from his previous defence of the Test, Dr. Ralph Lambert proceeded from chaplain to the Viceroy to Bishop of Dromore.

There is not a scrap of evidence that Swift at this moment behaved otherwise than with integrity and good faith. On what he considered the matters of vital principle — the rejection of the divine right of hereditary Kings, and the power of Parliament to settle the succession — he was a Whig: on the right and duty of the State to require adherence to the established religion as the condition of participating in political power he was a Tory. He thought he had a good claim upon moderate Whigs like Somers and Halifax to some sort of preferment, for services rendered. He frequently refers to these services, but what they were, beyond the *Discourse* of 1701, is not apparent; and Swift may have over-estimated them. But his chief mistake lay in a misunderstanding of Somers and Halifax. They were both moderate and affable men, highly intelligent, and with an appreciation of genius; but primarily they were Whig politicians, and as such, they had a still keener appreciation of the advantages of political discipline. In the last resort they always followed the lead of the brilliant and unscrupulous party-manager and tactician, Wharton. And Wharton had no doubt that if the Whigs were to achieve political power they must rely on the Dissenters to help them to it. For Nonconformity as a religious movement Wharton did not care a straw. Harley the Tory was infinitely more representative of the core of religious seriousness in Nonconformity than he, and perhaps equally aware of it as a political potentiality. But somewhere in Wharton's strange composition lurked a passion for liberty as well as libertinism; and he knew that on the basis of such a political doctrine as Swift professed the Tories would be in a perpetual majority.

It was at this time that Swift began to feel the fascinated loathing of Wharton to which he afterwards gave utterance. It was self-defeating. Swift was beaten by such a phenomenon, whom candour compelled him to represent as personally invulnerable to his attacks — a kind of genial rhinoceros who emerged from the fusillade with an exasperating and not unappreciative smile: who clapped Swift on the back and grinned that he had been 'damnably mauled'. One's strong impression is that Swift never felt against Wharton the intense personal resentment he felt against Godolphin. Godolphin treated Swift *de haut en bas*, which was unforgivable. Wharton never did that: probably he was incapable of it. He had merely declined Swift as chaplain, for reasons well known to them both.

For a little while Swift reverted to his thoughts of Vienna. It was a neutral appointment that would have taken him out of the way of a party feud into which he could not fit. But Berkeley did not go. What else remained for him to hope for? A comfortable minor Church preferment in England? But anything of adequate dignity and emolument — such as Dr. South's Westminster prebend and sinecure at Islip — would need to be approved by the Queen. To be approved by the Queen it needed to be approved by the Archbishop of York, her chief ecclesiastical adviser: and he had read *A Tale of a Tub* and disliked the smell of it. Swift resolved to do what he could to dissipate the odour; and at the same time to make his political position entirely clear.

CHAPTER IX

THE POLITICAL PHILOSOPHER: 1708-1709

IN the latter part of 1708 Swift was hard at work to clarify his position with regard to Church and State. On September 4 he wrote to Ambrose Philips repudiating the authorship of Shaftesbury's *Letter on Enthusiasm*, which had been fathered upon him. It was well written, and the affiliation did not annoy him in point of style; but the matter was (he said) too full of 'free Whiggish thinking'. Since Shaftesbury's *Letter* was innocent of politics, we have to ask what Swift meant. One of Shaftesbury's main arguments was that to profess a belief in the perfect goodness of God, and at the same time to be afraid of using our reason freely in matters of religious faith, is a moral contradiction. Such an argument was repugnant to Swift. If it appealed to him at all, it was as an insidious temptation. Shaftesbury may have touched home when he wrote:

> He must surely have an unhappy opinion of God, and believe him not so good by far as he knows himself to be, who imagines that an impartial use of his reason, in any matter of speculation whatsoever, can make him run any risk hereafter; and that a mean denial of his reason, and an affectation of belief in any point too hard for his understanding, can entitle him to any favour in another world. This is being sycophants in religion, mere parasites of devotion. 'Tis using God as the crafty beggars use those they address to, when they are ignorant of their quality.

Swift was never sure that he had not an unhappy opinion of God; at any rate he was always much less certain of the goodness of God than he was of the badness of man. The notion that God might delight (as Milton had averred he did) in the ferment of human minds freely speculating about his nature was one that Swift dared not entertain. With the example of the Commonwealth close behind him, he believed it was but one step from freedom of religious speculation to political anarchy, and but another to tyranny.

It is no wonder then that Swift said to Philips, concerning the *Letter*: 'Though I am every day writing by-speculations in my chamber, they are quite of another sort.' Possibly, he had specifically in mind the dazzling *Argument against Abolishing Christianity*, which would make an admirable ironic complement to Shaftesbury. Swift had now, after his long silence, entered on a period of intense and various intellectual activity. At first, in keeping with his mood of gaiety on his return to England, it had been the magnificent joke of Isaac Bickerstaff Esq.'s *Predictions for the Year 1708*, foretelling the death of Partridge, the almanac-maker, and its sequels. The test of congruity of mood would incline one to place the *Argument against Abolishing Christianity* next; and the wholly sedate *A Letter concerning the Sacramental Test, The Sentiments of a Church of England Man*, and *A Project for the Advancement of Religion*, afterwards, in that order. Leaving aside Bickerstaff, which is the pure high spirits of the comic genius, operating under a perfect gravity of expression, the other four pieces all contributed to the work of defining his position. Only one is precisely dated: *A Letter concerning the Sacramental Test*. That was finished on December 4, 1708. There is reason to believe that *A Project for the Advancement of Religion* was published in April 1709, and that it was immediately preceded by *The Sentiments of a Church of England Man*. Swift was incapacitated by what seems to have been the first really serious attack of his giddiness from December 5, 1708 — that is, just after he had finished *A Letter on the Sacramental Test* — to January 6, 1709.* On January 12 he wrote: 'I amuse myself sometimes with projects for the uniting of parties, which I perfect overnight, and burn in the morning.' *The Sentiments of a Church of England Man* and *A Project for the Advancement of Religion* both answer to this description. They are 'projects for the uniting of parties' which satisfied Swift sufficiently to escape burning. *The Sentiments* is a well reasoned argument for the formation of a Court 'party' of the centre, uniting moderate Tories and moderate Whigs.

A Letter concerning the Sacramental Test was finished a few days after Swift had announced to King, on November 30, that Lambert was going as chaplain to Wharton. Swift had made no attempt to conceal his opinions, while the affair was in the balance: now that it was decided, he took the further step of publishing them, with a characteristic alibi. The *Letter* purports to be from an Irish M.P. to an English one. There was, he said, only one clergyman in all Ireland in favour of repealing the Test; but there were two in London. One was Dr. Lambert; but surely he could not, consistently with his previous professions, support the repeal. The other was Dr. Swift; but his disappointment at not being Wharton's chaplain would 'cool his zeal that way if he had any before'.[1] This was neat, indeed; but its very neatness would prevent it from deceiving the elect. Lambert had no doubt from whom it

---

* The entries in his account-book show that he did not completely recover until the end of January. They are as follows: 'Decbr 5 Horrible sick 12 much better Thank Gd and MD's prayers 16 bad fitt at Mrs Barton's 24 better — but dread a fitt. Better still to the end. Janry 21 an ill fitt but not to excess 29 out of order 31 not well at times.'

came. Neither, we may be sure, had anybody else with a nose for Swift's manner.

There is nothing new in his argument against any proposal to repeal the Test in Ireland by an English Act. The Presbyterians in Ireland are so energetic and zealous, that if once they are admitted to positions of power, they will quickly establish Presbyterianism as the State religion. The notion that it is expedient to admit them to power in order to unite the Protestants of Ireland in face of the danger from the Papists is quite false: the Papists are completely broken, and 'as inconsiderable as the women and children'.[2] The real question at issue is the nature of Presbyterianism. It is inherently intolerant; and it regards the Episcopal Church of Ireland, or England, as 'three degrees worse than Popery'.

> We are fully convinced in our consciences, that *we* shall always tolerate them, but not quite so fully that *they* will always tolerate us when it comes to their turn; and *we* are the majority, and *we* are in possession.[3]

In the course of the argument Swift contradicts himself. At one point he says that the Irish clergy are impartial in the question because the repeal of the Test will qualify the Presbyterians only for lay employments and not for church-livings; but within two pages he is contemplating the time when 'these same Protestants have by their dexterity made themselves the national religion, and disposed the Church revenues among their pastors or themselves'.[4]

But to a modern sense, much the most striking part of the pamphlet for matter and manner is the outburst of Irish patriotism. No doubt it is a misnomer to call by the name of Irish patriotism Swift's fierce resentment of the subordination of the Anglo-Irish interest to the English; it is very remote from the Irish patriotism of the 19th century or today. Nevertheless, it is one of its ancestors. However paradoxical it may now seem that this peculiar note of passion should be sounded in an argument for keeping the Presbyterians out of the privileged circle of the Protestant ascendancy, it is authentic and minatory. One thrills to it as to the sound of a trumpet, or the voice of prophecy. And the note is new in Swift. The passage begins with urbane irony: 'I must begin by telling you, we are generally surprised at your wonderful kindness to us on this occasion, in being so very industrious to teach us to see our interest in a point where we are so unable to see it ourselves.' Then it gathers force.

> I do not frequently quote poets, especially English, but I remember there is in some of Mr. Cowley's love-verses, a strain that I thought

extraordinary at fifteen, and have often since imagined it to be spoken by Ireland:

> 'Forbid it Heaven my life should be
> Weigh'd with her least conveniency:'

In short, whatever advantage you propose by repealing the Sacramental Test, speak it out plainly, 'tis the best argument you can use, for we value your interest much more than our own: If your little finger be sore, and you think a poultice made of our vitals will give it any ease, speak the word and it shall be done; the interest of our whole Kingdom is at any time ready to strike to that of your poorest fishing towns; it is hard you will not accept our services unless we believe at the same time that you are only consulting our profit, and giving us marks of your love. If there be a fire at some distance, and I immediately blow up my house before there be occasion, because you are a man of quality, and apprehend some danger to a corner of your stable; yet why should you require me to attend next morning at your levee with my humble thanks for the favour you have done me?[5]

The germ of this is perhaps to be detected in a letter of Archbishop King to Swift, written shortly before. 'The good of Ireland', he said, 'had no weight at all' with an English ministry. It is folly, when we are pleading with them against a line of action in regard to Ireland, to point out to them its ill consequences for us, for as likely as not, those ill consequences will provide them with an insuperable argument for pursuing it. 'It moves one's spleen to find a clergyman pressing the ruin of the Church if a certain thing be done, when perhaps that is the reason that it is to be done.'[6] Swift in his pamphlet did this very thing; but with a difference. Whereas the naive clergyman assumed that England wished to do Ireland good, Swift brushes this simplicity aside. What King mutters, he proclaims. 'If your little finger be sore, and you think a poultice made of our vitals will give it any ease, speak the word, and it shall be done.'

2

The *Letter concerning the Sacramental Test* was a direct and telling onslaught on the policy of Wharton and Sunderland. If the Whigs were a solid phalanx, Swift had deliberately ruined his chances with them. But he was loth to believe that they were. And it was by no means certain that they were. They were more solid and disciplined than the Tories; but that was all. If an English-speaking and English-educated monarch had succeeded Anne, the Whigs would never have been able to get that exclusive grasp of the apparatus and emolument of power which enabled them to consolidate the party. Assuredly, in 1708, the formation of a strong and controlling Centre body of 'Queen's servants' was a practical policy. In *The Sentiments of a Church of England Man with respect to Religion & Government* Swift laid down its principles. That he approached the question primarily as a Churchman was not due to idiosyncrasy. Although it is true, up to a point, that Swift in his attitude to politics was a Churchman first and foremost, the attitude was not peculiar to him: there was a great multitude of laymen and clergy who thought much the same, and possibly they were a majority of the full citizens of England. The cry 'The Church is in danger' was one of the two most potent political slogans in England at that day; and the other, 'No Popery!' was its near relation. The almost universal assumption was that a state religion was necessary to society. The one slogan proclaimed what this religion should be, the other what it should not. There were very few minds to which the notion of a secular state was not repugnant or even inconceivable, and they were certainly not the best.

Swift's approach to the problem of politics by way of the Church of England was not only natural to the times; it was almost a necessity of thought. Swift, like Blake, believed that 'Man must, and will have some religion'; it followed that the English State must have one. Which form of Christianity was it to be? Popery had been rejected; so had Presbyterianism. Cromwell's effort to disconnect the State from any particular form of Christianity had required a tyranny to maintain it. Yet none of these threats to the Established Church was distant enough in the past to seem remote in the present. The Church of England remained, as the citadel of sanity, and the highest common denominator of religious sentiment. But under the Restoration its political doctrines had become extravagant. The cult of King Charles as the martyr of the Divine Right of Kings was gradually expanded to the quasi-deification of the reigning Monarch; which led to sheer absurdity when James II refused to play the game as the divinely appointed Head of the Church of England. With the monarch a declared Papist, it was dimly apparent that God was not providing for the Protestant succession. Somebody else had to. The Lords and Commons of England took the duty upon themselves. That involved a theological revolution for many High Churchmen, which they were loth to admit to consciousness. They hid their heads in the sand of a subtle and silly distinction between Kings *de jure* and *de facto*. The accession of Anne gave them the opportunity of burying their heads a little deeper. With the help of the famous warming pan, the good Queen could be the Queen she obviously was, both *de jure* and *de facto*. The Non-Jurors, who had a genuine scruple against forswearing their solemn oath to James II, smiled contemptuously at their endowed and embarrassed brethren

Swift swept all the nonsense away. The Church of England, he declared, could fit with any species of regular government. A purely elective monarchy was better in theory, but in practice a hereditary one was to be preferred, because it prevented the confusion and insecurity caused by rival competitors to the Crown. But the practical and rational compromise between the hereditary and the elective principle lay in the *limited* monarchy, whereby the King was compelled to govern according to law, and the law was determined by the King, the Lords and the Commons of England. Every such limited monarch is a monarch *de jure*, for his right is bestowed by the consent of the whole. But 'whoever argues in defence of absolute power in a single person ought in all free states to be treated as the common enemy of mankind'.[7]

The Legislature had established the Church of England as an essential institution of the State. That did not mean that the Church was merely an institution of the State, as the Tindals absurdly argued; but that the State had accepted the Christian Church, with a life and institutions of its own, as necessary to its own well-being. Thus it had accepted Episcopacy, both as a historical institution of the Church and as congruous with its own civil institutions. Undoubtedly, in pure theory the Legislature had the power to change the institutions of the State religion, but it would not have the desire to do so, so long as the right to legislate was confined, as it ought to be, to members of the Church. Since any great separation from the worship established by law, even to a new one more pure and perfect, might endanger the public peace, Dissenters should be tolerated as regards their religion, but excluded from the Legislature. 'A government cannot give them too much ease, nor trust them with too little power.'[8]

That section of the Tories which attributed to the monarch some 'divine' power which did not derive from the consent of the whole, and was not controlled by the laws which only the whole could enact or repeal, were enemies to the State; likewise that section of the Whigs which pressed for the admission to the privileges of full citizenship of those who refused even an occasional conformity to the established religion, were enemies to the Church. And both alike were enemies of the Constitution in which Church and State were enmeshed and interdependent. But (Swift maintained) the majority of men on either side were agreed in the fundamental principles he had formulated. It was the extremists, in each case, who maintained the party feud, and 'built their systems upon opposition, upon injurious appellations, charging their adversaries with horrid opinions and then reproaching them for the want of charity'.[9] His own effort had been to unbias his mind and moderate between the rival powers, and to show that 'in order to preserve the Constitution entire in Church and State, whoever has a true value for both, would be sure to avoid the extremes of Whig for the sake of the former, and the extremes of Tory on account of the latter'.[10] It followed from this conception of the Constitution and of the monarch, who was the head, under law, of both Church and State, and presided over the whole, that he 'ought not in any sort be under the guidance or influence of either party' because he thereby declined from his high office to be the head of a faction. Precisely this doctrine was at this moment being expounded by Harley to the grateful ears of the Queen, who had come to it by instinct, and the experience of ruthless party pressure.

3

It is easy enough after the event to say that Swift and Harley were dreaming, because English political evolution took a different course. But it does not follow, and it is not true. Exactly how far the different direction of our history was due to accident must be left to profounder historians to estimate. But that there were a great many accidents which helped to turn the current awry (or aright) is surely indubitable. Nor is it true, as many critics have urged, that Swift's conception was too static. It certainly allowed as much scope for constitutional development as did the Whig monopoly under the first two Georges. Much the most cogent criticism of Swift's political scheme was made by himself. He hints at it in the *Sentiments*, when he declares that 'few states are ruined by any defect in their institution, but generally by the corruption of manners, against which the best institution is no long security, and without which a very ill one may subsist and flourish';[11] but he developed it to its full force in the *Argument against Abolishing Christianity*. In the *Sentiments* there is but little irony, and without irony Swift seldom delivered himself of his deepest convictions. There is just a touch of it at the beginning of the second section of the *Sentiments*, where he passes from religion to government, and by way of introduction compares the violence of political feuds to the violence of religious feuds in England. The religious animosity is among men 'who agree in all fundamentals, and only differ in some ceremonies, or at most mere speculative points'. We all deplore it, and disagree only about who is to blame. But is not the case the same with political feuds?

The differences fairly stated, would be much of a sort with those in religion among us, and amount to little more than *who should take place* or *go in and out first*, or *kiss the Queen's hand*; and what are these but a few court ceremonies? Or, *who should be in the ministry?* And what is that to the body of the nation but a mere speculative point?[12]

What is he hinting? That the feuds and factions in Church and State are about trivialities, after all? That they arise not out of questions of import, but from the irresponsibility which makes mountains out of molehills for the sake of a fight? In the *Sentiments* this is suggested as a mere possibility. The weight of the argument tends in another direction. It is that the majority of men are well-meaning enough, but through lack or impatience of reason to discern the truth, allow themselves to be inveigled 'upon false representations, to serve the ambition or malice of designing men, without any prospect of their own'.[13] The purpose of the *Sentiments* is to lift the veil of party from the truth in order that men, misled into faction, may see that they do verily agree on fundamentals, and draw together: if it be possible.

But if that is not to be hoped for, my next wish should be, that both might think me in the wrong, which I would understand as an ample justification of myself and a sure ground to believe, that I have proceeded at least with impartiality, and perhaps with truth.[14]

Thus Swift, in the *Sentiments*, leaves the question undecided, whether the prevailing party violence is due to moral obliquity, or innocent ignorance. His conclusion recalls his beginning:

To sacrifice the innocency of a friend, the good of our country, or our own conscience to the humour, or passion, or interest of a party, plainly shews that either our heads or our hearts are not as they should be: Yet this very practice is the fundamental law of each faction among us, as may be obvious to any who will impartially and without engagement, be at the pains to examine their actions, which however is not so easy a task: For it seems a principle in human nature, to incline one way more than another, even in matters where we are wholly unconcerned.[15]

Which are wrong? Men's heads or their hearts? Or is there a third possibility: that it is a principle of human nature that men seek an occasion for quarrel, even in matters wholly indifferent? And is that an invincible defect of head and heart together?

The latter is the answer of the *Argument against Abolishing Christianity*. This is one of Swift's indubitable masterpieces. The coruscations of his mind at play are incessant. It is idle to ask whether he is wholly serious. In one obvious sense, the *Sentiments* is more serious than the *Argument*. It is what we now call 'a serious contribution' to the political thinking of his time, and therefore proceeds on the assumption that the majority of men are rational beings, though it concludes by suggesting that rationality may finally be found to be in a minority of one. To make the assumption of rationality is the rule of the game. In the *Argument* he discards it. Therefore, he ceases to be 'serious'. But, in fact, he is rather more serious than before. The question: Is man, in the main, rational or irrational? exercised Swift all his life. His answers, as his life went on, grew more sombre. The element of rationality seemed to dwindle more and more under his microscope. But so long as he felt that there was an appreciable leaven of rationality in men, he could be light-hearted in letting his mind explore and dilate upon the spectacle of their irrationality.

This he does in the *Argument*. One of the propositions has an immediate bearing on the theme of the *Sentiments*. It is argued in favour of the abolition of Christianity that it will do away with parties: there will be no more High Church *v.* Low Church. If this were true, he replies, he would submit. But it is false.

Are party and faction rooted in men's hearts no deeper than phrases borrowed from religion, or founded on no firmer principles? ... What, for instance, is easier than to vary the form of speech, and instead of the word Church, make it a question in politics, whether the Monument be in danger?[16]

Perhaps the savour of the joke is dulled by time; but it is prodigiously funny if one comes to it with the incessant debates on 'Whether or not the Church is in danger?' fresh in mind. The joke would have scandalized the Tories, and hardly have amused the Whigs. To see oneself as having moved heaven and earth and a bit of hell to get a majority vote that 'The Monument is *not* in danger' is not heartening. But this is venial compared to the enormity which Swift perpetrates when, among 'the inconveniences that may be caused', he blandly writes:

Nor do I think it wholly groundless, or my fears altogether imaginary, that the abolishing of Christianity may perhaps bring the Church into danger, or at least put the Senate to the trouble of another securing vote. I desire I may not be mistaken; I am far from presuming to affirm or think that the Church is in danger at present, or as things now stand, but we know not how soon it may be so when the Christian religion is repealed ... This may be intended as one politic step toward altering the constitution of the Church established, and setting up Presbytery in the stead, which I leave to be further considered by those at the helm.[17]

The vision he conjures up of the Whig majority in the Lords, having repealed the Christian religion, solemnly voting that the Church is *not* in danger, and thereby securing its safety, is fantastic and superb. Equally satisfying is the spectacle of High Church Tories digesting the implications of the idea that the abolition of Christianity might (or might not) endanger the Church. And how much is packed into the innocent-looking 'as things now stand'! The very premiss of this comic masterpiece is that, of course, he is not 'so weak to stand up in the defence of real Christianity such as used in primitive times (if we may believe the authors of those ages) to have an influence on men's belief and actions'.

> Every candid reader will understand my discourse to be intended only in defence of nominal Christianity; the other having been for some time wholly laid aside by general consent, as utterly inconsistent with our present schemes of wealth and power.[18]

But nominal Christianity is valuable. First, if the wits had not a God to rail against, they might rail against Ministers of State. Second, it does not oblige men to believe anything at all. Third, it keeps ten thousand parsons to the necessity of a low diet and plenty of exercise, which makes them cheap and sound sires of healthy stock. Fourth, it does not, as is said, deprive the community of one day in seven and of a number of buildings useful for trade and pleasure; on the contrary, Sunday is a very useful day — for physic, claps, accounts and briefs, and the churches are equally useful for gallantry, business appointments and sleep. Fifth, by employing men to bawl once a week against the activities universally pursued in the rest of it, it gives a precious piquancy to these activities: the pleasures of a refined age largely depend on the knowledge that they are forbidden. Sixth, the abolition of nominal Christianity will not really remove the grievous prejudices of education, in favour of virtue, honour, justice and the rest, as is supposed: they have been removed already. Neither, seventhly, will it contribute as much as it seems it might to the uniting of Protestants 'by opening a large noble gate, at which all bodies may enter'.

> To all this, I answer; that there is one darling inclination of mankind, which usually affects to be a retainer to religion, though she be neither its parent, its godmother, or its friend; I mean the spirit of opposition, that lived long before Christianity, and can easily subsist without it . . . What imports it how large a gate you open, if there will be always left a number who place a pride and a merit in not coming in?[19]

Is the *Argument* simply a magnificent *jeu d'esprit*? Surely not. The defence of nominal Christianity, however comical it may be in detail, is very close to a position which Swift actually did hold and put forward quite soberly at this time, in *A Project for the Advancement of Religion & Morality*: which begins by a declaration that 'the nation is extremely corrupted in religion and morals'.

> To deliver nothing but plain matter of fact without exaggeration or satire; I suppose it will be granted that hardly one in a hundred among our people of quality or gentry appears to act by any principle of religion; that great numbers of them do entirely discard it, and are ready to own their disbelief of all revelation in ordinary discourse. Nor is the case much better among the vulgar. . . . [20]

After pointing to the notorious prevalence of drunkenness and open sexual immorality, he continues:

> But all these are trifles in comparison, if we step into other scenes, and consider the fraud and cozenage of trading men and shopkeepers; that insatiable gulf of injustice and oppression, the law. The open traffic for all civil and military employments (I wish it rested there) without the least regard to merit or qualifications; the corrupt management of men in office; the many detestable abuses in choosing those who represent the people, with the management of interest and factions among the representatives. [21]

Swift really did believe he was not exaggerating. This was the state of the nation as he saw it, and which he offered a proposal to improve The difference of emphasis is notable. The lack of genuine religious belief, the drunkenness and lewdness, are venial in comparison with the corruption of public morality. He does not agree that this corruption of public morality is a consequence of the decay of religious belief. The corruption of private morality, he seems to suggest, may be; but the corruption of public morality is independent of it. And, of course, the most pernicious examples of that corruption, namely, in officers of State, were found exclusively among men who professed themselves members of the Established Church. The Sacramental Test was a condition of their office.

If nominal Christianity, of the kind required at present as a condition of office, is thus notoriously ineffective to prevent corruption, what is the remedy? To cease to require it will mend nothing: the corruption will remain. But if the Queen, in whose gift, directly or at a remove, are all the offices of state, would require from their holders, in addition to the nominal

membership of the Church of England required by law, decency in private
and public morals; if it were known that private vice and public corruption
would be immediately punished by loss of office, a reformation of manners
throughout the country would follow. 'Nor would the public weal be less
advanced; since of nine offices in ten that are ill executed, the defect is not in
capacity or understanding but in common honesty.'

After suggesting various particular reforms: as that the clergy should
cease to hold themselves apart, mix freely with the laity, and to this end wear
civilian dress except on specifically religious occasions; that 'trading magis-
trates' should be suppressed; and that a censor of the theatre be appointed,
Swift writes:

> Neither am I aware of any objections to be raised against what I have
> advanced; unless it should be thought, that making religion a necessary
> step to interest and favour might increase hypocrisy among us: and I
> readily believe it would. But if one in twenty should be brought over to
> true piety by this, or the like methods, and the other nineteen be only
> hypocrites, the advantage would still be great. Besides, hypocrisy is
> much more eligible than open infidelity and vice; it wears the livery of
> religion; it acknowledges her authority, and is cautious of giving
> scandal. Nay, a long continued disguise is too great a constraint upon
> human nature, especially an English disposition: men would leave off
> their vices out of mere weariness, rather than undergo the toil and
> hazard, and perhaps expense of practising them perpetually in private.
> And I believe it is often with religion, as it is with love; which by
> much dissembling, at last grows real.[22]

The argument for nominal Christianity is there quite positive. The *Project* is the 'serious' counterpart of the jesting *Argument*. Swift never indulged
the fancy that men could be compelled to an inward religious belief. As he
said, following Temple:

> To say a man is bound to believe, is neither truth nor sense. You may
> force men by interest or punishment, to say or swear they believe, and
> to act as if they believed: You can go no further.[23]

But thus far, he held, the State could and ought to go. There should be
punishment for the open advocacy of infidelity, that is, for casting doubt
upon those fundamental tenets of the Christian faith that were common to
all Christian sects. Beyond that, the motive of interest should be employed,
by the monarch who had power to employ it. The Legislature imposed the
Sacramental Test on every candidate for office; the Administration, of which
the Queen was the sole head, should impose, both directly and by deputy,

the test of decent and honest behaviour upon them all, from the highest to the lowest.

At this point Swift's argument rejoins that of the *Sentiments*. His *Project* is aimed at the correction of that corruption of manners which he had declared to be the prime cause of the ruin of states, rather than any defect in their institutions. The suppression of public corruption would be the best means to bring the war to a good conclusion; and it would powerfully contribute to the uniting of parties.

> All parties would be obliged to close with so good a work as this, for their own reputation: Neither is any expedient more likely to unite them. For the most violent party men, I have ever observed, are such, as in the conduct of their lives have discovered least sense of religion or morality; and when all such are laid aside, at least those among them as shall be found incorrigible, it will be a matter perhaps of no great difficulty to reconcile the rest.[24]

Swift then makes some more specific recommendations, this time to the Legislature: much more stringent regulation against legal and commercial and financial fraud, the practisers of which 'do surely deserve the gallows much better than the wretch who is carried thither for stealing a horse'; the closing of taverns at midnight, and making it an offence to serve a drunken person with more drink; the building of new churches to accommodate the vastly overgrown and largely heathen population of London. The first two of these proposals waited a hundred and fifty years for adoption, and were not really practicable until an efficient police-force had been formed. The third is said to have been the origination of the Act of 1712 whereby the produce of a tax on coal imported into London was applied to building of fifty new London churches.

5

Whenever Swift comes to be particular about the party-man, Wharton rises before his imagination. The picture above suggests him; and the suggestion is still more definite towards the end of the *Project*.

> It must be confessed as things are now, every man thinks that he has laid in a sufficient stock of merit, and may pretend to any employment, provided he has been loud and frequent in declaring himself hearty for the government. 'Tis true, he is a man of pleasure, and a freethinker, that is, in other words, he is profligate in his morals, and a despiser of religion; but in point of party he is one to be confided in; he is an

assertor of liberty and property; he rattles it out against Popery and
Arbitrary Power, and Priestcraft and High Church. 'Tis enough: He
is a person fully qualified for any employment, in the court or the navy,
the law or the revenue; where he will be sure to leave no arts untried,
of bribery, fraud, injustice, oppression, that he can practice with any
hope of impunity.[25]

No Tory would take that to himself. The slogans are Whig slogans. If
it is not Wharton alone, it is Wharton and his tribe that are envisaged. Swift,
though entirely sincere in his efforts for the reconciliation of the moderate
men in both parties, has already acquired a slight but perceptible bias towards
the Tories, while still reckoning himself an under-rate Whig. There is nothing
untoward in that. What is astonishing is that, in a very little while, he will be
consorting familiarly with Harry St. John, as dissolute in private and public
morals as Wharton himself. Can he so completely have forgotten the central
argument of the *Project*, or have been so beglamoured by the familiarity of
that brilliant rogue, that he could not recognize in him another epitome of
the vices against which he had inveighed? Even when the débâcle had happened, when the Queen was dead, and the Tories broken — not least through
Bolingbroke's unscrupulous ambition — when Swift knew his man through
and through, still he wrote to him that a great position was assured to him,
as 'the head of the Church party'. To a Churchman the spectacle of Bolingbroke at the head of the Church party should surely have been more disquieting than that of Wharton at the head of the Dissenters.

But at this moment, in the winter of 1708-9, Swift had not been exposed to
the temptations of proximity to power. He was still sufficiently detached and
politically insignificant to be able to think out his position with an unbiased
mind. On the surface it was coherent enough. To a well-ordered state,
religion was essential: of the English Constitution the Established Church
was an integral part. He, as a clergyman, must not suffer the position of the
Church in the Constitution to be weakened.

'I look upon myself,' he wrote in his *Thoughts on Religion*, ' in the capacity
of a clergyman, to be one appointed by Providence for defending a post
assigned to me, and for gaining over as many enemies as I can.'[26] Since the
position of the Church in the Constitution depended, not on any right
divine, but upon the will of the Legislature, it was imperative that the
Dissenters should be excluded from political power. (The converse proposition that, since the toleration of the Dissenters also depended upon the
Legislature, they needed political power to prevent it from being taken
away from them, hardly entered Swift's mind.) From the Tory high-flyers
Swift was sharply differentiated by his conviction that the succession to the

Crown was determined entirely by the Legislature, and that, though the Church itself was a divine institution, the Church 'by law established' was not. From the extreme Whigs he was distinguished by his refusal on principle to admit, either in England or Ireland, any mitigation of the Test. The full citizen of England must be a professed member of the Church of England. These he believed to be the principles of a rational politics, and upon them, he hoped, a unification of parties might be possible, whereby the extremists on either side might be isolated and made ineffective.

But in his satirical writing at this moment a deeper level of thought is apparent. Although he demonstrated that the party alignment was irrational, he suspected that the party-division might be pre-rational and instinctive, and that Englishmen like dogs delighted to bark and bite at each other. The injustice and extravagance of their party-cries was part of the sport, a congenial manifestation of the English passion for 'liberty'. Bolingbroke's description of the House of Commons, in his *Letter to Wyndham*, is in point: 'You know the nature of that assembly; they grow, like hounds, fond of the man that shows them game, and by whose halloo they are used to be encouraged.' Like most of Bolingbroke's observations, it was only partly true: the influence of St. John's oratory in the Commons was never equal to that of Harley's sober persuasions. But there was truth enough in it to make the party-feud appear extraordinarily dangerous to Swift in this transition period when the conventions of the party-system had barely begun to emerge. It must have been very hard for a detached mind to feel at all certain that this irrational English passion for a political dog-fight would not end in disaster; and quite impossible to foresee that, mellowed by time and experience and favoured by geography, it would turn out to be one of the most effective methods evolved in human history, of combining liberty with order and embodying the dialectic of growth.

Of the quiet instinctive faith in the destiny and essential soundness of England which was remarkable in Harley, Swift had nothing. Although he put forward a scheme for the uniting of parties which, at the intellectual level, was identical with Harley's actual policy, when it came to the test of action, his nerve failed. In a crisis he was one of Harley's devoted 'cowards'. Political experience and sagacity apart, he lacked the underlying religious conviction by which Harley was sustained. Swift's view of things was naturally desperate. In his moments of imaginative detachment, he could smile sardonically or laugh outright at the irrationality and baseness of man; but when his mind descended to the level of practical reality he was aghast at the precariousness of such order as there was. It was almost a paradox that there should be any at all. The menace of degeneration and disaster seemed to him incessant. Good government consisted in maintaining the dykes to prevent the further flood of irrationality, appetite and corruption.

The Constitution was a sort of miracle of providence with which it was dangerous to tamper; the Church an institution for ingeminating morality. The problem was how to maintain morality enough to save society from anarchy. The merit of Christianity was that it gave a supernatural sanction to a system of morals which otherwise had only the sanction of reason on which to depend, and reason was far too thinly distributed to maintain it. Since the value of religious faith consisted precisely in its supplying an anchorage for morality, 'enthusiasm' was almost as deplorable and dangerous as infidelity.

6

Thus Swift made his position clear, and it was one which left him little to hope for from the Whigs. He wrote to Ford on March 8, 1709: 'You are satisfied by this time that I am not grown great nor like to do so very soon, for I am thought to want the art of being thorough-paced in my party'; and to Hunter a fortnight later: 'I shall go for Ireland some time in the summer, being not able to make my friends in the Ministry consider my merits, or their promises, enough to keep me here; so that all my hopes now terminate in my bishopric of Virginia.' His friend, Colonel Hunter, was Lieu-tenant-Governor designate of Virginia. He proved to be an excellent one — brave, disinterested, capable and incorruptible, who left his Government a much poorer man than he entered it. The bishopric of Virginia was pro-bably more than a private joke between them. The appointment of such a bishop was contemplated at the time, and indeed it was urgently necessary if the Church of England in America was not to dwindle and die. From the terms of a later letter of Hunter's to him, it appears that Swift had seriously considered it as a possibility.[27]

Meanwhile, his mission regarding the First Fruits continued to plague him. Fortunately, Pembroke had informed Archbishop King as well as himself that the boon had been granted. When it transpired that nothing had been done, it was not Swift's credit, but Pembroke's that suffered. Pembroke lamely explained that 'he had been promised that he should carry over the grant when he returned to Ireland'. Swift went straightway to Wharton, who told him that he expected that an entirely fresh application should be made to himself as the new Lieutenant. Swift complained to Somers of this treatment, and Somers arranged a meeting between Swift and Wharton on March 27, 1709, at which Wharton received him 'as dryly as before'.[28] Thus the whole enterprise had ended in complete fiasco, and another black mark was scored against Wharton.

Nevertheless, the fact that Addison — 'le plus honnête homme du monde' — was going to Ireland as Wharton's Secretary must have helped, not only to reconcile Swift to a return to Ireland, but to keep him nominally a Whig. Besides that, he was reluctant finally to admit that his intimacy with Somers and Halifax was to be barren of advantage to himself. On his way back to Ireland in June he wrote to Halifax one of the most constrained and insincere letters of his whole correspondence. Swift cannot often be accused of being fulsome. But in telling Halifax that 'he had fifty times more wit than all of us together', he certainly was.[29] However, the point of his letter was that Halifax should keep Somers in mind of him, particularly when Dr. South's prebend and sinecure became vacant. Both, he emphasized, were in the Queen's gift. Perhaps he had fallen in with Berkeley's suggestion that he should give a copy of the *Project* to Sharpe, the Archbishop of York, to put before the Queen, and was hopeful of the effect.

Swift was keeping all his irons in the fire. In his preface to Part III of Temple's *Memoirs*, which he was now arranging for publication, and for which he received £40, he went well out of his way to pay all the compliments he could contrive.

> But as this author is very free in exposing the weaknesses and corruptions of ill ministers, so he is ready to commend the abilities and virtues of others, as may be observed from several passages of these Memoirs; particularly, of the late Earl of Sunderland, with whom the author remained in the most intimate friendship to his death; and who was father of that most learned and excellent Lord, now Secretary of State; as likewise, of the present Earl of Rochester; and the Earl of Godolphin, now Lord Treasurer, represented by this impartial author as a person at that time deservedly entrusted with so great a part in the Prime Ministry; an office he now executes again with such universal applause, so much to the Queen's honour and his own, and to the advantage of his country as well as of the whole Confederacy.

The compliment to Sunderland may pass, though his father's abilities were *not* commended in the *Memoirs*; but that to Godolphin was a *tour de force*. Swift's dislike of him was intense, and Temple's narrative contains nothing whatever in his favour. Indeed in the previous section he had definitely charged Godolphin with a heartless refusal to pay him £2200 due to him on account of his embassy at Nimuegen.

> Mr. Godolphin, after having both said and writ to me, that he would move to have my statue set up if I compassed that Treaty, has sat several

years since in the Treasury, and seen me want the very money I laid out of my own purse in that service, and which I am like to leave a debt on my estate and family.[30]

Halifax replied to Swift's letter: 'I am quite ashamed for myself and my friends . . . to see so much merit and so great qualities unrewarded by those who are sensible of them', and assured him that he would never rest content until they were. Swift afterwards endorsed the reply: 'I kept this letter as a true original of courtiers and court promises'.[31] Temple's experience should have warned him long ago. Probably it had.

7

Swift's witty baiting of Partridge, the almanac-maker, had been kept up by himself and his friends throughout 1708. In his almanac for 1709 Partridge protested that he was still alive, and Swift replied in his final *Vindication of Isaac Bickerstaff Esq.* with further proofs that he was dead, among them the unanimous declaration of above a thousand gentlemen who had read his almanac that 'they were sure no man alive ever writ such damned stuff as this'. The popularity of Bickerstaff was enormous. Steele, with Swift's approval and encouragement, cashed in upon it by issuing on April 12, 1709, the first number of *The Tatler*, by Isaac Bickerstaff Esq. It was an instant success. Steele gratefully and publicly acknowledged his indebtedness to Swift: first, in the dedication of the first volume.

But a work of this nature requiring time to grow into the notice of the world, it happened very luckily, that a little before I had resolved on this design, a gentleman had written Predictions, and two or three other pieces in my name, which had rendered it famous through all parts of Europe; and by an inimitable spirit of humour, raised it to as high a pitch of reputation as it could possibly arrive at. By this good fortune the name of Isaac Bickerstaff gained an audience of all with any taste of wit.

In the Preface to the collected edition of the whole four volumes he was still more explicit on the importance of Swift's inspiration to the venture.

I have in the dedication of the first volume made my acknowledgments to Dr. Swift, whose pleasant writings in the name of Bickerstaff created an inclination in the town towards anything that could appear in the same disguise. I must acknowledge also, that at my first entering upon this work, a certain uncommon way of thinking, and a turn in conversation peculiar to that agreeable gentleman, rendered his company very advantageous to one whose imagination was to be employed on obvious and common subjects, though at the time obliged to treat of them in a new and unbeaten method. His verses on the Shower in Town and the Description of the Morning are instances of the happiness of that genius, which could raise such pleasing ideas upon occasions so barren to an ordinary invention.

The acknowledgment could hardly have been more handsome. *A Description of the Morning* appeared in *The Tatler* (No. 9), on April 30, 1709.

> Now hardly here and there a hackney-coach
> Appearing, show'd the ruddy morn's approach
> Now Betty from her master's bed had flown
> And softly stole to discompose her own.[32]

It is still fresh and alive; it was Swift's parting present to the town before he retired to Ireland.

He left London on May 5. He stayed for six weeks with his mother at Leicester, working hard; and was back in Dublin on June 30. He had been away more than a year and a half, but not more than a year from 'the ladies', to whom he had written with great regularity once a fortnight, though, alas, none of the letters have survived. He had greatly increased his reputation as a wit — Bickerstaff was a household word — and as a political pamphleteer. He had moved, in politics, perceptibly nearer to Harley's centre position and his 'moderating scheme'. He can hardly have been unaware of the rapprochement.

CHAPTER X

MAKING ENEMIES: 1709-1710

THE *Apology* for *A Tale of a Tub* is dated June 3, 1709. It was therefore written during Swift's stay in or around Leicester, on his way
back to Ireland. It adds nothing to the strength of the book. Part of
it is indeed, simply, an apology for it. The attitude was uncongenial to
Swift, and his gesture was embarrassed. He was not altogether veracious,
either. He declared that he had not so much as read Shaftesbury's *Letter on
Enthusiasm*; whereas his correspondence proves that he had. And it is hard
to credit his assurance that in the original there were four oratorical machines,
one of which 'those who had the papers in their power blotted out'. It is
an unconvincing way of proving that he meant no blasphemy in his playing
with 'the profound number, THREE'. He would have done better to ignore a
charge which, if it was urged in good faith, was stupid.

Swift has two points to make. One is that his book is entirely original,
which he makes with ease. The other is that it is not irreligious. It is this
which embarrasses him. The best he can say is that the clergy of the Church
of England ought not be offended by it, because 'it celebrates the Church of
England as the most perfect of all others; it advances no opinion they reject,
nor condemns any they receive'. He hurries on to suggest that their dis-
pleasure would find a fitter object in the Deists; but they have never been
good at distinguishing enemies from friends. He then intimates that, if the
Tale had been better received by the influential dignitaries of the Church,
he would have employed himself in a critical attack on the Deists.

> But he has now given over these thoughts; since the weightiest men,
> in the weightiest stations, are pleased to think it a more dangerous
> point to laugh at those corruptions in Religion, which they them-
> selves must disapprove, than to endeavour pulling up those very
> foundations, wherein all Christians have agreed.[1]

Swift had just abandoned a reply to Tindal's *The Rights of the Christian
Church Asserted*; and he may have abandoned it because he felt that, even if
he went through with it, he would not be able to overcome the prejudice
that Archbishop Sharpe, the chief of the Queen's ecclesiastical advisers, had
conceived against the author of the *Tale*. This is just possible, but the evidence
of his unfinished reply to Tindal is that he dropped it because he was bored

by the task. As he himself said later in the *Apology*: 'To answer a book effectively requires more pains . . . than were employed in the writing of it.'[2] This corresponds exactly with what he says in the *Remarks* upon Tindal: 'I am now opening the book which I propose to examine. An employment, as it is entirely new to me, so it is that to which, of all others, I have naturally the greatest antipathy.'[3]

But before he laid it aside he had some fun, at Locke's expense as much as Tindal's. He quotes from Tindal: 'It will be necessary to show what is contained in the idea of government', and says:

> Now it is to be understood, that this refined way of speaking was introduced by Mr. Locke; after whom the author limpeth as fast as he is able. All the former philosophers in the world, from the age of Socrates to ours, would have ignorantly put the question, *Quid est imperium?* But now it seemeth we must vary our phrase; and, since our modern improvement of human understanding, instead of desiring a philosopher to describe or define a mouse-trap, or tell me what it is; I must gravely ask, what is contained in the idea of a mouse-trap?[4]

After quoting Tindal's unrewarding exposition of what *is* contained in the idea of government, he continues:

> Let us melt this refined jargon into the old style for the improvement of such who are not conversant in the new . . . Suppose he had thought it necessary (and I think it was as much so as the other) to show us what is contained in the idea of a mouse-trap, he must have proceeded in these terms. 'It would be vain for an intelligent being, to set rules for hindering a mouse from eating his cheese, unless he can inflict upon that mouse some punishment, which is not the natural consequence of eating the cheese. For, to tell her it may lie heavy on the stomach; that she will grow too big to get back into her hole, and the like, can be no more than advice: therefore, we must find out some way of punishing her, which hath more inconveniencies than she will ever suffer by the mere eating of cheese.' After this, who is so slow of understanding as not to have in his mind a full and complete idea of a mouse-trap?[5]

Apart from such admirable fooling, Swift was confessedly unwilling to spend the pains required to answer Tindal effectively. By suggesting that he would have persevered if he had not been discouraged by the episcopal reception of the *Tale*, he pleased himself and scored off his enemy.

But Swift, in the *Apology*, makes no reply at all to the main charge against the *Tale* brought by the devout. Wotton had put this simply and well in the third edition of his *Reflections*.

I confess, sir, I abhor making sport with any way of worshipping God, and he that diverts himself too much at the expense of the Roman Catholics and the Protestant Dissenters, may lose his own religion ere he is aware of it, at least the power of it in his heart.

Swift, though he replies to Wotton at length, does not touch upon this. Just as he had dismissed, by an amusing but unscrupulous trick, Wotton's polite and substantial reply to Temple's *Essay on Ancient and Modern Learning*, so he now evades Wotton's criticism of himself. He had previously turned the laugh against Wotton, very cleverly indeed, by incorporating his explanations as serious footnotes to the 1705 edition of the *Tale*. But the *Apology* itself is, for Swift, a lame and half-hearted performance. Some small part of him would like to conciliate the shocked religious sensibilities of men who, he knew, were not only influential but genuinely devout; a much larger part of him jibs at making any concession at all.

2

At about the same time he was correcting the proofs of Part III of Temple's *Memoirs*. The publication of these in 1709, without any preliminary consultation with the Temple family, outraged Lady Giffard. Rather hastily she inserted an advertisement in the *Postman* to say that the publication was both unauthorized and inaccurate. Since Swift's name appeared openly as editor, this was an ugly slur upon his reputation. Lady Giffard's second charge, at least, was untrue. But Swift had taken the high hand, and a serious risk as well.

The published text of the *Memoirs* was certainly not garbled, as Lady Giffard's advertisement suggested; but whether the publication was authorized by Temple is another matter. Swift himself had said in his preface to the last volume of Temple's remains that he had published (the last volume of the *Letters*, in 1703): 'The following papers are the last of this, or indeed of any kind, about which the author gave me his particular commands.' So that, on his own public confession, Temple had not given him instructions to publish the *Memoirs*, Part III. Since he further confessed that he knew the Temple family objected to their being published, it is pretty plain that he was acting in a high-handed way. He may have been legally in the right, as having a general title to act as Temple's literary executor; but he was morally in the wrong.

Temple, in his lifetime, had instructed Swift to make copies of his MSS., and these copies had been corrected under his supervision. Swift retained them, as he had a right to do. But the originals remained with the family, and the family had decided that the third part of the *Memoirs* ought not to be published during the lifetime of the dowager Lady Essex. Lady Essex had been Lady Giffard's life-long friend; and she was the aunt of the Duchess of Somerset, who was also a close friend of Lady Giffard. The third part of the *Memoirs* bore very hard on the character of her husband, the unfortunate Lord Essex, who had been sent to the Tower in 1682 for his complicity in Shaftesbury's plot, and there committed suicide. Rightly or wrongly, Temple represented him as a faithless, corrupt and meanly ambitious man, whose actions during the critical years from 1679 to 1682 had been entirely governed by his desire to return to the government of Ireland for the purpose of enriching himself. When he found his path to the Lieutenancy blocked, partly by Temple's disclosure of his plan for the financial exploitation of Ireland, he joined with Shaftesbury. 'Lord Shaftesbury [wrote Temple] told him in those shameless words: "My Lord, if you come into us, never trouble yourself, we'll make you Lieutenant of Ireland".'[6] A sense of personal injury may have darkened this ugly picture of Essex, for Temple complains of having been deliberately duped by him; but Essex far more than Shaftesbury is the villain of Temple's piece. With Shaftesbury he had no personal contact at all; but Essex was a seeming friend, who is represented as a sordid traitor to both Temple and his King.

The publication was thus bound to be deeply wounding to Lady Essex; to Lady Giffard it was a double outrage, as the revelation of her beloved brother's sentiments about the husband of her dear friend. Swift knew that she was utterly opposed to the publication. He ignored her opposition. When he wrote to her, reproaching her for the terms of her advertisement, he said: 'Knowing your Ladyship's opinion was against their publishing, I did it without your knowledge, on purpose to leave you wholly without blame.'[7] He contended that Lady Giffard ought to have done no more than publicly disclaim all responsiblity for the publication; she ought not to have said that the text was 'unfaithful'. In that he showed a crass lack of imagination, or of sympathy. What was the poor woman to do? She was concerned not only to spare the feelings of her friend, but to save the reputation of her brother with her friend. In both their eyes, Temple's delineation of Essex was cruel — a breach of friendship. When actual publication had occurred, what other refuge had she than to insinuate that the text was not authentic? To her the issue was simple. Swift had wantonly thrust her into an intolerable situation. Why should he not pay the price of saving her brother's reputation and her friend's feelings?

But far more serious, in its consequences for Swift, than Lady Giffard's indignation was that of the Duchess of Somerset. She was to become the blackest of Swift's *bêtes noires*, and he was to be unscrupulous in denigrating her. The evidence is that she was a spirited, generous and gracious woman.

3

The Lady Elizabeth Percy was Swift's exact co-eval. She was born in 1667, and was the only child of the eleventh and last Earl of Northumberland of the original line, who died while she was a child. She was thus the richest heiress in England, and the noblest born. At the age of four, she held in her own right six of the oldest baronies in the kingdom, namely, Percy, Lucy, Poynings, Fitz-Payne, Bryan and Latimer. The mere recital is like a fanfare. Inevitably, her marriage was the subject of plot and intrigue. She was contracted in childhood to Lord Ogle, the deformed son and heir of the Duke of Newcastle. He died in 1680, when the Lady Elizabeth was barely fourteen; and, although she had never left her grandmother's house for him, she was brought up to Whitehall in widow's weeds. Charles II called her 'the sad little heiress'.

Almost immediately, in October 1691, she was again contracted, this time definitely against her will, to the wealthy Thomas Thynne of Longleat — 'Tom o' Ten Thousand'. Being still in mourning, she had never even met him. As soon as her mourning was over, aided by Henry Sidney — the Earl of Romney who neglected Swift in 1699 and whom Swift lampooned — she managed to escape from her husband and from England. She took refuge with the Temples at the Hague, and instituted proceedings in the ecclesiastical court for the dissolution of her marriage with Thynne. Then she went to the Court of Hanover, where she made the acquaintance of Count Charles Königsmark, the elder brother of Philip, the story of whose fatal intrigue with the Princess Sophia Dorothea of Zell, the wife of the future George I, has been brilliantly, though not quite truthfully, told by Thackeray. Charles Königsmark, no doubt planning to secure the rich prize for himself, plotted the murder of Thynne, who was shot in his coach in St. James's Street, as he was coming from Northumberland House on the evening of Sunday, February 11, 1682. There is no reason whatever to believe that the little Lady Elizabeth had any foreknowledge of the crime, or any attachment to its instigator.

Shortly afterwards, she returned to England, and was married to Charles Seymour, the 6th Duke of Somerset, on May 30, 1682. She was then fifteen, and he was twenty. He was, after Norfolk, the senior Duke of England, handsome, and fantastically proud; but even he could not suppose the Lady Elizabeth's lineage less distinguished than his own, and he was her inferior in character and intelligence. Her life with her husband was not very happy. Swift himself describes her as suffering under 'a domestic tyranny';[8] and Dartmouth says that the Duke treated her 'without gratitude or affection, though he owed her all he had'.[9] Probably, his stupid pride was humiliated by this very fact; and he asserted himself by trying to humiliate her. In April 1692, ten years after their marriage, the Somersets gained the grateful friendship of the Princess Anne, by placing Sion House at her disposal when she was summarily ejected from the Cockpit. In return, ten years later still, at her accession, the Queen made Somerset her Master of the Horse. After the Marlboroughs, the Somersets stood next as personal servants and friends of the Queen; and when Sarah Marlborough was finally dismissed, Elizabeth Somerset was her natural successor. Except by Swift and the party-blinded, she was highly esteemed for her grace and courtesy in office. Peter Wentworth, himself a Tory, wrote of her in January 1712, just before the Tories had succeeded in getting rid of her husband:

> If the Duchess must out, she will leave the Court with a very good grace, for everybody is pleased with her good breeding and civility; and I believe that if her Duke had thought her what all the rest of the world thinks, capable of advising him, things would not be as they now are. Their case is the reverse of the Duke and Duchess of Marlborough, in the eye of the world 'tis she has been the ruin of him, and he the ruin of her.[10]

The judgment accords with the impression produced by her few surviving letters, written to Lady Giffard. They are delightfully easy and natural; and they are generous. She has a good word even for the Duchess of Marlborough, who had been furious with her for taking her place. When the Duke of Marlborough died, she wrote to Lady Giffard:

> I don't wonder she is in great affliction for him, for she married him for love, and tho' his ill health had much affected his understanding, yet he had still enough to be sensible of the care she had of him, and there is nothing touches so near as the death of an old friend.[11]

She herself died on June 26, 1722, only six days after writing this letter. On the evidence, the Duchess of Somerset was the reverse of vindictive. But she was shocked by Swift's deliberate publication of a book which outraged both her favourite aunt, Lady Essex, and her dear friend, Lady Giffard, who had stood by her when she fled as a girl bride to Holland, thirty years before. She wrote to Lady Giffard:

> I remember we both agreed with you that it was not proper to be made public during my Aunt Essex's life, and I am sure Dr. Swift has

too much wit to think it is, which makes his having done it unpardonable and will confirm me in the opinion I had before of him that he is a man of no principle either of honour, or of religion.[12]

Swift, she said, was too intelligent not to know that Temple's character of Lord Essex ought not to be published while his wife was alive. One cannot but agree with her. He had definitely failed in humanity, and in loyalty to the Temple family. One cannot excuse it as mere carelessness, for he admitted that he knew of the objection. It is inconceivable that the Duchess's judgment of him did not reach his ears; and it is certain that he cherished a fierce resentment against her for it.

The peculiar turpitude of his subsequent attack upon her in *The Windsor Prophecy* is not to be explained either by the compulsions of a desperate political situation, or even by the fact (if indeed it was then apparent) that her influence with the Queen was working against his preferment in England. Some deeper motive is required for a piece of malignity unique even in Swift. It is to be found in the consciousness that he had acted shabbily and disloyally, and the still more galling consciousness that a very great lady knew it, and had judged him accordingly. There was, indeed, a scarcely veiled threat in Swift's letter of protest and self-justification to Lady Giffard of November 10, 1709.

Is it agreeable to prudence, or at least to caution, to do that which might break all measures with any man who is capable of retaliating?

Retaliate he did; not upon Lady Giffard herself, but upon the Duchess of Somerset. It was not her reputation which suffered, but his own.

Presumably the chief reason why he published the *Memoirs* when he did was that he was hard pushed for money. No editing was required. It was a useful £40 for a manuscript he had ready in his drawer.

4

But now he was back in Ireland, while the Whigs in England were moving to their doom by impeaching Dr. Sacheverell. He was living quietly and frugally, and repairing his finances. His account books show that he was living on £80 a year. Two years later, when he was comforting Stella with the assurance that when he returned to Ireland he would keep no company but hers — meaning the circle of her friends in Dublin — he wrote: 'You know I kept my resolution last time; and except Mr. Addison, conversed with none but you and your club of Deans and Stoytes.'[13] He had arrived at Ringsend on June 30 and gone straight to Laracor; but he returned to

Dublin on July 4. He spent much time with Addison and, though he subsequently represented that he had practically no contact with Wharton, it is clear from his letters that he was fairly assiduous at Dublin Castle. He was in Ireland on this occasion from July 1, 1709, to August 31, 1710 — exactly fourteen months. Only eight of his letters of this period have survived, since two of these refer to conversations with Wharton at his levées, we must presume that his attendance was regular, at least when he was in Dublin. Probably it would have been difficult for him to avoid this, while his friend Addison was Secretary, even if he had wished to. But there is no evidence that he did wish. His subsequent account of his relations with Wharton is not to be trusted. It is coloured by an animus which he thought prudent to conceal at the time.

There was nothing reprehensible in Swift's relations with Wharton; and it does not conflict with his having lived for the most part in relative retirement. The Castle was the Castle; and it was his elementary duty to keep in with it, if he hoped for advancement. The Vice-regal Court was a replica of *the* Court; and the fact that Wharton was personally disreputable was irrelevant. The Court was the centre of power; and those who hoped to succeed must treat it as such. The attitude was traditional. Sir William Temple had taught him by precept and example that to withdraw from the Court was to abandon all ambition in Church or State. Temple could afford to withdraw; Swift could not.

Thus it would be preposterous to represent Swift as currying favour with Wharton. For Swift, when he was in Dublin, to attend Wharton at the levée was the most natural thing in the world. Only he was more assiduous than he cared to remember afterwards. But much of his time was spent in the real retirement of Laracor, where he loved to be in the spring. From April to June 1710 he was there, and 'the ladies of St. Mary's' stayed near by at Trim. Even when he was not there for a long stay, he went for a week-end every fortnight, and 'the ladies' rode out from Dublin with him. At Laracor he lived in a little cottage that he had had built for himself; there he preached to his congregation of fifteen people, 'most of them gentle and all simple'; there he enjoyed labouring to improve his tiny domain, planting willows and hedges, making a walk by the river, scouring his 'canal', lending a hand in fishing for eels and trout. He enclosed his glebe with a quick-set hedge, which did well on the bank and poorly on the flat. He was proud of his river-walk, and the cherry trees he planted beside it.

He was at Laracor when the news of his mother's death arrived. She died on April 24, 1710, but the letter did not reach him until May 10. 'I have now lost my barrier between me and death,' he wrote.[14] The phrase is eloquent of our common experience. So long as our parents live, we do feel that they stand between us and death; but the feeling lies deep, half-formed and seldom uttered. That Swift felt it so sharply at the age of forty-three was because 'he was often giddy and had fits this year'.[15] His incessant *memento mori* — or the warning of worse than death — had begun. 'God grant', his note runs on, 'I may live to be as well prepared for it as I confidently believe her to have been! If the way to heaven be through piety, truth, justice and charity, she is there!' In the case of another than Swift, one would accept the 'if' as merely rhetorical. But with him one is tempted to wonder, and to take the words less as a profession of faith, than an expression of his love and admiration for his mother.

5

At Addison's summons, he returned to Dublin on June 5, taking a lodging in Capel Street — the same street as 'the ladies'. Then came the news that Sunderland had been dismissed on June 13. At first, Swift felt that there was no mistaking the omen, and that the entire downfall of the Whigs was imminent. On June 29 he wrote to Tooke, his publisher, that he hoped to be seeing him soon, 'since it is likely to be a new world, and I have the merit of not complying with the old'. He had indeed definitely dissociated himself from the extreme Whigs by his arguments against the repeal of the Test, and in the only pamphlet he had written since his return to Ireland, *A Letter to a Member of Parliament, in Ireland, upon the choosing of a new Speaker there*, he had emphasized his position. But the piece may not have been recognized as Swift's; it is a perfunctory performance, and has little of his style. Anyhow, he did not feel that he had finally broken with the Whigs, or that he really understood what was happening at Court. His first interpretation of the political changes wavered. Even on August 22, when the news of Godolphin's dismissal had come, he wrote to Addison, who had gone to England:

Even the moderate Tories here are in pain at these revolutions, being what will certainly affect the Duke of Marlborough, and consequently the success of the war. My Lord Lieutenant asked me yesterday when I intended for England. I said I had no business there now, since in a little time I should have no friend there that had any credit, and his Excellency was of my opinion.

He goes on, in evident perplexity, to ask Addison's candid advice. 'Tell me freely whether it will be of any account for me to come to England. I would not trouble you for advice if I knew where else to ask it. We expect every day to hear of my Lord President's [Somers's] removal. If he were to continue I might perhaps hope for some of his good offices.' Since Addison had asked him to say definitely what place he would like to have, he replied that he had two things in mind: Dr. South's prebend and sinecure, or the place of Historiographer. 'But,' he continued, 'if things go on in the train they are now, I shall only beg you, when there is an account to be depended on for a new government here, that you will give me early notice to procure an addition to my fortunes.'

Thus, in spite of his previous notice to Tooke, Swift had now become entirely uncertain about going to England. At first sight it is puzzling that, with Tooke, he claims the merit of not complying with the old world; while, to Addison, he appears to put all his hopes on Somers's remaining in office. It was not duplicity, but perplexity. We must not apply to this situation, or Swift's behaviour in it, habits of thought which belong to a later age; we shall misconceive the reality and do injustice to him. At this moment Somers himself was equally perplexed. For some weeks after the fall of Godolphin, he was hoping that he would neither be dismissed nor have to resign. And Cowper, the Whig Lord Chancellor, was being positively pressed to remain in office. Behind all the uncertainty were two things. The first was that Harley and the Queen wanted 'a moderating scheme', a union of moderate Whigs and moderate Tories, who would regard themselves primarily as the 'Queen's servants'. They were only too willing to retain influential Whigs who would cut themselves adrift from the Junto, on condition they accepted Harley's leadership, and a policy of peace with France. The second was that Whigs were mortally afraid of a dissolution of Parliament and a new election while the Sacheverell boom was on; and Harley himself was not eager for one. He was, essentially, a man of moderation. He disliked Sacheverell, and the consequences of Sacheverell. His sentiments were well expressed by his shrewd sister Abigail, at the time of the trial. 'What is mankind,' she wrote on March 2, 1709, 'that a nonsensical harangue from a pragmatical insignificant man should make such terrible work!', and on March 11, after the Doctor's virtual acquittal: 'This business will in all probability break the Whigs; my foolish fears are it will raise the Tories to their old madness, the extravagance of every party is to be dreaded.'[16]

Harley's dilemma was plain. If he could not win over the moderate Whigs to his centre government for peace, he would be faced by a hostile Commons; and his only recourse must be to a new election to the dangerous tune 'The Church is in danger!' The Whigs would be routed, indeed, but a moderate Tory government would be forced into extreme courses by the triumphant backwoodsmen. What Harley hoped and tried to do was to induce the moderate Whigs, by the threat of an election which he feared only a little less than themselves, to join his centre government of Queen's servants. In the event they declined. It was Harley's policy of peace that stuck in their throats.

In a situation so confused Swift was all at sea. His letter to Addison of August 22 shows that he was at this time averse to peace. Indeed, one of his arguments for a moral reformation in *A Project for the Advancement of Religion* had been that, by removing abuses of administration, it would make for the more efficient conduct of the war. All the arguments he was to put forward three months later against continuing the war were discovered only after he had hitched his wagon to Harley's star. Plainly, the true political issue of the moment — War or Peace — had not really occupied his thoughts at all. Apart from his Whig 'principles' and strong feelings against the repeal of the Test, his politics were strictly personal, and concerned with his own career. Would any of 'the great men' with whom he had some credit be in power? That narrowed down to the question: Would Somers be able to hold on?

On the whole, Swift thought that he would not, and was inclined to stay in Ireland and wait for a new and perhaps more congenial Lieutenant. The reason why he suddenly changed his mind, without waiting for Addison's advice, was that the Irish bishops felt that the moment had come to renew their application for the First Fruits, which Godolphin and Wharton had blocked; and, guided mainly by King, reluctantly chose Swift for their envoy again. That gave him the opportunity he wanted, of making himself personally known to the great men of the new world, as a privileged and apparently disinterested ambassador. He went at a moment's notice, catching the Government yacht at the last minute on August 31. To 'the ladies' he averred that he went unwillingly, and was sure to be back by Christmas.

The real nature of his hesitation is revealed in his letter to King of November 23. 'Your Grace may remember that upon your telling me how backward the Bishops were in giving me a power, I was very unwilling to go at all, and sent the Dean of St. Patrick's to tell you so.' Swift was not in the least reluctant to go to England, provided he had the kind of commission from the Irish bishops which would enable him to make the contacts he desired. Armed with such a credential he was eager enough. But with anything less, he would not. Some of the bishops had demurred on the ground that he was too much tarred with the Whig brush; and Swift, through Dean Stearne and thence through King, had sent them a sort of ultimatum, which overcame their hesitations. Swift's commission was signed on August 31. He caught the yacht that day.

His fourteen months in Ireland had been another period of fallow. He had seen a great deal of Addison; he had written a few minor prose pieces for Steele's *Tatler*; a very minor political piece; and some equally minor verses. He had not seriously bestirred himself. He had written some letters to his young lady favourites in London: to Mrs. Barton in particular, and to Miss Hester Vanhomrigh. But he seems to have done very little, except to busy himself with his improvements at Laracor. His health had been none too good. He remembered this period, years after, as the one in which he was first seriously troubled with his giddiness.

CHAPTER XI

SWIFT AND HARLEY: 1710

SWIFT arrived in London on September 7, 1710. His first effort of business was to call upon Godolphin. It is hard to understand why. Godolphin was definitely 'out' since August 8; his previous attitude towards Swift's mission had been hostile, and his feelings toward the clergy, bitter enough before, had not been sweetened by what had happened at and since the trial of Sacheverell. He was tired with the strain of long years of responsible office, and soured by the gracelessness of his abrupt dismissal. In two years more, he would be dead. Presumably, Swift went to see him to get his advice and his own bearings in the confusing political situation. His reception was mortifying to his vanity. It was, he told King, 'altogether different from what I ever received from any great man in my life: altogether short, dry and morose'.[1] Although he was assured that Godolphin 'used nobody better' in his present mood, Swift took it as a personal insult and went away (he told Stella) 'almost vowing revenge',[2] which he straightway set himself to execute by drafting a verse lampoon upon him. Rather cryptically he told King that he thought he had, 'for some reasons, deserved much the contrary from his Lordship'. What services he had done Godolphin is not apparent. Not one of the pamphlets known to be his was of much use to the Godolphin ministry: rather the contrary. But Swift harped so on the Whigs' lack of gratitude towards him, that it is hard to believe that the nine years old *Conflicts and Dissensions* was in fact his sole title to it. Yet no other is known.

He was particularly stung by the contrast between his reception by Godolphin and that by the other politicians. He told Stella 'he was equally caressed by both parties'. While meditating his revenge, he reconnoitred the position. Harley, he reported, was in real command of the Treasury; Shrewsbury, who remained in office as Lord Chamberlain, regarded Harley as his leader: from both he had some reason to expect a favourable response to his mission. Harley, in particular, he said, had made advances to him in the past.

By September 20, it was clear that the Whig defeat was a rout. Somers, Devonshire and Boyle were all out, and Rochester, Buckingham and St. John in their places. Wharton and Orford were out the next day. Swift confessed he was 'almost shocked' at the cleanness of the sweep. By the end of the month, through the offices of his Kilkenny schoolfellow, Francis Stratford, now a prominent financier, he was in touch with Erasmus Lewis, an able civil servant devoted to Harley, who straightway arranged a meeting between Swift and his chief. That was all in the necessary way of business for a man bent on accomplishing the mission with which Swift had been charged. But he had also taken care to have himself represented to Harley as 'a discontented person that was used ill for not being Whig enough'.[3] In this there was some confusion between the ill success of his previous mission and his own lack of personal reward. On October 4 Harley received him 'with the greatest kindness imaginable'. He told Stella:

> He has appointed me an hour on Saturday at four, afternoon, when I will open my business to him; which expression I should not use if I were a woman. I know you smoked it; but I did not till I writ it.

2

Harley knew well what a prize was within his grasp, apter for his purposes than even Defoe, though he would need a different kind of treatment. Harley was naturally affable; Defoe's correspondence with him shows that he always treated that tough and battered journalist with courtesy and consideration, though their relations were always secret, for obvious reasons. Swift, as one of the reigning wits, with the pride of a Lucifer, would have to be publicly acknowledged — and more. How much more Harley had not yet rightly calculated. Indeed, considering his man, he took a considerable risk in sitting down to dinner with company at four o'clock on the fateful Saturday and instructing his famous lying porter, old Read, to tell Swift to return in an hour.

> Which I did, expecting to hear Mr. Harley was gone out; but they had just done dinner. Mr. Harley came out to me, brought me in, and presented to me his son-in-law Lord Doblane (or some such name) and his own son, and, among others, Will Penn the Quaker: we sat two hours drinking as good wine as you do; and two hours more he and I alone; where he heard me tell my business; entered into it with all kindness; asked for my powers and read them; and read likewise a memorial I had drawn up, and put it in his pocket to show the Queen; told me the measures he would take; and in short, said everything I could wish: told me he must bring Mr. St. John (Secretary of State) and me acquainted; and spoke so many things of personal kindness and esteem for me, that I am inclined half to believe what some friends have told me, that he would do everything to bring me over. He has

desired to dine with me (what a comical mistake was that!). I mean he has desired me to dine with him on Tuesday; and after four hours being with him, set me down at St. James's Coffee-house in a hackney-coach. All this is odd and comical, if you consider him and me. He knew my Christian name very well. . . .

They may talk of the you know what; but, gad, if it had not been for that, I should never have been able to get the access I have had; and if that helps me to succeed, then that same thing will be serviceable to the Church. But how far we must depend on new friends, I have learnt by long practice, though I think among great Ministers, they are just as good as old ones. And so I think this important day has made a great hole in this side of the paper. . . . [4]

On the next day (October 8) he added:

I must tell you a great piece of refinement [that is, a very subtle move] of Harley. He charged me to come to him often: I told him I was loth to trouble him in so much business as he had, and desired I might have leave to come at his levee; which he immediately refused, and said, that was not a place for friends to come to.

Within a few days Harley had shown Swift's memorial concerning the First Fruits to the Queen and obtained her consent. There were the usual delays, perhaps more than the usual, for at one moment the draft of the Royal grant was lost, and the affair was not finally concluded until the middle of the next year. But Swift never doubted Harley's entire good faith in the matter.

The reference to *A Tale of a Tub* at the end of Swift's account of his important day shows that it was one of the subjects of conversation and compliment from Harley. Harley had read it, as we have seen, and he had appreciated it. One of his ways of teasing Swift, when their familiarity was completely established, was to address him as Dr. Thomas Swift, the cousin who had allowed it to be thought that he was part-author of the *Tale*. Harley's admiration for Swift's literary genius was genuine, and his literary flair considerable. When Swift's lampoon on Godolphin, *Sid Hamet*, came out, Harley guessed the author immediately. At a dinner party at which Prior and Peterborough were present on October 15, he repeated part of it by heart; and, while Peterborough read it aloud, 'bobbed me at every time to take notice of the beauties'. Such intimate flattery had its effect. Swift was captivated. By the end of the month he had taken over the *Examiner*, which the Tories had begun just before Godolphin's fall. The previous thirteen numbers had been written by Prior, St. John, Atterbury and Freind. With the fourteenth Swift began. He had become the official chief of the

Tory polemists. There was no suggestion of any salary for Swift's work on the *Examiner*; but Harley promised him some preferment in England.*

It was an immense acquisition to the cause; and it was due entirely to Harley. Swift did not make the acquaintance of St. John until his second *Examiner* was out. Possibly, if the matter of the First Fruits had lain within St. John's department, he might have been the means of attaching Swift to the Tories. But it is less likely. Harley had a much more highly developed sense of the importance of what would now be called 'public relations'. No Secretary of State, it was said, since Walsingham, had spent so much in acquiring information concerning the temper of the people; and none had ever studied so carefully the art of estimating and influencing public opinion. What the advances were which, Swift says, he had made to him in the past, we do not know, nor why Swift refused them. But Harley had marked him out, just as he marked out Defoe, as a prize to be won. And in both cases he won something more than a splendid instrument; he inspired in both these so different men of genius, who moved in totally different worlds, a personal devotion to himself. It was an extraordinary achievement. There was nothing comparable to it on the other side. To none of the Whig statesmen did the Whig men of letters feel the same personal attachment.

3

It would be extravagant to pretend that Swift was ever wholly in Harley's confidence. Of Harley's contacts with the Pretender, to take the most conspicuous example, he was entirely ignorant. And it is plain from the *Journal to Stella* that there was a whole realm of Harley's political ideas and activities to which he had no access. No doubt he knew more than he dared to set down in his letters to Stella — it is difficult to believe, for instance, that he did not know all about Prior's secret mission to Paris in July 1711 — but his genuine ignorance of much of Harley's most cherished policy is manifest. Some of it he learned as he went on. Thus, in March 1711, he was mystified by Harley's reluctance to make a clean sweep of the Whig officials;[6] but five months later he wrote to King: 'I know particularly that he dislikes very much the notion of some people that every one is to be turned out.'[7] Plainly, in the interval Harley had instructed him on this principle of his policy. On the other hand, Harley seems never to have been explicit about his own rela-

---

* This is the plain meaning of Swift's account of the transaction in the *Memoirs*: 'He [Harley] added, that this province [of writing in support of the new ministry] was in the hands of several persons, among whom some were too busy, and others too idle to pursue it; and concluded, that it should be his particular care, to establish me here in England, and represent me to the Queen as a person they could not be without.'[5]

tions with the Queen. It was very slowly that Swift came to realize that the Queen had an obstinate will of her own, and that the art of handling her was one of which even Harley was never wholly master: since he had to let it appear that he was, he had to keep silent. This affected Swift personally. Harley never dared to tell him outright that he was *persona non grata* with the Queen, until the final crisis over his preferment in April 1713. It seems that the royal disapproval only became definite when the Duchess of Somerset succeeded the Duchess of Marlborough. That would explain why the plan of presenting Swift to the Queen and having him preach before her, which Harley and St. John were equally anxious to arrange in November and December 1710, was suddenly dropped.

On November 28 Swift told King that Harley had promised to present him to the Queen; on December 14 he told Stella that he had desired to be excused from preaching before her, because everybody would be disappointed by 'the plain honest stuff' he would preach; but the ministers would not hear of it. Stella was naturally pleased, and teasingly wrote to ask whether he had given his sermon, and if he was sure he could preach. On February 9 he replied:

> No, indeed, I put off preaching as much as I can. I am upon another foot: nobody doubts here whether I can preach, and you are fools . . . Mr. Harley of late has said nothing of presenting me to the Queen: I was overseen when I mentioned it to you. He has such a weight of affairs on him that he cannot mind all; but he talked of it three or four times to me, long before I dropped it to you.

The project had been quietly shelved. On January 18 the Duchess of Somerset had received the Gold Key. As a political move the new appointment was congenial to Harley, who was glad to see the high Tory influence of Mrs. Masham counterpoised by the moderate Whig influence of the Duchess: and it is unlikely that he knew beforehand of the Duchess's intimate and personal objection to Swift. But he soon realized that there was now an insuperable obstacle to his plan of drawing Swift to the personal attention of the Queen.

Swift affected to make light of it; but since he had been evidently gratified by the prospect, he must have been correspondingly disappointed. Indeed, one would think that in some of the sparsely attended and almost private Courts at Windsor at which Swift was present from August 1711 onwards, it would have been difficult for him *not* to be presented to the Queen. But it never happened. And we may perhaps measure Swift's disenchantment by the contrast between his charming fantasy to Stella, on November 7, 1710, when the horizon of his new favour seemed unlimited:

I was at Court today, where the Queen passed us by with all Tories about her; not one Whig . . . and I have seen her without one Tory. The Queen made me a curtsey, and said, in a sort of familiar way to Presto, 'How does M.D.?' I considered she was a Queen and so excused her —

and the unflattering portrait of her Majesty at Windsor on August 8, 1711, when he had learned the length of his tether:

There was a Drawing-room today at Court; but so few company, that the Queen sent for us into her bed-chamber, where we made our bows, and stood about twenty of us round the room, while she looked at us round with her fan in her mouth and once a minute said about three words to some that were nearest her, and then she was told dinner was ready, and went out.

By that time the limits of Swift's eligibility were common knowledge among his friends. They could tease him about them and he could make a joke of it. He was adept at concealing his emotions.

Lord Treasurer and the Secretary sought to mortify me; for they told me that they had been talking a great deal of me today to the Queen, and she said she had never heard of me. I told them that was their fault, not hers, etc., and so we laughed. (August 6, 1711)

That was two days before the Windsor portrait; it coloured the vision.

4

Queen Anne's court, now that she was emancipated from the Marl-boroughs, was a world of penumbra — of hints, suggestions and surmises. The *mana* of the Queen, her idiosyncrasy and unpredictability, shaded imperceptibly into the politic secretiveness of Harley to compose a realm of half lights and mystery. Harley had learned his habit of reserve in the hard school. He had seldom or never, he told Swift, made a political confidence to a friend but it had been betrayed. The tradition of loyalty of ministerial colleagues to the Prime Minister was still far ahead. He had to assume that they were caballing against him; and the only safeguard was to keep the intimate threads of policy close in his own hand. Thus, no one knew what were Harley's plans for dealing with the precarious financial situation, when he was laid low by Guiscard's penknife in March 1711: if the blow had been fatal, they would have perished with him. Similarly, at the same moment, he was unable to prevent the dispatch of the ill planned and mismanaged expedition to Quebec. In this matter he was by-passed by the roguery of Bolingbroke, and the ambition of Mrs. Masham.

Nevertheless, Harley seems never to have become really cynical; but rather to have accepted this twilight world of insecurity, caprice, disloyalty, and intrigue as the necessary medium of political action, and in some queer way to have been inspired by it. Perhaps it was the consequence and reward of his long and arduous apprenticeship in the House of Commons, where he had learned all the arts of political management, and the satisfactions of being a maestro. The contrast between his reputation among his political opponents as 'Robin the trickster' and the impression of indolent and lovable integrity he makes in the pages of Swift is singular and significant. Equally singular and equally significant is the enduring hatred felt against him by St. John. In the showy writings of that brilliant man, Harley is a veritable obsession: vile insinuations against his character, and vulgar sneers at his ancestry and breeding, are the paradoxical embroidery of his exposition of a policy which had been Harley's own, and which St. John had done his level best to sabotage. Much excuse may be made for the ill-temper of a politician cheated by fate of supreme power; but there are limits to what can be condoned, and St. John exceeds them. The meanness of his hatred is matched by the dishonesty of his thinking. His justification of himself against Harley is the justification of Harley against him.

Mystified by Harley Swift certainly was, more than once; and though he had an intellectual understanding of his policy of moderation, he did not heartily appreciate it. He had nothing of Harley's intimate contact with the instincts of the English nation, or his inherited sympathy with Dissent. Harley stood for the healing of the cleavage of the Civil War; Swift would have fought it again. He would have been staggered to discover that Defoe had more influence on Harley's policy than himself. One whole side of the man was concealed from him. And yet he knew him. For Harley revealed himself as a private man to Swift as he did to few. That private self of Harley Swift admired and loved. His agony of mind when he believed that Guiscard's stab might be fatal was that of a friend for a friend. There is no mistaking the accent of his words to Stella on Harley's recovery and promotion to Lord Treasurer and the Earldom of Oxford.

> This man has grown by persecutions, turnings out, and stabbing. What waiting, and crowding, and bowing will be at his levee! Yet, if human nature be capable of so much constancy, I should believe he will be the same man still, hating the necessary form of grandeur he must keep up. (May 22, 1711)*

* Swift, as it were formally, confirms this prophecy in his character of Harley written in 1715, in the first part of *An Enquiry into the Behaviour of the Queen's Last Ministry*. 'He is the only instance that ever fell within my observation of a person passing from a private life, through the several stages of greatness, without any perceivable impression on his temper or his behaviour.'[8]

'The same man still.' That perfectly describes him as he appears in Swift's letters; and it fits with his quiet calm and courage when he was in the Tower. It tells us more than Swift's more considered tribute to him in a letter to King, though that too is worth pondering.

The Treasurer is much the greatest minister I ever knew, regular in life, with a true sense of religion, an excellent scholar, and a good divine, of a very mild and affable disposition, intrepid in his notions and indefatigable in business, an utter despiser of money for himself, yet frugal, perhaps to an extremity, for the public. In private company he is wholly disengaged and very facetious, like one who has no business at all. He never wants a reserve on any emergency which would appear desperate to others; and makes little use of those thousand projectors and schematists who are daily plying him with their visions, but to be thoroughly convinced by the comparison that his own notions are best.[9]

One cannot help wishing that Oxford had made it clear to Swift that the English Deanery he had set his heart on was not to be compassed. But since Swift, whose capacity for resentment was great, cherished none, it is clear that he was convinced of Oxford's good will and good faith throughout. The explanation of his reticence to Swift must be that he hoped, rather characteristically, that something would turn up, and some way yet be found of outflanking the Royal opposition. In this, as in other things, Oxford was defeated by the Queen's tenacity.

Harley made only one mistake in his relations with Swift. It was a good-natured one, and he made it early on. On February 5, 1711, he sent him a banknote for £50. Swift promptly returned it and gave Harley to understand that that was not the way to reward him, and that he expected an apology. He received it. Harley had meant no worse than to relieve Swift's straitened finances. But Swift's fierce pride had taken alarm. To make honourable amends, Harley promptly persuaded Harcourt and St. John to admit him to the Saturday dinner-party of the inner Cabinet. Swift had reached the heights; but whether much high politics was talked on them is doubtful. However, the entrée into the sanctum was gratifying enough for him to indulge himself with the momentary happiness of being well-deceived; and in his elation he reported to the sceptical Peterborough that they seemed 'heartily to love one another'. He soon repented of that naivety.

5

Swift had to live very frugally in London. His income from his livings and his prebend was under £300 a year, of which a considerable amount went to 'the ladies', to Tom Warburton, his curate at Laracor, and to his sister, Jane. At least £100 a year went in this way. What was left had to be carefully husbanded to maintain him respectably in the society he kept. He had some savings, apparently about £500, partly invested in Bank Stock, on which he did not like to trench. His rooms cost him 8s. to 10s. a week, and Patrick his Irish manservant must have cost him at least as much again, for he needed to be fed. Fortunately he got plenty of invitations to dinner — so many indeed that he could report triumphantly to Stella, after three weeks in London: 'It has cost me but three shillings in meat and drink since I came here.' His breakfast was of the simplest — generally milk porridge, 'cheap and wholesome' — qualities to which he did not like to be beholden. At first, he was involved by his rich friend, Sir Andrew Fountaine, in heavy expenses at taverns: his share of 16s. for two bottles of wine among three; or 7s. for his dinner 'like a puppy', after being taken to the top of St. Paul's 'like a fool'. He was determined to protect young Harrison, his protégé, who had only £40 a year as a tutor, from such impositions.

The fine fellows are always inviting him to the tavern and making him pay his club. Henley is a great crony of his; they are often at the tavern at six or seven shillings reckoning, and he always makes the poor lad pay his full share. A colonel and a lord were at him and me the same way tonight: I absolutely refused, and made Harrison lag behind, and persuaded him not to go to them. I tell you this, because I find all rich fellows have that humour of using all people without consideration of their fortunes; but I will see them rot before they shall serve me so. Lord Halifax is always teasing me to go down to his country house, which will cost me a guinea to his servants, and twelve shillings coach hire; and he shall be hanged first. Is not this a plaguy silly story? But I am vexed at the heart; for I love the young fellow.... [10]

Swift had, as D. H. Lawrence used to say, 'to watch it'. Soon after his return to London he needed a new periwig. He paid only three guineas for it, at a time when a fashionable periwig might easily cost ten, and an ultra-smart one thirty or forty. A decorous clerical one was much cheaper. A country curate reckoned 30s. a fair price. Swift thought three guineas dear for his. 'I am undone,' he cried. 'London lickpenny: I find it true.' He had no watch of his own, though he was twice involved in ordering one from Tompion for Irish friends: they cost £38 apiece.* Coach hire was a burden to him in rainy weather — 'twelvepenny weather', he called it. Either his

---

* It is possible that the two watches were only one. The *Journal*, March 22, 1711, speaks of a watch for Parvisol. A letter to Staunton, February 10, 1711, of one for Percival. Deane Swift may have misread Percival as Parvisol.

periwig, or his purse must suffer; and his purse suffered sometimes as much as 10s. a week. Fires he permitted himself from the first of November to the first of April; but, though he greatly appreciated the convenience of small coals, he found them expensive. In the depth of winter his bill for coal and candles — of which he 'never burned fewer at a time than one' — amounted to 3s. a week. He carefully picked the coals off his fire before he went to bed. At Christmas he was undone with Christmas boxes.

> The rogues of the Coffee-house have raised their tax, every one giving a crown; and I gave mine for shame, besides a great many half-crowns to great men's porters, etc.[11]

The formation of the society of Brothers — the confraternity of Tory wits and Tory grandees — imposed a further strain on his economy. At first he had to entertain the whole Brotherhood in his turn; when that method was dropped, largely because of Harley's disapproval of their extravagance, and they clubbed for a more modest dinner, Swift's share amounted sometimes to 19s. It was still worse when, instead of recommending deserving writers to official reward (which was the original scheme), they passed the hat round among themselves. Swift, after one painful experience, had this put on a fair footing. The Brothers were assessed according to their fortunes: where the Duke of Ormond paid ten guineas, Swift paid seven shillings: 'at that rate, they may tax as often as they please'.

Yet, in spite of all this, by the end of 1711, Swift reckoned that he had spent £50 on books — all he mentions are Greek or Latin: Congreve's plays he borrowed from Patrick — and more than doubled his library. At one moment indeed he contemplated buying a whole library for £130. That would have made a big hole in his capital. Considering his relatively large outlay on books, it is amazing how Swift managed to keep within his slender income. It would have been much more difficult if he had not had the Vanhomrighs to depend on for a dinner, when other congenial invitations failed — or the weather.

> If you be wise then go not far to dine;
> You'll spend in coachhire more than save in wine.[12]

The times he mentions dining with the Vans are innumerable; and he does not mention them all. The extravagant Mrs. Vanhomrigh evidently kept open house for Swift and his more fashionable friends.. Nearly all those whom he affectionately calls his 'drabs of quality', he met there constantly — Lady Ashburnham, Lady Betty Butler, Lady Betty Germaine, Mrs. Anne Long (till debts forced her into hiding). He was splendid company; his reputation was that of 'the man of mirth'. To women who were not fools, young and old, he could be irresistible. Old Lady Orkney and young Hester Vanhomrigh were in agreement that no one ever thought as he did.

6

Those who read between the lines of the *Journal* can have no doubt that Swift got a subtle enjoyment from the combination of poverty and power. Anxious though he was to improve his situation, it was primarily for Stella's sake that he wanted more money. Besides that, he wanted a public acknowledgment of his own genius. That was not wholly personal to himself. He passionately believed in the rightful claims of genius, and set himself to vindicate them.

> If those who possess great endowments of the mind would set a just value upon themselves, they would think no man's acquaintance whatsoever a condescension, nor accept it from the greatest on unworthy or ignominious terms.[13]

So he wrote in Harrison's *Tatler* at this time. When he was engaged in pushing Berkeley as 'a very ingenious man and great philosopher' among the Ministry, he told Stella: 'This I think I am bound to, in honour and conscience — to use all my little credit toward helping forward men of worth in the world.'[14] This was the purpose, at any rate in Swift's view, of the society of Brothers. Further, he held strongly that literary distinction was a valid title to civil preferment which should not be taken away under a change of government. What the Whigs had given, the Tories should continue, provided the recipient did not indulge in violent party politics: and the Tories should make it their special merit to reward men of letters. But he did not regard himself as coming under this rubric. Of the whole group of 'wits' to which he belonged — Addison, Congreve, Prior, Steele, Pope and Gay — he and Congreve were the most averse to considering themselves in any degree professional men of letters. It was almost a point of honour with him not to take money for his writings. The £200 he got later in life for *Gulliver* was owing to Pope. He worked like a Trojan for the monster subscription to Pope's Homer; and equally hard, in his more restricted circumstances in Ireland, for the 4000 guinea subscription for Prior's poems. But he would not hear of anything of the kind for himself. He was offered a subscription of £500 for the collected *Examiners*. He refused it. In that case it may have been that he did not want to allow the Ministers to think he could be rewarded in that way. But it is too much of a piece with his constant attitude to call for a particular explanation. He was at once careful and contemptuous of money.

We may put it down to his pride. Much later in life, he told Pope that he had always cherished one ambition: on the strength of his intellectual gifts alone to be received and respected as an equal by the great ones of the earth

> All my endeavours from a boy to distinguish myself were only for want of a great title and fortune, that I might be used like a Lord by those who have an opinion of my parts — whether right or wrong, it is no great matter, and so the reputation of wit or great learning does the office of a blue ribbon, or of a coach and six horses.[15]

Much of the peculiar satisfaction he derived from his brilliant work for the Tories was that it showed the Whig grandees what a mighty mistake they had made in not treating him as an equal. Harley made no such mistake. Swift's ambition was then achieved. And it is plain that he savoured it the more because of his impecuniosity. His became a pure case. Wit, with only just enough to live on, had established its claim to be equal with the greatest. Reward, though not extravagant, he expected and desired — enough to show the world how he stood, and to make life comfortable for Stella and himself. But his pride would not permit him to press his claims. One imagines that after his brief note to Harley on the death of the Dean of Wells the subject was never mentioned between them again. But doubtless Harley knew that Swift was resolved, if a suitable preferment fell vacant and was not given to him, to return instantly to Ireland.

But it was not the hope of preferment that kept Swift in England, against the prickings of his conscience and the pull of his emotions. It was the sensation of power, of being at the centre of power. One does not doubt the sincerity of his longing to be at Laracor and with Stella again, or the reality of the malaise he felt at continually putting off his promised return, or the genuineness of his gratitude to Stella when she wrote to tell him she understood. Perhaps there is no passage in all the *Journal* more truly expressive of their relation.

> I am pleased that Stella the conjuror approves what I did with Mr. Harley [in relation to the £50 banknote]; but your generosity makes me mad; I know you repine inwardly at Presto's absence; you think he has broken his word of coming in three months, and that this is always his trick; and now Stella says she does not see possibly how I can come away in haste, and that MD is satisfied etc. An't you a rogue to over-power me thus? I did not expect to find such friends as I have done. They may indeed deceive me too. But there are important reasons

why they should not. I have been used barbarously by the late Ministry; I am a little piqued in honour to let people see I am not to be despised. The assurances they give me, without any scruple or provocation, are such as are usually believed in the world; they may come to nothing, but the first opportunity that offers, and is neglected, I shall depend no more, but come away. I could say a thousand things on this head, if I were with you.[16]

Would that we could hear them! But Swift's gratitude to Stella for her approbation was such that he straightway proposed to give her £50 to go to the Bath.

CHAPTER XII

THE TORY CHAMPION: 1711

SWIFT wrote the *Examiner* for seven months, from November 2, 1710, to June 7, 1711. His work upon it began and ended with the first session of the new Parliament, in which the Tories had a strong majority. By the time his last *Examiner* was written, the secret negotiations for peace with France were far advanced, and the time was ripe for him to undertake the new and even more important task of vindicating the mode and terms of the peace-making in which the Ministry had engaged.

In the *Examiner* the rôle Swift assumes is that of the non-party man, and his basic opinions are identical with *The Sentiments of a Church of England Man*. He maintains that Tory and Whig principles are quite consistent with one another; they are really emphases on different parts of a body of doctrine which is held, more or less consciously, by the great majority of the nation; and his avowed object is to rally this body of opinion to the Harley ministry, and in particular to the support of its policy of making peace at the first favourable opportunity. To the policy of peace he had himself been converted since his return to England by Harley, who had no doubt instructed him in the wanton rejection by Marlborough and the Whigs of the French peace-offer in 1709. The Whigs he castigates are those who supported the Godolphin ministry in its last exclusively Whig phase, when the Tories were eliminated and the members of the Whig Junto were thrust upon the reluctant Queen. From this behaviour he concludes, fairly enough, that the Junto Whigs and their followers are concerned with persons rather than principles.

In his last number he confessed (as he had confided to Stella at the time of his first) that the difficulties and dangers of so drastic a change in the government as the Queen and Harley had made had appeared to him insuperable in view of the apparent opposition. He did not allow himself to confess so much until his task was done. Very properly, he assumed a confidence that he did not feel, and set himself to reassure those who expressed the misgivings that he concealed. The opening of his first number is masterly for this purpose. His neat motto from Virgil —

Longa est injuria, longae
Ambages; sed summa sequar fastigia rerum —

is a reminder to what a select and educated audience the political argumentation of those days was directed. Then he begins:

> It is a practice I have generally followed, to converse with equal freedom with the deserving men of both parties; and it was never without some contempt, that I have observed persons wholly out of employment, affect to do otherwise: I doubted whether any man could owe so much to the side he was of, though he were retained by it; but without some great point of interest, either in possession or prospect, I thought it was the mark of a low and narrow spirit.
>
> It is hard, that for some weeks past, I have been forced, in my own defence, to follow a proceeding that I have so much condemned in others. But several of my acquaintance, among the declining party, are grown so insufferably peevish and splenetic, profess such violent apprehensions for the public [i.e. the *res publica*], and represent the state of things in such formidable ideas, that I find myself disposed to share in their afflictions, although I know them to be groundless and imaginary, or, which is worse, purely affected. To offer them comfort one by one, would not only be an endless, but a disobliging task. Some of them, I am convinced, would be less melancholy, if there were more occasion. I shall therefore, instead of hearkening to further complaints, employ some part of this paper for the future, in letting such men see, that their natural or acquired fears are ill-grounded, and their artificial ones as ill-intended. That all our present inconveniencies are the consequence of the very counsels they so much admire, which would still have increased, if those had continued: and that neither our constitution in Church or State, could probably have been long preserved, without such methods as have been lately taken.[1]

He goes on to argue that the continuance of the war, which was the only policy of the Godolphin ministry in its last phase, was steadily shifting the balance of power in the state from the owners of land to the owners of the financial obligations of the state. The former were taxed heavily to provide the interest due to the latter, who escaped taxation. Therefore, to have rejected, as the Whigs had rejected, terms of peace which would have secured all the essential objects for which the war was begun, showed them bent on subverting the constitution by subordinating the landed to the financial interest. He ends:

> Upon these considerations alone, it was the most prudent course imaginable in the Queen, to lay hold of the disposition of the people for changing the Parliament and ministry at this juncture, and extricating herself, as soon as possible, out of the pupillage of those who found their accounts only in perpetuating the war. Neither have we

the least reason to doubt, but the ensuing Parliament will assist her Majesty with the utmost vigour, till her enemies *again* be brought to sue for peace, and *again* offer such terms as will make it both honourable and lasting; only with this difference, that the Ministry perhaps will not *again* refuse them.[2]

At another time, in No. 24, he asks the question why, 'instead of aiming at peace, while we had the advantage of the war, which has been the perpetual maxim of all wise states, it has been reckoned factious and malignant even to express our wishes for it'? And the answer is substantially the same. If the war were to end, so would the process by which the balance of power was being shifted from the landed to the moneyed interest. Therefore, the Whigs resolved to disappoint all overtures of a peace, till they and their party should be so deeply rooted as to make it impossible to shake them.

2

That is the leading argument of Swift throughout the *Examiner*. It must be allowed that, even though it was a new discovery for Swift, it was sound. It rested on the premiss that the purposes for which the war had been begun had been achieved and could have been consolidated by a peace which France had been only too willing to conclude. That was and is undeniable. To later eyes his view that the growing preponderance of the moneyed over the landed interest was subversive, may seem archaic. But that also was sound. So long as it was administratively impossible to tax incomes derived from the funds or from trade, the moneyed interest entirely escaped its burden of financial responsibility for the national policy, and was therefore irresponsible; and in fact it was steadily accumulating the untaxed wealth which enabled it to corrupt the elections for years to come. The only corrective to this process until the distant time when a genuine income-tax was practicable was the attraction of landownership, whereby the fortunes made in finance and commerce were continually converted into landed estates.

The combination of the brilliant and successful general and the moneyed interest was thus to Swift, as it was to the Tory squires, highly sinister. The vast fortune being accumulated by Marlborough was symbolic of the silent and insidious revolution. That he should dictate the composition of a ministry in order to perpetuate the war was intolerable. So Swift fought for the principle of the complete subordination of the military to the civil power. For this it was necessary to lower Marlborough's popular prestige. Swift aimed two telling blows against it. In one *Examiner*, No. 17, he exhibited a formidable balance sheet comparing the rewards of a triumphant Roman general, £994.11.10., with those of the victor of Blenheim, £540,000.0.0. Thus Roman gratitude compared with British ingratitude. In another, No. 28, he ends a penetrating analysis of avarice with an imaginary letter to Crassus.

> How far that fatal greediness for gold may have influenced you, in breaking off the treaty with the old Parthian King Orodes, you best can tell; your enemies charge you with it, your friends offer nothing material in your defence; and all agree, there is nothing so pernicious which the extremes of avarice may not be able to inspire.
> The moment you quit this vice, you will be a truly great man; and still there will imperfections enough remain to convince us, you are not a god.[3]

But Swift does not press Marlborough very hard, partly from personal compunctions of his own — he was himself only a very recent convert to the necessity of peace — partly on instructions from the Ministry, who were making an attempt to reach a decent working agreement with Marlborough, whose presence at the head of the army was necessary to maintain the pressure on France. The aim of Swift's criticisms was to dissipate the aura which surrounded the great general, and to make him aware that the Ministry was determined to control policy. To the Whig party manager, Wharton, he was ruthless. Apart from his own personal grievance against him, the emphasis on his villainies — Wharton in Ireland is compared to Verres in Sicily — proceeds from Swift's effort to drive a wedge between the moderate and the extreme Whigs, in accord with Harley's policy. It was not until April, when presumably all Whig opinion that could be, had been detached, that he put the screw on the party as a whole, and arraigned them as a faction and not a national party, because of their internal incoherence. 'How could a Whig, who is against all discipline, agree with a Presbyterian, that carries it higher than the Papists themselves?'[4] Here, as continually, he harks back to the Civil War and the Protectorate to uncover the purposes of the extreme Whigs. They correspond to the Cromwellian army and the Independents. According as he is courting the moderate, or flaying the extreme Whigs, he acquits or accuses them of justifying the execution (which is, of course, the 'murder') of King Charles I. Such comparisons with the Civil War period were unhistorical. They conveniently obscured the fact that most of the descendants of the country gentlemen who fought on the Parliament side were the new Tories. But Swift had little of the true historian in his composition. His dominant conceptions were static and moralistic. Even if he could have recognized that the party system was to offer a practical solution of the problem of peaceful development, it would have been no recommendation to him. He felt that any development was best arrested, for it was bound to be for the worse.

But he was on solid ground in claiming that the Tories represented the bulk of the nation, and that in order to make head against them the Whigs had to seek a combination of heterogeneous interests. There was plenty of substance in his contention that the Tories were in fact the national party and the Whigs were not; and there was some justification for his view that the government of Britain was now established on a permanent footing, with Queen and Commons in a natural alliance, and the Lords in a fair way to be brought into harmony by the appointment of High Church bishops and the inevitable attractions of Court favour. The avowed Jacobites and the extreme Whigs would both be isolated: the moderates on either side would coalesce, with the Tories in a natural preponderance, and the party-system would be at an end almost before it had begun.

Unfortunately for this rosy prospect, the Tories were no more effectively homogeneous than the Whigs; for the Whigs made up by superior party discipline for their inferiority in common interest. And Swift's simple and specious argument that because the Church of England had made the Glorious Revolution, and the Church party the Act of Settlement, the Tories were solid for the Hanover Succession, did not correspond with the facts. The Tories were solid only for peace. Swift, in the *Examiner*, did not seriously look beyond that, and it was his duty as an effective Tory journalist not to do so. The necessity of peace was his positive theme and it was a sound one: and Swift expounded it well.

3

But the enjoyment a modern reader finds in the *Examiner* comes rather from his witty jibes at his opponents. They are still tremendous fun. He meets the Whig charge that the Tories have a design to bring in the Pretender, by turning the accusation upon themselves.

But further what could be more consistent with the Whiggish notion of a revolution-principle, than to bring in the Pretender? A revolution-principle, as their writings and discourses have taught us to define it, is a principle perpetually disposing men to revolutions: and this is suitable to the famous saying of a great Whig, 'That the more revolutions the better'; which how odd a maxim soever in appearance, I take to be the true characteristic of the party.

A dog loves to turn round often; yet after certain revolutions he lies

down to rest; but heads under the dominion of the moon, are for perpetual changes and perpetual revolutions: besides, the Whigs owe all
their wealth to wars and revolutions; like the girl at Bartholomew-
fair, who gets a penny by turning round a hundred times, with swords
in her hands.

To conclude, the Whigs have a natural faculty of bringing in pretenders,
and will therefore probably endeavour to bring in the great one at last:
How many *pretenders* to wit, honour, nobility, politics, have they
brought in these last twenty years? In short, they have been sometimes
able to procure a majority of pretenders in Parliament; and wanted
nothing to render the work complete except a Pretender at their head.[5]

This is not argument; but it is very funny, and very effective. Another
of his boutades about the Whig fondness for revolutions has a more serious
intention.

Why should not a revolution in the ministry be sometimes necessary
as well as a revolution in the crown? It is to be presumed, the former is
at least as lawful in itself, and perhaps the experiment not quite so
dangerous. The revolution of the sun about the earth was formerly
thought a necessary expedient to solve appearances, though it left many
difficulties unanswered; till philosophers contrived a better, which is
that of the earth's revolution about the sun. This is found upon
experience to save much time and labour, to correct many irregular
motions, and is better suited to the respect due from a planet to a
fixed star.[6]

Or he begins a serious remonstration with the Dissenters by a malicious
glance at the internal discrepancies of the Whigs.

I write this paper for the sake of the Dissenters, whom I take to be
the most spreading branch of the Whig party, that professeth Christianity, and the only one that seems to be zealous for any particular system
of it; the bulk of those we call the Low Church, being generally indifferent, and undetermined in that point; and the other sub-divisions
having not yet taken either the Old or New Testament into their
scheme.[7]

They suffer, he says elsewhere, under 'that grievous persecution of the
modern kind called want of power'. For their sakes the Whigs laid down the
grand maxim:

That no man, for the sake of a few notions and ceremonies, under
the names of doctrine and discipline, should be denied the liberty of
serving his country: as if places would go a begging, unless Brownists,
Familists, Sweet-singers, Quakers, Anabaptists and Muggletonians,
would take them off our hands.[8]

Or he jibes at the affected concern of the Whigs for the national credit, which they said would be disastrously shaken by the advent of the Harley ministry.

To hear some of those worthy reasoners talking of credit, that she is so nice, so squeamish, so capricious; you would think they were describing a lady troubled with vapours or the colic, to be only removed by a course of steel, or swallowing a bullet. By the narrowness of their thoughts, one would imagine they conceived the world to be no wider than Exchange Alley. It is probable they may have such a sickly dame among them, and it is well if she has no worse diseases, considering what hands she passes through.[9]

The tarnished and sickly lady, needing a course of steel pills, is even better than the girl twirling with the swords at Bartholomew Fair. They are the images of genius, implanting in the delighted mind the dependence of the Whigs on war.

Or again, when Swift affects to doubt whether the concern the Whig pamphleteers show for the honour of the previous ministry can be serious — 'at least whether their masters will thank them for their zeal in such a cause'.

It is I think, a known story of a gentleman who fought another for calling him 'son of a whore'; but the lady desired her son to make no more quarrels on that subject, *because it was true*.* For pray, Sir; does it not look like a jest, that such a pernicious crew, after draining our wealth, and discovering the most pernicious designs against our Church and State, instead of thanking fortune that they are got off safe in their persons and plunder, should hire these bullies of the pen to defend their reputations? I remember I thought it the hardest case in the world, when a poor acquaintance of mine, having fallen among sharpers, where he lost all his money, and then complaining he was cheated, got a good beating into the bargain, for offering to affront gentlemen.[10]

But no attitude Swift adopted in the *Examiner* could have been more exasperating to the Whigs than his steady refusal to reply to his critics. It was part of the literary strategy he had adopted long before, on the sound principle that to reply is to allow your enemy to dictate your dispositions. Swift never allowed himself to be beguiled from the offensive. 'When I have produced my facts and offered my arguments, I have nothing further to

* The story was told of Catharine Sedley, Countess of Dorchester, the ugly, brave and witty mistress of James II. She eventually married Sir David Collyer, later Earl of Portmore, by whom she had two sons, to whom she said: 'If any one calls you sons of a whore, you must bear it, for so you are; but if they call you bastards, fight till you die, for you are Sir David's sons.'

advance; it is their office to deny and disprove; and then let the world decide.'
He had the neatest apology for his conduct.

> This paper is not intended for the management of controversy, which
> would be of very little import to most readers, and only misspend time
> that I would gladly employ to better purposes. For where it is a man's
> business to entertain a whole roomfull, it is unmannerly to apply him-
> self to a particular person, and turn his back upon the rest of the com-
> pany.[11]

Never descending to his critics in particular, he enjoyed himself vastly at
their expense in general.

> I must needs confess (and it is with grief I speak it) that I have been the
> innocent cause of a great circulation of dullness: at the same time, I have
> often wondered how it has come to pass, that these industrious people,
> after poring so constantly upon the *Examiner*, a paper writ with plain
> sense, and in a tolerable style, have made so little improvement. I am
> sure it would have fallen out quite otherwise with me; for, by what I
> have seen of their performances (and I am credibly informed they are
> all of a piece) if I had perused them till now, I should have been fit
> for little but to make an advocate in the same cause.[12]

He pretends to find his answerers so intolerably dull that he threatens to
answer the *Examiner* himself, which he does in an amusing parody of a
Whig pamphlet in No. 23. It is mainly taken up with an ironical enumeration
of the services the Whigs had done the Church, which ends with a plain
reference to a drunken escapade of Wharton's youth.

> I have hitherto confined myself [the imaginary Whig concludes] to
> those endeavours for the good of the Church, which were common
> to all the leaders and principal men of our party; but if my paper were
> not drawing to an end, I could produce several instances of particular
> persons, who by their exemplary lives and actions have confirmed the
> character so justly due to the whole body. I shall at present mention
> only two, and illustrate the merits of each by a matter of fact.
> That worthy patriot and true lover of the Church, whom the late
> *Examiner* is supposed to reflect on under the name of Verres, felt a
> pious impulse to be a benefactor to the Cathedral of Gloucester, but
> how to do it in the most decent, generous manner was the question.
> At last he thought of an expedient: One morning or night he stole into
> the Church, mounted upon the altar, and there did that which in cleanly
> phrase is called disburthening of nature: He was discovered, prosecuted,
> and condemned to pay a thousand pounds ... to support the Church, as
> no doubt the benefactor meant it. .... [13]

A fortnight later, Swift ends No. 25 with this portentous apology:

> Being resolved publicly to acknowledge any mistakes I have been guilty of; I do here humbly desire the reader's pardon for one of mighty importance, about a fact in one of my papers, said to be done in the Cathedral of Gloucester. A whole Hydra of errors in two words: For as I am since informed, it was neither in the cathedral, nor city, nor county of Gloucester, but some other church of that diocese. If I had ever met any other objection of equal weight, though from the meanest hands, I should certainly have answered it.[14]

One suspects that the mistake was pre-arranged by Swift in order to make the correction; his tongue is visibly in his cheek while he makes it: and by this apparently simple legerdemain he at once drives home the horridness of Wharton's indecency and suffuses an unpleasant subject with our admiration for the wit with which he handles it.*

4

Not long before, Swift had published a separate pamphlet: *A Short Character of Thomas, Earl of Wharton*. It is dated: London, August 30, 1710: which is obviously fictitious, for Swift was still in Ireland on that day. But it was the day on which Wharton's regime ended. 'The people of Ireland', he says, 'have for some time been distinguished from all her Majesty's subjects' by the arbitrary power and oppression from which they suffer. 'Those who preside there . . . value themselves on every step they take towards finishing the slavery of that people, as if it were gaining a mighty point to the advantage of England.'[16] It is the attitude of Archbishop King more robustly expressed; but King did not approve the character of Wharton with which Swift embellished the narrative (from another hand) of his minor oppressions. It was uncharitable, he said; it was wounding a man in the dark. But it was a superb piece of portraiture: so excellent, indeed, that it really misses the intended effect.

> I have had the honour of much conversation with his Lordship, and am thoroughly convinced how indifferent he is to applause, and how insensible of reproach; which is not a humour put on to serve a turn or keep a countenance, not arising from the consciousness of innocence, or any grandeur of mind, but the mere unaffected bent of his nature. He is without the sense of shame or glory, as some men are without the

---

* The story which has been ascribed to Swift's scurrilous and scatological invention, is true; and part of Swift's correction is mistaken. The church Wharton defiled was that of Barrington in Gloucestershire.[16]

sense of smelling; and therefore a good name to him is no more than a precious ointment would be to those. Whoever were to describe the nature of a serpent, a wolf, a crocodile, or a fox, must be understood to do it for the sake of others, without any personal love or hatred for the animals themselves.[17]

And so Wharton is made to appear. He is beneath, or beyond, good and evil; a strange and, in a way, a splendid animal, whom it is hard to believe that Swift did not, in spite of himself, or in some part of himself, admire.

When these papers are public, 'tis odds but he will tell me, as he once did upon a like occasion, that 'he is damnably mauled'; and then with the easiest transition in the world, ask about the weather or the time of the day; so that I enter on the work with more cheerfulness, because I am sure neither to make him angry, nor any way hurt his reputation; a pitch of happiness and security his excellency has arrived to, which no philosopher before him ever could reach.[18]

Swift there acknowledges that his barbs will not penetrate. Resentment was one of his strongest emotions, and he was baffled by a man who felt none, and behaved as though nobody else should either. But he was fascinated, too. His portrait of Wharton is, by far, the fairest he ever drew of a political enemy; and it is the most valuable we possess of that extraordinary man. It helps us to understand the influence he wielded as a politician.

Swift's attacks on him in the *Examiner* are more effective, because he there regarded him purely as an unscrupulous party boss, and was neither perplexed nor inspired by the effort to be objective. From the angle of the *Examiner*, Wharton was simply the villain of the piece — the man who kept the Junto in battle order and made the Whigs dangerous. There was no need to spare him. No persuasion would ever bring him into a coalition of moderates. No one whose feelings Swift would have liked to consider, would be offended by his attacks upon him. Addison, who had been his Secretary, 'did not love him'.

5

Addison and Swift had become much more intimate by their constant contact in Ireland. Their pleasure in each other's company had been increased by Addison's appreciation of Stella. Now Swift's emergence as the champion of the Tories threatened to drag them apart. Swift's many despondent references to Addison in his letters to Stella seem always slightly apologetic, as though he were conscious of her desire that they should remain friends. Distinct from the unknown galaxy of Swift's new and powerful acquaintances, Addison was someone she personally knew and esteemed.

At first, on Swift's return to London, their friendship was undisturbed; and Swift wrote within a month two papers and a poem for the *Tatler*, because it was short of copy. The poem was a longer piece in the same vein as the *Description of the Morning*. Addison and Steele thought it even better than its predecessor. 'They say it is the best thing I ever writ, and I think so too.' Presumably, they and he meant the best of his verses, so far. Perhaps it was; though we confess a preference for both *The Humble Petition of Mrs. Frances Harris* and *Baucis and Philemon*. But the *Shower* is excellent; and the culminating picture of a downpour in Queen Anne's London is unforgettable.

> Now from all parts the swelling kennels flow,
> And bear their trophies with them as they go:
> Filth of all hues and odours seem to tell
> What street they sail'd from, by their sight and smell.
> They, as each torrent drives, with rapid force
> From Smithfield, or St. Pulchre's shape their course,
> And in huge confluent join at Snow-Hill ridge,
> Fall from the Conduit prone to London Bridge.
> Sweepings from butchers' stalls, dung, guts, and blood,
> Drown'd puppies, stinking sprats, all drench'd in mud,
> Dead cats and turnip-tops come tumbling down the flood.[19]

Swift was still willing to give his best to the *Tatler*.

He saw much more of Addison than Steele. They met, indeed, at least every other day. Just after his relations with Harley had become close, he received the news of Addison's successful election with unfeigned pleasure and outspoken admiration. 'I believe if he had a mind to be chosen King, he would hardly be refused.'[20] A momentary cloud appeared when, Steele having been turned out of his editorship of the *London Gazette*, Swift exerted himself to have him retained in another of his offices: as a commissioner for Stamped Papers.

> Leave was given me to clear matters with Steele. Well . . . in the evening I went to sit with Mr. Addison, and offer the matter at distance to him, as the discreeter person; but found party had so possessed him, that he talked as if he suspected me and would not fall in with anything I said. So I stopped short in my overture, and we parted very drily . . . When shall I grow wise? I endeavour to act in the most exact points of honour and conscience; and my nearest friends will not understand it so. (October 22, 1710)

What had happened? It would seem that Addison suspected Swift of trying to use him to buy Steele over; or Swift thought he did, and his hyper-sensitive pride was in arms. On the other side, Addison, though he was a less violent party-man than Steele, regarded his friend's independence as inviolable. The thought that he was expected to use his influence to persuade Steele to be at least neutral towards the new Ministry was offensive to him. On a point so delicate the danger of misunderstanding was obvious.

However, the cloud was dissipated. Swift quietly dropped his declared intention of 'growing bare acquaintance' with Addison, and on November 16, when he had written three *Examiners*, he reassured Stella: 'Mr. Addison and I meet a little seldomer than formerly, but we are still at bottom as good friends as ever; but differ a little about party.' Nevertheless, on December 12 he has to report that Addison and he 'hardly meet once a fortnight; his Parliament and my different friendships keep us asunder'. That was natural enough; and one may fairly interpret a passage in the *Examiner* of December 14 as an expression of regret for the situation that had arisen between them. In this, Swift, after deploring that literary judgment was corrupted by party prejudice on both sides, asserts that the Whigs, 'so ruined a faction . . . were never provided with pens more resembling their condition, or less suited to their occasions'.

This is the more to be wondered at [he continues], when we consider they have the full liberty of the press, that they have no other way left to recover themselves, and that they want not men of excellent parts to set their arguments in the best light they will bear. Now if two men would argue on both sides with fairness, good sense and good manners, it would be no ill entertainment to the town, and perhaps be the most effectual means to reconcile us. But I am apt to think that men of a great genius are hardly brought to prostitute their pens in a very odious cause. . . . [21]

Swift's explanation of Addison's silence — he had just given up the *Whig Examiner*, on October 12 — was hardly calculated to please him. Though he was not an extreme Whig, he was a convinced one, and he certainly did not regard the cause of the late Ministry as odious. But neither his temper nor his genius were suited to the violences of party journalism. It was thus to take an unfair advantage of him, under the disguise of high compliment, to impute his silence to a consciousness that the Whig cause was indefensible.

On the evening that this *Examiner* appeared, Addison, in company with an Irish friend of Stella's, paid Swift a surprise visit and took him out to supper. Possibly he hinted to Swift how embarrassing his compliment was, and that he would prefer not to be praised at the expense of his party. At any rate that would explain the tone of Swift's comment to Stella.

> Mr. Addison and I are different as black and white, and I believe our friendship will go off, by this damned business of party: he cannot bear seeing me fall in so with this Ministry: but I love him as well as ever, though we seldom meet. (December 14, 1710)

On the next day, Swift, irritated by Steele's failure to keep an appointment with Harley which he had arranged for him, vented his spleen on Addison.

> I believe Addison hindered him out of mere spite, being grated to the soul to think he should ever want my help to save his friend; yet now he is soliciting me to make another of his friends Queen's Secretary at Geneva; and I'll do it if I can; it is poor Pastoral Philips.

The suspicion was extravagant, and Swift thought better of it. On January 2 he was drinking punch with Addison, and confessing that Steele had never kept an appointment, except twice, since he had known him; but on January 14 he had veered about again.

> At night I called at the Coffee-house, where I had not been in a week, and talked coldly a while with Mr. Addison. All our friendship and dearness are off: we are civil acquaintance, talk words of course, of when we shall meet, and that is all. I have not been at any house with him these six weeks . . . Is not it odd? But I think he has used me ill; and I have used him too well, at least his friend Steele.

On February 4 they dined together 'as common acquaintance. Yet what have I not done for his friend Steele?' This was Swift's constant grievance: that Addison used him ill in spite of his services to Steele. It is not apparent in what the ill-usage consisted; unless in a certain coolness in Addison's behaviour to which Swift was sensitive. In Addison's eyes he was bound to appear something of a turncoat. Moreover, Swift's defection could not be compensated by his services to Steele; for, although Swift wanted to do Steele a good turn, and genuinely believed he had done it, he was mistaken in thinking that it was owing to his good offices that Steele kept his place in the Stamped Paper office. Harley was content to let Swift think so: it was the commonest of all Court 'refinements' to allow a friend to believe that you were doing for his sake what you were doing for your own. Swift was familiar with it, and in a less flattering context would have been quick to detect it. To Harley it was well worth the price of a minor office to keep Steele's pen neutral. The *Tatler*, soon after Sunderland's dismissal, had published a veiled attack upon Harley in the form of a letter purporting to come from Downes the prompter, complaining of the new and incompetent management in the theatre. For that Steele lost his editorship of the *Gazette*. To offer to let him retain his Stamp office if he would refrain from further attacks was reasonable in itself — for the *Tatler* had claimed to be non-political — and a good bargain for Harley.

Steele, though he failed to keep his first appointment with Harley, kept another, of which Swift knew nothing, and the interview was satisfactory to them both. Harley even offered Steele a more 'commodious' place.[22] Further, it is very probable that as the result of this interview Steele suddenly brought the *Tatler* to an end, and started the *Spectator*. It is remarkable that he dropped the *Tatler* without consulting or even warning Addison, and that in his last number (January 2, 1711) he blamed himself for having touched upon matters concerning Church and State. The *Spectator*, on the other hand, was once more avowedly non-political. Moreover, it positively aimed at softening the asperities of the party-feud. Addison's creation of Sir Roger de Coverley — the sympathetic Tory squire — was a precious contribution to the political civilization of England. But the first rough sketch of the character was Steele's. Thus the evidence is very strong that Steele came to an honourable understanding with Harley in his own right, and that he was not really beholden at all to Swift's advocacy. But only when Swift directly accused him of ingratitude, did he bluntly repudiate any obligation to him.

To return to Addison: apparently from February 4 to July 26, 1711, Swift and he did not meet at all. Swift's increasingly strong party line in the *Examiner* made contact difficult where it had been easy. Both were the losers. When they met again, however, at the Tonsons' in July, they talked as usual 'and as if we had seen each other yesterday'. Again, on September 14, they met by chance in the Park and supped together, and Swift was constrained to admit, in spite of all his new and glamorous acquaintance, 'I yet know no man half so agreeable to me as he is.' It may be that he was saying something which he knew would please Stella; but one feels that the friendship had been very real and important to Swift, and that it died hard. But the eager intimacy was over. Swift believed that the withdrawal was on Addison's side. And that may have been true. But his notion that Addison was guilty of ingratitude, in view of all Swift had done for the Whig wits, was based on self-deception. Swift greatly exaggerated, though in good faith, what he had done for Addison's particular friends. He claimed to have kept Steele in office, it was not true. He did nothing for Ambrose Philips. As for Addison himself, he told Stella: 'I set Addison so right at first that he might have been employed, and have partly secured him in the place he has.' Swift was talking big: Addison, as a convinced Whig, would not have accepted a political employment; and Harley (or Ormond) of their own mere motion, would have chosen rather to gratify Addison than exasperate him by depriving him of his Irish sinecure. Swift's tone of patronage on the strength of services which were illusory would have been justly resented by men who were his equals, if not in sheer genius, in contemporary standing and influence — supposing he had used it in conversation with them. There is no evidence that he did.

Swift's persuasion that Addison was ungrateful did not endure very long. Their great intimacy came to an end, but they cherished kind feelings towards each other. They met but seldom, but when they did, they met as friends. Looking back on this period, ten years later, Swift could say to Pope, that 'during all my Lord Oxford's ministry . . . Mr. Addison's friendship to me continued inviolable, with as much kindness as when we used to meet at my Lord Somers or Halifax, who were leaders of the opposite party'.[23]

6

Swift's work on the *Examiner* came to an end on June 14, 1711. The parliamentary session was over. Harley, recovered from Guiscard's stabbing, had reappeared in the Commons, and his scheme for funding the debts of the country had been received with enthusiasm, not least because it took for granted that the famous *Asiento* would be wholly in England's hands at the conclusion of peace. The new ministry was now successful and popular and apparently secure. By the end of May Harley had been made Lord Treasurer, and Earl of Oxford. But Swift was now aware that he had been altogether too sanguine in believing that Harley and St. John 'heartily loved one another'. He knew that St. John had deceived him into giving a misleading account of Guiscard's attempt on Harley in the *Examiner*, in order to steal the popularity, by making it appear that he himself was the intended victim;* he knew that St. John, by defending Brydges, the Whig Paymaster-General, against the suspicion of malversation, had deliberately deserted the party-line; and his forebodings of the ill success of the Quebec expedition, which St. John had forced through during Harley's illness against his wishes, show that he had absorbed Harley's views on this affair.

In the *Examiner* (Nos. 32 and 33) Swift had compared Guiscard's attempt on Harley's life with the previous effort of the Whig Lords to implicate him

* See Appendix V.

in Greg's treason. The Whigs had put out a pamphlet to exonerate them. To this Swift replied in August, in *Some Remarks upon a Pamphlet entitled A Letter to the Seven Lords of the Committee appointed to examine Greg*, by the author of the *Examiner*. The performance throughout is in Swift's best light-hearted style. The opening is delightful.

> Those who have given themselves the trouble to write against me ... do all agree in discovering a violent rage, and at the same time affecting an air of contempt towards their adversary; which, in my humble opinion are not very consistent; and therefore it is plain, that their fury is real and hearty, their contempt only personated. I have pretty well studied this matter, and would caution writers of their standard, never to engage in that difficult attempt of despising, which is a work to be done in cold blood, and only by a superior genius to one at some distance below him. I can truly affirm that I have had a very sincere contempt for many of those who have drawn their pens against me; yet I rather chose the cheap way of discovering it by silence and neglect, than be at the pains of new terms to express it: I have known a lady value herself upon a haughty disdainful look, which very few understood, and nobody alive regarded.[24]

After arguing, cogently enough, that the conduct of the Committee towards Greg was suspicious, he turns to deal with the pamphleteer's encomium upon the seven Whig Lords who composed it: Devonshire, Somerset, Bolton, Wharton, Townshend, Somers and Halifax.

> He hopes his seven correspondents 'will never want their places'; but is in pain for the poor kingdom, lest 'their places should want them'. Now I have examined this matter, and am not at all discouraged. Two of them hold their places still, and are likely to continue in them. Two more were governors of islands; I believe the author does not imagine those to be among the places which will want men to fill them. God be thanked, a man may command the Beef-eaters without being a soldier; I will at any time undertake to do it myself.[25]

In the course of his *Remarks*, Swift plainly hinted that he was now engaged on the detailed incrimination of the old ministry and vindication of the new one, which was *The Conduct of the Allies*.

He turned aside from it, however, to deal a witty and subtle stroke in favour of the Peace. By a blunder of the master of the packet-boats, Prior was arrested at Dover on his return from his secret mission to Paris, and his journey became generally known. Swift had the brilliant idea of writing what purported to be a narrative of Prior's doings by his French courier. To

Stella he described it merely as 'a project to bite the town', in which it was entirely successful; but *A New Journey to Paris*, 'translated from the French of the Sieur du Baudrier', was equally successful in a more serious purpose: namely, to indicate that the Ministry was taking the high hand with France over the peace, presenting an ultimatum rather than offering a negotiation. 'Sire, tout ou rien!' the imaginary courier overheard Prior say to Louis XIV. That was the language all Englishmen, whether Tory or Whig, liked to think their envoy spoke to the Great Monarch. And it was sufficiently near the truth to show that Swift knew more about the actual peace-moves than he dared to put in his letters to Stella.

7

The Conduct of the Allies is one of the two most famous political pamphlets in English. But the qualities which made it immediately effective make it disappointing to a modern reader. It has nothing of the eloquence, the exaltation and the prophetic power of Milton's *Areopagitica*. That was to be expected; the intellectual and religious climate had changed: and Swift's genius was of another kind. But it is also notably lacking in the incessant touches of gay humour which make Swift's slighter political pamphlets so exciting. It moves mainly within the realm of party politics, and within what seems to us nowadays a curiously restricted circle of economic ideas. Probably for these reasons it was enormously influential. It had what was for those days a prodigious sale — no less than 11,000 copies, mostly at a shilling apiece.

It is, of course, a piece of enviably lucid prose. Where it chiefly disappoints is in a certain disingenuousness. In spite of the admirable principles to govern the declaration and conduct of war which Swift propounds at the beginning, of which the first is that a war may be wisely begun 'to check the overgrown power of some ambitious neighbour', he manages to insinuate that the war had been entirely unnecessary and that the Church-party was always opposed to it. He then undertakes to show 'by plain matters of fact, that no nation was ever so long or so scandalously abused by the folly, the temerity, the corruption, the ambition of its domestic enemies; or treated with so much insolence, injustice and ingratitude by its foreign friends'. This is the familiar tone of party rhetoric.

This will be manifest by proving the three following points.
First, That against all manner of prudence, or common reason, we engaged in this war as principals, when we ought to have acted only as auxiliaries.

Secondly, That we spent all our vigour in pursuing that part of the war which could least answer the end we proposed by beginning of it; and made no efforts at all where we could most have weakened the common enemy, and at the same time enriched ourselves.

Lastly, That we suffered each of our allies to break every article in those treaties and agreements by which they were bound and to lay the burthen upon us.[26]

The first of these propositions was a mere Tory atavism: a reversion to the position held by the Tories in 1700-1701, previous to Louis XIV's proclamation of James III as King of England, and his occupation of the Spanish Netherlands — events which led most of the Tories to abandon it, and with it their contention that the interests of England were not involved in the fate of the Low Countries. However, to clinch his unconvincing point, Swift offers a singularly specious argument. Godolphin, he says, resigned the Treasurership (in 1702) because he disapproved of the war; but when Anne came to the throne, he took the office again, because the army was to be commanded by Marlborough.

So that, whether this war were prudently begun or not, it is plain, that the true spring or motive of it, was the aggrandizing a particular family, and in short, a war of the general and the ministry, and not of the prince and people; since those very persons were against it when they knew the power, and consequently the profit, would be in other hands.[27]

This is chicane, not argument. In the first place there is no evidence that Godolphin, who was then a Tory, resigned because he opposed the war. What he opposed was a new election, in which, because of Louis XIV's new provocations, the Whigs would regain much of the ground they had lost to the Tories in the previous one. King William's final 'war-election' was one of the great grievances the Tories cherished against him. And the reason why they were so enraged by it was that they had accepted the Grand Alliance, and resented being branded as pro-French. In the second place, even if Swift's statement about Godolphin had been true, it could not possibly have proved that the war was 'a war of the general and the ministry, and not of the prince and people'. Who was this Prince? King William had ardently desired the war, and chosen Marlborough to wage it. Queen Anne followed Marlborough. As for the people, they presumably spoke in the new evenly balanced House of Commons, which voted the generous supply of 40,000 men for the Flanders War. The whole contention is flimsy and false.

Swift's second proposition, that England should have made her main effort at sea, was indeed a favourite Tory maxim; but it had been quietly dropped after Blenheim. To revive it now was curiously inconsistent with his attack on the treaty with Portugal which, even if over-generous, was necessary to secure to the English navy the harbours without which it could not operate effectively in the Mediterranean.

By spending time on these two propositions, one patently false, the other archaic, Swift weakened the real strength of his case, in the eyes of posterity. His attempt to rehabilitate the High Tory prejudice against a continental war involved him in a flagrant contradiction. At one moment he argues that the British victories up to and including Ramillies put the country in a position to achieve all the purposes of the Grand Alliance, and something besides; and he argues this on the premiss that those purposes were legitimate and necessary. At another moment, he argues that the Grand Alliance was itself a mistake, and that the whole war was consequently unnecessary. In other words, all the Tories, no matter how divided among themselves, or how incoherent their views and policies, were always right, all the time. In the same strain, though possibly with more sincerity, he contends that the English war-effort ought to have been limited to what could have been paid for by the annual revenue. He professes to find the new practice of partly financing a war by loans on the national credit indisputably evil, and he affects to believe that it was a cunning invention of Dutch William to secure himself on the throne. All this, one imagines, was with the object of consolidating all the Tories behind the Ministry. It could hardly have converted the most moderate Whig.

To an impartial judgment Swift does not come near to proving either of his first two propositions; he does not make them even plausible. Fortunately for the abiding strength of his pamphlet, the third bulked much larger, was more practically important, and he proved it up to the hilt. The Dutch and the Austrians had consistently failed to fulfil their treaty obligations. And from this he might fairly conclude, as he did, that 'We who have borne the burthen of the war, ought in reason, to have the greater share in making the peace.' That is his real and cogent thesis, and its prime importance is emphasized in his title: *The Conduct of the Allies and the Late Ministry in beginning and carrying on the Present War*. The pamphlet is designed to stifle the criticism that England was letting down her allies, by proving with vigour and in detail, that her allies had let England down; and to deflect the opposition to the Peace by demonstrating that the reason why Godolphin, Marlborough and the Whigs had submitted England to this humiliating treatment was that the general and the clique surrounding him found it very profitable to make England submit.

In that whole chain of encroachments made upon us by the Dutch, which I have above deduced, and under those several gross impositions from other princes, if any one should ask, why our general continued so easy to the last? I know no other way probable, or indeed so charitable to account for it, as by that unanswerable love of wealth, which his best friends allow to be his predominant passion. However, I shall waive anything that is personal upon this subject. I shall say nothing of those great presents made by several princes, which the soldiers used to call winter foraging, and said it was better than that of the summer; of two and an half *per cent* subtracted out of all the subsidies we pay in these parts, which amounts to no inconsiderable sum; and lastly, of the grand perquisites in a long successful war, which are so amicably adjusted between him and the States.[28]

The trick of the trade is blatant. 'I shall say nothing of . . .' and he says it. But the accusation is justified, and it is deadly.

8

In spite of Sir Winston Churchill's brilliant defence of his ancestor, Swift's indictment prevails. The only rational object of waging war is to secure a just and reasonable peace. On this basic principle of sane politics Swift and the ministry were sound, and Marlborough was not. The peace could have been had after Ramillies. The carnage of Malplaquet was unnecessary, and unnecessary carnage is a crime. In the Barrier Treaty Marlborough's statesmanship revealed its bankruptcy. In that 'wild bargain' (as Swift justly called it) the interests of England in the Low Countries and in the Mediterranean and in the trade with Spanish-America were sacrificed to bribe the war-weary Dutch to fight on until Spain was conquered for the Hapsburg. Even if the Barrier Treaty was the work of the Junto rather than Marlborough himself, he has to bear the responsibility for it. That he avoided affixing his signature is immaterial.

But for all its political effectiveness, *The Conduct of the Allies* suffers in comparison with the most brilliant issues of the *Examiner*. One feels that Swift was too oppressed by his task to indulge his mordant wit. He found it irksome continually to submit his manuscript to the Ministers for approval. On the eve of publication St. John put it in his pocket and went off to Hampton Court. It took Swift five days to recover it; and then 'I must alter and undo and a clutter'. Two days later, on November 10, 1711, he complains: 'Three or four great people are to see there are no mistakes in point of fact; and 'tis so troublesome to send it among them and get their corrections that I am weary as a dog.' Even when it was printed, he had to make alterations in every edition, and complained that it cost him even more trouble than before. All this told upon the pamphlet itself, as it did upon his spirits. The defeat of the Ministry in the Lords on the issue of 'No peace without Spain' must have struck him as a proof that his pamphlet had failed, for his argument against the folly of making peace depend on the conquest of Spain is one of the most cogent parts of it.

It was on the Commons that it made its impression. But, although the Commons was already in fact the decisive assembly, it was not yet fully understood that it was. There was still a discrepancy between the outward paraphernalia and the inward reality of political power. Harley himself was indubitably the head of the Ministry for the crucial nine months that followed the fall of Godolphin; but not until he was made Lord Treasurer, and consequently a peer, was he generally recognized as Prime Minister.

> Yet he makes one difficulty [Swift had reported to Stella] which is hard to answer; he must be made a Lord, and his estate is not large enough, and he is too generous to make it larger; and if the Ministry should change soon by any accident, he will be left in the suds. Another difficulty is that if he be made a peer, they will want him prodigiously in the House of Commons, of which he is the great mover. (April 22, 1711)

Harley was at least aware of the danger of the Prime Minister not being in the Commons, and seems to have followed the tradition with misgiving, but as of necessity. More surprising was the choice of St. John. When Harley had gone to the Lords, he was left undisputed leader of the Commons: an inexpugnable position from which to wage his battle for power against Oxford. Yet in order not to be inferior to Oxford in outward prestige, he followed him to the Lords and threw his advantage away. Plainly, it was not yet apparent to the statesmen of that day that the Commons was in fact the seat of power. Walpole seems to have been the first clearly to recognize it, and to take his measures accordingly.

Swift's arguments did much to rally the Tories in the Commons, and the nation behind them, and thus to strengthen Oxford's hand in pressing the Queen to make the Lords come into line. How far the arguments were his own is doubtful. Previous to his taking over the *Examiner* he had no definite views on the issue of war and peace: and the note of his letters to Stella, even after he had joined the Tories, is rather that a peace was necessary to secure the new Ministry, than that the *raison d'être* of the new Ministry was to make peace. It looks as though in the *Examiner* he was briefed chiefly by Harley, and in the *Conduct* by Bolingbroke. The important contention that the essential objects of the war as defined in the treaty of the Grand Alliance did not include the expulsion of Philip of Anjou from Spain was probably Bolingbroke's; it was certainly the main argument of his brilliant defence of the Treaty of Utrecht in his *Letters on the Study and Use of History*, written in 1735-6, where he contended, convincingly, that the Treaty fulfilled, even in detail, the wise designs of William III.

CHAPTER XIII

SWIFT AND PREFERMENT: 1711-1713

WHILE Swift was painfully engaged in the composition of *The Conduct of the Allies*, the Whig forces were being marshalled for an attack on the Peace. Right up to the autumn of 1711, Marlborough seems to have been undecided. Oxford had no desire to humiliate him. On the contrary, once his political influence at Court was overthrown and the Duchess dismissed, Oxford was willing to come to a decent working arrangement with him, on condition he made no attempt to sabotage the Peace. Obviously, it would greatly strengthen the hands of the Ministry in the final negotiations, if they were on fair terms with the victorious and unconquerable general, and could hold over the French the threat of another campaign. Any such understanding involved a diminution of the extraordinary position Marlborough had occupied, which was virtually that of Generalissimo and Prime Minister combined; but since he had failed in his responsibility as statesman, and thrust away the opportunity of Peace, the choice before him now was simple enough. Either he must accept and collaborate with Oxford's policy of Peace, or he must make a last desperate effort to break the Ministry. Since Marlborough was a shrewd politician, and was well aware that the country as a whole — as represented in the Commons — was eager for Peace, and that there was no chance, without another palace revolution, of getting a House of Commons of a different complexion, we need to seek for the motives that determined him to the choice he made.

The chief of these is to be found in the violent opposition of the Electoral Prince to Peace. The future George I, neither then nor at any other time, was capable of thinking as a King of England. First, he thought as the ruler of Hanover; next, as a prince of the Empire. In both capacities he was for continuing the war, and letting England pay for it. As a brave, but not very intelligent commander, he enjoyed the glory of war; as an impecunious kinglet, he enjoyed it much more when England paid his troops and he commanded them; as a prince of the Empire he wanted to see France in ruin, and to have the satisfaction of helping to dictate peace to her. By the autumn Marlborough had determined to keep in with Hanover. He did so demonstratively. He returned to England in November in company with Bothmar, the Hanover envoy, and instigated, or at least connived at, the publication of the Elector's protest to the British government against the Peace on November 29, 1711. Sir Winston Churchill, who applauds his ancestor's conduct, believes that he helped to draft it.

2

That was the final signal for the Whig assault. But a great deal of mining had been going on before. How far Marlborough had been concerned with this is uncertain. Perhaps not at all, and it was merely a convergence of independent forces. The chief instrument in preparing the attack at home was the Duke of Somerset. His jealousy of the Marlboroughs had led him to join Harley in his effort to overthrow them. When he found that his exorbitant pretensions were disregarded by Harley, he turned against him, and began to intrigue for his overthrow. The breach between Somerset and the Ministry became open on August 12, 1711, at Windsor, when St. John refused to sit at council if he were present. Swift, whose information on this matter must have been exceptionally good, gives a guarded but very interesting account of it, in his *Letter to the October Club*. This he wrote on January 13, 1712, immediately after the main crisis was over: when Marlborough was out and the twelve peers had been created; but Somerset was still in office.

Upon the opening of this session an incident had happened, to provide against the consequences whereof will require your utmost vigilance and application. [That is, the defeat of the Ministry in the Lords.] All this last summer the enemy was working under ground, and laying their train; they gradually became more frequent and bold in their pamphlets and papers, while those on our side were dropped, as if we had no farther occasion for them. [That is, the *Examiner*.] Some time before an opportunity fell into their hands, which they have cultivated ever since [that is, the appointment of the Duchess of Somerset]; and thereby have endeavoured, in some sort, to turn those arts against us, which had been so effectually employed to their ruin: A plain demonstration of their superior skill at intrigue; to make a stratagem succeed a second time, and this even against those who first tried it upon them. I know not whether this opportunity I have mentioned could have been prevented with any care, without straining a very tender point, which those chiefly concerned avoided by all means, because it might seem a counterpart of what they had so much condemned in their predecessors. Though it is certain the two cases were widely different; and if policy had once got the better of good nature, all had been safe, for there was no other danger in view: But the consequences of this were foreseen from the beginning, and those who kept the watch had early warning of it.[1]

This veiled language refers to the appointment of the Duchess of Somerset as Groom of the Stole in place of the Duchess of Marlborough. The assertion is that at her husband's instigation she was influencing the Queen against the Ministry as Mrs. Masham had influenced her at Harley's, and that the Ministry hesitated to press for her dismissal, because they had previously condemned the Marlboroughs for bringing pressure on the Queen. However, they were aware of the danger that threatened them.

It would have been a masterpiece of prudence, in this case, to have made a friend of an enemy. [That is, to have satisfied the claims of the Duke of Somerset.] But whether that were possible to be compassed, or whether it were ever attempted, is now too late to enquire. All accommodation was rendered desperate, by an unlucky proceeding some months ago at Windsor, which was a declaration of war too frank and generous for that situation of affairs, and, I am told, was not approved by a certain great minister.[2]

The reference to the incident at Windsor is plain; and it is in character that Oxford should have thought St. John's forthrightness imprudent.

It was obvious to suppose, that in a particular where the honour and interest of a husband were so closely united with that of a wife, he might be sure of her utmost endeavours for his protection, though she neither loved nor esteemed him. The danger of losing power, favour, profit, and a shelter from domestic tyranny, were strong incitements to stir up a working brain, early practised in all the arts of intriguing. Neither is it safe to count on the weakness of any man's understanding, who is thoroughly possessed with the spirit of revenge to sharpen his invention. Nothing else is required besides obsequiousness and assiduity, which as they are often the talents of those who have no better, so they are apt to make impressions on the best and greatest minds.[3]

Though all this is skilfully veiled, the meaning is clear. To the Duchess of Somerset her position at Court was particularly precious, because it afforded her a shelter from her husband's domestic tyranny. Since the Duke threatened to take her away if he was dismissed from his position as Master of the Horse, the Duchess was virtually blackmailed into becoming the instrument of his plans. Swift cannot refrain from a jab at her as 'early practised in the arts of intriguing'.

Then Swift becomes even more diplomatic in his narrative; but the substance of it is that the Duchess's intimacy with the Queen enabled Somerset plausibly to represent to certain peers, who were dependent on the Queen for pensions, that they would incur no danger in following him in voting against Peace.

That this was the actual situation is borne out by other evidence. On December 1 Oxford wrote a strong and sensible letter to Somerset, plainly warning him of the consequences of opposing the Peace.

> I am confirmed in the opinion that I had in 1706 when I was in place, and afterwards in 1709 when I was out of place, that it is our interest and that of all the Protestant states to get out of this ruinous war as soon as we can with safety and honour, and I am the more fixed in this judgment by observing how often and how industriously a good peace has been thrust from us . . . There is nothing plainer than that the outcry against a peace at this time is raised by the art and cunning of some who are against any peace, and others who are angry so good a peace may be made by those persons they do not like. I will add one thing more, that no honest or wise man will take upon him the consequences which will follow the defeating of this opportunity, for if the arts or restlessness of any here should wrest this treaty out of the Queen's hands, there will be a peace, but such a one whenever it is as Britain will have no share in either of honour, safety, or profit.[4]

It produced no effect. Somerset's concern was revenge for his injured pride, not the interest of the nation. Relying on the Queen's attachment to his Duchess for his own impunity, he went his way. The forces against the Peace converged.

What happened then is obscure in detail, though the main events are clear. The Whig Lords tried to do a deal with Oxford. On December 2 Halifax wrote to Oxford offering to support a bill against Occasional Conformity if he would drop the Peace. On the day before the crucial debate of December 7 he wrote again to say that there would be a majority in the Lords against the peace-terms. All Oxford had to do was to bow gracefully to the coming vote of the Lords of 'No Peace without Spain', and say to the House: 'If their Lordships think the nation in a condition to insist on higher terms, and that their resolutions will obtain them, he wishes it as much as anybody.'[5] In return presumably, the Whigs would pass the Occasional Conformity bill, and thus show their deference to the Queen's zeal for the Church. It was a poor inducement to offer Oxford, who had nothing of the Tory eagerness to heap disabilities on the Dissenters, and was determined to stand or fall by the Peace. The bait had been previously swallowed, however, by 'Dismal' Nottingham, the High Church leader in the Lords. He agreed to move the amendment to the Address against the Peace. Was he acting on consistent principle, as Mr. Trevelyan believes, or was he furious, as Swift averred, at not being brought back into office by Oxford? 'I will quit my best friends, while I'm *Not-in-game*.' There is evidence for both; and probably both were true. The stupid slogan 'No Peace without Spain' was an article of faith with him, and he was openly opposed to Marlborough's continental strategy. In the Lords' debate Marlborough duly subscribed to the formula, in which he did not at all believe.

So nicely balanced were the parties that the persuasions of Somerset and the defection of Nottingham were enough to turn the scale. The motion was carried on December 7 by 62 votes to 54 that 'No Peace could be safe or honourable to Great Britain or Europe if Spain and the West Indies were allotted to any branch of the House of Bourbon'. The Queen listened to the debate. Peter Wentworth records:

> They say the Duke of Somerset, just by the Queen, called out louder for the question than anybody, and was not content only with that and a proxy he gave that way, but pulled the Duke of Cleveland with him.[6]

Yet at the end, the Queen, when asked by Shrewsbury, the Lord Chamberlain, whether he or Lindsey, the hereditary Lord Chamberlain, should lead her from the House, refused them both and chose Somerset.

Of a gesture so surprising at a moment so tense, only two explanations seem possible. One is that Anne was unconscious of the interpretation which would be put upon it: which is to say that she was really stupid. The other is that she enjoyed the sensation of power that such a gesture gave her. Anne was not really stupid; therefore the second explanation is to be preferred. And presumably she was also indicating that she did not regard a vote against the peace policy of the Ministry as a reason why her personal courtiers should be dismissed. But if she stuck to that view and insisted on retaining Somerset, the position of the Ministry would obviously become untenable. Somerset would be at his persuasions again, more plausibly than before, because he could now prove that the royal favour was not forfeited by opposition to the policy of the royal ministers.

3

The Whigs were jubilant at the vote and the royal gesture; and the Tories were in despair — all save one: Oxford himself. Even St. John was in perplexity. But Oxford, as he had striven to avoid this head-on conflict, had at last come to the conclusion that it was inevitable. As at other great crises in his life, he remained calm. He had decided that three things must be done. The Queen must be asked to create twelve new Tory peers, to dismiss Marlborough, and to dismiss Somerset. It speaks volumes for the difference in values between that day and ours that the dismissal of Somerset was regarded as more important and more difficult than the dismissal of Marlborough. If the Queen refused, then Oxford would accept the consequences as the fiat of Destiny, or the will of God. Never did his genuinely religious nature more evidently sustain him than at this moment of creative crisis. To make a dozen peers in order to conform the House of Lords to the will of the nation seems simple enough today, when the mere threat is sufficient to achieve the end. But once it had actually to be done, and it was a revolutionary innovation. To insist upon it with the scrupulous and obstinate Queen required great courage and conviction, for the consequences of failure were likely to be grim. When Wharton, during the Lords' debate, put his fingers round his neck to signify to Oxford that the block awaited him, it might have come true. 'I told Lord Treasurer,' Swift wrote to Stella the day after the Lords' vote, 'I should have the advantage of him; for he would lose his head, and I should only be hanged, and so carry my body entire to the grave.' The risks of decisive political action at that moment of our history were incalculable.

That is the peculiar fascination of the period. The transition from the ways of violence to the ways of Peace was still uncertain. We look back and persuade ourselves that the ways of Peace were preordained and the tranquil development of the British constitution was always assured. We cannot easily believe that statesmen were called upon to risk their lives for this very achievement. But so it was. They were called, and they responded to the summons. Swift's picture of Oxford's response is unforgettable. Swift was certainly not without courage himself; but he appears as a nervous and apprehensive child beside the imperturbable assurance of Oxford, who told him on December 11, 'You had better keep company with me, than with such a fellow as Lewis, who has not the soul of a chicken, nor the heart of a mite.' A week later, on December 19, Swift reported: 'Things do not mend at all. Lord Dartmouth despairs, and is for giving up; Lewis is of the same mind, but Lord Treasurer only says "Poh, poh, all will be well." '

All was well, though Swift 'did very much dislike' the means of salvation. On December 29 the twelve peers were created; on December 31 Marlborough was turned out; but the Duke of Somerset not until January 19. That had been the hardest point to carry, and it was not until the Queen had extorted from Somerset the promise that he would not take the Duchess away that it could be accomplished.* What persuasions Oxford used on the

---

* A curious evidence of Swift's strain and suspense while waiting for Somerset's dismissal is his extraordinary statement in June 1715 that 'he was not removed from her [the Queen's] service but with exceeding difficulty many months after' the Lords' vote. The actual period was six weeks. Yet he wrote this when the events must still have been vivid in his memory.[7]

Queen are unknown. But by his tenacity, by his instinctive knowledge of what, beneath the clamours of faction, the ordinary decent Englishman desired, by his readiness to hazard all at the pinch for what he felt to be the true interest of the nation, Oxford helped the British polity to birth, and established two cardinal principles of viable democracy. If in 1950 a President Truman could call a General MacArthur to order and subordination, it was partly because in 1711 Oxford had told Marlborough that he must obey or be dismissed. If in 1832 the will of the nation for parliamentary reform could peacefully prevail over the resistance of the Lords, it was because in 1711 Oxford had insisted that Queen Anne must either create twelve Tory peers or let him break his White Staff.

4

Swift was convinced that the Duchess of Somerset was the villain of the piece. There is no real evidence that she was; and Swift's own account indicates rather that her influence on the Queen was used simply to prevent the Duke from being dismissed — and that solely in order to retain her own position, and so escape the discomforts of her married life. Certainly this enabled the Duke to prosecute his own intrigues against Oxford; but that the Duchess herself was caballing against the Ministry or the Peace is, to say the least, not proven. When the Duke was finally dismissed, and the Duchess remained with the Queen, as far as the evidence goes, she behaved with a correct neutrality;* and it is hard to believe that Dartmouth, who was devoted to Oxford, would have cherished his high opinion of the Duchess if he had believed she was intriguing against his chief. The position was obviously delicate; and so long as the Duke was in office, and the Duchess was the means of keeping him there, it was natural that the supporters of the Ministry should desire that the Duchess too should be superseded. It was equally natural that the Queen, who loved and respected her, should be adamant against the suggestion. Apart from the purely personal motive, she dreaded a return of the durance from which, with Harley's help, she had freed herself in April 1710 — conditions wherein her intimate personal servants were imposed or deposed by the exigencies of politics. Probably, too, she clung to the Somersets as symbols of her pathetic and human longing to be free from party and above it, as emblems of that 'moderating scheme'

* This is borne out by Swift himself when describing the Queen's resentment at the jubilation of the Whigs over her serious illness in December 1713. He says: 'The women of both parties who then attended her Majesty [i.e. the Duchess of Somerset and Lady Masham] were well disposed to represent the behaviour of the Whigs in the strongest light.'[8] If the Duchess had been an active Whig partisan she would have done just the opposite.

which she and Oxford had at heart. But, so soon as Somerset began to behave like a vindictive Whig partisan, that dream was over.

The Queen's relation to the Duchess of Somerset was essentially different from her relation to Mrs. Masham. The Duchess was as nearly the Queen's equal as it was possible for a subject to be. On the perfection of her breeding and her courtesy the witness is unanimous. Even Swift himself was constrained to describe her behaviour at court, on the day after the Duke had been dismissed, as 'extremely courteous'. We may believe Dartmouth when he says that 'the Queen thought herself justified in her favour to her, when she was ashamed of it elsewhere'.⁹ Mrs. Masham was the Queen's personal maid; the Duchess was her personal friend.

Mrs. Masham was jealous of her; but Swift hated her. She was a veritable obsession with him. She had committed the unpardonable offence of judging his behaviour over the Temple *Memoirs* as ill-bred and disloyal. She had despised him as a character. Hating her, he had come to the conclusion that she was, necessarily, *the* evil influence working upon the Queen. As we have seen, he was probably quite mistaken. But Swift needed no evidence to convince him that the Duchess was the root of the evil: she was already cast for the rôle. 'We must certainly fall,' he wrote to Stella, 'if the Duchess of Somerset be not turned out; and nobody believes the Queen will part with her.' In the extremity of his fear and hatred, on December 23, he composed a truly vicious lampoon against her, which he called *The Windsor Prophecy*. Following a pattern he himself had set three years before, during the Bickerstaff jest, he had it printed in black letter, as purporting to be a prediction made two hundred years before and discovered during an excavation at Windsor. The diabolical part of it was this:

> And dear Englond, if ought I understond,
> Beware of Carrots from Northumberlond.
> Carrots sown Thyn a deep root may get,
> If so be they are in Sommer set:
> Their Conyngs mark thou, for I have been told,
> They assassine when young, and poison when old.
> Root out these Carrots, O Thou, whose name
> Is backwards and forwards always the same;
> And keep close to thee always that name,
> Which backwards and forwards is almost the same.
> And Englond, wouldst thou be happy still,
> Bury those Carrots under a Hill.¹⁰

The doggerel is horribly clever. 'Carrots' was the Duchess, who was red-haired. Thynne, Königsmark and Somerset — all the names of the painful story are there: followed by the vile accusation: 'They assassine when young, and poison when old.' The appeal to Anne to uproot Carrots and cling to Masham; and to England to bury the Carrots under a Hill (Mrs. Masham's family name) was not seriously meant. If the Queen had read the production, she would have been outraged by it. It could not possibly have achieved its political purpose; and Swift must have known it.

His motives were fear and revenge; and the revenge was of such a kind that it completely justified the Duchess in her opinion of Swift. Once more he revealed himself to her as 'a man of no principle either of honour or religion'. But it points almost to a kind of possession by hatred that he should not have sensed the danger before he sent the lampoon to the press. He knew that everybody would guess it to be his. Yet it was not till Mrs. Masham herself warned him that it would anger the Queen, that he wrote to the printer to stop publication. The printer did not receive the letter, and brought up 'dozens apiece' to the members of the society of Brothers at their dinner on December 27. None of the original edition were actually published. But there must have been fully two hundred copies of it in circulation. And, of course, it was not long before other editions were printed and sold in the streets. ''Tis an admirable good one,' said Swift complacently to Stella, 'and people are mad for it.' Peter Wentworth sent one to his brother, Lord Strafford. Lady Strafford reported to her husband: 'I hear there is a most scandalous lampoon come out against the Duchess of Somerset, but I have not seen it, for I am very cautious who I inquire for things of that nature of, and particularly of her.'

5

We need look no further for the reason why Swift's preferment in England was resolutely blocked. *A Tale of a Tub* was a minor impediment compared to this. Unless the Duchess of Somerset were actually dislodged, *The Windsor Prophecy* was bound to be fatal to his pretensions. As soon as Swift realized that the Queen did not intend to part with the Duchess, he must have known his chance of an English Deanery was desperate. Such evidence as there is indicates that Oxford did his best for Swift. It is hard to conceive any other reason why the appointments to the three English Deaneries which fell vacant in the first half of 1712 — Wells, Ely and Lichfield — were held up for a whole year, except that Oxford took seriously Swift's threat that he would pack up and return to Ireland the moment a suitable preferment was given away from himself. Nor is there any ground for supposing that Oxford was not anxious to satisfy the double claim of friendship and service.*

Where Oxford offended, if he did offend, was in not making it quite clear to Swift that his desire for an English Deanery was likely to meet with a stubborn refusal from the Queen. What seems to have happened is that Oxford, rather than bring the matter to an issue with the Queen, procrastinated as long as he could, and kept all three Deaneries vacant. On February 5, 1712, that is, within three weeks of Somerset's dismissal, when perhaps it still seemed possible that the Duchess might be forced to leave the Queen, Swift wrote to Oxford: 'I humbly take leave to inform your Lordship that the Dean of Wells died this morning at one o'clock. I entirely submit my poor fortunes to your Lordship.' It is impossible to suppose that Oxford simply kept silence. Perhaps he told Swift that, if the Duchess retired, and the Queen were left to the persuasions of Mrs. Masham, it might be done. Throughout the year, the report was current that Swift was to be appointed to Wells. It reached Ireland. Archbishop King heard it; Stella heard it. Applicants began to put in for Swift's Irish livings. In November 1712, immediately after the incident of the band-box containing an amateurisn infernal machine addressed to Oxford, which Swift suspected and opened for him, an amusing ballad was published, which ended:

> Now God preserve our gracious Queen,
>   And for this glorious deed,
> May she the Doctor make a Dean,
>   With all convenient speed.
>
> What tho' the Tub hath hindered him,
>   As common story tells,
> Yet surely now the Bandbox whim
>   Will help him down to Wells.

It did not. The Deanery of Wells went at last to Dr. Brailsford, the chaplain to the Duchess of Newcastle, whose service consisted in having smoothed the negotiations between Oxford and the Duchess concerning the marriage of Lord Harley to the Duchess's red-haired daughter. That Brailsford's appointment was a job is indubitable: but everything was a job of some sort or other in those days. Swift's own Deanery of St. Patrick's was a job. But there is no evidence at all that Oxford ever had it in his power to give Swift the Deanery of Wells, or any other in England.

* See Appendix VI.

6

Even when the decisive moment came, on April 13, 1713, and Erasmus Lewis showed Swift the order to draw the warrants for the three Deaneries — 'but none of them to me' — his only complaint was of Oxford 'not giving me timely notice as he promised to do, if the Queen would do nothing for me'. But it is clear from his letters to Stella that the disappointment did not come to him as a surprise; and that he had previously laid plans on the assumption that his chance of an English Deanery was remote. Six months before, on October 28, 1712, he had told Stella that Dr. Coghill had suggested that he should get the bishopric of Raphoe for Dean Stearne of St. Patrick's, and the Deanery for himself. 'I shall indeed,' he replied ironically. 'I have such obligations to Stearne. But however, if I am asked who will make a good bishop, I shall name him before anybody.' That is to say, while appearing to turn down the suggestion, he was entertaining it. But his reply to Coghill was so guarded that it was misinterpreted, and Coghill gave Stella to understand that Swift had said he would not accept preferment in Ireland. This misunderstanding Swift corrected in his letter to Stella of February 4, 1713.

> I did not write to Dr. Coghill that I would have nothing in Ireland, but that I was soliciting nothing anywhere, and that is true. I have named Dr. Sterne to Lord Treasurer, Lord Bolingbroke and the Duke of Ormond, for a bishopric and I did it heartily. I know not what will come of it; but I tell you as a great secret that I have made the Duke of Ormond promise me to recommend nobody till he tells me, and this for some reasons too long to mention.

On April 7, he sent Stearne a letter enclosed in his own to Stella, 'which he must not have but upon condition of burning it immediately after reading, and that before your eyes . . . You shall only know in general that it is an account of what I have done to serve him in his pretensions on these vacancies etc. But he must not know that you know so much.'

From all this it is clear that Swift was in fact working hard to get Stearne promoted, on the tacit understanding that he would succeed him as Dean of St. Patrick's. This scheme had the immense advantage that the consent of the Queen was not directly necessary to his appointment. It lay with Ormond; and the Queen could acquiesce with a quiet conscience. She was not preferring a wicked man in her beloved Church of England. Even so, it was not achieved without a struggle. At the last minute, Oxford, loth to lose Swift to Ireland, pressed the Queen to make him a prebendary of Windsor — a post which Swift had always regarded as desirable — but in vain. The Queen and the Duchess were resolute that he should receive no post of distinction in the Church of England.

During the final period of suspense, Swift became nervously irritable and unjust. He was angry with Oxford for his eleventh-hour effort to get him to Windsor instead of St. Patrick's. 'Thus he perplexes things,' he complained to Stella. 'I expect neither; but I confess, much as I love England, I am so angry at this treatment that, if I had my choice, I would rather have St. Patrick's.' Two days later, on April 18, everything appeared settled.

This morning Mr. Lewis sent me word that Lord Treasurer told him the Queen would determine at noon. At three Lord Treasurer sent to me to come to his lodgings at St. James's, and told me the Queen was at last resolved that Dr. Sterne should be Bishop of Dromore, and I Dean of St. Patrick's; and that Sterne's warrant should be drawn immediately. You know the deanery is in the Duke of Ormond's gift; but this is concerted between the Queen, Lord Treasurer and the Duke of Ormond, to make room for me. I do not know whether it will yet be done; some unlucky accident may yet come. Neither can I feel joy at passing my days in Ireland, and I confess I thought the Ministry would not let me go; but perhaps they can't help it.

But even now, the scrupulous Queen demurred. She must know whether Ormond fully approved of Stearne's promotion; and Swift discovered that he did not. Let Swift choose any other Deanery in Ireland, said Ormond — one that did not involve his making Stearne a bishop. But Swift was firm. It was St. Patrick's or nothing. Indeed, no other Deanery in Ireland was comparable to it in dignity and prestige. At last Ormond agreed. After one more day of suspense, it was finally settled. 'I think 'tis now passed,' he wrote to Stella on April 23, 'and I suppose MD is malicious enough to be glad, and rather have it than Wells.' There was, of course, no malice in Stella's undoubted pleasure. She did not want to be uprooted again. Her roots were now in Ireland; her friends were Irishmen. And Swift himself was not without his satisfaction. 'This affair was carried with great difficulty, which vexes me,' he wrote. But equally there was something in it which gratified his pride. 'But they say here 'tis much to my reputation that I have made a bishop, in spite of all the world, to get the best deanery in Ireland.'

7

It is a fascinating episode in Swift's career. Thanks to the *Journal*, we live through the ambition, the anxiety, the suspense with him. More even than the political crisis of December 1711, it gives the tension of drama to that record, unique in its expansiveness and its reticence. But the two crises are intimately connected; the latter personal drama grows out of the former impersonal one. By *The Windsor Prophecy*, Swift was condemned to St. Patrick's. And some, who care for justice, may feel that Swift got off lightly, and that his punishment was hardly adequate to his crime. But Swift does not lend himself to such simple judgments. At the very moment that he was making his dastardly attack on the Duchess of Somerset, he was showing his tenderness in his grief for Mrs. Anne Long, who died while in hiding from the bailiffs at King's Lynn. She had been a favourite of his, but she had offended him by what he thought was a double entendre in a letter, and he had broken off correspondence. When she heard the reason, she, very charmingly, protested her innocence and gently intimated that she had been ill. He wrote back a delightful letter, denying that she had offended him. Before it reached her she was dead. 'I was never more afflicted by any death,' he told Stella; and straightway wrote to the clergyman at Lynn asking that she should be buried close to the church wall where a marble plaque could be fixed, at his expense, to her memory. 'She had,' he told the parson, 'every valuable quality of body and mind that could make a lady loved and esteemed.'

I had the honour of an intimate acquaintance with her, and was never so sensibly touched with any one's death as with hers. Neither did I ever know a person of either sex with more virtues or fewer infirmities: the only one she had, which was neglect of her own affairs, arising wholly out of her goodness of temper.[11]

He gave exactly the same character of Anne Long to Stella, and said that he had ordered an honourable notice of her to be put in *The Postboy*, 'which is all I can do to serve her memory'; characteristically he added that 'one reason was spite; for her brother would fain have her death a secret, to save the charge of bringing her up her to bury her, or going into mourning'.[12] As usual, he made the worst of his own motives. To try to defeat the mean plans of Mrs. Long's callous relatives by paying a public tribute to her, was entirely laudable.

The contrast between his brutality towards the Duchess of Somerset and his tenderness towards Mrs. Long is striking. But the Duchess had wounded him in his pride, and looked down upon him from above. He had tried to take revenge — so basely that it came near to ruin his career. The punishment would have been excessive: for there was much more generosity than baseness in Swift. The Deanery of St. Patrick's was a nice adjustment of reward.

That the Duchess was the prime cause of his disappointment is fairly certain. The Archbishop of York, the Queen's chief ecclesiastical adviser, had been scandalized by *A Tale of a Tub* and did not favour him; but that resistance might have been overcome. The decisive influence on the Queen was the Duchess. Swift himself had no doubt about it. In the verses, *The Author on Himself*, which he wrote at Letcombe in 1714, the Duchess comes first of the villains, and at the head of the piece.

> By an old [red-hair'd, murd'ring hag] pursued,
> A crazy prelate, and a royal prude ... [13]

The missing words, supplied by Orrery, are obviously authentic; and in the body of the poem, the crucial influence is again ascribed to the Duchess.

> Now angry Somerset her vengeance vows
> On Swift's reproaches for her murdered spouse:
> From her red locks her mouth with venom fills:
> And thence into the royal ear instils.

Here in place of 'angry Somerset', Orrery read 'Madam Coningsmark', no doubt correctly. Swift's hatred was still blazing when he wrote his poem. It was indeed common knowledge among the circle of Swift's London friends that the Duchess was his implacable enemy. On the day when Oxford was finally put out of office, Bolingbroke, eager to retain Swift's services if he could, told Barber the printer to give him a message, which Barber passed on after the Queen was dead.

> Lord Bolingbroke told me last Friday, that he would reconcile you to Lady Somerset, and then it would be easy to set you right with the Queen, and that you should be made easy here, and not go over.[14]

Bolingbroke in his extremity promised much more than he could have performed, when he spoke of reconciling Swift and the Duchess. Even an apology far more abject than Swift was ever known to make would not have accomplished that. And he was so far from repenting his offence that at Letcombe he was repeating all his calumnies against her — though not, this time, in print.

But something, it would seem, was at work subsequently to obliterate the shameful episode from Swift's memory. Twenty years later his friend Ford was diligently collecting his past writings for publication in the Dublin edition, and sent Swift a list of titles. Swift replied, on November 4, 1733:

> In your catalogue of pamphlets there are some I do not remember, I mean, *Journey to Paris, Remarks about Greg, Peace & Dunkirk, Windsor Prophecy, Pretender's Letter to a Whig Lord.* I fancy I did not write any of these.

We may reasonably ascribe his forgetfulness of the other papers to a failing memory. But in the case of *The Windsor Prophecy*, this seems impossible. It had played too potent a part in Swift's destiny to be simply forgotten. This was something which Swift wanted to raze from his memory, because he was ashamed of it.

CHAPTER XIV

SUSPENSE: 1712-1713

THE prolonged suspense had some indirect but marked effects upon Swift. At the end of February 1712 he wrote to Stella: 'I have now nothing to do . . . I can sit and be idle now, which I have not been above a year past.'[1] That was immediately after he had written to Oxford about the vacancy at Wells. It was not a good moment for Swift to be unoccupied. Until then he had been hard at work. He had followed *The Conduct of the Allies* with a business-like appendix, *Some Remarks on the Barrier Treaty*; he had written the able *Letter to the October Club*; he had given the finishing touches to the only pamphlet to which he ever attached his name: *A Proposal for Correcting, Improving and Ascertaining the English Tongue*, in the form of a letter to Oxford. This was finished on February 22. On February 24 he wrote to Stella:

> I sometimes sit up very late at Lord Masham's, and have writ much for several days past, but I will amend both; for I have now very little business: and hope I shall have no more, and I am resolved to be a great rider this summer in Ireland.

In November 1711 he had said he hoped to be home soon after Christmas: he was weary of courts, and felt the need of his rides to Laracor, which 'did him more good than all the Ministries these twenty years'. In January 1712, he would set out in March; at the beginning of February, it was the beginning of April; at the end of February, he must wait till the end of the session, which he supposed would end in April. At the end of March began a violent and painful attack of the shingles, which incapacitated him for two months and pulled him down. The journal letters now dwindled into ordinary ones, and the buoyancy went out of them. No doubt, he was in considerable pain, and he did not care to write letters which would depress Stella; but even when he had recovered, he did not resume his daily talk with her. Nor did he until the end of the year.

Something was wrong. Partly it was ill-health; but much of the ill-health was due to his determination to keep close to the centre of power until some decision was reached about his preferment. On May 31 he wrote to Stella:

> I believe I have lost credit with you in relation to my coming over; but I protest it is impossible for anyone who has anything to do with this

ministry to be certain when he fixes any time. There is a business which, till it takes some turn or other, I cannot leave this place in prudence or honour. And I never wished so much as now that I had stayed in Ireland; but the die is cast, and is now a spinning, and till it settles, I cannot tell whether it be an ace or a sise. I am confident by what you know yourselves, that you will justify me in all this. The moment I am used ill, I will leave them; but know not how to do it while things are in suspense. — The session will soon be over (I believe in a fortnight), and the peace, we hope, will be made in a short time; and then there will be no further occasion for me, nor have I anything to trust to but Court gratitude, so that I expect to see my willows a month after Parliament is up; but I will take MD in the way, and not go to Laracor like an unmannerly spreenekish ferrow [splenetic fellow].

That seems an odd assurance: that he will see Stella, and not go straight to Laracor. But it was what he had done in June 1709, when his mission over the First Fruits and his hopes of preferment from the Whigs had failed. And what he was now saying was that he will not let his new disappointment make him so boorish again.

A fortnight later he wrote:

The worst thing [for his health] is my evenings at Lord Masham's, where Lord Treasurer comes, and we sit till after twelve, but it is convenient I should be among them for a while as much as possible; I need not tell oo why. But I hope that will be at an end in a month or two one way or another: and I am resolved it shall ... But how affectedly Ppt talks of my being here all summer; which I do not intend; nor to stay one minute longer in England than becomes the circumstances I am in. (June 17, 1712)

Lady Masham kept her rooms insufferably hot, and that, together with the late hours, did Swift no good. And his soul was divided. 'I wish,' he wrote to Stella, 'I had never come here as often and heartily as Ppt. What had I to do here?' He knew perfectly well what he had to do. But the suspense was making him sick at heart. And though he had told himself and her, again and again, that his object in making this long siege to preferment was to make MD easy, he knew it was only half-true.

In this condition of suspense and strain and ill-health, his letters to Stella became perfunctory: even nervy and short-tempered. On August 7 he wrote to her, after receiving a letter in which she had mentioned the report that he was to be Dean of Wells.

I had your N. 32 at Windsor; I just read it, and immediately sealed it up again, and shall read it no more this twelvemonth at least. The reason of my resentment at it is, because you talk as glibly of a thing as if it were done, which for aught I know is further from being done than ever, since I hear not a word of it; though the Town is full of it, and the Court always giving me joy and vexation. You might be sure I would have let you know as soon as it were done. . . .

He was as good as his word; he refused to open her letter again. Not only so; but his brief reply was followed by nearly six weeks' silence. He did not write again until September 15. 'I never was so long without writing to MD as now, since I left them, nor ever will again while I am able to write.' The letter ends affectionately enough, and contains a kind of explanation of his own perfunctoriness. 'See how my style is altered by living and thinking and talking among these people, instead of my canal and river-walk, and willows.'

2

There was more to be said about the alteration in his style towards Stella than that; but before we consider it, we may glance at his writings during this year, 1712, for they also show signs of strain and weariness. *Some Remarks on the Barrier Treaty* needs no comment; it was a business-like setting out of facts. The *Letter to the October Club* we have already discussed in so far as it is concerned with the Somersets. That affair was now settled. The Duke was out and the Duchess in; and Swift knew that she was irremovable. But the *Letter* has another political interest. It needs to be read in conjunction with the pamphlet he wrote in June 1712, soon after he had recovered from his illness: *Some Reasons to Prove that no Person is obliged by his principles as a Whig to oppose Her Majesty or her present Ministry, in a Letter to a Whig Lord.*

In both of these, Swift restates, in a new historical perspective, the position he had taken three years before: that there was no real difference of political principle separating Whigs and Tories. He now points out that the original party distinction was between Court and Country, and that the old Whigs belonged to the Country party. (The old Tories were Court: those who on principle, or interest, upheld the 'high prerogative' and 'the divine right'.) The revolution of 1688 had made obsolete the old distinction, because the title of the monarch was now parliamentary. Parliament had bestowed the Crown and settled the succession, thus making possible the situation which now existed, wherein Court and Country were on the same side. 'It has been the old complaint of your party,' says Swift to the Whig Lord, 'that the body of country gentlemen always leaned too much (since the Revolution) to the Tory side.'² By the same process the rump of the Whigs, who had not developed into the new Tory party, had become an independent faction with an anti-national policy: namely, to oppose the Peace and continue the war, in order to weaken the landed interest; and to oppose and weaken the Church. Allowing for the partisan exaggeration, this historical analysis, which is common to both pamphlets, is substantially sound.*

To the October Club Swift urges that they should be resolute to preserve the new unity of Court and Country, and so defeat the new faction. The real obstacle to the clean sweep of all the Whigs which they demanded (and to which, he not very truthfully suggests, Oxford was personally inclined) was the reluctance of the Queen. They were mistaken in thinking that, because Oxford had prevailed with the Queen to make the twelve peers, his power with her was absolute. He had to pretend that it was, in order to preserve the authority necessary to his office as Lord Treasurer; but sometimes he even 'has to forbear what *is* in his power, for fear of discovering [i.e. revealing] how far the limits extend of what *is not*'.³ The fact is that the Queen, having recovered her personal authority from the clique which had deprived her of it, is now doubly suspicious of any encroachment upon it. He hints plainly enough that the failure to remove the Somersets — the Duke was still in office when he wrote — was due to the Queen's insistence on keeping them. The burden of the pamphlet is that it is the duty and the interest of the October Club to be loyal to Oxford. They are wrong to suspect him of playing a double game. Let them remember that it is to him alone, his extraordinary patience and skill, that they owe it that Tories are in power at all. Oxford has, perhaps, two failings: a scrupulous loyalty which impels him to take responsibility for all the Queen's hesitations and prejudices and to be silent about them; and a reluctance to delegate authority. As Swift put it in a poem at this time,

> Suppose then Atlas ne'er so wise;
> Yet, when the weight of kingdoms lies
> Too long, upon his single shoulders,
> Sink down he must or find Upholders.⁴

In the *Letter to a Whig Lord*, whom he supposes to be one of the old Whigs who, through a sense of party loyalty, has followed the Junto, he declares that there are only two real questions at issue between them: first, whether the Queen shall choose her own servants; second, whether she shall keep her prerogative of declaring war and making peace. No Whig in England, he says, will openly deny her power in either.

* See Appendix VII.

As to the latter, which is the more avowed, Her Majesty has promised that the Treaty shall be laid before her Parliament; after which, if it be made without their approbation, and proves to be against the interest of the kingdom, the ministers must answer for it at their extremest peril.[5]

As to the former, Swift himself was rather in difficulties; for, although he had defended Oxford to the October Club by saying that the Queen insisted on choosing her own servants, he had not concealed his opinion that it was a pity that she did, and had implied that he was in sympathy with their demand for what was in effect party government. Two incompatible notions of constitutional government were jostling in his mind: one, that the Queen should freely choose her own ministers, and that these should be liable to impeachment for either her or their own acts which Parliament subsequently condemned; the other, that Parliament, and primarily the Commons, should impose upon the Queen a team of ministers whom they approved and would support. The first of these he had previously condemned in *Contentions and Dissensions*, on the reasonable ground that it did not make for good government if a statesman had to work with a halter round his neck. Yet at the second, he hesitated. Though he was more and more drawn towards it as the reign of the Queen neared its close, it was not because he accepted the idea of the two-party system, but because he believed that the Tories would be in a permanent majority, if the grosser forms of corruption were eliminated. It was the idea of one-party government which appealed to him. In this, as in other things, the static quality of his thinking was apparent. His conception was that, by a sort of miracle, chiefly of Oxford's working, England had regained her true constitution. All that mattered was to preserve it — to prevent any further undermining of the landed interest, and any disruption of the homogeneity of Church and State.

For all his admiration of Oxford, Swift did not really accept his idea of a ministry which should be genuinely above party: which would recruit itself from the able and honest men of either side, and thus, by a continuous assimilation of the political talent of the nation, prevent the emergence of party-faction. Oxford had none of Swift's conviction that the moneyed interest and the nonconformists ought to be ostracized. The more comprehensive the national society and the government, the better, he felt. Although his idea, in the circumstances of his time, was unrealizable, it may yet, after the lapse of two centuries and a half, prove to have been prophetic. We have already learned that in the emergency of modern war a national, non-party government is indispensable; we may yet discover that it is necessary in the emergency of modern peace.

3

Swift was particularly pleased with his *Letter to the October Club*; twice he assured Stella that it was 'finely writ'. It is, indeed, excellently done: a capital piece of delicate innuendo. In its more forthright manner the *Letter to a Whig Lord* is equally good. There is plenty of zest, too, in the verses: *Toland's invitation to Dismal to dine with the Calves' Head Club*:

> Who, by disgraces or ill fortune sunk,
> Feels not his soul enliven'd when he's drunk?
> Wine can clear up Godolphin's cloudy face,
> And fill Jack Smith with hopes to keep his place.
> By force of wine, ev'n Scarborough is brave,
> Hal grows more pert, and Somers not so grave:
> Wine can give Portland wit, and Cleveland sense,
> Montague learning, Bolton eloquence:
> Cholmondeley, when drunk, can never lose his wand;
> And Lincoln then imagines he has land.[6]

This was one of a bundle of 'Grub Street papers', at a penny each, which Swift put out in the last fortnight of July 1712, just before the new, prohibitive tax of a halfpenny on a half-sheet was imposed. Others which have survived are the ballad *Peace & Dunkirk*, and the *Letter from the Pretender to a Whig Lord* — neither of which are more than mediocre — and *A Hue and Cry after Dismal*, which is a comic story of the dark-visaged Nottingham appearing as a chimney-sweep in Dunkirk.

A Letter of Thanks from my Lord W [harto]n to the Lord Bishop of St. Asaph was written at about this time, and is of a higher order than the 'Grubs'. Fleetwood, the Whig bishop of St. Asaph, had published a volume of sermons, with a preface attacking the Ministry, which the Commons ordered to be burned. Steele promptly published it in the *Spectator* (May 21, 1712), in breach of his undertaking to his readers, to keep the *Spectator* free from politics. Swift countered this, in a letter of appreciation to the Bishop which purported to be written by Wharton. It is extremely funny. The Bishop had written, reflecting on the doctrine of 'passive obedience':

Although in the constant course of my ministry, I have never failed, on proper occasions, to recommend, urge, and insist upon the loving, honouring and the reverencing the Prince's person, and holding it, according to the laws, inviolable and sacred ... yet did I never think myself at liberty, or authorized to tell the people, that either *Christ*, St. *Peter*, or St. *Paul*, or any other holy writer, had, by any doctrine delivered by them, subverted the *Laws* and *Constitutions* of the country in which they lived, or put them in a worse condition, with respect to their civil liberties, than they would have been if they had not been Christians.

On which the imaginary Wharton writes approvingly:

'You have never failed, on proper occasions, to recommend the loving, honouring, and reverencing the prince's person', so as never to break his royal shins, or tread upon his heels; yet you never intended men should pay any submission or obedience to him any longer than he acted according to the will and pleasure of his people. This you say is the opinion of Christ, St. Peter and St. Paul: and faith I am glad to hear it; for I never thought the prigs had been Whigs before.[7]

That, though funny, is a little unscrupulous towards the Bishop. The following is both funny and just. The Bishop had written, nominally in eulogy of the Queen, but in fact of Marlborough, Godolphin and the Junto:

Such was the fame of her administration of affairs at home, such was the reputation of her wisdom and felicity in choosing ministers, and such was then esteemed their faithfulness and zeal, their diligence and great abilities in executing her commands; to such a height of military glory did her great general and her armies carry the British name abroad; such was the harmony and concord betwixt her and her allies, and such was the blessing of God upon all her counsels and undertakings, that I am as sure as history can make me, no prince of ours was ever yet so prosperous and successful, so loved, esteemed, and honoured by their subjects and their friends, nor near so formidable to their enemies. We were, as all the world imagined then, just entering on the ways that promised to lead to such a peace as would have answered all the prayers of our religious queen, the care and vigilance of a most able ministry, the payments of a willing and obedient people, as well as all the glorious toils and hazards of the soldiery; when God, for our sins, permitted *the Spirit of Discord* to go forth, and by troubling sore the camp, the city, and the country (and oh that it had altogether spared the places sacred to his worship!) to spoil for a time this beautiful and pleasing prospect, and give us in its stead, I know not what —

On which the imaginary Wharton rhapsodizes:

Here your Lordship rises, if possible, above yourself. Heavens! Such force, such energy in each pregnant word! Such fire, such fervour, in each glowing line! One would think your Lordship was animated with the same spirit with which our hero fought. Who can read, unmoved, these following strokes of oratory? 'Such was the fame, such was the reputation, such was the faithfulness and zeal, to such a height of military glory, such was the harmony and consent, such was the blessing of God' etc. O! the irresistible charm of the word 'such'! Well, since Erasmus wrote a treaty in praise of Folly, and my Lord Rochester an excellent poem on Nothing, I am resolved to employ the *Spectator*, or some of his fraternity (dealers in words) to write an encomium upon Such. But whatever changes our language may undergo (and everything that is English is given to change) this happy word is sure to live in your immortal preface. Your Lordship does not end yet, but to crown all, has another *such* in reserve, where you tell the world, 'We were just entering on the ways that lead to such a peace ... And give us in its stead, I know not what — ' Oh exquisite! How pathetically does your Lordship complain of the downfall of Whiggism, and Daniel Burgess's meeting-house! The generous compassion your Lordship has shown upon this tragical occasion, makes me believe your Lordship will not be unaffected with an accident that had like to have befallen a poor whore of my acquaintance about that time, who being big with Whig, was so alarmed at the rising of the mob that she had like to have miscarried upon it; for the logical jade presently concluded (and the inference was natural enough) that if they began by pulling down meeting-houses, it might end in demolishing those houses of pleasure, where she constantly paid her devotion; and, indeed, there seems a close connection between extempore prayer and extempore love. I doubt not, if this disaster had reached your Lordship before, you would have found some room in that moving parenthesis, to have expressed your concern for it.[8]

It is admirable criticism, admirable fooling, and a just retribution. It was, presumably, written in June. Plainly Swift's new illness had no immediate effect upon his spirits. But afterwards he began to droop.

4

Some months before, however, he had written a piece clean outside his political concerns: *A Proposal for Correcting, Improving and Ascertaining the English Tongue.* This had been in his mind ever since he gave up the *Examiner* in June, 1711; but he had had to put it aside to work on *The Conduct of the Allies.* He took it up again and finished it on February 22.

It has been common form in the critics of Swift from Dr. Johnson onwards to deride his project for the foundation of an English counterpart to the French Academy, as being antipathetic to the national genius. That may be so; though it really is not self-evident. But it has also been common form to misrepresent what he actually proposed. He spoke, indeed, of 'fixing' the language; but by that he did not mean that the English language should not be enlarged. He is explicit to the contrary. What he sought to ensure is that good expressive English should never become obsolete. The real purpose of the proposed society is to try to keep sound words and expressions in currency, so that good books should never become antiquated for the ordinary Englishman. It does not appear that the idea was in itself either reactionary or Utopian, or that, if the society had been founded with a modest official endowment, it would not have endured and done good work. Moreover, as Swift conceived it, its influence would have been liberal. Unlike the society of the Brothers, which was avowedly a fraternity of Tory wits, the proposed society was above party. It was to include Whig and Tory men of letters; and he went out of his way to pay the *Spectator* in general and Steele in particular a compliment as one 'who has tried the force and compass of our language with so much success'. And young writers in the difficult circumstances of today may feel more sympathetic than their Victorian predecessors used to be towards Swift's appeal to the Lord Treasurer to grant a number of small pensions to writers of 'true genius': which he thus defines:

> I do not mean by a true genius, any bold writer, who breaks through the rules of decency to distinguish himself by the singularity of his opinions; but one who upon a deserving subject, is able to open new scenes, and discover a vein of true and noble thinking, which never entered into any imagination before; every stroke of whose pen is worth all the paper blotted by hundreds of others in the compass of their lives.⁹

Nor should it be forgotten that in the fifty years that followed Swift's abortive proposal the economic condition of the writer of genius in England was pitiable in the extreme. The treatment by the English ruling class of Fielding and Goldsmith and Johnson and Collins is an indelible stain upon our civilization. Swift would have spared us that.

5

By the middle of July he had begun work on the historical narrative of the making of the Peace of Utrecht, which was not published till ten years after his death, and then under the rather misleading title, *The History of the Four Last Years of the Reign of Queen Anne*. The narrative has not the personal interest of the other accounts he wrote of the same period; but it has one marked peculiarity; that it gives much the largest credit for the peace-making to Oxford, almost to the exclusion of Bolingbroke. This may have been one of the motives behind his decision to keep it from the press, which he communicated to Stella.

> Did I tell you that I forbear printing what I have in hand till the Court decides something about me? I will contract no more enemies, at least I will not embitter worse those I have already, till I have got under shelter; and the Ministers know my resolution. (December 29, 1712)

The reference is there primarily to his own Whig enemies. A little later he reported:

> My large treatise stands stock-still. Some think it too dangerous to publish, and would have me print only what relates to the peace. (January 18, 1713)

One of the obviously dangerous statements it contained was that Prince Eugène had proposed that Oxford should be assassinated.

Whether because the work itself was unduly burdensome — Swift complained that it involved reading a host of official documents to 'squeeze out a line' — or because the Ministers were half-hearted about it, or because he himself was becoming depressed by the continual uncertainty of his prospects — or most probably for all three reasons, the history is distinctly dull, and lacking in fire. Only on rare occasions does he let fly a typical shaft, as when he says of Wharton: 'He hath imbibed his father's principles in government; but dropped his religion, and took up no other in its stead: excepting that circumstance, he is a firm Presbyterian.'[10]

By the end of the year Swift had shelved his history for the time being. He turned aside to write what is in effect an elaborate parody of Anthony Collins's *Discourse of the Grounds and Reasons of the Christian Religion* under the title, *Mr. Collins's Discourse of Freethinking put into plain English by way of Abstract for the Use of the Poor.* Critics have given it high praise as a piece of sustained irony. It does not deserve their superlatives. Swift, one feels, was tired. One of the occasional flashes which relieve the tedium is the complete absurdity of the answer of the imaginary Collins to an objection which is Swift's own chief objection to the Deists.

> It is again objected, that freethinking will produce endless divisions in opinion, and by consequence disorder society. To which I answer; When every single man comes to have a different opinion every day from the whole world, and from himself, by virtue of freethinking, and thinks it his duty to convert every man to his own freethinking (as we freethinkers do) how can that possibly create so great a diversity of

opinions as to have a set of priests agree among themselves to teach the same opinions in their several parishes to all who will come to hear them? Besides, if all people were of the same opinion, the remedy would be worse than the disease; I will tell you the reason some other time.[11]

That does, indeed, faintly recall the *désinvolture* of *A Tale of a Tub*, and the argument that, without a tincture of madness, 'even all mankind would unhappily be reduced to the same belief in things invisible'; but the reminiscence serves chiefly to remind us that Swift's gusto is flagging.

6

The change of style towards Stella which Swift admitted in his letter of September 15 and the silence which preceded it are capable of another explanation than that which he gave to her. At the very moment that he could not bring himself to write to Hester Johnson, he was writing to Esther Vanhomrigh. She even came to visit him at Windsor. Again the evidence is that it was at this time that he wrote the first draft of the longest and most elaborately worked of all his poems, *Cadenus & Vanessa*, which carefully and sympathetically describes the birth of Vanessa's ill-starred passion for him. Yet again, at this time, references to the Vanhomrighs' house, which had previously been frequent in his letters to Stella, almost entirely disappear. In a court of law the verdict would certainly go against him. He was off with the old love and on with the new.

But the case is not so simple. Whatever may have been his original motive in persuading Stella and Dingley to settle in Ireland in 1701, Swift had, since the affair with Tisdall, been forced to realize that he must take some real responsibility for Stella. He had been instrumental in depriving her of marriage, in order that he might have her companionship; and he recognized the obligation to give her his in return. So he had stayed in Ireland for three years and a half, and returned to England, not at his own caprice, but on an official mission the compulsiveness of which she recognized. During his long stay in Ireland he had come to depend more and more upon her companionship. When he returned to England on August 30, 1710, once more upon the same official mission, whatever his less conscious purposes may have been, the rational picture he set before himself and her was clear enough. He was going reluctantly; he would be absent at most for a few months. Either his mission would succeed or it would fail: in either case, he would be back by Christmas. But the attractions of power had been too great for him. His mission had succeeded, but he did not return. The new situation also was fairly easy to rationalize in relation to his duty to Stella. First, because the success of his mission was a personal favour from Harley, which he must requite by his services; second, because the advancement which Harley promised in return for those services, would serve to make Stella and himself easy. As he put it, 'MD's felicity is the great end I aim at in all my pursuits.' For all this, his conscience was not at rest; and his sigh of relief and gratitude is audible when Stella told him that he did quite right to stay.

As his separation from her was prolonged, and the tension of his anxieties increased, he was increasingly a prey to the conflict between his obligation and his ambition. The ambition was twofold: in so far as it was a desire to improve his financial position, it was partly a desire to make Stella more comfortable; but it was more importantly a desire, by right of genius, to wield power and to mix on terms of equality with the world's 'great men', and to have that position 'acknowledged by some mark of distinction. Stella shared this second ambition on Swift's behalf. She knew his uniqueness, and desired it should have its reward; she took pleasure in the knowledge that the man she knew so intimately was a power among the powerful. Her attitude was entirely generous.

Partly because it was so generous, Swift was uneasy; and his uneasiness increased with the intensification of his own anxieties. His malaise impelled him to seek relaxation in the society of women. He always loved the conversation of women; and he was very attractive to them. His bevy of 'drabs of quality' responded to his sense of fun, but still more to his fundamental esteem for them. Swift at this time really did regard women as at any rate potentially his intellectual equals. The attitude was unusual, and women appreciated it. He did not expect or desire them to be blue-stockings, though he wanted them to be educated. He not only admired the feminine quality of a woman's mind; but he enjoyed the underlying sex-attraction. In his unfinished *Hints towards an Essay on Conversation* he deplores the corruption of manners caused by the degeneracy of conversation.

> In default of which we are forced to take up with those poor amusements of dress and visiting, or the more pernicious ones of play, drink, and vicious amours, whereby the nobility and gentry of both sexes are entirely corrupted both in body and mind, and have lost all notions of love, honour, friendship, generosity; which, under the name of fopperies, have been for some time laughed out of doors.
> This degeneracy of conversation ... hath been owing, among other causes, to the custom arisen, for some time past, of excluding women from any share in our society, further than in parties at play, or dancing,

or in the pursuit of an amour. I take the highest period of politeness in England (and it is of the same date in France) to have been the peaceable part of King Charles the First's reign; and from what we read of those times, as well as from the accounts I have formerly met with from some who lived in that court, the methods then used for raising and cultivating conversation, were altogether different from ours. Several ladies, whom we find celebrated by the poets of that age, had assemblies at their houses, where persons of the best understanding, and of both sexes, met to pass the evenings on whatever agreeable subjects were occasionally started; and although we are apt to ridicule the sublime platonic notions they had, or personated in love and friendship, I conceive their refinements were grounded upon reason, and that a little grain of the romance is no ill ingredient to preserve and exalt the dignity of human nature, without which it is apt to degenerate into everything that is sordid, vicious and low.[12]

The little grain of the romance was the spice of life to Swift. It entered into his relations with young women and old. The longer he was separated from Stella, the more he sought it in the society of other women. The list of his 'favourites' at this time is impressive: the two Lady Bettys, old Lady Kerry, Mrs. Barton, Lady Bolingbroke, the Duchess of Shrewsbury. The depth of his feeling for them is apparent in the case of the two who had died: Lady Ashburnham and Mrs. Long. At the same time that his relation with Vanessa was becoming intimate, he was becoming bosom friends with Elizabeth Villiers, Lady Orkney, the mistress of King William III, ten years older than himself. About her he could speak freely to Stella. She was 'the wisest woman he ever saw'.

> Lady Orkney is making me a writing-table of her own contrivance, and a bednightgown. She is perfectly kind, like a mother. I think the devil was in it the other day, that I should talk to her of an ugly squinting cousin of hers, and the poor lady herself, you know, squints like a dragon. The other day we had a long discourse with her about love; and she told us a saying of her sister Fitz-Hardinge, which I thought excellent, that in men, desire begets love, and in women, love begets desire. (October 30, 1712)

The grain of the romance was obviously there. Lady Orkney was wise, and a woman. Swift found solace in such an *amitié amoureuse*.

And now the extraordinary convention he had established to safeguard himself in his relation with Stella helped to betray him. His strange practice of writing to Stella, as though she were not personally herself, but an impossible compound of herself and Dingley, as it led him to abound in the substitute for intimacy which 'the little language' really is, so now it interposed a veil of false neutrality when intimacy was his need. A greater honesty in his relation with Stella would have made him less vulnerable to Vanessa's admiration and sympathy and devotion. The absurd and unnatural constraints he had imposed upon Stella and himself helped to deprive him of the solace of her friendship and anchorage of her love when he needed them most.

Nevertheless, to regard Vanessa simply as a substitute for a Stella, frustrated of her true function towards him by his own elaborate defensive mechanisms, is inadequate. That may have been the root of the matter; but other motives entered in. Swift was living in an ever-increasing tension of anxiety and nervous excitement, on the surface sedulously controlled. It is a commonplace of experience that in such a condition a man often seeks and finds relief in a kindred excitement in his relation with a woman. The decisive attraction of the affair with Vanessa was that it was dangerous. Stella was safe. Swift had taken prodigious care about that. Vanessa was thrilling in a way Stella had never been allowed to be.

CHAPTER XV

VANESSA

ESTHER VANHOMRIGH (Vanessa) was born in Dublin on February 14, 1688. She was thus twenty years younger than Swift, and nearly seven years younger than Stella. She was the eldest of four children of a Dutch merchant, Bartholomew Vanhomrigh, who had done eminent service to King William III as Commissary-General during his Irish campaign, and subsequently, in 1697, become Lord Mayor of Dublin. Vanhomrigh had settled in Dublin some years before King William's accession, and had married the daughter of John Stone, a commissioner of the Irish revenue. He himself was appointed one of the chief commissioners when his service with the army was over. He died on December 29, 1703, leaving an estate of some £20,000 to be divided equally among his wife and children. The children, in order, were Esther, Bartholomew, Ginkel and Mary. Esther was the eldest by at least four years.

Much of their father's estate consisted in claims on the Irish government for money advanced, which took four years to settle. When these were cleared, Mrs. Vanhomrigh with her children left Dublin in December 1707 for London, bent on making a figure there. She kept open house for the friends she had made in Dublin Castle society; she sent Bartholomew to the aristocratic college of Christ Church; and she quickly got into financial difficulties. In less than two years Mr. Peter Partinton, her husband's executor and now her Irish agent, was refusing to meet a bill she had drawn on him, for lack of funds to meet it, and remonstrating forcibly with her and her sons' refusal to mend their extravagant ways. 'Mr. Ginkell and Mr. Barty will not confine themselves within their allowance . . . and Madam Van Homrigh still goes on in the old road, never considering the reckoning that must at last be made.' Her fatal profuseness, he told her, was due to her desire 'to keep up your credit in a strange place'; Mr. Barty's 'to keeping bad company and striving to imitate those far above him'.[1] In consequence, when Mrs. Vanhomrigh died in 1714, the estate was seriously embarrassed with debts, and Vanessa had to spend years in the effort to straighten her and her sister's affairs. Her two brothers were dead by July 1715.

Vanessa was nineteen at the time of the migration. When Swift first met the family is uncertain. He may have made their acquaintance in Dublin before he left it for London at the end of November 1707. He certainly met them in the course of that journey, in an inn at Dunstable, where Vanessa spilt some coffee in the chimney. This incident was always remembered by them both as the beginning of their friendship. Probably it was Swift's first meeting with Vanessa. It happened at the end of December 1707.*

2

In London Swift very quickly became intimate with the family. When he reached town, he stayed for a few weeks at Sir Andrew Fountaine's house in Leicester Fields, and it was while he was living there — probably in January 1708 — that a 'treaty' of acquaintance with Mrs. Anne Long, the famous and charming young beauty and a cousin of Vanessa's, was drawn up, nominally by Ginkel Vanhomrigh, Mrs. Vanhomrigh's younger son, Vanessa's junior by six years, but in fact by Swift himself. The terms of the 'treaty' show that Swift was now completely at home in the family; it twice refers to 'Mrs. Vanhomrigh and her fair daughter Hessy', who are humorously charged with aiding and abetting Mrs. Long in her refusal to derogate from her dignity as a 'toast' by making the first advances to Swift.

It is remarkable, and revealing, that precisely at this time Stella and Dingley were staying in London, for it shows that Stella was completely outside the Vanhomrigh circle. Three years later Stella betrayed a certain jealousy of Swift's assiduity at the Vanhomrighs'. 'You say they are of no consequence,' Swift wrote to her on February 26, 1711. 'Why, they keep as good female company as I do male; I see all the drabs of quality at this end of the town with them. I saw the two Lady Bettys there this afternoon.' The two Lady Bettys were Lady Betty Germaine, Lord Berkeley's daughter, and Lady Betty Butler, the Duke of Ormond's: both, so to speak, daughters of Dublin Castle. With that 'official' Anglo-Irish society, with which Swift was a favourite and which Mrs. Vanhomrigh gathered about her in London, Stella seems never to have mixed. Her friendship with Addison in 1709-10 was private and personal. It is difficult at this distance of time to discern the nature of the barrier which separated Stella from the Dublin Castle society, but one senses its existence. The Vanhomrighs had the entrée to it, and Stella had not. Very naturally, she could not resist a dig at them.

It is treacherous ground to tread, but one cannot avoid venturing on it. There was a difference between the social status of Stella and Vanessa, which, though it is almost invisible today, was (one suspects) considerable then.†
Vanessa was well-connected, relatively wealthy, and moved in an aristocratic society. Swift was never entirely oblivious of worldly considerations, and

* See Appendix VIII. † See Appendix IX.

it is possible that Vanessa had other attractions for him than her prettiness, her intelligence, and her eager appreciation of his wit. When their friendship began she was not quite twenty, and she must have looked less than her age; for it appears to have been an established and plausible convention in her family that she was at least two years younger than she actually was, perhaps in order to preserve the youth of her fashionable mother. She seemed more of a girl than she was; but even seventeen was very much a marriageable age in those days.

How far their friendship progressed during Swift's stay in London during 1708-9 it is impossible to say. There is no evidence of any kind. But by the time he returned to Ireland in May 1709, she had become one of his favourites. There were others. He corresponded with Misshessy from Ireland; but he wrote, more frequently, to Mrs. Barton and Mrs. Long — both toasts, both young, both unmarried, and both in the Vanhomrigh circle. When he returned to London in September 1710, he was assiduous at the Vanhomrighs' house, and then, if not before, his relation with Vanessa became really intimate and in some sense secret. He was now almost an inmate of the house. The visits actually recorded in his letters to Stella are innumerable; and it is obvious that he did not mention them all. When he went to lodge in Chelsea (from April 26 to July 5, 1711), their house was his daily port of call. He kept his best gown and periwig there, to change into — and back again — whenever he came to town; there he deposited St. John's present of some dozens of Florence wine; and there he had a little study assigned to him. At this time if not before, he began educating Vanessa, as he had educated Stella fifteen years before. At Chelsea, too, Vanessa visited him probably more than once — in retrospect he recalls a 'chapter of Chelsea'. But the first definite evidence that we have of the nature of their relation is in the first of his letters to her which survives. It was written on December 18, 1711, and enclosed a letter to Mrs. Long — now lying perdu and ill at Lynn — which Vanessa was to forward, after she had read it.

To little Misessy,
I have writ three or four lies in as many lines. Pray seal up the letter to Mrs. L, and let nobody read it but yourself. I suppose this letter will lie two hours before you awake. And pray let the outside starched letter to you be seen, after you have sealed up that to Mrs. L. See what art people must use, though they mean ever so well. Now are you and Puppy lying at your ease, without dreaming anything of all this. Adieu till we meet over a pot of coffee or an orange and sugar in the Sluttery, which I have so often found to be the most agreeable chamber in the world.[2]

The 'starched letter', to be shown to any inquisitive person who asked what the Doctor had written, has not survived. It may have been the one which contained the lies, though there are a few white ones at the beginning of the letter to Mrs. Long. But there was more art in Swift's letter than this. The letter for Mrs. Long contained a passage about Vanessa, which she was to read. That was in reply to some words of Mrs. Long about her, in the letter which Swift was answering.

If Miss Hessy keeps company with the eldest Hatton, and is still a politician, she is not the girl I took her for; but to me she seems melancholy. Sure Mr. St. John is not so altered but he will make returns; but how can I judge of anything, when my poor cousin [Vanessa] is taken for an hermaphrodite — a thing I as little suspected her for as railing at anybody: I know so little cause for it that I must be silent.[3]

Interpretation of that must be guess-work. But if, as it seems, there is a connection between Mrs. Long's opinion that Vanessa seemed sad, and her belief that St. John would not fail to reward Swift for his services, the train of thought is possibly this.

If Vanessa has Mrs. Hatton for her bosom friend and is taken up with politics, she is not the girl Mrs. Long took her for; but the truth Mrs. Long feels is that she is sad, and in love. Surely, Swift will get preferment and be able to marry her. But how can she judge of anything when Vanessa is now supposed to be more boy than girl? She would no more have suspected her of that than she would of being quarrelsome; and she knows so little cause for the opinion, that she must be silent. The gist of it, then, will be that Mrs. Long knows Vanessa too well not to be persuaded that she is very much a woman, and in love, and sad because of it, and hoping that Swift will offer to marry her.

If this was the insinuation, Swift glanced it off. Vanessa's sadness had another cause. He replied:

Misessy is but like her neighbour — she is a politician because everybody else is so, and a Tory out of principle without hopes of an employment. Mistress Hatton visits there, but is not her companion. The poor girl, between sickness, domestic affairs, and state speculations, has lost a good deal of her mirth. But I think there is not a better girl on earth. I have a mighty friendship for her. She had good principles, and I have corrected all her faults; but I cannot persuade her to read, though she has an understanding, memory and taste that would bear great improvement. But she is incorrigibly idle and lazy — she thinks the world was made for nothing but perpetual pleasure; and the deity she most adores is Morpheus. Her greatest favourites at present are Lady Ashburnham, her dog, and myself. She makes me of so little consequence that it almost distracts me. She will bid her sister go downstairs before my face, for she has 'some private business with the Doctor'. In short, there would be no end of telling the hardships she puts on me, only because I have lived a dozen or fifteen years too much.

Swift was telling Vanessa, obliquely, to be more discreet in her public behaviour with him; but at the same time he was telling her, directly, that her company was sweeter than any other to him. Perhaps, by some casuistry, he persuaded himself that this was not his meaning when he said he had so often found the Sluttery the most agreeable chamber in the world; but this was how his ardent admirer was bound to take it. This, with the arrangement for secrecy, was heady stuff for Vanessa.

There are allowances to be made for him. His letter was written at a moment when his anxiety as to the fate of the Harley ministry was at its height — at the moment when the government had been defeated in the Lords. The tendency of a highly strung man who leads a public life of excitement and strain is to seek relief in a similar excitement in his private life. He was playing with fire by entering into such a relation with Vanessa; but the enchantment of it lay precisely there. Perhaps, had Stella been at hand, it would never have gone so far; but from the world in which it was Swift's ambition and delight to move she was debarred. Vanessa was at least on the fringe of it. She became the confidante of his political concerns and anxieties. Where he had to express himself — if only because of the unreliability of the post — guardedly to Stella, he could speak freely to Vanessa.

But, over and above all this, his relation to Vanessa gives out a different note from his relation to Stella. It is not merely that the one is attuned to a period of intense excitement, and the other to one of calm. With Vanessa the unmistakable emotion of love enters in. With Stella Swift is affectionate, playful, concerned, devoted; but, so far as we can tell, he never comes near losing his head. With Vanessa he did. Although the exact significance of the various episodes in his retrospect of 1720 is impenetrable, the tone which pervades the whole catalogue is that of a love affair.

There would be the chapter of the blister; the chapter of Madam going to Kensington; the chapter of the Colonel's going to France; the chapter of the wedding, with the adventure of the lost key; of the strain; of the joyful return; two hundred chapters of madness; the chapter of long walks; the Berkshire surprise; fifty chapters of little times; the chapter of Chelsea; the chapter of swallow and cluster; a hundred whole books of myself and *so low*; the chapter of hide and whisper; the chapter of 'who made it so?' My sister's money.[4]

That is not the accent of placid and paternal affection; and the imaginative women-novelists who have represented Swift as Vanessa's physical lover have some justification.

Nevertheless, it is very improbable. He may have come perilously near it. There were many kisses and embraces. He was disturbed as he had never been before, and he took delight in the disturbance. But he managed to keep control of himself.

3

The cardinal document for his relation with Vanessa is the poem *Cadenus & Vanessa*. This was intended as a personal and secret gift for Vanessa's eyes alone. The ambiguity of the famous lines which conclude the account of her declaration of love — an ambiguity which has been judged highly reprehensible — has a quite different quality according as they were addressed to her or to the world. Swift represents himself as taken aback by Vanessa's frank avowal of her love, and as making a somewhat embarrassed offer of romantic devotion: to which she replies that they must now change places. In the matter of love she must be the tutor, he the pupil, although it is obvious he is not an apt one.

> But what success Vanessa met
> Is to the world a secret yet.
> Whether the nymph, to please her swain,
> Talks in a high romantic strain;
> Or whether he at last descends
> To like with less seraphic ends;
> Or to compound the business, whether
> They temper love and books together,
> Must never to mankind be told,
> Nor shall the conscious Muse unfold.[5]

Addressed to Vanessa, and to Vanessa alone, the lines are harmless enough. To say less to her would have been a kind of brutality. What strikes the dispassionate reader of the poem is that Swift has been very successful in suffusing the whole of it with a tender playfulness. He has got the affair into proportion.

Cadenus & Vanessa was written, according to two definite statements of Swift made in 1726, at Windsor in 1712. It has been argued that he must have been mistaken, because he could not have called himself Cadenus (Decanus) when he was not yet a Dean. The argument is not compulsive.

To call himself Cadenus in a private poem to a girl with whom he must certainly have discussed whether he would really get his Deanery, at a time when common report had given him Wells, seems a very natural joke; and, even if it were not, it is by no means certain that the name Cadenus figured in the original draft of the poem, which bears marks of having been revised in 1713, after Swift had been appointed to St. Patrick's. For example, when, in the poem, Vanessa confounds her fashionable suitors by telling them

> That, present times have no pretence
> To virtue, in the noblest sense,
> By Greeks and Romans understood,
> To perish for our country's good . . .[6]

one suspects that Swift took the hint from Vanessa's letter to him of June 23, 1713.

> I wish you had been here last Thursday, I am sure you could have prevented the Bills being lost. Are you not prodigiously surprised at Sir Thomas Hanmer and Lord Anglesey? Lord, how much we differ from the ancients, who used to sacrifice everything for the good of the commonwealth; but now our greatest men will, at any time, give up their country out of a pique and that for nothing.

Not that there is anything greatly original in the sentiment, but it is a little excessive where it comes in the poem. One feels that Swift added it from the life. Again, the manner in which Cadenus is introduced into the poem is curiously awkward, and suggests that he had not made up his mind between alternative versions when he gave the manuscript to Vanessa.

We conclude then that Swift's retrospective account is accurate in the main, and that the poem was at least drafted at Windsor in 1712, though it was revised in the next year, and afterwards. He was at Windsor, with intervals, from the end of July to the end of September. His journal-letters to Stella had been dropped since his attack of shingles; he wrote only briefly, though affectionately: but from August 7 to September 15 he did not write at all. On Friday, July 31, he wrote to Vanessa from Windsor:

> I will come as early on Monday as I can find opportunity, and will take a little Grub Street lodging, pretty near where I did before, and dine with you thrice a week, and tell you a thousand secrets, provided you will have no quarrels to me.

This he appears to have done, and to have returned to Windsor on August 10. On August 15 he wrote to her, and obliquely suggested that the Vanhomrigh family should visit Windsor. Vanessa jumped at the idea, and proposed to come with only her brother as escort. To this Swift made no reply, nor to two other letters which Vanessa wrote him, but told her through Erasmus Lewis, half-seriously, that as soon as she arrived, he would leave. At the end of September she came, and Swift wrote to her immediately after: 'Why then you should not have come; and I know that as well as you.' That is not a serious reproach; Swift had wanted her to visit him, but was a little apprehensive of indiscretion on Vanessa's part. It all chimes with the tone of *Cadenus & Vanessa*. If, as we suppose, the love-declaration described in the poem was made at some time previous to Swift's going to Windsor, it seems fairly clear that Swift was not taking the situation too seriously. And that is the impression made by the poem itself on the reader who comes to it without prepossession.

4

Cadenus & Vanessa is an important poem, but it is not important in the way imagined by those who have read back into it the strain and suffering of Vanessa's subsequent hopeless and hapless passion for Swift: *Venus toute entière à sa proie attachée*. That was to come later: but there is no suggestion of it in Swift's verses, or in Vanessa's letters of this time.

The machinery of the poem is conventional. Venus is sitting in judgment. Before her the women indict the men, the men the women, as the cause why true love is no more. The men's case is set out much more fully than the women's. Love, they say, is no longer

> A fire celestial, chaste, refin'd,
> Conceiv'd and kindled in the mind,
> Which having found an equal flame,
> Unites, and both become the same,
> In different breasts together burn,
> Together both to ashes turn.
> But women now feel no such fire,
> And only know the gross desire . . .
> Hence we conclude, no women's hearts
> Are won by virtue, wit and parts.[7]

Venus calls in the Muses and Graces to assist her, appears to consult the authorities, defers judgment, and by one device and another defers it for sixteen years. For, in fact, as soon as the case had begun, she had decided to make an experiment. She had picked on a new-born girl in whom she would unite all the virtues and graces.

Since men allege they ne'er can find
Those beauties in a female mind
Which raise a flame that will endure
For ever, uncorrupt and pure;
If 'tis with reason they complain,
This infant shall restore my reign.[8]

Then, with the Graces' aid, she sprinkles the child.

From whence the tender skin assumes
A sweetness above all perfumes:
From whence a cleanliness remains,
Incapable of outward stains;
From whence that decency of mind,
So lovely in the female kind,
Where not one careless thought intrudes
Less modest than the speech of prudes;
Where never blush was call'd in aid,
That spurious virtue in a maid,
A virtue but at second-hand;
They blush because they understand.[9]

That leaves little for the Graces to do; but they give her her name, Vanessa, and

That gentle, soft, engaging air,
Which in old times adorn'd the fair.[10]

But Venus, not content with this, hoodwinks Pallas into the belief that Vanessa is a boy; and Pallas accordingly

Then sows within her tender mind
Seeds long unknown to womankind,
For manly bosoms chiefly fit,
The seeds of knowledge, judgment, wit.
Her soul was suddenly endu'd
With justice, truth and fortitude;
With honour, which no breath can stain,
Which malice must attack in vain;
With open heart and bounteous hand.[11]

Pallas also bestows a nicely adjusted fortune of £5000.

Venus now has no doubt that the girl will be universally admired. Pallas, annoyed at having been deceived, wants to take back her gifts, but knowing this is impossible, consoles herself with the foreknowledge that Venus' plan must fail, and tells her so.

> For how can heav'nly wisdom prove
> An instrument to earthly love?
> Know'st thou not yet that men commence
> Thy votaries for want of sense?[12]

Pallas has no need to interfere; she will leave things to their natural course.

5

Then Vanessa, at sixteen, enters the world. (Since Swift and her family always made her two or three years younger than she was, this refers to her coming to London at nineteen in December 1707.) The fashionable fops attend her. She listens to their town-talk in silent scorn; then gives them her own views,

> And said she valued nothing less
> Than titles, figure, shape and dress;
> That merit should be chiefly plac'd,
> In judgment, knowledge, wit and taste;
> And these, she offered to dispute,
> Alone distinguish'd man from brute.[13]

They retire, persuaded that she is a little crazy. Then comes a crowd of women. Vanessa is reading Montaigne, while her hair is brushed, when they arrive. They talk fashions and scandal: and again Vanessa is silent. They depart, and pass their judgment.

> She's not so handsome in my eyes:
> For wit, I wonder where it lies.
> She's fair and clean, and that's the most;
> But why proclaim her for a toast?
> A baby face, no life, no airs,
> But what she learnt at country fairs.[14]

So Venus' project failed. Pallas, she realized, had done more harm than good. Still, Vanessa attracts and admits a small and select company of friends: among them Cadenus,

> Whom Pallas, once Vanessa's tutor,
> Had fix'd on for her coadjutor.[15]

Cupid, eager to avenge his mother's defeat, since he cannot punish Pallas, vows to take vengeance on Vanessa's heart. He shoots at 'colonels, lords and beaux' — in vain, because Cadenus always interposes a book. Cupid thinks of a new plan.

I find, says he, she wants a doctor,
Both to adore her, and instruct her:
I'll give her what she most admires
Among those venerable sires.
Cadenus is a subject fit.
Grown old in politics and wit,
Caress'd by ministers of state,
Of half mankind th' dread and hate.
Whate'er vexations love attend.
She needs no rivals apprehend.[16]

This introduction of Cadenus is clumsy, or at least confusing. He has first been named as the tutor, chosen by Pallas for Vanessa; he has then been represented as interposing books between Cupid's shafts and her potential suitors' hearts; he seems to be appointed to her yet a third time by Cupid himself. The apparent confusion is, perhaps, defensible. The first may apply to Cadenus' general co-operation with Pallas, in stimulating Vanessa by his conversation; the second to the books he induced her to read, which deflected her eyes; and the third to his definite undertaking of her education. But this interpretation can hardly be made to square with the passage which follows, where Cupid's arrow strikes her while she is reading Cadenus' 'poetic works'.

And while the book was in her hand,
The urchin from his private stand
Took aim, and shot with all his strength
A dart of such prodigious length,
It pierc'd the feeble volume thro',
And deep transfix'd her bosom, too.
Some lines, more moving than the rest,
Stuck to the point that pierc'd her breast,
And, borne directly to the heart,
With pains unknown increas'd the smart.[17]

It is difficult to think of any passage in Swift's verses that could have produced such an effect. Presumably, it is a flight of fancy, meaning that Vanessa came to love his person through writings. In consequence,

Vanessa, not in years a score,
Dreams of a gown of forty-four;
Imaginary charms can find
In eyes with reading almost blind:
Cadenus now no more appears
Declin'd in health, advanc'd in years.

She fancies music in his tongue,
Nor farther looks, but thinks him young.

Swift was, indeed, forty-four in 1712; and his health had been particularly bad that year; but Vanessa was twenty-four. However, the need of contrast (or of rhyme) induced Swift to make her even younger than he believed her to be.

Cadenus is so intent upon her quick progress in learning —

Ideas came into her mind
So fast, his lessons lagg'd behind[18] —

and so inexpert in the signs of love, that he is blind to what is happening. He ascribes the distraction of her mind to her being tired of his teaching, and offers to give it up; comes, indeed, to say goodbye. Vanessa is indignant with him for supposing that his lessons were wasted on her. On the contrary, she was just about to act on the maxims he had taught her:

That virtue, pleas'd by being shown,
Knows nothing which it dare not own . . .
That common forms were not design'd
Directors to a noble mind.[19]

Whereupon she tells him that his lessons 'aim'd at the head' had 'reach'd the heart'. At this avowal,

Cadenus felt within him rise
Shame, disappointment, guilt, surprise.[20]

He tries to persuade himself she is not serious, for, if she is, the scandal-mongers will be busy.

So tender of the young and fair?
It show'd a true paternal care —
Five thousand guineas in her purse?
The Doctor might have fancy'd worse . . .[21]

After an embarrassed silence he tries to laugh it off. He always knew she rallied well; but her entirely serious manner was against the rules, by which a hint of the jest must be given.

Vanessa dismisses this evasion. She had meant what she said; and her love was grounded not in impulse but in reason. She had absorbed his values, and was convinced that they were true. They were incorporate in him.

> The utmost her desires will reach
> Is but to learn what he can teach:
> His converse is a system, fit
> Alone to fill up all her wit;
> While ev'ry passion of her mind
> In him is center'd and confin'd.[22]

Love makes her so eloquent on the theme, that Cadenus 'insensibly came on her side', and

>   to his grief and shame,
> Could scarce oppose Vanessa's flame;
> And, though her arguments were strong,
> At least could hardly wish them wrong.
> Howe'er it came, he could not tell,
> But, sure, she never talk'd so well.
> His pride began to interpose;
> Preferr'd before a crowd of beaux!
> So bright a nymph to come unsought!
> Such wonder by his merit wrought![23]

The innocent flattery of her declaration has captivated him. He cannot indeed offer her love — or what is understood by love,

> But friendship in its greatest height,
> A constant, rational delight . . .
> Which gently warms, but cannot burn;
> He gladly offers in return;
> His want of passion will redeem
> With gratitude, respect, esteem:
> With what devotion we bestow,
> When goddesses appear below.[24]

Vanessa rejects these lofty sentiments. She tells him that by professing respect and devotion to her he has abdicated his position. Now he must be her pupil, and she will teach him how to love.

> But what success Vanessa met,
> Is to the world a secret yet . . .

Finally, the scene shifts to Venus' court again. Her experience with Vanessa, though disappointing, has enabled her to give judgment. She decrees the cause against the men.

> She was at Lord knows what expense,
> To form a nymph of wit and sense,

A model for her sex design'd,
Who never could one lover find.
She saw her favour was misplaced;
The fellows had a wretched taste;
She needs must tell them to their face,
They were a stupid, senseless race;
And were she to begin again,
She'd study to reform the men.[25]

6

That there is, in the poem, a solid core of factual truth is self-evident. As an account of how Vanessa came to fall in love, of how she declared it, and of Swift's reaction — the mixture of dismay and secret satisfaction — one feels it is substantially veracious. He was taken by surprise, and he experienced an authentic thrill, of tenderness, compassion — and pride.

But the poem itself is, essentially, not a love poem. It is charming, it is tender, it is truthful; but Swift is evidently in control of his verses and himself. The equivocal finale, to which so much exception has been taken, and so much importance given, is no more than a piece of playful ambiguity. He could not have said less without hurting Vanessa. That he might have hurt her less in the long run if he had hurt her more now may be true, but it is beside the point.

In the poem he does the best he can to put the situation in a true perspective — or at least one which would at once gratify Vanessa and reconcile her to her disappointment. The moral of the poem is that the ideal woman, which he represents Vanessa to be, does not inspire love because men are incapable of appreciating her. She falls in love, indeed, but hopelessly, because her supreme value is intellectual integrity and emotional sincerity. She can love only where she respects and admires, and — short of a miracle — this is possible only with a much older man, who by reason of his integrity, sees the moral impossibility, or solecism, of marriage. In woman, 'love begets desire', and he cannot give her what she will naturally come to need. The consequence would be an ignominious relation.

And he must fall a prey to Time
While she continues in her prime.[26]

In three of his later letters to Vanessa, Swift glanced over past scenes between them. In all of them he refers to 'the Colonel's going to France'. The 'Colonel' was the nickname of her brother, Bartholomew, who went to Paris in the early spring of 1713. Two of them refer to 'Ryder Street':

Swift lodged in Little Ryder Street when he returned from Windsor at the end of September 1712, and stayed there till December. We must imagine the relation between Swift and Vanessa developing into greater intimacy, as his anxiety concerning his preferment increased. At the same time, at the other end of the scale of *amitié amoureuse*, he was meeting Lady Orkney frequently, sometimes dining *tête à tête*, and discussing love. At the same time, too, he resumed his journal-letters to Stella, as freely as before. There is no sign of any constraint. One must infer that Swift believed that his loyalty to Stella was unimpaired, and that he was managing his delicate, embarrassing and exciting relation with Vanessa with a proper combination of firmness and tenderness; but as happens with sensitive men in such a situation, to Vanessa his tenderness was more apparent than his firmness.

Other things conspired to bring that side of him uppermost at this moment. His heart was wrung by the pathetic death of his 'creature', the brilliant and affectionate 'little Harrison', whom he had had made Queen's Secretary at the Hague. On February 12, 1713, he found him 'mighty ill' and penniless. Straightway, he got thirty guineas for him, and an order for £100 on the Treasury: which must have cost him much pains. On the next day, he took money to Diaper, another gifted young poet, 'in a nasty garret, very sick'. The day after:

> I took Parnell this morning, and we walked to see poor Harrison. I had the hundred pounds in my pocket. I told Parnell I was afraid to knock at the door; my mind misgave me. I knocked, and his man in tears told me his master was dead an hour before. Think what grief this is to me!... I could not dine with Lord Treasurer, nor any-where else; but got a bit of meat towards evening. No loss ever grieved me so much: poor creature!

Under such strains his tenderness would seek expression, and comfort. And Vanessa was at hand for both.

7

So, when the affair of the Deanery was at last over, and Swift was setting out for Dublin to be installed, his last act in London was to write Vanessa a note:

> I promised to write to you; and I have to let you know it is impossible for anyone to have more acknowledgments at heart for all your kind-ness and generosity to me. I hope this journey will restore my health. (June 1, 1713)

He wrote to her again from Dunstable, but the letter has been lost; and to Mrs. Vanhomrigh from Chester. Then there was silence. Vanessa learned, through Lewis, that he was ill; and then her concern burst through the effort she made to restrain it. There is no mistaking the tone of her letter to him of June 27. It is that of a woman deep in love.

'Tis unexpressible the concern I am in ever since I heard from Mr. Lewis, that your head is so much out of order. Who is your physician? For God sake do not be persuaded to take too many slops. Satisfy me so much as to tell me what medicines you have taken and do take. How did you find yourself while a ship-board? I fear 'tis your voyage has discomposed you, and then so much business following so immediately before you had time to recruit — 'twas too much. I beg, make all the haste imaginable to the country, for I firmly believe that air and rest will do you more good than anything in the world besides. If I talk impertinently, I know you have goodness enough to forgive me, when you consider how great an ease 'tis to me to ask these questions, though I know it will be a great while before I can be answered — I am sure I shall think it so. Oh! what would I give to know how you do at this moment. My fortune is too hard, your absence was enough without this cruel addition. Sure the powers above are envious of your thinking so well, which makes them sometimes strive to interrupt you; but I must confine my thoughts, or at least stop from telling them to you, or you'll chide, which will still add to my uneasiness. I have done all that was possible to hinder myself from writing to you, till I heard you were better, for fear of breaking my promise, but 'twas all in vain, for had I vowed neither to touch pen, ink, nor paper, I certainly should have had some other invention; therefore I beg you will not be angry with me, for doing what is not in my power to avoid. Pray make Parvisol write me word what I desire to know, for I would not for the world have you hold down your head. I am impatient to the last degree to know how you are. I hope I shall soon have you here.

It is the letter of a woman who had been ministering to Swift in depression or sickness. One imagines her stroking his forehead when he had a headache, as he so often had; or 'kissing it away'. And he had been glad to surrender himself to her ministrations. This is 'the kindness and generosity' which his heart acknowledged when he left her. But her position is painfully insecure; she dreads offending him by the importunacy of her concern. He has erected an artificial and arbitrary barrier between his life in London, and his life in Ireland; in the former he admits her claim to share, from the latter she is excluded. He had told her before he left England that 'he would endeavour to forget everything there, and write as seldom as he could'.[27] For him, no doubt, the difference between life in Windsor and London and life in Laracor and Dublin was enormous; they were different orders of existence. To pass from the former to the latter was a psychological convulsion. When, at last, he did answer Vanessa's letters on July 8, he told her:

At my first coming I thought I should have died with discontent, and was horribly melancholy while they were installing me; but it begins to wear off and change to dullness.

That may be by way of answer to Vanessa's last letter to him (June 30), in which she says Lewis had told her he was better, gently reproaches him for not having told her himself, and says: 'If you are very happy, it is ill-natured of you not to tell me so, except it is what is inconsistent with mine.' It has been supposed that this refers to Stella, and it may be so; but it ought not to be strained into a glance at the possibility of his marrying Stella. The most it will bear is an apprehension lest another woman has taken Vanessa's place. And Swift appears to reply that, so far from being very happy, he has been in a slough of despond; but he allows no hint to escape that it is on her account. She is merely a part — though perhaps the sweetest part — of the life of excitement and glamour and power that he has been compelled to resign.

Depression and sickness worked on Swift together at this moment. He wrote to Ford from Laracor:

I stay'd there [in Dublin] no longer than business forced. I received no visits but one day, for I was very ill, and I pay'd none at all, but stole down here to ride and drink bitter draughts. I am somewhat better, I thank God, but have still a very disordered head. (July 9, 1713)

What is remarkable is that there is no sign of any satisfaction at seeing Stella again. There is no mention of 'the ladies' in his letter to Ford, who knew Stella well; and in both his last two letters to them from London he had been emphatic that they should not take any rooms for him in Dublin.

Take no lodging for me. What? At your old tricks again? I can lie somewhere after I land, and I care not where, nor how. (May 16, 1713)

The brusqueness is disconcerting. If Vanessa was merely part of the excitement that had to be resigned, Stella had become part of the dullness that had to be accepted.

Swift's stay in Dublin was as short as he could make it. He was installed on June 13 and hurried off to Laracor on June 25. He was unwell, depressed, mortified, and worried about money. His installation — including the purchase of Stearne's new Deanery house — had cost him £1000, most of which he still owed. In the margin of his account book for these weeks occur more than once the words *Ubi nunc?* — 'Where am I now?' It did not apply solely, or even primarily, to his finances. He felt all at sea. And though his extreme melancholy wore off, it changed only to dullness. There was bound to be a constraint between himself and Stella. One cannot help wondering whether Archbishop King, who was habitually well-informed, knew the Vanhomrighs and had a vein of dry maliciousness, was entirely innocent when he wrote to Swift from the Bath:

> An odd thought came into my head on reading that you were among willows, imagining perhaps that your mistress had forsaken you, and that was the cause of your malady. If that be the case, cheer up, the loss may be repaired, and I hope the remedy easy.[28]

Swift had made up his mind to return to London in October, if only to put Oxford in mind of a grant of £1000 (which, he said, had been promised him) to clear his Deanery debt. But, during his absence, the relations between Oxford and Bolingbroke had catastrophically deteriorated. Erasmus Lewis wrote three times to him, pressing him to return, and help to reconcile the antagonists. Rather reluctantly, Swift set out on August 29. He arrived in London on September 8.

CHAPTER XVI

SWIFT *versus* STEELE: 1713-1714

ON October 1, 1713, only three weeks after he had returned to London, Swift wrote to Archdeacon Walls jumping at the suggestion that he should be elected Prolocutor of the Lower House of Convocation in Ireland. He would (he said) willingly let his name go forward, provided his election was certain. He gave two reasons. 'One is that I am heartily weary of Courts and Ministers for reasons impossible to tell you, and I have a mind to be at home since the Queen has been pleased that Ireland shall be my home.' To some extent he had anticipated his own impotence to heal the breach between Oxford and Bolingbroke; now he had realized that it was quite past mending. He had learned, too, that neither his own influence nor Oxford's power were as great as he had once imagined. As for himself, though his position as Oxford's personal friend was undiminished, and though he went with him to Windsor every week, he was now definitely on the periphery of the great affairs. His political narrative, the publication of which he (rather fondly) believed might have averted the Tory split over the commercial part of the Utrecht treaty, had been shelved. He was really not much use, nor likely to be, except as a personal relaxation to Oxford.

His first piece of writing was purely personal. He dunned Oxford for his £1000 in a way he would appreciate: a charming 'imitation' of Horace's charming story of the auctioneer, Volteius Mena, and his patron Marcius Philippus.

> Harley, the nation's great support,
> Returning home one day from court,
> (His mind with public cares possesst,
> All Europe's business in his breast)
> Observed a parson near Whitehall,
> Cheap'ning old authors on a stall.[1]

He sends Erasmus Lewis — 'a cunning shaver' — to inquire who he is.

> It was Doctor Swift:
> A clergyman of special note
> For shunning those of his own coat;
> Which made his brethren of the gown
> Take care betimes to run him down:

No libertine, nor over nice,
Addicted to no sort of vice;
Went where he pleas'd, said what he thought;
Not rich, but ow'd no man a groat;
In state opinions à la mode,
He hated Wharton like a toad;
Had given the Faction many a wound,
And libell'd all the Junta round.
Kept company with men of wit,
Who often father'd what he writ:
His works were hawk'd in ev'ry street,
But seldom rose above a sheet:
Of late, indeed, the Paper-Stamp
Did very much his genius cramp;
And, since he could not spend his fire,
He now intended to retire.[2]

The details of this picture are, of course, not historical: he was friends with Harley long before the paper-stamp was introduced. However, Swift depicts himself, like Horace's original, as refusing the first invitation to dinner and accepting the next.

The doctor now obeys the summons,
Likes both his company and commons;
Displays his talent, sits till ten:
Next day invited, comes agen;
Soon grows domestic, seldom fails,
Either at morning or at meals;
Came early and departed late:
In short, the gudgeon took the bait.
My Lord would carry on the jest,
And down to Windsor take his guest.
Swift much admires the place and air
And longs to be a Canon there;
In summer round the park to ride,
In winter — never to reside.[3]

That is authentic. Swift had been enchanted by Windsor; he had found the place 'delicious', and the prebendary's house in which he lodged, enviable. Harley objects:

A Canon! — that's a place too mean:
No, Doctor, you must be a Dean;
Two dozen Canons round your stall,
And you the tyrant o'er them all:

You need but cross the Irish seas,
To live in plenty, power and ease.[4]

Swift borrows money and goes off to Dublin.

Suppose him, now, a Dean complete,
Demurely lolling in his seat,
And silver virge, with decent pride,
Stuck underneath his cushion side.
Suppose him gone through all vexations,
Patents, instalments, abjurations,
First-fruits, and tenths, and chapter-treats,
Dues, payments, fees, demands and cheats
(The wicked laity's contriving
To hinder clergymen from thriving.)
Now all the doctor's money's spent,
His tenants wrong him in his rent,
The farmers, spitefully combin'd,
Force him to take his tithes in kind,
And Parvisol discounts arrears,
By bills for taxes and repairs.
  Poor Swift, with all his losses vex't,
Not knowing where to turn him next,
Above a thousand pounds in debt,
Takes horse, and in a mighty fret,
Rides day and night at such a rate,
He soon arrives at Harley's gate.

Like Mena, he begs Harley to put him back where he found him.

It is pleasantly surprising to think that this poem was hawked about the London streets for threepence; and three editions sold. The details Swift gives of his financial position are exact. 'You see what a condition I am in,' he had written to Stella on April 23, 1713.

I thought I was to pay but £600 for the house; but the Bishop of Clogher says £800; first fruits £150, and so, with patent, £1000 in all ... I hope in some time they will be persuaded here to give me some money to pay off these debts ... They expect I shall pass next winter here, and then I will dun them to give me a sum of money.

The imitation of Horace, published as a threepenny broadside, was a neat way of doing it

His political pamphlets now give the impression of being no longer inspired by the Ministry — there was no longer a united Ministry to inspire them — but chiefly by his own determination to have his revenge on Steele. To understand their origination, we must return to the irritable period in the spring when Swift's chagrin about the Deaneries was extreme. At that moment he had a violent quarrel with Steele. The occasion was a rather tasteless joke in the *Examiner* of April 24, 1713, against Nottingham's daughter, Lady Charlotte Finch.

No sooner was Dismal among the Whigs, and confirmed past retrieving, than Lady Char—te is taken knotting in St. James's Chapel, during Divine service, in the immediate presence both of God and Her Majesty, who were affronted together, that the family might appear to be entirely come over.

Steele was indignant at this, and with an exaggerated chivalry (which was one of his weaknesses) declared in the *Guardian* that 'Every man that hopes for a virtuous woman to his wife, that would defend his child, or protect his mistress, ought to receive this insolence as done to himself.' Further, he said of the author that 'It is very visible which of those powers [i.e. God and her Majesty] (which he has put together) he is the more fearful of offending'; and denounced him as a 'miscreant'. The *Examiner* made a slight apology but retorted that Steele himself had indulged in personalities in the *Tatler*. To this Steele replied, in a letter over his own name in the *Guardian*, that it was indifferent to him whether the *Examiner* wrote against him in the character of 'an estranged friend or an exasperated mistress' — that is, whether Swift or Mrs. Manley was the author.

Swift, whose responsibility for the *Examiner* had ceased two years before, now took offence and wrote to Addison, protesting that Steele had 'insinuated with the utmost malice' that he was the author of the *Examiner*, and 'abused him in the grossest manner he could possibly invent'.

Now, Sir, if I am not the author of *The Examiner*, how will Mr. Steele be able to defend himself from the imputation of the highest degree of baseness, ingratitude and injustice? Is he so ignorant of my temper and of my style? Has he never heard that the author of *The Examiner* (to whom I am altogether a stranger) did, a month or two ago, vindicate me from having any concern in it? Should not Mr. Steele have first expostulated with me as a friend? Have I deserved this usage from Mr. Steele, who knows very well that my Lord Treasurer has kept him in his employment upon my treaty and intercession? (May 13, 1713)

Addison simply passed the letter on to Steele, who replied:

They laugh at you, if they make you believe your interposition has kept me thus long in my office. If you have spoken in my behalf at any time, I am glad I have always treated you with respect: though I believe you an accomplice of the *Examiner* . . . You do not in direct terms say you are not concerned with him; but make it an argument of your innocence that the *Examiner* has declared you have nothing to do with him. I believe I could prevail on the *Guardian* to say there was a mistake in putting my name in his paper; but the English would laugh at us, should we argue in so Irish a manner.
I am heartily glad of your being made Dean of St. Patrick's.

Even the congratulations were irritating to Swift at this moment; and the insinuation that his disavowal of responsibility for the *Examiner* was casuistical touched his *amour propre* both as a man of honour and a man of genius. Most irritating of all was the assertion that he had been gulled if he supposed that his influence had kept Steele in his place. It happened to be true.

Swift did not know that. He was taken aback by Steele's forthright repudiation of any cause for gratitude. In his reply to Steele, he deliberately mistook his meaning. 'If your interpretation were true,' he retorts, 'I was laughed at only for your sake; which, I think, is going pretty far to serve as a friend.'⁵ But that was not to the point. Swift had founded his charge of 'baseness and ingratitude' on his assertion that Steele 'knew very well' that Oxford had kept him in his employment upon Swift's 'treaty and intercession'. On the contrary, Steele knew that he had been kept in it as the result of a gentleman's agreement between Oxford and himself. It speaks well for him that he did not attempt to enlighten Swift any further.

On the other hand, Steele had no effective reply to make to the reproach that he had not inquired from Swift himself whether he was the writer of the *Examiner*, before reflecting on him. And Swift's final letter of May 27, which deals with this, and with Steele's refusal to accept his disavowal of responsibility, is unanswerable. He takes up Steele's reference to the aspersion as a mere 'allusion'.

This allusion was only calling a clergyman of some little distinction an infidel: a clergyman who was your friend, who always loved you, who had endeavoured at least to serve you; and who, whenever he did write anything, made it sacred to himself never to fling out the least hint against you . . . And, in short, I solemnly affirm, that with relation to every friend I have, I am as innocent, as it is possible for a human creature to be. And whether you believe me or not, I think, with submission, you ought to act as if you believed me, till you have demonstration to the contrary.

The tone is very different from that of his first letter to Addison. He drops the charge of ingratitude, and insists on offence against friendship.

3

Swift now regarded the obligations of friendship between himself and Steele as at an end. His first piece of prose-writing on his return to London was a pamphlet to punish his disloyal friend: *The Importance of the Guardian Considered in a Second Letter to the Bailiff of Stockbridge.* The first letter to the Bailiff was a production of Steele's: *The Importance of Dunkirk considered . . . in a Letter to the Bailiff of Stockbridge.*

During Swift's absence in Ireland Steele had taken a deeper plunge into Whig politics. He had resigned his place in the Stamp Office and his pension as Gentleman-Usher to Prince George, and stood for Parliament for the rotten borough of Stockbridge, where he was duly elected by 70 votes to 21 on August 5. His rather pretentious letter to the Bailiff was mainly to insinuate that the delay in demolishing the fortifications of Dunkirk was highly suspicious, and pointed to a secret and dangerous understanding between the Oxford ministry and France.

That gave Swift his opportunity. No doubt he was genuinely angry with Steele for criticizing the Treaty of Utrecht, with which he identified himself; but he was much more deeply annoyed by Steele's repudiation of any obligation to him, which he chose to regard as a breach of friendship. That is the ironical point of describing his pamphlet on the title page as *By a Friend of Mr. St — le.* He is bettering the instruction given him by Steele as to the duties of friendship. Steele's florid assumption of civic virtue gave him an ample target. 'You will observe in reading', he drily remarks to the Bailiff, 'that the letter called *The importance of Dunkirk* is chiefly taken up in showing you the importance of Mr. Steele.'

Wherein it was indeed reasonable your borough should be informed, which had chosen him to represent them. . . .
I would therefore place the importance of this gentleman before you in a clearer light than he has taken the trouble to do; without running into his early history, because I owe him no malice.[6]

This is one of Swift's familiar gambits. The rest of the pamphlet is packed with references to Steele's early history. One of the most deadly thrusts is based on it. Swift affects to be disposing of Steele's complaint that the Government had taken proceedings against the Whig *Flying Post* and let the Tory *Examiner* go free.

Now, Sir, we reckon here, that supposing the persons on both sides to be of equal intrinsic worth, it is more impudent, immoral and criminal to reflect on a majority in power, than a minority out of power.[7]

Quite likely Swift seriously believed this. The doctrine of the freedom of the press in political comment was very far from being firmly established; and he could plausibly appeal to the thought and practice of the local magistrate.

Put the case, that an odd rascally Tory in your borough should presume to abuse your worship who, in the language of Mr. Steele, is first minister, and the majority of your brethren, for sending two such Whig representatives up to Parliament: And on the other side that an honest Whig should stand in your defence and fall foul on the Tories; would you equally resent the proceedings of both, and let your friend and enemy sit in the stocks together? Hearken to another case, Mr. Bailiff; suppose your worship, during your annual administration, should happen to be cuffed and kicked by a parcel of Tories, would not the circumstance of your being a magistrate, make the crime the greater, than if the like insults were committed on an ordinary Tory shopkeeper, by a company of honest Whigs? What bailiff would venture to arrest Mr. Steele, now he has the honour to be your representative? What bailiff ever scrupled it before?[8]

Scott thought the jibe ungenerous; but it is very funny, and it caps a legitimate argument.

For the rest, Swift is ruthless to his victim.

To take the height of his learning, you are to suppose a lad just fit for the university, and sent early from thence into the wide world, where he followed every way of life that might least improve or preserve the rudiments he had got. He hath no invention, nor is master of a tolerable style; his chief talent is humour, which he sometimes discovers both in writing and discourse; for after the first bottle he is no disagreeable companion. I never knew him taxed with ill nature, which hath made me wonder how ingratitude came to be his prevailing vice; and I am apt to think it proceeds rather from some unaccountable sort of instinct, than premeditation. Being the most imprudent man alive, he never follows the advice of his friends, but is wholly at the mercy of fools or knaves, or hurried away by his own caprice; by which he hath committed more absurdities in economy, friendship, love, duty, good manners, politics, religion and writing, than ever fell to one man's share.

It is horribly near the truth; it is, indeed, the fact seen by a cold, piercing and unfriendly eye. The literary judgment is not necessarily in conflict with the praise Swift had previously bestowed upon him as one 'who hath tried the force and compass of our language with so much success'. Nor is this, again, necessarily belied by Swift's criticism of his style later in the pamphlet — 'for studying cadence instead of propriety, and filling up niches with words before he has adjusted his conceptions to them'. Steele's writing was, too often, hurried, verbose and vague. And Swift had, though not publicly, criticized his lack of invention before, when he complained to Stella that Steele used up the hints he gave him too quickly and superficially.

But the real motive-force of Swift's indictment of his former friend comes from his resentment of what his vanity compelled him to believe was Steele's ingratitude. It is, he says, his prevailing vice; and this is mysterious, because he is not ill-natured; it springs from levity, rather than from malice, of character. It is a pity that Swift did not stick to that explanation; but he drops it for something worse, when he warns Steele's new political friends not to reward him too liberally.

> For, as it was said of Cranmer, 'Do the archbishop an ill turn, and he is your friend for ever:' So I do affirm of your member, 'Do Mr. Steele a good turn, and he is your enemy for ever.'[9]

4

Immediately after Swift's attack had appeared, a new political pamphlet by Steele was announced. It was to be called *The Crisis*, and was advertised repeatedly from October 22, 1713 onward, rather in the style of Mr. Snodgrass who so frequently proclaimed that he 'was going to begin'. This was fair game for Swift. Pending the delivery of the mountain, he produced what he called a paraphrase of the Ode which Horace addressed to Asinius Pollio, the tragic dramatist, when he temporarily abandoned the drama for a history of the civil wars. Horace's ode was serious; Swift's was not.

> Dick, thou'rt resolv'd, as I am told
> Some strange arcana to unfold,
> And with the help of Buckley's pen,
> To vamp the good old cause again:
> Which thou (such Burnet's shrewd advice is)
> Must furbish up, and nickname *Crisis*.
> Thou pompously will let us know
> What all the world knew long ago . . .
> That we a German prince must own
> When Anne for heav'n resigns her throne.[10]

It is Steele's marked, though harmless vanity, that Swift shoots at — on the whole with more good-humour than might have been expected; and his judgment that Steele's genius was not suited to politics was true.

> Dick, we agree — all's true thou'st said.
> As that my Muse is yet a maid.
> But, if I may with freedom talk,
> All this is foreign to thy walk:
> Thy genius has perhaps a knack
> Of trudging in a beaten track,
> But is for state affairs as fit
> As mine for politics and wit.
> Then let us both in time grow wise,
> Nor higher, than our talents, rise.[11]

'Vamping the good old cause again' was an apt description, by anticipation, of *The Crisis*. It may have been momentarily effective when it appeared in early January, 1714 — indeed the incredible number of 40,000 copies are said to have been sold — but it was, in every way, a shoddy and pretentious production, which deserved the punishment Swift promptly gave it in *The Public Spirit of the Whigs*, published on February 24.

There are (he says) but three writers 'of any great distinction' on the Whig side, 'which are *The Flying Post*, Mr. Dunton, and the author of *The Crisis*'. Having thus fixed Steele in Grub Street, he continues:

> The third and principal of this triumvirate is the author of *The Crisis*; who although he must yield to *The Flying Post* in knowledge of the world, and skill in politics, and to Mr. Dunton in keenness of satire, and variety of reading, hath yet other qualities enough to denominate him a writer of a superior class to either, provided he would a little regard the propriety and disposition of his words, consult the grammatical part, and get some information on the subject he intends to handle.[12]

He then has some thoroughly good fun with the fact that Steele's shilling pamphlet was, extraordinarily, published by subscription. More extraordinarily still, it had been announced on December 28 that at the desire of several ladies of quality, the publication was postponed 'till the female world had expressed their zeal for the public by a subscription as large as that made by the other sex': on which Swift remarks:

> I should be glad to have seen a printed list of the fair subscribers prefixed to this pamphlet; by which the Chevalier might know he was so far from pretending to a monarchy here, that he could not so much as pretend to a mistress.[13]

To the subscription itself Swift riposted by a comic advertisement of *The Public Spirit of the Whigs* as 'Price 6d but to the subscribers half a crown'.

With all the persiflage is mingled some trenchant literary criticism. He fairly riddles Steele's opening paragraph, in which he adopts a famous simile from Virgil describing the calming effect of a wise grave man (*vir pietate gravis*) upon an excited mob, claims that he had frequently seen it happen, and offers it as the origin of civil institutions.

> To which I answer with great phlegm, that I defy any man alive to show me in double the number of lines, though writ by the same author, such a complicated ignorance in history, human nature, or politics, as well as in the ordinary proprieties of thought or of style.[14]

Then he lets himself go on Steele's really nonsensical eulogy of Liberty.

The weighty truths which he endeavours to impress upon the reader are such as these. That, 'Liberty is a very good thing'; That, 'Without liberty we cannot be free'; That, 'Health is good, and strength is good, but liberty is better than either'; That, 'No man can be happy, without the liberty of doing whatever his mind tells him is best'; That 'Men of quality love liberty, and common people love liberty'; even women and children love liberty; and you cannot please them better than by letting them do what they please. Had Mr. Steele contented himself to deliver these and the like maxims in such intelligible terms, I could have found out where we agreed and where we differed. But let us hear some of these maxims as he has involved them. 'We cannot possess our souls with pleasure and satisfaction except we preserve to ourselves that inestimable blessing which we call liberty: By liberty, I desire to be understood, to mean the happiness of men's living,' &c. — 'The true life of man consists in conducting it according to his own just sentiments and innocent inclinations.' — 'Man's being is degraded below that of a free agent, when his affections and passions are no longer governed by the dictates of his own mind.' — 'Without liberty, our health' (among other things) 'may be at the will of a tyrant, employed to our own ruin and that of our fellow-creatures.' If there be any of these maxims, which is not grossly defective in truth, in sense, or in grammar, I will allow them to pass for uncontrollable [i.e. incontrovertible]. By the first, omitting the pedantry of the whole expression, there are not above one or two nations in the world, where any one man can 'possess his soul with pleasure and satisfaction.' In the second he 'desires to be understood to mean'; that is, he desires to be meant to mean, or to be understood to understand. In the third, 'the life of man consists in conducting' his life. In the fourth, he affirms, That 'men's beings are degraded when their passions are no longer governed by the dictates of their own mind'; directly contrary to the lessons of all moralists and legislators, who agree unanimously that the passions of men must be under the government of reason and law; neither are laws of any other use than to correct the irregularity of our affections. By the last, 'Our health is ruinous to ourselves and other men, when a tyrant pleases'; which I leave him to make out.

Though severe, it is just criticism; and the passages which Swift demolishes are good examples of what he had in mind when he twitted Steele for 'putting words together with no regard but to their cadence'. Both in the literary and the political argument, Swift was an easy victor. But that does not imply that *The Public Spirit of the Whigs* was more politically effective than *The Crisis*. Not only was the vague and verbose rhapsody about liberty the kind of thing that has always been popular in England, but the very indefiniteness of Steele's indictment of the Government corresponded to the diffused sense of alarm in the country. Was the ministry in correspondence with the Pretender or not? Nobody knew. Swift himself was certain that it was not. That was fortunate for his peace of mind; but he was mistaken. That Oxford meant nothing serious by his communications with St. Germains is pretty plain; but Bolingbroke cannot so easily be acquitted. Steele's alarmism about the Hanover Succession, though it makes dull reading today, was more justified than Swift knew. He might indeed have applied to it what he says about Steele's report of 'a strict and secret alliance' between Savoy and the house of Bourbon:

> This is one of those facts wherein I am most inclined to believe the author, because it is what he must needs be utterly ignorant of, and therefore might possibly be true.[15]

5

By an irony of justice, both Swift and Steele came under condemnation for their pamphlets. Steele was expelled from the House of Commons for his; while the House of Lords took into custody the publisher and printer of Swift's and offered a reward of £300 for the discovery of the author. Oxford managed to extricate the publisher and printer from the Lords' jurisdiction; and sent Swift secretly £100 — ostensibly for their defence — but probably to supply him with ready money in case he needed to escape. Swift was scared.

In fact he had become rather reckless. He must have known that the sarcasms about the Scots peers in *The Public Spirit of the Whigs* would enrage them all, and Argyll in particular, at whom he was obviously hitting in the last sentence of the passage which was the ground of the Lords' proceedings. He quotes Steele's words: 'The late kingdom of Scotland had as numerous a nobility as England.'

They had indeed; and to that we owe one of the great and necessary evils of the Union upon the foot it now stands. Their nobility is indeed so numerous, that the whole revenues of their country would hardly be able to maintain them according to the dignity of their titles; and what is infinitely worse, they are never likely to be extinct till the last period of all things, because the greatest part of them descend to heirs general. I imagine, a person of quality prevailed on to marry a woman much his inferior, and without a groat to her fortune, and her friends arguing, she was as good as her husband because she brought him as numerous a family of relations and servants, as she found in his house. Scotland in the taxes is obliged to contribute one penny for every forty pence laid upon England; and the representatives they send to parliament are about a thirteenth: Every other Scotch peer has all the privileges of an English one, except that of sitting in parliament, and even precedence before all of the same title that shall be created for the time to come. The pensions and employments possessed by the natives of that country now among us do amount to more than the whole body of their nobility ever spent at home: And all the money they raise upon the public is hardly sufficient to defray their civil and military expenses. I could point to some with great titles, who affected to appear very vigorous for dissolving the Union, though their whole revenues before that period would have ill maintained a Welsh justice of the peace; and have since gathered more money than ever any Scotchmen, who had not travelled, could form an idea of.[16]

The Scots peers had always been a thorn in Oxford's side, who regarded their demands as inordinate. His refusal of one of Argyll's led that ambitious Duke to support a motion for the dissolution of the Union, of which he had been a prime mover, and by which he greatly profited, really in order to blackmail Oxford into surrender. Oxford, outwardly shocked, was secretly pleased by Swift's outburst.

CHAPTER XVII

FAREWELL TO GREATNESS: 1714

SWIFT'S increasing recklessness accompanied a growing despair at the irreconcilable antagonisms which had developed within the Ministry. When Oxford finally resigned on July 27, 1714, he wrote to Swift that he 'had had no power since July 25, 1713'; and he made frequent references to that date in his own memoirs.[1] Though the details of the struggle between himself and Bolingbroke are obscure, it is fairly clear that two main issues (other than the purely personal) were involved. One was the issue of party government, for which Bolingbroke was now pressing, and to which Oxford was by conviction opposed. This was complicated with another issue: the choice between the Hanover succession and the return of the Stuart. The complication was inevitable, because a great many of the Tories were at least sentimental Jacobites, and a purely Tory government must have been largely hostile to the Hanover succession. Moreover, since a purely Tory government, as conceived by Bolingbroke, involved the replacement of Whigs or moderates by high-flying Tories not only in the armed services, but even in the minor posts of the administration (to which again Oxford was opposed on principle), such a policy held the menace of civil war. Though probably a majority of the Tories were sentimental Jacobites, the active Jacobites among them were few; and there is no doubt that a majority of the nation as a whole was definitely opposed to a return of the Stuart unless he would turn Protestant, which he honourably refused to do. In such a situation, the danger was that the rash and violent men would get control of the apparatus of power.

To this end Bolingbroke, even before July 25, 1713, was intriguing. His principal associates were Harcourt and Atterbury, who had been made Bishop of Rochester and Dean of Westminster against Oxford's wishes. Oxford regarded July 25 as the date on which his loss of power began, because on that day he sent a letter to Bolingbroke. What it actually contained is not known; but one may surmise that it unmasked Bolingbroke's intrigue against him. The details of this fall rather into the historian's province than ours; but some knowledge of them is necessary to the understanding of Swift's anomalous position. Bolingbroke's plan was to create 'a Tory Junto' (his own phrase) and reduce Oxford to a mere figure-head. Accordingly Oxford had been made the object of a whispering attack as 'no sincere

Churchman'. Under cover of strengthening the High Church interest in the ministry, active Jacobites were to be introduced into it. Dartmouth, Oxford's loyal supporter, was to be forced out of his Secretaryship of State for the South, and replaced by an instrument of Bolingbroke's. Thus Bolingbroke, who already held the Secretaryships of the North and of Scotland, would be in control of the administrative machine. At the same time Atterbury was to be made Lord Privy Seal, and Wyndham Chancellor of the Exchequer. In July 1713 Oxford countered this plot. He proposed to the Queen to revive the independent Secretaryship of Scotland, and give it to the Earl of Mar; to promote Dartmouth to the vacant Privy Seal; and to appoint Bromley, a High Church leader indeed but no Jacobite, to the Secretaryship vacated by Dartmouth. All this he succeeded in carrying through.[2] It was his last victory. His mistake appears to have been in making Lady Masham privy to his plans by showing her his letter and Bolingbroke's reply. Anyhow, from that time onward, Lady Masham was won over by Bolingbroke. According to Oxford and the Harley family she was bribed by a share in the Asiento company, and in other illicit profits arising from articles inserted in the Spanish treaty.[3] It is probably true.

The defection of Lady Masham was perhaps the immediate occasion of Oxford's attempt to resign in November 1713. Moreover, the Queen had refused a personal favour which he had asked.[*] He was convinced that his star was waning. However, he was dissuaded from resigning by his close friends, and by the moderate Whigs with whom he maintained contact: both dreaded an increase of Bolingbroke's power. Even the Queen still regarded Oxford as irreplaceable, since Bolingbroke's private reputation made him impossible as her Lord Treasurer. But Oxford's real influence with the Queen was now gone. Hitherto, the Queen and he had been at one on the desirability of a moderate policy and a centre government, if it were possible. But the unconcealed rejoicing of some of the Whigs at the Queen's dangerous illness in December and January, 1713-14, definitely turned her against them, and made her willing to fall in with Bolingbroke's scheme of an extreme Tory government. Besides this, her feminine reluctance to consider realistically the problem of the succession made it impossible for Oxford to set at

* Oxford's reference to this is cryptic, but emphatic. He dates it precisely on September 16, 1713, after his return from Wimpole, where he had been from August 18 to September 5 for the final arrangements for his son's wedding to the only daughter of the late Duke of Newcastle, Lady Henrietta Cavendish Holles. 'After my return,' he says, 'advantage was taken of my never enough to be lamented folly in mentioning to H.M. the titles. I never did this to anyone else except Lady Masham, and have kept my word never to speak of it directly or indirectly ... but this was made my crime.'[4] It has been suggested that his request was that the Dukedom of Newcastle should be revived for his son. Oxford's words seem to imply that Lady Masham was guilty of a breach of confidence, and provided the ammunition for his enemies.

rest the suspicions of Hanover, and indeed of the country at large. It was all he could do to prevent the Queen from an overtly anti-Hanover gesture. In April 1714 a writ of summons to the House of Lords was demanded for the Electoral Prince (the future George II), who had been made Duke of Cambridge. Anne was furious, and wished to refuse the writ. Bolingbroke encouraged her in this breach of the law. Oxford opposed them both, and his loss of favour was complete.

The breach between Oxford and Bolingbroke had thus become irreparable while Swift was absent in Ireland, at the moment when Oxford was convinced that Bolingbroke was intriguing against him with success. Nothing in Swift's various accounts of the period suggests that he was aware of this. One can only assume that this was one of the matters on which Oxford did not confide in him. In consequence, Swift's views of the situation are oddly superficial. He was captivated by Bolingbroke's apparent policy of pure Tory government, and a clean sweep of the Whigs and Trimmers; but since he assumed that the Tories were practically solid for the Hanover succession, he had no notion of the dangers attending it, or of the reasons for Oxford's dogged opposition to it. He was acutely conscious of the personal antagonism between them, but the real causes of it were a mystery. His personal friendship to both did not, in these circumstances, endow him with any capacity to reconcile them as politicians.

2

The evidence of Swift's correspondence is that after his return to London his political (as distinct from his personal) contacts were with Bolingbroke rather than Oxford. Hitherto, in Irish affairs, Swift had been in accord with Archbishop King. King was opposed to the policy and practices of the ultra-Tory Lord Chancellor Phipps who, encouraged by Bolingbroke, was trying to make a clean sweep of the Irish Whigs. Nevertheless, the Whigs secured a majority in the Irish Commons and proceeded to demand that Phipps should be dismissed. Shrewsbury was sent by Oxford as Lord Lieutenant to calm the uproar. He arrived in Dublin on October 27, 1713, and acted in accord with King. Roughly speaking, one may say that at this moment Phipps was Bolingbroke's man, and Shrewsbury Oxford's. Swift was on Phipps's side. Not merely did he lend a too ready ear to Phipps's effort to make bad blood between him and King, by reporting that the Archbishop intended to compel him to reside in his Deanery; but he actually exerted his influence (whether it was great or small) to prevent King from being appointed Primate of Ireland, although he knew well that both for political capacity and pastoral conscientiousness King was the rightful choice. This was a serious aberration from the line of Swift's own convictions. To Bishop Stearne, his friend and predecessor at St. Patrick's, who was a loyal supporter of King, he explained: 'I should be thought a very vile man if I presumed to recommend ... my own brother if he were the least disinclined to the present measures of her Majesty and the Ministry here' (December 19, 1713). Doubtless, he was sincere; but he was begging the question. He was assuming that the policy of the Ministry was Bolingbroke's, not Oxford's; and Bolingbroke, we know, was pressing on the reluctant Oxford an extreme policy in Ireland, and even suggesting that the Irish House of Commons should be permanently dissolved.[5]

One can only conclude that Oxford was disinclined to talk politics with Swift any more. By the end of the year the famous Saturday dinners were abandoned. But the personal friendship between Swift and Oxford rather increased than diminished. Conscious that his power was waning, deeply affected by domestic grief at the death of his daughter, Lady Carmarthen, Oxford sought in Swift's company a release from his cares and his insoluble problems. It is this period of their relation that Swift describes in the 'imitation' of Horace's *Hoc erat in votis* — which he wrote at Letcombe. He tells how Oxford

> Would take me in his coach to chat,
> And question me of this and that;
> As 'What's o'clock?' And, 'How's the wind?'
> 'Whose chariot's that we left behind?'
> Or gravely try to read the lines
> Writ underneath the country signs;
> And mark at Brentford how they spell
> *Hear is good Eal and Bear to cell.*
> Or, 'Have you nothing new today
> From Pope, from Parnell, or from Gay?'
> Such tattle often entertains
> My lord and me as far as Staines,
> As once a week we travel down
> To Windsor, and again to town;
> Where all that passes, *inter nos*,
> Might be proclaimed at Charing Cross.[6]

To this period, too, belong the meetings of the Scriblerus Club, of which the three poets named were members, with Swift and Arbuthnot. Oxford was a member, or the honoured guest, but not Bolingbroke. He replied cheerfully to Swift's invitation:

Come then, my Lord, and take your part in
The important history of Martin — [7]

with some characteristic doggerel of his own:

> I honour the men, sir
> Who are ready to answer,
> When I ask them to stand by the Queen;
> In spite of orators,
> And bloodthirsty praters,
> Whose hatred I highly esteem.
> Let our faith's defender
> Keep out every pretender
> And long enjoy her own;
> Thus you four, five,
> May merrily live
> Till faction is dead as a stone. [8]

To this period, finally, belongs the well-known picture by the able Whig bishop of Peterborough, White Kennett, of Swift in the ante-chamber at Windsor, acting as 'a sort of Master of Requests' to Oxford. Kennett had the vivid memory of an alert enemy.

He was soliciting the Earl of Arran to speak to his brother the Duke of Ormond, to get a chaplain's place established in the garrison of Hull for Mr. Fiddes, a clergyman in that neighbourhood, who had lately been in gaol, and published sermons to pay fees. He was promising Mr. Thorold to undertake with my Lord Treasurer, that, according to his petition, he should obtain a salary of two hundred pounds per annum as Minister of the English Church at Rotterdam. He stopped F. Gwynn Esq., going in with the red bag to the Queen and told him aloud that he had something to say to him from my Lord Treasurer. He talked with the son of Dr. Davenant to be sent abroad, and took out his pocket-book and wrote down several things, as memoranda, to do for him. He turned to the fire, and took out his gold watch, and telling him the time of day, complained it was very late. A gentleman said he was too fast. 'How can I help it,' says the Doctor, 'if the courtiers give me a watch that won't go right?' Then he instructed a young nobleman, that the best poet in England was Mr. Pope (a Papist), who had begun a translation of Homer into English verse, for which he must have them all subscribe. 'For,' says he, 'the author shall not begin to print till I have a thousand guineas for him.' Lord Treasurer, after leaving the Queen, came through the room, beckoning Dr. Swift to follow him; both went off just before prayers. [9]

We know, from his correspondence, that Swift was engaged in doing good turns to Fiddes and Davenant at this time: so that the Bishop's memory can be relied on. It is the convincing evidence of a hostile witness to the truth of Swift's claim that he was a better solicitor for others than himself. It is quite likely that he never spoke another word (beyond his poem) about the thousand pounds, for which he was going to dun the Ministers. But one of them had, at least, given him a gold watch. Two years before he had to ask Bolingbroke the time.

3

The welcome and privileged solicitor and the political confidant are two different rôles; and there is no evidence that Oxford ever made Swift share the burden of his cares of state, or his difficulties at Court. In all Swift's various accounts of the political events of this period, he gropes after an explanation of Oxford's behaviour. He cannot answer the simplest questions about it. Was Oxford's reluctance to make a clean sweep of the Whigs his own policy, or deference to the Queen's? Why did he reject the idea of annihilating the Whig opposition, which seemed so obviously sensible to Swift? Why did he maintain relations with the moderate Whigs? These questions, and others like them, Swift answers now one way, now another, with an uncertainty which proves that he never received any authoritative information from Oxford on any of them. In the most careful of his narratives: *An Enquiry into the Behaviour of the Queen's last Ministry*, he reveals his ignorance of the real situation in the autumn and winter of 1713. He was indeed aware that Oxford was losing favour with the Queen, and says so.

> I am very confident [he continues] that this alteration in the Queen's favour towards the Earl of Oxford, could never have appeared, if he had not thought fit to make one step in politics which I have not been able to apprehend.[10]

This incomprehensible step of Oxford's was that he did not exert himself either to maintain Lady Masham in favour with the Queen, or to cultivate Lady Masham's favour for himself. The idea that Bolingbroke was bribing Lady Masham away from Oxford (as indeed he had previously done over the Quebec expedition) did not enter Swift's head. Because he himself was on frank and friendly terms with Lady Masham, he imagined her incorruptible and incapable of duplicity. He gives her a character without blemish as 'a person of a plain sound understanding, of great truth and sincerity, without the least mixture of falsehood or disguise; of an honest boldness and courage, superior to her sex; firm and disinterested in her friendship, and full of love, duty, and veneration for the Queen her mistress'.[11] Lady Masham, alas, was not that. Oxford was not willing to pay the price of conciliating her: that expensive mode of propitiation went against the grain. But he seems to have respected Swift's friendship for her, and refrained from even hinting at the true causes of the coldness between himself and her.

The nature of Swift's Tory pamphleteering at this time confirms the evidence of his historical writings that he was only on the periphery of events at Court. As far as the political content of his pamphlets is concerned, he was as guilty as Steele of 'vamping the good old cause again'; he confined himself to asserting the absurdity and disloyalty of suggesting that the Hanover succession was in any danger at all. The two attacks on Steele are essentially personal; so is the onslaught on Burnet for beating the big No Popery drum: *A Preface to the B — p of S — m's Introduction &c*, the merits of which are not great. None of them advocates any positive policy, and the best of them might have been written by a Swift who had no personal contact with the ministers at all.

He was more positive in the pamphlet he wrote immediately after his retirement to Letcombe: *Some Free Thoughts on the Present State of Affairs*, which Barber the printer submitted to Bolingbroke, and Bolingbroke delayed till it was made obsolete by the Queen's death. This is, first, a criticism of Oxford's secrecy and his moderation towards the Whigs, and, secondly, a criticism of the Ministers as a whole for not unitedly and vigorously pursuing what Swift considered a commonsense Tory policy. This policy is twofold. The first part of it consists in maintaining the Church of England 'in all its powers and privileges', and consequently of resolutely excluding all Dissenters from any kind of political power. This necessitates permanently disabling the Whigs, which is the more imperative because they have succeeded in convincing Hanover that they are the only people he can trust. Measures must therefore be taken so 'that it shall not be in the power of the Crown, although in conjunction with any rich and factious body of men, to choose an ill majority in the House of Commons'.[12] Presumably, what Swift had in mind was to purge the Corporations — such as Steele's Stockbridge — most of which were in some degree rotten boroughs of which the moneyed interest could easily gain control at a price, and to throw the balance of political power permanently into the hands of the forty-shilling freeholders of the shires. He also pressed for a purge of Whigs from all controlling positions in the army. The second part of the policy was to remove the suspicions of Hanover by inviting one of the family to reside in England, on condition that Hanover ceased all correspondence with the Whig opposition.

The policy was logical enough; but it had singularly little relation to the political realities. It assumed that the Tories were solid for the Hanover succession, and that the Queen's refusal to have the Electoral Prince in England could be overcome; and it allowed no weight to the fact that the situation had degenerated into an envenomed struggle for power between Oxford and Bolingbroke. Not that Swift ignored this: on the contrary, he describes it vividly, though he admits his ignorance of the cause.

> On the one side very great reserve, and certainly very great resentment on the other, if we may believe general report (for I pretend to know no farther) have inflamed animosities to such a height, as to make all reconcilement impracticable ... A ship's crew quarrelling in a storm, or while their enemies are within gunshot, is but a faint idea of this fatal infatuation.[13]

But the policy he proposed as one which 'on principles of general reason' they ought to have unitedly pursued was not one they could have pursued. Oxford, who did not believe in disfranchising the Dissenters or trying to annihilate the Whigs, would have been false to himself had he adopted it. The policy was practically identical with Bolingbroke's, as far as domestic affairs were concerned; but quite impossible for Bolingbroke to follow, as far as Hanover was concerned. Not only was he more suspect to Hanover than Oxford, but he was engaged in exploiting against Oxford the Queen's resentment at any practical measure to secure the Hanover succession. And, as a matter of fact, it is to be doubted whether, even in domestic affairs, Bolingbroke's policy aimed at anything more than securing power for himself; for on the evening of the day (July 27) on which he compassed Oxford's downfall, he invited the younger Whig leaders — Stanhope, Craggs, Pulteney and Walpole — to dine with him, with the obvious intention of forming, if he could, a coalition with the Whigs: precisely the manœuvre for which he had sowed suspicion of Oxford among the Tories.

One cannot avoid the conclusion that Bolingbroke was completely unprincipled, and solely concerned to establish himself in power. Whereas in Oxford's stubborn resistance to Bolingbroke's extreme measures one can, without undue partiality, discern a sense of responsibility to the nation as a whole; in the case of Bolingbroke himself no such saving grace is perceptible. No doubt, towards the end, Oxford's resentment against Bolingbroke was as fiercely personal as Bolingbroke's against him; but the causes of the resentment were morally different. Oxford felt that Bolingbroke had been guilty of treachery; Bolingbroke that Oxford stood between him and power.

4

All through the winter the sense that his good intentions and good offices were powerless to effect a reconciliation between the two leaders grew upon Swift. His personal friendship with Oxford, as we have said, increased rather than diminished. Oxford was always more congenial to him than Bolingbroke. However secretive he may have been as a politician, as a human being he was without reserve. Indeed, he seems to have regarded the world of politics as different in kind from the world of human relations: an attitude which was probably wise, but had the paradoxical effect of making him doubly scrupulous when it came to advancing his personal friends. It was known among them as a bad sign when Lord Treasurer spoke well of any suitor. This idiosyncrasy they accepted, and rather ruefully admired, as the consequence of his admitted uncorruptibility where public money was concerned. In the noble letter Swift wrote to him on July 3, 1714, he said: 'In your public capacity you have often angered me to the heart, but, as a private man, never once.' The letter was written just after Swift had finished *Some Free Thoughts*, and was, perhaps, immediately inspired by the fact that the abortive pamphlet was in the main a severe criticism of Oxford's policy.* It is the more impressive that, at the moment he was declaring himself, in politics, on Bolingbroke's side, he told Oxford that he wished him 'a private man tomorrow ... and then you would see whether I should not with much more willingness attend you in a retirement ... than ever I did at London or Windsor'. When he wrote he knew that Oxford's downfall was imminent, and that Bolingbroke was bound (if the Queen survived) to succeed him in power, if not in office. He was committing himself in advance, not to follow Bolingbroke. The simple nobility of Swift's language, the emotion which it communicates by constraining, recalls the words of Enobarbus:

> He that can endure
> To follow with allegiance a fall'n lord,
> Doth conquer him that did his master conquer
> And earns a place i' the story.

Swift's letter sustains the comparison. There could be no higher praise.

At the end of April Swift was making preparations to retire. He sent down some wine to an old acquaintance of Moor Park days, the Rev. John Geree, who was now the parson of Letcombe Bassett in Berkshire, and arranged to be lodged and boarded for a guinea a week. An allusion in a letter from the

* See Appendix X.

Duchess of Ormond to Æsop's famous fable, incited him to a last forlorn appeal for unity in the ministry. The wands of office were the sticks in Swift's verses *The Fagot*.

> Come, courtiers: every man his stick!
> Lord Treasurer, for once be quick:
> And that they may the closer cling,
> Take your blue ribbon for a string.
> Come, trimming Harcourt, bring your mace;
> And squeeze it in or quit your place:
> Dispatch, or else that rascal Northey
> Will undertake to do it for thee:
> And be assured, the court will find him
> Prepared to leap o'er sticks, or bind them.
>   To make the bundle strong and safe,
> Great Ormond, lend thy general's staff:
> And if the crosier could be cramm'd in,
> A fig for Lechmere, King and Hampden!
> You'll then defy the strongest Whig
> With both his hands to bend a twig;
> Though with united strength they all pull,
> From Somers, down to Craggs and Walpole.[14]

The reference to 'trimming Harcourt' is peculiar: for the Lord Chancellor was regarded (with Atterbury, 'the crozier') as a member of Bolingbroke's Tory Junto. It must refer not to his political attitude at the moment, but to his character as Swift knew it.*

5

On May 31 Swift left London abruptly. He stayed in Oxford for two days and left for Letcombe, with a conspicuously big portmanteau, on June 3. On June 8 he wrote to Vanessa. 'This', he said to her, 'is the first syllable I have writ to anybody since you saw me.' He described his mode of life.

I am at a clergyman's house, an old friend and an acquaintance, whom I love very well; but he is such a melancholy thoughtful man, partly from nature, and partly from a solitary life, that I shall soon catch the spleen from him. Out of ease and complaisance, I desire him not to alter any of his methods for me; so we dine exactly between twelve and one, at

---

* On July 17, 1714 Lewis described him contemptuously to Swift as 'the great Attorney who made you the sham offer of a Yorkshire living'. And a year later Swift wrote to Chetwode: 'I always knew my friend, Mr. Attorney, would be as great as he could, in all changes.' (December 17, 1715)

267

eight we have some bread and butter and a glass of ale, and at ten he goes to bed. Wine is a stranger, except a little I sent him, of which, one evening in two, we have a pint between us . . . I read all day, or walk, and do not speak as many words as I have now writ in three days; so that, in short, I have a mind to steal to Ireland, unless I feel myself take more to this way of living, so different, in every circumstance, from what I left.

Swift always claimed that he was by nature a stranger to the spleen — or, as we should say, to depression. He deceived himself: for it is evident, here and elsewhere, that he needed society and conversation to keep it away. But, in spite of Geree's taciturnity, he stayed on at Letcombe until August 16. It was hardly to be expected that he would steal away to Ireland until he knew the issue of the struggle at Court. So he worked away on *Some Free Thoughts*, which he had begun in London.

As to Vanessa herself, it is clear that he had been seeing her constantly since his return to London. Looking back on the past, eight years later, he spoke of it to her as 'the joyful return'. She had resumed her position as his chief solace in strain and anxiety. Latterly, she had needed his practical help: for her mother had died and left her affairs in confusion and debt. Swift, who was a good man of business, had been trying to straighten them out and going through her papers. One of his last acts before leaving town had been to send them back to her in a bandbox. She was short of ready money: he stood security for a loan of £30. She was frightened by a visit from the bailiffs: he reassured her. Finally, when she knew that he was going back to Ireland, she paid him a surprise visit in Berkshire, early in August. As before, it both gratified and alarmed him.

I think [he wrote] since I have known you, I have drawn an old house on my head. You should not have come by Wantage for a thousand pounds. You used to brag you were very discreet: where is it gone? (August 12, 1714)

It was not her coming, but her coming conspicuously through the post town, that made him remonstrate.

The anxieties and efforts of the last nine months had affected his health. He gradually recovered it at Letcombe; but the contemplation of the approaching doom of all his hopes, and the severance of precious friendships, engendered a strange mood in him. Never, perhaps, did Swift come nearer to the emotional nakedness of a breakdown; never was his constant effort after control more evident or more admirable. We have already spoken of the restrained emotion of his letter to Oxford, and compared the effect of it to a speech of Enobarbus. He himself described it to Arbuthnot as 'very odd and serious'; and that again recalls a phrase of Enobarbus: it was 'one of those odd tricks that sorrow shoots out of the mind'. And over the whole of his correspondence at this time (which was copious) is the atmosphere of a Roman tragedy of Shakespeare. It is no less in the letters he received than in those he sent; for there was a rare quality in the other two members of the little triumvirate of Oxford's devoted friends who watched the decline of their master and the decay of the Queen. A whole world is crumbling to ruin, and they are moved to the depths. For this alone we may be grateful that Swift was moved to retire: that we can hear them speak. They write to him, and he to them, more frequently than ever before, or ever again. At this moment they cannot help themselves. 'Writing to you much,' says Swift to Arbuthnot, 'would make me stark mad.' But he goes on writing.

> Judge his condition who has nothing to keep him from being miserable but endeavouring to forget those for whom he has the greatest value, love and friendship. But you are a philosopher and a physician, and can overcome by your wisdom and your faculty those weaknesses which other men are forced to reduce by not thinking on them. Adieu, and love me half so well as I love you. (June 16, 1714)

Arbuthnot, in return, tries to distract him with details of his suggestions for the Memoirs of Martinus Scriblerus, tells him what he knows of the progress of the struggle at Court, and offers to lend him all his ready money — for Swift was in temporary straits. Swift replies:

> And so you will lend me all your money. The mischief is, I never borrow money of a friend. You are mightily mistaken: all your honour, generosity, good nature, good sense, wit, and every other praiseworthy quality, will never make me think one jot the better of you. That time is now some years past, and you will never mend in my opinion. But really, Brother, you have a sort of shuffle in your gait; and now I have said the worst that your most mortal enemy could say of you with truth. (July 25, 1714)

When the final blow had fallen and the Queen was dead, Swift wrote him a letter which has not survived. Arbuthnot's reply began with his memorable words upon the Queen's death. 'My dear mistress's days were numbered even in my imagination, and could not exceed such certain limits; but of that small number a great deal was cut off by this last troublesome contention among her servants. I believe sleep was never more welcome to a tired traveller, than death was to her.' So it began; it ended thus:

Dear friend, the last sentence of your letter quite kills me. Never repeat that melancholy tender word, that you will endeavour to forget me. I am sure I never can forget you, till I meet with, what is impossible, another, whose conversation I can delight so much in as Dr. Swift's, and yet that is the smallest thing I ought to value you for. That hearty sincere friendship, that plain and open ingenuity in all your commerce, is what I am sure I can never find in another man. I shall want often a faithful monitor, one that would vindicate me behind my back, and tell me my faults to my face. God knows I write this with tears in my eyes. (August 12, 1714)

It is the noblest tribute Swift ever received as a man. It must never be forgotten, for it was paid to him by the one of all his friends who was best fitted to judge a man.

The double drama of the falling minister and the failing Queen, as it appears in Swift's correspondence, is the more affecting because the 'three honest counsellors' had each a different emphasis in their loyalty. The loyalty of Lewis, the able, upright, and devoted civil servant, was exclusively towards Oxford himself. He profoundly mistrusted Bolingbroke, who in turn despised him for not being a 'man of parts'; and he had no faith at all in Lady Masham. The worst of his pain was that he was compelled to recognize that Oxford's powers, as well as his power, were declining: he was now fuddled, dilatory, and obstinate. Lewis's one desire was that Oxford should quit his post with dignity; and he felt himself to blame, because he had joined with those who persuaded him not to resign some months before. That his master should be humiliated, and should humiliate himself; that he should suffer the shrill denunciations of Lady Masham, and still worse, the pathetic reproaches of the Queen, was torture to him. The loyalty of Arbuthnot was primarily to the Queen herself. He too mistrusted Bolingbroke; he too wanted Oxford to resign with dignity: but most of all he desired that his mistress should be spared the appalling strain, and end her sad life in peace. Of Arbuthnot's personal feeling for the woman, Anne, Swift had nothing. He knew her only at second-hand, or from a distance. For him she was, to the fall of the curtain, 'the royal prude' who had excluded him from her familiarity and frowned upon his advancement. The woman of the Court who had his loyalty was Lady Masham. He dreaded her falling completely under the influence of Bolingbroke, and constantly called upon his friends to stand by her and advise her. Arbuthnot, wisely, declined the dangerous assignment. She was not likely to listen to him, anyhow, for she had abused him for his loyalty to Oxford.

With all these differences of attitude, the three trusted one another completely. They wrote to one another without reserve. Common to them all, besides the trust in each other's integrity, was a distrust of Bolingbroke's — 'the man of Mercury'. In Lewis, this reached positive detestation. Arbuthnot was more detached and philosophical. In Swift it was a malaise. He was inclined to be beglamoured by Bolingbroke — 'you, not the other, were my hero', he told him years afterwards, choosing his word nicely, and without reminding him that he mistrusted 'heroes' — and he had guarded himself against temptation by committing himself beforehand to follow Oxford into retirement. That decision would have involved breaking with Lady Masham also, if the Queen had lived. For, although Swift was loth to admit it, the Bolingbroke-Masham combination was a fact, as Lewis warned him. In concert, they addressed urgent appeals to him, when Oxford had fallen, to return to London to help them. Swift did not respond.

> I am not of your opinion [he wrote to Vanessa] about Lord Bolingbroke; perhaps he may get the staff, but I cannot rely on his kindness to me ... I am writ to earnestly by somebody to come to town, and join with these people now in power, but I will not do it. Say nothing of this, but guess the person. I told Lord Oxford I would go with him when he was out, and now he begs it of me, and I cannot refuse him. I meddle not with his faults, as he was a Minister of State; but you know his personal kindness to me was excessive. He distinguished me above all other men while he was great, and his letter to me t'other day was the most moving imaginable. (August 1, 1714)

When that was written, the Queen was already dead, although Swift did not know it. Bolingbroke's moment of power was past; 'like the lightning which doth cease to be, Ere one can say "It lightens".' For a little while he dreamed fantastic dreams of what, with the help of Swift's pen, he could yet accomplish. 'The Whigs are a pack of Jacobites: that shall be the cry in a month, if you please.'[15] Oxford, more reasonably, entertained some hopes of being recalled to power, or to a share of it, and postponed his retirement into the country, so that Swift was no longer called to follow him. Since he had to take the oaths to the new King, his return to Ireland was obligatory. Before he left, he sent Bolingbroke a letter demolishing all his hopes of power, and consoling him with the prospect of being a leader of the Church party in opposition. He put his finger on one fatal weakness of Bolingbroke's policy.

> It might reasonably be expected that this quiet possession might convince the successor of the good dispositions of the Church party towards him; and I ever thought that there was a mighty failure somewhere or other, that this could not have been done in the Queen's life. (August 7, 1714)

Since that had been one of the two main suggestions in *Some Free Thoughts*, which Bolingbroke had suppressed; since Bolingbroke's final effort to undermine Oxford had been to encourage the Queen in her aversion to making any concession to Hanover, the shot, whether deliberately aimed or not, must have gone home.

The quietness in which the new King succeeded surprised Swift and his friends. 'We are ill prognosticators,' wrote Lewis to him. 'Everything goes on with a tranquillity we dared not hope for.'[16] It is not clear what they apprehended. A rising in Scotland? A French fleet and army? Riots in the west country? But men's nerves were on edge. Swift had been living on his. He ended his imitation of *Hoc erat in votis*:

> Thus in a sea of folly toss'd,
> My choicest hours of life are lost:
> Yet always wishing to retreat;
> O, could I see my country seat!
> There, leaning near a gentle brook,
> Sleep, or peruse some ancient book;
> And there in sweet oblivion drown
> Those cares which haunt the court and town.[17]

That is a pretty exact translation of *O rus, quando ego te aspiciam*; but it expressed the longing of one half of Swift — but only of one half. For the other half the Court had a fearful fascination. At Letcombe he had been lingering on, to watch the last scene of the last act of the Tory tragedy. He had sent off his books, six cases of them, by long sea to Ireland — 'all old, and half very bad, to make a show as the Dean of St. Patrick's should'; he had sent off even his clothes and linen. The big portmanteau he carried from Oxford to Letcombe had contained chiefly papers. His mind played incessantly on the events in which he had participated. On August 9 — just a week before he left Letcombe — he began an account of them: *Some Considerations upon the Consequences hoped and feared from the Death of the Queen*. It got no further than the introduction. Now the curtain had fallen and he departed. He talked of coming back in the winter — to Oxford, to Bolingbroke, to Vanessa; but he did not really believe in it. His last letter in England was to Oxford. 'I set out tomorrow morning, and shall have no thoughts of returning, unless some juncture of affairs shall make my friends think it may be of any use.'[18] To Vanessa, naturally, but less seriously, he was more encouraging:

It is probable I may not stay in Ireland long, but be back by the beginning of winter. When I am there, I will write to you as soon as I can conveniently, but it shall always be under a cover; and if you write to me, let some other direct it; and I beg you will write nothing that is particular, but what may be seen; for I apprehend letters may be opened, and inconveniences will happen. If you are in Ireland while I am there, I shall see you very seldom. It is not a place for any freedom, but where everything is known in a week, and magnified a hundred degrees. These are rigorous laws that must be passed through; but it is probable we may meet in London in winter, or, if not, leave all to fate, that seldom cares to humour our inclinations. I say all this out of the perfect esteem and friendship I have for you. These public misfortunes have altered all my measures and broke my spirits. I shall, I hope, be on horseback in a day after this comes to your hand. I would not answer your questions for a million, nor can I think of them with any ease of mind. Adieu. (August 12, 1714)

CHAPTER XVIII

VANESSA AND STELLA

SWIFT arrived in Dublin on August 24, 1714. The reaction to the excitement and strain of the past was immediate. Ireland seemed to him weary, stale, flat and unprofitable. He complained to Ford of his 'perfect lazyness, and listlessness, and anneantissement . . . I cannot think or write in this country'. Bolingbroke (he said) was pressing him to return, but he will not, until he is fully convinced that his return will be of use; and for that he will rely on the judgment of Ford and Lewis. It would be foolish for him to return otherwise, for 'being in England only renders this place more hateful to me, which habitude would make tolerable'. The prospect of taking part in a forlorn struggle has no allurement: 'for I care not to fight against sea and wind so late in my life; and having been beaten with all advantages on our side makes me a greater coward than ever'. Whether the new regime intended to be at all indulgent towards the Tories would be apparent from the steps taken to manage the elections. 'Without much pains or pence the Whigs cannot have a majority.'[1] He wrote to the same effect to Bolingbroke.

> I know not what motions your Lordship intends; but if I see the old Whig measures taken in the next elections, and that the Court, the Bank, East India and the South Sea, act strenuously and procure a majority, I shall lie down and beg of Jupiter to heave the cart out of the dirt. (September 14, 1714)

The old Whig measures were taken; the pains and pence were spent; and the disaster was complete. If he had cherished a spark of hope of return, it was finally extinguished.

In the depth of his despondency he wrote to Arbuthnot. Then he fell ill. Arbuthnot replied:

> Even in affliction, your letter made me melancholy, and communicated some of the spleen which you had when you wrote it, and made me forfeit some of my reputation of cheerfulness and temper under afflictions . . . The Queen's poor servants are, like so many poor orphans, exposed in the very streets, and those, whose past obligations of gratitude and honour ought to have engaged them to have represented their case, pass by them like so many abandoned creatures,

without the possibility of ever being able to make the least return for a favour, which has added to my theory of human virtue. (October 19, 1714)

With these words of Arbuthnot's ringing in his mind Swift wrote the verses, *In Sickness.*

> 'Tis true — then why should I repine
> To see my life so fast decline?
> But, why obscurely here alone,
> Where I am neither loved nor known?
> My state of health none care to learn;
> My life is here no soul's concern.
> And, those with whom I now converse
> Without a tear will tend my hearse.
> Removed from kind Arbuthnot's aid,
> Who knows his art but not his trade,
> Preferring his regard for me
> Before his credit or his fee.
> Some formal visits, looks, and words,
> What mere humanity affords
> I meet perhaps from three or four,
> From whom I once expected more;
> Which those who tend the sick for pay
> Can act as decently as they:
> But, no obliging, tender friend,
> To help at my approaching end.
> My life is now a burthen grown
> To others, ere it be my own.[2]

The attitude to Stella implied in these verses is astonishing. She might not have existed. They indicate a breach of sympathy and contact between them which cannot be fully explained by the morbidity of illness and dejection. One must invoke Vanessa.

Of her tender concern for Swift's state of health there is no doubt; she had all the anxiety of a lover about it. It throbs through the letters she wrote him when he was in Ireland the year before. And very soon after Swift had written his verses she arrived in Dublin, perhaps drawn by the news of his illness, though she also had business there. On November 5 Swift replied to a letter of hers, asking him to come to see her at Cellbridge, where she had a house. But Swift was then on his way to stay with a new Tory acquaintance, Knightley Chetwode, twelve miles north of Laracor. He told her that he would stay there about a fortnight, after which he would call on her in Dublin, as presumably he did.

It is difficult to suppose that Stella was still ignorant of Swift's friendship with Vanessa. It was not very secret. Even a recent acquaintance like Chetwode knew something of it.[3]

2

The verses alone are evidence enough that Swift on his return to Ireland was, at least, disenchanted with Stella. His letter to Vanessa on his departure from England, for all its reticence, shows that she was very near his heart. That Stella knew something of the affair is probable; if she behaved coldly to Swift in consequence it would have been only natural. Even if it were not so, it would have made no difference to Swift's attitude at the moment. Vanessa was a part of the thrilling life he had left: Stella was consubstantial with the dullness to which he was now exiled. But, beyond that, Vanessa was thrilling in herself to him; Stella was not. That implies no comparison between the two women as women. Stella's beauty and merit may have been greater than Vanessa's. She may have been, in her heart, just as deeply in love with Swift as Vanessa. But Vanessa had stirred something in Swift which Stella had never been allowed to stir. He had been touched by the passion of love.

That is the difference — and it is a mighty one — between Swift's relation to Vanessa and his relation to Stella. Stella had been trained, from girlhood, by Swift to play the part in his life that he desired her to play. Vanessa had broken through his plans and defences, and set a chord in him vibrating that never stopped, and that in his heart of hearts he did not want to stop. It was not, as Vanessa was one day pathetically to fear, merely to give her pleasure that he recalled again and again, in the vivid secret language of lovers — so strangely different from 'the little language' of the *Journal* — all the scenes of their past intimacies. It was because he also took pleasure in dwelling upon them. There is nothing remotely like them in all the *Journal* to Stella, or in his birthday poems to her, or in the restrained account of her which he wrote on her death.

Why then did he not marry Vanessa, as she had hoped, and others had expected? We need not embark upon barren speculations concerning a possible physical incapacity. There is no real evidence for them at all; and it is plain enough that when, as a man of nearly thirty, he wanted to marry Varina, no thought of such an obstacle entered his head. After that momentary aberration, he barricaded himself as thoroughly as a man of strong purpose and consuming ambition can, against the possibility of falling in love. He settled in his mind that all he wanted from a woman could be had from Stella on his own terms, which he was unconscious of having imposed on her. Neither was she conscious of it. She wanted just what he wanted. Perhaps she would never have wanted anything else, if Vanessa had never appeared. But Vanessa did appear. She fell in love with Swift, and he to some degree with her. When she avowed her passion, he did not, because he could not, repudiate it. And, had there been no Stella, we believe he would have married her, in spite of all his plans and resolutions.

But, if his reason told him he was free to do so, his conscience did not admit it. He had shaped and trained Stella to his purposes, or what he had thought his purposes. He could not discard her now. But neither could he discard Vanessa. That his heart forbade. The thrilling intimacy was precious to him. If only he had felt towards Stella, what he felt towards Vanessa, things would have been simple enough. He would have married her, and been impregnable to the appeal of the younger woman.

When he returned to Ireland after the death of the Queen, his mind was made up. His duty towards Stella forbade him to think of marrying Vanessa. But he felt a kind of resentment towards Stella, both for what she made him resign, and for what she was. Why had she not Vanessa's magic? Why were her ministrations and Vanessa's so different? The memory of Vanessa's fingers on his dizzy and aching head was one thing; Stella's constrained condolence quite another. And, for her part, Stella, with vague or definite reports of Vanessa beating in her mind, would at the least refrain from pressing her attentions on him, or more likely withdraw into wounded silence. Even if she had been praeternaturally generous and forgiving, she would have found him as unapproachable as an injured bear.

3

That, it seems, is the explanation of the verses *In Sickness*. The illness, in so far as it was physical, did not last long. It was primarily a mental condition. Swift was sick in heart and mind: for the moment at least, utterly disenchanted, with the collapse of all his great hopes, with the prospect of permanent exile, with Stella herself, who became the symbol and scapegoat of his discomfiture; depressed, too, by the enforced resignation of his intimacy with Vanessa. While he was in England he could temporize, live in the moment, put off the evil day of decision. But now it had come and he loathed it.

It is easy for the moralist to say what he ought to have done. He ought to have told Vanessa clearly that his obligation to Stella made it imperative for him to break with her. But Swift's fundamental tenderness and need of tenderness was far greater than is usually believed. Beyond a certain point he could not go, either in hurting her or hurting himself. He could not really break with Vanessa. He needed her, almost as much as she needed him. And her need of him was extreme. She was now almost alone in the world. Her mother and brothers were dead, her young sister was ailing, and she was involved in protracted litigation to secure her inheritance. She had a real claim to his protection. One has but to picture her, moping with her elbows on her knees in the sad great house at Cellbridge, echoing with the roar of the Liffey that foams through the garden, to feel how humanly impossible it was for Swift to abandon her now.

So the relation lingered on. How often Swift saw her we do not know though on one occasion she complained of a ten-week interval as inordinate. But she lived by the memory of their last meeting and the anticipation of their next, appealing continually — and never altogether in vain — to the tenderness she knew was in him.

On the other side, Stella endured the torment of uncertainty. Somewhere about this time she wrote the heartfelt lines *On Jealousy*:

> O shield me from his rage, celestial Powers!
> This tyrant that embitters all my hours.
> Ah, Love, you've poorly played the monarch's part;
> You conquer'd, but you can't defend my heart:
> So bless'd was I throughout thy happy reign,
> I thought this monster banish'd from thy train;
> But you would raise him to support your throne,
> And now he claims your empire as his own.
> Or tell me, Tyrants, have you both agreed
> That where one reigns, the other must succeed?

They may have been written before, or after Swift's secret marriage to Stella. Of the fact of the marriage, there can be little reasonable doubt. It was asserted by Orrery; it was accepted as unquestionable by Delany, who if he could have controverted Orrery on the point would not have hesitated to do so; it was accepted by Deane Swift; it was accepted by the younger Sheridan, and by his father. It is, indeed, compassed by a cloud of witnesses: all Swift's Irish friends and contemporaries are agreed upon it. That they wrote after his death is true, because they could not have written about it while he was alive. And there is, besides, the letter of the Bishop of Meath to Archbishop Wake on July 27, 1723 on the occasion of Vanessa's death: 'In April last she discovered the D. was married to Mrs. Johnson (a nll. daughter of Sir W. Temple, a very good woman) . . .'[4] That the Bishop was Swift's bitter enemy is beside the point. He does not reckon his marriage to Stella as one of Swift's misdeeds, and he sets it down as a plain matter of fact. The tradition is that the marriage ceremony was performed by Swift's old friend St. George Ashe, the Bishop of Clogher, in the garden of the Deanery at Clogher, some time in 1716.*

The story, as told by Sheridan, is that 'oppressed by love, jealousy and disappointment', Stella's health began visibly to decline. Whereupon Swift employed the Bishop of Clogher, as a common friend, to find out the cause of her dangerous dejection.

> Upon this application Mrs. Johnson opened her mind fully to this friend. She told him that from the peculiarity of her circumstances and the singular connection she had with Swift for so many years, there had been great room given for the tongue of slander to exert itself. That she had learned to bear with this patiently, as she had reason to expect that all reports of that sort would be effaced by marriage, as soon as Swift should be in circumstances to make her a proposal of that nature. That she saw now with the deepest concern, ever since his promotion, his behaviour to her had been wholly changed, and a cold indifference had succeeded to the warmest professions of eternal affection. That the necessary consequence would be, an indelible stain fixed upon her character, which was much dearer to her than life.[5]

To this, Sheridan says, Swift replied that he had early in life laid down two maxims about marriage: the first, not to marry unless he were possessed of a decent provision for a family; the second, not to marry unless this should happen while he could reasonably expect to have children. As to the first, he was still in debt; and he was now too old. (He was forty-eight or forty-nine.) If he could have married consistently with these maxims, Stella would have been his choice. As things were, he was prepared to go through the ceremony on two conditions: that they should live as before, and their marriage should be kept an absolute secret. Stella accepted marriage on these conditions: it would at least remove the fear of his marrying Vanessa.

Sheridan claims to have had these details from Mrs. Sican, who was a friend of Stella's and Swift's. If they are authentic, they must have come from Stella herself. But, details apart, we accept Sheridan's story as substantially true: not only because of the unanimity of the competent witnesses, but equally because the marriage seems necessary to account for the subsequent catastrophe in the relations of Swift and Vanessa. Swift married Stella, against his real inclination, in order to calm her apprehensions and

* See Appendix XI.

secure her against uncertainty. That it was a marriage which did not change their actual relations stands in the nature of the case. Nevertheless, it was something more than an empty form. If it was not, in the true sense, a marriage, it was at least a solemn and binding renunciation of his right to marry any other woman. Having made it (says the moralist), he should have told Vanessa. But — what good would it have done? Why hurt Vanessa, as it were wantonly? To a marriage that was a real marriage with him, Vanessa had as true a claim as Stella. If, in order to give Stella some feeling of security, he had married her only in form, justice required that he should not take the last comfort from Vanessa, and drive her to despair. It was better, much better (he could say to himself) that Vanessa should know nothing at all of what he had done. That she, after she had come to Ireland, veritably believed or hoped that Swift might marry her, is unlikely. There is not one of her letters that indicates, or hints at, any such hope; and the letter he wrote to her on leaving England offers not a gleam. What she did hope for was a continuation of their intimacy: and that, so far as he could, he gave her. What she did expect was that he would not marry another woman, simply because she believed he loved her. In this belief she was not mistaken. There are letters of his which make it clear that he did.

4

There is a brief group of letters between Swift and Vanessa which appears to belong to the winter of 1714-15; then there is nothing till July 1719, when there is another group of letters which ends ten months before Vanessa's death on June 2, 1723. From the first group of letters it is difficult to say whether Swift was really trying to bring the relation to an end, as is often supposed. Swift's position during the months that followed her coming to Ireland in November 1714 was inordinately difficult. Besides his own depression, he had to contend with a very real hostility in Dublin. He was believed to have been hand in glove with a ministry suspected of trying to bring in the Pretender; and the Anglo-Irish were almost solid in their detestation and fear of Jacobitism. Swift sincerely believed that there was no ground for suspicion of the Oxford ministry; but he was mistaken. There was ground for suspicion, and when Ormond and Bolingbroke joined the Pretender, suspicion became certainty to the ordinary man. Swift was inevitably involved in it. Even Archbishop King (who had been made one of the new Lords Justices) believed that it might turn out that Swift was deeply implicated in a Jacobite plot. Swift had an exceedingly difficult path to tread, at the best. King was both his political and ecclesiastical superior.

It would have been fatal for Swift to compromise himself in a matter of moral conduct. It took him five years of circumspect behaviour to get into a position from which he could safely emerge as the Anglo-Irish champion.

Therefore it was imperative that, in the winter of 1714-15, he should behave distantly towards Vanessa, and urge the necessity of extreme discretion in their contacts. It is unlikely that his behaviour to Vanessa was influenced by any feeling of disloyalty to Stella. Indeed, it is unlikely that Swift thought his loyalty to Stella was in any way involved. In his own eyes, his relations to both women were perfectly compatible. Neither of them had, by his 'rational' standards, any right to be jealous of the other. What he had to overcome, if he was to respond to Vanessa's pathetic appeals for advice and help, was his fear of being dangerously compromised as the unpopular and suspected Dean of St. Patrick's. The evidence is that, in this respect, he behaved with a good deal of courage. He appears to have met Vanessa frequently, if not regularly, in Dublin: so frequently indeed that it was common gossip that he was in love with her.[6] At this Stella took alarm, and prevailed on him to enter into formal marriage with her.

From Swift's point of view it was an unreasonable demand, for he had no intention of marrying Vanessa. Having given way to it, he had no intention of abandoning Vanessa. But Vanessa was, in her different way, even more importunate. She wanted more of him than he could give. She had come to depend on him in a way Stella had never done. He recognized the claim, indeed he was not displeased by it, but for sheer self-preservation tried to prevent the web from being too tightly drawn round him.

> I ever feared the tattle of this nasty town [he wrote to her] and told you so, and that was the reason why I said to you long ago, that I would see you seldom while you were in Ireland, and I must beg you to be easy, if for some time I visit you seldomer, and not in so particular a manner. I will see you at the latter end of the week if possible. These are accidents in life that are necessary and must be submitted to, and tattle, by the help of discretion, will wear off.[7]

That was written at the height of his embarrassment by rumours, and at a guess, near the time when he was married to Stella. Nevertheless, he intends to see her soon. But a woman, in Vanessa's position, cannot make the effort to be fair. What seems to be her reply to this letter is a mixture of anguish and reproach.

> Well! now I plainly see how great a regard you have for me. You bid me be easy, and you would see me as often as you could; you had better have said as often as you could get the better of your inclinations

so much, or as often as you remembered there was such a person in the world. If you continue to treat me as you do, you will not be made uneasy by me long. It is impossible to describe what I have suffered since I saw you last; I am sure I could have borne the rack much better than those killing, killing words of yours. Sometimes I have resolved to die without seeing you more, but those resolves, to your misfortune, did not last long; for there is something in human nature which prompts one so to find relief in this world, I must give way to it, and beg you would see me, and speak kindly to me, for I am sure you would not condemn anyone to suffer what I have done, could you but know it. The reason I write to you is because I cannot tell it you, should I see you; for when I begin to complain, then you are angry, and there is something in your look so awful that it strikes me dumb. Oh! that you may but have so much regard for me left, that this complaint may touch your soul with pity. I say as little as ever I can. Did you but know what I thought, I am sure it would move you. Forgive me, and believe me, I cannot help telling you this, and live.[8]

It pierces the heart still; and there is not much doubt that Swift's heart was pierced, though he tried to stop her from writing to him. At this period he was always afraid of her letters miscarrying, and it was not until his position in Dublin had radically changed that he at all encouraged her to write. By sending him a letter, it is plain, she was disobeying orders. Thus the absence of any correspondence between them for at least three years is rather an indication of frequent meetings than of the opposite.

But there is some external evidence that for some time after Swift's marriage with Stella, when, according to Deane Swift, he became 'abundantly more sparing of his visits' to Vanessa, she, oppressed by the ultimate hopelessness of her situation, tried to bring herself to return to England. From a letter of Archbishop King it appears that towards the end of 1717 Vanessa contemplated selling her entangled property in Ireland.

I have seen Mrs. Vanhomrigh and her sister several times, and gave them the best advice I could. It seems to me there has been a great deal of ill management in the family, and that the consideration thereof should make them more cautious for the future. I confess I did not approve their resolution of selling their estate and turning it into money in order to their living in London, which seemed the notion and design; that way of living succeeded so ill with their mother that in my opinion it was advisable for them to change it.[9]

And, eighteen months later, Erasmus Lewis wrote to her, commiserating with her on the delays in her lawsuit, and suggesting a composition. 'Your removal into this country of which you have so often given me hopes would have at least one good effect that it would make you forget the disagreeable scene of Ireland and Law.'[10] But, however often she spoke of returning to England, she could not tear herself away. And the absence of any 'complaining letter' from Vanessa tells heavily against any unbearable interruption of her contact with Swift. That she should have dreamed of escaping from the bondage of her love is as intelligible as that she lacked the strength to do it.

The question has been asked — as though it were a problem — why Vanessa kept copies of her letters to Swift; and it has been suggested that it was in order to be able to bring pressure to bear upon him. The suggestion is unnecessary and unjust. The implication that Vanessa kept copies of her letters in order, virtually, to blackmail Swift into marrying her is absurd. Vanessa knew Swift far too well to imagine that such a proceeding would have any other effect than to close his heart against her for ever. Besides, the letters in themselves supply the obvious reasons why she preserved her drafts of them. Not only were they precious to her; but she took great pains with them. She was Swift's pupil, as well as his lover. She was always conscious of him as a critic of her performances — of

> The master's secret joy
> To hear in school the finest boy.

She was equally conscious of the possibility of a not so secret frown. She drafted her letters, and copied them again. She was never quite unafraid of him. Much of the peculiar pathos of her letters comes from this.

5

When on May 12, 1719, their letters begin again, Swift is pouring out praise upon her in bad French, in reply to a letter of hers in French which has not survived. It looks as though he wrote with the idea of setting up Vanessa's morale while he was absent on one of the long country journeys for his health's sake — half visit, half tour — which became part of the pattern of his life in Ireland. In any case, the eulogy of Vanessa was extraordinary. 'Croyez moi [he wrote], s'il y a chose croyable au monde, que je pense tout ce que vous pouvez souhaiter de moi, et que tous vos désirs seront toujours obéi, comme de commandements qu'il sera impossible de violer.' He then hopes that she will spend part of the summer in her country house at Cellbridge: which shows that she lived chiefly in Dublin. 'Vous aurez vos vers à revoir', he continues. 'Quand j'aurai mes pensées et mon temps libre; la muse viendra.' This must refer to *Cadenus & Vanessa*; and it probably means not that Vanessa is to revise the poem (as the French suggests) but that she shall have it back again when Swift has done so.

His letter continues with a high compliment on the excellence of the French in hers, compared to which his own is pitiable. 'Il faut vous connoître long-tems de connoître toutes vos perfections; toujours en vous voyant et entendant, il en paroissent des nouvelles qui estoient auparavant cachées.'

> Que je suis sot moy de vous repondre en même langage, vous qui estes incapable d'aucune sottise; si ce n'est l'estime qu'il vous plait d'avoir pour moy; car il n'y a point de merite ni aucune preuve de mon bon goût de trouver en vous tout ce que la nature a donnée à un mortel, je veux dire l'honneur, la vertue, le bon sens, l'esprit, le douceur, l'agrément, et la fermeté d'ame. Mais en vous cachant comme vous faites, le monde ne vous connoit pas, et vous perdez l'eloge des millions de gens. Depuis que j'avois l'honneur de vous connoitre, j'ai toujours remarqué, que, ni en conversation particulière ni generale, aucun mot a echappé de votre bouche qui pouvoit etre mieux exprimé; et je vous jure qu'en faisant souvent la plus severe critique, je ne pouvois jamais trouver aucun defaut en vos actions, ni en vos parolles: la coquetrie, l'affectation, la pruderie sont des imperfections que vous n'avez jamais connu.
>
> Et avec tout cela, croyez-vous qu'il est possible de ne vous estimer au dessus du reste du genre humain? Quelles bestes en jûppes sont, les plus excellentes de celles, que je vois semées dans le monde, au prix de vous; en les voyant, en les entendant, je dis cent foix le jour ne parle, ne regarde, ne pense, ne fait rien commes ces miserables. Sont ce du même sexe — de meme espece de creatures? Quelle cruauté! de fair mépriser autant de gens, qui, sans songer de vous, seroient assez supportables. Mais il est tems de vous delasser, et de vous dire adieu. Avec tout le respecte, la sincerité et la estime du monde, je suis, et seray toujours.

What was Vanessa to make of that? What, indeed, are we? Are we to suppose that, by some tacit convention with himself, Swift excluded Stella from the comparison? Are we to suppose that he was entirely insincere. Whether the eulogy was extravagant, we have no means of telling — no one except Swift himself seems to have known Vanessa intimately.

That is often forgotten. From what we can gather — and it is implicit in the description of her in *Cadenus & Vanessa* — she seems to have maintained an impenetrable reserve towards the rest of the world, and to have lived aloof and withdrawn. She mixed with society with reluctance; and society retaliated by imputing her aloofness to conceit. More likely, it was shyness. Orrery claims to describe her.

Vanessa was excessively vain ... She was fond of dress: impatient to be admired: very romantic in her turn of mind: superior, in her own opinion, to all her sex: full of pertness, gaiety, and pride: not without some agreeable accomplishments, but far from being either beautiful or genteel: ambitious, at any rate, to be esteemed a wit; and with that view always affecting to keep company with wits: a great reader, and a violent admirer of poetry: happy in the thoughts of being reputed Swift's concubine: but still aiming and intending to be his wife. By nature haughty, and disdainful, looking with the pity of contempt upon her inferiors, and with the smiles of self-approbation upon her equals: but upon Dr. Swift with the eyes of love. Her love was founded in vanity, or, to use a more fashionable phrase, in taste.[11]

The description is worthless. Orrery had never known her, and did not come to Ireland until ten years after her death. His picture is palpably based on a hostile and perverted reading of *Cadenus & Vanessa*. To the Bishop of Meath she was 'a pretended vain wit'; but he did not know her at all. Erasmus Lewis knew her and gave an eye to her affairs in London; but none of her letters to him (or indeed to any other person than Swift) have survived. Charles Ford knew her, but never mentions her in his letters; but neither does he mention Stella, whom he knew even better. The subject of his women friends was *tabu* in Swift's correspondence with others.

The truth is that all that we really know about Vanessa comes from the poem and the letters. The letters show that, at least after coming to Ireland, she had no friends save Swift and her younger sister. She refers to nobody, and we can refer to nobody for her, except Swift himself. If his praise of her in his French letter seems inordinate, we must acknowledge that it is entirely in tune with the eulogy in his poem.

We must, therefore, regard the tribute paid to Vanessa in the French letter as Swift's sincere opinion of her. But, though it must have been intoxicating to receive, it is not fair to describe the letter as a love-letter. That Swift felt that he could safely write it indicates rather that he thought they had reached a basis of mutual understanding and had established a relation midway between friendship and love, in which they could speak the truth to each other. The balance may have been precarious, and even perilous. But, at any rate for a time, they both believed in its stability, and there followed a period in which Vanessa was contented and happy. Her next letter, which belongs to the following year, 1720, is blithe and gay.

Is it possible that again you will do the very same thing I warned you of so lately? I believe you thought I only rallied when I told you the other night that I would pester you with letters. Did not I know you very well, I should think you knew but little of the world, to imagine that a woman would not keep her word whenever she promised anything that was malicious. Had you not better a thousand times throw away one hour at some time or other of the day, than to be interrupted in your business at this rate? For I know 'tis as impossible for you to burn my letters without reading them, as 'tis for me to avoid reproving you when you behave yourself so wrong.[12]

She then gaily promises to use black art upon him, if he is recalcitrant, to compel him to come to her: which will be very inconvenient for him, if he is brought by force, 'perhaps at a time when you have the most agreeable engagement in the world'. However, she is in no hurry for her revenge, so that it is still in his power to turn all this fury of hers into good humour — 'and more, I assure you'. 'Come at what time you please, you can never fail of being very well received.' Swift replied, just as gaily:

If you write as you do, I shall come the seldomer, on purpose to be pleased with your letters, which I never look into without wondering how a brat who cannot read can possibly write so well . . . But raillery apart, I think it inconvenient for a hundred reasons, that I should make your house a sort of constant dwelling place. I will certainly come as often as I conveniently can, but my health, and the perpetual run of ill weather hinders me from going out in the morning; and my afternoons are taken up, I know not how, that I am in rebellion with a dozen people beside yourself, for not seeing them. For the rest you need make use of no other black art besides your ink. It is a pity your eyes are not black, or I would have said the same of them; but you are a white witch and can do no mischief. If you have employed any of your art on the black scarf, I defy it for one reason: guess.[13]

No doubt Vanessa guessed, but we cannot. None of the many cryptic allusions in Swift's letters were lost on her. But it is plain enough that she was happy at this moment, and that they were seeing one another frequently, always in Dublin. By this time, it is true, Swift's position in the city, and in Ireland, had completely changed. He was popular in the liberty of St. Patrick's and beyond, for his practical benevolence and his identification with the Irish interest. The little group of loyal and devoted Irish intimates had formed itself round him. The need for excessive circumspection was gone. He was well on the way to having established his right to be a law unto himself. The evidence points to a relative freedom of intercourse between him and Vanessa. Two years later, when he was on one of his country journeys, plagued with bad weather, he wrote to her:

It would have been infinitely better once a week to have met Kendall and so forth, where one might pass three or four hours in drinking coffee in the morning, or dining tête à tête and drinking coffee again until seven. (June 1, 1722)

A little later, he fills out the picture:

I see you this moment as you are visible at ten in the morning, and now you are asking your questions round, and I am answering them with a great deal of affected delays, and the same scene has passed forty times, as well as the other, from two to seven, longer than the first by two hours, yet each has ses agremens particuliers. (August 8, 1722)

Mr. Ball discovered that one Kendall carried on business as a bookbinder in the Dublin parish where Vanessa lived and supposed that they met at his house. At any rate, it is clear that they met once a week when Swift was in Dublin, either for three hours in the morning, or for five in the afternoon; and this had evidently happened for a long period. The phrase 'drinking coffee' had always been hovering about their relation. Now, it begins to recur insistently. From Horace Walpole onwards critics have often put a sinister interpretation upon the phrase. It is true that Swift's cryptic and allusive mode of expression makes this possible; but it is mistaken. 'Drinking coffee' in their private language means no more, and no less, than the whole happening of their meetings together — their delight in each other, their conversation, their kisses. No doubt, as someone has said, if these phrases had been produced in evidence against Swift in a law court — what happened to Mr. Pickwick through 'chops and tomato sauce'? — they would have told against him. Nevertheless, they are innocent. Even though nine hundred and ninety-nine men out of a thousand would find it impossible not to be thrown off their balance in such a relation, it is no argument against Swift. He was the man in a thousand.

6

To return to 1720. In July Vanessa left Dublin for Cellbridge. She had seen Swift just before she left, and he had promised to write to her by the end of the week and to send her some verses he had written to her. He sat down to perform his promise, but did not finish in time; perhaps because he wrote to her sister Molkin as well. Moreover, there were delays in getting the letter delivered.

I am now writing on Wednesday night [he said] when you are hardly settled at home, and it is the first hour of leisure I have had, and it

may be Saturday before you have it, and then there will be Governor
Huff, and to make you more so, I here enclose a letter to poor Molkin,
which I will command her not to show you because it is a love-letter . . .
Your friend sent me the verses he promised, which I here transcribe.

> Nymph, would you learn the only art
> To keep a worthy lover's heart;
> First, to adorn your person well,
> In utmost cleanliness excel:
> And though you must the fashions take,
> Observe them but for fashion's sake:
> The strongest reason will submit
> To virtue, honour, sense and wit.
> To such a nymph, the wise and good
> Cannot be faithless, if they would,
> For vices all have different ends,
> But virtue still to virtue tends;
> And when your lover is not true
> 'Tis virtue fails in him, or you:
> And either he deserves disdain,
> Or you without a cause complain.
>   But here Vanessa cannot err,
> Nor are those rules applied to her:
> For who could such a nymph forsake,
> Except a blockhead or a rake;
> Or how could she her heart bestow
> Except where wit and virtue grow . . .

The questions which you were used to ask me you may suppose to be
all answered, just as they used to be after half an hour's debate: *Enten-
dez-vous cela?* You are to have a number of parsons in your neighbourhood, but not one that you love, for your age of loving parsons has
not yet arrived . . .
I hold a wager, there are some lines in this letter you will not understand, though you can read them; so drink your coffee, and remember
you are a desperate chip, and that the lady who calls you bastard, will
be ready to answer all your questions. (July 13, 1720)

The questions, we may suppose, were the traditional questions of the
woman in love: 'Do you love me? Do you love me still? Do you really and
truly love me?' and it was part of the ritual of their meetings that Swift
should fence and tantalize in his reply. He was a master of affectionate
raillery. 'Governor Huff' is exquisite in its way. The last sentence, in
isolation, is cryptic indeed; but the subsequent letters supply a clue. In her
reply, Vanessa says: 'I have asked — all the questions I used, ten thousand

times, and don't find them answered at all to my satisfaction' (July 29, 1720): which Swift misread. 'You do not find' he replied, 'I answer your questions to your satisfaction: prove to me first that it was ever possible to answer anything to your satisfaction, so as you would not grumble in half an hour' (August 4, 1720). Vanessa retorted: 'You wrong me when you say, I did not find that you answered my questions to my satisfaction; what I said was, I had asked those questions as you bid, but could not find them answered to my satisfaction. How could they be answered in absence, since Somnus is not my friend?' (August 8, 1720). Obviously then, 'the lady who called Vanessa bastard' was to answer her questions during sleep. Perhaps the reference is to Pallas in *Cadenus & Vanessa*, where Vanessa is palmed off upon her by Venus as a boy.

It was difficult for Swift to keep the relation tender and affectionate and light-hearted, when the weekly meetings were interrupted, and Vanessa was at Cellbridge. Although there is, as usual, no definite evidence of it, it is pretty certain that both she and her sister were tubercular. Molkin was now in an evident decline, and died in March 1721; Vanessa lasted only two years longer. The situation recalls that of Tom and John Keats. No doubt Vanessa, while she tended her sister, was haunted by the same premonitions of early death as John Keats and was a prey to a twofold melancholy. 'I own,' she replied to Swift's letter with the verses, 'I never expected to have another letter from ,you, for two reasons: first, because I thought you had forgot me, and because I was so very ill that I thought I should have died.' She added but crossed out: 'which if I had, it would have made both you and I easy' (July 29, 1720). The first reason was unjust to Swift: the second has been interpreted in a way unjust to Vanessa, as though it were a pretended illness to elicit his sympathy. There is no reason at all to suppose it was not true.

On the whole, however, Vanessa made a brave effort to keep up her spirits, and tried hard not to worry Swift with letters. He kept up the note of affectionate raillery. If, as it seems, he did not realize how very precarious was her health, he did not add to her worries by telling her the truth about his own, which was beginning to deteriorate.

> If you knew how many little difficulties there are in sending letters to you, it would remove five parts in six of your quarrel . . . It [the letter to Molkin] was the first love-letter I have writ these dozen years [that is, since he met Vanessa], and since I have such ill success I will write no more. Never was a *belle passion* so defeated, but the Governor I hear is jealous, and upon your word you have a vast deal to say to me about it. Mind your nurse-keeping, do your duty, and leave off your huffing.

One would imagine you were in love, by dating your letter August 29th, by which means I received it just a month before it was written . ... I am glad my writing puzzles you, for then your time will be occupied in finding it out; and I am sure it cost me a great many thoughts to make my letters difficult . . . I wish your letters were as difficult as mine, for then they would be of no consequence if they were dropped by careless messengers. A stroke thus — — — — signifies everything that may be said to Cad, at the beginning or conclusion. It is I who ought to be in a huff that anything written by Cad is difficult to Skinage. (August 4, 1720)

At this letter, Vanessa was overjoyed, partly by the sufficient reason he gave for not having kept his promise of a letter to the day, but chiefly because of the opening he gave her to express her endearments in a secret language.

— — — — Cad, you are good beyond expression, and I will never complain again if I can help it; but, with submission, it is you who are so hard to be pleased, though you complain of me. I thought the last letter I wrote you was obscure and constrained enough. I took pains to write it after that manner; it would have been much easier for me to have wrote otherwise . . . Molkin is better, though in a very weak way. Though those that saw me told you nothing of my illness, I do assure you that I was for twenty-four hours as ill as 'twas possible to be, and live . . . We have had a vast deal of thunder and lightning: where do you think I wished to be then, and do you think that was the only time I wished so, since I saw you? I am sorry my jealousy should hinder you from writing more love-letters; for I must chide sometimes, and I wish I could gain by it this instant, as I have done, and hope to do. Is my dating my letter wrong the only sign of my being in love? . . . I am mightily pleased that you talk of being in a huff; it is the first time you ever told me so. I wish I could see you in one. I am now as happy as I can be without seeing — — — Cad. I beg you will continue happiness to your own Skinage. (August 8, 1720)

In his next letter, written almost by return, he tried to continue her happiness. 'Glassheel [Ford] talks of going to see you, and taking me with him, as he goes to his country house.' This was Swift's way of announcing that he had arranged with Ford to pay her a visit. Actually, he had hinted it, even more obliquely, in his previous letter. 'Glassheel is come over . . . Molkin will be so glad to see Glassheel: ay, Molkin?' But Vanessa had not dared to pick up the hint.

Why should Cad's letters be difficult [he goes on]. I assure you ——'s are not at all. I am vexed that the weather hinders you from any pleasure in the country, because walking, I believe, would be of good use to you and Molkin. I reckon you will return a prodigious scholar, a most admirable nurse-keeper . . . and a great drinker of coffee.

I have asked and am assured there is not one beech in all your groves to carve a name on, nor a purling stream for love or money, except a great river which sometimes roars, but never murmurs, just like Governor Huff. We live here in a very dull town, every valuable creature absent, and Cad says he is weary of it, and would rather drink his coffee on the barrenest mountain in Wales, than be king here.

> A fig for partridges and quails —
> Ye dainties, I know nothing of ye;
> But on the highest mount in Wales
> Would choose in peace to drink my coffee.

And you know very well that coffee makes us severe, and grave, and philosophical.

What would you give to have the history of Cad and ———, exactly written, through all its steps, from the beginning to this time? I believe it would do well in verse, and be as long as the other [i.e. *Cadenus & Vanessa*]. I hope it will be done. It ought to be an exact chronicle of twelve years from the time of spilling the coffee to drinking of coffee, from Dunstable to Dublin, with every single passage since. There would be the chapter of the blister; the chapter of Madam going to Kensington; the chapter of the Colonel's going to France; the chapter of the wedding, with the adventure of the lost key; of the strain; of the joyful return; two hundred chapters of madness; the chapter of long walks; the Berkshire surprise; fifty chapters of little times; the chapter of Chelsea; the chapter of swallow and cluster; a hundred whole books of myself and *so low*; the chapter of hide and whisper; the chapter of who made it so; my sister's money.

Cad bids me tell you, that if you complain of his puzzling you with difficult writing, he will give you enough of it . . . (August 13, 1720)

Part of this catalogue of memories has been discussed before; much of it remains entirely obscure. It is, obviously, not consistently chronological. The only part of which one is reasonably certain is that which begins with 'the strain' and ends with 'the Berkshire surprise'. That refers to a sequence of incidents beginning with Swift's journey to Dublin in June 1713 to be installed as Dean. The strain, we learn from a later reference, was the strain by a box of books at London. It was Swift's habit, when he left a London lodging, to put the books he had accumulated into a box and store it. He had six such boxes when he finally left London in August 1714. We imagine that Vanessa helped him with his box in June 1713. The joyful return was his return in September 1713; and the 'two hundred chapters of madness' followed that. This natural interpretation accords with the impression made by Vanessa's letters to Swift during his absence in Ireland in 1713, that it was at this time that their relation came nearest to a love-affair, that Vanessa's hopes and happiness were at their highest, and Swift himself most dependent on their intimacy.

The recital of the memories, and the promise of a visit, had their effect. Vanessa was in ecstasy.

— — — Cad, is it possible that you will come and see me? I beg for God's sake you will; I would give the world to see you here (and Molkin would be extremely happy). Do you think the time long since I saw you? I did design seeing you this week, but will not stir in hopes of your coming here. I beg you will write two or three words by the bearer, to let me know if you think you will come this week. I shall have the note tonight. You make me happy beyond expression by your goodness. It would be too much once to hope for such a history; if you had laid a thousand pounds that I should not understand your letter, you had lost it. Tell me sincerely did those circumstances crowd on you, or did you recollect them only to make me happy? (August 14, 1720)

Perhaps the best answer to Vanessa's pathetic question is some words of Swift to Ford years before: 'I think upon what St. Evremont says of Devotes that when they call their sins to mind in order for repentance, the truth of the matter is they take a delight in remembering them.'[14]

Swift went to Cellbridge, for the first time, soon after. Vanessa was now tethered there by the needs of her dying sister, and could make only flying visits to Dublin. Swift wrote to her on October 15:

I sit down with the first opportunity I have to write to you, and the Lord only knows when I can find conveniency to send the letter; for all the morning I am plagued with impertinent visits or impertinent business below any man of sense or honour to endure, if it were any way avoidable. Dinners and afternoons and evenings are spent abroad, and in walking to help and avoid spleen as far as I can; so that when I am not so good a correspondent as I could wish, you are not to quarrel and be Governor, but to impute it to my situation; and to conclude infallibly that I have the same respect, esteem, and kindness for you I ever professed to have, and shall ever preserve, because you will always merit the utmost that can be given you, especially if you go on to read and still further improve your mind, and the talents that nature has given you . . .

I am in much concern for poor Molkin, and the more, because I am sure you are so too. You ought to be as cheerful as you can for both your sakes, and read pleasant things that will make you laugh, and not sit moping with your elbows on your knees on a little stool by the fire. It is most infallible that riding would do Molkin more good than any other thing, provided fair days and warm clothes be provided ...

Swift had a fanatical belief in the efficacy of violent exercise; but Molkin, by this time, was beyond the scope of such drastic remedies. Continuing his letter on October 18, he wrote:

I am getting an ill head in this cursed town for want of exercise. I wish I were to walk with you fifty times about the garden, and then — drink your coffee. I was sitting last night with half a score of both sexes for an hour, and grew as weary as a dog ... Everybody grows silly and disagreeable, or I grow monkish and splenetic, which is the same thing. Conversation is nothing but South Sea, and the ruin of the Kingdom, and scarcity of money. I had a thousand times [rather] hear the Governor chide two hours without reason.

Two days later, he concludes the same letter with this:

The Governor was with me at six o'clock this morning, but did not stay two minutes, and deserves a chiding, which you must give when you drink your coffee next. I hope to send this letter tomorrow. I am a good deal out of order in my head after a little journey I made and ate too much I suppose, or travelling in a coach after it. I am now sitting at home alone, and will go write to Molkins — — So adieu
— — — —

Presumably, Vanessa had appeared to him in a dream — too briefly.

So ends the correspondence which can be certainly assigned to 1720. It is intimate and genuinely affectionate. Their relation may not have been all that Vanessa desired; but she must have felt that Swift was giving her all he could — and that not from öbligation or enforcement, but from the desire of his heart.

CHAPTER XIX

THE DEATH OF VANESSA

MEANWHILE, Stella's situation was not enviable. She must have known that Swift was seeing Vanessa regularly, and seeing her alone: an intimacy which he never permitted himself with her. Swift, being what he was, and having convinced himself that Stella had no rational cause for jealousy, would have thought it beneath him to conceal from her his continued relation with Vanessa; and probably beneath her as well. That Stella was not wholly the rational creature into which he had tried to fashion her was a difficulty he chose to ignore. He had had to surrender something to womanly reality, or weakness, by marrying her: he would not surrender more.

On March 13, 1719 — that is, just two months before his French eulogy of Vanessa — he wrote the first of his birthday poems to Stella. At the time he composed it he was engaged in re-working *Cadenus & Vanessa.* Perhaps that put into his head that he must celebrate Stella as well; and that again, by some engaging scruple of even-handed justice, was the stimulus to the panegyric on Vanessa. 'I write nothing but verses of late,' he told Ford, 'and they are all panegyrics' (December 8, 1719). He was smiling to himself at his own ambiguous occupations.

In his poem to Stella, he made her, as he had made Vanessa, four years younger than she really was. Actually, at this date, Stella was thirty-eight, and Vanessa thirty-one.

> Stella this day is thirty-four,
> (We shan't dispute a year or more.)
> However, Stella, be not troubled,
> Although thy size and years are doubled
> Since first I saw thee at sixteen,
> The brightest virgin on the green;
> So little is thy form declined;
> Made up so largely in thy mind.
> 　O, would it please the gods to split
> Thy beauty, size, and years, and wit!
> No age could furnish out a pair
> Of nymphs so graceful, wise, and fair;
> With half the lustre of your eyes,
> With half thy wit, thy years, and size.

> And then, before it grow too late,
> How should I beg of gentle fate,
> (That either nymph might have her swain,)
> To split my worship too in twain.[1]

Was it some ironic impulse to veracity which engendered the odd conceit of dividing Stella into two nymphs? One feels that the idea of splitting his worship in twain was too close to his actual condition to have been pure accident. And one thing more is noticeable when we come to the verses fresh from the Vanessa correspondence: they lack immediacy.

The verses *To Stella, visiting me in my sickness*, which belong to 1720, strike us as much more considered, and more heartfelt. The opening lines are curiously reminiscent of *Cadenus & Vanessa*.

> Pallas, observing Stella's wit
> Was more than for her sex was fit,
> And that her beauty, soon or late,
> Might breed confusion in the state,
> In high concern for human kind,
> Fix'd honour in her infant mind.[2]

Vanessa's soul, in *her* poem, had likewise been by Pallas

> suddenly endued
> With justice, truth, and fortitude
> With honour which no breath can stain,
> Which malice must attack in vain —

and honour is the first of her attributes in the French encomium. But in Stella's poem Swift defines it; at first, rather obscurely, as answering in things natural to faith in things divine; then, as comprehending all the virtues; finally, and more usefully, as the power of disinterested choice of the good — not what is good for me, but what is objectively good. One might call it moral integrity. By virtue of her honour Stella cannot fail her promise, or her friends, and is immune from affected feminine fears. After this expatiation on Stella's honour, which is the main theme of the poem, he reaches more familiar ground.

> Her hearers are amazed from whence
> Proceeds that fund of wit and sense;
> Which, though her modesty would shroud,
> Breaks like the sun behind a cloud;
> While gracefulness its art conceals,
> And yet through every motion steals.

> Say, Stella, was Prometheus blind,
> And forming you mistook your kind?
> No, 'twas for you alone he stole
> The fire that forms a manly soul;
> Then, to complete it every way,
> He moulded it with female clay;
> To that you owe the nobler flame,
> To this the beauty of your frame.[3]

We are on the look out for nuances; and there is a nuance of difference between this eulogy of Stella, and that of Vanessa. Vanessa's manly qualities are given by Pallas only; they are qualities of intelligence. To Stella is also attributed manly courage, in a physical sense. There is no suggestion that Vanessa's 'fortitude' or *fermeté d'âme* included this. Stella took deliberate aim with a pistol out of the window and killed a burglar; Vanessa was frightened by thunder and lightning, and longed to be in Swift's arms in a thunderstorm. That, presumably, is the reason why Swift could say it was for Stella *alone* that Prometheus stole the fire that forms a manly soul.

This may appear a refinement; but Swift was trying to satisfy a peculiar, but peculiarly scrupulous, conscience while he was composing these concurrent tributes to Stella and Vanessa. One must not really conflict with the other. By precisely what intellectual and moral casuistry he managed to reconcile the last paragraph of his French prose *éloge* on Vanessa with what he was now saying about Stella may be hard to understand; but at least the poems to each are reconcilable. That Stella's concludes with an expression of his gratitude for her tendance of him.

> Best pattern of true friends, beware!
> You pay too dearly for your care,
> If, while your tenderness secures
> My life, it must endanger yours.[4]

The language of the third poem: *To Stella, who collected and transcribed his verses* (1720) suggests that Swift had chosen his words carefully when he wrote of her as 'best pattern of true friends'.

> Thou, Stella, wert no longer young,
> When first for thee my harp was strung
> Without one word of Cupid's darts,
> Of killing eyes, or bleeding hearts;
> With friendship and esteem possesst,
> I ne'er admitted Love a guest.
> In all the habitudes of life,
> The friend, the mistress, and the wife,

> Variety we shall pursue,
> In pleasure seek for something new . . .
> But his pursuits are at an end,
> Whom Stella chooses for a friend.[5]

There were many words about Cupid's darts in *Cadenus & Vanessa*; and there was no such peremptory exclusion of love. In Stella's poem Swift goes on, at length but not very convincingly, to declare that whereas false poets glorify the transient, true ones celebrate the permanent qualities of those they praise.

> Your virtues safely I commend;
> They on no accidents depend:
> Let malice look with all her eyes,
> She dares not say the poet lies.[6]

But now comes the rub: the criticism which appears to be the main purpose of the verses.

> Stella, when you these lines transcribe,
> Lest you should take them for a bribe,
> Resolv'd to mortify your pride
> I'll here expose your weaker side.
>   Your spirits kindle to a flame,
> Mov'd with the lightest touch of blame;
> And when a friend in kindness tries
> To show you where your error lies,
> Conviction does but more incense;
> Perverseness is your whole defence;
> Truth, judgment, wit, give way to spite,
> Regardless both of wrong and right;
> Your virtues, all suspended, wait,
> Till time has opened reason's gate;
> And, what is worse, your passion bends
> Its force against your nearest friends,
> Which manners, decency, and pride,
> Have taught you from the world to hide;
> In vain; for see, your friend has brought
> To public light your only fault.[7]

'Your nearest friends' is a poetic plural. It is Swift alone on whom the passion is vented; otherwise it could not have been hidden.

It is a fault, he admits, that is often found in a generous mind; and he who suffers from it may be compared to one who endures a southern sun, and, like him,

Must own that pain is largely paid
By generous wines beneath a shade.
   Yet, when I find your passions rise,
And anger sparkling in your eyes,
I grieve those spirits should be spent
For nobler ends by nature meant . . .
   You think this turbulence of blood
From stagnating preserves the flood,
Which, thus fermenting by degrees
Exalts the spirits, sinks the lees.
   Stella, for once your reason wrong;
For should this ferment last too long,
By time subsiding you may find
Nothing but acid left behind. [8]

Whether just or not, it is a memorable criticism of Stella; the more memorable because it is unique. Moreover, it is in striking contrast to his praise of her 'honour' — her disinterestedness and objectivity in pursuit of the good and the true, which he had just been commending. Stella's outbursts of anger, at this particular moment, one feels, must have had their origin in jealousy.

2

   Stella's gusts of passion synchronized with the increased tenderness of Swift's concern for Vanessa which is evident in their correspondence in the autumn of 1720. At least the outlines of the situation are visible. Vanessa's situation would have wrung the heart of a sensitive man. Her younger sister was now dying, and she could not leave her. Apparently, even the weekly meetings with Swift, by which and for which she lived, had to be abandoned. 'Never (she wrote to him) was human creature more distressed than I have been since I came [to Cellbridge]. Poor Molkin has had two or three relapses, and is in so bad a way, that I fear she will never recover. Judge now what a way I am now in, absent from you, and loaded with melancholy on her score.' [9] On the other side Stella's discontent was such that Swift was constrained to withdraw; for it is difficult to find any other explanation for the ten weeks' neglect of which Vanessa complained so bitterly in her next letter.

   Believe me 'tis with the utmost regret that I now complain to you, because I know your good-nature such, that you cannot see any human creature miserable without being sensibly touched. Yet what can I do?

I must either unload my heart, and tell you all its griefs, or sink under the inexpressible distress I now suffer by your prodigious neglect of me. 'Tis now ten long weeks since I saw you, and in all that time I have never received but one letter from you, and a little note with an excuse. Oh! — — — how have you forgot me! You endeavour by severities to force me from you, nor can I blame you; for with the utmost distress and confusion, I behold myself the cause of uneasy reflections to you, yet I cannot comfort you, but here declare, that 'tis not in the power of art, time or accident to lessen the unexpressable passion which I have for — — — Put my passion under the utmost restraint, send me as distant from you as the earth will allow, yet you cannot banish those charming ideas which will ever stick by me while I have the use of memory. Nor is the love I bear you seated only in my soul, for there is not a single atom of my frame that is not blended with it. Therefore, don't flatter yourself that separation will change my sentiments; for I find myself unquiet in the midst of silence, and my heart is pierced with sorrow and love. For Heaven's sake, tell me what has caused this prodigious change on you that I have found of late. If you have the least remains of pity for me, tell me tenderly. No, don't tell it, so that it may cause my present death, and do not suffer me to live a life like a languishing death, which is the only life I can lead, if you have lost any of your tenderness for me.[10]

Vanessa had been trying her best to obey Swift's injunction not to write to him. At this moment he shrank from receiving her letters. They tortured him: the more because he felt he was impotent to relieve her distress. All he could do was to hide himself from it. The attitude was to recur when it was Stella's turn to die. It is not a lovely attitude; but one will judge it according to one's experience. Swift's apparent lack of feeling derived from a fear of being overwhelmed by feeling.

He kept silence; he did not dare to reply to Vanessa's letter. She, for her part, could not hold fast to her partial understanding of him. Her misery demanded the relief of expression, and she wrote to him again.

Tell me sincerely, if you have once wished with earnestness to see me, since I last wrote to you. No, so far from that you have not once pitied me, though I told you how I was distressed. Solitude is insupportable to a mind which is not at ease. I have worn out my days with sighing, and my nights with watching and thinking of —, —, —, — — —, who thinks not of me. How many letters must I send before I shall receive an answer? Can you deny me in my misery the only comfort which I can expect at present? Oh, that I could hope to see you here, or that I could go to you. I was born with violent passions, which terminate all in one — that inexpressible passion which I have for you. Consider the killing emotions which I feel from your neglect, and show some tenderness for me, or I shall lose my senses. Sure, you cannot be so taken up, but you might command a moment to write to me and force your inclinations to do so great a charity.[11]

Vanessa knew, in her heart, that neither tenderness nor charity were lacking in Swift; it was, indeed, they which kept him silent. That was how he was made. But Vanessa's understanding of him was engulfed in the sharpness of her own suffering. Now, having made him a devil, she reacted against her own injustice and raised him again to a god.

I firmly believe, could I know your thoughts (which no human creature is capable of guessing at because never anyone living thought like you) I should find you have often in a rage wished me religious, hoping then I should have paid my devotions to heaven; but that would not spare you, for was I an enthusiast, still you'd be the deity I should worship. What marks are there of a deity, but what you are to be known by? You are at present everywhere; your dear image is always before mine eyes. Sometimes you strike me with that prodigious awe, I tremble with fear; at other times a charming compassion shines through your countenance which revives my soul. Is it not more reasonable to adore a radiant form one has seen, than one only described?

That is not the fancy of a distressed and exalted imagination. It is the most penetrating description of Swift that we have. No one saw him more nearly and clearly than Vanessa, or better comprehended the strange combination of overwhelming compassion and ruthless repression that worked within him.

This time he replied by going to see her. Within a day or two she wrote him a hurried note to say Molkin was dead.

I am surprised and grieved [he wrote] beyond what I can express. I read your letter twice before I knew what it meant, nor can I yet well believe my eyes. Is that poor good creature dead? I observed she looked a little ghastly on Saturday, but it is against the usual way for one in her case to die so sudden. For God's sake, get your friends about you to advise, and to order everything in the forms. It is all you have to do. I want comfort myself in this case, and can give little. Time alone must give it you. Nothing is now your part but decency. I was wholly unprepared against so sudden an event, and pity you most of all creatures at present. (February 27, 1721)

She was no longer tied to Cellbridge, and he began to meet her regularly again. But, apart from her meetings with him, she moped in solitude now that Molkin was gone. He tried to persuade her to go out into society. He wrote to her from Gaulstown where he was staying with the Rochforts, and obeying his own prescription.

> It was not convenient, hardly possible, to write to you before now, though I had a more than ordinary desire to do it, considering the disposition I found you in last, though I hope I left you in a better. I must here beg of you to take more care of your health by company and exercise or else the spleen will get the better of you, than which there is not a more foolish or troublesome disease, and what you have no pretences in the world to, if all the advantages in life can be any defence against it. Cad — assures me, he continues to esteem and value and love you above all things, and so will do to the end of his life, but at the same time entreats you that you will not make yourself or him unhappy by imaginations. The wisest men in all ages have thought it the best course to seize the minutes as they fly, and to make every innocent action an amusement. If you knew how I struggle for a little health; what uneasiness I am at in riding and walking, and refraining from everything agreeable to my taste, you would think it a small thing to take a coach now and then, and converse with fools and impertinents, to avoid spleen and sickness. Without health you will lose all desire of drinking your coffee, and *so low* as to have no spirits. (July 5, 1721)

Swift did not exaggerate; his life had to a large extent become a sheer struggle for health. Increasing dread of the final outcome of his disease gave a desperate energy to his effort to live in the moment. Why should Vanessa not do the same? It was the best; it was all there was to do. He seems not to have realized that she was radically ill, and that much of her depression had a physical origin. 'I am *so low*' was one of her constant expressions, on which he teased her. No doubt she increased her unhappiness by 'imaginations'; but they too were incident to her disease. What were they? Generally, they have been interpreted in a matter-of-fact way as a hope that she might yet be married to Swift. The real evidence for this amounts to nothing. Much more likely the imaginations with which she distressed herself and him were fears that his love and tenderness for her were fading, and that their meetings would be at an end.

> I answer all your questions that you were used to ask Cad — [he continues] and he protests he answers them in the affirmative ... What is this world without being as easy in it as prudence and fortune can make it? I find it every day more silly and insignificant, and conform myself to it for my own ease. I am here as deep employed in other folks ditchings and plantations as if they were my own concern; and think of my

absent friends with delight, and hopes of seeing them happy and being happy with them. Shall you, who have so much honour and good sense, act otherwise to make Cad and yourself miserable? Settle your affairs and quit this scoundrel island, and things will be as you desire. I can say no more, being called away; mais soyez assurée que jamais personne du monde a été aimée, honorée, estimée, adorée par votre ami que vous. I drunk no coffee since I left you, nor intend till I see you again; there is none worth drinking but yours, if *myself* may be the judge. Adieu.

How things could have been as Vanessa desired had she left Ireland is not apparent; nor was Swift wholly serious in the suggestion, since he looked forward to seeing her again. But the substance of his recommendation to her is: 'Be like me! Come to terms with this disappointing life. I should be happier in England; why not you?'

He did not return from Gaulstown to Dublin until October; and there are no other letters, on either side, during his absence. If we may judge of Vanessa's attitude from that during his similar absence in the next year, she was making a valiant effort to be as independent as she could. Their regular meetings were resumed when he returned. It would appear that Stella, by a like effort, had conquered her jealousy. His birthday verses to her were on the familiar theme that the qualities of her mind more than repair the decay of her beauty. They are a little ruthless, as his verses to her always were; but they are reassuring.

> All travellers at first incline
> Where'er they see the fairest sign
> And if they find the chambers neat
> And like the liquor and the meat,
> Will call again, and recommend
> The Angel Inn to every friend.
> And though the painting grows decayed
> The house will never lose its trade
> Nay, though the treacherous tapster, Thomas,
> Hangs a new Angel two doors from us
> As fine as daubers' hands can make it,
> In hopes that strangers may mistake it,
> We think it both a shame and sin
> To quit the old true Angel Inn.[12]

In the circumstances Stella must have read this, and been meant to read it, as an assurance that she could not be displaced by Vanessa; and that perhaps is the reason why she responded with verses on his own birthday.

When men began to call me fair
You interposed your timely care:
You early taught me to despise
The ogling of a coxcomb's eyes;
Showed where my judgment was misplaced;
Refined my fancy and my taste . . .
    You taught how I might youth prolong,
By knowing what was right and wrong;
How from my heart to bring supplies
Of lustre to my fading eyes;
How wit and virtue from within
Send out a smoothness o'er the skin:
Your lectures could my fancy fix
And I can please at thirty-six.[13]

She was, in fact, forty. For the rest, Stella's verses faithfully reflect Swift's praises of her, and impute them all to his teaching. There are lines in them which, at first, sound almost like echoes of *Cadenus & Vanessa*: in particular,

O turn your precepts into laws,
Redeem the women's ruin'd cause,
Retrieve lost empire to our sex,
That men may bow their rebel necks.[14]

But, on reflection, we realize that these were the commonplaces of his 'lectures' to both his women: that they should aim to be the intellectual equals and companions of men. Both had imbibed and obeyed his instruction.

3

Stella's verses were written for his birthday on November 30, 1721, by which time he was meeting Vanessa regularly in Dublin again. He gave her what he had written of *Gulliver* to read, and departed into the country at the end of April 1722. The tone of his letter to her suggests that he felt that, by his mixture of tenderness and firmness, he had brought Vanessa to a more stable frame of mind.

This is the first time [he wrote from Clogher] I have set pen to paper since I left Dublin, having not been in any settled place till ten days ago, and I missed one post by ignorance, and that has stopped me five days. Before that time, I was much out of order by the usual consequences of wet weather and change of drink, neither am I yet established, though much better than I was. The weather has been so constantly bad, that I have wanted all the healthy advantages of the country, and it seems likely to continue so. It would have been infinitely better once a week to have met Kendall and so forth, where one might pass three or four hours in drinking coffee in the morning, or dining *tête à tête* and drinking coffee again till seven. I answer all the questions you can ask me in the affirmative. I remember your detesting and despising the conversation of the world. I have been so mortified with a man and his lady here two days, that it has made me as peevish as — I want a comparison. I hope you are gone, or going to your country seat, though I think you have a term [of the Law Courts] on your hands. I shall be here long enough to receive your answer, and perhaps to write to you again; but then I shall go farther off, if my health continues, and shall let you know my stages. I have been for some days as splenetic as ever you was in your life, which is a bold word. Remember I still enjoin your reading and exercise for the improvement of your mind, and health of your body, and grow less romantic, and talk and act like a man of this world. It is the saying of the world, and I believe you often say, I love myself, but I am *so low* I cannot say it, though your new acquaintance were with you, which I heartily wish for the sake of you and myself. God send you through all your law and reference; and remember that riches are nine parts in ten of all that is good in life, and health is the tenth — drinking coffee comes long after, and yet it is the eleventh, but without the two former you cannot drink it right; and remember the china in the old house, and Ryder Street, and the Colonel's journey to France, and the London wedding, and the sick lady at Kensington, and the indisposition at Windsor, and the strain by the box of books at London. Last year I writ you civilities and you were angry; this year I will write you none, and you will be angry; yet my thoughts are still the same, and I give you leave to be carver. I hope you will let me have some of your money when I see you, which I will honestly pay you again. Repondez moy si vous entendez bien tout cela, et croyez que je serai toujours tout ce que vous desirez. Adieu. (June 1, 1722)

His emphasis that it was the first letter written on his journey was meant to gratify her; so was the assurance that, if the weather prevented the success of his pursuit of health by his country journey, then it was 'infinitely better' to be meeting her. To confess, too, that company had made him (in spite of all his sage advice to her) inexpressibly peevish, and that he had been as melancholy as she ever was, was an acknowledgement that, for all his efforts to struggle against his, their natures were akin. And he certainly did not expect her to believe him serious when he, of all people, declared that riches were nine parts in ten of what was good in life, and health only the tenth. The money she was to pay him, and he was to repay, when they met again, was kisses.

Vanessa, in reply, reproached him for not writing sooner — she had been five weeks without a letter — and rubbed home his confession of the tedium of his company, with pertinent references to *Gulliver*.

Since I saw you, I have gone more into the world than I did for some time past, because you commanded me; and I do protest that I am more and more sick of it every day than other. One day this week I was to visit a great lady that has been a-travelling for some time past, where I found a very great assembly of ladies and beaux dressed (as I suppose) to a nicety. I hope you'll pardon me now I tell you I heartily wished you were a spectator, for I very much question if in your life you ever saw the like scene, or one more extraordinary. The lady's behaviour was blended with so many different characters, I cannot possibly describe it without tiring your patience. But the audience seemed to be a creation of her own, they were so very obsequious. Their forms and gestures were very like those of baboons and monkeys; they all grinned and chattered at the same time, and that of things I did not understand. The room being hung with arras, in which were trees very well described, just as I was considering their beauty and wishing myself in the country with — — —, one of these animals snatched my fan, and was so pleased with me, that it seized me with such a panic that I apprehended nothing less than being carried to the top of the house and served as a friend of yours was, but in this one of their own species came in, upon which they all began to make their grimaces, which opportunity I took and made my escape.
I have not made one single step in either law or reference since I saw you. I meet with nothing but disappointments, yet am obliged to stay in town attending Mr. P. etc., which is very hard. I do declare I have so little joy in life, that I do not care how soon mine ends. For God's sake write to me soon, and kindly, for in your absence your letters are all the joy I have on earth, and sure you are too good-natured to grudge one hour in a week to make any human creature happy. — — — — Cad, think of me and pity me. (June 1722)

It is not the letter of a woman who entertained the faintest hope of marrying him. If ever her passion tended that way, she was now resigned to its inevitable disappointment. Even so, she asks more than he thinks wise to give. Their meeting once a week when he is in Dublin he will allow and enjoy; but not a letter a week in absence. It was a full month before he wrote again, this time from Loughgall.

I have received yours, and have changed places so often since, that I could not assign a place where I might receive an answer from —; and if you be now in the country, and this letter does not reach you in due time after the date, I shall not expect to hear from you, because I leave this place the beginning of August. I am well pleased with the account of your visit, and the behaviour of the ladies. I see every day as silly things among both sexes, and yet endure them for the sake of amusements. The worst thing in you and me is that we are too hard to please, and whether we have not made ourselves so, is the question; at least I believe we have the same reason. One thing I differ from you in, that I do not quarrel with my best friends. I believe you have ten angry passages in your letter, and every one of them enough to spoil two days apiece of riding and walking. We differ prodigiously in one point: I fly from the spleen to the world's end, you run out of your way to meet it. I doubt the bad weather has hindered you much from the diversions of your country house, and put you upon thinking in your chamber.

Swift's oblique compliment is notable. They both find society foolish, because they have been accustomed to each other's; but she quarrels with him, not he with her. Each one of her reproaches is enough to spoil the effect of two days of his riding and walking.

The use I have made of it [the bad weather] is to read I know not how many diverting books of history and travels. I wish you would get yourself a horse, and have always two servants to attend you, and visit your neighbours — the worse the better. There is a pleasure in being reverenced, and that is always in your power, by your superiority of sense and an easy fortune. The best maxim I know in life is, to drink your coffee when you can, and when you cannot, to be easy without it; while you continue to be splenetic, count upon it, I will always preach. Thus much I sympathise with you, that I am not cheerful enough to write, for, I believe, coffee once a week is necessary for that. I can sincerely answer all your questions, as I used to do, but then I give all possible way to amusements, because they preserve my temper as exercise does my health; and without health and good humour I had rather be a dog. I have shifted scenes oftener than I ever did in my life, and I believe, have lain in thirty beds since I left the town; and always drew up the clothes with my left hand, which is a superstition I have learnt these ten years ... Be cheerful and read and ride and laugh, as Cad — used to advise you long ago. I hope your affairs are in some better settlement. I long to see you in figure and equipage; pray do not lose that taste. Farewell. (July 13, 1722)

Whether or not he stretched a point to comfort her, the implication is that he needed her company once a week to keep him cheerful. But when that is not possible, by reason of the quest of health, then one must try to be easy, by seeking distraction as much as possible. To give way to melancholy is the sin against which he will always preach. If in this he did not speak to Vanessa's condition — and how could he have done? — he was nevertheless most certainly sincere. The melancholy he had to fight was at least as deep as hers. The cryptic reference to drawing up the bed-clothes with his left hand has been supposed to be connected with Vanessa's visit to him at Windsor in the summer of 1712.

—, —, —, Cad [Vanessa replied], I am, and cannot avoid being in the spleen to the last degree. Everything combines to make me so. Is it not very hard to have so good a fortune as I have, and yet no more command of that fortune, than if I had no title to it ... Here am I obliged to stay in this odious town, attending and losing my health and humour. Yet this and all other disappointments in life I can bear with ease, but that of being neglected by —, —, —, Cad. He has often told me that the best maxim in life, and always held by the wisest in all ages, is to seize the moments as they fly, but those happy moments fly out of the reach of the unfortunate. Pray tell — — — Cad I do not remember any angry passages in my letter, and I am sorry if [they] appeared so to him. Spleen I cannot help, so you must excuse it. I do [all] I can to get the better of it; and it is too strong for me. I have read more since I saw Cad, than I did in a great while past, and chose those books which required the most attention, on purpose to engage my thoughts, but I find the more I think the more unhappy I am.
I had once a mind not to have wrote to you, for fear of making you uneasy to find me so dull, but I could not keep to that resolution, for the pleasure of writing to you. The satisfaction I have in you remembering me, when you read my letter, and the delight I have in expecting one from — — — Cad, makes me rather choose to give you some uneasiness than to add to my own.

This time Swift answered promptly, for his reply is dated August 7, 1722. He does not take her to task for breaking the rules by writing to him. As before, by promising to let her know his next settled address, he rather invites her letters. The delay in her law affairs, he says, is due to her disdaining to exercise her power and skill to expedite them. He continued his letter the next day.

Yesterday I rode twenty-nine miles without being weary, and I wish little Heskinage could do as much. Here I leave this letter to travel one way while I go another, but where I do not know, nor what cabins and bogs are in my way. I see you this moment as you are visible at ten in the morning, and now you are asking your questions round, and I am answering them with a great deal of affected delays, and the same scene has passed forty times, as well as the other from two to seven, longer than the first by two hours, yet each has ses agremens particuliers. A long vacation, law lies asleep, and bad weather; how do you wear away the time? Is it among the fields and groves of your country seat . . . or thinking in a train that will be sure to vex you, and then reasoning and forming teasing conclusions from mistaken thoughts. The best company for you is a philosopher, whom you would regard as much as a sermon. I have read more trash since I left you than would fill all your shelves, and am abundantly the better for it, though I scarce remember a syllable. Go over the scenes of Windsor, Cleveland Row, Ryder Street, St. James's Street, Kensington, the Sluttery, the Colonel in France etc. Cad thinks often of these, especially on horseback, as I am assured. What a foolish thing is time, and how foolish is man, who would be as angry if time stopped as if it passed. But I will not proceed at this rate; for I am writing and thinking myself fast into a spleen, which is the only thing I would not compliment you by imitating. So adieu till the next place I fix in, if I fix at all till I return, and that I leave to fortune and the weather. (August 8, 1722)

'Especially on horseback.' Surely it is, as Leslie Stephen thought, a reminiscence of Hotspur to Kate.

> And when I am o' horseback I will swear
> I love thee infinitely.

4

Then the correspondence ceases, and we pass into the realm of story, legend and conjecture. The only positive facts we know are these. Vanessa died on June 2, 1723. On May 1 she had made her will. It contains no mention of Swift; he does not even figure in the list of friends to whom she bequeathed 'twenty-five pounds to buy a ring'. And one of the chief beneficiaries, to his own astonishment, was George Berkeley, the philosopher and future Bishop of Cloyne. He wrote to Sir John Perceval:

Something that will surprise your Lordship as much as it doth me; Mrs. Hester Van Omry, a lady to whom I was a perfect stranger, having never in the whole course of my life, to my knowledge, exchanged a single word with her, died on Sunday night; yesterday her will was opened, by which it appears that I am constituted executor, the advantage whereof is computed by those who understand her affairs to be worth £3000, and if a suit she had be carried, it will be considerably more. (June 4, 1723)[16]

He adds that it comes as a providential help towards his scheme for establishing a college in the Bermudas.

The unexpectedness of this bequest certainly supports the tradition that Vanessa in making her will revoked one previously made in favour of Swift; and it is possible that the bequest to Berkeley was intended as an actual demonstration against Swift, who viewed the Bermuda scheme with sympathetic scepticism. But even without this impressive corroboration, the breaking off of the correspondence at a point and on a note which suggests no likelihood of a rupture of relations is presumptive evidence of a catastrophic change.

Swift's last letter to Vanessa is as intimate and tender as any. From it one would have expected that on his return to Dublin their meetings would have been resumed. And probably they were. What then was the catastrophe? The familiar story is that some two or three months before her death, Vanessa heard a report that Swift was married to Stella. She wrote to him to ask if it was true. Another version (given by Sheridan) is that she wrote to Stella herself, and that Stella sent the letter to Swift. Swift rode straightway to Cellbridge, flung the letter on the table before her, and rode away without a word.

One can, too easily, imagine it all: Vanessa, now in the last stage of phthisis, summoning up the courage of extremity to write her letter, foreboding the worst, and above all that 'something in your look so awful that it strikes me dumb'; Swift's dark anger at what he conceived to be a trespass on the secrets of his soul — a trespass the more fiercely resented because his marriage to Stella was, in truth, a wrong done to both women.

If the story is an invention, it is a magnificent one. But it is hard to conceive Swift telling it to any mortal soul. And who, save himself and Vanessa, can have witnessed the scene? Thus, the more probable of the two versions of the story is that Vanessa's letter was written to Stella; for in that case Swift could hardly have avoided telling her what he had done.

We may approach the story from the other side, along the high *a priori* road. If we ask ourselves what conceivably could have happened to cause the total change in Vanessa's attitude to Swift that is manifest in her will, it is hard indeed to think of anything adequate to such a convulsion, except the certain knowledge that he was married to Stella. Rumour would not have been sufficient to one who trusted him so absolutely as Vanessa. She needed to *know*. Only Swift or Stella could have given her the certain know-ledge. Whether she found in herself the courage to demand the truth from him, or more pitifully wrote to Stella — one or other was necessary.

Thus, we are driven to accept the story told by Sheridan as substantially true. It is confirmed by the Bishop of Meath, writing shortly after Vanessa's death, who says that she heard of Swift's marriage in April.[16] Sheridan also tells us that Stella herself replied to Vanessa's letter by a simple 'Yes', before sending it on to Swift, 'after which she immediately went out of town, without seeing him, or coming to any explanation, and retired to Mr. Ford's country seat at Woodpark'; and that Vanessa, in her final illness 'laid a strong injunction upon her executors that immediately after her decease, they should publish all the letters which passed between Swift and her, together with the poem *Cadenus & Vanessa*'.

Accordingly, they were put to the press, and some progress made in the letters, when Dr. Sheridan getting intelligence of it . . . applied so effectually to the executors that the printed copy was cancelled, but the originals still remained in their hands. The poem *Cadenus & Vanessa* was however sent abroad into the world.[17]

The Bishop of Meath, writing at the time of the event, told the same story except that he said 'the Archbishop of Dublin and the whole Irish posse' were responsible for the suppression of the letters, 'lest one of their own dear joys should be trampled over by the Philistines'. Manuscript copies of the poem were certainly circulated in the year of Vanessa's death; and it is obviously from first-hand knowledge that Delany tells how at a dinner at Woodpark a guest who was ignorant of Stella's situation, remarked that Vanessa must have been an extraordinary woman to inspire the Dean to write so finely upon her: to which she replied that 'she thought that point not quite so clear, for it was well known that the Dean could write finely on a broomstick'. Would one like Stella better if she had not said it?

Swift went into the country at the end of March. It is supposed that this was immediately after his last visit to Vanessa. He was back in Dublin in May; but he left again on June 3, the morning after Vanessa's death, pre-sumably because he had learned that Vanessa's death might lead to dis-closures and scandal. He took a long journey into the remote South of Ireland, eventually reaching Clonfert. There he received a letter from Sheri-dan, which he answered on August 3. In it he asked if 'the ladies' were in the town or in the country. If he knew, he would write to them. Plainly there had been no communication between Stella and himself.

What effect did the tragedy of Vanessa have upon him? Visibly, of course, none. He was a master of repression. But the wound must have been deep and lasting. As far as he could know he had precipitated the death in misery of a woman whose only offence had been that she loved him; and this he had done by an act which did not come from his true self. If one thing shines out from the correspondence between him and Vanessa, it is that he could not be deliberately cruel to her. Finally trapped between two valid claims upon his heart, which he dared neither concede nor reject, he had acted like a man distraught, and struck at Vanessa in a paroxysm of anger. She was, no doubt, already doomed to die; and he may not have shortened her life by a single day. But he would never be able to convince himself of that. His sense of guilt would be abiding.

'Tis generally believed [wrote the vindictive Bishop of Meath] that she lived without God in ye world. When Dean Price (the Minister of her Parish) offered her his services in her last minutes: she sent him word no Price no Prayers, with a scrap out of the Tale in the Tub . . . and so she dyed.[18]

One admires that spirited end. She had not lived without a God, though she died without one. Her god had betrayed her.

CHAPTER XX

IRELAND: 1714-1723

FOR the six years following his return to Ireland in August 1714 Swift was virtually silent as a writer, except for two attempts to record and reconsider the political events in which he had been implicated. In October 1714 he wrote his *Memoirs Relating to that Change which happened in the Queen's Ministry in the year 1710;* in June 1715 he began *An Enquiry into the Behaviour of the Queen's Last Ministry.* They were conceived in very different moods. In writing the *Memoirs,* which largely deal with the overthrow of the Godolphin ministry, of which he had no personal knowledge, he was irritated by Oxford's failure to give him the information he desired. He had pressed for it repeatedly — not only from Oxford himself, but from Lady Masham and Erasmus Lewis. Rather naively, he was surprised that they put him off; with equal naivety, he had thought that, if only he had been appointed Historiographer, their reluctance would have yielded perforce.

The *Memoirs* are singularly incomplete and careless. He proposes to give an account of events from September 1710 — that is from his own participation in affairs after meeting Harley; but the greater part of his actual narrative is concerned with the events preceding the fall of Godolphin. Of these Swift's account is culpably inaccurate. His failure to elicit definite information from Oxford is no excuse for his wild mistakes in chronology, or for his preposterous assertion that the Duchess of Marlborough was Godolphin's mistress. Since the exacter part of his story ends abruptly with the Guiscard affair in March 1711, the historical value is very small. Except for some autobiographical particulars concerning his early indifference to party politics and his relations with the Whig grandees, the most interesting passage is the confession of his own shortcomings as a writer of historical memoirs.

One circumstance I am a little sorry for, that I was too negligent (against what I had always resolved, and blamed others for not doing) in taking hints or journals of everything material as it passed, whereof I omitted many that I cannot now recollect, though by a thousand instances, I was convinced of the weakness of my memory. But, to say the truth, the nearer knowledge any man has in the affairs at court, the less he thinks them of consequence or worth regarding. And those kind of passages which I have with the greatest curiosity found or searched for in memoirs, I wholly neglected when they were freely communicated to me from the first hand, or were such wherein I acted myself.[1]

The *Memoirs* appear to have been abandoned at the time of Swift's illness in October 1714. The *Enquiry* is much superior. It falls into two parts, of which the second is a reasoned argument to prove that the Oxford ministry could not have had any serious intention of bringing in the Pretender. But this, though begun in 1717, was not finished until 1721. The first part was written in June 1715, when the report of the Secret Committee on the negotiations which led to the Utrecht treaty was published. It was conceived in a spirit of generous and indignant defence of Oxford, and was probably inspired by admiration of his courage in calmly awaiting the charge of high treason. The character of Oxford is admirably drawn; and Swift exonerates him from blame for the final failure of the ministry. The real cause, he maintains, was the character of the Queen, whose vacillation and purely personal attitudes Oxford thought it his duty to cover, and for which he assumed responsibility. Although Swift praises Bolingbroke's abilities very highly, he dissociates himself entirely from his criticism of Oxford, and attributes the hostility between them first to Bolingbroke's attempt to snatch the credit of Guiscard's attempt, and secondly, to his belief that Oxford's influence had cheated him of an earldom: a belief which Swift is positive was mistaken. The total impression of Bolingbroke which Swift conveys is that which history has endorsed — a man of superb abilities, yet lacking in fundamental integrity of character. The picture of him is indeed more damning than Swift intended, for he credits him with a frank and open nature by which 'he seldom gave himself the trouble of disguising, or subduing his resentments, although he was ready enough to forget them'.[2] Of the latter virtue, we know, and Swift was to learn, Bolingbroke was incapable. His resentment against Oxford was enduring, venomous, and repulsive in its extremity.

The *Enquiry* contains one delightful ironic touch. Following the Sacheverell trial, says Swift, the Queen, convinced that the sentiment of the nation had turned against the Godolphin ministry, 'resolved to take Mr. Harley into her councils'.

This was brought about, as the charge against that minister says, 'by the basest insinuations'; upon which, being a determination of parliament, I shall not dispute: Although I confess to have received a very different account of that matter from a most excellent lady [Lady Masham], upon whose veracity I entirely depend; and who, being then in chief confidence with her mistress, must needs know a particular fact, wherein she was immediately concerned and trusted, better than any one man, or number of men, except the majority of a House of Commons.[8]

The *Memoirs* were avowedly not intended for publication. The general style and tone of the *Enquiry* suggest that Swift in writing it had in mind that it might be published, or at least circulated among the Tories, as a vindication of Oxford from their criticisms of him. Indeed, at one point, Swift definitely contrasts the *Enquiry* with the *Memoirs* and *The History of the Four Last Years of The Reign of Queen Anne*, 'neither of them fit to see the light at present'. But, on second thoughts, he made no attempt to publish it, and when he wrote to Oxford, on hearing that he had been committed to the Tower, he was content to renew his offer of service and attendance, and to say:

I do not conceive myself obliged to regulate my opinions by the proceedings of a House of Lords or Commons; and therefore, however they may acquit themselves in your Lordship's case, I shall take the liberty of thinking and calling you, the ablest and faithfulest Minister, and truest lover of your country, that this age hath produced. And I have already taken care that you shall be so represented to posterity, in spite of all the rage and malice of your enemies . . . You suffer for a good cause, for having preserved your country, and for having been the great instrument under God, of his present Majesty's peaceable accession to the throne. This I know, and this your enemies know; and this I will take care that all the world shall know, and future ages be convinced of. (July 19, 1715)

Swift was referring to the *Enquiry*; and his language, though it does not preclude the idea of immediate publication, does not suggest it. The letter itself, which would certainly have been opened, was courageous enough.

2

Thus, for six years after his return to Ireland Swift maintained a discreet silence on public affairs. He wrote very little, and published nothing at all. When the Duke of Ormond fled abroad, for a moment he thought of bolting too. The flight of Bolingbroke and Ormond was bewildering to one who so genuinely believed in the innocence of all the Oxford ministry; and it made him doubly suspect. For a time he was held virtually *incommunicado*. His correspondence was intercepted. He wrote to Prior:

Will you tell our friends I am just alive, and that is all? Since I came here I never received one line from any friend of consequence and some of mine tho sent with caution I hear have been opened, so that I know nothing further with relation to you than what those people tell me who read newspapers. (March 1, 1715)[4]

He turned away from politics and devoted himself to consolidating his position at St. Patrick's.

I hear they think me a smart Dean; and that I am for doing good. My notion is, that if a man cannot mend the public, he should mend old shoes if he can do no better; and therefore I endeavour in the little sphere I am placed to do all the good it is capable of. (January 3, 1715)

So he wrote to Knightley Chetwode, the high Tory Irish landowner, with whom he now commenced a friendship. High Tories were scarce in Ireland, and though Chetwode eventually became a nuisance to Swift, his political sympathy was welcome for a while.

Looking back on this period of his life in 1723, when his whole position was changed, Swift told Gay that it had taken him three years to reconcile himself to the scene and business to which fortune had condemned him, 'and stupidity was what I had recourse to'.[5] By stupidity he meant, not the rather childish amusements he indulged in with Sheridan — these came later — but simply an abstention from intellectual activity. There was nothing stupid about his activities as Dean. He disciplined his Chapter, defended his privileges against encroachment, put the finances and fabric of the Cathedral into careful order, gave a new dignity and regularity to the services, and made a beginning with his system of practical help to the inhabitants of the Liberty of St. Patrick's by establishing from his own resources a fund of £500 for small loans to hardworking tradesmen. When, in 1729, the corporation of Dublin gave him the freedom of the city,

He reflected a little on the severe treatment he had met with on his return to Ireland after her Majesty's death and for some years after. 'That being forced to live retired, he could think of no better way to do public service, than by employing all the little money he could save, and lending it, without interest, in small sums to poor industrious trades-men, without examining their party or their faith. And God hath so far pleased to bless his endeavours, that his managers tell him he hath recovered above two hundred families in this city from ruin, and placed most of them in a comfortable way of life.'[6]

His help was given to Catholics as freely as to Protestants; and thus he laid a solid local foundation for the immense popularity and veneration which he subsequently enjoyed. In the same spirit he looked after Laracor. With the help of the Trustees for the First Fruits, which he had got for the Irish Church, he purchased twenty acres of glebe; he carefully reset the tithes, and took great pains to find an equally competent successor to his excellent curate, Tom Warburton. He sharply reprimanded one of his wealthy parishioners for building a Presbyterian meeting-house, and told the Bishop of Meath roundly that he refused to attend his visitation unless he was treated with proper courtesy.

At the end of his period of reconciliation, he wrote to Chetwode, who chafed at his own enforced residence in Ireland:

> I doubt you will make a very uneasy change from Dukes to Irish squires and parsons, wherein you are less happy than I who never loved great company, when it was most in my power, and now I hate everything with a title except my books, and even in those the shorter the title the better. (September 2, 1718)

It was not affectation. Great company — or most of it — put a great strain on Swift. The extraordinary freedom and forthrightness which he adopted in it was a deliberate technique which required a constant effort; it put him under a compulsion to be always at the top of his form, in order to seem as formidable as he was. His abiding affection for Oxford was based on the fact that with him this strain was unnecessary; Swift also could relax and be himself. But Oxford was the exception. With the rest of the great men Swift had to pay a heavy price for his proximity to power; and he experienced a real relief in returning to a little kingdom of his own wherein he could be free, and it did not matter what he said. As he put it to Ford:

> I am very confident that in the whole year I do not speak to above a dozen persons, and make choice only of such with whom it is no manner of consequence what I say to them, or what they say to me. When it happens otherwise, I am not at my ease, and that is the true reason why I cannot think of a journey to England till I get more health and spirits. (December 8, 1719)

He began to make new friends: chief among them Thomas Sheridan and Patrick Delany. Though they were, of course, men of the Protestant ascendancy, their Irish names are indicative. Both were Trinity men, and both parsons. Sheridan was twenty, Delany eighteen years, younger than Swift, who was fifty in November 1717. By that time, they had become his friends. The first memorial of their friendship that remains is some Latin verses Swift wrote to Sheridan, dated October 1717, praising his wit, his scholarship, his sense of fun, and his great gifts as a schoolmaster, and laughing gently at his slight physique ('a spindle-shanked hoddy-doddy') and his weak chest. Pallas had stood by his cradle and prophesied:

> Heu puer infelix! nostro sub sidere natus;
> Nam tu pectus eris sine corpore, corporis umbra;
> Sed levitate umbram superabis, voce cicadam,
> Musca femur, palmas tibi mus dedit, ardea crura.
> Corpore sed tenui tibi quod natura negavit
> Hoc animi dotes supplebunt, teque docente,
> Nec longum tempus, surget tibi docta juventus
> Artibus egregiis animas instructa novellas.[7]*

The friendship with Delany is first celebrated in some verses to him, dated October 10, 1718.

> To you whose virtues I must own
> With shame, I have too lately known;
> To you, by art and nature taught
> To be the man I have long sought,
> Had not ill Fate, perverse and blind,
> Placed you in life too far behind:
> Or, what I should repine at more,
> Placed me in life too far before . . . [8]

They imply a friendship with them both of some standing, for they request Delany to drop a hint to Sheridan that some of his facetious poems about Swift overstepped the bounds of legitimate raillery. Swift referred to the incident later in a rather caustic character-study of Sheridan: *The History of the Second Solomon*, which he wrote in 1729, when his temper was soured after the death of Stella, and irritated by Sheridan's fecklessness.

> He became acquainted with a person distinguished for poetical and other writings, and in an eminent station, who treated him with great kindness on all occasions, and he became familiar in this person's house. In three months' time Solomon, without the least provocation writ a long poem describing that person's muse to be dead, and making a funeral solemnity with asses, owls etc. and gave the copy among all his acquaintance.[9]

But, at the time, Swift did not take it very seriously. Neither decorum, nor common sense, was Sheridan's strong point; and he often exasperated Swift

---

* 'Unhappy child, born under my star: for you will be a chest without a body, the shadow of a body. You will be lighter than a shadow, shriller than a grasshopper. A fly has provided you with thighs, a mouse with hands, a heron with legs. But what Nature has denied you in a thin body, the riches of your mind will supply. Taught by you, in a little while will arise a race of educated youth — new souls instructed in distinguished arts.'

by his maddening neglect of his sound advice, and of his own best interests. But Swift had a great affection for him, and Stella had even more.

Delany was a steadier character: as fitted by nature to advance (from very humble origins) as Sheridan was to decline. Swift exaggerated his merits as a poet, but not as a friend. His admiration for Swift was deep and lasting, and his defence of him, after his death, against the superficiality, the smartness and the spite of Orrery is a proof of his loyalty. Delany was not afraid of the Dean; and he even had the courage to remonstrate with him over the concealment of his marriage with Stella.*

It was the companionship of these two men, and their friends, John and Robert Grattan and John and Daniel Jackson, the Grattans' cousins, all parsons bred at Trinity College, which set Swift's pen in motion again; or, at least, it played an important human part in the reconciliation of Swift to the scene and business of Ireland which was needed to release his genius.

3

Meanwhile the political suspicions of Swift had died down. The impeachment of Oxford had faded out in June 1717. Archbishop King had become friendly again. He had had a legitimate grievance against Swift, for it was partly on Swift's advice that he had been passed over for the Primacy of Ireland; and it was only human that when, on the accession of George I, he was made a Lord Justice, he strongly suspected Swift of complicity in Bolingbroke's Jacobitism. Nevertheless, the two men drew together again; and when in 1719 the English Parliament passed an act depriving the Irish House of Lords of its powers as a court of final Appeal, and next year in another act affirmed the entire subordination of the Irish to the English legislature,† they were united in a common indignation.

> I believe myself not guilty [Swift wrote to Ford] of too much veneration for the Irish House of Lords, but I differ from you in politics, the question is whether people ought to be slaves or no. It is like the quarrel against Convocations; they meet but seldom, have no power, and for want of those advantages, cannot make any figure when they

---

* The actual words are: 'I am assured that a friend of his had the courage . . .'[10] But this is the way Delany often reports his own experiences of Swift; and it is reasonably certain that he is speaking of himself.

† *An Act for Securing the Political Dependency of Ireland* (1720): 'That the said Kingdom of Ireland, hath been, is, and of right ought to be subordinate unto and dependent upon the imperial crown of Great Britain, as being inseparably united and annexed thereunto; and that the King's majesty, by and with the advice and consent of the lords spiritual and temporal and commons of Great Britain in parliament assembled had, hath, and of right ought to have power and authority to make laws and statutes of sufficient authority to bind the Kingdom and people of Ireland.'

are suffered to assemble. You fetter a man seven years, then let him loose to show his skill in dancing, and because he does it awkwardly, you say he ought to be fettered for life. (April 4, 1720)

At this moment, Swift published his pamphlet: *A Proposal for the Universal Use of Irish Manufacture in Clothes and Furniture of Houses etc., utterly rejecting and renouncing everything wearable that comes from England.* There was nothing new in the proposal itself. In 1703 the Irish Commons unanimously resolved that 'it would greatly conduce to the relief of the poor and the good of the Kingdom, if the inhabitants thereof would use none other but the manufacture of this Kingdom in their apparel and the furnishing of their houses', and it had passed similar resolutions in 1705 and 1707. But a glance at the title-page of Swift's pamphlet reveals a new animus behind it. The penultimate six words of the title are in very small type, so that it looks like: UTTERLY REJECTING AND RENOUNCING . . . ENGLAND.

And that is the tone of it. The proposed boycott of English manufactures occupies a relatively small place, though it is the occasion for one of the most dangerous of his sallies:

> I heard the late Archbishop of Tuam mention a pleasant observation of somebody's: 'that Ireland would never be happy till a law were made for burning everything that came from England, except their people and their coals'. Nor am I even yet for lessening the number of those exceptions.[11]

Not that Swift took his own proposal lightly: he was to return to it again and again. But the actual occasion of this incursion into Irish politics appears to have been the ominous behaviour of the Irish Commons during the previous session. At the instigation of the Whig government they had passed one bill removing some minor disabilities of the Presbyterians — a measure hateful to Swift — and of their own motion had rejected another enforcing a small proportion of tillage on every landowner. Thus the technique, to be more fully developed later, for keeping Ireland in subjection was clearly adumbrated. In return for strengthening the English interest in the country the landlords would be given a free hand to exploit and depopulate it by converting tillage to pasture at will.

Swift's aim was to arouse popular indignation against this maleficent combination of the Irish Parliament and the English government. How far he was impelled by his detestation of the English Whigs, how far by a positive sympathy with the appalling conditions of the native Irish, it is impossible to define. Originally his position hardly went beyond a conviction that the Church of Ireland ought to be recruited from Anglo-Irishmen, and that it ought to be prosperous. That required the prosperity of Irish agriculture, since the Irish Church depended on its tithes. But cattle paid no tithe. Therefore the conversion of tillage to pasture was as prejudicial to the Church as it was oppressive to the peasantry. In this vital matter the interests of the Protestant Church and the Catholic peasants were identical.[12] Further, as in England the Whig hegemony depended upon systematic corruption, so corruption was necessary to ensure the subordination of the Anglo-Irish interest to the English one in Ireland: and Swift genuinely hated corruption. Almost in spite of himself, he was drawn to take broader ground than a mere defence of the Church of Ireland.

Here lies the interest of his pamphlet of 1720. Compared to his former political pamphlets it is a shapeless, almost a crude piece of work. One feels that he is uncertain of his audience: he is no longer confidently addressing himself to the select ten thousand of the politically important as he had in England, but feeling his way to the attention of a very different public. Evidently, the last thing he has in mind is to attempt to persuade the Irish House of Commons. His contempt for their proceedings is undisguised.

> I could wish the Parliament had thought fit to have suspended their regulation of Church matters, and enlargements of the prerogative till a more convenient time, because they did not appear very pressing (at least to the persons principally concerned) and instead of these great refinements in politics and divinity, had amused themselves and their committees a little with the state of the nation.[13]

The irony here and elsewhere is of the simplest. He will, for example, add a few to the many grievances poor England suffers by impositions from Ireland.

> That the governing of this kingdom costs the Lord Lieutenant two thousand four hundred pounds a year [i.e. in salaries to the Lords Justices], so much *net* loss to poor England. That the people of Ireland presume to dig for coals in their own grounds; and the farmers in the county of Wicklow send their turf to the very market of Dublin, to the great discouragement of the coal trade at Mostyn and Whitehaven. That the revenues of the post-office here, so righteously belonging to the English treasury, as arising chiefly from our own commerce with each other, should be remitted to London, clogged with that grievous burthen of exchange, and the pensions paid out of the Irish revenues to English favourites, should lie under the same disadvantage to the great loss of the grantees. When a divine is sent over to a bishopric here, with the hopes of five-and-twenty hundred pounds a year; upon his arrival he finds, alas! a dreadful discount of ten or twelve *per cent.*[14]

He openly raises the question — he pretends, as a mere point in moral theology — whether laws to bind men without their own consent are obligatory upon conscience; and he ends with an onslaught on the Irish landlords:

> Who by unmeasurable screwing and racking their tenants all over the kingdom, have already reduced the miserable people to a worse condition than the peasants in France, or the vassals in Germany and Poland; so that the whole species of what we call substantial farmers will in a very few years be utterly at an end ... I know not how it comes to pass (and yet perhaps I know well enough) that slaves have a natural disposition to be tyrants; and that when my betters give me a kick I am apt to revenge it with six upon my footman; although perhaps he may be an honest and diligent fellow. I have heard great divines affirm, that 'nothing is so likely to call down an universal judgment upon a nation as universal oppression'; and whether this be not already verified in part, their worships the landlords are now at full leisure to consider. Whoever travels this country, and observes the face of nature, or the faces, and habits, and dwellings of the natives, will hardly think himself in a land whether either law, religion, or common humanity is professed.[15]

The pamphlet is much less concerned with commending the use of Irish manufactures than with indicting oppression. As the audience is uncertain, so the object of his indictment is not single. Though England is the arch-oppressor, the Irish landlords run it close: and these last are practically identical with the Irish Parliament. By incriminating both, Swift was moving beyond the familiar circle of his former political ideas: almost insensibly slipping into a new rôle — of a rebel appealing to the rabble, as he would call it affectionately to the end. And that twofold change is probably the cause of the roughness and unevenness of his first great Irish pamphlet.

The indictment was too true. Waters, the printer, was immediately prosecuted for publishing a 'scandalous, seditious, and factious' pamphlet. The Lord Chancellor, Broderick, seems to have acted reluctantly, rather in fear of censure from England than of his own inclination; but the Chief Justice, Whiteshed, was passionately bent on a conviction. The Grand Jury, chiefly composed of landowners, returned a true Bill, but the City jury, although, according to Swift, it was deliberately packed with Whigs, refused to convict. The Chief Justice sent it back nine times, till partly from sheer weariness it yielded so far as to bring in 'a special verdict', whereby the printer could be tried again. But Swift applied himself to an old friend, Sir Thomas Hanmer, who was the father-in-law of the Lord Lieutenant, the Duke of Grafton, and the prosecution was eventually dropped.

Between the presentment of the Grand Jury and the trial before Whiteshed Swift put out a ballad:

> Brocados, and damasks, and tabbies, and gauzes
> Are by Robert Ballantine lately brought over,
> With forty things more: now hear what the law says,
> Whoe'er will not wear them, is not the King's lover.
> Tho' a printer and Dean
> Seditiously mean
> Our true Irish hearts from old England to wean,
> We'll buy English silks for our wives and our daughters,
> In spite of his Deanship and journeyman Waters.[16]

This was his typical technique: definitely to ascribe the authorship to himself in an anonymous ballad, which was no evidence. In the pamphlet itself he had given a plain hint, where he tells how Wharton told Addison to ask him his opinion of one of his speeches. That would have been quite enough to enable most people to identify him; while the vigour of the ballad put it beyond doubt.

> And as for the Dean,
> You know whom I mean,
> If the printer will peach him, he'll scarce come off clean.

But Swift was disappointed by the lack of response to his appeal for a boycott of English goods, and both disappointed and alarmed by the failure of the jury to hold out to the end against Whiteshed's intimidation. If the Government were to take direct action against him for sedition, he would be left very exposed. He drew in his horns. Chagrined and apprehensive, he turned aside from his provocative championship of Ireland for four whole years, while he devoted himself in the main to a satire on human nature in general and Walpole's government in particular. Only when that was finished, and then rather reluctantly, did he enter the Irish battle again.

4

During the years 1720-1723 his main preoccupation was with *Gulliver*; and in the last of them the strain of the affair with Vanessa reached a climax. It is not surprising that his other writings were rather desultory, though plentiful compared to the production of the preceding period. One's impression is that, quite apart from his politic silence on public affairs, he had been absorbed in getting the manifold affairs of the Deanery into such excellent order that they ran upon wheels. Now, he had energy to spare.

He wrote several prose pieces. He took up his *Enquiry into the Behaviour of the Queen's last Ministry* and finished the second part, in which his experience of the intervening years is reflected in his contention that, although only an insignificant fraction of the English people were Jacobites under Queen Anne, George I and the Whig tyranny had increased them to millions.

A Letter of Advice to a Young Poet is an unsatisfactory piece: a long ironical essay, admirable in form, yet in substance surprisingly pointless. If its main purpose was to deride the empty facility of contemporary Dublin poetry, it is hopelessly entangled by constant ridicule of Sidney's *Defense of Poesie*, of which the fine excess seems particularly to have annoyed Swift. But that is not all: some parts of it are so strongly reminiscent of *A Tale of a Tub*, and others of the *Argument against Abolishing Christianity*, yet so lacking in the verve and gusto of the originals, that they read like clever imitations of Swift by somebody else. The phenomenon is difficult to account for, except perhaps by supposing that Swift, after his years of silence, was engaged in writing himself in, and that it was a detached exercise in an older manner.

A Letter to a Young Gentleman lately entered into Holy Orders, on the other hand, is an effective piece of work, which sets out clearly and cogently Swift's practical ideal for the manner, the matter, and the delivery of sermons. He had made it a practice to listen critically to the sermons preached by others in his cathedral; and his own sermons, of which too few have survived, show that he followed his own precepts. Let there be, he says, clarity in exposition of the formal opening summary, strict adherence to plain language, the minimum of appeal to the emotions, a rigorous exclusion of all theological subtleties and technicalities, an avoidance of elaborate eloquence on the one side and man-of-the-world slanginess on the other; if the sermon must be read, at least cultivate the appearance of not reading it, by writing it out big and clear; and for the matter chiefly expound with concrete applications the simple moral duties of ordinary Christian men, in plain and natural words.

> For a divine has nothing to say to the wisest congregation of any parish in this Kingdom, which he may not express in a manner to be understood by the meanest among them.[17]

And let this be done without any of the conventional humbug of running down the Pagan moralists. The one great difference between the morals of the best ancient philosophers and those of Christianity, is that the rules of the ancients lacked a divine sanction: that difference will give a parson field enough to enlarge on. But, for the ancient moralists themselves, not only 'give them quarter, but make their works a considerable part of your study', for they are the best commentary on Christian morals.

In this letter of sound sense Swift comes as near as he ever did to giving explicit instruction on the prose style of which he was a master.

It would be endless to run over the several defects of style among us; I shall therefore say nothing of the mean and paltry (which are usually attended by the fustian), much less of the slovenly and indecent. Two things I will just warn you against: the first is the frequency of flat unnecessary epithets, and the other is the folly of using old threadbare phrases, which will often make you go out of your way to find and apply them, are nauseous to rational hearers, and will seldom express your meaning as well as your own natural words.

Although . . . our English tongue is too little cultivated in this kingdom; yet the faults are nine in ten owing to affectation, and not to the want of understanding. When a man's thoughts are clear, the properest words will generally offer themselves first, and his own judgment will direct him in what order to place them, so as they may be best understood. Where men err against this method, it is usually on purpose, and to shew their learning, their oratory, their politeness, or their knowledge of the world. In short, that simplicity without which no human performance can arrive to any great perfection, is nowhere more eminently useful than in this.[18]

Memorable, too, is his recommendation of the manner of reading that 'maketh a full man', or woman (for Swift spent much of his time urging his women-friends to read). After inveighing against the compilation and use of common-place books by clergymen who only read 'in order to transcribe wise and shining remarks, without entering into the genius and spirit of the author', he says:

If a rational man reads an excellent author with just application, he shall find himself extremely improved, and perhaps insensibly led to imitate that author's perfections, although in a little time he should not remember one word in the book, nor even the subject it handled: for books give the same turn to our thoughts and way of reasoning, that good and ill company do to our behaviour and conversation; without either loading our memories, or making us even sensible of the change.[19]

In part, *A Letter to a very young Lady on her Marriage* drives home the same lesson. If she wants to retain her husband's affection, she must fit herself for good company and conversation by reading good books. Good company is the company of educated men, and women who have educated themselves to share in it. 'I never knew a tolerable woman to be fond of her own sex.' Whatever her female friends recommend her to do, let her do the opposite, and she will be fairly safe. It is the advice to Stella and Vanessa put in forcible prose; there is nothing new in it; except the sombre tone of his anticipations of the effect of marriage on the husband.

> You have but a very few years to be young and handsome in the eyes of the world; and as few months to be so in the eyes of a husband who is not a fool; for I hope you do not still dream of charms and raptures, which marriage ever did, and ever will, put an end to. Besides yours was a match of prudence and common good liking, without any mixture of that ridiculous passion which has no being but in play-books and romances.[20]

He protests too much. He believes what he wants to believe: that physical intimacy between man and woman is the end of the illusion of love.

He enlarges on this theme in his verses of this time. *A Quiet Life and a good Name* (1719) is a picture of a shrewish wife, presumably Sheridan's; *Phyllis, or the Progress of Love* (1719) exhibits the consequences of an elopement under the influence of the 'ridiculous passion':

> They keep, at Staines, the Old Blue Boar,
> Are cat and dog, and rogue and whore.[21]

This is one panel of a triptych. The other two are *The Progress of Beauty* (1719), and *The Progress of Marriage* (1722). The first describes, unpleasantly enough but with great restraint compared to his future exercises in this kind, the efforts of the unfortunate Celia to repair the ravages of time and disease; the second, the consequences of the marriage of a reverend Dean of fifty-two to a handsome, aristocratic and imperious girl. (The Dean in question was Benjamin Pratt, two years younger than Swift, and his contemporary at Trinity, where he became Provost from 1710-1717.) He and his young wife have no common interests, except in bed where he is inadequate. She is all that Swift has warned the young wife not to be: she makes her maid her confidant, spends all her husband's money in dress and all her time in cards and gossip. After a year he dies (as Dean Pratt fortunately had done) and Swift concludes with the amiable wish:

> Oh, may I see her soon dispensing
> Her favours to some broken ensign.
> Him let her marry for his face,
> And only coat of tarnish'd lace;
> To turn her naked out of doors
> And spend her jointure on his whores:
> But for a parting present leave her
> A rooted pox to last for ever.[22]

What now appears to be absolutely excluded by Swift from the range of human possibilities is married love.

> Outliving beauty's outward, with a mind
> That doth renew swifter than blood decays.

The power which Shakespeare believed to be inherent in the 'winnow'd purity' of true love Swift now denies utterly, although (if we trust his letter to Varina) he had believed in it once. The only chance of enduring mutual esteem between a man and woman lies in the formation of a friendship which, excluding all physical relation, is based on the commerce of two rational minds. Everything comprehended in the idea of love that does not fall within this notion of rational friendship is a mere illusion, which exists only in 'play-books and romances'. In short, there is animal desire, and there is rational friendship: they are entirely heterogeneous, and by nature mutually destructive; and the belief that love is a power which refines the one and intensifies the other is an insidious and degrading fallacy, which it is Swift's mission to destroy.

To speak of his mission, in this respect, is hardly to exaggerate. He could not let the subject alone. It does not call for much psychological acumen to be aware that a very personal maggot was working in his brain. He was engaged in justifying his own behaviour; or the enforced victory of the rational over the emotional part of him. It was a specious victory. It was not rational friendship which held him to Stella and Vanessa alike. There were, even in him, moments of clarity when he had to allow that 'a spice of the romance' was required to give the true perfection even to conversation. And even he could not be so blind as not sometimes to know that he needed, not imaginary neuters, but flesh-and-blood women for his most intimate friends.

Although his radical scepticism of married love was rooted enough in the abstract, there was at least one moment when he could not maintain it in the concrete. To this period belongs something unique in his writings: a poem which is a gracious and graceful compliment to a happily married woman on her domestic felicity. *The First of April*, besides being remarkable enough in the context of his general attitude to demand attention, is an entirely charming poem in itself.

Apollo sends the Muses to the house of Mrs. Robert Cope. Each is charged to take care of one of the nine children. Thalia is suspicious of the mission, and thinks they are being sent to take them off the hands of some 'flaunting dame'. They had better peep in and observe.

They peep'd and saw a lady there
Pinning on coifs and combing hair;
Soft'ning with songs to son and daughter
The persecution of cold water;
Still pleas'd with the good-natur'd noise
And harmless frolics of her boys;
Equal to all in care and love,
Which all deserve and all improve.
To kitchen, parlour, nurs'ry flies,
And seems all feet, and hands, and eyes.
No thought of hers does ever roam
But for her 'squire when he's from home;
And scarce a day can spare a minute
From husband, children, wheel, or spinet.
The Muses when they saw her care
Wonder'd the God had sent them there;
And said, 'His worship might ha' told us,
This house don't want, nor will it hold us.
We govern here! where she presides
With virtue, prudence, wit besides;
A wife as good as heart could wish one,
What need we open our commission?
There's no occasion here for us;
Can *we* do more than what *she* does?'[23]

Then they remember the day. They have been made April fools.

Two letters of Swift refer to this happy household. One is to Ford, written from Loughgall, where the Copes lived:

I have been here three weeks with your old friend Mr. Cope, who is the most domestic man you ever saw, with a wife whom he is so silly as to love, and who deserves it as well as a wife can; and with nine children with whom he troubles himself as much and his friends as little as possible. (July 22, 1722)

A year later he wrote to Cope himself:

I will put the greatest compliment on you that ever I made, which is, to profess sincerely that I never found anything wrong in your house, and that you alone of all my Irish acquaintance have found out the secret of loving your lady and children, with some reserve of love for your friends, and, which is more, without being troublesome; and Mrs. Cope, I think, excels even you, at least you have made me think so, and I beg you will deceive me as long as I live. The worst of it is, that if you grow weary of me, and I wonder why you do not, I have no other retreat. The neighbours you mention may be valuable, but I never want them at your house; and I love the very spleen of you and Mrs. Cope, better than the mirth of any others you can help me to . . . My most humble service to Mrs. Cope, and pray God bless your fire-side. (May 11, 1723)

The conjunction is very strange. It would be hard, probably impossible, to find even a faint echo of the particular note that is sounded in this poem and this letter in the whole of Swift's writings. (The note is gathered, as it were, into a single musical phrase, in the lovely couplet:

> Soft'ning with songs to son and daughter
> The persecution of cold water.)

Yet the letter is the one in which he first announced his intention to go on the long southern journey which he took, on the death of Vanessa, to distract himself and escape the rumours of evil tongues. Three weeks later she died. Was it pure coincidence that this solitary, spontaneous recognition of the reality of married love and of domestic happiness occurred at the moment when the inhuman consequences of his own stubborn denial of it were most painfully apparent?

CHAPTER XXI

'GULLIVER': THE PATTERN

THE discovery of Swift's letters to Charles Ford has finally disposed of the old notion that *Gulliver's Travels* was written between 1715 and 1720, that is to say, during the period of withdrawal which ended with Swift's entry into the domestic politics of Ireland. It is now certain that the composition of *Gulliver* synchronized with his new political pre-occupations and a revival of his old ones. The return to vigorous intellectual activity was general for Swift. At the same time that he wrote the first of his Irish nationalist pamphlets, and completed his vindication of the Oxford ministry, he took up the outline or first sketch of *Gulliver*, which he had begun as a contribution to the Memoirs of Martin Scriblerus. The Scriblerus Club, consisting of himself and Arbuthnot, Pope, Gay and Parnell, and occasionally of Oxford, had served to distract the Tory wits during the anxious winter of 1713-14. To Swift and Arbuthnot it had been a compensation for their political despondency.

The original idea of composing the memoirs of this prodigious and absurd polymath was ascribed by Swift to Pope: perhaps Pope himself derived or adapted it from the imaginary author of *A Tale of a Tub.* Swift's contribution was to have been an account of Martin's voyages into various remote nations of the world. He seems to have done a little work on what afterwards became the voyage to Lilliput, and on 'the projects of Laputa', when he suddenly retired to Letcombe. On June 26, 1714, Arbuthnot wrote to him giving some account of Martin's investigations into medicine, which he himself was writing to which Swift replied:

> To talk of Martin in any hands but yours is a folly. You every day give better hints than all of us together could do in a twelvemonth; and to say the truth, Pope who first thought of the hint has no genius at all to it, in my mind. Gay is too young; Parnell has some ideas of it, but is idle; I could put together, and lard, and strike out well enough, but all that relates to the sciences must be from you. (July 3, 1714)

There, apparently, dissatisfied with what he had written about the sciences, Swift seeks to hand that department entirely over to Arbuthnot, and to confine himself to a general editorship of the proposed Memoirs. In any case, he tells Arbuthnot, his mind is now preoccupied. Shortly afterwards the Club was finally broken up by the death of the Queen and Swift's enforced retirement to Dublin. A year later he wrote to Pope: 'I must be a little easy in my mind before I think of Scriblerus.'[1] What he had actually written did not amount to much — perhaps some small part of a voyage to the Pygmies, and rather more of the material subsequently incorporated in Book III.

Stimulated possibly by *Robinson Crusoe*, which appeared in 1719, Swift took up these fragments again in 1721, and from his letters to Ford we know, pretty exactly, how the new work progressed. The first two books of *Gulliver* — Lilliput and Brobdingnag: the children's classic — were written in 1721 and 1722. Well before June 1722 Vanessa had read the capture of Gulliver by the monkey which occurs in Book II, chapter v. By the end of 1723, Swift had finished Book IV — the Yahoos and the Houyhnhnms — and had turned back to Book III — Laputa and the rest. For this book the material he had from 1714 was more substantial than for Book I. The internal evidence agrees with the external on this point. Book III makes the impression of being a collection of scraps. Only one part of it — namely, the Struldbrugs — is conceived with the same intensity of imagination as Book IV. In a letter of January 19, 1724, Swift rebukes Ford affectionately for betraying secrets to Bolingbroke.

> You are a traitor into the bargain: else how should he know anything of Stella or of Horses. 'Tis hard that folks in France will not let us in Ireland be quiet. I would have him and you know that I hate Yahoos of both sexes, and that Stella and Madame de Villette are only tolerable at best, for want of Houyhnhnms . . . I have left the country of Horses and am in the Flying Island, where I shall not stay long, and my two last journeys will be soon over: so that if you come here this summer you will find me return'd.

Within a week or two of writing this he had turned aside to the first of *The Drapier's Letters*. How much he had added to Book III before and how much after this diversion is pure conjecture. He worked on *Gulliver* and on *The Drapier's Letters* at the same time, for he told Ford on April 2, 1724: 'I shall have finished my Travels very soon if I have health, leisure and humour.' Probably there was a good deal of intermittent revision of the whole book all through the struggle over Wood's Halfpence. And if, as some believe, the description of the King of Laputa's method of suppressing insurrections on Balnibarbi is a parable of that struggle, it was added at this time. Anyhow, in August 1725 he told Ford (who seems to have been his only confidant in the matter) that he had finally finished the *Travels* and was making a fair copy.

The most important facts that emerge from all this are that the substance

of Book IV was written in 1723 — the year of Vanessa's death, of Swift's
long solitary journey to the South and West of Ireland, and Stella's long
stay with Ford at Woodpark — and that he turned to Book III afterwards.

2

No one would deny two facts about the *Travels*: the first, that it is Book IV
— the Yahoos and the Houyhnhnms — which make the book really formidable. To a lesser degree this holds of the Struldbrugs: at least they contribute
to the final effect of intensity. The second undeniable fact is that Book III
as a whole is definitely inferior to the others. It is diffuse; it lacks focus.
Were it not that we should lose the Struldbrugs, it might have been entirely
suppressed without much loss to the *Travels* as a whole. From the moment
of publication its weakness was remarked. Arbuthnot pounced upon it
immediately. To explain this inferiority by the fact that Swift was largely
incorporating, without re-creating, old material is not an artistic defence —
artistically, Book III remains a serious blemish on one of the world's great
books — but an explanation of any sort is worth having. Whereas, if we
had to suppose that the books were composed in the order they are printed,
the contrast between the aimlessness of Book III and the masterly directness
of Books I, II and IV would almost compel the hypothesis of some psychological disturbance, the knowledge that Book III is virtually a subsequent
interpolation into a process of creation which primarily consisted of Books I,
II and IV is reassuring. A reluctance to waste old material is comprehensible.
Laputa as the creative successor to Brobdingnag and the creative predecessor
to the land of the Houyhnhnms is not.

For the impression made by Book III in the sequence is bewildering.
The focus of attention is incessantly being changed. The initial absurdity of
the inhabitants of the Floating Island is fairly amusing; but it does not stand
up to close inspection. Absorption in the abstract sciences has induced in
the Laputans a complete inability to cope with the practical concerns of
life: their clothes do not fit, their absence of mind is such that their wives
find no piquancy in their infidelities. Yet, in spite of this practical incompetence, their telescopes are so excellent that they have vastly extended the
catalogue of the stars. Why (one asks), if the Laputans can make good telescopes, can they not make a good suit of clothes? Then comes a tedious
account of the way the Floating Island is used to enforce obedience on the
subject land of Balnibarbi, and of its recent failure owing to intelligent
resistance. This is plausibly supposed to be a parable of the Irish resistance

to Wood's Halfpence. That may explain, but cannot excuse, its inconsequence. For, when Gulliver descends to Balnibarbi, there are no indications of any such successful resistance to Laputa. On the contrary, the whole country has been for forty years infected with the contagion of 'scientific' enthusiasm caught from the Laputans. All the inhabitants of Balnibarbi, with the exception of those on the estates of a few of the old-fashioned nobility, are in frenzied pursuit of absurd projects in what would elsewhere be the useful arts. Productive agriculture is entirely neglected, the people are in rags, and the cities in ruins, not by the oppression of Laputa, but by their own madness. Academies of projectors, modelled on the central academy in Lagado, are everywhere. How (one asks) do the people maintain themselves at all, and how do the Laputans derive any revenue from them?

We pass to the central Academy itself. The 'useful' artists are engaged in extracting sunbeams from cucumbers, resolving human excrement, calcining ice into gunpowder, and softening marble for pillows. The projectors in speculative learning are busy with a preposterous machine for composing books; those in the school of languages with abolishing words and conversing by means of things; those in the mathematical school with acquiring theorems by ingurgitation. It may have been quite funny at the time of the South Sea Bubble; it is not very funny now. About science, abstract or applied, Swift knew nothing. He merely falls in with the fashion among the wits of guying the virtuosi; the energy of his original mind is not engaged.

In the school of political projectors he comes nearer to his real concerns, and more sinew comes into his writing. Most of the professors Gulliver reckons stark mad, for they are busy with schemes for wise and honest government. But a few of them are not so visionary. One proposes medical treatment for all members of political assemblies; physical methods — 'a tweak by the nose, a kick in the belly, or tread on his corns' — to prevent forgetfulness in ministers; that all senators, after delivering their opinions, should be bound to vote contrary; and that, to abate the violence of parties, one hundred leaders on either side whose heads are of a size, should have them cut in half and one half exchanged, so that the issues should be debated in one skull. 'As to the difference in brains in quality or quantity among those who are directors in faction; the doctor assured us from his own knowledge, that it was a perfect trifle.' All these proposals Gulliver greatly approves. He has some improvements to offer, however, from his knowledge of practice in Langden [England], on the method proposed for discovering plots by scrutiny of the diet and excrement of the suspect. This, so far as it goes, seems excellent to him. But the English methods were worthy of inclusion.

It is first agreed and settled among them, what suspected persons shall be accused of a plot; then, effectual care is taken to secure all their letters and papers, and put the criminals in chains. These papers are delivered to a set of artists, very dexterous in finding out the mysterious meanings of words, syllables and letters. For instance, they can discover a close-stool to signify a privy council; a flock of geese, a senate; a lame dog, an invader; a codshead, a — ; the plague, a standing army; a buzzard, a prime minister; the gout, a high priest; a gibbet, a secretary of state; a chamber pot, a committee of grandees; a sieve, a court lady; a broom, a revolution; a mouse-trap, an employment; a bottomless pit, the treasury; a sink, the court; a cap and bells, a favourite; a broken reed, a court of justice; an empty tun, a general; a running sore, the administration.

When this method fails, they have two others more effectual, which the learned among them call acrostics and anagrams. First, they can decipher all initial letters into political meanings. Thus *N.* shall signify a plot; *B.* a regiment of horse; *L.* a fleet at sea; or secondly by transposing the letters of the alphabet in any suspected paper, they can discover the deepest designs of a discontented party. So, for example, if I should say in a letter to a friend, *Our brother* Tom *has just got the piles*, a skilful decipherer would discover, that the same letters which compose that sentence, may be analysed into the following words; *Resist, a plot is brought home; The tour.* And this is the anagrammatic method.[2]

This is Swift's satire on the treatment of his friends, Oxford, and Prior, and now of Atterbury, by the Whig investigators.

The account of the political projectors is much more cogent and effective than the account of the others; and the difference in tone and attitude is notable. One cannot suppose that Swift regarded a scheme for good government as equally absurd with a project for extracting sunshine from cucumbers. Even if we say that the scientific and political projectors equally ignore reality, the reality is so different — in the one case, physical nature, in the other, the moral nature of man — that to expose the two kinds of people to a common ridicule is itself ridiculous. But this is not what Swift does. With the political projectors his irony, which has previously been in abeyance, comes into action. The schemers of honest government are, *ipso facto*, visionaries; whereas the professor who devises impossible techniques for amending the vices of government is practical. Neither the one nor the other is really exposed to ridicule. The object of ridicule is the absurdity of human government. The remedies are absurd, indeed; but if they could be used, the result would be an improvement. If senators could be given purges and vomits, compelled to vote contrary to their own arguments, exchange half their heads with the opposite party, and raffle for employments, government would be better than it is. The detection of treason might as well be based on the colour of the excrement as on the methods actually employed. The absurdity of the reforms is a function of the absurdity of the system. This is one of Swift's favourite techniques of irony. In the *Modest Proposal* he was to use it with terrible effect. But the schemes of the scientific projectors have nothing of this ironic quality, which depends upon a fundamental earnestness of purpose.

Here, then, are two radically inconsistent attitudes in the single account of Lagado. When we pass to Glubbdubdrib, the land of the Magicians, we are equally disappointed, but in another way. All we derive from the fantasy of calling up historical figures from the dead is the knowledge that Swift's prejudice in favour of the Greeks and the Romans (prior to the Empire) is as robust and unreasoning as his prejudice against science. He naively idealizes the city-state of classical antiquity.

> I desired that the senate of Rome might appear before me in one large chamber, and a modern representative ... in another. The first seemed to be an assembly of heroes and demi-gods; the other a knot of pedlars, pickpockets, highwaymen and bullies ... I had the honour to have much conversation with Brutus; and was told, that his ancestor Junius, Socrates, Epaminondas, Cato the younger, Sir Thomas More, and himself were perpetually together — a sextumvirate to which all the ages of the world cannot add a seventh.[3]

Homer and Aristotle appear, to disown their commentators; Aristotle predicts the eventual rejection of the Newtonian system. A view of the more recent illustrious confirms Gulliver in his conviction of universal corruption, the utter falsity of modern history, and the physical degeneracy (largely through venereal disease) of contemporary man. Once more one can only pronounce it boring, and ask why, if modern history is false, it is assumed that classical history is true, and why, in spite of that, the depressing evidence of the greatest of all the historians of classical antiquity, Thucydides, is totally ignored.

3

With the passage to Lugnagg the narrative picks up again. Gulliver's encounter with the Struldbrugs is impressive indeed. But the content and quality of this episode is strangely unrelated to anything else in Book III, while it does appear to be intimately related to the sequence of Books I, II and IV. The relation is immediately manifest in this: if we leave out Laputa,

Balnibarbi, and Glubbdubdrib — countries in which he appears to wander aimlessly, but without constraint, like a mere sightseer — there is an evident progression in Gulliver's attitude towards his return home from the countries in which he is successively caught. From Lilliput he deliberately plans his escape from the imminent danger of a treacherous death; from Brobdingnag he is liberated by a happy accident. Though he is treated with kindness there, he longs to return home, because his position was unworthy of human dignity and he 'wanted to be among people with whom he could converse upon even terms and walk about the streets and fields without fear of being trod to death like a frog'. But in Lugnagg, as soon as he hears of the immortal Struldbrugs, he for the first time in his travels desires to stay for ever.

> In one thing I was determined, that his Majesty having frequently offered me an establishment in this country, I would with great thankfulness accept the favour, and pass my life here in the conversation of those superior beings the *Struldbrugs*, if they would please to admit me.[4]

But the discovery that the Struldbrugs are not superior but inferior beings, because of their immortality, cures him of this desire. Once more he is eager to return home. Finally, in the land of the Houyhnhnms he meets with beings who are superior indeed; and the longer he stays among them, the more deeply he desires to be with them for ever. He returns only because he is actually expelled; and the shock of the sentence is such that he faints away.

The progression is evident. Gulliver, in his travels, is the human being in search of wisdom. He is other things as well. But he is certainly that. The encounter with the Struldbrugs represents the shedding of a final illusion. At first Gulliver thinks he has found in them, because they are not liable to death, repositories of accumulated wisdom: 'who being exempt from that universal calamity of human nature have their minds free and disengaged without the weight and depression of spirits caused by the continual apprehension of death'. He is sadly disillusioned. The immortality of the Struldbrugs consists in a perpetuation of the infirmities of age. Their highest happiness is a total escape from consciousness into the oblivion of dotage.

Gulliver thus learns two things: first, that so far from being a universal calamity, death is a merciful release. As Swift put it in his *Thoughts on Religion*:

> It is impossible that anything so natural, so necessary, and so universal as death, should ever have been designed by Providence as an evil to mankind.[5]

The second lesson he learns is that the wisdom he seeks is not to be found through the prolongation of any specifically human experience. Accordingly, the Houyhnhnms are a totally different species from the human, and they are, in truth, the 'superior beings' he thought he had found in the Struldbrugs. They are not, and do not dream of being, immortal; but they have made their peace with death. For them it is a natural, easy, and welcome event.

> They live generally to seventy or seventy-five years, very seldom to fourscore: some weeks before their death they feel a gradual decay, but without pain. During this time they are much visited by their friends, because they cannot go abroad with their usual ease and satisfaction. However, about ten days before their death, which they seldom fail in computing, they return the visits that have been made them by those who are nearest in the neighbourhood, being carried in a convenient sled drawn by *Yahoos* . . . And therefore when the dying *Houyhnhnms* return those visits, they take a solemn leave of their friends, as if they were going to some remote part of the country, where they designed to pass the rest of their lives.[6]

The Struldbrugs are thus an important link between the first two books and the last of the *Travels*, and they are the only portion of Book III that is. The greater part of it is unsatisfying and disturbs the pattern we can discern in the *Travels* as a whole.

4

Roughly the pattern appears to be this. In Lilliput human society is represented in miniature. There is no substantial exaggeration of the absurdity of the human scene, as Swift himself knew it. It is the Court of George I rather than that of Queen Anne of which he makes fun, naturally enough — for he had feelings about Queen Anne's Tory ministers;* but he has an effective dig at the 'royal prude' for her supposed squeamishness about *A Tale of a Tub*, when he represents Gulliver's saving of the palace by pissing on the fire in the Empress's apartments as a cause of his loss of favour. The detailed political allusions are, no doubt, as irrelevant to the modern reader as those in Dante; but the main purport of the book remains as valid as the charm of the narrative. The incursion of Gulliver into Lilliput is analogous to the vast accession of physical strength which has accrued to

---

* Not that Swift in his Irish detachment now made much distinction between the courts of Anne and George. 'If all Courts have a sameness in them, as the parsons' phrase is,' he wrote to Gay, 'things may be as they were in my time, when all employments went to Parliament-men's friends, who had been useful in elections, and there was always a huge list of names in arrear at the Treasury.' (January 5, 1723)

the industrial nations by the power-machine. The Lilliputians, like the nations, regard this accession of strength primarily as a means to overcome their rivals. But Gulliver, unlike the power-machine, is a conscious and responsible person. Though he is willing to defeat the aggressive intentions of the Blefuscans by capturing their navy, he draws the line firmly at being used to subjugate and enslave them. To punish him for this the Lilliputian statesmen resolve to kill or blind him. Thus, in comparison with the Lilliputians, Gulliver is their moral superior.

In Brobdingnag, Gulliver's nature changes. He becomes morally a Lilliputian, but he retains the analogue of his former giant strength by his knowledge of the technique of firearms. He proposes to the King that he should manufacture a modern armament of muskets and cannons, and thus make himself the absolute master of 'the lives, the liberties and fortunes of his people'. The King rejects the proposal with indignation; but Gulliver, unabashed, regards the King's abhorrence as 'a strange effect of narrow principles and short views'.[7] If the *Travels* were a novel, the inconsistency of Gulliver's character would be shocking. But the *Travels* are not a novel, but a parable; and Gulliver among the Brobdingnagians merely sinks to the condition of a Lilliputian; or, Gulliver is to the Lilliputians as the King of Brobdingnag is to Gulliver. In Lilliput Gulliver belongs to the superior beings; in Brobdingnag to the inferior. But there is a perceptible increase in the violence of the scorn for the inferior beings as we pass from Lilliput to Brobdingnag. Gulliver in Lilliput is fairly contemptuous of Lilliputian behaviour, but he does not dream of expressing himself with the vehemence of the King of Brobdingnag's famous verdict: 'I cannot but conclude the bulk of your natives to be the most pernicious race of little odious vermin that nature ever suffered to crawl upon the surface of the earth.'[8]

Not that all the Brobdingnagians are superior beings. The treatment of Gulliver by his farmer captor is pitiless and inhuman; he intends, without a qualm, to work him to death, much as contemporary society treated negro slaves. The superiority of Brobdingnag consists primarily in the moral superiority of the King himself, and secondarily in the superiority of its institutions. The Brobdingnagians, as Gulliver explains in his epilogue, are the least corrupted of the Yahoo species, and their 'wise maxims in morality and government it would be our happiness to observe'.[9] The society of Brobdingnag is agricultural and feudal. The country is defended by a militia, 'where every farmer is under the command of his own landlord, and every citizen under that of the principal men of the city, chosen after the manner of Venice by ballot'.[10] The science of the Brobdingnagians is eminently practical, and applied chiefly to the improvement of agriculture and those mechanical arts which advance it, in accordance with the King's maxim that 'whoever could make two ears of corn, or two blades of grass to grow upon a spot of ground where only one grew before, would deserve better of mankind, and do more essential service to his country than the whole race of politicians put together'.[11] They have been through the same civil dissensions to which, according to Swift's reading of history, all civilized mankind is subject: 'the nobility often contending for power, the people for liberty, and the King for absolute domination'.[12] But the last of these outbreaks was in the time of the King's grandfather, since when, after 'a general composition', there has been domestic peace. And the King of Brobdingnag is on Swift's side about the Test Act. 'He said, he knew no reason, why those who entertain opinions prejudicial to the public, should be obliged to change, or should not be obliged to conceal them.'[13]

From these glimpses of the polity of Brobdingnag we may fairly conclude that it represents Swift's vision of a practicable ideal — roughly, an England whose 'glorious Revolution' was not nullified, as Swift believed it had been, by the development of party-faction, court-corruption, a moneyed interest, and the establishment of a standing army. Gulliver does his patriotic best to conceal the political deformities of his own country; but the King examines him severely, and elicits the truth. Indeed, in his long series of leading questions, his Majesty shows a detailed knowledge of the seamy side of English society that would hardly be plausible in a realistic fiction, unless we were to regard Brobdingnag as having emerged from a similar corruption. But the willing suspension of disbelief comes easy enough. The main point to grasp is that the King of Brobdingnag extracts the truth from a reluctant Gulliver, or rather compels him to assent to the truth of his own unflattering deductions from Gulliver's evidence.

5

When he comes to the land of the Houyhnhnms, Gulliver's attitude changes radically. It takes him a long while to adjust to the new and astonishing society of truly rational beings. He stays longer in Houyhnhnm land than in any other; and he needs to do so. For he has to undergo a mental and spiritual revolution, of which the consequence is that he becomes incapable of saying 'the thing which is not'. Now, it is of his own motion that he tells his master the truth concerning English society. And a crucial factor in his spiritual purgation is his realization that he belongs to the species of the Yahoos. The picture of these repulsive brutes has been resented as a blasphemy on humanity. In one important respect, which shall be considered, it is. But in so far as the qualities of the Yahoo are to be 'cunning, malicious, treacherous and revengeful' and unteachable, it would be hard for a detached observer of the behaviour of the human race during the last fifty years to deny that there is sufficient likeness between mankind and the Yahoos to give us food for thought. At least it would not be wholly unjust to describe mankind, on the evidence of this behaviour, as a race of sophisticated Yahoos. Notably, it is when Gulliver describes the happenings in a European war, that the Houyhnhnm his master experiences 'a disturbance in his mind, to which he was wholly a stranger before'.

> Although he hated the *Yahoos* of this country, he no more blamed them for their odious qualities, than he did a *gnnayh* (a bird of prey) for its cruelty, or a sharp stone for cutting his hoof. But when a creature pretending to reason, could be capable of such enormities, he dreaded lest the corruption of that faculty might be worse than brutality itself. He seemed therefore confident, that instead of reason, we were only possessed of some faculty fitted to increase our natural vices.[14]

The possibility which so disturbs the Houyhnhnm is that the faculty which the sophisticated Yahoos possess may be a corruption of 'reason'. But he comes to rest in the confidence that it is a different faculty altogether.

Quite rightly, for it is evident that the 'reason' which the Houyhnhnms possess, and which Gulliver in their society and by force of their example comes partly to acquire, is not the faculty of ratiocination at all. It is the gift of discerning and doing what is good. It is because Swift uses 'reason' in this distinctive sense in Book IV that he could say to Pope that *Gulliver's Travels* was based on the proposition that man is not an *animal rationale* but only *rationis capax*. Capable of 'reason', in this sense, can only mean capable of developing in oneself a discernment of the good, and a devotion to pursuing it, and simultaneously of developing an incapacity to pursue evil. This is what Swift asserts when Gulliver says of the 'reason' of the Houyhnhnms:

> Neither is reason among them a point problematical as with us, where men can argue with plausibility on both sides of the question; but strikes you with immediate conviction, as it needs must where it is not mingled, obscured or discoloured by passion and interest.[15]

This 'reason' exists, according to Swift, as a mere latent potentiality in humans, and only becomes operative when the mind is free from passion or interest, that is to say, when it is purged of what Santayana calls 'animal egotism'. And this purgation happens to Gulliver in consequence of his discovery that he belongs to the Yahoo species. It is a painful process of self-discovery and self-annihilation. For the only difference between a human such as himself and a Yahoo consists in the addition of the faculty of ratiocination, which, being morally neutral, becomes in the human being merely an intrument in the service of the fundamental animal egotism of the Yahoo. But besides this there is a gleam or germ: the possibility of the emergence of 'reason' when the radical vice of animal egotism is discerned in oneself and overcome. When man has seen himself in the mirror of the Yahoo, he may be purged. Then 'reason', or the true self, may be liberated from its animal bondage.

It is highly characteristic of Swift that he should represent the society of purged and liberated spirits as a community of horses. The peculiar cast of his mind is nowhere more simply evident. The device not only enables him to avoid the difficulty of representing a community of entirely good human beings, without insipidity, but enables him to make visible, in a concrete and vivid symbol, the almost generic difference between the animal and the spiritual, the enslaved and the liberated man. The element of dullness and monotony which would otherwise be inseparable from an attempt to depict a society of completely virtuous humans becomes in a sense natural when they are horses. We do not expect them to be idiosyncratic; or talkative, trivial or mean. Moreover, since the distinguishing feature of regenerated humans is that they are instinctively and spontaneously good, the use of the 'noblest' animal to represent them is appropriate and effective. On the other hand, it enables Swift to suggest a specious solution to a problem which deeply concerned him: the reconciliation of reason and sex. That solution, in its turn, is intimately connected with what has been justly felt to be excessive savagery of his picture of the Yahoos. This is too important a question to be considered in passing. Here we are concerned solely with what is positive and profound in the parable of Book IV.

The substance of it is that moral goodness, or 'reason', is a second and better nature, achieved by means of a ruthless self-purgation; but there is a change in kind — a rebirth. Perhaps the most notable of the marks of this change is the one on which Gulliver insists in chapter XII, at the very end of his narrative.

My reconcilement to the *Yahoo*-kind in general might not be so difficult, if they would be content with those vices and follies only which nature hath entitled them to. I am not in the least provoked at the sight of a lawyer, a pickpocket, a colonel, a fool, a lord, a gamester, a politician, a whoremaster, a physician, an evidence, a suborner, an attorney, a traitor or the like; this is all according to the due course of things: but when I behold a lump of deformity, and diseases both in body and mind, smitten with *pride*, it immediately breaks all the measures of my patience; neither shall I ever be able to comprehend how such an animal and such a vice could tally together . . . But the *Houyhnhnms*, who live under the government of reason, are no more proud of the good qualities they possess, than I should be for not wanting a leg or an arm, which no man in his wits would boast of, although he must be miserable without them.[16]

It recalls St. Paul's rebuke to the Corinthians: 'What hast thou that thou didst not receive? Now, if thou didst receive it, why dost thou glory as if thou hadst not received it?' That is the specifically Christian version of the same spiritual truth. Goodness, when really achieved, is known not to have been achieved by our own efforts. Reason, when it is true reason, is not a personal acquisition; it is not a faculty of which it can be said, 'I possess it': it possesses me.

This naturalness of the reason and goodness of the Houyhnhnms is the cause of Gulliver's delay in recognizing it for what it is. 'At first, indeed, I did not feel that natural awe, which the Yahoos, and all other animals, bear towards them; but it grew upon me by degrees.' It is as though Gulliver had at first to grope his way in an unfamiliar dimension, or be gradually initiated into a mystery. But once he is there, his values change. In consequence of the same inward revolution, the impulse to defend his own human society, as he had done before the King of Brobdingnag, abandons him completely before the Houyhnhnms. He is ruthlessly veracious about it, and he explains why.

The reader may be disposed to wonder how I could prevail on myself to give so free a representation of my own species, among a race of mortals who are already too apt to conceive the vilest opinion of human kind, from that entire congruity betwixt me and their Yahoos. But I must freely confess, that the many virtues of these excellent quadrupeds placed in opposite view to human corruptions, had so far opened my eyes and enlarged my understanding, that I began to view the actions and passions of man in a very different light, and to think the honour of my own kind not worth managing . . . Let me deal so candidly with the reader as to confess, that there was a yet much stronger motive for the freedom I took in my representation of things. I had not been a year in this country, before I contracted such a love and veneration for the inhabitants, that I entered on a firm resolution never to return to human kind, but to pass the rest of my life among these admirable Houyhnhnms in the contemplation and practice of every virtue; where I could have no example or incitement to vice.[17]

When we consider the general drift and pattern of *Gulliver's Travels* as a whole in the light of Book IV, a sort of hierarchy of moral progression finally emerges. At the bottom are the Yahoos; then in ascending order come, first, the Lilliputians, to whom Gulliver (Brobdingnagian among them) is morally as well as physically superior; second, the Brobdingnagians, who are morally as well as physically superior to Gulliver (Lilliputian among them); and third and topmost comes Gulliver himself when he has been reconciled to death by the Struldbrugs, and finally humiliated by the Yahoos and regenerated by the Houyhnhnms. To go beyond that requires passing into another species altogether. Whether the Houyhnhnms are credible or plausible embodiments of the new moral dimension, which is *totaliter aliter*, is a question of individual taste; but it can hardly be denied that they make a dramatically powerful contrast. For the contrast which Swift desires to drive home is not that between the Houyhnhnms and Gulliver (who is now regenerate), but between them and the Yahoos. The contrast between the Houyhnhnms and Gulliver, if indeed it amounts to one, is of small importance, because they are incommensurable: it is the difference between the goodness of Innocence, and the goodness of Innocence regained after painful experience, which must always carry the stains and scars of battle. But the contrast between the Yahoos and the Houyhnhnms symbolizes the dreadful one between the sophisticated brutishness of man and animal innocence. The Yahoos make visible the judgment of the King of Brobdingnag on the human race; but the judgment is now passed with an added intensity of moral aversion, so that we feel much the same shudder of revulsion which overcame the Houyhnhnm when Gulliver described to him a war among mankind.

It is Book IV which gives the others a new and unexpected depth of significance, or puts them in a new spiritual perspective. The total effect is as though Swift were trying to find the focus of truth in his contemplation of mankind. With his instrument he first diminishes, then he magnifies the object; then, he discards his instrument altogether, and uses the spiritual eye. This description is metaphorical, and over-simplified besides; but it may serve as an indication of the new dimension of which we are made sensible in Book IV. It is a mistake to see in the picture of the Yahoos only the evidence of a deepened savagery of hatred of his kind in Swift. The Yahoos are there to make his parable profound, and to prevent us from taking Lilliput and Brobdingnag as a good-humoured fantasy. They shatter the complacency which lurks beneath our habit of laughing at satire. The vision is appalling. But ought we not to be appalled? Is the vision so different from Shakespeare's in *King Lear*?

> If that the heavens do not their visible spirits
> Send quickly down to tame these vile offences,
> It will come,
> Humanity must perforce prey upon itself,
> Like monsters of the deep.

And if it be urged that in *King Lear* the baseness of humanity is redeemed by loyalty and love in Kent and the Fool, and supremely in Cordelia, we may reply that it is likewise redeemed in *Gulliver's Travels*. When allowance is made for the lowered tone and the total absence of poetry in Swift's story, is not Don Pedro, the Portuguese captain's behaviour to Gulliver almost as astonishing in its generosity as that of Shakespeare's heroine? Even the common seamen treat the rescued Gulliver 'with great humanity', and the courtesy, the patience and the kindness of their captain are worthy of the good Samaritan himself. Indeed, when we compare the account of Gulliver's final homecoming with his previous returns, we see that Swift has gone out of his way to describe in unusual detail the beautiful humanity of Don Pedro. He treats Gulliver not merely with courtesy and consideration, but with such sensitive sympathy as a friend might treat a friend who had just emerged from some shattering experience. This emphasis must be deliberate. What impression does it make?

At the very least it is an intentional demonstration of the more comforting part of Swift's ambivalent attitude. When he had finished the *Travels*, he wrote to Pope:

> I have ever hated all nations, professions, and communities; and all my love is towards individuals: for instance, I hate the tribe of lawyers, but I love Counsellor Such-a-one, and Judge Such-a-one; so with physicians — I will not speak of my own trade — soldiers, English, Scotch, French and the rest. But principally I hate and detest that animal called Man, although I heartily love John, Peter, Thomas and so forth. This is the system upon which I have governed myself many years, but do not tell, and so I shall go on till I have done with them.

And later in the same letter he said:

> Mr. Lewis sent me an account of Dr. Arbuthnot's illness, which is a very sensible affliction to me, who, by living so long out of the world, have lost that hardness of heart contracted by years and general conversation . . . Oh! if the world had but a dozen Arbuthnots in it, I would burn my Travels! (September 29, 1725)

Don Pedro is an Arbuthnot. He may be *the* Arbuthnot: for he behaves to Gulliver more like a generous and sympathetic physician than a ship's captain. That would help to explain the subtler impression made by the episode and the character of Don Pedro. It is as though, without departing from the tone of straightforward matter of fact which is the peculiar charm of the *Travels*, Swift were hinting that Gulliver's experiences among the Houyhnhnms and the Yahoos had been an excursion beyond the bounds of 'sanity'; that he had gone too far, and, like Keats at one moment, seen too far.

> But I saw
> Too far into the sea; where every maw
> The greater on the less feeds ever more:
> But I saw too distinct into the core
> Of an eternal fierce destruction,
> And so from happiness I far was gone.
> Still am I sick of it.

It is as though Gulliver were unhinged by the dreadful vision he has seen. And this condition of Gulliver arouses all the tenderness of the Portuguese stranger. Tenderness is certainly the word to describe his patient ministration to the castaway.

If this is to read too much into the episode of Don Pedro (which is often ignored by commentators on the *Travels*), at the very lowest, it is a successful demonstration of Swift's hearty love for individuals, and the existence of individuals worthy of it. It is too much the custom to write as though Book IV consisted of nothing but Yahoos and Houyhnhnms, and chiefly of Yahoos. There are Gulliver and Don Pedro besides, and they are important.

And, even if we regard the episode of Don Pedro as no more than an expression of Swift's avowed love for individuals amid his avowed detestation of the animal called man, we cannot but remark that the precise reverse of this condition obtains among the Houyhnhnms. Whereas in Swift reason prompts him to detest his species and to love individuals, the Houyhnhnms 'will have it that nature (which in them is identical with reason) teaches them to love the whole species'. The contrast is logical enough, supposing that the individuals whom Swift loves are those rare members of the human species in whom 'reason and nature' have won the victory. But the absoluteness of the antithesis indicates the completeness of the transvaluation of values of which the Houyhnhnms are the symbols.

How far they are effective symbols of this transvaluation is questionable, because Swift was attempting what is impossible on the plane of realism to which he affects to keep. We cannot enter into Gulliver's transport of despair at the sentence of expulsion from the Houyhnhnms; we cannot regard their life as particularly desirable, or help finding Don Pedro a more pleasant companion, with as much of reason and nature and goodness as the best of them. They may be satisfactory symbols of the negative — of the need to pass beyond the human altogether to attain pure goodness; but as symbols of the positive — of goodness itself, they are almost ludicrously inadequate. One may admit that, however, without admitting that Book IV is a failure. It is not. It is enormously impressive. It has a kind of nightmare quality which abides in the mind, and makes it uneasy. To pin this effect of nightmare down to the Yahoos does not correspond to the impression, which emanates just as powerfully from the Houyhnhnms themselves. They are more weird than the Yahoos, though they are not repulsive like them. Or they are repulsive in a quite different way.

CHAPTER XXII

'GULLIVER': THE PERSONAL EQUATION

W E have said that the impression made by Don Pedro is that of a generous physician ministering from kindness to a mind diseased, and that he calls up the image of Dr. Arbuthnot. That there was some real connection in the mind of Swift between Arbuthnot and the import of the *Travels* is evident from his remark to Pope: 'Oh, if the world had but a dozen Arbuthnots in it, I would burn my Travels!' At least it registers Swift's opinion that in the character of Arbuthnot humanity was redeemed from the indictment he had brought against it.

Arbuthnot's character was very relevant. A radical criticism of *Gulliver* was implicit in it. He was a distinguished mathematician as well as a physician; he was a leading fellow of the Royal Society. He was a living refutation of Laputa. That is relatively unimportant beside the fact that he was also a standing criticism of the Houyhnhnms in a more vital matter. He loved his children dearly and was not afraid to own it, even to Swift. When, in November 1713, Oxford lost his beloved daughter, Lady Carmarthen, Arbuthnot advised Swift not to attempt to give him rational or religious consolation, but to try to turn his mind to other thoughts.

> I have a true sense of his present condition, for which I know philosophy and religion are both too weak, and I believe it is the will of God that it should be so. I have lost six children. If I am not deceived, I believe I could have been content to have ransomed the lives of every one of them even at the hard terms of begging their bread.[1]

Swift did not take his wise and humane advice. His letter of consolation to Oxford was very much what Arbuthnot told him *not* to write.

The Houyhnhnms are immune from Arbuthnot's irrational weakness.

> They have no fondness for their colts and foals, but the care they take in educating them proceeds entirely from the dictates of reason. And I observed my master to shew the same affection to his neighbour's issue that he had for his own.[2]

Love, as a concomitant of the sexual relation between male and female, is unknown to the Houyhnhnms. The couples for copulation are chosen by parents and friends, on the grounds of the stockbreeder; and this is entirely acceptable to the couples themselves, who regard the act of copulation 'as one of the necessary actions of a reasonable being'. Consistently with this, they have no 'fondness' — that is, particular affection — for their offspring; nor is there any 'fondness' between the couples after their marriage.

There is a close similarity between this and some of the institutions of Lilliput, which Gulliver admired. They are, in fact, incongruous in that corrupt society, and Gulliver has, very cavalierly, to explain that he is describing the original laws abstracted from the subsequent corruptions.

> Their notions relating to the duties of parents and children differ extremely from ours. For, since the conjuction of male and female is founded upon the great law of nature, in order to propagate and continue the species, the Lilliputians will needs have it, that men and women are joined together like other animals, by the motives of concupiscence; and that their tenderness towards their young proceeds from the like natural principle; for which reason they will never allow, that a child is under any obligation to his father for begetting him, or to his mother for bringing him into the world, which, considering the miseries of human life, was neither a benefit in itself, nor intended so by his parents, whose thoughts in their love-encounters were otherwise employed. Upon these, and the like reasonings, their opinion is, that parents are the last of all others to be trusted with the education of their own children . . . [3]

The difference between the sexual institutions of the Houyhnhnms and the Lilliputians reduces to this: that the founding fathers of Lilliput had realized that love, whether between male and female, or parent and child, is merely an illusion attendant on the workings of animal desire, which must be prevented from influencing the education of children; whereas the Houyhnhnms are immune from the desire and the illusion together. They do not have to bring in reason to correct the workings of nature, because nature and reason are identical in them. Their thoughts are not 'otherwise occupied in their love-encounters', because they have no 'love-encounters'. They are simply engaged in 'one of the necessary acts of a reasonable being', who recognizes the necessity of propagating the species. The sexual institutions of the Houyhnhnms are ideal, the institutions of completely rational beings who have no need of government: those of the Lilliputians are the nearest practical approximation to them among partly rational beings who need government. But the attitude to sex common to them both is fundamental to Swift's thinking at this period of his life.

In so far as this repudiation of the claims of animal affection between man and woman, and parents and children, as irrational, was motivated by the desire to prevent the corruption of education by false parental claims, it is reasonable enough. But Swift is creating a subtle confusion. He is insinuating that love between parents, or between parents and children, is the cause of unreasonable demands for gratitude from children, and of the corruption of education. This is not true; and it can be made to appear true only by his tacit and preliminary reduction of love to a fantasy attendant on animal desire and animal affection.

But love is not this fantasy. Love between man and woman is the mutual election of two reasonable beings. A man and a woman choose one another for permanent union. The consequence, not the purpose, of that mutual choice is the birth of a child. If the parents love one another they do not dream of demanding gratitude from the child for being born; he is an independent being with a claim to their love, which expresses itself as a concern that his own, and only his own, true interests shall be considered. Possessive animal affection from parents to children is indeed a curse. But in order to repudiate it, we do not have to repudiate love. Love itself repudiates it, much more emphatically than reason. Parental love differs from man-woman love, in that, whereas the man and woman choose each other, they do not choose their children; but the difference is immaterial, for the child is the consequence of their choice of each other. The essential independence of the child does not arise from the fact that the sexual union of its parents is an animal and sub-rational relation which can confer no rights over a potentially rational being; it arises from the fact that their sexual union is not an animal and sub-rational relation, but a supra-rational one.

Swift, for reasons of his own, wished to make a chasm between love (which he therefore called friendship) and the sexual relation. The sexual relation, he held, was an animal and sub-rational connection, which reason accepted only because it was necessary to the propagation of the species. He was by no means sure that propagation of the species was itself a rational purpose. It certainly did not commend itself as such to his own reason; but he was prepared to allow that this might be 'a mystery of Providence'. But the only excuse for the sexual relation was the desire to propagate the species. For this purpose reason permitted man to enter into this essentially degrading animal relation, in which he put off his rationality. If he did not want to have children, he was spared this degradation. The idea that the sex-relation was a natural and beautiful fulfilment of the relation of love between a man and a woman was excluded from his mind.

The choice of horses as the exemplars of the rational life enabled him to make this plausible. That horses should be mated at the will of others than themselves, and solely for the propagation of the species; that the affair of propagation should not be complicated and confused by the emotion of love of individual for individual; that they should be animated by a kind of diffused affection for the species: all this strikes us as eminently natural and reasonable — for horses. Then we remember that they are being put before us as exemplars of the life of reason for humans, and we recoil. Swift is pulling the wool over our eyes, and over his own.

2

We cannot say Swift is not in deadly earnest in this matter. It is not merely that the practices of the Houyhnhnms accord with the laudable institutions of Lilliput. They are at one with the attitude which he himself now constantly manifested. He had conceived a profound mistrust of love as the motive of mating between man and woman. This may have had its origin in his early reflections on his own misery as a youth. There is obvious significance in his condemnation of the marriage of his father and mother.

> This marriage was on both sides very indiscreet: for his wife brought her husband little or no fortune, and his death happening so suddenly before he could make a sufficient establishment for his family, his son (not then born) hath often been heard to say, that he felt the consequences of that marriage not only through the whole course of his education, but during the greatest part of his life.[4]

Was that the judgment of his early years? One can imagine a sensitive schoolboy, more isolated, poorer, more dependent on the grudging assistance of his relatives than his fellows, coming to such a conclusion. But there is nothing in Swift's few direct recollections of his schooldays to suggest that he was more than averagely miserable, or averagely impecunious at Kilkenny. It is more likely that it belongs to his years at Trinity, when his uncle Godwin's fortunes were declining, and he himself more sensitive to his poverty among his fellow-pensioners. It is clear enough that by the time his college days were over he had made up his mind not to marry until he had some secure position in the world. But it is equally clear that, as soon as he had such a position, he felt free to fall in love, and he did so. Up to this crucial point the most we can say is that his experience as the child of an 'improvident' marriage had made him prudent—but not unreasonably or excessively so.

But when he wrote in the autobiographical *Fragment* that he had felt the consequences of his parents' marriage 'not only through the whole course of his education, but during the greatest part of his life', he implied much more than this. The *Fragment* itself ends with his final settlement in Dublin in 1714; but it was written much later. In 1753, Deane Swift, in presenting the

MS. to Trinity, said it was written 'six or eight and twenty years ago': which would place it in 1725-27. Thus it may have been contemporary with the finishing of the *Travels*, or even with the last months of Stella's life. And he may have been implying that his parents' marriage had had a disastrous effect upon his own attitude to marriage.

Whether or not he was actually suggesting this, it seems to have been true. A galling experience of poverty and neglect at the university sowed in him the seeds of a distrust of a love-marriage. That his parents married for love may fairly be presumed, not from their 'improvidence', but from the devotion which Swift felt and showed to his mother. She was obviously a lovable woman.* This radical mistrust of a love-marriage was momentarily overcome by his passion for Varina. When that passion was disappointed, the mistrust took possession of him again, more strongly than before from its apparent justification by Varina's behaviour. If he married now (he seems to have said to himself) his marriage should be purely rational. It should be for the propagation of children only, and it should wait till his financial position was entirely secure. For a man who had discarded love for ambition this was really to postpone it to the Greek Kalends. Unfortunately, the relative immunity to Stella's physical attraction produced by his acquaintance with her from a child conspired with the reaction of his pride to Varina's irresolution, to make possible a substitute and equivocal relation with Stella. He could convince himself and her that he was only waiting to make his fortune to marry her. Perhaps there was this much truth in it, that if Stella's fortune had been larger he might have married her long before he did, and in a different and far better way. And it may have been partly because Vanessa's fortune was considerable that he allowed himself to be drawn into his equivocal relation with her. If he could have obeyed his reason — or his prudence — alone, he might have married Vanessa, not from mercenary motives, but because her fortune would have removed the barrier set by his reason (in the case of Stella) against surrender to the emotion of love. But when it came really to the pinch, he had to recognize that his obligation to Stella forbade.

By the time he came to write the *Travels* he had fought the battle of reason against emotion so long and with such steely determination — he was nearly

* And if one delightful story is true, a gay and vivacious one. It has very good authority, for Dr. Lyon said he had it from Swift himself. His mother came to visit him in Dublin. She took a lodging with Mrs. Brent (who subsequently became his housekeeper); and, as soon as she was settled in, asked her landlady 'Whether she could keep a secret?' Then she told her in strict confidence that she had a lover in the city, who would be coming to see her. Mrs. Brent, who was a Presbyterian, was scandalized — and intrigued. The lover duly came, was admitted with becoming secrecy, and on this footing continued for some time to visit his mistress, until shocked and bewildered Mrs. Brent was let into the joke. This happened, presumably, in 1700.

fifty at the time of his formal marriage — that physical attraction itself created no disturbance in him. He was now immune. But he was not immune from regret for an experience which, at the dictates of reason, he had refused, or even from regret for the barren lives of two rare women either of whom he could have loved, and both of whom in his thwarted and distorted way he had loved. This regret, in a man of such overweening pride in the rightness of his own reason, took the form of a will to annihilate the sexual relation, and with it every animal function of the body (and above all of the female body). It was unclean, it was loathsome, it was Yahoo.

His extremity of loathing of the physical — and primarily the sexual — functions of humanity was self-induced; and arose from his deliberate and prolonged repression of the emotion of love in the name of reason. It is doubtful whether he ever knew quite what he had done. His power of self-repression and consequently of self-ignorance, was almost superhuman. Besides, the impression made by his creation of the Yahoos is of an elemental upsurge giving demonic strength to an effort to annihilate the physical nature of humanity. In the picture of these creatures there is a fierce and terrible exaggeration, which breeds the conviction that Swift has overreached himself. For though it is well, painful but salutary, that we should have a vision of ourselves and our kind as 'the veriest human animals', we cannot see our animal selves as disgusting as the Yahoos: and this is not for lack of courage and veracity, but simply because no animals are. And if it is said, as Swift in effect says, that the *human* animal is more horrible than any simple animal, because he has the faculty of reason to make his animality sophisticated, the reply is obvious. It may be true; but it is irrelevant: first, because it is not as sophisticated brutes that the Yahoos are depicted; they are specifically denied the faculty of speech and reason. Gulliver alone possesses that. And, secondly, because the peculiar horror of the Yahoos consists not in their savagery but in their filth.

> Several of this cursed brood getting hold of the branches behind, leapt up into the tree, from whence they began to discharge their excrements on my head; however, I escaped pretty well, by sticking close to the stem of the tree, but was almost stifled with the filth, which fell about me on every side.[5]

In the same fashion they treat the discarded favourites of the herd leader. Their natural stink is horrible. When sexually excited the she-Yahoo emits an even more offensive stench. They are instinctively abhorred, because of 'their strange disposition to nastiness and dirt', by all other animals, which have a natural love of cleanliness. Unlike other animals the she-Yahoo admits the male while she is pregnant; and is fought by and fights the males. Cunningly, Swift appears to create the Yahoo merely by stripping the human of his reason, his speech, his laws, his clothes, and his cleanliness. But this is an illusion: for even if we carry the process of stripping the human to the limit of imaginative possibility, we do not arrive at the Yahoo. We might arrive at his cruelty and malice; we should never arrive at his nastiness and filth. That is a gratuitous degradation of humanity; not a salutary, but a shocking one.

Our recognition of this should not perturb our judgment. Book IV of the *Travels* is a masterpiece of concentration and control. The fact that Swift has given a repulsive exaggeration to his picture of the human animal does not invalidate or weaken his satire on human society. It is not the Yahoo, *in puris naturalibus*, who should and does disturb us (unless with concern for the mental health of Swift); it is the Yahoo endowed with reason and speech, with discovery and invention, clothed and cleansed, the creature whose institutions and practices as expounded by Gulliver roused in the Houyhnhnm a malaise of soul he had never experienced before. The natural Yahoo, as Swift depicts him, might be washed and deodorized; the civilized Yahoo would still be as dreadful to contemplate.

3

It is because the filthiness of the Yahoo is quite eccentric to Swift's satiric or moral purpose that we are compelled to ask why it is there at all, and why it is so dominant in the picture. If physical nastiness were an adequate and forceful symbol of moral corruption, we could accept it. But it is not. It is a totally misleading one. When we say the Yahoos make the impression of an elemental upsurge from the unconscious, we do not imply it is not deliberate; and when we say that Swift may not have known what he was doing, we mean simply that he may not have known why he was doing what he did. That his loathing of the physical being of man, and above all of the sexual being of woman, was now intense, is indubitable. It was now veritably a nightmare. But why had it become a nightmare? For there is no trace of this peculiar nausea in his earlier writing. He is coarse; but this is not a question of coarseness. In particular, there is no trace of it in the *Journal to Stella*. There he makes not a few intimate sexual jokes, but they are healthy jokes such as any lover not oppressed with false delicacy might make, with pleasure on both sides. One may fairly say that Swift's attitude in the *Journal* is that of a man who looks forward to marrying Stella — in his own good time indeed — without any misgiving about physical intimacy, much less any nausea at the idea of it. In ten or a dozen years this attitude has totally and catastrophically changed. The change is foreshadowed, as we have seen, in some of his verses in 1719-20, but it is first fully manifest in his Book IV of the *Travels*; and that was written in 1723, in the months following the death of Vanessa. At that time, unless he was much more inhuman than there is any reason to suppose he was, Swift's conscience must have been deeply disturbed by what had happened. He must have asked himself whether he was to blame. The Yahoo — and in particular the she-Yahoo — is the answer: and perhaps the only answer compatible with his pride in his 'reason'. No, he was not to blame. It was the women — the women who did not obey 'reason' and would not recognize that their pressure for sex-fulfilment in love proceeded from an animality which 'reason' must repudiate. Love was a relation of minds, not of bodies; nor could it be exclusive. If Stella had understood that, she would not have forced him into marriage, and the disaster would not have happened. If Vanessa had understood it, she would never have put the ill-starred question, and the disaster would not have happened. Vanessa was dead; Stella was alive.

But Woman — or that ineradicable element in her nature which worked to convert love into sexual intimacy — was the root of the evil and the cause of his own distress. He would put her where she belonged. Now, in Book IV, the sex-relation between humans must be degraded and annihilated; he presents it to his mind and to ours, as unspeakably disgusting. In chapter VIII he remarks that among the Yahoos 'the red-haired of both sexes are more libidinous and mischievous than the rest' (which may be a reminiscence of his hateful insinuations against 'Carrots', the Duchess of Somerset); and he goes on to relate his own particular encounter with a she-Yahoo.

Being one day abroad with my protector the sorrel nag . . . I entreated him to let me bathe in a river that was near. He consented, and I immediately stripped myself stark naked, and went down softly into the stream. It happened that a young female *Yahoo*, standing behind a bank, saw the whole proceeding, and inflamed by desire, as the nag and I conjectured, came running with all speed, and leaped into the water, within five yards of the place where I bathed. I was never in my life so terribly frighted; the nag was grazing at some distance not suspecting any harm. She embraced me after a most fulsome manner; I roared as loud as I could, and the nag came galloping towards me, whereupon she quitted her grasp, with the utmost reluctancy, and leaped upon the opposite bank, where she stood gazing and howling all the time I was putting on my clothes.
This was a matter of diversion to my master and his family, as well as of

mortification to myself. For now I could no longer deny that I was a real *Yahoo* in every limb and feature, since the females had a natural propensity to me, as one of their own species. Neither was the hair of this brute of a red colour (which might have been an excuse for an appetite a little irregular), but as black as a sloe, and her countenance did not make an appearance altogether so hideous as the rest of the kind; for, I think, she could not be above eleven years old.[6]

The insistence on the relative comeliness, the youth, and above all, the jet-black hair of this she-Yahoo causes as strange a malaise in us, as Gulliver's account of war did in his master. It is impossible to suppress the notion that Swift is engaged in annihilating Stella herself as a sexual being; as it were cauterizing out of his mind, and that retrospectively, as from the moment when he first became conscious of her beauty, the possibility of a sexual relation with her.

This urge to personal justification underlies the obsessive emphasis on that character of the Yahoo which is irrelevant equally to Swift's indictment of humanity and to Gulliver's self-purgation. In so far as Gulliver himself is affected by it, he behaves on his return like a man afflicted with mania: his abhorrence of physical contact with his own wife and children is a disease.

When I began to consider that by copulating with one of the *Yahoo* species I had become a parent of more, it struck me with the utmost shame, confusion and horror.[7]

This physical loathing of the human-Yahoo adds nothing to Gulliver's spiritual stature; it diminishes it. Neither has it any sanction in his experience of the Houyhnhnms, for they, after all, took sex in their stride, and regarded copulation as one of the necessary acts of a rational being. In this matter Gulliver leaves Houyhnhnm land more deeply irrational than he came to it.

And so did Swift. In the last resort we must pronounce that his vision lacks integrity. Its profound spiritual truth struggles against the egoistic power that makes for its corruption, and the truth cannot wholly prevail. Neither Gulliver, nor his creator, can really be reborn. The regaining of innocence is beyond the power of Swift or his manikin, for the urge to justify himself is too strong. Reason itself, which is the faculty whereby man, freed from the distortions of self-interest, simply recognizes and pursues the good, and is potentially universal in all men, is finally constrained to be the endorsement of Jonathan Swift.

Reason, therefore, must submit to the distortions he has suffered, and which his pride has magnified and indurated. Reason must be the mirror of a mind which abhors sexual love. Swift, in his Christian persona, had glimpses that the paradox was intolerable.

> Although reason were intended by Providence to govern our passions, yet it seems that in two points of the greatest moment to the being and continuance of the world, God hath intended our passions to prevail over our reason. The first is the propagation of the species, since no wise man ever married from the dictates of reason. The other is, the love of life, which from the dictates of reason, every man would despise, and wish it at an end, or that it never had a beginning. [8]

The Houyhnhnms are ostensibly an answer to both misgivings: they neither love life nor despise it; and they marry at the dictates of reason. They make the answer plausible because they are not human. Therefore they are no answer at all. The human predicament — Swift's predicament — remains precisely where it was. His real answer is the Yahoo. Whether or not God intended men's passions to prevail over their reason, Swift's sentence is that it is an abomination if they do. Who, save a Yahoo, would copulate with a Yahoo — even with a black-haired one, not too uncomely? Gulliver is horror-struck at what he has done. Swift is triumphant at what he has not done. He has saved Stella from becoming a Yahoo, as she would like to have been.

Even though Swift allows it to appear through the behaviour of Don Pedro that, in spite of the corruption of the mass, individuals are capable of loving one another, he draws the line at married love. For no obvious reason at all, we are informed that Don Pedro has no wife. If Arbuthnot was the model for the Don, Swift was falsifying the original; if he was not, still he serves as the criterion which Swift has admitted. But Arbuthnot was a Christian; and Swift, whenever he is giving unfettered expression to the workings of his spirit, must drop the Christian persona, and reveal the Manichee.

CHAPTER XXIII

THE DRAPIER: THE FIRST FOUR LETTERS

SWIFT did not intervene in the famous struggle over Wood's Half-pence until the resistance to the new coinage had already become formidable. Wood's patent was issued on July 12, 1722, and protest was almost immediate; it was finally surrendered on August 19, 1725. The agitation thus lasted three years. But it was not until half-way that Swift appeared upon the scene, in the disguise of the Drapier. Nor do his letters of 1722 and 1723 indicate that he was paying much attention to the movement that was developing.

The inattention was not due to indifference. But he had been disheartened by the reception of his *Proposal for the Universal Use of Irish Manufactures*; and now he was preoccupied. Up to the end of May 1723 the affair with Vanessa was gathering to its climax; and the satire of *Gulliver* was much more congenial to his condition than an attempt to arouse a spirit of unity and resolution in a mass of corruptible and contemptible humans.

For the first year and a half of the agitation Swift was withdrawn. When he first emerged from his lonely journey into the South and West of Ireland, he wrote to Sheridan that he hoped to be back in Dublin at the beginning of September: 'though it will be a bad time in the hurry of your lousy Parliament' (August 3, 1723). Yet that was the Parliament which was to act with some boldness in the matter of Wood's Halfpence. Swift may have been stimulated by their doings; but his letters show no sign of it. If we may trust a letter to Pope he was afraid of some action against him by the authorities. 'I am every day persuading myself that a dagger is at my throat, a halter about my neck, or chains about my feet, all prepared by those in power' (September 20, 1723). That was an exaggeration of his fears; but the violence of Chief Justice Whiteshed against Waters and the final surrender of the jury made him hesitate to involve another printer and possibly himself in a futile martyrdom. Until as late as January 19, 1724, he stuck to *Gulliver*. Shortly after that he turned to the first of the *Drapier's Letters*. It was published at the end of February.

2

Wood's patent empowered him to coin into pennies, halfpence and farthings 360 tons of copper over a period of 14 years, at a rate of not more than 30d. to the pound of copper. He was allowed to coin 100 tons in the first year, and 20 tons during each of the following 13 years. His coinage was 'to pass and be received as current money by such as will, voluntarily and wittingly, and not otherwise receive the same'. Nobody in Ireland had been consulted about the patent, and it was universally believed that Wood had paid £10,000 to the Duchess of Kendal, George I's German mistress, to get it. In consequence, it was so designed that he could recoup himself, and more. Whereas in England a pound of copper was coined into 23d., Wood was to make 30d. of it. Since his copper, when prepared into fillets for minting, was worth 1s. 6d. a pound, the gross profit of coining 360 tons of copper on these terms was nearly £40,000. That is putting the transaction at its best. It was a shameless piece of jobbery.

As soon as they heard of the patent, the Commissioners of the Irish Revenue took alarm and addressed a memorial to the Lord Lieutenant, on August 7, 1722, declaring that such a patent 'would be highly prejudicial to the trade and welfare of this Kingdom, and more particularly to His Majesty's revenue', to which they received no reply. On September 19 they addressed another memorial to the Commissioners of the Treasury in England, again without reply. A whole year now elapsed before the next important move, which was made when the 'lousy' Parliament met on September 9, 1723. What happened in the interval is not clear, beyond that the general apprehension steadily grew, and that by August 1723 Wood was busy making arrangements to import his Halfpence in large quantities. In that month James Maculla published a pamphlet expressing *Ireland's Consternation* 'in the losing of two hundred thousand pound of their gold and silver for brass money'.

The discontent was now so general that, immediately on meeting, the Irish Commons resolved themselves into a Committee of the whole House to consider the patent. They asked the Lord Lieutenant for a copy of it, and were told that he had none. However, one was produced on September 16. After examining witnesses they passed resolutions to the effect that the patent was prejudicial to the revenue, destructive of trade, and dangerous to property; that Wood had obtained it by falsely representing the state of the nation; that the coinage was fraudulent in itself; that the nation would lose 150 per cent (of what?) by it; and finally that it always had been and always would be highly dangerous to permit coinage by private persons. An address to the King in accordance with these resolutions was voted on September 27; and a similar address and resolutions by the Lords on September 28. This time a reply was sent, assuring them that 'if there have been any abuses committed by the patentee, His Majesty will give the necessary

orders for inquiring into those abuses and punishing them, and will do everything in his power for the satisfaction of his people'. This reply was laid
before the Commons on December 12. It did not satisfy them, and on
December 26 they made the definite request that the officers of the revenue
should be ordered not to receive or utter Wood's coinage.

3

Two months later Swift intervened with *A Letter to the Shop-keepers,
Tradesmen, Farmers and Common-people of Ireland* . . . by M. B. Drapier.
His pamphlet had been carefully prepared: even though he had a legal friend
to help him, he needed time for his accumulation of statutes and legal precedents to show that only gold and silver were lawful money which the King's
subjects were bound to accept; and, as the subsequent *Letters* were to show,
it was not easy for him to constrain himself within the disguise of a draper.
His indignation with his fellow-countrymen for their slavishness always
threatened to run away with him.

At the very outset he upbraids his audience for their lack of public spirit,
as shown in their treatment of his *Proposal* of 1720.

> It is a great fault among you, that when a person writes with no other
> intention than to do you good, you will not be at the pains to read his
> advices: One copy of this paper may serve a dozen of you, which will
> be less than a farthing apiece. It is your folly that you have no common
> or general interest in your view, not even the wisest among you, neither
> do you know or enquire or care who are your friends, or who are your
> enemies. About three years ago, a little book was written, to advise all
> people to wear the manufactures of this our own dear country: It had no
> other design, said nothing against the King or Parliament, or any man,
> yet the POOR PRINTER was prosecuted two years with the utmost
> violence, and even some WEAVERS themselves for whose sake it was
> written, being upon the JURY, FOUND HIM GUILTY. This would be
> enough to discourage any man from endeavouring to do you good,
> when you will either neglect him or fly in his face for his pains, and
> when he must expect only danger to himself and loss of money,
> perhaps to his ruin.[1]

That is, in part, the explanation of Swift's reluctance to enter into the
controversy. Swift's aim was to awaken a sense of Irish patriotism, or at
least of public spirit. This time his task was easier. The boycott of English
goods, combined with a conscientious improvement of Irish manufactures,
which he had previously proposed, required more disinterestedness and
determination than the Irish — or, indeed, any other — people were capable

of at that period, when the nationalist consciousness was only beginning to emerge. But a debasement of the coinage appeared to threaten the self-interest of everybody. How far Wood's Halfpence did so in fact is not clear. As a copper coinage it was distinctly superior in design and quality to what Ireland had been used to; and there was a serious shortage of small change in the country. It is not impossible that if Wood's coinage had been limited, as he afterwards proposed, to £40,000, it would have been economically beneficial. But the manner in which the patent had been obtained was an insult to Ireland — no greater, indeed, than the established practice of bestowing all the most lucrative offices in Ireland upon Englishmen; and rather less outrageous than the practice of giving English favourites huge pensions on the Irish establishment. The insult alone could not have aroused popular feeling. The native Irish would not have felt it; and the Anglo-Irish stood on too shaky a foundation to indulge their discontents. They depended upon the power of England to maintain them in their privileged position. It was not for them to be indignant if England treated them with a little of the contempt they showed towards the native Irish.

Swift hardly dared to think out his own position clearly. He took Protestant ascendancy for granted. What was really involved in the independence which he claimed for the Anglo-Irish; how far it was conceivable without a revolutionary change in the attitude of the Anglo-Irish towards the Irish natives, were questions he shut out from his conscious mind. But he seized upon a grievance which, precisely because it was universal enough to affect the Protestant rank and file, was also universal enough to bring the native Irish into the movement of resistance. Indeed, what could be purchased for a farthing or a halfpenny concerned them even more nearly than it did the Protestant tradesmen.

However mixed Swift's motives may have been — the bare idea of creating embarrassment for Walpole and the Whigs was not without its attractions for him — and however little he may have envisaged the consequences if he had been successful in persuading the Anglo-Irish to assert their independence, his immediate objective was plain and clear: to inspire enough determination in Irishmen of every kind to boycott Wood's Halfpence. To this end he became the perfect demagogue. His first *Letter* is packed with wild exaggerations. His great care over the statutes and precedents which he quotes to prove that the people are entirely within their rights in refusing the new copper, is matched by a complete recklessness about figures. He does not even trouble to get the amount of Wood's coinage right. He repeatedly says it is £90,000 instead of £100,800. (Never once in all the *Letters* does he give the correct figure: it simply dances about.) At one moment the new halfpence are intrinsically worth one-twelfth of their nominal value; at another one-ninth; at yet another one-sixth. All that matters is to create the impression that the new money is, to all intents and purposes, utterly worthless. He draws an absurd picture, based on ostensibly sober calculations, of the two hundred and forty horses it would require to bring a half-year of Squire Conolly's rents in halfpence to Dublin.* But with all his demagogic extravagances, he drives home his two main points: that the new money will mean ruin to the average man, if he is fool enough to accept it; and that the King himself has not the power to compel him to do so.

Therefore, my friends, stand to it one and all, refuse this filthy trash. It is no treason to rebel against Mr. Wood. His Majesty in his patent obliges nobody to take these halfpence, our gracious prince hath no so ill advisers about him; or if he had, yet you see the laws have not left it in the King's power, to force us to take any coin but what is lawful, of right standard gold and silver. Therefore you have nothing to fear.[2]

An essential part of Swift's technique in the *Letter* is to profess an unbounded faith in the benevolence of King George I towards Ireland. That enables him to hint, very broadly indeed, that the patent has been obtained by bribery and chicane: the generous monarch has been malignantly deceived into believing that the patent was for the advantage of Ireland. In a later *Letter* he was to use this ironical device with a subtlety which no credible draper could employ: for the present, it serves to fill out a convincing picture of the nominal author. M. B. Drapier is a shrewd, homely and downright man, and a passionate Hanoverian loyalist. But the best touch of all, both for propaganda and portraiture, is the postscript.

N.B. The author of this paper is informed by persons who have made it their business to be exact in their observations on the true value of these halfpence, that any person may expect to get a quart of twopenny ale for thirty-six of them.[3]

4

Having launched his *Letter*, Swift turned back to *Gulliver*. On April 2 he wrote to Ford: 'I shall have finished my Travels very soon if I have health, leisure and humour.' His health in fact was poor at this time. But at the

---

* William Conolly, Speaker of the Irish Commons and Chief Commissioner of the Irish Revenue, was reputed the richest man in Ireland. In July 1723 he had purchased the Rathfarnham lands of the Duke of Wharton for £62,000, which would not have endeared him to Swift, who had a weakness for that extravagant and unstable young man. Conolly was a devoted adherent of the English interest. In 1722 he had begun to build himself the superb house at Castletown, co. Kildare.

same time he told his friend in England of the *Letter*. He was dubious of the effect. 'One can promise nothing from such wretches as the Irish people.' Even Archbishop King, he said, was nervous.

I came just now from a Commission with the Chancellor, Abp Dublin &c. I spoke very severely to the knaves about the farthings. I told them the baseness and pusillanimity when they and others were sent for by the L? on that subject, they all talked as much against the thing as I. But people are more in fear than ever.

Meanwhile, on March 10, Carteret as Secretary of State had written to tell the Lieutenant, the Duke of Grafton, that a Committee of the English Privy Council had been appointed to inquire into Wood's patent and to request that the Irish Parliament should send over witnesess and documents. The request was disregarded, really on the ground that the address of both Houses of Parliament against the coinage made compliance derogatory to themselves; and, obviously, since neither house was in session, it was both invidious and dangerous for any members of either to undertake such a mission. Apparently, Grafton's failure to persuade Parliament to send witnesses was regarded in London as a final proof of his incompetence to handle the situation. He was recalled on April 9, and Carteret himself appointed in his place. As soon as this was known, Swift wrote to him on April 28, at the request, he said, 'of many of the principal persons in the Kingdom', who knew that he was personally acquainted with Carteret, to inform him of the universal opposition to the patent, and asking him to employ his influence to have it surrendered. Carteret, diplomatically, delayed to reply; for he knew that the object of his appointment was to break down the resistance. A week before his letter to Carteret, Swift had inserted in a newspaper issued by Harding, the printer of the *Drapier*, a comment on a London report that the Committee of Inquiry had met on April 10; but no witnesses against the patent had appeared.

Mr. Woods, the Patentee was heard in his own defence, and orders are given for an essay to be made of its fineness, value and weight, compared with the former coinage of Ireland.

The comment upon this is undoubtedly Swift's:

We hope the Kingdom will observe that the impudence of this same Woods is equal in its kind to the perniciousness of his project. Here he gives us a scene in the Committee of the English Council putting the unanimous representation of the Parliament of Ireland into one balance, and his halfpence into another . . . And what is the result?

Orders are given for an essay to be made of the fineness, value and weight of the halfpence. To what end? To compare it with the former coinage in Ireland. So that, if upon any great emergency in recent times when silver and gold were rare, under the pressure of war or any other difficulties, base coin hath been uttered, this man would insinuate that the precedent will be allowed in times of peace and plenty and under so happy an administration as ours, and so his business and ours be done. But God be thanked, we live under a gracious King; the patent does not pretend to oblige us to take this coin, and the pamphlet lately published entitled *A Letter to the Shop-keepers, Tradesmen, Farmers, &c* upon this subject, shews: *That by the Law no man is bound in payment to take any money but gold and silver*; so that unless we contribute to our own destruction, Mr. Wood's trash may lie upon his own hands.

But after all, is it possible without some indignation to conceive a whole Kingdom kept in a fright for so many months by one *obscure, inconsiderable, insignificant, ill-designing mechanic?*[4]

The publication of the report from London which was the cause of Swift's outburst, moved the Irish Privy Council, as representing Ireland when Parliament was not sitting, to draw up an address to the King repeating the request made by the Commons that the officers of the revenue should be instructed to refuse the Halfpence.

The full report of the English Committee was not published in Dublin until August 19. But in the meantime some particulars of the proceedings had leaked out, in the form of a paragraph from London (no doubt inspired by Wood) which appeared on August 1. It said that various merchants on examination had agreed that there was an urgent need of new copper money in Ireland; and that the assay had proved that Wood had in all respects performed his contract. Nevertheless, the Patentee now proposed to limit his coinage to £40,000, 'unless the exigencies of trade' required more; and, in order to relieve the apprehensions that Ireland would be drained of its gold, he would take manufactures in exchange; and nobody should be obliged to take more than 5½d. at one payment. Finally, a note stated that no evidence appeared to prove any of the mischiefs and abuses complained of.

In his second *Letter — to Mr. Harding the Printer*, dated August 4, the Drapier pulverizes this statement sentence by sentence. He adjusts himself a little to the finding of the assay by now saying that the Halfpence are only seven times above their intrinsic value, instead of the previous twelve and nine times. Apart from that insignificant concession, he is entirely aggressive. Who are these merchants? Wood's confederates who are making their profit. Wood has satisfactorily performed his contract. 'His contract! With whom? Was it with the parliament or people of Ireland? Are they not to be the purchasers?' The assay is a fake: Wood picked out a few decent coins for the purpose. The exigencies of trade! Who is to judge them? Wood! And he will judge of our exigencies by his own. He will accept our manufactures! That is the very misery we complain of. He will buy 6s. worth of wool for 6d. No one will be obliged to take more than 5½d. Sheer high treason? No one can be obliged to take any but legal money of silver or gold.

Good God! Who are this wretch's advisers? Who are his supporters, abettors, encouragers or sharers? Mr. Wood will *oblige* me to take fivepence halfpenny of his brass in every payment! And I will shoot Mr. Wood and his deputies through the head, like highwaymen or housebreakers, if they dare to force one farthing of their coin upon me in the payment of one hundred pounds. It is no loss of honour to submit to the lion, but who, with the figure of a man, can think with patience of being devoured by a rat?[5]

No evidence appeared! The impudence of this exceeds all the rest. The unanimous voice of the Irish Parliament and the Privy Council is not evidence? 'If his copper were diamonds, and the Kingdom were entirely against it, would that not be sufficient to reject it?'

Having torn the statement to shreds, he turns to his audience. You are becoming fearful of a Royal proclamation commanding that the Halfpence be accepted. It will never be issued; 'and if it should, yet upon this occasion will be of no force'. Wood is trying to wear you down. And I am trying to keep up your spirits.

When the evil day is come (if it must come) let us mark and observe those who presume to offer these halfpence in payment. Let their names, and trades, and places of abode be made public, that every one may be aware of them, as betrayers of their country, and confederates with Mr. Wood.[6]

He then suggests that 'some skilful judicious pen' should draw up a declaration, to be signed by two or three hundred principal gentlemen of estates, that they will refuse to accept the Halfpence and will order their tenants to do likewise. He gives a draft of such a declaration, which is forcibly and admirably phrased, and must have finally disposed of any lingering belief that the author was a draper. In the third *Letter – to the Nobility and Gentry of the Kingdom of Ireland*, which is dated August 25, it can hardly be said that he even pretends to be one. At any rate it is entirely out of character. It is a careful and reasoned reply to the full report of the

Committee of the English Privy Council, which reached him on August 18. Swift set to work upon it immediately.

5

The Report of the London Committee is said to have been drafted by Walpole himself. It rehearsed the substance of the addresses of the Irish Parliament, and the Lieutenant's difficulty in getting witnesses, which it pronounced 'very strange'; and it incorporated the result of the assay, which was that the coinage satisfied the conditions of the patent, and was greatly superior to any previous copper coinages for Ireland. (However, the Committee omitted the important fact that 'the single pieces were not so equally coined in the weight as they should have been'.) It reported therefore that there was no possibility of vacating the patent on the ground of fraud. It went on to declare that it was undoubtedly within the royal prerogative to issue a patent to a private person for coining copper in Ireland, and that previous patents had not imposed such strict conditions as those imposed on Wood. (They had indeed been fixed by Sir Isaac Newton.) Neither had the patent been obtained by false representations of the state of Ireland: there was no doubt that there was a real want of small money in the country.

> The Committee cannot discover the least pretence to say, this patent was passed or obtained in a clandestine or unprecedented manner, unless it is to be understood, that your Majesty's granting a liberty of coining copper money for Ireland, under the Great Seal of Great Britain, without referring the consideration thereof to the principal officers of Ireland, is the grievance and mischief complained of . . . The Lords of the Committee hope it will not be asserted that any legal orders or resolutions of your Majesty can or ought to be called in question or invalidated, because the advice or consent of your chief governors of that Kingdom was not previously had upon them.[7]

If, as Wood complains, the officers of the revenue in Ireland have on their own authority given 'orders, directions, signification, or insinuations' to their subordinates not to accept the coinage, it is 'a very extraordinary proceeding'. It is contrary to the terms of the patent, and the Committee advises against giving any such directions as the Irish Commons and Privy Council have requested. It concludes by advising that Wood's proposal to limit the coinage to £40,000 should be accepted, and that it should be transmitted to the Irish government, when 'it will give them a proper opportunity to consider whether', after that reduction, 'anything can be done for the further satisfaction of the people of Ireland'.

Swift begins by insinuating that the publication of the report, because it had not appeared in the *London Gazette*, was a manœuvre of Wood's. He doubts whether it is a genuine report of the Privy Council, because it is 'written with the turn and air of a pamphlet'. Having thus freed his hands to deal with it, he says that if it is genuine, Wood has treated the Committee with great rudeness, in publishing it without authority; and, anyhow, such a report is not a law, and remains disputable by every subject. All of which is obviously beyond the scope of any imaginable draper.

This (may it please your lordships and worships) may seem a strange way of discoursing in an illiterate shopkeeper. I have endeavoured (although without the help of books) to improve that small portion of reason which God hath pleased to give me, and when reason plainly appears before me, I cannot turn my head away from it. Thus, for instance, if any lawyer should tell me that such a point were law, from which many gross palpable absurdities must follow, I would not, I could not believe him. If Sir Edward Coke should positively assert (which he nowhere does, but the direct contrary) that a limited prince could by his prerogative oblige his subjects to take half an ounce of lead, stamped with his image, for twenty shillings in gold, I should swear he was deceived or a deceiver, because a power like that, would leave the whole lives and fortunes of his people entirely at the mercy of the monarch. [8]

He proceeds to name and dismiss the witnesses for Wood: two are criminals, one is a banker who hoped to make a profit out of the Halfpence, the fourth is one 'whose name 1 know not'. Wood himself had been a collector of taxes in Shropshire, and dismissed for embezzlement.

He then turns to the passage of the report which said it was 'very strange' that no witnesses against Wood appeared from Ireland 'in a matter which had raised so great a clamour'. The committee had prejudged the whole case by calling the united sense of both Houses of Parliament a 'universal clamour'.

I desire to know how such a style would be resented in England from a committee of Council to a Parliament, and how many impeachments would follow upon it. But supposing the appellation to be proper, I never heard of a wise minister who despised the universal clamour of a people, and if that clamour can be quieted by disappointing the fraudulent practice of a single person, the purchase is not exorbitant. [9]

Suppose this had happened in England, would His Majesty debate half an hour what he had to do? Would the matter be referred to the Privy Council or Westminster Hall, the two Houses of Parliament plaintiffs and William Wood defendant?

> And is there even the smallest difference between the two cases? Were not the people of Ireland born as free as those of England? How have they forfeited their freedom? Is not their Parliament as fair a representative of the people as that of England? Are they not subjects of the same King? Does not the same sun shine upon them? And have they not the same God for their protector? Am I a freeman in England, and do I become a slave in six hours by crossing the Channel?[10]

That is why no witnesses appeared against Wood. How could they dare to represent the representatives of the nation?

When the Irish Parliament said that the patent was passed in a clandestine manner, surely the Committee did not imagine that they meant that it had not passed in the common forms 'and run through every office where fees and perquisites were due'. No, they meant that it was kept secret from the people and government of Ireland. The Committee admits this, but argues that such a patent is none the less good in law, and in the power of the prerogative.

> God forbid that so mean a man as I should meddle with the King's prerogative: But I have heard wise men say, that the King's prerogative is bounded and limited by the good and welfare of his people. I desire to know whether it is not understood and avowed that the good of Ireland was intended by this patent. But Ireland is not consulted at all in the matter, and as soon as Ireland is informed of it, they declare against it; the two Houses of Parliament and the Privy-council addresses His Majesty on the mischiefs apprehended by such a patent. The Privy-council in England takes the matter out of Parliament's cognizance; the good of the Kingdom is dropped, and it is now determined that Mr. Wood shall have the power of ruining a whole nation for his private advantage.[11]

Nevertheless, it is the least forcible of the *Letters*; it is even rather tedious. Swift's style was always cramped, as he frequently acknowledged, by the necessities of a detailed reply to an argument. Its tone and content show that it was primarily aimed (as indeed the title indicates) to prevent the Irish ruling class from being intimidated by the formal report of the English Privy Council in Wood's favour. At the end he confesses his embarrassment, and turns his own apology for it into a splendid flight of humorous denunciation.

> I am very sensible that such a work as I have undertaken might have worthily employed a much better pen. But when a house is attempted

to be robbed it often happens that the weakest in the family runs first to stop the door. All the assistance I had were some informations from an eminent person, whereof I am afraid I have spoiled a few by endeavouring to make them of a piece with my own productions; and the rest I was not able to manage: I was in the case of David who could not move in the armour of Saul, and therefore I rather chose to attack this 'uncircumcised Philistine (Wood I mean) with a sling and a stone'. And I may say for Wood's honour as well as my own, that he resembles Goliath in many circumstances, very applicable to the present purpose; for Goliath had 'a helmet of brass upon his head, and he was armed with a coat of mail, and the weight of the coat was five thousand shekels of brass, and he had greaves of brass upon his legs, and a target of brass between his shoulders'. In short he was like Mr. Wood, all over brass; And 'he defied the armies of the living God'. Goliath's conditions of combat were likewise the same with those of Wood. 'If he prevail against us, then shall we be his servants:' But if it happens that I prevail over him, I renounce the other part of the condition, he shall never be a servant of mine, for I do not think him fit to be trusted in any honest man's shop.[12]

6

The English Privy Council had ordered the Irish Lords Justices to revoke any instructions given by government officials to refuse the coins. None had been given. But it also ordered them to issue positive orders that the money be permitted to pass 'without any let, suit, trouble, molestation or denial of any of his Majesty's officers or ministers whatsoever'. Without definitely refusing to do this, the Lords Justices did nothing. The excitement was now intense. Declarations on the pattern Swift had given in his second *Letter* were published daily; tradesmen suspected of having made arrangements to distribute the coin hastened to issue advertisements protesting their innocence; corporate repudiations by trade-guilds, signed with long lists of names were circulated and posted up. The most intriguing of these, at this distance of time, is that of the flying stationers, or newsboys.

We the Flying Stationers of the City of Dublin (commonly call'd Newsboys) hearing the report of the Vile Practices of William Wood's Design of Ruining this Kingdom. Do hearby give Notice to all Gentlemen, Ladies, and others who shall have Occasion to buy News, Poems, Songs, Letters, Lampoons, &c. That we will not Receive or Offer in Change any of WILLIAM WOODS Drossy Half Pence or Farthings, because we can neither get News, Ale, Brandy, Tobacco nor Snuff for such cursed Stuff.[13]

There are fifty-two names to this, and all but two or three are native Irish. Their attitude is good evidence how deep and wide the movement was.

In the meantime, on July 13, Lindsay, the Tory Primate, had died; and on August 31 Hugh Boulter had been appointed from England: a capable and resolute man whose life was to be devoted to promoting and consolidating the English interest in Ireland. Between him and Walpole there was a close understanding, whereas between Walpole and Carteret there was bitter rivalry. Swift was now working hand in glove with Archbishop King; and both knew well what Boulter's appointment meant. The iron net was closing on the Anglo-Irish. The idea of possibly breaking through it by a bold thrust inspired the fourth *Letter to the Whole People of Ireland*. It is dated October 13 and was published just in time to greet Carteret on his arrival on October 22.

Swift made cunning use of his title-page. 'The Whole People of Ireland' suggests, and was meant to suggest, Protestants and Papists combined; yet in the text of his *Letter* he explicitly repudiates any appeal to the Papists. He repels the charge that the Papists have entered into an association against the Halfpence: it is 'notoriously known that they never once offered to stir in the matter'. That is on the first page; but at the end he shifts his ground again. It is not the Irish who refuse the Halfpence, but 'the true English people of Ireland although we take it for granted that the Irish will do so too whenever they are asked'. The support of the Irish was, of course, indispensable to the boycott he was inspiriting; and by his title-page he appealed to them, while pretending not to in his text.

After emphasizing once again that the King's prerogative is limited by law and cannot extend to compelling his subjects to take copper as lawful money, he ironically expatiates on the 'unexampled loyalty' of the Irish.

Now, here you may see that the vile accusation of Wood and his accomplices, charging us with 'disputing the King's prerogative' by refusing his brass, can have no place, because compelling the subject to take any coin which is not sterling is no part of it, and I am very confident if it were so, we should be the last of his people to dispute it, as well from that inviolable loyalty we have always paid to His Majesty, as from the treatment we might in such a case justly expect from some who seem to think, we have neither common sense or common senses. But God be thanked, the best of them are only our fellow-subjects and not our masters. One great merit I am sure we have, which those of English birth can have no pretence to, that our ancestors reduced this Kingdom to the obedience of England, for which we have been rewarded with a worse climate, the privilege of being governed by laws to which we do not consent, a House of Parliament without jurisdiction, almost an incapacity for all employments; and the dread of Wood's halfpence.[14]

The combination of 'inviolable loyalty' and the fear of inhuman treatment, the nuance of contempt in his conviction that if the prerogative did include the right to enforce the currency of Wood's Halfpence the Irish would be the last to resist it, are the purest Swift. So is the consummate impertinence of his next paragraph.

But we are so far from disputing the King's prerogative in coining, that we own he has power to give a patent to any man for setting his royal image and superscription upon whatever materials he pleases, and liberty to the patentee to offer them in any country from England to Japan, only attended with one small limitation. That nobody alive is obliged to take them.[15]

He turns to a report that Carteret is coming over 'to settle Wood's half-pence'. It is unbelievable that the Lord Lieutenant should be sent over suddenly 'to put a hundred thousand pounds into the pocket of a sharper'. But, suppose it true, what can he do? He will have to convert Parliament, and he has not the means to do it. Swift then gives a list of the great Irish employments in the hands of absentee Englishmen. There is really nothing left to bribe the Irish parliament. And even if there were, can you expect them to accept payment in Wood's brass at 80 per cent discount? Even the Englishmen sent over to fill our posts are on our side.

Money, the great divider of the world, hath by a strange revolution, been the great uniter of a most divided people. Who would leave a hundred pounds a year in England (a country of freedom) to be paid a thousand in Ireland out of Wood's exchequer.[16]

Boulter himself will be a good Irishman on this article.

But we are accused of trying to 'shake off our dependence on the crown of England'. People who come from England and the faint-hearts among ourselves often shake their heads and say we are 'a depending Kingdom'.

I have looked over all the English and Irish statutes without finding any law that makes Ireland depend on England, any more than England does upon Ireland. We have indeed obliged ourselves to have the same King with them, and consequently they are obliged to have the same King with us. For the law was made by our own Parliament, and our ancestors then were not such fools (whatever they were in the preceding reign) to bring themselves under I know not what dependence, which is now talked of without any ground of law, reason, or common sense.[17]

This was a direct challenge to England. Only four years before the English parliament had formally declared that it had and ought to have the right to make laws which were binding upon Ireland; and it had frequently made such laws and enforced them in matters of vital importance to Ireland. Indeed, the right of the English parliament to make laws for Ireland had not been questioned until 1698, when William Molyneux published *The Case of Ireland's being bound by Acts of Parliament in England stated*, in which he argued that, in order to be binding, such acts must have the consent of the Irish parliament. Seeing that the English Commons promptly and unanimously voted his book 'of dangerous consequence to the Crown and Parliament of England' and ordered it to be burned, the Drapier was asking for trouble.

> Let whoever think otherwise [he went on], I M. B. Drapier desire to be excepted, for I declare, next under God, I *depend* only on the King my sovereign, and on the laws of my own country; and I am so far from *depending* upon the people of England, that if they should ever rebel against my sovereign (which God forbid) I would be ready at the first command from His Majesty to take arms against them, as some of *my* countrymen did against *theirs* at Preston. And if such a rebellion should be so successful as to fix the Pretender on the throne of England, I would venture to transgress that statute so far as to lose every drop of my blood to hinder him from being King of Ireland.[18]

This was subtle, though hardly scrupulous. He insinuates that the English were Jacobites, because some Irish troops had been sent over against the rebels in 1715; and he supposes a Jacobite parliament, under a restored Stuart, in England. Would resistance then be lawful or not? If lawful, where is the dependency? If not, where is the Protestant succession? The dilemma would exasperate, but not convince. He then admits that the English parliament had in fact assumed the power of enacting laws for Ireland, and that Molyneux was the first to challenge it.

> But the love and torrent of power prevailed. Indeed the arguments on both sides were invincible. For in reason, all government without the consent of the governed is the very definition of slavery. But in fact, eleven men well armed will certainly subdue one single man in his shirt. But I have done. For those who have used power to cramp liberty have gone so far as to resent even the liberty of complaining, although a man on the rack was never known to be refused the liberty of roaring as loud as he thought fit.[19]

Like a man in a consumption, Ireland sways between unreasonable fear and unworthy hopes; it has grasped at a third-hand rumour that a great English minister has said 'we shall be no more troubled with those halfpence'. But this matter does not rest with English ministers.

> The remedy is wholly in your own hands, and therefore I have digressed a little in order to refresh and continue that spirit so seasonably raised among you, and to let you see that by the laws of GOD, of NATURE, of NATIONS, and of your own COUNTRY, you ARE and OUGHT to be as FREE a people as your brethren in England.[20]

This was a direct repudiation in terms of the English declaratory Act of 1720.

When the argument was lifted to this level, only a sleight of mind could confine it to the Anglo-Irish. If the Irish Papists were not free by the laws of Ireland, by the laws of God and Nature they certainly were. If the fact that eleven men well armed would subdue one single man in his shirt was the cause of the slavery of the Anglo-Irish, it was ten times more the cause of the slavery of the Irish natives: unless, of course, the laws of God and Nature prescribed that in order to be free a man must belong to the Church of England. Only half of Swift believed that.

He concluded with an ironical attack on Walpole, who had been reported to have said that he would make the Irish swallow the Halfpence 'in fireballs'. This he counters with one of his absurd calculations. Allowing two Halfpence to each fireball, it would mean seventeen fireballs to be swallowed by every single person in Ireland, which would require fifty thousand operators to administer. The trouble and charge of the experiment would exceed the profit. The report therefore is probably untrue.

> But I will now demonstrate beyond all contradiction that Mr. Walpole is against this project of Mr. Wood, and is an entire friend to Ireland, only by this one invincible argument, that he has the universal opinion of being a wise man, an able minister, and in all his proceedings pursuing the true interest of the King his master: And that as his integrity is above all corruption, so is his fortune above all temptation. I reckon therefore we are perfectly safe from that corner, and shall never be under the necessity of contending with so formidable a power, but be left to possess our brogues and potatoes in peace, as remote from thunder as we are from Jove.[21]

CHAPTER XXIV

THE DRAPIER: THE BARREN VICTORY

IT is not surprising that others than Carteret thought the fourth *Letter* seditious; and Carteret had not much difficulty in persuading a majority of the Irish Privy Council on October 27 to prosecute the printer, and to issue a proclamation offering a reward of £300 for the discovery of the author. But Archbishop King refused to sign either the order for Harding's prosecution, or the proclamation, declaring that

> If his excellency would secure us from the brass money, I would sign it, or any other, tending only to the disadvantage of private persons; but, till we had that security, I would look upon this proclamation no otherwise than as a step towards passing that base and mischievous coin, and designed to intimidate those who opposed the passing it.[1]

Three others joined him in refusing to sign the proclamation. Some of those who signed it, notably Broderick, now Lord Middleton, the Lord Chancellor, had previously signed a declaration against the Halfpence; and they salved their consciences by asking that the proclamation should make it clear that the author was not being pursued 'for what he writ against the Halfpence'. The proclamation itself was a compromise; it described the *Letter* as 'a wicked and malicious pamphlet ... in which are contained several seditious and scandalous paragraphs highly reflecting upon His Majesty and His Ministers, tending to alienate the affections of his good subjects of England and Ireland from each other, and to promote sedition among the people'.

The proclamation was issued on October 27. On October 30 Archbishop King had an interview with Carteret, in which he told him that the author of the *Letter* 'had some thoughts of owning and even declaring himself to be the author of it;' he further said that 'he believed in the present conjuncture the author might safely put himself upon his country and stand his trial, since it was generally understood his crime was writing against the Halfpence'. Carteret replied that 'no man in the Kingdom, how great and considerable soever he might think himself, was of weight enough to stand a matter of this nature'. And, in writing an account of the conversation to the ministry in London, Carteret declared his intention, 'if the author was so bold as to declare himself', of taking him into custody without bail. He ended:

My Lord Shannon was the first person who acquainted me, that he had received intelligence that this matter was under the deliberation of several considerable persons in this city; but neither he nor I could give entire credit to it till I received this visit from the Archbishop. 'Tis the general opinion here, that Doctor Swift is the author of the pamphlet, and yet nobody thinks it can be proved upon him; though many believe he will be spirited up to own it. Your Grace by this may see what opinion the Archbishop of Dublin and Swift have of the humour of the people whose affections they have exceedingly gained of late by inveighing against the halfpence.[2]

On November 1, Tickell, now in Addison's former post as Secretary to the Lieutenant, wrote to a friend in England: 'The printer is run away, the hawkers dare not cry it, and the author is now writing an answer against himself.'

Tickell was referring to the pamphlet which was first published in Faulkner's 1735 edition of Swift's works, entitled *A Letter to the Lord Chancellor Middleton*. It was then printed with the signature J. S. and dated from the Deanery House, October 26, 1724. It may have been begun on that day, but the greater part of it was written after the appearance of the proclamation, which it quotes in detail. It bears signs of having been written in great haste. Since the Archbishop was engaged in sounding Carteret to discover what his reaction would be if Swift owned to the fourth *Letter*, it seems that Swift, on hearing from King what Carteret's attitude would be, thought better of any intention he may have had of avowing his authorship. For that is precisely what he does not do in the *Letter to Middleton*. Tickell's description of it as 'an answer against himself' is accurate: and it sounds very like what Swift's own description of it would have been.

At any rate, it is a mistake to suppose that the *Letter to Middleton* contains any avowal of Swift's authorship of the fourth *Letter*. No lawyer — and Swift had lawyers in mind — could possibly have extracted such an admission from it. Indeed, much of the brilliance of the pamphlet lies in the extraordinary skill with which Swift, while consistently treating the *Drapier* as a third person, of whom he has no knowledge, leaves no doubt in any reader's mind that he *is* the Drapier. Swift's purpose, in fact, is clear enough: he intended, at the moment when he was composing the *Letter to Middleton*, to write no more under the disguise of the Drapier, to identify himself only with those of the Drapier's opinions which the Government could not attack, and to appear in person as the leader of the movement against the Halfpence.

I do think it my duty [he wrote], since the Drapier will probably be no more heard of, so far to supply his place as not to incur his fortune:

For I have learnt from old experience that there are times wherein a man ought to be cautious as well as innocent.[3]

His technique is superb. He counters the intimidating effect of the proclamation by boldly endorsing the first three *Letters*; and at the same time, under cover of allowing that in his fourth *Letter* the Drapier was carried perhaps a little too far by his zeal in a good cause, he seizes the opportunity to restate his case, and to reduce to trivialities all the charges brought against him. On the charge of promoting sedition, for instance, Swift says:

> I must confess that with many others, I thought he meant well; although he might have the failing of better writers, to be not always fortunate in the manner of expressing himself.
> However, since the Drapier is but one man, I shall think I do a public service by asserting that the rest of my countrymen are wholly free from learning out of *his* pamphlets to reflect on the King or his ministers, to breed sedition.[4]

The equivoque is brazen. It is capable of an innocent interpretation; but the real meaning is unmistakable. The Irish people *are* seditious and do not need to be inspired to it by the Drapier. As for reflecting on the King and his ministers, although it has been reported that Mr. Walpole has said uncomplimentary things about the Irish people, the Drapier, 'wholly clears Mr. Walpole of this charge by very strong arguments'. Anyhow, the reports obviously emanated from Wood. 'Thus I have sufficiently justified the people of Ireland from learning any bad lessons out of the Drapier's pamphlets with regard to the King and his ministers'. As to the charge of alienating the affections of the people of England and Ireland from each other, 'I believe the Drapier, whatever his intentions were, hath left that matter just as he found it.' The English know little more about Ireland than they do about Mexico: only that

> It is a country subject to the King of England, full of bogs, inhabited by wild Irish Papists, who are kept in awe by mercenary troops sent from thence: And their general opinion is that it were better for England if the whole island were sunk into the sea.[5]

Since the first three *Letters* have not received any public censure, he regards them as unexceptionable. The people should read them often to keep up their spirit.

As for this last letter, against which a proclamation is issued; I shall only say that I could wish it were stripped of all that can be any way exceptionable; which I would not think it below me to undertake, if my abilities were equal; but being naturally somewhat slow of comprehension, no lawyer, and apt to believe the best of those who profess good designs, without any visible motive either of profit or honour, I might pore for ever, without distinguishing the cockle from the corn.[6]

In this strain the letter continues, extolling the first three *Letters*, and, while ostensibly condemning the Fourth, making its points over again. He apologises for the dullness and insipidity of his present letter; but that is inevitable,

For a man of the most superior understanding will find it impossible to make the best use of it, while he writes in constraint; perpetually softening, correcting, or blotting out expressions, for fear of bringing his printer, or himself, under a prosecution from my Lord Chief Justice Whiteshed.[7]

Therefore all the public can expect in future is an occasional warning to beware of Mr. Wood's Halfpence, and to refer themselves to the Drapier's first three letters for reasons. Unless, of course, authority shall think to forbid all writings on the subject, except in favour of Wood: in which case,

I will obey as it becomes me; only when I am in danger of bursting, I will go and whisper among the reeds, not any reflection upon the wisdom of my countrymen; but only these few words, BEWARE OF WOOD'S HALFPENCE.[8]

There was nothing in the *Letter to Middleton* which could possibly have justified legal proceedings against Swift as the author of the fourth *Letter*. His motive for suppressing it must have been that, on second thoughts, he felt nothing would be gained by his coming forward in person to lead the movement. Everybody knew, or everybody believed, that he *was* the author of the fourth *Letter*. Nobody could prove it; it is doubtful whether the printer himself could have proved it, so careful was Swift to employ intermediaries. It was worth the sacrifice of some brilliant irony to preserve his enormously effective anonymity. To have appeared in person would not, because it could not, enhance his popularity; and his concealment probably strengthened the movement. The participants felt that they were united in a conspiracy to hide him. When a Quaker supporter had the bright idea of circulating a fly-sheet simply containing a passage from Samuel I. xiv (which, Tickell reported, men, women and children had by heart) Swift's popularity reached a zenith.

And the people said unto Saul, Shall Jonathan die, who hath wrought this great salvation in Israel? God forbid: as the Lord liveth, there shall not one hair of his head fall to the ground, for he hath wrought with God this day. So the people rescued Jonathan that he died not.

In this situation the publication of the *Letter to Middleton* would have been almost an anti-climax. Wisely Swift turned himself to securing the acquittal of the printer.

2

Harding was arrested on November 7. On November 11 Swift wrote some *Seasonable Advice*, which was sent to all who were likely to be chosen members of the Grand Jury to consider the bill against him. It called on them to consider, first, the service done by the first three *Letters*; second, that the one incriminated was by the same author, whose innocent intentions had never been doubted; third, whether the expressions charged were really liable to just exception; fourth, what effect finding a true bill would have on the Irish people, who would imagine that Dublin had changed its mind and now intended to take the Halfpence; fifth, that the members of the jury, being merchants and shopkeepers, had nothing to lose by rejecting it.

They do not expect any employments in the state, to make up in their own private advantage, the destruction of their country. Whereas those who go about to advise, entice, or threaten them to find that bill, have great employments, which they have a mind to keep, or to get greater, which was likewise the case of all those who signed to have the author prosecuted. And therefore it is known that his grace the Lord Archbishop of Dublin, so renowned for his piety, and wisdom, and love of his country, absolutely refused to condemn the book or the author.[9]

Lastly, let them think of the effect upon the innocent printer, who could not possibly be expected to know what expressions lawyers might pick upon as exceptionable, 'where no other man is able to find any'.

This Carteret regarded, or affected to regard, as 'insolent, scandalous and seditious', and ordered the law-officers to apply to the Grand Jury to present it. The Jury refused. Chief Justice Whiteshed discharged it and ordered a new one. Whereupon Swift circulated a resolution of the English House of Commons of November 13, 1680.

Resolved, that the discharging of a Grand Jury by any Judge, before the end of the Term, Assizes, or Sessions, while matters are under their consideration, and not presented, is arbitrary, illegal, destructive to public justice, and a manifest violation of his oath, and is a means to subvert the fundamental laws of the Kingdom.[10]

When, on November 23, the new jury likewise refused to present *Seasonable Advice*, Whiteshed did not dare to discharge it. It met again, on November 28, and turned the tables by making a presentment of its own: 'of all such persons as have attempted, or shall endeavour, by fraud or otherwise, to impose the said Halfpence upon us'. Carteret told the Government that he suspected that Swift was the author of this also; which may have been true, though it is rather difficult to suppose him, in his then mood, writing 'Whereas His Majesty hath been graciously pleased to leave his loyal subjects of this Kingdom at liberty to take or refuse the said halfpence'; for that surrendered Swift's main contention: that the King's prerogative in this matter was limited by law.

Still, the Jury's attitude must have satisfied him. 'The Government and Judges', he wrote to Ford, 'are all at their wit's end.'[11] Carteret reported to England that a banker juryman, who had been in favour of presenting *Seasonable Advice*, had such a violent run on him afterwards that it was feared he would have to stop payment. He now positively advised that the patent should be withdrawn. While public opinion was in its present ferment, he said, any treason could be published under cover of writing against the Halfpence, and no jury would convict. But the English government was reluctant to climb down.

Swift now wrote the fifth of the Drapier's *Letters*, dated December 14, 1724, and addressed to Lord Molesworth, whom, in 1713, he had been instrumental in removing, as a Whig, from the Irish Privy Council. But they had been reconciled again, at least since 1717. The *Letter to Middleton* had been hurriedly written; this to Molesworth was a more polished, but less vigorous production, which makes most of the points in the discarded *Letter*. The Drapier pretends to be a tradesman again, and describes all his previous pamphlets under the figure of various stuffs which he has had woven for his customers. He was, he says, so mortified by the failure of his effort to revive the woollen manufacture (i.e. the *Proposal*) that he resolved to sit quiet in his shop:

> Till it happened some months ago considering with myself that the lower and poorer sort of people wanted a *plain strong coarse stuff to defend them against cold easterly winds, which then blew very fierce and blasting for a long time together*, I contrived one on purpose, which sold very well all over the Kingdom, and preserved many thousands from agues. I then made a second and third kind of stuffs for the gentry with the same success, insomuch that an ague hath hardly been heard of for some time.[12]

He then ventured on a fourth; but of late some great folks complain 'that when they had it on, they felt a shuddering in their limbs'. But now he has woven one piece more, especially for Lord Molesworth, though he must confess it is made only of the shreds and remnants of wool from his former pieces.

The offence the fourth *Letter* has given comes chiefly from what he said on the subject of Ireland's being 'a dependent Kingdom'. He could not understand what it meant; nor can he now. He himself would be content to depend only upon God and his prince and the laws of his own country.

> But since my betters are of a different opinion and desire further dependencies, I shall readily submit, not insisting on the exception I made of M. B. Drapier.[13]

But to say the point he made did not belong to his subject is false and foolish. The Irish people were accused of trying to shake off their dependency. He therefore showed that the only dependency they had — that which comes from the statute, passed by the Irish Parliament, declaring that they have the same King as England — could not be shaken off. The trouble with himself is that he was brought up in England, and believed that, in coming to Ireland, he had only changed one free country for another.

> But I shall in time grow wiser, and learn to consider my driver, the road I am in, and with whom I am yoked. This I will venture to say, that the boldest and most obnoxious words I ever delivered, would in England only have exposed me as a stupid fool, who went to prove that the sun shone in a clear summer's day.[14]

All he now desires is that Ireland shall not suffer by any inadvertency of his. 'Whether Ireland depends upon England, or only upon God, I hope no man will assert it depends upon Mr. Wood.' Provided Ireland has security against Wood's money, he will cheerfully renounce every syllable of his *Letters*. But since it is very unlikely that any relief will come from England, there is nothing to be done but to persevere with the boycott. As for his own part in the agitation, his mistake has been to begin and pursue it on a wrong foundation.

> I foolishly disdained to have recourse to whining, lamenting and crying for mercy, but rather chose to appeal to law and liberty and the common rights of mankind, without considering the climate I was in.[15]

The note is perceptibly lowered. Swift is mindful that he will not be followed where he would like to lead.

On the day the *Letter to Molesworth* was published, December 31, 1724, Swift told Ford that he had been confined by his deafness to the Deanery garden for four months. Carteret had sent him only 'one cold compliment'; nevertheless, he intended to visit him as soon as he could hear him. His retirement had been partly politic; and one reason for his going to see Carteret now was that he knew the Lieutenant was now pressing the revocation of the patent. He paid his visit in January, and wisely avoided politics. Perhaps Carteret excused himself by his famous quotation from Virgil:

> Res dura, et regni novitas me talia cogit Moliri.

It would have made a neat dismission of the thorny subject.

During the spring of 1725 Swift's relations with Carteret became friendly enough. He wrote a pleasant *Apology to Lady Carteret* for a blunder he had made over an invitation to dine at the Castle, in verses which tell how he walked her about in his newly walled garden, Naboth's Vineyard. Just as the unaccustomed exercise and the spring air chilled and tired her, so the unwonted civility from the Castle had made him awkward.

> Can it be strange if I eschew
> A scene so glorious and so new?
> Or is he criminal that flies
> The living lustre of your eyes?[16]

And Swift felt free enough to ask Carteret to give Sheridan some preferment, which he did.

He had intended to go to England for the summer, perhaps to arrange for the publication of *Gulliver*; but his Dublin friends were against it, thinking he might be in danger for his activities in Dublin. Swift believed their fears exaggerated, but he asked Ford's advice. Whether Ford advised against it, or Swift found his deafness too troublesome, or *Gulliver* in need of more revision, he arranged to spend the summer with 'the ladies' at Sheridan's house at Quilca, seven miles from Kells. There he worked hard, 'improving' Sheridan's little estate, transcribing *Gulliver*, cursing and making friends with the Irish servants, and writing another *Letter*, to be published on the day Parliament met.

3

Parliament had been successively prorogued until September 7, for Carteret knew that, unless he could open it with an announcement that the patent had been surrendered, there would be an uproar, and supplies would not be voted. Swift also knew it and thought to take advantage of the indignation, by spiriting up the Parliament to remedy ills that went much deeper than the Halfpence. He wrote, once more as the Drapier, *A Humble Address to Both Houses of Parliament*, in which he set out 'the universal desires of the nation'.

The nation desires (he says) that Parliament should begin by strictly inquiring into Wood's detestable fraud, in spite of the opposition of members bribed by places. How powerful are such motives is shown by the recent proceedings of the judges. It is therefore the nation's wish that the powers and privileges of juries should be declared and confirmed by the legislature, and that Parliament should refuse any composition or compromise over the Halfpence and trust entirely to the general aversion. The question is not, and never has been, whether we want halfpence — we do, and a great many other things — but whether a whole kingdom should be at the mercy of a single sordid adversary.

Secondly, it is the nation's wish that we should be allowed to coin copper for ourselves. We have a title to some indulgence from England, seeing the enormous profits she derives from Ireland, which amount in all to at least £700,000 a year.

> There is not one single article in the essentials, or circumstances of trade, whereby a country can be a loser, which we do not possess in the highest perfection; somewhat, in every particular, that bears a kind of analogy to William Wood; and now the branches are all cut off, he stands ready with his axe at the root.[17]

Absentee landlords are one great cause of our misery. Their absence from Parliament has produced, besides rack-renting and depopulation, such fatal results as the removal of appeals from the Irish to the English House of Lords. Second-rate Englishmen take all our places. But our extremity has brought us one benefit. All the bases of party have been destroyed. The issues on which Whig and Tory are divided are now palpably meaningless in Ireland.

> However we may dislike the causes; yet this effect of begetting an universal concord among us in all national debates, as well as in cities, corporations and country neighbourhoods, may keep us at least alive, and in a condition to eat the little bread allowed us in peace and amity.[18]

A firm union in any country will supply the defect of power in some important matters. If Parliament will declare the universal wish of the nation on any point — even if its votes do not receive the royal assent — it might well be regarded by the nation as obligatory. For example, let it declare that any one who uses Wood's Halfpence, or refuses to boycott foreign fabrics (which is the nation's third wish), is an enemy of the King and the nation.

Of course all such suggestions for the good of the country will be stigmatized as disloyal. The *Proposal* was 'a design to bring in the Pretender'. His own efforts against Wood are called 'flying in the King's face' by 'those softeners, sweeteners, compounders and expedient-mongers who shake their heads so strongly that we can hear their pockets jingle'.

Besides the three wishes of the nation already set out, there is, fourth, the wish that some effectual steps be taken to civilize the native Irish; fifth, that proper encouragement be given to agriculture, and an end put to the practice of engrossing arable land for grazing; sixth, that the acts for planting timber-trees be enforced, and premature felling forbidden; seventh, that the cutting of turf should be regularized; and, finally, that the paring of grass be forbidden.

On the estates of perpetual absentees no improvement is possible. Their tenants are more cruelly rack-rented by merciless agents than by the severest resident landlord. Nevertheless, an improved agriculture is Ireland's only hope of prosperity. He ends with the same opinion as the King of Brobdingnag.

> That few politicians, with all their schemes, are half so useful members of a commonwealth as an honest farmer; who, by skilfully draining, fencing, manuring, and planting hath increased the intrinsic value of a piece of land; and thereby done a perpetual service to his country; which it is a great controversy, whether any of the former ever did, since the creation of the world; but no controversy at all, that ninety-nine in a hundred, have done abundance of mischief.[19]

But on August 25 Carteret received an official intimation that the patent had been surrendered. Dublin was jubilant. Swift wrote to his friends to suppress the *Humble Address* and break up the type. The struggle was over, and the Drapier the national hero.

4

The Drapier's victory had been more apparent than real. On the particular issue of Wood's coinage, the English government had given way; but it had done so on the advice of those who, like Primate Boulter who now led them, were determined to eradicate all resistance to complete English control of Ireland. The English government had been pressed to yield, simply because under cover of the agitation against Wood, Irish autonomy could be advocated and asserted with impunity. To yield on the relatively minor matter of the Halfpence was *reculer pour meiux sauter*.

Swift's decision not to publish the *Address to Both Houses of Parliament* was not made because the victory had been won; but because he knew that the Irish parliament had not the conviction, the courage, or the patriotism to take the further measures which he urged or hinted in it. He was in the position of a commander who had inspirited some faint-hearted troops to a local success, but knew only too well that they had not the endurance to fight on towards the more important objective. The local success had been won under exceptionally favourable conditions. Four years later he wrote:

> My printers have been twice prosecuted, to my great expense, on account of discourses I writ for the public service ... and the success I had in those of the Drapier, was not owing to my abilities, but to a lucky juncture, when the fuel was ready for the first hand that would be at the pains of kindling it.[20]

Swift was conscious of failure rather than success. In his eyes the agitation against Wood was a momentary blaze, not a steady fire. His positive proposals for creating a unity of spirit in Ireland, by concerted measures which would call for some patriotic self-sacrifice, had been ignored. Far more important to him than the boycott of Wood's Halfpence had been his twofold proposal to boycott English woollen manufactures, and improve the quality and reliability of the Irish ones. It had failed, for lack of public spirit, and he had been disheartened. He was a prophet and pioneer not so much of Irish nationalism as of co-operation (which alone gives nationalism a moral value): the forerunner of Horace Plunket and A. E. To this previous disheartenment more than any other single cause was due his delay in entering the battle. The agitation had grown of itself until his scepticism and reluctance had been overborne by his sense that it offered an opportunity not to be missed to invigorate the morale of the Irish people.

His aim, throughout, had been to extend the scope and raise the moral significance of the agitation. 'I was ever averse,' he wrote in the fourth *Letter*, 'against all recourse to England for a remedy against the present impending evil.' His purpose was to spur the Irish people to help themselves: then God might help them. And in the *Address to Both Houses of Parliament* there is a plain hint of the bold strategy he would have had them pursue. Parliament should constitute itself the mouthpiece of the needs of 'the whole people of Ireland', and the people should obey the votes of Parliament, irrespective of whether they received the royal assent (as of course they would not). In other words, Ireland was, without actually declaring itself independent, to behave as though it were. The loyalty to the King which he had tactically and ironically professed here goes by the board: unless the King behaved as the constitutional monarch of an independent Ireland, the Irish parliament and the Irish people were simply to ignore him. They were to assert their fredom not in words but in deed.

Swift's revolutionary suggestion called for a degree of disinterested patriotism in parliament and people of which they were incapable. The Irish parliament (like the English) was mainly composed of men too concerned with their own selfish interests to legislate for the welfare of the country as a whole; and without that it was inconceivable that the Irish people would regard its legislation as morally obligatory upon themselves. Swift's proposal was a dream; but it was a noble dream. The *Address to Both Houses of Parliament* justifies the conviction that the apparent narrowness of his Irish patriotism, its apparent restriction to the Protestant Irish, was an appearance only. For, if the Irish parliament could have had the moral courage to follow Swift's lead, nothing could have prevented it from becoming the representative of the Papists as well as the Protestants. Swift may have closed his conscious mind to that inevitability; but it was inherent in his proposals. It is not a paradox that the Irish people salute in him the prophet of an independent Ireland.

But he turned from the dream to the reality. He suppressed his *Address*. It was not published till 1735. In that year he wrote his final withering invective on the Irish House of Commons: *The Legion Club*. Between the dream and the reality there was an abyss — almost as great as that between the Houyhnhnms and the Yahoos. It was not till he had finished the book of the Yahoos that he wrote the first *Drapier*. Though he may have indulged a momentary optimism in the excitement of the battle, in his heart he believed it was a forlorn hope. The régime of Boulter and the Undertakers was at hand.

CHAPTER XXV

STELLA'S LAST YEARS: 1723-1728

DELANY says that, shortly before Vanessa's death, Swift proposed to Stella that they should live as man and wife. She refused, because Swift's temper had deteriorated.

> I well knew a friend to whom she opened herself upon that head; declaring that the Dean's temper was so altered, and his attention to money so increased; (probably increased by his solicitude to save for her sake) her own health at the same time gradually impaired; that she would not take upon herself the care of his house and economy; and therefore refused to be publicly owned for his wife, as he earnestly desired she should. It was then, she said, *too late*; and therefore better that they should live on as they had done.
> Her resolutions on this head were (not very long after) fully confirmed; and, I fear, embittered by the publication of the poem *Cadenus & Vanessa*.[1]

'Publication' is not used here in the modern sense, but in the contemporary one of 'making public'. Manuscript copies of *Cadenus & Vanessa* were circulated shortly after Vanessa's death. Swift's offer and Stella's refusal therefore apparently took place in the winter of 1722-23, within the obscure period between Swift's final letter to Vanessa of August 8, 1722, and her death, and perhaps throws some light upon it. The friend to whom Stella unburdened herself was, almost certainly, Sheridan.

To Stella the shock of reading Swift's poem to Vanessa must have been painful. Swift must have known that it would be. His sudden 'earnest desire' that she should let herself be acknowledged as his wife may well have sprung from a desperate effort to forestall the disclosure which he feared if Vanessa should die; and it may have been tinged with a fleeting sense of the blessedness of domesticity.

Vanessa died and the disclosure came. In anticipation of it Swift had arranged that Ford should invite 'the ladies' to stay some time with him at Wood Park, his country house some eight miles from Dublin. Ford was the only one of Swift's friends who was intimate with both Stella and Vanessa: he was 'Don Carlos' to the one, and 'Glassheel' to the other, and he understood the situation which it was his function to redress.

Meanwhile, Swift rode into the south-west, 'where I never was before, without one companion, among people where I know no creature'. He did not write to Stella, nor she to him for more than two months. Of Stella's attitude we know, as usual, nothing directly. Ford entertained her royally, and installed her as mistress of his house. Sheridan visited her frequently and, according to Delany, 'used his utmost efforts to relieve, support and amuse her in this sad situation'. We have one glimpse of her, making a brave show as a woman of the world, in her remark about Vanessa and the broomstick. It is the wittiest of all Stella's recorded *bons mots*; but it was a rash one, for she was now nearly a broomstick herself. Perhaps the high living at Wood Park had put some flesh on her.

On August 2 Swift wrote to Sheridan from Clonfert to say that, if he knew whether the ladies were in town or in the country, he would write to them. That seems to have been his first approach; but by the end of the summer, the breach was healed. Swift himself stayed some days at Wood Park at the end of September, and when Stella returned to Dublin on October 3 he wrote her some charming verses of reconciliation.* He contrasted her regal entertainment as the châtelaine of Ford's house with her restricted housekeeping at Ormond Quay, and told how on her return she tried to keep up the lordly style.

> She strove in vain to ape Wood Park.
> Two bottles call'd for, (half her store;
> The cupboard could contain but four;)
> A supper worthy of herself,
> Five nothings in five plates of Delph.
> Thus, for a week the farce went on
> When, all her country savings gone,
> She fell into her former scene,
> Small beer, a herring, and the Dean.²

He apologizes for his raillery: it was too severe. But Stella's good taste is such that she will certainly forgive.

> And you must know in what I writ
> I had some anger in my wit.³

Which, presumably, means that he had been annoyed by her burst of extravagance.

> Yet granting all I said were true
> A cottage is Wood Park with you.⁴

* A week later Swift, for some unknown reason, gave Dingley a note for £100, dated October 10, 1723 and payable on demand, which Dingley, for some reason equally mysterious, never cashed. She made particular mention of it in her will, and bequeathed it to Dr. Lyon. It may have been for services rendered during this difficult time.

The compliment is a gracious one; and a still sweeter was to follow. In the spring of the next year, 1724, Swift fell ill, and Stella nursed him. Instead of her birthday verses, which, he said, he could not write for pain, he wrote a poem of gratitude.

> She tends me, like a humble slave;
> And when indecently I rave,
> When out my brutish passions break,
> With gall in ev'ry word I speak,
> She with soft speech my anguish cheers,
> Or melts my passions down with tears;
> Although 'tis easy to descry
> She wants assistance more than I;
> Yet seems to feel my pains alone
> And is a Stoic in her own.[5]

We can see the scene. Swift, in pain, saying cruel and wounding things, till Stella suddenly bursts into tears, at which he becomes all tenderness.

> Whatever base returns you find
> From me, dear Stella, still be kind.
> In your own heart you'll reap the fruit,
> Tho' I continue still a brute.
> But when I once am out of pain,
> I promise to be good again.[6]

Her devotion to him was very real; for by this time she herself was declining fast. She grew thinner and thinner, and could scarcely bring herself to eat any solid food at all. Her stomach was disordered; and milk and broth were her main sustenance. What her precise ailment was there is no record.

In the following spring, 1725, when he contemplated going to London, he wrote some verses urging her to go to Quilca for the summer. She was, he said, like a Scottish cow, reduced to skin and bone during the winter — winter-roots were still a new-fangled invention of advanced husbandry — and waiting for the summer grass.

> Why, Stella should you knit your brow,
> If I compare you to a cow?
> 'Tis just the case; for you have fasted
> So long till all your flesh is wasted;
> And must against the warmer days
> Be sent to Quilca down to graze.[7]

In the event, Swift postponed his journey to England for a year, and went with her to Quilca to superintend her cure. Sheridan's ramshackle house was hardly ideal for the cure. Swift's description of it in *The Blunders, Deficiencies, Distresses and Misfortunes of Quilca* is grimly amusing. The grate in Stella's bedroom was broken so that she could have no fire, and Swift's great-coat had to be used to stop the wind from coming down the chimney. There was no lock to the door, a great hole in the floor, and another hole in the wall just behind Stella's head, enough to blow out a candle on the calmest day.

Mrs. Dingley full of cares for herself, and blunders and negligence for her friends. Mrs. Johnson sick and helpless. The Dean deaf and fretting; the lady's maid awkward and clumsy; Robert lazy and forgetful; William a pragmatical, ignorant and conceited puppy; Robin and nurse the two great and only supports of the family.

Then there was:

Bellum lacteum: or, The milky battle, fought between the Dean and the crew of Quilca; the latter insisting on their privilege of not milking till eleven in the forenoon; whereas Mrs. Johnson wanted milk at eight for her health. In this battle the Dean got the victory; but the crew of Quilca begin to rebel again; for it is this day almost ten o'clock, and Mrs. Johnson hath not got her milk. [8]

So things were at the end of April. With the summer conditions improved. The Dean managed to impose some discipline on the crew of Quilca, and Stella appeared to regain something of her health and spirits, though Swift's panacea of violent exercise cannot have been good for her. She could not ride; but he reported her as walking sometimes three or four miles. He had a miniature pickaxe made for her to help him with his improvement of Sheridan's estate. But the weather was bad all through the summer. One feels that Stella's apparent improvement was a combination of wishful thinking on Swift's part and a great effort to cheer him up on hers.

2

We learn of her only through Swift's letters from Quilca, from which two things emerge. The first is that Rebecca Dingley was more a burden than a help to her in sickness. She was scatter-brained, immersed in trivialities and neglectful. The second is that Stella was deeply and affectionately concerned for Sheridan's welfare. Carteret, in response to Swift's request, had made him a chaplain at the Castle and given him a living of £200 a year at Rincurran in co. Cork. The advice which Stella sent him, through Swift, as to how he was to behave, was admirable, and one piece of it unexpected from a woman. She remembered that the Bishop of Cork had a theological scruple against the practice of drinking to the dead, and she begged him not to propose any toast if he dined at the Bishop's table.

But all the good advice was unavailing. An impish fate pursued Sheridan. He already had the reputation of a Tory; and he was called to preach, in Cork, on the day of thanksgiving for the accession of King George I. He was taken by surprise, or forgot his engagement, and he went off to the church with the first sermon that came to his hand, without looking at it. Its text was 'Sufficient for the day is the evil thereof', and he had not the presence of mind to change it. That, at least, is the story as told by Swift, who made a gallant effort to retrieve the situation when he heard of the disaster. For disaster it was. Richard Tighe, a violent Whig and an old enemy of Swift, happened to be in the church and posted off to Dublin to raise a storm over Sheridan's indiscretion; and Carteret felt obliged to dismiss him from his chaplaincy.[9]

'She loved you well, and a great share of the little merit I have with you is owing to her solicitations', Swift wrote to Sheridan on July 27, 1726, when he was away in England and in anguish over what he believed to be a fatal turn in Stella's illness. The words reveal Swift's eagerness to assume that Stella was dead — to have done with the agony; and they reveal how loyally she had striven to explain and excuse Swift to Sheridan. Sheridan's nature was affectionate and spontaneous, and his admiration of Stella was great. So too was his admiration of Swift. Stella could and did give him her confidences, in the knowledge that she was not betraying Swift. For her to speak her woman's truth to Swift was impossible. The iron curtain was drawn over his soul. She spoke it to Sheridan; and Sheridan inevitably took her side, and became hostile to Swift. Then she pleaded with Sheridan on Swift's behalf. How many times, in the history of human hearts, has this situation recurred! What is strange is that Swift should have been aware of it, and, in a moment of exceptional stress, should have confessed so humbly to Sheridan that it was Stella's pleading on his behalf that had kept Sheridan his friend.

So it was in Sheridan's charge that he placed Stella when he left her, dying as he believed, to go to England. In fact, he was leaving Sheridan to do what he could not and dared not do — minister to her as a loving man to a beloved woman. But it was not to Sheridan that he sent his strange and repellent injunction that Stella must not be allowed to die in the Deanery, for fear of evil tongues. He wrote that only to Worrall, who was Swift's slave, and he ordered him burn the letter. He was deliberately concealing it from Sheridan, knowing that he would have found it hard to forgive.

3

How far Swift's journeys to England in 1726 and 1727 were really motivated by business and the desire to see his old friends again; how far by a desperate desire to escape from the torment of watching Stella die, omniscience only knows. But Swift's ostensible business was, in fact, not very urgent: to get from the new Lord Oxford, Harley's son, those of Oxford's papers which would enable him to write an authoritative vindication of the man; and to arrange for the publication of *Gulliver*. About the former he did nothing at all on his first visit, and very little on his second; and the publication of *Gulliver* could have been perfectly well arranged through the agency of Ford and Pope and Lewis (as to all intents and purposes it was). Revisiting his friends, which had waited so long, could have waited a little longer. And the evidence of his letters is that he definitely desired to be far away when Stella died. It was only when Sheridan, in September 1727, finally and bravely took upon himself the responsibility of writing to Pope to tell Swift that if he wished to see the living Stella once again he must return immediately, that he conquered his own terrified reluctance and set out.

It would be monstrous to blame him for this. Perhaps most men, of deep affections, even though quite differently constituted from Swift, would choose if they could, not to be present at the lingering death of a beloved woman. The difference is that they cannot choose. He could: for other motives than the simply human operated upon him. Not many men have striven with such iron determination to keep their emotions under the control of their reason. Swift's grief was passionate — that is undeniable — and his fear of breaking down was extreme. Other men have not his reason to be afraid of that. The thought that he might lose control of himself was dreadful to him; the thought that he might keep control perhaps more dreadful still. He did not know what he might do or say in the presence of the dying Stella. All the elaborate construction of his willed relation might collapse; still worse, in his desperate effort to maintain his attitude, he might say or do something brutal, inflict a final and irreparable wound, the guilt of which would haunt him to the grave.

Primarily, we believe, it was in order to escape this ordeal that he went to England in March 1726. He expected and indeed hoped that Stella would be dead before he returned. He was convinced that she had not long to live. The strain was telling on him. His own giddiness and deafness were increasing; and the prospect of living on, after Stella's death, was bleak indeed. Under the strain, he showed himself, just before he left Ireland, at his best and worst. At his best, in his efforts to encourage Sheridan from his depression after his blunder; at his worst in two deliberately offensive letters to the recently ennobled head of the Temple family, Viscount Palmerston.

No one can know Swift, or Sheridan, who has not studied his letter to him of September 11, 1725. After agreeing that it was against common-sense to suppose him to have intended any disloyalty by his unfortunate sermon, he goes on:

> But what will that avail? Therefore sit down and be quiet, and mind your business as you should do, and contract your friendships, and expect no more from man than such an animal is capable of, and you will every day find my description of Yahoos more resembling.
>
> You should think and deal with every man as a villain, without calling him so, or flying from him, or valuing him less. This is an old true lesson. You believe, every one will acquit you of any regard to temporal interest, and how came you to claim an exception from all mankind? I believe you value your temporal interest as much as anybody, but you have not the arts of pursuing it. You are mistaken. Domestic evils are no more within a man than others, and he who cannot bear up against the first, will sink under the second, and in my conscience I believe this is your case; for being of a weak constitution, in an employment precarious and tiresome, loaden with children, a man of intent and abstracted thinking, enslaved by mathematics, and complaint of the world, this new weight of party malice had struck you down, like a feather on a horse's back already loaden as far as he is able to bear . . .
>
> I will hear none of your visions. You shall live at Quilca but three fortnights and a month in the year; perhaps not so much. You shall make no entertainments but what are necessary in your interests; for your true friends would rather see you over a piece of mutton and a bottle once a quarter. You shall be merry at the expense of others. You shall take care of your health, and go early to bed, and not read late at night, and laugh with all men, without trusting any; and then a fig for the contrivers of your ruin, who have now no further thoughts than to stop your progress, which perhaps they may not compass, unless I am deceived more than usual.

This is affectionate, wise and penetrating. It *is* the weakness of supersensitive men, who cannot cope with the world, to deceive themselves into believing that they are disinterested, because they lack the hardness necessary to pursue their interests. It is an amiable and harmless illusion. Swift merely shows that it does not deceive him in Sheridan. And towards such men — like Harrison, and Diaper, and Gay — he always felt a tender and tonic sympathy. Their condition he had known in himself; and, for better or worse, he had conquered it. His hardness, unlike that of the average human animal, had been bought at a price.

What moved him to show it, with such offensive truculence, in his letter to Palmerston? Ostensibly he wrote to beg a favour for a friend. A set of rooms in Trinity belonged to the Temple family, and Palmerston had granted them at Swift's request many years before to a Fellow, who as he ascended in the College hierarchy, had left them for better ones. Instead of handing his rooms back to Palmerston, he had pretended they were his by a tenancy for life, and had let them to another, who in turn had let them to Swift's friend. Swift's friend had no just title to them, and Palmerston had claimed them back again. The last tenant had been, as Swift said, 'unjustly and injuriously treated': but not by Palmerston. Nevertheless, Swift wrote to him as though no decent man could behave as Palmerston was behaving. One has but to imagine Swift's wrath if such a trick had been tried upon him, to realize that Swift was deliberately picking a quarrel with Palmerston. His letter was written with studied insolence; and the only effect it could have had was to make Palmerston certainly refuse what he might have granted as a matter of grace to a less provocative letter. Swift's letter ends:

> I will say nothing of Mr. Curtis's character, because the affair is a matter of short plain justice; and besides I would not willingly do the young man an injury, as I happened to do to another whom I recommended to your Lordship merely for your own service, and whom you afterwards rejected, expressing your reason for doing so, that I had recommended him, by which you lost the very person of the whole kingdom who by his honesty and abilities could have been most useful to you in your offices here. But these are some of the refinements among you great men, which are above my low understanding. (January 1, 1726)

Palmerston replied that if Swift had taken the trouble to inquire into the matter, he would have seen that no injustice had been done.

> I fear you hugged the false report to cancel all feelings of gratitude that must ever glow in a generous breast, and to justify what you declared, that no regard to my family was any restraint to you. These refinements are past my low understanding, and can only be comprehended by you great wits. (January 15, 1726)

The rebuke was deserved; and it stung Swift to fury, to which he gave full vent in a letter which Palmerston disdained to answer.

But what caused him to make his original onslaught on Palmerston at this moment? Was his old grudge against the family over the *Memoirs* still smouldering? Or had it been rekindled by his Irish patriotism, which made him think of them as lifeholders of great sinecures that drained the wealth of Ireland? At the head of the list in the fourth *Drapier* he had put Palmerston, who had been appointed joint Chief Remembrancer at £2000 a year at the age of seven, and Lord Berkeley of Stratton, his brother-in-law, who was absentee Master of the Irish Rolls, at an even bigger salary. But Sir William Temple had held the same office on the same terms. Or was he still exasperated that his recommendation of his lawyer-friend, Staunton, to be Palmerston's deputy had failed?[10] All these motives may have been at work together. But the flaring up of his grudge against the family had one strange consequence. Two years later it led Swift so to distort his written memories of Stella that no one reading them would dream that she had ever lived in Sir William Temple's household, or been indebted to him for her small fortune.

4

By a fatality, the moment Swift had left Dublin in March 1726, *Cadenus & Vanessa* was printed and published. Although the wound had scarred, it was one that would not cease to ache; and it must have been hateful to Stella to know the poem was being hawked about the Dublin streets. On July 8 Swift received from Sheridan a dubious account of her condition, and a week later a definitely pessimistic one from Worrall.

What you tell me of Mrs. Johnson [he replied] I have long expected, with great oppression and heaviness of heart . . . And indeed ever since I left you, my heart has been so sunk, that I have not been the same man, nor ever shall be again; but drag on a wretched life, till it shall please God to call me away.
I must tell you, as a friend, that if you have reason to believe Mrs. Johnson cannot hold out till my return, I would not think of coming to Ireland.

For in that case, he says, he must go into retirement till he is capable of appearing in public again. Could some one see to it that she makes her will? She intends to leave her estate for life to her mother and sister, and then to Dr. Steevens's Hospital for certain purposes.

I would not for the universe be present at such a trial of seeing her depart. She will be among friends that upon her own account and great worth, will tend her with all possible care, where I should be a trouble to her, and the greatest torment to myself.

He then gives the instruction that, if she comes to town — she was apparently at Laracor — she should not be lodged in the Deanery. But he was not to tell this to any living soul.

> I am determined not to go to Ireland to find her just dead, or dying. Nothing but extremity could make me so familiar with those terrible words, applied to such a dear friend. Let her know I have bought her a repeating gold watch, for her ease in winter nights. I designed to have surprised her with it; but now I would have her know it, that she may see how my thoughts were always to make her easy. I am of opinion that there is not a greater folly than to contract too great and intimate a friendship, which must always leave the survivor miserable. (July 15, 1726)

The pathos of it! And the naivety! As though one could evade 'l'engrenage terrible de la responsabilité et de la souffrance humaine' by refusing to love; as though one were not the richer for having loved and been loved, in spite of mortality.

Five days later, he writes in the same strain to his young relation, James Stopford, who knew Stella.

> I think there is not a greater folly than that of entering into too strict and particular a friendship, with the loss of which a man must be absolutely miserable, but especially at an age when it is too late to engage in a new friendship . . . Dear Jim, pardon me, I know not what I am saying; but believe me that violent friendship is much more lasting, and as much engaging, as violent love. (July 20, 1726)

What unreal distinction was this the distracted man was making? This friendship was love; only it had been denied its fruition. In order to preserve his own independence inviolable, he had degraded the idea of love, and fastened the name to mere animal passion. It availed him less than nothing now. To the anguish of approaching loneliness, was added the unspoken pang of conscience that he had cheated her of that which was hers by right, both human and divine.

A week later he wrote to Sheridan.

> The account you give me is nothing but what I have some time expected with the utmost agonies, and there is one aggravation of constraint, that where I am, I am forced to put on an easy countenance . . . I look upon this to be the greatest event that can ever happen to me; but all my preparations will not suffice to make me bear it like a philosopher, nor altogether like a Christian. There hath been the most intimate friendship between us from her childhood, and the greatest merit on her side, that ever was in one human creature toward another.

Nay, if I were near her now, I would not see her; I could not behave myself tolerably, and should redouble her sorrow. Judge in what temper of mind I write this. The very time I am writing, I conclude the fairest soul in the world hath left its body. Confusion! that I am this moment called down to a visitor, when I am in the country, and not in my power to deny myself.

I have passed a very constrained hour, and now return to say I know not what. I have been long weary of the world, and shall for my small remainder of years be weary of life, having for ever lost that conversation, which only could make it tolerable. (July 27, 1726)

Why, one asks in despair, had he to pretend to his English friends that no such person as Stella existed, or that, if she did exist, she was a mere acquaintance for whom he felt no deep concern? Why this presumptuous façade of invulnerability? It almost deserved the punishment it was receiving. But towards Sheridan he is humble; to him he can acknowledge that Stella's love had merited a better return than he had ever given. Sheridan knew it; and Swift knew that he knew.

Stella did not die that year. The immediate danger passed, and Swift returned, according to his plan, on August 15. On October 15 he could write to Stopford that 'Mrs. Johnson is much recovered since I saw her first, but still very lean and low'. She rallied a little during the winter, and in the spring Swift wrote her the tenderest of his birthday poems; and he was sufficiently confident of her health to have her lodge at the Deanery just before he left again for England. He arrived at Pope's at Twickenham on April 22, 1727. Soon after, he received bad news from Sheridan: Stella had caught a dangerous cold. Then came one of those strange exhibitions of insensitiveness which perplex the most sympathetic of his chroniclers. Pope was putting together a second volume of *Miscellanies*. On July 1 Swift wrote to Sheridan:

Pray copy out the verses I writ to Stella on her collecting my verses, and send them to me, for we want some to make our poetical Miscellany large enough, and I am not there to pick what should be added.

At the end of the letter, bethinking himself that Sheridan would not approve the publication at this time of a poem written for Stella's eyes alone, and avowedly 'to expose her weaker side', he added: 'I do not want that poem to Stella to print it entire, but some passages out of it, if they deserve it, to lengthen the volume.' Nevertheless, the whole of the poem was printed in the *Miscellany*, and indeed all the poems save one that he had ever written to her. The publication of *Cadenus & Vanessa* in the previous year he could not have prevented; but the publication of these was entirely his own act.

Can he really have been so obtuse as not to realize that the publication of
these private poems would wound her? Or was he so determined that she
must fulfil the rational persona he had imposed upon her as not to admit it?
Or was he simply so infatuated with Pope that he trusted to his discretion?

If Stella was now too ill even to be hurt by it, we may be sure Sheridan
resented it on her behalf. Her solicitations would have been needed again;
unless he generously supposed that Swift's own illness was now so severe
that he was barely responsible for what he did. For, in reply to a letter of
bad news from Sheridan, Swift had written on August 29:

> I have had your letter of the 19th and expect before you read this to
> receive another from you with the most fatal news that can ever come
> to me, unless I should be put to death for some ignominious crime.
> I continue very ill with my giddiness and deafness, of which I had
> two days intermission, but since worse, and I shall be perfectly content
> if God shall please to call me away at this time . . . I beg, if you have not
> writ to me before you get this, to tell me no particulars, but the event
> in general; my weakness, my age, my friendship will bear no more . . .
> I am strongly visited with a disease which will at last cut me off, if I
> should this time escape. . . .

Two days afterwards he left Pope's house and placed himself in charge
of his cousins, Patty and Lancelot Rolt, at their house in London: whence
he wrote again to Sheridan:

> I know not whether it be an addition to my grief or not, that I am now
> extremely ill; for it would have been a reproach to me to be in perfect
> health, when such a friend is desperate. I do profess upon my salvation,
> that the distressed and desperate condition of our friend makes life so
> indifferent to me, who by course of nature have so little left, that I do
> not think it worth the time to struggle; yet I should think, according
> to what hath been formerly, that I may happen to overcome this
> present disorder; and to what advantage? Why, to see the loss of that
> person for whose sake only life was worth preserving. I brought both
> those friends over, that we might be happy together as long as God
> should please; the knot is broken, and the remaining person, you know,
> has ill answered the end, and the other, who is now to be lost, is all that
> was valuable. You agreed with me, or you are a great hypocrite. What
> have I to do in the world? I never was in such agonies as when I
> received your letter and had it in my pocket. I am able to hold up my
> sorry head no longer. (September 2, 1727)

His physical and mental condition was pitiful. He wrote to Worrall yet
again to ensure that Stella should not die in the Deanery, again keeping this

injunction secret from Sheridan; and he proposed, when the news came, to go to France. But now Sheridan took the brave step of writing to Pope to rouse him out of his paralysis of fear. If he wanted to see Stella again in this world, he must come without delay. Swift pulled himself together and set out on September 18. The journey itself improved his condition. He reached Holyhead on September 24, only to be delayed for a week by contrary winds. Of his discomfort and misery he has left a vivid record in the *Holyhead Journal*. He wrote it to distract his mind, concentrating on the tiny events of the day to stave off the thought of Stella.

> I shall say nothing upon the suspense I am in about my dearest friend, because that is a case extraordinary, and therefore by way of amusement, I will speak as if it were not in my thoughts, and only as a passenger who is in a scurvy unprovided comfortless place without one companion, and who therefore wants to be at home, where he hath all conveniences there proper for a gentleman of quality.[11]

Swift was no novice at such feats of suppression; his relation with Stella had come to be composed of them. It is with a sort of surprise that we find in one of the sets of verses that he wrote:

> Before, I always found the wind
> To me was most malicious kind,
> But now the danger of a friend,
> On whom my hopes and fears depend,
> Absent from whom all climes are curst,
> With whom I'm happy in the worst,
> With rage impatient makes me wait
> A passage to the land I hate.[12]

One cannot forget that he had deliberately left her two years in succession although, or because, he believed she was dying.

5

He reached Dublin in the first week of October. Stella's strength was now ebbing steadily away. Swift composed some prayers for himself to use at her bedside. They are grim and formidable; as was Swift's faith. They are informed much less by any sense of gratitude for a life and love that had been dedicated to him, than by a horror of the bleak and lonely years that lay before him. They contain one tell-tale phrase:

> Forgive the sorrow and weakness of those among us, who sink under the grief and terror of losing so dear and useful a friend.[13]

'Terror' is as strange a word in that human context as 'useful'. How did they strike on Stella's ear? Had she absorbed so much of Swift's peculiar religion that she accepted them? Or did she feel a pang of almost maternal pity for the self-enclosed and self-tormented man? Let us believe, at least, that her Christian faith was warmer, more intimate and personal, than was his; and that the great asseveration that God is Love had a meaning for her that it never had for him.

On December 30 she made her will. It was in the terms Swift had fore-shadowed more than a year before; and part of it is couched in language which must have come from him. She left £1000 to endow an unmarried chaplain for Dr. Steevens's Hospital — the simple and satisfying building that stands next to St. Patrick's Hospital — with this qualification.

> If it shall happen (which God forbid) that at any time hereafter the present Established Episcopal Church of this Kingdom shall come to be abolished, and be no longer the Established Church of the said Kingdom, I do, in that case, declare wholly null and void the bequest above made.

She provided for the apprenticeship of a child 'who now lives with me and whom I keep on charity'. She disposed of her personal belongings carefully: to Dingley she gave her 'little watch and chain and twenty guineas'. Curiously, there is no mention of the gold repeating watch that Swift meant to give her. Perhaps it was in the strong-box which she left him together with all her papers. When the strong-box was opened it was found to con-tain £150 in gold.

There is thus conclusive evidence against one part of the famous story told by Sheridan's son.

> A short time before her death a scene passed between the Dean and her, an account of which I had from my father, and which I shall relate with reluctance, as it seems to bear more hard on Swift's humanity than any other part of his conduct in life. As he found her final dissolution approach, a few days before it happened, in the presence of Dr. Sheri-dan, she addressed Swift in the most earnest and pathetic terms to grant her dying request. That as the ceremony of marriage had passed be-tween them, though for sundry considerations they had not cohabited in that state, in order to put it out of the power of slander to be busy with her name after death, she adjured him by their friendship to let her have the satisfaction of dying at least, though she had not lived, his acknowledged wife. Swift made no reply, but turning on his heel, walked silently out of the room, nor ever saw her afterwards during the few days she lived. This behaviour threw Mrs. Johnson into unspeak-

able agonies, and for a time she sunk under the weight of so cruel a disappointment. But soon afterwards, roused by indignation, she inveighed against his cruelty in the bitterest terms; and sending for her lawyer, made her will, bequeathing her fortune by her own name to charitable uses. This was done in the presence of Dr. Sheridan, whom she appointed one of her executors. Upon this occasion the Doctor gave an instance of his disinterested spirit: for when Mrs. Johnson mentioned his name to the lawyer, annexing a very handsome legacy, the Doctor interposed and would not suffer it to be put down, saying, that as she disposed of her fortune to such pious uses, he should think he defrauded the charity if he accepted of any part of it. During the few days she lived after this Dr. Sheridan gave her constant attendance, and was in the chamber when she breathed her last. His grief for her loss was not perhaps inferior to the Dean's. He admired her above all human beings, and loved her with a devotion as pure as that which one would pay to angels. She on her part had early singled him out from all the Dean's acquaintance as her confidential friend. There grew up the closest amity between them, which subsisted, without interruption, to the time of her death. During her long illness he never passed an hour from her which could be spared from business; and his conversation, in the Dean's absence, was the chief cordial to her drooping spirits. No wonder therefore if the Doctor's humanity was shocked at the last scene which he saw pass between her and the Dean, and which affected him so much, that it was a long time before he could be thoroughly reconciled to him.[14]

The younger Sheridan is plainly wrong in his statement that Stella made the will she did in consequence of Swift's refusal to acknowledge the marriage. She made her will just as she had previously arranged with Swift to make it. Moreover, she made it a full four weeks before she died, which is not 'a few days'. Indeed, this legend of Stella's will looks strangely like an unconscious repetition of the story of Vanessa's. But this does not invalidate the rest of the story. For the account Thomas Sheridan gives of the confidential intimacy between Stella and his father is explicitly confirmed by Swift's own letters. Therefore, unless there is positive evidence to the contrary, as in the matter of the will, we are bound to regard anything coming from the elder Sheridan as probably true. The only question is whether the son can be trusted as reporting the father correctly. It is not easy to see why, regarding the main event, he should have been mistaken. He was nineteen when his father died in 1738 and perfectly capable of appreciating the importance of what he was told. The chief reasons for rejecting the story are a reluctance to impute to Swift behaviour apparently so cruel; and a desire to discredit the story of Swift's secret marriage, for which this is part of the evidence. The first of these reasons only concerns us here. It is based on a radical misconception. Swift was not being cruel in denying Stella's request. However shocking his behaviour may have appeared to Sheridan at the time, and to others since, it was the necessary consequence of the conditions on which he had married Stella, and of his own confessed psychology. There was nothing for the unhappy man to do, when faced with Stella's pitiful and unexpected demand, but to go away and to keep away from her. For what she asked was now humanly impossible for him to grant. Five years before, in 1722, he might have acknowledged the marriage. There was still a prospect of a life together before them. But to acknowledge it now would have ruined his position as a dignitary of the Church, by revealing him as having entered into a mockery of Christian marriage, and it would have created an entirely false impression of their true relation. However painful it might be, he had every right to regard the pathetic request as a sudden weakness of Stella's to which he ought not to yield. And since, as his letters make quite clear, he was terrified of losing control of himself in her presence, he did right also to keep away from her.

To have been the witness, as Sheridan was, of a scene so lamentable was beyond the endurance of his sensitive and affectionate nature. Nothing in his character stands out more clearly than that he was at the mercy of his emotions. Of course, in his eyes Swift ought to have done what Stella asked. How could he refuse? But Sheridan acted always in reckless disregard of consequences. Swift did not. And in this case Swift was right, and Sheridan was wrong.

Stella died at about 6 p.m. on Sunday, January 28, 1728. Swift received the news at eight o'clock. Sunday was his night for company. He waited, impassive, till his guests had gone, at eleven. Then he began to write an account of 'the truest, most virtuous, and valuable friend that I, or perhaps any other person, was ever blessed with'. He told how 'she had a gracefulness somewhat more than human, in every motion, word, and action. Never was so happy a conjunction of civility, freedom, easiness and sincerity'. She was buried, as her will directed, in the great aisle of St. Patrick's, on the night of January 30. Then Swift took up his narrative again.

This is the night of the funeral, which my sickness will not suffer me to attend. It is now nine at night; and I am removed into another apartment, that I may not see the light in the church, which is just over against the window of my bedchamber.
With all the softness of temper that became a lady, she had the personal courage of a hero . . . [15]

Stella was forty-six when she died. In spite of all effort, she remains a shadowy figure. Swift is to blame for that. It is not even certain that the traditional portrait is really of her. What little survives of her writing is on impersonal matters: a book of her copies of Swift's poems (which he gave away), a few signatures to legal documents, and one solitary brief letter of business. Yet her actual handwriting makes a curiously definite impression: as though it were a child's, or rather a pupil's. It is so upright, so carefully formed, so obviously not fluent. One could almost believe that, whenever Stella took pen in hand, she unconsciously became her writing master's pupil again. That she was beautiful and brave — both physically and mentally — intelligent and vivacious, we take at second-hand rather than by any direct apprehension. Swift's collection of her *bons mots* is pitifully meagre: it contains only two which offer a glimpse of character; and both belong to the period of her final illness. When the doctor said to her: 'Madam, you are near the bottom of the hill, but we will endeavour to get you up again', she replied: 'Doctor, I fear I shall be out of breath before I get to the top.' And again when a Quaker apothecary sent her a phial of medicine, which had a broad rim and a paper label tied round its neck, she said: 'What is that? My apothecary's son?'[16] They are the words of a brave and smiling woman.

It is become a convention to praise highly Swift's own account of her. In truth it is a poor portrait of a human being, and it is distorted by repressions. The detachment it affects is at moments fantastic. No one knew Stella's finances better than Swift, for he managed them for her: yet he wrote 'Her fortune, with some accession, could not, *as I have heard say*, amount to more than two thousand pounds.' The phrase is preposterous. For whom, except himself and posterity, was Swift writing? It is as though he were constrained to play some extravagant comedy of remoteness and indifference. The excuse that he is trying to keep control of himself will not serve. One feels that he is also trying to thrust Stella away. The general tone is such that it is hard to be satisfied that his animus against the Temple family was the sole cause of his silence concerning their friendship at Moor Park: we feel he had other reasons too for wanting to put it out of his mind. Throughout, his effort is to make Stella much more masculine than there is any reason to believe she was. But there are a few faint cracks in this varnish of masculinity. Thus, he says that she disliked arguing, and rather than controvert an opinionated man she would (like Addison) gently encourage him to abound in his own sense. She said, 'it prevented noise and saved time'. 'Yet', Swift says, 'I have known her very angry with some whom she much esteemed, for sometimes falling into that infirmity.' He means himself. At a guess the reason for what seemed to him an inconsistency in Stella is that she did not like his way of doing it: he would have egged on his victim with a malicious irony which she did not enjoy. And this is in accord with his former statement that her anger was reserved for him.

> Your spirits kindle to a flame
> Moved by the slightest touch of blame ...
> And, what is worse, your passion bends
> Its force against your nearest friends
> Which manners, decency and pride
> Have taught you from the world to hide.[17]

Her nearest friends, besides himself, were Sheridan and Delany: and they are unanimous that the most remarkable of her many virtues was the sweetness and gentleness of her temper.

But Swift tried it too hard. Her patience with him, almost infinite as it was, sometimes gave way under the frequent harshness of his attitude; and she reacted sometimes with fiery indignation, sometimes with tears. In a moment of humility Swift could admit to Sheridan that in their lifelong friendship there had been 'the greatest merit on her side that ever was in one human creature towards another'. In fact she had spent her life in loving and bearing with and championing one of the most difficult men that ever God created. Yet of this there is not a trace in Swift's account of her. It conceals, not reveals her: and he meant it to do so.

That is not to deny that there was in her the element of the docile pupil which appears in her handwriting. In her own poem to Swift she represents herself as all that Swift would have had her be. She had been obedient to the teaching of 'her early and her only guide', and learned his lesson

> How soon a beauteous mind repairs
> The loss of changed or falling hairs.[18]

No doubt Swift's influence upon her was immense and overwhelming. But there was an intractable element as well. It peeps out in her remark about Vanessa and the broomstick; it shines in the 'anger sparkling in her eyes'. The grateful pupil sometimes rebelled, and refused to be cramped within the master's mould. It was this element in her which gave her the feminine charm which she undoubtedly possessed. For the evidence of others than Swift is again unanimous that she was, with all her courage, the reverse of a masculine woman. And it was Stella the woman, who, in turn, had more influence over Swift than any other human being. To some extent she could and did control him. If she could not prevent, she mitigated the steady deterioration of his temper. Her death was doubly disastrous to him. As Delany put it,

His infelicities of temper were remarkably augmented after the death of Mrs. Johnson: whose cordial friendship, sweet temper, and lenient advice, poured balm and healing into his blood: but as soon as he was deprived of that medicine of life, his blood boiled, fretted and fermented beyond all bounds.[19]

It seems almost a malignant miracle that not one of all the many letters she wrote to Swift has survived. Yet the reason is clear. Just as Swift carefully preserved them, so he must have deliberately destroyed them. It is as though he were determined that only so much of her as he willed should survive. He set up no tablet to her memory. In not one of his letters is she ever mentioned again. Was it to annihilate an importunate and tormenting memory? Was it to make her his secret and exclusive possession? What escaped his censorship is but the abstract of a living woman.

CHAPTER XXVI

TWO NOBLE LADIES

SWIFT'S ostensible motives for going to England in 1726 were to arrange for the publication of *Gulliver* and to examine Harley's papers, now in the keeping of his son, for the history he still, rather vaguely, proposed to write. He totally neglected the former, and postponed the latter till the last week of his stay. A much stronger motive was his desire to escape from the torment of watching, or rather not daring to watch, Stella die; and at the same time to mitigate the loss by renewing old friendships. He was on much more intimate terms with Pope and Gay by the end of his visit than he had been before. Probably, too, he had in mind the possibility of a permanent settlement in England. With Stella gone, Dublin would be a ghost-ridden city. But for Swift to escape from it to a snug English preferment was, in 1726, to escape to a castle in the air. Nothing less than a Deanery would have done; for he could not have borne to sacrifice his position of dignity and power: and there was no chance that Walpole would let him have one, except on terms which he was bound to reject.

Nevertheless, both Swift and Walpole seem to have thought the ground worth exploring. Walpole took the initiative of arranging to meet him at a dinner-party soon after he arrived in London. Arbuthnot had previously taken him to see the Princess of Wales — Swift subsequently insisted that he went only at the ninth time of asking — and to meet the dissident Whigs, of whom Pulteney was the chief, and Chesterfield a leading figure. They had now struck up an alliance with Bolingbroke and Wyndham. Though Walpole, as the artificer of the change, knew better than anybody that the situation was now totally different from the fluidity of Queen Anne's time, in which Swift's pen was so dangerous, he would have thought it worth an English Deanery to prevent the new opposition of 'Patriots' from gaining such a formidable recruit. If a deal was at all possible, he was ready to do it. And so was Swift. After the meeting at dinner, at which their intercourse was non-political and friendly, he sought, through Peterborough, a private interview with Walpole.

At the interview, Swift confined himself to Ireland. He had made up his mind that, if he could secure a radical change of English policy towards Ireland, or the Anglo-Irish interest, honour would be satisfied. Honour would have been more than satisfied. It would have been a triumphant close to the second phase of Swift's political career, if he could have persuaded Walpole to agree to the programme which, after the interview, he set out in a memorandum for Peterborough to transmit to him. But by that time Swift knew his case was hopeless, and the real purpose of the memorandum was to serve as a historical justification for his approach to Walpole and a safeguard against Walpole's misrepresenting it. The hostile gossips were busy with rumours that he was turning his coat again. It had not been true before, and it was not true now. He was willing to make peace with Walpole on terms; but his terms were high, and Walpole was not willing to consider them. He had no intention of changing his Irish policy, of complete subordination of Ireland to English interests: and, from his own point of view, it would have been political suicide for him to do so. No serious body of opinion in England opposed his Irish policy; it represented the average Englishman's view of how Ireland ought to be treated. And that view was common to Whig and Tory. Swift must at least have suspected that, even if the new opposition were to succeed in overthrowing Walpole, there was precious little chance of the new ministry treating Ireland any better than the old one. The notion that a Pulteney or a Carteret in power would remedy the grievances of Ireland was chimerical.

Whether Swift admitted this fully to consciousness may be doubtful. He realized that Walpole at least was adamant. There was no possibility of making terms with him without becoming a renegade. But perhaps the excitement of renewed proximity to the Court induced him to indulge some vague hope that, if Walpole were removed, everything would be different. At any rate, he became loosely attached to the entourage of the Prince and Princess of Wales, like most of his friends. The chief link between Gay and Pope and the Prince's Court was Mrs. Howard, Lady of the Bedchamber to the Princess, and mistress of the Prince of Wales: a charming, wise and witty woman, whom Swift's friends greatly and justly admired. She behaved with humanity and dignity in an exceedingly uncomfortable situation. A royal mistress is supposed to have some influence on her royal lover. Mrs. Howard had none. She had to deal with the able and cynical Princess Caroline, who had learned how to manage her stupid husband, but for all her enlightenment had enough of the vixen in her to find satisfaction in subtly humiliating his gentle mistress. She, being married to a brute, clung desperately to her position at Court, which kept her out of his power. The insensitiveness of the Prince, and the tyrannies of the Princess, were preferable to the society of Mr. Howard.

Mrs. Howard is an attractive and pathetic figure. The difficulties of her position were great. The Princess had a sort of half-liking for her as a woman who did not try to take advantage of her position. It was reassuring to her that the Prince should have so disinterested a mistress. At the same time, she despised her for having so much less influence over the Prince than she herself would have had in the same position. When Mrs. Howard retired from the Court in 1734, the Queen said to Hervey: 'I have always heard a great deal of her great sense from other people, but I never saw her, in any material great occurrence in her life, take a sensible step since I knew her . . . All her behaviour to the King while she was at Court was as ill-judged as her behaviour to me on leaving it.' One would like to know what Caroline understood by 'sensible' in this context. One cannot imagine her, as a mistress, not doing her utmost to establish the kind of ascendancy over her lover that she had over her husband. The effort was quite alien to Mrs. Howard. She desired the quiet happiness of love; and she eventually found it, when, on the death of her husband, she married George Berkeley, Lady Betty Germaine's brother, who had been in love with her for years. Her letters to him have the authentic note of deep and trustful yet anxious affection.

How she ever imagined she could find anything of the kind in her relation with the Prince is the problem. Perhaps his very simplicity was more beguiling than it now appears.* Hervey and Chesterfield, no bad judges in the matter, were agreed that, if love-letters alone were in question, a lover could have no more dangerous rival than the Prince. Perhaps she succumbed to these. Anyhow, he was at least a refuge from her intolerable husband. As a mistress, she was loyal and long-suffering, and she quickly learned not to wear her heart upon her sleeve. Men found her appreciative, kind and sympathetic, but quietly reserved. But her fellows in the Queen's service — maids of honour like the brilliant and beautiful Lepell and Bellenden — admired, trusted and loved her. 'I have kept the same grave unmeaning face I used to wear,' she wrote to Bellenden, who had left the Court, 'which, to compliment me, you may call philosophical.' There is a well-known engraving of her which shows exactly what she meant. The expression is curiously grave; but it is far from unmeaning. It is wistful, reserved and

---

* When Mrs. Howard married George Berkeley, the King wrote to Queen Caroline: 'J'étois extrèmement surpris de la disposition que ma vieille maîtresse a fait de son corps à ce vieux goutteux George Berkeley, et je m'en réjouis fort. Je ne voudrois faire de tels presens à mes amis; et quand mes ennemis me volent, plût à Dieu que ce soit de cette façon.' A characteristic utterance.

sad. Perhaps the wistfulness was partly due to the deafness from which she suffered. But the face is haunting.[1]

The ageing Peterborough imagined that he was madly in love with her, and addressed to her the charming lines:

> I said to my heart, between sleeping and waking,
> Thou wild thing, that always art leaping or aching,
> What black, brown, or fair, in what clime or what nation
> By turns has not taught thee a pit-a-pat-ation?

His heart denies the imputation. Do not Celia, Sappho, Prudentia — the reigning beauties — leave it unperturbed?

> But Chloe so lively, so easy, so fair,
> Her wit so genteel, without art, without care;
> When she comes in my way, the emotion, the pain,
> The leapings, the achings, return all again.

> O wonderful creature! a woman of reason!
> Never grave out of pride, never gay out of season!
> When so easy to guess who this angel should be,
> Would one think Mrs. Howard ne'er dreamt it was she?

And he bombarded her with love-letters, which which she turned smilingly aside, with replies full of gravity and humour, of wit and wisdom. Peterborough had been extravagantly laudatory of her sincerity, as the quality he most valued and was proudest to possess. She answered:

To convince your Lordship that I have some pretensions to that uncourtly quality you seem so fond of, I venture to advise you against these strong professions of sincerity; because those who are ever recommending a particular virtue, give occasion to believe they have been very often suspected of the want of it.[2]

And again:

I think a woman has reason to suspect a person that has it in his power abruptly to declare his passion. Love discloses itself without design, and by such imperceptible degrees, that I believe it is generally very difficult to determine which of the lovers made the first declaration.[3]

Mrs. Howard was not now to be easily deceived by professions of sincerity in a lover. Moreover, she was in a position in which men would pay court to her from ulterior motives, believing that she had an influence which she did not possess. Still worse, when she felt they were sufficiently trustworthy to be told that in fact she had no influence, they suspected her own sincerity, and blamed her for making a courtier's excuse to cover her own indifference. Pope subsequently accused her of having no heart.

> 'With ev'ry pleasing, ev'ry prudent part,
> Say, what can Chloe want?' — she wants a heart.
> She speaks, behaves, and acts just as she ought;
> But never, never, reached one gen'rous thought.
> Virtue she finds too painful an endeavour,
> Content to dwell in decencies, for ever.
> So very reasonable, so unmov'd,
> As never yet to love, or to be lov'd.
> She, while her lover pants upon her breast,
> Can mark the figures on an Indian chest:
> And when she sees her friend in deep despair,
> Observes how much a chintz exceeds mohair.
> Forbid it, Heav'n, a favour or a debt
> She e'er should cancel! — but she may forget.
> Safe is your secret still in Chloe's ear;
> But none of Chloe's shall you ever hear.
> Of all her dears she never slander'd one,
> But cares not if a thousand are undone.
> Would Chloe know if you're alive or dead?
> She bids her footman put it in her head.
> Chloe is prudent — Would you too be wise?
> Then never break your heart when Chloe dies.

Pope was mistaken — if not worse — about her character. And so was Swift.

3

Mrs. Howard was the central figure in Swift's new relations with the new Court. In spite of his own better knowledge, in spite too of Stella's misgivings lest he should compromise his reputation by becoming a courtier again, he indulged in hopes of 'a new world' when the Prince and Princess should come to the throne. Since his friends of the old Scriblerus days — Arbuthnot, Pope and Gay — were already Mrs. Howard's friends, it would not have been possible for him to avoid her. In fact, he laid himself out to please her; and when he did that, he was irresistible. By the time he returned to Ireland in August 1726 they were on terms of familiar friendship. She made him promise to write to her, and at his request gave him a ring as a keepsake. He sent her some Dublin-woven silk plaid, partly as a personal present, partly in order to get an Irish manufacture into vogue at the Prince's court — an ulterior motive which he avowed and she heartily approved. Characteristically, the Princess appropriated it; still, she ordered some more. Meanwhile, *Gulliver* had come out. Mrs. Howard read it with more than ordinary intelligence and care, and passed on the royal order in terms of art taken from the book. Swift, in turn, paid her the pretty compliment of persuading Captain Gulliver in person to send her the crown of Lilliput, which he had found in his waistcoat pocket after his escape from Blefuscu. Presumably he had the trinket made for her. Just before returning to England in April 1727, he wrote to her:

> I expect to find you are not altered by flattery or ill company. I am glad to tell you now, that I honour you with my esteem, because when the Princess grows a crowned head, you shall have no more such compliments . . . Besides, it so happens that the King is too tough a person for me to value any reversion of favour after him, and so you are safe. (February 1, 1727)

Swift went out of his way from Chester to London to visit Gooderich in Herefordshire, where his stout royalist grandfather had been vicar. He presented the church with a chalice which had belonged to him, and arranged for a tablet to be set up in his memory. He also ordered a supply of local cider to be sent to his friends in London and to himself in Dublin. When he got to Twickenham he showed his design and inscription for the tablet to Pope and Mrs. Howard, and he was so full of reminiscences of his ancestral home and of his pious commemorations that Pope suggested an alternative inscription:

> Jonathan Swift
> Had the gift
> By fatheridge, motheridge
> And by brotheridge
> To come down from Gutheridge.
> But now is spoil'd clean
> And an Irish Dean.
> In this Church he has put
> A stone of two foot
> With a cup and a can, sir,
> In respect of his grandsire.
> So, Ireland, change thy tone
> And cry: O hone, O hone,
> For England has its own.

The doggerel is very witty, and it has a particular point. Swift was feeling that his moorings had given way. He was adrift, and reaching out for an anchorage in his ancestry and in England. Pope was aware of it. Just after Swift had gone back, reluctantly, to Ireland the year before, he had reported to him that he had had a conversation with Walpole.

> He said he observed a willingness in you to live among us, which I did not deny, but at the same time told him, you had no such design in your coming this time, which was merely to see a few of those you loved; but that indeed all those wished it, and particularly Lord Peterborough and myself, who wished you loved Ireland less, had you any reason to love England more. (September 3, 1726)

In June, 1727, however, Swift was preparing for a short visit to France, where *Gulliver* was already famous, for health or distraction from his underlying anxiety, or both together. No sooner had he reached London from Twickenham to begin his journey than the news of the King's death arrived, on June 15. Bolingbroke immediately urged him to stay. 'There would not be commonsense in your going to France at this juncture,' he wrote on June 17; 'the opportunity of quitting Ireland for England is fairly before you.' After a day or two of hesitation, Swift once more prepared to go to France. Then, 'upon some new incidents', he wrote to Sheridan on June 24, 'I was with great vehemence dissuaded from it by certain persons, whom I could not disobey . . . Here is a strange world,' he added, and Stella would reproach him for taking part in it. But the talk was of a moderating scheme, where nobody should be used worse or better, for being called Whig or Tory. The King was behaving with equal civility to both.

> I prevailed with a dozen, that we should go in a line to kiss the King and Queen's hands. We have now done with repining, if we shall be used well, and not baited as formerly; we all agree in it, and if things do not mend, it is not our faults — we have made our offers, if otherwise, we are as we were. It is agreed the Ministry will be changed, but the others will have a soft fall.

A week later, his precarious optimism was shaken. He had left London and was now staying a week at Twickenham, he told Sheridan.

> Then I shall go thither again, just to see the Queen, and so come back hither. Here are a thousand schemes, which I embraced but coldly, because I like none of them . . . I desire it may be told that I never go to Court, which I mention because of a passage in Mrs. Dingley's letter. (July 1, 1727)

The brief fiasco of Sir Spencer Compton as Prime Minister was almost over. Compton felt so inadequate that he had to ask Walpole's help in drafting the King's declaration of his accession to the Privy Council; and when Walpole promised to get from the Commons an addition of £100,000 to the Civil List, the King took Caroline's advice and kept him.

Whatever hopes Swift may have entertained of a change of minister were dashed. A year before, Pope had shrewdly warned him against putting any faith in the new Opposition.

> I had a glimpse of a letter of yours lately, by which I find you are, like the vulgar, apter to think well of people out of power, than of people in power; perhaps it is a mistake, but however there is something in it generous. Mr. Pulteney takes it extreme kindly, I can perceive, and he has a great mind to thank you for that good opinion, for which I believe he has only to thank his ill fortune; for if I am not in an error, he would be rather in power than out. (September 3, 1726)

Pope's view plainly was that Swift would do better to apply himself to Walpole. But that was hopeless, unless Swift was prepared to recant about Ireland. His own hope appears to have been of an appointment direct by royal favour, mediated through the Princess and Mrs. Howard. There is no evidence that he took seriously the schemes of Pulteney and Bolingbroke, whatever they were; and, as we have seen, though Bolingbroke's advice may have made him hesitate for a day or two, he had resumed his intention of going to France. But before finally deciding he asked Mrs. Howard for her advice.

> I writ to her for her opinion; and particularly conjured her, since I had long done with Courts, not to use me like a courtier, but give me her sincere advice; which she did, both in a letter and to some friends. It was, by all means not to go; it would look singular, and perhaps disaffected; and to my friends, [she] enlarged upon the good intentions of the Court towards me. (January 8, 1733)

That was written six years later, when Swift was expatiating on his grievance against Mrs. Howard to Lady Betty Germaine, who, like most women who knew her, admired and trusted her.[4] Swift's case against her, even when he had time to brood over and exaggerate it, is quite astonishingly flimsy. He does not say that Mrs. Howard made him a promise of any kind; merely that she advised him strongly not to go to France, for reasons obviously sound, and spoke to his friends of the good intentions of the Court towards him, meaning Queen Caroline. She had grounds for believing they were good. The Queen, as Princess, had received Swift graciously, enjoyed *Gulliver*, promised him a present of medals (which he never got) in return for his silk plaid, and told Mrs. Howard that she had enjoyed talking to the 'very odd' man. There is not a scrap of evidence to show that Mrs. Howard did not behave towards Swift with complete integrity and good faith. Nor was Swift at the time in the least suspicious of her, for frequent and friendly letters were passing between them in August 1727, up to the moment when his deafness and giddiness forced him to leave Pope's and go to his cousins in London to be nursed. On the day he left for Ireland, in response to Sheridan's summons, he sent Mrs. Howard a parting letter, explaining that his illness compelled him to return to Dublin. 'I am,' he wrote, 'infinitely obliged to you for all your civilities, and shall preserve a remembrance of them as long as I have any memory left;' and he asked her to make his excuses to the Queen. 'I shall pass the remainder of my life with the utmost gratitude for her Majesty's favours.' (September 18, 1727.) The last was courtiers' humbug; but it shows that Swift himself was inclined to believe that the Queen's intentions towards him were good.

What seems to have turned him against Mrs. Howard was the disappointment of Gay's hopes of a decent post at Court. Gay was a particular friend of Mrs. Howard's, and he is said to have helped her in some of her witty replies to her embarrassing correspondents. She did her best for him, and the Queen told her that she intended to do something for him when her new household was being settled. But all she did was to give him the trivial post of Gentleman Usher to the two-year old Princess Louisa at £100 a year, which he declined. Swift ascribed this to the influence of Walpole, who believed that Gay was the author of a lampoon against him, of which he, in fact, was innocent. Gay himself never dreamed of blaming Mrs. Howard in the matter; even Pope completely exonerated her. But Swift persisted that Mrs. Howard had deceived Gay — and himself. He wrote to Pope:

> With all the partiality of my inclination, I cannot acquit the characterized person. It is against my original fundamental maxims . . . Neither will your *mutato nomine* etc. satisfy me unless things are monstrously changed from what you taught me. For I was led to believe that the present unexpected situation or confirmation of things was brought about over two years ago by the intervention of the person whose character was drawn. (November 23, 1727)

The fundamental maxims concerning a Court which forbade him to acquit Mrs. Howard were set out in the letter. They were 'the insincerity of those who would be thought the best friends', and 'sacrificing those whom we wish well to a point of interest or intrigue'. The assumption necessary to make these maxims relevant was that Mrs. Howard had decisive influence with the King. He made out that Pope had instructed him that she had.

It was Swift's own fault if he believed it. He had plenty of opportunity of forming his own judgment of Mrs. Howard's influence. He had become sufficiently intimate with her to write a 'character' of her, and to present her with it, just before the news of the old King's death. It was to this he referred when he spoke of her to Pope as 'the characterized person'. It is not, on the whole, very perspicacious; but on the point at issue — her influence with the King — it is clear enough.

> I shall say nothing of her wit or beauty, which are freely allowed by all persons of taste or eyes ... As to her history, it will be sufficient to observe that she went, in the prime of her youth, to the Court of Hanover, and there became of the Bedchamber to the present Princess of Wales, living with the rest in expectation ... of the Queen's death [i.e. Anne's], after which she came over with her mistress, and hath ever since continued in her royal highness's service; where from the attendance duly paid her by all the ministers, as well as others who expect advancement, [she] hath been reckoned for some years to be the great favourite of the Court at Leicester Fields, which is a fact that of all others she most earnestly wishes might not be believed.[5]

In other words, she had tried hard to convince Swift that she had no real influence. She indeed told him so plainly enough in one of her letters. 'I have been a slave twenty years', she wrote to him on August 16, 1727, 'without ever receiving a reason for any one thing I was obliged to do.' She could not have gone further without positively confiding in him. If Swift, because of his perverse adherence to his maxim 'of the insincerity of those who would be thought the best friends,' refused to believe her, he had only himself to blame. He would not even believe himself, for his 'character' goes on to say:

> The credit she hath is managed with the utmost parsimony, and whenever she employs it, which is as seldom as possible, it is only upon such occasions where she is sure to get more than she spends. She would readily press Sir Robert Walpole to do some favour for Charles Churchill, or Mr. Doddington; the Princess for some mark of grace to Mrs. Clayton, or his Royal Highness to remember Mr. Schutz.[6]

That is wittily expressed; but the plain meaning of it is that Mrs. Howard dared only use her supposed influence on behalf of those who could get what they wanted without it.

Swift knew this; he also knew that Walpole was Gay's enemy, just as, with much better reason, he was Swift's. What did he expect Mrs. Howard to have done? To prevent Walpole from getting back into power? He was back already. To obtain preferment for Gay and himself in defiance of Walpole, now that he was in power again? Such expectations were so extravagant that it is hard to believe that Swift entertained them. But it seems that he did, and that he was both credulous and obtuse. If it had been a temporary lapse, it might be ascribed to the perturbation caused by his despair about Stella and his own illness. But it was not temporary. He went on cherishing this fictitious grievance against Mrs. Howard for years. Her imagined duplicity became almost as great an obsession with him as Oxford's conduct was with Bolingbroke.

5

It is a satisfaction to record that in the event Mrs. Howard punished him neatly for his boorish behaviour. Three years later, on November 21, 1730, having heard a false report that Mrs. Howard had retired or been discarded from Court, he wrote her a letter which could only have been intended to hurt her. He recapitulated his grievances, protested his own disinterestedness and continued in terms which to a sensitive woman in her position must have seemed deliberately offensive.

As to yourself, Madam, I most heartily congratulate you for being delivered from the toil, the envy, the slavery, and vexation, of a favourite; where you could not always answer the good intentions that I hope you had ... Mr. Pope has always been an advocate for your sincerity; and even I, in the character I gave you of yourself, allowed you as much of that virtue as could be expected in a lady, a courtier, and a favourite. Yet, I confess I never heartily pledged your health as a toast, upon any other regards than beauty, wit, good sense and an unblemished character. For as to friendship, truth, sincerity and other trifles of that kind, I never concerned myself about them, because I knew them to be only parts of the lower morals, which are altogether useless at Courts ... I could have been a better prophet in the character I gave you of yourself, if it had been good manners in the height of your credit, to put you in the mind of its mortality, for you are not the first, by at least three ladies, whom I have known to undergo the same turn of fortune.

Mrs. Howard did not reply. But not long after, Swift had need of her good offices. He had taken up a mediocre poetess, Mrs. Barber, the wife of a Dublin woollen-draper, and had been lavish with his recommendations of her to his English friends. Some enemy had the clever idea of writing letters to the Queen in Swift's name, in one of which the inability of Mrs. Barber to gain access to her Majesty was represented as a supreme example of the injustice of the English Court to Ireland. Though it was hardly a plausible imitation of Swift's style, it was good enough to deceive the average intelligence, to annoy the Queen, and to make Swift appear ridiculous. His only remedy was to write to Mrs. Howard, nominally to congratulate her on becoming the Countess of Suffolk — her husband had succeeded to the earldom in 1731 — but really to beg her to exculpate him with the Queen. Yet, even when appealing for her help, he could not refrain from charging her with having deceived him and, by preventing his journey to France, with the responsibility of his subsequent illness. Mrs. Howard took a delicious revenge.

> You seem to think [she wrote] that you have a natural right to abuse me, because I am a woman, and a courtier. I have taken it as a woman and as a courtier ought, with great resentment, and a determined resolution of revenge. The number of letters that have been sent, and thought by many to be yours, and thank God they were all silly ones, has been a fair field to execute it. Think of my joy to hear you suspected of folly; think of my pleasure when I entered the list for your justification. Indeed, I was a little disconcerted to find Mr. Pope took the same side; for I would have had the man of wit, the dignified divine, the Irish Drapier, have found no friend but the silly woman and the courtier. Could I have preserved myself alone in the list, I should not have despaired that this monitor of Princes, this Irish patriot, this excellent man at speech and pen, should have closed the scene under suspicions of having a violent passion for Mrs. Barber . . . Now, to my mortification I find everybody inclined to think you had no hand in writing those letters; but I every day thank Providence that there is an epitaph in St. Patrick's Cathedral, that will be a lasting monument of your imprudence. I cherish this extremely; for, say what you can to justify it, I am convinced I shall as easily argue the world into the belief of a courtier's sincerity, as you, with all your wit and eloquence, will be able to convince mankind of the prudence of that action.*

(September 25, 1731)

* Swift had asked the Schomberg family to pay for a memorial to the Duke of Schomberg, who was killed at the Boyne and buried in St. Patrick's, with nothing to mark the place. He had received no reply, and had carried out his threat of erecting a tablet at the expense of the chapter reflecting on the family's neglect. 'Decanus et Capitulum maxim opere etiam atque etiam petie-

For once, Swift had met his match. Her delicate and witty rebuke was richly deserved. Her further defence of herself against his ill-natured insinuations was entirely convincing, and admirably expressed.

I expect to hear if peace shall ensue, or war continue between us. If I know but little of the art of war, yet you see I do not want courage; and that has made many an ignorant soldier fight successfully . . . If you send honourable articles, they shall be signed. I insist that you own you have been unjust to me, for I have never forgot you, but made others send my compliments, because I was not able to write myself. If I cannot justify the advice I gave you from the success of it, yet you know I gave you my reasons for it: and it was your business to have judged of my capacity by the solidity of my arguments. If the principle was false, you ought not to have acted upon it. So you have only been the dupe of your own ill judgment, and not to my falsehood. Am I to send back the crown and the plaid, well packed up, in my own Characters, or am I to follow my inclination, and continue
Very truly and very much your humble servant,
H. SUFFOLK

It seems fantastic that Swift should have continued after this to grumble his accusations of Lady Suffolk to his friends. But so he did. A year later Lady Betty Germaine mentioned casually that Lady Suffolk was coming to visit her. He seized the occasion to complain to Lady Betty of her insincerity. She replied that she was surprised to find Lady Suffolk dwindle in his opinion, while she was rising infinitely in her own, the longer and better she knew her.

But you say, 'you will say no more of Courts, for fear of growing angry'; and indeed, I think you are so already, since you level all without knowing them, and seem to think that no one who belongs to a Court can act right. I am sure this cannot be really and truly your sense, because it is unjust; and, if it is, I shall suspect there is something of your old maxim in it, which I ever admired and found true, that you must have offended them, because you do not forgive. (November 7, 1732)

It was a shrewd remark, and it went home. To justify himself, Swift set out once more his familiar and tedious grievance to Lady Betty. The letter

runt, ut haeredes Ducis monumentum in memoriam Parentis erigendum curarent; sed postquam per epistolas, per amicos, diu ac saepe orando nil profecere, hunc demum lapidem statuerunt, saltem ut scias, hospes, ubinam terrarum Schombergenses cineres delitescunt. Plus potuit fama virtutis apud alienos quam sanguinis propinquitas apud suos.' Swift's action was resented by the Court of Prussia, where Schomberg had been generalissimo after his explusion from France as a Protestant in 1685. It was also interpreted as a reflection on the English Court. 'God damn Dr. Swift,' said George II, 'whose design was to make me quarrel with the King of Prussia.'

reached her while she was sitting with Lady Suffolk at dinner. 'She knew your hand, and inquired much after you, as she always does; but I, finding her name frequently mentioned, not with that kindness I am sure she deserves put it into my pocket with silence and surprise.' Lady Betty pointed out, with vigour, that, on his own showing, there was no substance in his charge and ended with a declaration of loyalty that rings gratefully in our ears across two centuries. In her house, she said, members of both parties met as friends; she disregarded their labels and esteemed them according to their human qualities.

And those of them that have great and good qualities and virtues I love and admire, in which number is Lady Suffolk, and I do like and love her, because I believe, and as far as I am capable of judging, know her to be a wise, discreet, honest and sincere courtier, who will promise no further than she can perform, and will always perform what she does promise: so now, you have my creed as to her. (February 8, 1733)

And there we may leave this episode in Swift's later life. It was not trivial, either in itself, or in the place it occupied in his mind; and it is illuminating. Swift was becoming a very poor judge of character: at once unjustly suspicious and unreasonably credulous. He was becoming impatient of integrity and independence in others, and a prey to obsequiousness and flattery. In him begin to be visible the outlines of a resemblance to King Lear, who will not find his Cordelia again, even in prison.

6

In fairness, as a counterpoise to his deplorable misjudgment of Lady Suffolk we may set his friendship with the Duchess of Queensberry. She was, in circumstance, the opposite of Lady Suffolk; in character, akin: and she was Lady Suffolk's friend.[7] She had the supreme merit, in Swift's eyes, of having been dismissed from the Court for championing Gay. The prodigious success of *The Beggars' Opera* had compensated for the disappointment of Gay's hopes of royal favour. He finished it in the autumn of 1727, at the moment that his appointment as Gentleman Usher was announced and declined. It was produced on the following January 29. It was instantly popular. But, though Gay was probably innocent of any intention to satirize the Court or Walpole, his humorous comparisons of the thieves' kitchen with the corruptions of politicians were badly taken; his refusal of the Ushership predisposed people to look for allusions, and of course they found them. Polly was regarded as a hit at Miss Dolly Skerrett, Walpole's bouncing mistress, whom he afterwards married. At the same time the spirited, independent and beautiful young Duchess of Queensberry — Prior's Kitty, 'beautiful and young, And wild as colt untam'd,' now twenty-seven — who had long been Gay's friend, decided that, if he could not have a worthy and congenial post in the Royal household, he should have one in hers. As Arbuthnot put it, Gay, of all people, was become, *invita Minerva*, the second Sacheverell.

To take advantage of his success, Gay promptly wrote a sequel, *Polly*, which he finished by the end of the year. It was just going into rehearsal, when Rich, the manager of Drury Lane, received notice from the Lord Chamberlain, first, that it must not be rehearsed until he had read it, then that it was absolutely forbidden. At that moment Gay became seriously ill, and the Duchess took him away from his lodgings to her house in Burlington Gardens, where she nursed him back to health. He remained with the Queensberrys to his death. She then took the war into the enemy's camp by persuading him to print *Polly*, and canvassing the Court, under the very eyes of their Majesties, for subscriptions. For this, she was forbidden the Court — 'a thing', as the admiring Mrs. Pendarves said, 'never heard of before to one of her rank'. The Duchess's reply to the Vice-Chamberlain is famous.

The Duchess of Queensberry is surprised and well pleased that the King has given her so agreeable a command as forbidding her the Court, where she never came for diversion, but to bestow a very great civility on the King and Queen. She hopes that by so unprecedented an order as this, the King will see as few as she wishes at his Court, particularly such as dare to think and speak truth.
I dare not do otherwise, nor ought not; nor could I have imagined but that it would have been the highest compliment I could possibly pay the King and Queen, to endeavour to support truth and innocence in their house.

Nothing could have endeared her more to Swift than this spirited defiance of the Court on behalf of his friend Gay, and a delightful correspondence developed between them. She made a practice of writing postscripts to Gay's frequent letters. To meet her taste, he even went so far as to promise to use three-pronged instead of two-pronged forks, in order to avoid using his knife to get mashed turnips into his mouth: a promise which he apparently performed, for there is an entry in his account-books for the purchase of new forks.

The Queensberrys had the imagination and humanity to treat Gay as an equal. They prevented him from wasting his money, put a general curb on his amiable fecklessness, and gave him security. The friendship between him and the Duchess was deep and touching. She honoured him for his transparent and artless sincerity. When he died, fairly suddenly but in pain, on December 4, 1732, she was in great distress; and her first impulse was to commence a correspondence of her own with Swift, as the one of Gay's friends in nature most like himself, and the one for whom Gay himself had the deepest regard. But she checked it, and waited for a message from him. It did not come immediately, for Swift took Gay's death much to heart. He could not bring himself to open Pope's letter telling the news for five days, through a foreboding of what it contained.

If you are acquainted with the Duchess of Queensberry [he eventually wrote to Pope] I desire you will present her my most humble service. I think she is a greater loser by the death of a friend than either of us. She seems a lady of excellent sense and spirits. I had often postscripts from her in our friend's letters to me, and her part was sometimes longer than his, and they made up a great part of the little happiness I could have here. This was the more generous, because I never saw her since she was a girl of five years old, nor did I envy poor Mr. Gay for anything so much as being a domestic friend to such a lady. (January, 1733)

Pope showed the letter to the Duchess, and at that she wrote. She was now (she said) encouraged to hope that Swift and she might converse together as usual.

By which advantage I will not despair to obtain in reality some of those good qualities, you say, I seem to have. I am conscious of only one, that is being an apt scholar; and if I have any good in me, I certainly learned it insensibly of our poor friend, as children do any strange language. It is not possible to imagine the loss he is to me; but as long as I have any memory, the happiness of ever having such a friend will never be lost to me.

The simple humility in so great and beautiful a lady is touching. She had sensed what lay behind the reticence of Swift's letter.

Your letter touched me extremely. It gave me a melancholy pleasure. I felt much more than you wrote, and more than, I hope, you will continue to feel . . . Nothing is more pleasant than to believe what one wishes. I wish to be your friend; I wish you to be mine; I wish you may not be tired with this; I wish to hear from you soon; and all this in order to be my own flatterer. (February 21, 1733)

The Duchess was in a position to throw down an open challenge to the Court for its treatment of Gay: Mrs. Howard was not. She was totally dependent on it, not only for her livelihood, but for keeping her safe from her husband. Not until he was dead did she dare to break away. But she also was Gay's loyal friend, and Gay was equally loyal to her. Though he was devoted to Swift, he would never admit that there was a grain of truth in his charges against her. Swift called him a simpleton, but he stuck to it. And it is certain that, if there had been any ground whatever for suspicion of Mrs. Howard's conduct towards Gay, the Duchess would have been the first to resent it. On the contrary, there was not a moment's interruption in their close and affectionate friendship. When Mrs. Howard, now the Countess of Suffolk, had gone to the Bath, preliminary to retiring completely from Court, the Duchess wrote to her from Amesbury:

> I cannot leave off till I have told you some very strange things. Know then that for four or five years last past we had set our minds on a certain hill that I am sure you have heard me mention; and now not only of that, but of the whole estate, we are in possession, and as yet I have not felt delighted, only mighty well satisfied. Is not this astonishing? I often want poor Mr. Gay, and on this occasion extremely. Nothing evaporates sooner than joy untold, or even told, unless to one so entirely in your interest as he was, who bore at least an equal share in every satisfaction or dissatisfaction which attended us. I am not in the spleen, though I write thus; on the contrary, it is a sort of pleasure to think over his good qualities: his loss was really great, but it is a satisfaction to have once known so good a man. As you were as much his friend as I, it is needless to ask your pardon for dwelling so long on this subject. Adieu, my d — d — L. S. if any words could express it, I would tell you how sincerely and affectionately I am yours.[8]

It is an appropriate epilogue to this account of the relations between the ageing Swift and two noble ladies whose beauty of face was matched by their beauty of mind. Swift had never met the Duchess of Queensberry, since the time he saw her 'in hanging sleeves'. Probably, if he had, he would have managed to pick a quarrel with her too.

CHAPTER XXVII

THE LAND OF SLAVFS

WHEN Stella died, a restraining influence on Swift was removed. This is first perceptible in his Irish political writings, in which a new violence against women makes its appearance. This was of minor importance in the political writings themselves; it did not seriously distort the argument, though it made it less persuasive: but it is very marked, and it is the symptom of worse to come.

It appears in connection with his constant proposal that the Irish should by a self-denying ordinance restrict themselves to the use of home manufactures. When he first put it forward in 1720 he had been chagrined by the lack of positive response; infuriated by Whiteshed's vindictive proceedings against the printer; and disheartened by the failure of the jury to maintain their refusal to convict. His pessimism concerning what could be expected from the human animal had since grown steadily. It had not been checked by the popularity of the Drapier. That, he felt, was a flash in the pan. His mood on his final return from England had been one of deep disgust with Ireland. Had it not been for Stella, he wrote at Holyhead, he would rather stay for ever on the inhospitable shores of Wales; rather

> go in freedom to my grave
> Than rule yon Isle, and be a slave.[1]

And in the verses entitled *Ireland* he wrote bitterly:

> Remove me from this land of slaves,
> Where all are fools, and all are knaves;
> Where every knave and fool is bought,
> Yet kindly sells himself for nought;
> Where Whig and Tory fiercely fight
> Who's in the wrong, who in the right;
> And, when their country lies at stake,
> They only fight for fighting sake,
> While English sharpers take the pay,
> And then stand by to see fair play.[2]

He drew a withering picture of the Anglo-Irish politician, flattered and cajoled by the empty politeness of the Lord Lieutenant, and rushing round to his friends to persuade them to surrender every Irish interest — for nothing.

'I think they justly ought to share
In all employments we can spare.
Next, for encouragement of spinning,
A duty might be laid on linen.
An act for laying down the plough —
England will send you corn enough;
Another act that absentees
For licences shall pay no fees.
If England's friendship you would keep,
Feed nothing in your lands but sheep;
But make an act severe and full,
To hang up all who smuggle wool.
And then he kindly gave me hints
That all our wives should go in chintz.
Tomorrow I will tell you more,
For I'm to deal with him at four' . . .
Yet should this blockhead beg a place
Either from Excellence or Grace,
'Tis pre-engaged, and in his room
Townshend's cast page or Walpole's groom.[3]

In that list of measures which the slavish M.P. recommends, each single one of Swift's positive proposals for the recovery of Ireland is sacrificed. He demanded the enforcement of a proportion of tillage; a tax on the rents and salaries of absentees; an act against dispossessing tenants by graziers; and a voluntary embargo on the import of foreign cloth.

Stella's illness apart, these things filled his mind. He used them, no doubt, in part to distract himself at this moment; but his concern with them was real and lasting. While Stella lay dying he wrote one of his most carefully considered surveys of the whole Irish situation: *A Short View of the State of Ireland*, wherein he set out the fourteen conditions requisite to the prosperity of any country, and showed how they were all denied to Ireland. The fourteenth is 'a disposition of the people of a country to wear their own manufactures' and to import as few luxuries as possible.

We take special care to act diametrically contrary to it in the whole course of our lives. Both sexes, but especially the women, despise and abhor to wear any of their own manufactures, even those which are better made than in other countries, particularly a sort of silk plaid, through which the workmen are forced to run a sort of gold thread that it may pass for Indian.[4]

(This, by the way, was the silk plaid, or poplin, for which he had, through Mrs. Howard, sought the patronage of the Princess of Wales.) Now, for the first time, he puts the chief blame for the neglect of home manufactures on the women.

It is a gentle reproof compared to what followed; but it coincides with the removal of Stella's restraining hand. That she exercised a restraining influence, may fairly be deduced from his account of her:

> She had a true taste of wit and good sense . . . and was a perfect good critic of style; neither was it easy to find a more proper and impartial judge, whose advice an author might better rely on, if he intended to send a thing into the world, provided it was on a subject that came within the compass of her knowledge. Yet perhaps she was sometimes too severe, which is a safe and pardonable error.[5]

That her influence was operative in moderating his strictures on women may be gathered from his surprising admission that 'she made little ceremony in discovering her contempt of a coxcomb . . . but the follies of her own sex she was rather inclined to extenuate or pity'. One likes Stella the better for it; and it is oddly at variance with the masculine picture of her he seeks to give.

Stella, we may be sure, would never have let pass the general onslaught on women which he made the year after her death in *An Answer to Several Letters from Unknown Persons.*

> Is it not the highest indignity to human nature that men should be such poltroons as to suffer the Kingdom and themselves to be undone, by the vanity, the folly, the pride and the wantonness of their wives who, under their present corruptions, seem to be a kind of animal, suffered, for our sins, to be sent into the world for the destruction of families, societies, and kingdoms; and whose whole study seems directed to be as expensive as they possibly can, in every useless article of living; who, by long practice, can reconcile the most pernicious foreign drugs to their health and pleasure, provided they are but expensive, as starlings grow fat with henbane; who contract a robustness by mere practice of sloth and luxury; who can play deep several hours after midnight, sleep beyond noon, revel upon Indian poisons, and spend the revenue of a moderate family to adorn a nauseous, unwholesome living carcase?[6]

Yet again, in the *Letter to the Archbishop of Dublin concerning the Weavers,* written in the same year, 1729, he declares that the real and probably insuperable opposition to any reduction in the import of foreign luxuries comes from 'the cowardly slavish indulgence of the men to the intolerable pride, arrogance, vanity and luxury of the women'. If the virtuosi could discover a passage to the moon, the women would insist on wearing only what came from it.

It is absolutely so in fact that every husband of any fortune in the Kingdom is nourishing a poisonous, devouring serpent in his bosom with all the mischief but with none of its wisdom.[7]

Such violence is pathological. It may have been accumulating in him, and merely been repressed out of deference to Stella. Or, more deviously, it may have been the expression of a resentment against Stella herself for her womanly demand upon him which he had ignored and denied. That explanation, we confess, would seem far-fetched were it not for the unforgettable episode of Gulliver's encounter with the black-eyed girl Yahoo. That cannot be dismissed. It haunts the memory, and opens a forbidding vista on the seething reactions of Swift's suppressed emotional nature to the reality of woman.

2

To speak less speculatively, after Stella's death Swift's misogyny became the deeper and more irrational part of his growing misanthropy. Much of his general misanthropy was not unreasonable. The situation of Ireland filled him with despair. There was much that the Irish could not do. It was beyond their power to extort freedom of trade from England. They could not compel the return of the absentees, or repeal the Navigation Act. But what they could do to save themselves, they would not.

Since he was determined, as he declared, never again to be the instrument of leaving an innocent man to the mercy of the Irish bench, he is reticent about some of the things he believed they could do, if only they had the public spirit. He merely hints at them, as when he suggests that they should apply to the King 'in a national way' for the right of coinage. If they were to do that, there is no fear that the request would meet with 'refusal or the least delay'. What underlies the innocent phrase 'in a national way' is apparent from its consequences. Swift was still dreaming of a nation-wide movement of 'non-co-operation' with England, and co-operation among themselves. So, in the matter of the coinage, he finally suggests that a company of ten public-spirited men should coin copper tokens of high intrinsic value and not bother about His Majesty's permission. They would limit themselves to a fixed rate of interest on the capital employed, act as trustees for the public, and thus take upon themselves one of the essential functions of an honest government. But, having expounded his plan, he reflects despondently:

I do not doubt but there may be ten such persons in this town, if they had only some visible mark to know them at sight. Yet I just foresee another inconveniency; that knavish men are fitter to deal with others of their own denomination; while those who are honest and best-intentioned may be the instruments of as much mischief to the public, for want of cunning, as the greatest knaves; and more, because of the charitable opinion they are apt to have of others. Therefore, how to join the prudence of the serpent with the innocency of the dove, in this affair, is the most difficult point. It is not so hard to find an honest man, as to make this honest man active, and vigilant, and skilful; which, I doubt, will require a spur of profit greater than my scheme will afford him, unless he will be contented with the honour of serving his country, and the reward of a good conscience. [8]

The effort of co-operation on which his heart was chiefly set was the formation of the woollen weavers and drapers into a guild to impose stand-ards of manufacture and a just price upon its members, and guarantee the buyer against shoddy workmanship and overcharging. He returned to this again and again (for, as he said, 'the woollen manufacture of this Kingdom sat always nearest my heart') but with ever-increasing despondency and exasperation, because his suggestion was ignored. No attempt was ever made to put his promising scheme into practice. And Swift reluctantly had to admit that even the women had a sound reason for preferring English to home-made stuffs: the quality was more dependable. There are, he says, a few honest shopkeepers,

But as to handicraftsmen, although I shall endeavour to believe it possible to find a fair dealer among their clans, yet I confess it hath never been once my good fortune to employ one single workman, who did not cheat me at all times to the utmost of his power in the materials, the work and the price . . . This I must own, is the natural consequence of poverty and oppression. These wretched people catch at anything to save them a minute longer from drowning. [9]

That was the vicious circle which he strove to break. The poverty of the Irish was such that they were completely demoralized, and thus incapable of acting together for their mutual protection and advantage. It was a universal *sauve qui peut*. If they were honest, they would starve. If they tried to improve their wretched holdings, their rents were screwed up a few shillings higher. The simple human basis for the improvement of agriculture which was Ireland's chief way to salvation was totally lacking. After setting out a few of the improvements he thought necessary, in road-making, the manage-ment of bogs and tree-planting, he says:

The common objections against all this, drawn from the laziness, the perverseness, or the thievish disposition of the poor native Irish, might be easily answered, by shewing the true reasons for such accusations, and how easily those people may be brought to a less savage manner of life: but my printers have already suffered too much for my speculations. However, supposing the size of a native's understanding just equal to that of a dog or a horse, I have often seen those two animals to be civilised by rewards, at least as much as by punishments.[10]

The rapacity of the Irish landlords was not, indeed, in Swift's eyes the only cause of the misery of the Irish people. But it was one that was remediable by Irishmen; whereas they could do nothing to remove the repression of Irish trade with England, or the draining of the Irish revenues by great salaries paid to absentee officials. Swift therefore proposed to strike at both absentee officials and absentee landlords by imposing a tax of five shillings in the pound in their revenues, while absent, and so to bring pressure on the landlords to reside. That, he believed, would relieve some of the oppression of the Irish peasant, for the worst of it came from the middlemen to whom the absentee landlords let their estates. But even if 'landlords should by a miracle become less inhuman', there would still be plenty of reasons why the wretched Irish should look for any opportunity to escape to unknown misery abroad. The exactions of the landlords, however, made the vast majority of them too poor to dream of emigration. It was only the relatively well to do — therefore mainly the Protestants — who could afford to emigrate.

If labour and people are the true riches of a nation, what must be the issue where one part of the people are forced away, and the other part have nothing to do?[11]

Though his proposals were many and various, and though for reasons both politic and personal he refrained from too openly championing the cause of the native Irish, it was their condition which, almost in spite of himself, preoccupied him. At times, he is furious with them for the importunacy with which they disturbed his mind. There is a touch of positive brutality in his proposal to whip out of the city all the beggars of Dublin save those who were resident and consented to wear badges issued by the parish to which they belonged; but this is really the violence of a mind made desperate by the sight of misery that is unmanageable. Superficially, he oscillates between blaming the moral deficiencies of the Irish for their wretchedness, and finding the reason for it in causes over which they have no control. Thus, in one sermon, he declares that there is 'hardly one in a hundred among them who doth not owe his misfortunes to his own laziness, or drunkenness, or worse vices';[12] but in another sermon this is only one cause among five, of which the other four are hardships in every branch of trade, the absenteeism of landlords and officials, male and female vanity that will not use Irish goods, and

> That Egyptian bondage of cruel, oppressing, covetous landlords, expecting that all who live under them should make bricks without straw, who grieve and envy when they see a tenant of their own in a whole coat, or able to afford one comfortable meal in a month, by which the spirits of the people are broken and made for slavery; the farmers and cottagers, almost through the whole kingdom, being to all intents and purposes as real beggars as any of those to whom we give our charity in the streets. And these cruel landlords are every day unpeopling their Kingdom, by forbidding their miserable tenants to till the earth, against common reason and justice, and contrary to the practice and prudence of all other nations, by which numberless families have been forced either to leave the Kingdom, or stroll about, and increase the number of our thieves and beggars.[13]

It is not to be believed that Swift was unaware of the contradiction. It was simply that, according to his mood, he picked upon now one, now another segment of the vicious circle which drove him to fury: the economic causes of the poverty, or the moral degeneration which it engendered, and which in turn made it doubly impossible to contend against those causes.

3

But the groundswell of his indignation was against the rapacity of the landlords and their agents. That was made plain when his anger and despair had accumulated to such a point that the rational moralizing was overborne by the passion of pity and indignation. The full force of the creative irony of *A Modest Proposal for Preventing the Children of Poor People from being a Burthen to their Parents and for Making them Beneficial to the Public* (1729) can be appreciated only in the context of all the positive proposals he had been putting forward, repeatedly and in vain, in the previous years. The macabre proposal itself, that one hundred thousand children should be sold annually for eating at a year old, is too famous to need more than mention. But the mood in which he makes it is the consequence of the rejection of all his practical suggestions.

> But as to myself, having been wearied out for many years with offering vain, idle, visionary thoughts, and at length utterly despairing of success, I fortunately fell upon this proposal, which as it is wholly new, so it hath something solid and real, of no expense and little trouble, full in our own power, and whereby we can incur no danger in *disobliging*

ENGLAND. For this kind of commodity will not bear exportation, the flesh being of too tender a consistence to admit a long continuance in salt, *although perhaps I could name a country, which would be glad to eat up our whole nation without it.*[14]

The last clause is an artistic mistake; instead of clinching the impression, it weakens it by introducing a discordant image and a conflicting train of thought. Swift's fury against England for an instant got the better of his craft.

For the appalling impact of this masterpiece comes chiefly from the fact that the proposal really was the best solution, in the abstract: that is to say, if it had not been made impracticable by unfortunate and unnecessary scruples against cannibalism. These scruples were arbitrary: a mere *tabu*, without any basis in charity and human kindness. The adult Irish natives were already treated like cattle, except in two respects: that they were not eaten, and they were not fed. Then, why not abolish both these anomalies, which caused so much misery, by eating them as they were weaned? The advantages were manifest: even in morals.

Men would become as fond of their wives, during the time of their pregnancy, as they are now of their mares in foal, their cows in calf, or sows when they are ready to farrow, nor offer to beat or kick them (as it is too frequent a practice) for fear of a miscarriage.[15]

And it would obviously increase the sum total of happiness.

I desire those politicians, who dislike my overture, and may perhaps be so bold to attempt an answer, that they will first ask the parents of these mortals, whether they would not at this day think it a great happiness to have been sold for food at a year old, in the manner I prescribe, and thereby have avoided such a perpetual scene of misfortunes as they have since gone through, by the oppression of landlords, the impossibility of paying rent without money or trade, the want of common sustenance, with neither house nor clothes to cover them from the inclemencies of the weather, and the most inevitable prospect of entailing the like, or greater miseries upon their breed for ever.[16]

Why not? is the reaction to the proposal in any mind that looks squarely at the reality which Swift was confronting; and a convincing answer to Why not? is diabolically hard to find, except on a plane equally macabre. There was no effective demand for the commodity Swift proposed to supply.

But it is the rational solution: and it takes us into a realm of lucid nightmare. And that is where Swift had got to. Since there was no earthly chance of his previous remedies being applied, why not adopt the simplest and most radical of all: of reducing the population by profitable euthanasia? Very seldom does his blue eye twinkle during this superb performance. But once it visibly does.

> It would greatly lessen the number of Papists, with whom we are yearly over-run, being the principal breeders of the nation, as well as our most dangerous enemies, and who stay at home on purpose with a design to deliver the kingdom to the Pretender, hoping to take their advantage by the absence of so many good Protestants, who have chosen rather to leave their country than stay at home, and pay tithes against their conscience to an Episcopal curate.[17]

Above all, the *Modest Proposal* is the expression by his own peculiar art, of the bitterness of his experience as an Irish patriot. His efforts had ended in smoke. As he put it in a sermon, 'no people ever appeared more utterly devoid of what is called a public spirit'. He was then, of course, addressing Protestants, and he drew a sharp and absolute distinction between their loyalty to the King, which was abundant and effusive, and their concern for the common weal, which was non-existent. 'A man may be very loyal, in the common sense of the word, without one grain of public good at his heart.' That was the case with the Protestants of Ireland. The public spirit which he had required of them, in vain, would have showed itself, chiefly, in two things: an attitude of resolute independence towards England, and an attitude of common humanity towards the native Irish. They were incapable of either. They behaved like slaves to the one, and like tyrants to the other.

So, in the *Modest Proposal*, he dismisses all the measures which he had specifically urged them to adopt. They had refused them; he now discards them, one by one.

> I desire the reader will observe that I calculate my remedy *for this one individual Kingdom of Ireland, and for no other that ever was, is, or, I think, ever can be upon earth.* Therefore let no man talk to me of other expedients: *Of taxing our absentees at five shillings a pound: Of using neither clothes, nor household furniture, except what is of our own growth and manufacture: Of utterly rejecting the materials and instruments that promote foreign luxury: Of curing the expensiveness of pride, vanity, idleness, and gaming in our women: Of introducing a vein of parsimony, prudence, and temperance: Of learning to love our Country, wherein we differ even from* LAPLANDERS *and the inhabitants of* TOPINAMBOU: *Of quitting our animosities and factions, nor act any longer like the Jews, who were murdering one another at the very moment their city was taken: Of being a little cautious not to sell our country and our consciences for*

nothing: Of teaching landlords to have at least one degree of mercy toward their tenants. Lastly of putting a spirit of honesty, industry and skill into our shopkeepers, who, if a resolution could now be taken to buy only our native goods, would immediately unite to cheat and exact upon us in the price, the measure, and the goodness, nor could ever yet be brought to make one fair proposal of just dealing, though often and earnestly invited to it. Therefore I repeat, let no man talk to me of these and the like expedients, till he hath at least some glimpse of hope that there will ever be some hearty and sincere attempt to put them into practice.[18]

Swift had lost whatever hope he had had. The *Modest Proposal* was the projection of his complete despair, and the expectoration of his anger against the Irish landlords, who were for him doubly the villains: because of their cruelty as landlords, and because of their cowardice and selfishness as the chief members of both houses of the Irish parliament.

I grant this food will be somewhat dear, and therefore very proper for landlords, who, as they have already devoured most of the parents, seem to have the best title to the children.[19]

4

An Answer to the Craftsman (1730) is a variation on the same ironical theme: that any means of reducing the population of Ireland is beneficial to the country. The *Craftsman*, the brilliant journal in which Bolingbroke and Pulteney concealed themselves behind Caleb D'Anvers, had attacked the Government for permitting France to recruit soldiers in Ireland. This opposition, says Swift, is frivolous and uncalled for.

It is well known that about sixty years ago, the exportation of live cattle from hence to England was a great benefit to both kingdoms, until that branch of traffic was stopped by an act of Parliament on your side, whereof you have had sufficient reason to repent. Upon which account, when another act passed your Parliament, forbidding the exportation of live men to any foreign country, you were so wise as to put in a clause, allowing it to be done by his Majesty's permission, under his sign manual, for which, among other great benefits granted to Ireland, we are infinitely obliged to the British legislature. Yet this very grace and favour you, Mr. D'Anvers, whom we never disobliged, are endeavouring to prevent; which, I will take it upon me to say, is a manifest mark of your disaffection to his Majesty, a want of duty to the Ministry, and a wicked design of oppressing this kingdom and, a traitorous attempt to lessen the trade and manufacture of England.[20]

How monstrous is this hostility to his Majesty's graciousness! Let us rather export not six, but fifty thousand. Let us turn the whole country to grazing, and keep one family on every two thousand acres. That will make 67,200. Besides these we shall only need

> A standing army of twenty thousand English, which together with their trulls, their bastards and their horseboys, will, by a gross computation, very near double the count, and be very sufficient for the defence and grazing of the Kingdom, as well as to enrich our neighbours, expel popery, and keep out the Pretender. And, lest the army should be at a loss for business, I think it would be very prudent to employ them in collecting the public taxes for paying themselves and the civil list.[21]

Any annual excess over the quota of 67,200 natives shall be exported. No goods of any kind shall be exported except to England, and those only raw materials; none imported, except from England, and at their own prices. Tithe will be vastly diminished — that 'insupportable burden to all true Protestants, and to most churchmen'.

> So that the industrious shepherd and cowherd may sit every man under his own blackberry bush, and on his own potato bed, whereby this happy island will become a new Arcadia.[22]

We will have only leather money, manufactured in England. Indeed, the multitude of advantages which the scheme will produce for England is its great recommendation, since to live in amity with that country is the desire of the writer's heart. England has 'a just claim to the balance of trade with the whole world', and it is only just that she should have all our goods as raw materials, and send some of them back manufactured. But this will be of great benefit to Ireland also, for the graziers will be too busy to make anything.

But Swift's bolt was shot. Substantially, his effort as an Irish patriot culminates in the *Modest Proposal*, which is at once a despondent confession of his own failure and an effort to shock his audience into awareness of the evil for which their pusillanimity and supineness were to blame. That England's injustice to Ireland was monstrous, he well knew; but he would have had Irishmen look upon that as irremediable: as a calamity of nature, or an act of God. Within the narrow limits thus imposed upon them, they could, if only they had the imagination and the will, act like a united nation and a self-respecting community. There could be justice among them. Justice did not include equality of citizenship between Papist and Protestant. But in that exclusion, there was, in that age, no felt injustice. Justice in

England itself did not include equality of citizenship for Papists and Dissenters. But simple human justice towards the Papists was, in Swift's eyes, perfectly compatible with Protestant rule; and it would follow if only the Protestant Irishmen would show some self-respect and public spirit. To this he had tried to inspirit them, and he had failed. All his enormous popularity as the Drapier was empty: it was the expression of an emotional release, not of an acknowledgment of leadership, or a determination to follow it. His true position was symbolized in the action of the City of Cork which, when it bestowed the freedom of the city upon him in 1737, sent it in a silver box without a word to show for what services it was given.

CHAPTER XXVIII

THE EXCREMENTAL VISION: 1729-1731

WITHIN a few months of Stella's death, Swift made some new friends. Sir Arthur Acheson, a man of forty, whose estate was at Market Hill, between Armagh and Newry, was a Tory of Scottish descent. His wife, apparently in her early thirties, was the daughter of a Chancellor of the Irish Exchequer who had been a friend of Swift's. They were, at least at first, congenial company. Sir Arthur was well read, inclined to philosophical speculation, something of a recluse, and sufficiently inactive as a landlord to allow Swift a free hand in his favourite occupation of improvement. Lady Acheson, who seems like so many of Swift's women friends to have been tubercular, was intelligent and eager and submitted herself willingly to his inevitable tutelage. More rashly, she submitted herself to his universal prescription for every ailment — violent exercise. With an easy-going host, and a hostess who was willing to be corrected, Swift was in his element. He went to stay at Market Hill for the summer of 1728; but, deciding that his presence was required through the season of planting and pruning, he did not return to Dublin (except for a fleeting visit) until February 1729, when he reported on his sojourn to Pope:

> I lived very easily in the country. Sir Arthur is a man of sense, and a scholar, has a good voice, and my Lady a better. She is perfectly well bred and desirous to improve her understanding, which is very good, but cultivated too much like a fine lady. She was my pupil there, and severely chid when she read wrong. With that, and walking, and making twenty little amusing improvements, and writing family verses of mirth by way of libels on my Lady, my time passed very well and in very great order, infinitely better than here. (February 13, 1729)

The voices were important, for he was troubled with deafness during his stay at Market Hill. He stayed there again for the summers of 1729 and 1730.

He seems to have made his new acquaintance through Sheridan, who for some time contemplated transferring his school to Hamilton's Bawn on Sir Arthur's estate. Swift encouraged the plan; and he himself was so charmed with his company that he bought a few acres from Sir Arthur at Drumlack for £100, with the idea of building a house upon them. It was one of those amiable castles in the air which new friends, in the flush of enthusiasm, are apt to construct — a community of congenial spirits. Sheridan would have his school in the unoccupied building at Hamilton's Bawn, the Dean would have his country house nearby, and they and the Achesons 'would fleet the time carelessly as in the golden world'.

The dream sprang from the desire to begin again, far away from Dublin. Lady Acheson was to be the surrogate for Stella. The dream faded, as it was bound to do. Such a new beginning was impossible for a man of sixty-one, whose bodily and temperamental infirmities were increasing. But it speaks highly for the Achesons that Swift ever entertained it at all. His contact with them was stimulating as well as enjoyable: a notable group of poems had its origin in his life at Market Hill — they included, besides the verses generally grouped under that name, *A Portrait of a Modern Lady*, and *An Epistle to a Lady*. Lady Acheson was the Egeria to most of them. None of them belong to a high order of poetry; but they are lively and entertaining. They give us a picture of Swift during the last period when his enjoyment of life can be said to have predominated over depression, sickness, and indignation. They show him making fresh butter in a morning in a bottle; toiling away at his improvements in a rusty cassock and dirty bands, joking with Neil and Dermot and Sheelah, and the rest of 'the parcel of Teagues'; scolding everybody in general; and Lady Acheson in particular for not getting on with her lessons; and, in all, making an amiable and privileged nuisance of himself.

It is easy to misinterpret the verses. They were intended for the private diversion of the Achesons and himself. The raillery is incessant, and for the most part of the simple but deceptive kind which goes by opposites. If one were to take them literally one would conclude that Lady Acheson was a scarecrow, an unwilling and restive pupil, wrong-headed, opinionative, obstinate, resentful of interference, a devotee of dress and cards, who quickly grew weary of so difficult and domineering a guest; and that, after two years of gradually dwindling friendship, Swift and she parted with coldness on both sides. One might also conclude that she was at last justifiably offended by his incessant jibes at her, which passed beyond the limits of the tolerable. In *Death & Daphne* Death himself, of whom she is enamoured, is represented as shrinking from the touch of her hand, 'as cold and dry as lead'. A very tolerant woman might have felt outraged by that. But we have Orrery's explicit, though astonished, testimony that she was not.[1] On the contrary, she herself read it aloud one day in his and Swift's presence, and was rather pleased than otherwise that she was Daphne. That was at the earliest in the autumn of 1732, when Swift's visits to Market Hill had ceased for more than two years. And Swift wrote her an April fool letter in that year which shows that they were still good friends. Obviously there was a private understanding between them. She encouraged Swift to make a butt of her and enjoyed the result. He was chidden for idleness, he says, if he did not produce a lampoon at regular intervals.[2] We conclude that his raillery of Lady Acheson belongs to the kind that obviously makes no pretence to truth.

> No raillery gives just offence,
> Where truth has not the least pretence.[3]

If Lady Acheson was notoriously pretty, as she probably was, she would not mind being laughed at as Skinnybonia, and more skeletal than Death. On the same principle, we are not to take seriously Swift's complaints of her conversation. Even the verses in which he appears to take final leave of her as a friend (the *Twelve Articles*) and undertakes to let her have her foolish head in everything, end with the assurance

> Thus we both shall have our ends,
> And continue special friends.[4]

He probably meant it, and it was what happened. When the plan of Sheridan's taking Hamilton's Bawn for a school had been dropped, and the question arose whether it should be let to the Government for a barracks, or converted into a maltings, Swift wrote the very amusing poem *The Grand Question Debated*, in which Lady Acheson listens eagerly to her maid's picture of the glories of having smart officers for neighbours to put the rusty parsons in their places. Her Ladyship hears Hannah to the end, pretends to scold her, but gives her a gown. It would be as preposterous to infer that Lady Acheson really preferred the conversation of a stupid officer to Swift's as it would be to conclude from *The Revolution at Market Hill* that a pair of Parisian shoes would have been enough to distract her from her duty of defending Market Hill against the Dean's attack from Drumlack. These things go by contraries. And if Swift's baiting of Lady Acheson appears to become rather more ruthless as the friendship grows older, it is as much evidence of greater familiarity as of diminishing regard.

With Sir Arthur the case is different. Swift never makes him the butt of his raillery. We may suppose that he was entirely serious (though not necessarily entirely candid) in giving as his reason for not building at Drumlack, the discrepancy he had discovered between their tastes. Sir Arthur is speculative, absent-minded and silent.

> Who keeps his wisdom out of sight;
> Whose uncommunicative heart
> Will scarce one precious word impart:

Still rapt in speculations deep,
His outward senses fast asleep;
Who, while I talk a song will hum,
Or, with his fingers beat the drum.
But, as for me, who ne'er could clamber high
To understand Malebranche or Cambray;
Who send my mind (as I believe) less
Than others do, on errands sleeveless;
Can listen to a tale humdrum,
And, with attention, read Tom Thumb;
My spirits with my body progging,
Both hand in hand together jogging;
Sunk over head and heels in matter,
Nor can of metaphysics smatter;
Am more diverted with a quibble
Than dreams of words intelligible;
And think all notions too abstracted
Are like the ravings of a crackt head.
What intercourse of minds can be
Betwixt the Knight sublime and me?
If when I talk, as talk I must,
It is but prating to a bust.[5]

The idyll is over as regards the Knight of Gosford; but at least we owe to it the most vigorous of all Swift's expressions of a dislike of philosophical speculation which was first conceived when he was a student at Trinity and remained constant throughout his life. If he liked Berkeley, as he did, it was in spite of his philosophic genius.

According to Orrery, Lady Acheson separated from her husband[6] and apparently went to live with her mother at Baldoyle, where Swift was a frequent visitor. She died in 1737. One would gladly know more of her. The few direct glimpses of her character are attractive. She refused to drink Dr. Helsham's health after Swift had described him to her as one who took life so easily that he took the deaths of his friends easily too. In *An Epistle to a Lady*, she is made to defend herself against the Dean.

Am I spiteful, proud, unjust?
Did I ever break my trust?
Which, of all our modern dames,
Censures less, or less defames?
In good manners, am I faulty?
Can you call me rude, or haughty?
Did I e'er my mite withhold
From the impotent or old?

When did ever I omit
Due regard for men of wit?
When have I esteem express'd
For a coxcomb gaily dress'd?
Do I, like the female tribe,
Think it wit to fleer and gibe?
Who with less designing ends,
Kindlier entertains her friends?
    Think not cards my chief diversion,
'Tis a wrong, unjust aspersion:
Never knew I any good in 'um
But, to doze my head, like laudanum.
We, by play as men by drinking,
Pass our nights, to drive out thinking.
From my ailments give me leisure,
I shall read and think with pleasure:
Conversation learn to relish,
And with books my mind embellish.[7]

It was one of Swift's grievances against her that she was addicted to late
nights and cards. She was very ill, he wrote in August 1735, 'of her asthma
and other disorders, got by cards, and laziness, and ill hours.'[8] Swift was
obstinately stupid in diagnosis. Her 'laziness' was merely her reluctance to
stick to his prescription of violent exercise, which did her as little good as it
did Stella.

To lengthen my breath
He tires me to death . . .
And, say what I will,
Haul'd up every hill
Till daggled and tatter'd
My spirit's quite shatter'd.[9]

2

But underneath his friendship with Lady Acheson, Swift's animus against
woman was accumulating, and giving a touch of venom to the 'libels' he
wrote against her. They were, he insisted, harmless family mirth, and she
wisely accepted them at that. But if she read the prose tracts he wrote in
1729 — the year following his first and longest stay at Market Hill — she may
have wondered whether, beneath the raillery, there was not some lurking
hatred. 'Every husband of any fortune in the Kingdom is nourishing a
poisonous devouring serpent in his bosom, with all the mischief, but none

of its wisdom.' Under the circumstances that might have seemed addressed to herself, *par excellence*. Which was the real Swift? The man of friendship and mirth, or the obsessed misogynist?

Swift's attitude to women was always ambivalent. He attracted them and was attracted by them. He spent endless pains in trying to change them into what they were not, and in suppressing his fear of what they were. Lady Acheson was the last with whom he had a prolonged and intimate contact. More female 'pupils' were to come; but his contact with them was fleeting and occasional. Perhaps it is only coincidence that it was not until his visits to Market Hill had ceased that his animus against woman burst forth uncontrolled. Perhaps it is not, and the Market Hill verses really represent a last and on the whole a successful effort to keep a curb upon himself.

What is certain is that in 1731 there was an upsurge of peculiarly revolting coarseness in Swift's writing. Delany put it down to the influence of Pope during their close intercourse four years before. But the explanation does not explain — why was the effect delayed for four years? It would not be worth mentioning except to show that Delany, who knew Swift well at this time, felt that some external influence must be invoked to account for the astonishing contrast between the Swift he knew, whose piety he believed in and whose charity he admired, and the author of the scatological verses of 1730-2. But one of Delany's remarks is interesting.

> In all the long time I had the honour to be known to him, antecedent to this aera [i.e. his long visits to Pope in 1726-7], his ideas, and his style throughout the whole course of his conversation, were remarkably delicate and pure: beyond those of most men I was ever acquainted with. And I well remember his falling into a furious resentment with Mrs. Johnson, for a very small failure of delicacy on this point.[10]

The statement about Stella is so categorical that it must be true; and we must conclude that Swift was insanely capricious in his attitude to her in this matter: for one of her *bons mots* which he records with approval would surely have seemed shocking to Delany, whose standards were almost prudish. He regarded the amusing *Pastoral Dialogue* between Dermot and Sheelah, when they sat weeding Sir Arthur Acheson's courtyard, as the first instance of Swift's indecency after his return from Pope.

Dermot
No more that brier thy tender leg shall rake:
(I spare the thistle for Sir Arthur's sake).
Sharp are the stones; take thou this rushy mat;
The hardest bum will bruise with sitting squat.

JONATHAN SWIFT

Sheelah

Thy breeches, torn behind, stand gaping wide;
This petticoat shall save thy dear backside;
Nor need I blush, although you feel it wet,
Dermot, I vow, 'tis nothing else but sweat.

The *Pastoral Dialogue* is entirely harmless (as indeed is Stella's joke to Sheridan).* But if Delany found Dermot and Sheelah shocking, Stella's offence, over which Swift exploded, must have been ridiculously slight. His capriciousness over such things was pathological.

A sharp distinction must be made. There is a perfectly healthy coarseness which, however much it may offend the conventions of a particular time, is not in the least reprehensible. For some reason the harmless words 'bum' and 'arse', which are immediately in point, have been *tabu* now for generations, even on the music-hall stage. That Swift used them freely is nothing against him. Again, it would surely be unhealthily fastidious not to be able to laugh at his solemn fantasy on human turds in *An Examination of Certain Abuses, Corruptions & Enormities in the City of Dublin* (1732). The imaginary author is a Whig and Protestant fanatic on the look out for evidences of Jacobite machinations in the city.

Every person who walks the streets must needs observe the immense number of human excrements at the doors and steps of waste houses, and at the sides of every dead wall; for which the disaffected party have assigned a very false and malicious cause. They would have it, that these heaps were laid there privately by British fundaments, to make the world believe, that our Irish vulgar do daily eat and drink; and, consequently, that the clamour of poverty among us, must be false, proceeding only from Jacobites and Papists. They would confirm this by pretending to observe, that a British anus being more narrowly perforated than one of our own country; and many of these excrements upon a strict view appearing copple-crowned, with a point like a cone or a pyramid, are easily distinguished from the Hibernian, which lie much flatter and with less continuity. I communicated this conjecture to an eminent physician, who is well versed in such profound speculations; and at my request was pleased to make trial with each of his fingers, by thrusting them into the anus of several persons of different

---

* 'Dr. Sheridan, famous for punning, and intending to sell a bargain, said, he had made a very good pun. Somebody asked, what it was? He answered, My a — . The other taking offence, she insisted the doctor was in the right, for everybody knew that punning was his blind side.'[11]

'Selling a bargain' seems to have come into fashion under Charles II. The game, says Sir Charles Petrie, consisted in the seller naming his or her backside in answer to the question 'What?' which the buyer was artfully led to ask. 'For example, a girl, apparently frightened, would rush into a room full of people exclaiming "It is white, and follows me." On being asked "What?" she would sell the bargain by saying "Mine arse!" '[12]

nations, and professed he could find no such difference between them as those ill-disposed people allege. On the contrary, he assured me, that much the greater number of narrow cavities were of Hibernian origin. This I only mention to show how ready the Jacobites are to lay hold of any handle to express their malice against the government.[13]

But, although this is really funny and entirely legitimate, one cannot read Swift's writings of 1729 to 1732, without feeling that he is positively obsessed by human excretion. The subject occupies nearly one half of the otherwise amusing verses, *A Panegyric on the Dean* (1730). They are supposed to be written by Lady Acheson, which makes the expatiation the more offensive. Still, Swift might retort that he found the indiscriminate and ubiquitous evacuations of his time equally offensive. Why should he not represent Lady Acheson as commemorating his own sanitary achievement in building two privies for the Dermots and Sheelahs? It would be but half-convincing at the best: the tribute is excessive.

3

Nevertheless, it is not his direct obsession with ordure which is the chief cause of the nausea he arouses. It is the strange and disquieting combination of his horror at the fact of human evacuation with a peculiar physical loathing of women. It is an unpleasant subject; but it cannot be burked by any honest critic of Swift. The conventional excuses made for him are ridiculous. It has been said, for example, that in his loathsome picture of the diseased body of a poor prostitute he was merely castigating the horrors of sexual vice, and that his writings on sex have the merit of not exciting the lascivious appetite. To which one can only reply that it would be much better if they did. Lust is natural and wholesome compared to the feeling Swift arouses. Moreover, the horror of such a 'poem' as *A Beautiful Young Nymph going to Bed* is not confined to the nausea evoked by the hideous detail; it proceeds equally from the writer's total lack of charity, his cold brutality, towards the wretched woman who is anatomized. It is utterly inhuman.

Such religious and moral defences of Swift are quite untenable, and one can only suppose that those who make them have shrunk from looking steadily at the writings they excuse. In any case they entirely ignore the fact that this group of verses is not essentially concerned with sexual vice at all; the loathing is not of the syphilitic prostitute as such, but of woman as a physical being. Betty the grisette, and Corinna, the pride of Drury Lane, pass imperceptibly into Celia the healthy but filthy mistress of Strephon (*The Lady's Dressing Room*), and thence to Chloe, the newly married wife

(*Strephon & Chloe*) and back again to another Celia, the Cambridge freshman's sweetheart (*Cassinus & Peter*). It is not, as *The Lady's Dressing Room* makes clear, because the woman is filthy, or because she uses unpleasant artificial aids to beauty, that she is abominable, but because she is guilty of physical evacuation.

When it is taken out of physical nightmare in which Swift envelops it, the proposition he advances is at once nonsensical and intolerable. It is that no lover who has seen his mistress, no husband who has seen his wife, performing her natural functions can possibly remain in love with her. The sight, according to Swift, must inevitably put an instant end to woman's power of physical attraction, where the man has begun to feel it, and is an absolute prophylactic against it when he has not.

> O Strephon, ere that fatal day
> When Chloe stole your heart away,
> Had you but through a cranny spy'd
> On house of ease your future bride,
> In all the postures of her face,
> Which nature gives in such a case;
> Distortions, groanings, strainings, heavings,
> 'Twere better you had licked her leavings,
> Than from experience find too late
> Your goddess grown a filthy mate.
> Your fancy then had always dwelt
> On what you saw, and what you smelt;
> Would still the same ideas give ye
> As when you spy'd her on the privy;
> And, spite of Chloe's charms divine,
> Your heart had been as whole as mine.[14]

One jibs even at copying it. It is so perverse, so unnatural, so mentally diseased, so humanly *wrong*. Yet Swift labours it again and again. Another Strephon, peeping through his lady's bedroom, discovers the commode.

> Disgusted Strephon slunk away
> Repeating in his amorous fits
> Oh! Celia, Celia, Celia shits![15]

To the same refrain, after the same discovery, the undergraduate Cassinus loses his wits.

Criticism cannot escape the duty of trying to disentangle the nature of Swift's obsession. It is notable that, when the obsession becomes perceptible, there is one matter he studiously avoids: that is, the sexual act itself. He has many references to the consequences of venereal disease. But that is not the same thing; and, anyhow, though Swift's jokes about bridgeless noses and the other sequelae of syphilis are repulsive enough to a modern taste, they may have proceeded from a desperate reaction to the appalling moral and metaphysical problem presented by the appearance of the disease in Europe. The shock of the coming of syphilis must still have been reverberating in the European soul: and the psychic bewilderment may have found release in trying to make a joke of it. Shakespeare was sensitive enough for a million, and he made quite a few jokes about it. Swift's are much grimmer. But they ought not be reckoned against him.

But of Shakespeare's light-hearted and healthy jesting about the sexual act itself there is practically nothing in Swift. There is a certain amount — more than enough, some would say, for a clergyman — up to and including the *Journal to Stella*; but then it ceases. The essence of this healthy bawdy is that it regards the sexual act as a natural function. At some point in his life, apparently soon after the *Journal to Stella*, this capacity of regarding sex as a natural human function abandoned Swift. By the time he was writing the last book of *Gulliver* he had discarded it from true human nature and relegated it to the constitution of the Yahoos. It is the young female Yahoo who assails and horrifies Gulliver, while he is in process of being mentally and morally emancipated from his Yahoo nature, with her sexual advances. It is the emancipated Gulliver who, on his return to his own country, shudders with revulsion at the fact that he has propagated children by his Yahoo wife. And, as we have noted, the young female Yahoo who lecherously embraces him while he bathes, is horribly like Stella at the time that Swift first became conscious of her beauty. Yet again, it is an essential part of the physical contrast between the Yahoos and the Houyhnhnms that the former are as it were bathed in human excrement — it is the element in which they live and move and have their being; they squirt it, automatically, as infants; they use it as a deliberate weapon of offence as adults; they dabble and wallow in it — while the horses' excreta are compact, cleanly and inoffensive.

Evidently, the whole 'complex' was working in Swift's mind when he wrote the fourth book of *Gulliver*, which it partly corrupts and vitiates. That was in 1723. Its emergence at that moment may have been the outcome of a deep emotional upheaval caused by the death of Vanessa. Something of the sort is indicated by the physical degradation of Stella which was accomplished by Swift's imagination in the bathing-scene.

After Stella's death, and the removal of her restraining influence, Swift's animus against woman became more and more disproportioned, vituperative, and shrill. In the verses of 1730-2 his loathing reaches a condition of paroxysm. The female body is vile, it is loathsome, it is unspeakably horrible.

> His foul imagination links
> Each dame he sees with all her stinks;
> And if unsavoury odours fly
> Conceives a lady standing by.
> All women his description fits,
> And both ideas jump like wits;
> By vicious fancy coupled fast
> And still appearing in contrast.[16]

In vain Swift attempts an alibi. This creature driven into a frenzy of foulness by his contemplation of woman as a physical reality, *is* Swift; and, by some queer justice of the imagination, the symbol that insists on entering the reader's mind to describe him is his own picture of the Yahoos squatting in the trees discharging their excrement on Gulliver beneath. The wheel has turned full circle. It comes finally to rest in the condition described by Chancellor Yorke in a letter of 1742.

> Dean Swift has had a statute of lunacy taken out against him. His madness appears chiefly in most incessant strains of obscenity and swearing — habits to which the more sober parts of his life were not absolutely strangers.[17]

4

Then the rational part had completely lost control, and the preoccupation of his unconscious dribbled out. But in what sense and to what degree had the rational part control in his effusions of 1730-32? The answer partly depends upon what we understand by reason. What Swift understood by it, in this particular connection, emerges from one of his *Thoughts on Religion*:

> Although Reason were intended by Providence to govern our passions, yet it seems that in two points of the greatest moment to the being and continuance of the world, God hath intended our passions to prevail over reason. The first is, the propagation of the species, since no wise man ever married from the dictates of reason.[18]

Reason is there conceived as a power which should not merely control but suppress sexual passion. Yet Swift has to admit that the Deity appears to require that sexual passion should suppress reason. However, he had no intention of obeying the Deity. He insisted that reason, in the narrow sense in which he understood it, must prevail over passion in himself. God's command was not for him. What then did he mean by 'reason' here? Partly no doubt mere prudence, which impels a worldly-wise man, who has passed the heyday in the blood, to avoid marriage. 'Matrimony has many children: Repentance, Discord, Poverty, Jealousy, Sickness, Spleen, Loathing &c.'[19] But this, like the former, was a maxim of his middle age. The 'dictates of reason' which forbid marriage were certainly not operative in him in 1696 when he sought so ardently to marry Varina. Yet he was then nearly thirty, at the height of his genius, and assuredly he did not regard himself as irrational. Either he changed his notion of reason from something which approved his marrying to something which forbade it, or — as he became older, and more doubtfully wiser — he looked back upon himself as a man in whom (as God intended) the passions had momentarily prevailed over reason. He was aware of the reversal of his attitude towards love and marriage.

If a man would register all his opinions upon love, politics, religion, learning &c., beginning from his youth, and so go on to old age, what a bundle of contradictions and inconsistencies would appear at last!

Love comes first in the list. And that 'thought' is followed by:

What they do in heaven we are ignorant of; what they do *not* we are told expressly, that they neither marry nor are given in marriage.[20]

The question is not really the nature of reason. Swift was emphatically a man who, at all periods of his life, would claim that his conviction of the moment was the product of reason. The question is the cause and consequences of the abrupt change in his attitude towards marriage. That it was abrupt and even violent is evident from a comparison between his letter to Varina in 1696 and his maxims 'When I come to be old' in 1699. In the former he is eager to marry, and passionately eloquent on the felicity of marriage between true lovers; in the latter he assumes that he will remain unmarried till his old age. It is by no means impossible that he was not merely sincere at the moment in his solemn asseveration to Varina that 'he was resolved to die as he had lived all hers'; but that he was making a firm resolve, which he kept. Swift's powers of will were extraordinary.

In any case, the effect upon him of Varina's refusal (or her hesitation) was profound. It was a fearful blow to the pride of a very proud man. In the main his pride was legitimate: it was the proper pride of a noble nature, conscious of its worth and its integrity. His words to Varina: 'The little disguises and affected contradictions of your sex were all, to say the truth, infinitely beneath persons of your pride and mine; paltry maxims that they are, calculated for the rabble of humanity', are nobly spoken. This man, we feel, was capable of true love. That Varina did not respond, or was afraid to respond, was a tragedy.

The proud man had humbled himself in love to a woman, and his gift of himself had been refused. He withdrew into the citadel of his pride, and remained there for ever. At first he would not, at last he could not, emerge: because he had imposed a life-pattern upon himself, and also on the next woman who loved him and whom he loved. Because he had imposed it on her, he was bound in honour to impose it on the third woman, whom he loved and who loved him. He was fast bound by an iron system of human relations which his pride had forged.

The pity of it is that it was not in origin an evil pride, but a noble one: the pride of an intensely sensitive, intensely reserved man, with an unusual power of self-repression, and an unusual need and capacity for affection. He did not impose his pattern upon Stella deliberately; he did not foresee the effects upon himself and her of his withdrawal into the citadel of his own ego, in combination with his need of a woman's love and his capacity for evoking it. His pride had been intolerably hurt, and he reacted and acted instinctively. After his repulse by Varina he resolved that he would never again expose himself to such an humiliation: his inmost self should thenceforward be inviolable by woman. But his need of woman remained. So he turned instinctively to Stella, and called her to be his companion for life — on terms which another and a lesser man would have realized to be inhuman (or superhuman) and pregnant with disaster. Confident that she would respond, he summoned her to enter into the bonds of a life-companionship in which 'he ne'er admitted love a guest'. He was deceiving himself with words. What but love brought them together? Stella's child-love was bound to flower into woman-love. He himself felt more than brother-love for her. For all his careful and cunning words, when Tisdall sought to marry her, he deliberately queered the pitch for his friend. Yet he committed himself to nothing with Stella. At that point his excusable pride had begun insensibly to pass into an unimaginative and cruel egotism. He deliberately shut his eyes to the truth he recognized when Lady Orkney set it before him, that 'in women love begets desire'. The pathos and the irony of reporting that to Stella as a wise woman's wisdom! But, he said to himself, if he could resist desire at the command of his pride — and now of his ambition as well — why not she?

He had immunized himself from Stella's physical attractions, partly because he had known her from a child, but more by his own rigid precaution of never being with her alone. It may sound decorous and prudent; but in fact it was ignoble and unjust, for the opportunity he withheld from Stella, he gave to Vanessa. Vanessa indubitably penetrated his defences, and had it not been for the outrage to Stella he would have committed he would probably have married Vanessa, and sent 'the dictates of reason' to the place where they belong. Now he was caught in a trap created by his own egotism. To marry Vanessa would have been the blackest treachery to Stella. As it was, he was treacherous enough to her. What right had he, when he returned to Ireland, to allow Vanessa innumerable meetings with him alone, which were denied, by his own rigour, to Stella? Yet, on the other hand, what right had he to deny them to her? In England he had deliberately sought the intimacy.

The repression he had practised with Stella and imposed upon her came near to breaking down with Vanessa. It was, moreover, of not quite the same nature: the gap made by the weakening of 'the dictates of reason' was supplied by a belated sense of justice to Stella. But Swift resented his own obedience to this. There was resentment, too, in his submission to the formal ceremony of marriage with Stella.

5

During the long period of ten years between Vanessa's love-declaration and her death in 1723 there was a gradual accumulation of resentment against woman in Swift's psyche. Woman, in the person of Stella and Vanessa, was making two claims upon him, the justice of which he felt, but which he passionately repudiated as invasions of the rational, independent, uncommitted personality he had constructed for himself. That free and self-sufficient personality was continually threatened by his disease. Whether he interpreted his recurrent fits of vertigo rightly or wrongly, there is no doubt that he did interpret them as foreboding the possibility of an eventual lapse from rationality; and he strove the more desperately to preserve his own pseudo-rational inviolability. Yet perhaps few men have felt a deeper need of intimate relation with a woman. To satisfy the need yet keep the woman from invading the citadel: this was the conflict. He wanted to awaken love in his women, and he knew that love awakened desire in them: and from that, or at least from the fulfilment of it, he shrank. For a man so constituted physical love was an act of vital surrender: and with all the strength of the personality he had constructed from his reason and his will he repudiated it. But he was repudiating nature, and with nature, God. In his depths, he knew, well enough, that there was nothing wrong or evil in Stella's and Vanessa's mute demand. Even his reason compelled him to allow that the inscrutable wisdom of God seemed to require the surrender of man to woman. Still, he repudiated it. His own inviolability must have the precedence, and it must be justified.

As the resentment accumulated, so did the consciousness of guilt, and a process of self-justification began. It took the sinister form of steadily degrading woman as a physical being in his imagination. After the death of Vanessa, this process became catastrophic. It was natural that it should be so; for Vanessa's death was a sign that the injustice done to a loving woman whom he had sacrificed to his egotism was now irreparable. 'Nor God, nor demon, could undo the done.' The need of self-justification became the more clamant. To satisfy it the image of the female Yahoo was spawned.

When Vanessa was dying he could convince himself that loyalty to Stella and the dignity of his position required that he should keep away from her. When Stella in turn was dying, no such escape was offered to his rationality. He had to face the truth that he was afraid to confront her, for fear his persona would collapse. His plea of defence was reduced to the sorry one that his distress would distress her. That may well have been true; but it was a pitiful confession of the precariousness of his constructed character, built by violence done to his deeper nature, and by cruelty to hers.

If, as we believe, the story is true that he took his last sight of Stella when he was refusing, by silence, her pathetic request that he should acknowledge their marriage, the human drama was played out to the bitter end between them in conscious and rational terms. The specious and unreal concession he had made to her woman's nature he was compelled to withdraw, under peril of the annihilation of his public character. But even without that pitiful dénouement, he could not escape the knowledge that with Stella's death a second and more protracted wrong that he had done to a loving woman had become irreparable.

With all the perverted passion of his egotism he repudiated the idea that he had offended. Nature and God were wrong; and Jonathan Swift was right. Four years before Stella died his unconscious genius had contrived his own complete vindication by granting him the vision of the Yahoo: the special revelation that men and women, in their physical reality, were utterly abominable. They were not a little, or a good deal, lower than the angels; they were infinitely below the brute creation, separated from them by an impassable gulf in which animal innocence and animal cleanliness together were swallowed up. Man, and above all woman, in their animal nature were unclean and untouchable. Love shrank, because it must, in a paroxysm of horror from the physical relation of sex; and, in so far as woman did not, she was incapable of love. To the extent that love begat desire in a woman's nature she relapsed into the Yahoo. Injustice to his beloved Stella? The charge was the invention of the Devil. What he had rejected in her, killed in her, was what was utterly unclean. Behold and see!

6

What the influence of the living Stella had partly controlled in him, the dead could not. The revelation that had been confined to a parable must now be uttered directly. The repudiation of the conditions of human existence was so entire, its source so intimate, the collateral doubt so profound, the sense of guilt so ineradicable, that his loathing worked itself out like a destiny. It crept, inevitably, towards a consummation in public paroxysm: to a sort of prolonged incantation, with its own appalling refrain

Celia, Celia, Celia shits!

One listens to it with a kind of hateful fascination, as it were to the drooling of genius, or the chant of one of his own Bedlamite academy while he dabbles in his excrement.

It is somehow congruous that this peculiar self-absolution should have been accompanied by one more profound. *The Day of Judgment* is generally dated 1731 — the year of Chloe and Celia and Strephon and Cassinus. Swift was sixty-four.

> With a whirl of thought oppress'd
> I sink from reverie to rest.
> A horrid vision seiz'd my head;
> I saw the graves give up their dead!
> Jove, arm'd with terrors, bursts the skies
> And thunder roars and lightning flies
> Amaz'd, confus'd, its fate unknown,
> The world stands trembling at his throne!
> While each pale sinner hangs his head,
> Jove, nodding, shook the heav'ns and said:
> Offending race of human kind,
> By nature, reason, learning, blind;
> You who thro' frailty, stepp'd aside;
> And you who never fell — *thro' pride*:
> You who in different sects have shamm'd
> And come to see each other damned;
> (So some folks told you, but they knew
> No more of Jove's designs than you;)
> — The world's mad business now is o'er

And I resent these pranks no more.
I to such blockheads set my wit!
I damn such fools! — Go, go, you're *bit*.[31]

Certainly it was impossible to reconcile any conceivable form even of the peculiar brand of Christianity which Swift professed with the frenzied exorcisms of his excremental verses. But there is nothing frenzied or obsessive about *The Day of Judgment*. It would seem to have sprung from a moment of calm, when the poisonous ferment had been discharged from his system, and with some part of him he could look down, from a height, upon the strange condition of Jonathan Swift, 'who never fell — *through pride*'. The victory, he saw, was worthless. God damned such fools and such triumphs. Indeed, he did. But in a way more visible and more humiliating than Swift intended.

CHAPTER XXIX

THE DEAN ON THE DEAN: 1730-1733

THE process recorded in the last chapter belongs to the deep emotional nature of Swift, which was now in absolute rebellion against the very condition of human existence. It burst into expression at a time when his power of self-control was weakening. A kind of *cacoethes scribendi* had seized him. 'Finding it troublesome to read at night, and the company here growing tasteless,' he told Bolingbroke, 'I am always writing bad prose or worse verses, either of rage or raillery'.[1] And that corresponds to the total effect of his very considerable production at this time. Restlessness of mind quite as much as genuine creative impulse was responsible for this outburst of expression. It is spasmodic, capricious, and incoherent, owing to internal conflict and decaying powers; but there is not much of Swift that did not find utterance of some sort in the years 1730-1733.

The most distinctive strain in it, besides the one discussed in the last chapter, is an effort to establish the pattern of his own character and his career. In 1730, when he wrote the first of his excremental verses, he also wrote *A Panegyric on Dr. Swift*; and in the next year he wrote two separate poems in which he supposed himself to be dead and passed judgment on his life. In all three poems Swift tried, with varying success and confusions of perspective, to turn his sardonic humour upon himself, at a moment when he anticipated death. Death was now, he told Bolingbroke, never out of his thoughts, but it terrified him less than it did.[2] He had now reached the grand climacteric, the age of sixty-three; and he looked apprehensively forward to a probably rapid decline of his faculties, and perhaps a period of 'posthumous existence'. His giddiness, though much less violent, was chronic, indeed practically continuous. His mind was now busy with his plan for endowing a hospital for the insane. He looked before and behind him. His vision of the past was confused and changeable.

His peculiar delight in mystification remained. The ostensible author of *A Panegyric on Dr. Swift* is an Irish Whig, pretending to write as Delany. Swift described the piece to Lord Bathurst as 'a very scrub libel' upon himself;[3] he had sent it to a Whig printer, who was completely deceived, and printed it as a genuine attack upon both the Dean and Delany. Indeed, it must have been highly embarrassing to Delany, for it came at the end of a sequence of rather mortifying verse-comments by Swift (writing anonymously) on a poetic application by Delany to Carteret for more preferment. Delany had not the delicacy of touch required, and his verses were the butt of Sheridan and others as well as Swift. He had ended his *Epistle*:

> My Lord, I'd wish — to pay the debts I owe —
> I'd wish besides — to build and to bestow.[4]

To this Swift had replied by *An Epistle upon an Epistle*: in which he, not unfairly but rather gallingly, criticized Delany's building extravagances at Delville.

> Take this advice then from your friend;
> To your ambition put an end.
> Be frugal, Pat: pay what you owe
> Before you build and you bestow,
> Be modest: nor address your betters
> With begging, vain, familiar letters.[5]

He followed this up with *A Libel on Dr. Delany and Lòrd Carteret*.

He begins with some general satire on the folly of men of letters expecting preferment for their literary merit from statesmen whose rewards are given for political services. Granted Carteret is better than the common run of politicians, and would like to promote Delany, he is in Ireland to carry out Walpole's more than royal will: he cannot give his plums to independent Irishmen. So Delany, who 'until his fortune's made must be a sweetener by his trade',[6] must compare him with a kind-hearted angel sent by God as a minister of wrath. But Swift himself —

> in politics grown old
> Whose thoughts are of a different mould,
> Who from my soul sincerely hate
> Both kings and ministers of state — [7]

must make a harsher comparison. In truth, an English viceroy comes to Ireland as a devil from hell.

> For no imaginable things
> Can differ more than God and kings:
> And statesmen, by ten thousand odds,
> Are angels, just as kings are gods. [8]

2

In this engagement *A Panegyric on Dr. Swift* was the third broadside. Swift now pretends to be the *tertius gaudens*, an imaginary and witty Whig who chuckles over the quarrel between himself and Delany and pretends to

be Delany addressing a remonstrance to Swift. The idea and the execution
are equally clever, and it must have deceived many besides the Whig printer
who issued it. It begins:

> Could all we little folks that wait
> And dance attendance on the great,
> Obtain such privilege as you,
> To rail, and go unpunished too;
> To treat our betters like our slaves,
> And all mankind as fools, or knaves;
> The pleasure of so large a grant
> Would much compensate all we want.
> Mitres and glebes could scarce do more
> To scratch our endless itch of pow'r.
> For next to being great ourselves
> It is to think all great ones elves,
> And when we can't be tête à tête
> Their fellows, turn their dread and hate.
> How amply then does pow'r provide
> For you to gratify your pride!
> Where'er the wind of favour sits
> It still your constitution fits.
> If fair it brings you safe to port,
> And when 'tis foul, affords you sport.
> A deanery you got, when in,
> And now you're out, enjoy your grin.[9]

Continually in the *Panegyric* the imaginary Whig quotes Swift's previous
verses to Delany. In *The Libel* he had assured him that wits are used by
statesmen as 'a kind of panders to a vicious mind' to gratify their lust of pride.
Now Delany asks Swift:

> But hark'ee, is it truly so
> (And you of all mankind should know)
> That men of wit can be no more
> Than pimps to wickedness in pow'r?
> Then pray, dear Doctor, condescend
> To teach the science to your friend.[10]

All that Delany has been capable of in that direction is trivial.

> Lampoons on Whigs, when in disgrace,
> And vile submissions when in place,
> Poems addressed to great men's whores
> And other lap-dog cures for sores.[11]

The Dean works on a grander scale altogether. He even invented the band-box plot.

> Oh, wond'rous box! my lyre unstrung
> Shall be, when thou art left unsung;
> More precious far than ev'n the gift
> Of one metropolis to Swift.
> The gift (Good Heav'ns preserv't from thieves)
> Or Lord May'r, Aldermen, and Shrieves,
> Where if the curious list to read 'em
> They'll find his acts, and life, and freedom,
> And the great name engrav'd most fairly
> Of him that Ireland sav'd, and Harley;
> With quaint inscription, which contains
> Laid out with no less art than pains,
> Most of his virtues, all my brains.[12]*

In the *Libel* Swift had praised Pope for being 'of heart too great, though fortune little, To lick a rascal statesman's spittle'. This the imaginary Delany next takes up.

> No wonder you should think it *little*
> To *lick a rascal statesman's spittle*.
> Who have, to shew your great devotion,
> Oft swallow'd down a stronger potion,
> A composition more absurd,
> Bob's spittle mixed with Harry's t — .
> Oh, could'st thou teach us how to zest
> Such draughts as this and then digest,
> Then we might also have in time
> More beneficial ways than rhyme.[14]

Swift was invulnerable to the arrows he had so far launched against himself. Whether or not the bandbox plot was serious, he had not invented it, and he had surprised himself by his own presence of mind in dealing with what he honestly believed to be an infernal machine; and his manner towards Harley and St. John had been the reverse of obsequious. But the next shaft — which again refers back to the *Libel* — he sends more nearly home.

* Early in 1729 the City of Dublin had presented Swift with his freedom in a gold box. In accepting it, he acknowledged his authorship of *The Drapier's Letters*, and denounced Joshua, Lord Allen, who had criticized the proposed act of the City, and charged Swift with being 'a Tory, a Jacobite, an enemy to King George, and a libeller of the Government'. Swift made a vigorous defence of himself before the Lord Mayor, and lampooned Allen as Traulus in the verses of that name. At the end of his speech, he said that he had himself asked that there should be an inscription on the box, setting out the reasons for which the honour had been conferred upon him. The text of the inscription was written by Delany.[13]

Rightly you shew, that wit alone
Advances few, enriches none,
And 'tis as true, or story lies,
Men seldom by their good deeds rise:
From whence the consequence is plain,
You never had commenc'd a Dean,
Unless you otherways had trod
Than those of wit, or trust in God.
'Twas therefore cruel hard, by Jove,
Your industry no better throve
Nor could achieve the promis'd lawn,
Though Robin's honour was in pawn,
Because it chanc'd an old grave Don
Believ'd in God, and you in none.
Be this, however, your relief,
Whene'er your pride recalls your grief,
That all the loss your purse sustain'd
By that rebuff, your honour gain'd.
For must you not have often ly'd
And griev'd your righteous soul beside,
The Almighty's orders to perform,
Not to direct a plague, or storm,
But, 'gainst the dictates of your mind,
To bless, as now you curse mankind?[15]

Then he comes still closer. You tell me, says Delany, that until my fortune's made I must take up the sweetening trade. If I had the wit of Congreve or Addison — examples to which you pointed me — the advice might be good.

But, form'd by you, how should their model
E'er enter any mortal's noddle?
Our thoughts, to suit your nicer taste,
Must in a diff'rent mould be cast,
The language Billingsgate excel,
The sentiments resemble Hell.[16]

I should have, to praise my patron, to liken him to a horse.

Then show how statesmen oft are stung
By gnats, and draw the nation's dung,
The stinking load of all the crimes
And nastiness of modern times,
Not only what themselves have sh — ,
For that were not unjust a bit,
But all the filth, both spiss and sparse,
Of every rogue that wears an a — .[17]

When my invention flags, I should need, like you, to have the Devil always there to give it a lift.

> Is this the art, good doctor, say,
> The true, the genuine sweet'ning lay?
> Then must it truly be confest;
> Our ministers are void of taste,
> When such adepts as you, and I,
> So long unbishoprick'd lie by,
> While dunces of the coarsest clay,
> That only know to preach and pray,
> Devour the Church's tiddest bits,
> The perquisites of pimps and wits,
> And leave us naught but guts and garbage.[18]

The powers that be have no taste for the language of Billingsgate and the sentiments of Hell and this is the reason why 'you so sincerely hate both kings and ministers of state'.

> For once there was a time, God wot,
> Before our friends were gone to pot,
> When Jonathan was great at court,
> The ruin'd party made his sport,
> Despis'd the beast with many heads,
> And damn'd the mob, whom now he leads.
> But things are strangely chang'd since then,
> And kings are now no more than men;
> From whence 'tis plain, they quite have lost
> God's image, which was once their boast.
> For Gulliver divinely shows
> That humankind are all Yahoos.[19]

3

These vigorous and effective verses, which set out the case of the *advocatus Diaboli* against him, probably gave Swift the hint for *The Death of Dr. Swift*. On December 1, 1731 he told Gay he had been working several months, very slowly, on five hundred lines 'on a pleasant subject, only to tell what my friends and enemies will say on me after I am dead'. Although the poem traditionally published as *The Death of Dr. Swift* is 486 lines long, it is demonstrably a conflation by Pope of two poems: 61 lines being taken from another independent poem on the same subject, *The Life & Character of Dr. Swift*, which was published in London, with an ironical preface dated

April 1, 1733. Swift was fond of making April fools. We have, thus, two distinct poems treating the same theme quite differently. The longer one, which contains a surprising amount of self-eulogy, was not originally intended to be published during Swift's life-time. That it was eventually published in 1739, before his death, was probably due to the clouding of Swift's faculties.

What seems to have happened is that when it was finished in the summer of 1732, Swift read it to a number of friends. When the appetite of the public was whetted by rumour, he launched the second one instead, with a preface which, precisely because it vouched for the poem as authentic, would be taken by the knowing ones as a proof that it was either a pirated copy, based on a mere memory of the original, or a deliberate parody of it. The more discriminating of his friends were not deceived by his disclaimers. Pope must have been well aware that it was Swift's, or he would never have incorporated 60 lines from it into the version of the longer poem. But to the ordinary reader nothing could well be more unlike *The Death of Dr. Swift* than *The Life & Character.* Except that they both presuppose his death and are both based on the maxim of Rochefoucauld: 'Dans l'adversité de nos amis, nous trouvons toujours quelquechose qui ne nous déplaît pas', the poems have little in common save the style. The temper is entirely different.

The longer one begins with a vindication of Rochefoucauld's sentence. It is true. Whatever we may pretend, we cannot help envying the success of our friends, when it exceeds our own.

> The strongest friendship yields to pride,
> Unless the odds be on our side.[20]

Swift turns this into a deft compliment to his particular friends.

> In Pope I cannot read a line,
> But with a sigh, I wish it mine;
> When he can in one couplet fix
> More sense than I can do in six;
> It gives me such a jealous fit,
> I cry, Pox take him and his wit!
> Why must I be outdone by Gay
> In my own hum'rous biting way?
> Arbuthnot is no more my friend
> Who dares to irony pretend,
> Which I was born to introduce,
> Refin'd it first, and show'd its use.
> St. John, as well as Pultney knows
> That I had some repute for prose;

> And till they drove me out of date,
> Could maul a minister of state.
> If they have mortify'd my pride
> And made me throw my pen aside;
> If with such talents Heav'n has blest 'em
> Have I not reason to detest 'em?[21]

So much by way of prologue.

In the not far future (Swift goes on) he must die, by the nature of things; by the nature of things his friends will find some satisfaction in this misfortune. Even now he can hear them:

> See, how the Dean begins to break!
> Poor gentleman, he droops apace!
> You plainly find it in his face.
> That old vertigo in his head,
> Will never leave him till he's dead.
> Besides, his memory decays,
> He recollects not what he says;
> He cannot call his friends to mind:
> Forgets the place where last he din'd;
> Plies you with stories o'er and o'er;
> He told them fifty times before.
> How does he fancy we can sit
> To hear his out-of-fashion'd wit?
> But he takes up with younger folks
> Who for his wine will bear his jokes.[22]

Already, they make him out even older than he is; they say he can hardly last till the spring. In fact, they hope what they pretend to fear; and, though they may be out in their reckoning, one day they are bound to be right.

> Behold the fatal day arrive!
> 'How is the Dean?' — 'He's just alive.'
> Now the departing prayer is read.
> 'He hardly breathes.' — 'The Dean is dead.'[23]

His will? Everything to public uses. What affectation! He took good care to wait till he was dead. Lady Suffolk runs laughing to tell the Queen. Walpole wishes it had been Bolingbroke or Pulteney. Curll produces three volumes of *Remains*.

> Poor Pope will grieve a month, and Gay
> A week, and Arbuthnot a day.
> St. John himself will scarce forbear
> To bite his pen, and drop a tear.[24]

But the only friends who mourn in earnest are those a little younger than himself, to whom his life was a screen between themselves and death.

> My female friends, whose tender hearts
> Have better learn'd to act their parts
> Receive the news in doleful dumps:
> 'The Dean is dead: (and what is trumps?)
> Then Lord have mercy on his soul!
> (Ladies, I'll venture for the vole.)
> Six Deans, they say, must bear the pall.
> (I wish I knew what king to call.)'[25]

A year passes. He is no longer even talked of. A country squire goes to Lintot's bookshop for Swift's *Verse & Prose*. Lintot tells him to look in the second-hand shops. His way of writing is out of fashion now. He offers Cibber, Duck and Woollaston instead.*

4

The poem should have ended there. Instead it wanders off into what is virtually another poem, in the sense that it is an incongruous addendum to what has gone before. What set Swift's mind wandering was his unnecessary expatiation on Woollaston's latitudinarian writings, and their popularity at Court. This launched him on a train of garrulous and inconsequent political reminiscence, with the repetitive and absurd beginning:

> Suppose me dead; and then suppose
> A club assembled at the Rose.[26]

One member 'impartially' draws Swift's character. It turns out to be — in flat contradiction to the first part — an unqualified eulogy. Swift's writings, says this impartial judge, were entirely original and immensely popular; their purpose the moral reformation of mankind. He never courted the great, chose only the wise and good for his friends, used all his influence to help them, and to succour virtue in distress. Swift then anticipates his own epitaph (which perhaps was drafted at this moment).

> Fair LIBERTY was all his cry,
> For her he stood prepared to die;
> For her he boldly stood alone;
> For her he oft exposed his own.[27]

---

* Actually the text has Woolston. But this was a confusion of Swift's, by which he mistook Woolston, the Deist, for Woollaston, the moral philosopher, the author of *The Religion of Nature Delineated*, who was greatly admired by Queen Caroline. Significantly, in spite of Dr. William King's correction, the confusion was retained in Swift's note to the Dublin edition. It indicates that Swift was, in 1739, quite incapable of revision or correction.

Then he turns back to the good times of Queen Anne:

> Had he but spared his tongue and pen
> He might have rose like other men:
> But power was never in his thought,
> And wealth he valued not a groat.[28]

The first two lines are true enough; the second two are not. He then tells the familiar story of his abortive attempts to reconcile Oxford and Bolingbroke, of his retirement to Letcombe, of the downfall of the Tories, and the furious rage of the Whigs against them, and against himself on his return to Ireland. Here again his memory or his self-knowledge played him false: for in a note he says that 'nothing could have driven him to Ireland but the Queen's death, who had determined to fix him in England, in spite of the Duchess of Somerset'.[29] He was now weaving a fantasy about the past. The only grain of truth in it was that Bolingbroke told Barber on the day Oxford was dismissed that 'he would reconcile Swift to Lady Somerset, and then it would be easy to set him right with the Queen'. Even if Bolingbroke had succeeded in the first difficult task, and then in the second, Swift would have been faithless to his promise to Oxford by joining him. There is no evidence at all that the Queen ever changed her mind and 'determined to fix him in England'. But by this time he had forgotten even that he ever wrote *The Windsor Prophecy*. His actual memory of the past had become quite unreliable.

A eulogy of the Drapier follows, and a denunciation of Whiteshed. He then tells of his contempt for the Irish Lords and Commons:

> Biennial squires to market brought;
> Who sell their souls and votes for naught;
> The nation stript, go joyful back,
> To rob the Church, their tenants rack,
> Go snacks with rogues and rapparees
> And keep the peace to pick up fees;
> In every job to have a share,
> A jail or barrack to repair;
> And turn the tax for public roads
> Commodious to their own abodes.[30]

At long last a qualification to the catalogue of virtues appears.

> Perhaps I may allow the Dean
> Had too much satire in his vein.[31]

But it is immediately withdrawn. He gave full vent to his satire, because no age ever deserved it more.

> Yet, malice never was his aim;
> He lashed the vice, but spar'd the name.
> No individual could resent,
> Where thousands equally were meant.[32]

Shade of the Duchess of Somerset! Presumably Swift now believed it; but it is almost incredible that he did. Even Dr. William King, his great admirer, to whom the poem was entrusted for publication in 1739, felt that his respect for Swift's reputation forbade the printing of this. He told Mrs. Whiteway that in the opinion of Swift's London friends, 'these lines might be liable to some objection, and were not strictly speaking part of his character; because several persons have been lashed by name . . . Charteris and Whiteshed in this particular poem.'[33]

> His satire points at no defect
> But what all mortals may correct.[34]

Again, it is not true. Half the satire of the Yahoos is directed against the inescapable physical conditions of human existence. As for his being 'cheerful to his dying day', Swift certainly had often claimed that the spleen was foreign to his nature; but if it had been true once, it was true no longer. The evidence of his writings, his letters and the accounts of his friends for his latter years is peremptory. The fits of violent irritability in which he was unapproachable were now notorious.

> He gave what little wealth he had
> To build a house for fools and mad;
> And show'd by one satiric touch,
> No nation wanted it so much.[35]

That, at any rate, is characteristic. The rest of the second half of the poem is not. Dr. William King, in his letter, said that Swift's English friends feared that 'it might be thought by the public a little vain, if so much were said of himself by himself'.

In truth the latter part of this famous poem is unworthy in every way. It lacks the vitality and vividness, and above all the humour, of the former; and it is morally incongruous with it. The sardonic objectivity gives place to an extravagance of self-laudation. So striking a lapse from decorum must be ascribed to a radical weakening of Swift's vigour of mind.

5

Perhaps it was an awareness of this weakness which set him on writing *The Life & Character of Dr. Swift*. That comes much nearer to objectivity, and it is, if not the better poem, at least the less incoherent and unequal one. The defects and qualities of the Dean's character are bandied between the two disputants in lively interchange. Swift takes care, indeed, that his champion shall have the best of it; but he allows his detractor to get in some shrewd blows.

> I envy not the wits who write
> Merely to gratify their spite.
> Thus did the Dean: his only scope
> Was to be held a misanthrope.
> His zeal was not to lash our crimes
> But discontent against the times.[36]

Difficilis, querulus, laudator temporis acti. There was now a good deal of this in Swift; and his advocate rebuts the charge by defending not his misanthropy, but his discontent against the times, which was caused (he says) by his apprehensions for the Church. Swift truly believed

> That Church and State had suffer'd more
> By Calvin than the Scarlet Whore ...
> The Pope would of our faith bereave us,
> But, still our monarchy would leave us.[37]

This is the main defence of Swift in the poem: that his disgust was due to his despair at the weakening of the Church, and the despair was genuine (as indeed it was). He is not represented as a pattern of all the virtues, but as one whose defects are more than outweighed by his qualities.

The incoherence of *The Death of Dr. Swift* was due to the weakening of his faculties which he describes in the earlier and better part of the poem. The same kind of incoherence is manifest in two other considerable poems of this time. *An Epistle to a Lady who desired the author to write some verses to her in the heroic style* (1732) likewise divides into two independent halves, of which the second is weaker than the first. Again the poem begins with vivid and objective self-criticism and tails off inconsequently into a violent denunciation of Walpole and the Court. Yet again, in *On Poetry: a Rhapsody* (1733), he is carried away by the same ungovernable itch for invective against the Court and Ministry. All three poems begin well, and degenerate; and all would be much improved by the drastic amputation (though not the grafting) which Pope applied to *The Death of Dr. Swift*.

On Poetry: A Rhapsody, in particular, has been so extravagantly praised that it calls for brief examination. True poets are excessively rare, Swift begins; yet by a perversity of nature peculiar to man, a host of fools persist in writing verses.

Not empire to the rising sun
By valour, virtue, conduct won;
Not highest wisdom in debates,
For framing laws to govern states;
Not skill in sciences profound
So large to grasp the circle round,
Such heavenly influence require
As how to strike the Muse's lyre.
    Not beggar's brat, on bulk begot;
Not bastard of a pedlar Scot;
Not boy brought up to cleaning shoes,
The spawn of Bridewell or the stews;
Not infants dropt, the spurious pledges
Of gipsies littering under hedges;
Are so disqualified by fate
To rise in Church, or Law, or State,
As he whom Phoebus in his ire
Hath blasted with poetic fire.[38]

That is powerful; but it is already obscure. What is Swift saying, or meaning
to say? That poetic genius by nature incapacitates its owner from other
eminence? Or that it does so, in fact, because of the political corruption of
society? These are very different assertions. Yet it is quite uncertain which
Swift is making. If he is saying that in a well-ordered society poets ought to
rise 'in Church, or Law, or State', but do not in the existing one — and that
is what he says in a kindred passage in *A Libel on Dr. Delany*, where he
quotes the examples, in turn, of Congreve, Steele, Gay, and Addison — it is
not true, for Congreve, Addison and Steele did get places, and so did Prior.
And, one may add, Swift himself got a Deanery.

He then proceeds to advise the poetic aspirant. Let him publish anonymously and listen to what the critics say. To an unknown author they will
be impartial. If he fails even at the third attempt — and it is not clear in
what success consists: presumably in critical applause and remuneration
from the bookseller — he need not throw his pen away; he can turn party-
poet and royal panegyrist. If that trade seems too base, he may turn critic
and connoisseur. Or become famous for writing badly: a master of the low
sublime. Then comes a mildly amusing description of Grub Street, followed
by a long satirical eulogy on the royal family. With that the poem abruptly
ends. Its incoherence is remarkable. It is impossible to say with any
certainty what it is all about. No doubt this was half-implied by Swift when
he called it a 'rhapsody'. But that does not make it less confused or more
impressive.

Swift's power of self-control in his writing was now capricious and un-dependable. Intermittently he recognized the fact. At one moment, in the midst of his angry denunciation in *An Epistle to a Lady*, he is fully conscious of his own extravagance. He makes the lady (Lady Acheson) say:

> Deuce is in you, Mr. Dean.
> What can all this passion mean?
> Mention courts, you'll ne'er be quiet;
> On corruptions running riot.[39]

Yet, at another moment, in flat defiance of the surrounding context, he declares:

> As my method of reforming
> Is by laughing, not by storming.
> (For my friends have always thought
> Tenderness my greatest fault).[40]

When he had been storming more furiously than ever, this strikes almost as strangely as the prolonged and complacent self-eulogy into which *The Death of Dr. Swift* descends. His power of self-criticism was decaying with his memory.

The total effect of his poetic production in these years, 1730-33, is pathetic. In it all we sense the working, at different levels of consciousness, of an elemental urge for self-justification, an uncontrollable impulse to vindicate the whole of his public and private character. It overpowers all his efforts at objectivity. Anger continually carries him away; and it is the anger of the one righteous man. Corruption, in every sense of the word, he shouts, is everywhere. And his fury at it continually undermines his own power of concise and coherent expression. In his memory a strange fantasy of the past begins to displace the historical reality, and he becomes for himself the victim of malign accident. So that the final impression is of one who has been radically infected by the corruption he universally discovers. If he is a victim, he suffers under the law propounded by William Blake: 'We become what we behold.'

6

In the same mood of finality and frustration, Swift in 1733 began to encourage the proposal of Faulkner — 'the prince of printers' in Dublin — to issue a collected edition of his works. He shared his friend Ford's just annoyance at the manner in which Pope had indiscriminately used his writings to bump out his *Miscellanies*, and welcomed the opportunity of disentangling his own productions. In spite of his politic disclaimers of any direct responsibility for Faulkner's edition, there is no doubt that Swift co-operated in the work of selection and correction. Faulkner for his part did his utmost to make the edition worthy. It is still the most beautiful edition of Swift's works.

But there was one striking omission. It did not contain *A Tale of a Tub*. This exclusion demands an explanation, though it can only be conjectural. Granted that Swift was always chary of acknowledging his authorship of this book, that was no reason why he should have forbidden Faulkner to include it, for he took the greatest care not to give the edition any overt imprimatur. He would not have been committed in any way; and his public position with regard to the *Tale* would have remained precisely the same as before. It was just as well known that he was the author of the *Tale* as that he was the author of *Gulliver*. And its publication could not have been more discreditable to him than that of many of his other works. What harm could it possibly have done him? He had long since given up hopes of any further advancement in the Church.

Why then did he behave as though he wanted it to be forgotten, or at least concealed? Two motives suggest themselves, which are not mutually exclusive. One is that the attitude to sex in the *Tale* is Rabelaisian. (The spirit of Rabelais *habitans in sicco*, as Coleridge said.) The fun it makes of a man as a sexual animal is coarse, but healthy. This attitude may now have become abhorrent to Swift. The other, more powerful and more probable, is that the *Tale* was an intimate part of the real sequence of his life. It had been the first cause of his disfavour with Queen Anne. It was, so to speak, a solid lump of reality which could not be incorporated into the fantasy of the past which his mind had woven. It (with *The Windsor Prophecy*) — not the death of the Queen — was the cause of his exile to Ireland, which he professed to regard as unjust and iniquitous. His genius had made no bones about acknowledging this in the imaginative fiction of *Gulliver*, when the Captain incurs the Empress's implacable hostility by his manner of extinguishing the fire in her palace. But to admit this to his conscious mind was intolerable. That craved for the legend he had created of his own career, whereby he was the entirely innocent victim of malign accident, not the responsible architect of his own misfortunes. *A Tale of a Tub*, set in the place where it should have been, at the head of his collected works, would have made nonsense of the legend.

CHAPTER XXX

THE LAST YEARS: 1734-1745

'I HAVE lost half my memory and all my invention,' Swift told Ford on April 5, 1733; and, eighteen months later, Pope: 'I have lost by these diseases much of my memory, which makes me commit many blunders in my common actions at home by mistaking one thing for another, especially in writing' (November 1, 1734). It was not merely a day-to-day forgetfulness and confusion in little things that ailed him; but, as we have seen, a radical unreliability in his recollection of the past. Thus, he wrote to a correspondent on December 1, 1734: 'I had the honour to be for some years a student at Oxford, where I took my master's degree.' It was quite untrue. He was a student there at most for a few weeks in the summer of 1692. His Oxford years belong to his fantasy of the past.

The decay of his memory was not more conspicuous than that of his judgment, of which there are clear signs in his verses. He was liable to start aside, when provoked by the thought of any of his political or religious bugbears, into reminiscence, repetitive, disordered and untrustworthy. He could not trust himself to revise his narrative of *The Four Last Years of the Queen*, which accordingly had to be suppressed at the urgent instance of his friends in London, to whom he grudgingly submitted it. He showed his irresponsibility in taking Mrs. Barber and Mr. and Mrs. Pilkington under his wing. Stella would have saved him from those blunders.

Probably the Pilkingtons — a young and diminutive couple with literary aspirations and some literary ability — were more attractive than they appear in retrospect. Lætitia Pilkington was only seventeen and newly married to her young parson husband, 'Little Matthew', when they sought and obtained, through Delany, an introduction to Swift. Swift took to her: she was pretty, vivacious, intelligent, and admiring. We owe to her some of the few vivid glimpses we have of Swift in his habit as he lived.

Soon after her first meeting with Swift at Delany's, apparently in 1729, the Pilkingtons were invited to dinner at the Deanery.

The bottle and glasses being taken away, the Dean set about making the coffee; but the fire scorching his hand, he called to me to reach him his glove, and changing the coffee-pot to his left hand, held out his right one and ordered me to put the glove on it, which accordingly I did; when taking up part of his gown to fan himself with, and acting

in character of a very prudish lady, he said: 'Well, I do not know what
to think; women may be honest that do such things, but, for my part,
I never could bear to touch any man's flesh — except my husband's,
whom, perhaps,' says he, 'she wished at the Devil.'

'Mr. Pilkington,' says he, 'you would not tell me your wife's faults;
but I have found her out to be a damned insolent, proud unmannerly
slut.' I looked confounded, not knowing what offence I had committed. Says Mr. Pilkington, 'Ay, Sir, I must confess she is a little
saucy to me sometimes, but what has she done now?' 'Done! Why
nothing, but sat there quietly, and never once offered to interrupt me
in making the coffee, whereas had I had a lady of modern good breeding
here, she would have struggled with me for the coffee-pot till she had
made me scald myself and her, and made me throw the coffee in the
fire, or perhaps at her head, rather than permit me to take so much
trouble for her.'[1]

That is convincing. She tells too how he took her into his study and made
her read to him *The Four Last Years of the Reign of Queen Anne*, and how on
another occasion he employed her in pasting letters from his English friends
in the elegant Turkey-leather covers of a presentation book, from which he
had cut the text. She asked if she might read them, which he allowed; and she
says she could not avoid remarking to him that 'notwithstanding the friendship Mr. Pope professed for Mr. Gay, he could not forbear making a great
many satirical, or envious, remarks on the success of *The Beggars' Opera*':
to which Swift replied that 'he did not think Mr. Pope was so candid to the
merits of other writers as he ought to be'.

Mrs. Pilkington never saw the Dean laugh. 'When any pleasantry passed
which might have excited it, he used to suck in his cheeks, as folks do when
they have a plug of tobacco in their mouths, to avoid risibility.'[2] That was
part of Swift's technique: in conversation, as in writing, he proffered enormities with a solemn face. At this time, it was more solemn than ever; by
his increasing use of strenuous exercise and his sparing diet, he had become
very thin. His backside was so nearly skin and bone that he could not ride
more than two days in the week. He made up for the deficiency by violent
walking. Quite early in their acquaintance Mrs. Pilkington depicts him, on
a day when he was defeated of his walk by rain, as running up one flight of
stairs and down another so furiously that she was afraid he would injure
himself. His face, says Mrs. Pendarves, who first met him at this time, had
deep lines which gave it 'a hard look'. This is apparent in the portrait which
Bindon painted in 1735; that also shows this complexion as distinctly dark.
Lyon described it as 'light olive or pale brown'. Swift himself confirms this;
in 1732 he wrote of,

His tallow face and wainscot paws;
His beetle brows and eyes of wall.[3]

By 'tallow' (as the poem *Betty the Grisette* shows) he meant not the pale and
waxy white we now associate with the word, but yellow-brown. One of his
lampooners describes his face as 'bronze'. Dr. Johnson said it was 'muddy'.
This may have been due to constant exposure, for the portrait painted by
Jervas in 1710, at a time when his life in London debarred him from his
wonted exercise, shows his complexion as fresh enough.

His beetle-brows are familiar. What he meant by his 'eyes of wall' — a
nonce-phrase, borrowed from *Hudibras*, which, Mrs. Pilkington says, he
knew by heart — is obscure. 'Wall-eyed' has many meanings. The one most
frequent in Swift's time connoted an excess of white in the iris. None of his
portraits show that. The evidence of pictures and descriptions is that they
were large, prominent eyes of bright blue.

On the whole, he must have looked rather grim. But in spite of his
abomination of the sex, young and attractive ladies found the way to his
heart fairly easy. If they were prepared to put up with a good deal of bully-
ing, and submit to his constant correction of their speech and behaviour —
Mrs. Pilkington says he frequently pinched her arm black and blue for mistakes — underneath they might be assured of his kindness. Besides Lætitia
Pilkington, at this time, there were Anne Donnellan, Mrs. Pendarves —
Mary Granville that was, and Mrs. Delany to be — and Frances Kelly: all
socially superior to Lætitia. Then, on her own level, were the other wits
and poetesses: Mrs. Grierson, Mrs. Barber and Mrs. Sican. These constituted
what Orrery, at a safe distance in time, called Swift's 'constant seraglio of
virtuous women'. Of them Miss Kelly most nearly touched his heart, and
came nearest to falling in love with him. She was beautiful, the child of an
unhappy marriage, and consumptive. 'I have given up the trial with Kelly,'
wrote Mrs. Pendarves in March 1733. 'Her beauty and assiduity has dis-
tanced me . . . At present she is disabled, poor thing, for she is confined to
bed with a pleuritic disorder, but the Dean tends her bedside; his heart must
be old and cold indeed if that did not conquer.' Still, she offended him in
some way; and there is a pathetic letter from her to him which recalls the
agonies of Vanessa. 'For God's sake, sir, look upon me as you were wont
to do, for I cannot bear your coldness.'[4] She was on the point of leaving
Dublin for England, in the vain search for health. Swift relented. Within
five months she was dead. Her sad and lovely little shade flits across the
background of his ageing life to remind us of the devotion he could still
inspire in women.

To the Pilkingtons he was extremely generous. He prevailed with his old friend Barber, now Lord Mayor of London, to make Pilkington his chaplain for his year of office, and so gratify his desire to make his début as a wit in London. He assigned him the rights in a batch of his recent writings that he might make money out of them, and he lent him cash as well. Mrs. Pilkington he frequently helped. That they turned out to be unworthy protégés cannot detract from his kindness to them. To Mrs. Barber, whom he recommended in extravagant terms to his London friends, he gave the rights in his *Polite Conversation*.

2

For all its constancy, Swift's seraglio did not see him often. He described his manner of life to Pope. After explaining that he could not read in the evenings because of his eyes — he stubbornly refused to wear spectacles — he wrote:

> I dine tête à tête five days a week with my old Presbyterian housekeeper, whom I call Sir Robert [*sc.* Walpole] ... I am in my chamber at five, there sit alone till eleven, and then to bed. I write pamphlets and follies merely for amusement, and when they are finished or I grow weary in the middle, I cast them in the fire, partly out of dislike, and chiefly because I know they will signify nothing. I walk much every day and ride once or twice a week, and so you have the whole state of my life. (January 15, 1731)

That was the general pattern. He allowed himself two days for company. On Thursdays he went to Delany at Delville (until he was incapable of going so far), and on Sunday he entertained at the Deanery. But he made the picture a little bleaker than it actually was. Sheridan was often at the Deanery, and they spent an unconscionable amount of time over schoolboyish amusements after the pattern of *Is ab ille eris ago: Fortibus es in ero* (I say, Billy, ere's a go: Forty buses in a row). Much of this stuff has survived, with innumerable variations, some recondite, but none amusing now. Between them they scraped the bottom of the barrel of *la bagatelle*.

Swift also occupied himself with more sustained efforts at self-distraction. On August 28, 1731, he wrote to Gay from the country:

> I retired hither for the public good, having two great works in hand: one to reduce the whole politeness, wit, humour and style of England into a short system for the use of all persons of quality, and particularly the maids of honour; the other is of almost equal importance, I may call it the Whole Duty of Servants, in about twenty several stations, from the steward and waiting woman down to the scullion and pantry boy.

The *Complete Collection of Genteel & Ingenious Conversation*, by Simon Wagstaff, was published in 1738. It is the custom to praise the dialogues highly; but 'the satirical and imaginative genius' attributed to them is less apparent than a perverse ingenuity. That Swift had the perseverance to make such a collection of trivialities and inanities is certainly impressive; but the compilation itself is tedious in the extreme. His determination never to let the conversation deviate into sense shows the intensity of his detestation of fashionable small talk, but it does not make for the reader's entertainment. The arrival of Sir John Linger, with his rough country manners and forthrightness, is a blessed, but too brief, relief; and for a moment the dialogue is really amusing. The Derbyshire squire is, at least, something more than a mere mouthpiece for vapidity. Accordingly, Mr. Wagstaff introduces him as an awful warning of provincial vulgarity.

In his preface Mr. Wagstaff claims that all his characters are distinct 'to a degree, that, whenever any judicious person shall read my book aloud, for the entertainment of a select company, he need not so much as name the particular speakers; because all the persons, throughout the several subjects of conversation, strictly observe a different manner, peculiar to their characters, which are of different kinds'.[5] But this is ironical; the fact is the precise opposite. The words of Sparkish, Smart, Atwit and even Neverout might be interchanged without detection. This may be the effect Swift intended; and it might be argued that if his characters had been differentiated he would have defeated his own purpose. But it is a failure of art when the representation of insipidity is itself insipid.

From these strictures Mr. Simon Wagstaff's introductory essay is wholly immune. This is consistently amusing precisely because it is pontifical and portentous. Mr. Wagstaff is a character: and one can easily imagine him carrying through to the excruciating end his self-imposed task of collecting every item of approved conversation. But it would surely have been much more effective if three-quarters of the results of his patient investigations had been left to the imagination. A dozen, or at the outside, twenty pages of actual conversation would have been ample for the ironic purpose; and Swift's old device of a *hiatus*, or *cetera desunt*, would have served him well. But he no longer knew when to stop; perhaps no longer cared to stop. Partly it was an exercise of the same perverse pertinacity he displayed in his competitions with Sheridan; partly because he was so nauseated by human stupidity that it seemed to him a kind of weakness to make it amusing. It must appear what it is: an interminable bad joke, which slowly petrifies the smile on the reader's face.

In a letter to Pope Swift indicates that both the *Polite Conversation* and

the *Directions to Servants* had been begun in or about 1704.⁶ Very probably
most of the preface to the *Polite Conversation* was actually written at much
the same time as the specimens of fashionable talk in the *Tatler* (No. 31).
It has much more of the urbanity of Bickerstaff than one would expect if it
had been written when the dialogues were finished, about 1737. Their
composition may well have been spread over years. The *Directions to Servants*, which were never actually finished, lent themselves to the same
desultory method. As Swift's detailed knowledge of the villainies of servants
grew, so new items were added to their various instructions. Perhaps a lifetime of observation was required for the following pregnant paragraph.

> The servants' candlesticks are generally broken, for nothing can last
> for ever. But you may find out many expedients; you may conveniently
> stick your candle in a bottle, or with a lump of butter against the
> wainscot, in a powder-horn, or in an old shoe, or in a cleft stick, or in
> the barrel of a pistol, or upon its own grease on the table, in a coffee
> cup, or a drinking glass, a horn can, a tea-pot, a twisted napkin, a
> mustard pot, an ink-horn, a marrowbone, a piece of dough, or you may
> cut a hole in the loaf, and stick it there.⁷

Which of those methods had he actually witnessed, and which, if any, is
the product of the vigorous fancy? On the other hand, when it comes to
putting out candles, he surely gives rein to hilarious invention.

> There are several ways of putting out candles, and you ought to be
> instructed in them all: You may run the candle end against the wainscot,
> which puts the snuff out immediately; you may lay it on the floor, and
> tread the snuff out with your foot; you may hold it upside down, until
> it is choked with its own grease; or cram it into the socket of the
> candlestick; you may whirl it round in your hand till it goes out: when
> you go to bed, after you have made water, you may dip the candle-end
> into the chamber-pot: you may spit on your finger and thumb, and
> pinch the snuff until it goes out. The cook may run the candle's nose
> into the meal-tub, or the groom into a vessel of oats, or a lock of hay,
> or a heap of litter; the housemaid may put out her candle by running
> it against a looking-glass, which nothing cleans so well as candle-snuff;
> but the quickest and best of all methods is to blow it out with your
> breath, which leaves the candle clear, and readier to be lighted.⁸

Swift, being a life-long bachelor and always practising economy, had an
unusual knowledge of servants' ways. In his earlier life he had had much
patience with them. The *Journal to Stella* shows that he put up with a great
deal from the vagaries of Patrick, before he sacked him. When he found a
really faithful servant in Alexander McGee ('Saunders') he took him to his

heart, tended him in his fatal illness, and when he died on March 24, 1722, put a tablet in the Cathedral to his memory, and was only deterred by those who thought it beneath his dignity as Dean, from describing him upon it as his 'friend'. In a letter he was unconstrained. Saunders was 'one of my best friends as well as the best servant in the kingdom . . . He was the first good one I ever had, and I am sure will be the last. I know few greater losses in life'.[9]

He did not find another Saunders; and as the years went on he became a more exacting and difficult master. Mrs. Pilkington describes her acute discomfort at his sarcastic and tyrannical behaviour to his servants during a meal. But Delany is emphatic that his churlishness towards them was only superficial, and that he was, in fact, 'one of the best masters in the world' — a martinet, but generous.

3

His circle of activity was steadily narrowing. By the beginning of 1735 he had finally given up hope of revisiting England, and recalled £200 which the Duke of Queensberry held for him, 'which I had set apart to maintain me amongst you'. Gay had held it for him before; and he was dead. Arbuthnot also was now dead. It would have been a sad revisitation. But there were even more compulsive reasons for abandoning the dream. He was now mortally afraid of falling seriously ill far from home. Even in Ireland, he now did not venture more than a half-day's journey from the Deanery, except to Sheridan, who was fully aware of his disabilities. He explained to Barber that he seldom dared to go to Church for fear of being seized with vertigo during the service. In June 1736 he told Ford: 'I have not enjoyed a day of health for twenty months past, with continual giddiness, though not so violent.'

His exasperation with the course of public events grew apace. Three measures in particular, which he believed to be directed against the Irish Church, roused his anger and contempt. Two were bills, promoted by the bishops in 1732: one giving them power to compel country clergymen with livings of more than £50 a year to build a parsonage where one did not exist; the other enabling them to divide livings of more than £300 a year. The motives were laudable in theory; they aimed at enforcing residence. But the first bill could have been terribly oppressive; and the second would have been more plausible if the bishops had imposed a like sacrifice upon themselves. Swift thought them both iniquitous: 'abominable bills for beggaring and enslaving the clergy'. He was particularly violent against

Edward Tenison, cousin of the Archbishop of Canterbury and Bishop of Ossory, whose cathedral was the dove-grey beauty at Kilkenny. He had come to Ireland as chaplain to the Duke of Dorset in 1730, and he had been appointed to the first vacant bishopric. That alone was enough to make Swift angry with him; when he supported the obnoxious bills, he was promptly pilloried as 'the baboon of Kilkenny'. In this case, the Irish Commons rejected the bills.

> So God bless the Church, and three of our mitres;
> And God bless the Commons, for biting the biters.[10]

But a good deed of the Irish Commons towards the Irish Church was exceptional in Swift's eyes. And in 1734 it passed resolutions against the clergy's legal claim to the tithe of agistment, that is to say, tithe on the produce of grazing land. Considering the nature of Irish agriculture and the steady encroachment of pasturage on what little tillage there was, this was a serious attack on the revenues of the clergy. When the Commons agreed to a petition of the graziers against the tithe in March 1736, Swift broke out into *A Character, Panegyric and Description of the Legion Club*. Lecky criticized these famous verses on the Irish Commons very severely; yet in a different context he wrote:

> The heaviest burden of the tithes lay on the class least able to bear it.
> It was quite a common thing for a parish to consist of some 4000 or
> 5000 acres of rich pasture land, held by a prosperous grazier, who had
> rapidly been amassing a large fortune through the increased price of
> cattle, and of 300 or 400 acres of inferior land occupied by a crowd of
> miserable cottiers. In accordance with the vote of the House of Com-
> mons in 1735, the former was exempted from the burden which was
> thrown on the latter.[11]

Swift's wrath was justified. The Irish Commons, zealous enough in retaining the Test to keep the Presbyterians out of office, were ruthless against the just claims of the Church of Ireland where they conflicted with their interests as landowners.

4

The Legion Club has been represented as almost an outburst of delirium. Orrery implies that its composition brought on a vertigo, and that Swift had to leave it unfinished. This is nonsense. The emotion of the verses is violent, but the verse itself is perfectly controlled; and the end is quite calm.

Swift returns to his old vision of the Academy of Bedlam, and gives it a local
and particular habitation: it is the Irish House of Commons.

> As I stroll the City, oft I
> Spy a building large and lofty,
> Not a bowshot from the College,
> Half the globe from sense and knowledge.[12]

If only the Devil could drop on the roof with a mighty red-hot poker!

> Crack the stones, and melt the lead,
> Drive them down on every skull,
> While the den of thieves is full,
> Quite destroy that harpies' nest.
> How might then our isle be blest![13]

But, since Swift is endowing an asylum for his lunatics and fools, the
Commons house may be allowed to stand on condition it too is turned into
an asylum for its members. Keep them in cells, with a peep-hole.

> Let them, when they once get in,
> Sell the nation for a pin;
> While they sit a-picking straws,
> Let them rave of making laws;
> While they never hold their tongue,
> Let them dabble in their dung;
> Let them form a grand Committee
> How to plague and starve the city.
> Let them stare and storm and frown
> When they see a clergy-gown.
> Let them, ere they crack a louse,
> Call for th' orders of the House;
> Let them with their gosling quills
> Scribble senseless heads of Bills;
> We may, while they strain their throats,
> Wipe our arses with their votes.[14]

The force of it is tremendous; and it moves with a speed never touched by
Swift's verses before; it pours like molten lead. So far from suggesting madness in the author, the impression it makes is that all the force of Swift's
accumulated and scathing indignation was, in a final effort, focused on one
point. There is no spluttering in this amazing torrent of invective, neither
is there any vestige of irony: but there is a wild and fiery humour.

> Let Sir Tom, that rampant ass,
> Stuff his guts with flax and grass![15]

Most readers have forgotten, if they ever knew, that Sir Thomas Prendergast was conspicuous in support of the reduction of the tithe on flax, and the abolition of the tithe on pasture. Nevertheless, even without the gloss, it is wildly funny.

Clio backs out of the job of exhibiting the inmates to Swift.

> When she saw three hundred brutes
> All involved in wild disputes;
> Roaring, till their lungs were spent,
> Privilege of Parliament![16]

But Swift resolves to see it through, tips the keeper, and makes the round. Thirteen of the members come by name under his lash. Some of them are old *bêtes noires*: Tighe, Bettesworth, the Allens; one or two are men to whom, up to this moment, he had not been unfriendly. With one of these he ends: Dr. Marcus Antonius Morgan.

> Bless us, Morgan! Art thou there, man?
> Bless mine eyes! Art thou the Chairman?
> Chairman to yon damned Committee!
> Yet I look on thee with pity.
> Dreadful sight! What, learned Morgan
> Metamorphos'd to a Gorgon![17]

How he sighs for 'humourous Hogarth'!

> Thou, I hear, a pleasant rogue art.
> Were but you and I acquainted,
> Every monster should be painted;
> You should try your graving tools,
> On this odious group of fools;
> Draw the beasts as I describe 'em,
> Form the features, while I gibe 'em;
> Draw them like, for I assure you,
> You will need no *Car'catura*;
> Draw them so that we may trace
> All the soul in every face.[18]

It would have been a memorable collaboration.

The keeper has two hundred more inmates to show him. But Swift has had enough. 'The noise, the sight, the stench' have been too much for him.

> Taking then a pinch of snuff,
> I concluded, looking round 'em,
> May their God, the Devil, confound 'em.

Unlike most of the verses discussed in the previous chapter, *The Legion Club* is sustained. It never deviates, and never flags. He did not tire in the middle, as he told Pope he mostly did. Delany was almost justified in calling it the finest of all Swift's poems. It is not that; but more than any other it directly communicates the volcanic force of Swift's emotions. His fierce and contemptuous indignation at human baseness when clothed in office, and power, and pride, becomes almost a physical sensation in *The Legion Club*. It reveals what was behind the words of the last chapter of *Gulliver*.

> My reconcilement to the Yahoo-kind in general might not be so difficult, if they would content themselves with those vices and follies only which Nature hath entitled them to . . . But when I behold a lump of deformity, and diseases both in body and mind, smitten with pride, it immediately breaks all the measures of my patience: neither shall I ever be able to comprehend how such an animal and such a vice could tally together.[19]

5

Swift said — and the surviving correspondence bears it out — that he had little or no contact with those of rank or authority in Ireland. He saw himself as squatting like a toad in a corner of his great Deanery; he looked forward to dying like a poisoned rat in a hole. The pictures are not to be taken too seriously. Swift could turn his grim humour upon himself. He valued his enormous popularity with the 'rabble', and he felt that the mutual affection was sincere. The mob loves a strong man who is kindhearted; who does not sentimentalize over it, but does his best for it; who strives to be just. And the Irish mob loved his wit, and he was not averse to theirs. Sheridan described him (at Quilca in 1725):

> So far forgetting his old station
> He seems to like their conversation.
> Conforming to the tatter'd rabble,
> He learns their Irish tongue to gabble.
> And what our anger more provokes,
> He's pleased with their insipid jokes.[20]

Swift did not find their jokes insipid. 'I have found the poor cottagers here, who could speak our language, to have a much better natural taste for good sense, humour and raillery, than I ever observed among people of the like sort in England.'[21] So he wrote in 1732; and in 1736 he told his old friend Sir John Stanley: 'As to this country, I am only a favourite of my old friends, the rabble, and I return their love because I know none else who deserve it.'[22]

The little, incessant, systematic charities of the great man to them were an honour to the recipients. Even his meannesses were more significant than the largesse of the unimaginative. He was saving up for the public good. Every one knew what he intended to do with his money. It was accumulating fast. In 1725 he had saved only £1250; in 1736, he had £7500 invested in various mortgages. That is, in eleven years, he had saved at the rate of nearly £600 a year, always with his purpose in view.* His mind was continually preoccupied with the problem of securing his trust against abuses. He solved it eventually to good effect.

He was an incessant thorn in the flesh of the authorities. He was virtually an independent sovereign power. His legal jurisdiction over the little liberty of St. Patrick's was a symbol in miniature of the sway of his genius. To risk a public humiliation of the Dean was to risk a riot. But all the vast power of government patronage was against him. The few recommendations he made to the Lieutenant, the Duke of Dorset, were politely but firmly put aside. Dorset was a close friend of Lady Betty Germaine, and she appears to have done what she could to second Swift's efforts with the Lieutenant. But she may have felt that Swift's judgment was unreliable (as it had been in the case of Lady Suffolk) and her assistance may have been half-hearted. In any case, the hope was slender. Dorset was in Ireland as the instrument of the English interest, and Boulter was there to report on any deviations. Swift's recommendations were of men in the Anglo-Irish interest. They were bound to fail.

His final failure, to secure some small preferment for the Grattans' cousin, the Rev. John Jackson (to which he alludes bitterly in his will) led to a breach with his oldest woman friend. In a letter which he drafted and re-drafted, as conscious of its finality, he wrote to Lady Betty:

> I now dismiss you, Madam, for ever from being a go-between upon any affair I might have with his Grace. I will never more trouble him either with my visits or application. His business in this kingdom is to make himself easy; his lessons are all prescribed him from the Court, and he is sure at a very cheap rate to have a majority of most corrupt idiots and slaves at his devotion. (January 29, 1737)

It was a sad ending to a long friendship, which had triumphed over party differences. Neither Swift nor Lady Betty are to be blamed for it. The

---

* His income from the Deanery appears to have been about £700 a year, and he had about £200 a year from Laracor. The Lunacy Commission in 1742 returned his private estate as £800 a year. He started as Dean with at most £500 of his own. Considering his allowances to Stella, to Dingley, and to his sister, his economy was extraordinary. The rate of saving notably increased after Stella's death.

huge political machine of Walpole's creation was hostile to human relations. To the Dorset entourage, Swift was a turbulent priest, fortunately ageing, and manifestly a little mad. He had at least one big bee in his bonnet. Any regulation of the coinage was anathema to him. He was very angry at the importation, in February 1737, of £10,000 of copper, minted at the Royal Mint in England, though it is not apparent that it was anything but beneficial. The Primate had too much commonsense to invite a repetition of the commotion over Wood. Later in the same year, the nominal value of the gold guinea was lowered by threepence, also on Boulter's initiative, to bring it nearer to the actual exchange value. When the order in Council was published, the Dean ran up a black flag on St. Patrick's steeple, and the bells tolled a muffled peal all day. Since Swift had been dangerously ill but a few days before, it was supposed that he was dead. But the knell was a sign of his recovery.

Such a demonstration endeared him to the people as much as it annoyed the Castle. The Primate, indeed, was so afraid of an attack on his house by the mob, that he had a military guard quartered in it. Soon after, Swift was well enough to attend an official dinner given by the retiring Lord Mayor. Boulter was also there. Tactlessly, but boldly, he raised the question of lowering the gold and charged Swift with inflaming the mob against him. 'I inflame the mob!' Swift is said to have replied. 'Were I to lift but a finger, they would tear you to pieces.' The story is true. Swift's own verses, *Ay and No*, substantially confirm it.

> Quoth Hugh of Armagh, 'The mob is grown bold.'
> 'Ay, ay,' quoth the Dean, 'the cause is old gold' ...
> 'Go tell your friend Bob and the other great folk
> That sinking the coin is a dangerous joke.
> The Irish dear joys have enough commonsense
> To treat gold reduc'd like Wood's copper pence.
> It's a pity a prelate should die without law;
> But if I say the word — take care of Armagh!'[23]

That is certainly Swift's. He is also credited with a lively ballad, *Patrick astore*, against the lowering of the gold. It was first printed by Scott, 'as taken down from recitation by my friend, Mr. Hartstonge'. It is his, therefore, only by oral tradition. But if it is really his, it is much more like an authentic folk-ballad than any other he wrote. And it ends with some recognizable Gaelic, the inaccuracy of which may be due to transmission.*

* The last line is *'Och ma ceade millia mollighart*, on the feeders of swine'. *Mo chead mile mallacht ort* means 'A hundred thousand curses on thee.' We have quoted above Sheridan's

If it is his, it more closely identifies him with the native Irish than any other of his writings.

> Patrick astore, what news upon the town?
> By my soul, there's bad news, for the gold she was pull'd down.
> The gold she was pull'd down, of that I'm very sure,
> For I saw'd them reading upon the Towlsel door.
> Sing Och, och, hoh, hoh.

> Arrah! Who was him reading? 'Twas a *jauntleman* in ruffles;
> And Patrick's bell she was ringing all in muffles;
> She was ringing very sorry, her tongue tied up in rag;
> Lorsha! and out of her shteeple there was hung a black flag.
> Sing Och, och, hoh, hoh.[24]

There are two more verses, equally good.

6

Swift's last years were largely under the care of Martha Whiteway, a first cousin, and daughter of that uncle Adam who, long ago, had been concerned about his intentions towards Varina. There is a letter from Swift to her in 1730 which shows that they had met seldom, and never corresponded, though she had lived in Dublin for fourteen years, but that he had a better opinion of her than of most of his relations. When in 1732 her second husband died, she began to visit him frequently, and gradually took over the function of keeping a general eye on his household economy. She was in the late forties, the mother of three children, when she became Swift's chief intermediary in his dealings with the outer world; so indispensable to him that he looked upon any interruption of her regular visits to the Deanery as a calamity. She also acted as his confidential secretary.

She has been violently criticized. Delany accused her of keeping Swift away from his friends. But, on the evidence of her own correspondence, we see no reason to withhold from her the benefit of the doubt. Her one perceptible failing is an attitude of excessive deference to Orrery and Pope, to whose intrigues to recover Pope's letters she lent her assistance. But she may well have been their flattered but innocent tool. Whether or not her

testimony: 'He learns their Irish tongue to gabble.' That was at Quilca. Swift describes his behaviour at Market Hill in much the same way.

> He's all the day sauntering,
> With labourer's bantering,
> Among his colleagues,
> A parcel of Teagues.

That he wanted Erse to die out is irrelevant. He had probably picked up a good many phrases. But this is the only ballad in which he uses one.

motives were partly interested in taking virtual charge of Swift, it is certain that Swift needed, and knew he needed, someone to take care of him; and that she filled the position to his satisfaction. It was an invidious one, at the best.

Like Stella, she was on the best of terms with Sheridan, whose companionship and unflagging drollery were so precious to Swift. By now his fecklessness and his unhappy marriage had made havoc of his worldly fortunes. Persuaded by Dublin friends unwilling to lose his company, he had refused the offer of the school at Armagh, which Swift had procured for him, and had stayed on, living beyond his means, in the capital. His school dwindled, because a rival one had been established to which Delany, for some reason, had given his influential support.* The convivial Sheridan ran heavily into debt and, partly to escape the attentions of his creditors, took over the school at Cavan in 1734. In the autumn of 1735 Swift stayed with him there, in order, as he said, to avoid being in Dublin when the Legion Club met. But Swift was by now a very difficult guest, and his temper was frayed by the disorder and unquiet of the Sheridan menage. The younger Sheridan was then sixteen, of an age to remember the visit well, and he found it oppressive. The Dean, he says, was morose, irritable and capricious, and looked gaunt and emaciated. Still, there were plenty of intervals of good humour in which he could laugh, and allow others to laugh, at his own pernicketiness. The amusing triangular correspondence between Mrs. Whiteway and Swift and Sheridan is that of friends who still found it easy to laugh with, and at, one another.

But Sheridan himself, always of slight and delicate physique, was now in poor health. His breathing was badly affected. The affairs of his school were quickly entangled — Swift busied himself in chasing after at least one of his bad debts — and it was a burden to him. After a little more than two years he sold it, and returned to Dublin. During his vacations from Cavan he had been a constant guest at the Deanery, where he had a room of his own. While a house was preparing for him, he stayed at the Deanery. There he fell seriously ill. When he had recovered sufficiently to get up from bed, he apologized to Swift.

'I fear, Mr. Dean, I have been an expensive lodger to you this bout.' Upon which Mrs. Whiteway . . . briskly said, 'It is in your power, Doctor, easily to remedy this, by removing to another lodging.' Swift was silent. The poor Doctor was quite thunderstruck. As this lady

* Delany had been one of the most popular and successful tutors in Trinity College until he resigned his fellowship in 1728. He retained his Professorship of Oratory and History. His discriminating and generous help to an unusual pupil is recorded in Burdy's *Life of Skelton*. In 1732 he married a lady with £1600 a year, which did not diminish his influence.

had always professed great friendship for him and lay under considerable obligations to him, he quickly saw that this must have been done by Swift's direction. He immediately left the house . . . Nor did he ever enter it again.[25]

In a few weeks more Sheridan was dead. Like Falstaff's, 'his heart was fracted and corroborate'. His dismissal did not cause his death; but it did not help him to live. Swift's most intimate friendships were fated to grim conclusions, as though he were driven to crush in others what he had crushed in himself. But there is no good reason to believe that Mrs. Whiteway's part was other than reluctant and under compulsion. 'Briskly' was probably the imagination of Sheridan's wounded heart when he told the story to his son; 'quickly' may be the truth. Mrs. Whiteway had had to bear with Swift's tirades against his expensive and burdensome friend, and took the unpleasant office upon herself for fear of worse.

Sheridan died on October 10, 1738. He was just over fifty. Soon afterwards Swift wrote an account of him which, though not positively unjust, is marmoreal in its coldness and detachment. No one, reading it, would dream that most of the happiness he had had, since the death of Stella, had come from his friendship with Sheridan.

7

Where Sheridan was rejected, his other old friends had little hope of favour. They tended to avoid the Deanery. And Swift was now seldom to be met outside it. Delany believed that his new intimates deliberately kept his old ones away; and it may have been true that some of them were trying to establish a monopoly of the great man in decay. Deane Swift, who married Mrs. Whiteway's daughter, his cousin, in 1739, certainly makes that impression in his unpleasant narrative, in which his vendetta against Delany is obvious; and Dr. Wilson's assiduity was not for a good end. But the truth seems to be that, so far as Mrs. Whiteway discouraged visitors, it was for Swift's and their own good. His behaviour had now become incalculable; and his friends were afraid of arousing his fury.* It would have been an ordeal for them, and might have been disastrous to him.

Indeed, by the end of 1738, and perhaps at the beginning, Swift was not fully responsible for his own actions. Even the year before, on May 31,

---

* There is independent evidence that this was the situation, even in 1737, in the preface to Michael Clancy's play *The Sharper*. He tells how Dr. Helsham and Dr. John Grattan, though willing to help him, absolutely refused to put his MS. before Swift, for fear of an outburst. Dr. Robert Grattan, however, had the courage to put it on Swift's table when he was out of the room. The stratagem was successful. Swift wrote Clancy a kind note about his play and sent him £5. But all three — old friends of Swift — were obviously scared.

1737, he told Pope that he had made three attempts at the letter he then wrote to him and was not able to finish it for weakness. His reluctance to submit the MS. of *The Four Last Years* to Oxford's son or to Lewis and his apparent inability to understand their concern; the lapse of memory by which he believed that, on his installation as Dean in 1713, he had stayed in Ireland only a fortnight, instead of the three months in reality; an attack of illness so serious that his 'life was despaired of' at the end of August — were all indications of a condition in which entire lucidity was only intermittent. In one such interval he added twenty lines to his imitation of Horace's Satire: *I often wished that I had clear* . . . They are an excrescence on the poem; but they add to it a pathetic prayer, for

> Only what my station fits,
> And to be kept in my right wits.[26]

For what he did under the terrible and now imminent menace of imbecility he cannot fairly be criticized. On January 17, 1738, he wrote to Barber, addressing him as 'My dear old friend': 'I have for almost three years been only the shadow of my former self with age and sickness . . . I have entirely lost my memory except when it is roused by perpetual subjects of vexation.' He had, he said, not been out of doors beyond his own garden for several months. He was afraid of a seizure away from home. In the summer, apparently while Sheridan was in the house, he told Barber: 'I seldom walk less than 4 miles, sometimes 6, 8, 10 or more, never beyond my limits; or if it rains, I walk as much through the house up and down stairs . . . I have not written as much this many a day. I have tired myself much; but in revenge, I will tire you.'[27] Even though the fabric of the Deanery, save for the cellars, is new since Swift's time, it should still reverberate to the vehemence of that ghastly tramping. Swift spoke kindly and sympathetically to Barber of Sheridan — 'the best scholar in both Kingdoms' — and of his illness; yet he was writing only a few days before the final quarrel. The inhumanity of Swift's parting gesture towards him did not come from his veritable self.

Swift's fierce and fanatical exercise was a desperate effort to ward off the approaching disaster; but it exhausted him so much that his brain, even when relatively free from giddiness, could not function properly. Hence proceeded the overwhelming mental indolence which Mrs. Whiteway described in him, even when, she said, his health seemed to be improved. He was 'so indolent in writing that he will scarce put his name to a receipt for money' (March 6, 1739). More and more she became the channel of communication between him and the outer world on matters of business, whenever she could seize the rare opportunity of his attention. On May 4, 1740, shortly after an attack in which he suffered great pain, he made his will. Apart from the careful instructions for the endowment, construction and constitution of his hospital, and his chosen epitaph, it is notable for some whimsical bequests — particularly to the Grattans:

> *Item*, I bequeath to the reverend Mr. Robert Grattan . . . my gold bottle screw, which he gave me, and my strong box, on condition of his giving the sole use of the said box to his brother Dr. James Grattan, during the life of the said Doctor, who hath more occasion for it, and the second best beaver hat I shall die possessed of.
> *Item*, I bequeath to Mr. John Grattan . . . my silver box in which the freedom of the city of Cork was presented to me; in which I desire the said John to keep the tobacco he usually cheweth, called pigtail.

His third best beaver hat went, with all his horses, to Mr. John Jackson; and his best one, with nothing else, to Mr. John Worrall. The repeating watch which he had bought for Stella in her last illness was given to Mrs. Whiteway. To Pope he gave his miniature of Harley; to Harley's son two antique seals, 'because they belonged to her late most excellent Majesty Queen Anne, of ever glorious, immortal, and truly pious memory, the real nursing mother of all her kingdoms'. The 'royal prude' had undergone apotheosis. Bolingbroke was not mentioned. There were substantial bequests to Mrs. Whiteway and her children.

A fortnight later Mrs. Whiteway explained to Pope that Swift's memory was now so impaired that he had completely forgotten the existence of a letter from him in a few hours after receiving it, and his judgment was no longer sound enough to permit him to correct or finish any of his writings. On July 26 Swift sent her a note:

> I have been very miserable all night, and today extremely deaf and full of pain. I am so stupid and confounded, that I cannot express the mortification I am under both in body and mind. All I can say is, that I am not in torture, but I daily and hourly expect it. Pray let me know how your health is and your family. I hardly understand one word I write. I am sure my days will be very few; few and miserable they must be. I am, for those few days,
>
> Yours entirely,
> J. SWIFT

For all the misery of his condition, Swift was at that moment in control of his faculties. Mrs. Whiteway told Orrery he could 'hear no reason'; but that may have been because he was not entirely deceived, as she plainly was, by Pope's devious intrigue (in which Orrery was implicated) to get hold of his letters to Swift. Swift's obstinacy over this may have come from better knowledge. But his general condition was now pitiable: he was contending with an almost entire loss of memory, almost impenetrable deafness, and extreme exhaustion. But he fought to the last. On January 28, 1742, he wrote a remarkable charge to the Sub-Dean and Chapter. In it he first recited that

> Whereas my infirmities of age and ill-health have prevented me to preside in the chapters held for the good order and government of my Cathedral Church of St. Patrick in person,

he had appointed Dr. Wynne his Sub-Dean — an appointment which he now confirmed.

> And whereas it hath been reported, that I gave a licence to certain vicars to assist at a club of fiddlers in Fishamble Street, I do hereby declare that I remember no such licence to have been ever signed or sealed by me; and that if ever such pretended licence should be produced, I do hereby annul and vacate the said licence; intreating my said Sub-Dean and Chapter to punish such vicars as shall ever appear there, as songsters, fiddlers, pipers, trumpeters, drummers, drum-majors, or in any sonal quality, according to the flagitious aggravations of their respective disobedience, rebellion, perfidy and ingratitude.
> I require my said Sub-Dean to proceed to the extremity of expulsion, if the said vicars should be found ungovernable, impenitent, or self-sufficient ...
> My resolution is to preserve the dignity of my station, and the honour of my Chapter; and, gentlemen, it is incumbent on you to aid me and to show who and what the Dean and Chapter of St. Patrick's are.[28]

Apparently, Swift (or the Chapter) had second thoughts, for a chastened version is extant, from which the flourishes have been eliminated. The Cathedral is no longer his own, the possibility that he had signed a licence is admitted, and the final fanfare dropped. But as the last authenticated composition of Swift the original is worthy of his genius. Even up to April 18, 1742, he kept an exact account, in one of his little notebooks, of the charity money collected in the Cathedral. 'Samson hath quit himself like Samson.'

8

A miserable episode preceded, and perhaps precipitated, the petition of his friends for a commission of lunacy upon him. Dr. Wilson, one of his prebendaries, who had become for his own ends a familiar in the Deanery, took Swift for a drive during which he tried to extort from him the dismissal of Dr. Wynne as Sub-Dean and his own appointment in his place. He deposed, when charged with cruelty to Swift, that Swift had made a violent attack upon him, from which he merely defended himself. There was no witness other than a servant riding behind the coach, who said he heard Wilson demand the Sub-Deanship and Swift refuse it, and then 'Wilson began to curse, and in loud tones swore that "no man should strike him".' Apparently, under Wilson's insistence, Swift's exasperation became ungovernable. That was on June 14, 1742.

Early in August the petitioners for the Commission deposed that Swift 'hath for these nine months past been gradually failing in his memory and understanding, and of such unsound mind and memory that he is incapable of transacting any business, or managing, conducting, or taking care either of his estate or person'. The petition was granted on August 12, and the Commission found that he had been incapable since May 20: which would exculpate Wilson from having precipitated his imbecility, though not from the villainy of having tried to take advantage of his condition.

On November 22 Mrs. Whiteway wrote to Orrery:

> I was the last person whom he knew, and when that part of his memory failed, he was so outrageous at seeing anybody, that I was forced to leave him, nor could he rest for a night or two after seeing any person, so that all the attendance which I could pay him was calling twice a week to inquire after his health, and to observe that proper care was taken of him, and durst only look at him while his back was towards me, fearing to discompose him. He walked ten hours a day, and would not eat or drink if his servant stayed in the room. His meat was served up ready cut, and sometimes it would lie for an hour on the table before he would touch it, and then eat it walking.

It is not clear to what period Mrs. Whiteway is referring; but presumably, since she would have been called by the Commissioners as a chief witness, he was incapable of recognizing even her at the end of May. It may be that Wilson was telling the truth when he deposed that Swift 'declared he was the Devil, and bid him go to Hell'.

She further told Orrery that in October Swift's left eye swelled as large as an egg, great boils appeared on his body, and for a month he was in an extremity of torture, such that for one week 'five persons could scarce hold him from tearing out his own eyes'. (The swelling of the eye is mysterious, and not quite credible.) Nevertheless,

> The last day of his illness, he knew me perfectly well, took me by the hand, called me by my name, and showed the same pleasure as usual in

seeing me. I asked him whether he would give me a dinner. He said, 'To be sure, my old friend.' Thus he continued that day, and knew the doctor and the surgeon and all his family so well, that Mr. Nichols thought it possible he might return to a share of understanding, so as to be able to call for what he wanted, and to bear some of his old friends to amuse him.

But it proved, she thought, to be only pain that had aroused him. He was now quiet and apathetic, and could not, without great difficulty, be persuaded to walk a turn about his room. It was before this torture of pain, and the subsequent lethargy, that the 'incessant strains of swearing and obscenity' were manifest.

In this condition of apathy he lingered on for three years. The desire for fierce exercise had abandoned him, with the rest of his rational purposes. His emaciated body filled out again, the hard lines of his face were softened, his hair grew soft and white. Once, on his servant's moving a knife away from him, at which he tried to snatch, he shrugged his shoulders and said 'I am what I am', and, after an interval, repeated it. Sheridan says that on his birthday, November 30, 1743, his housekeeper told him that bonfires and illuminations were preparing, as usual, to celebrate it, and that he replied: 'It is all folly — they had better leave it alone.'

On October 19, 1745, he died. During the three days which, according to the precise instructions of his will, were to elapse before he was buried, people crowded to see him as he lay. Sheridan has a macabre story that, in less than an hour after his death, his head was entirely stripped of hair by people who bribed his servants to obtain locks of it.[29]

He was buried at midnight on October 22, 1745, in the great aisle of St. Patrick's on the south side. Seven feet above the ground the black marble tablet was fixed, bearing a Latin inscription 'in large letters deeply cut and strongly gilded', as he had commanded: of which this is the English:

The body of Jonathan Swift, Doctor of Divinity, Dean of this Cathedral Church, is buried here, where fierce indignation can lacerate his heart no more. Go, traveller, and imitate if you can one who strove his utmost to champion liberty.

It is silent on any Christian hope. It might be the epitaph of one of his Roman heroes — a Brutus or a Cato: except perhaps for the fierce indignation that tears at his heart no more. Death is not the opening of a gate, but the closing of a wound.

NOTES AND REFERENCES

The following abbreviations are used in the references

W.   The Prose Works of Jonathan Swift, edited by Temple Scott (Bell, 1897-1908)

P.   The Poems of Jonathan Swift, edited by Harold Williams (Clarendon Press, 1937)

Corr.   The Correspondence of Jonathan Swift, edited by F. Elrington Ball (Bell, 1910-1914)

Delany   Observations upon Lord Orrery's Remarks (1754)

Ford   The Letters of Swift to Charles Ford, edited by D. Nichol Smith (Clarendon Press, 1934)

Longe   Martha, Lady Giffard: a Memoir, by Julia C. Longe (George Allen, 1911)

Moore Smith   Early Essays & Romances of Sir William Temple, edited by G. C. Moore Smith (Clarendon Press, 1930)

Orrery   Remarks on the Life & Writings of Dr. Jonathan Swift (3rd edition corrected, 1752)

Sheridan   The Life of the Rev. Dr. Jonathan Swift (Dublin, 1785)

Temple   The Works of Sir William Temple (2 vols. folio, 1750)

CHAPTER I

[1] W. XI. 376.

[2] Ford, November 12, 1708.

[3] Corr. IV. 76.

[4] Sheridan, p. 402.

[5] Mrs. Delany in 1745 put it at £40; Swift himself in 1724 at £50, but this was for the son of a rich man (Corr. III. 218).

[6] W. XI. 376.

[7] W. I. 287.

[8] Delany, pp. 48, 258.

[9] W. XI. 377.

[10] Moore Smith, p. 194.

[11] W. XI. 127.

[12] Orrery, p. 14.

[13] W. XI. 132.

[14] Longe, p. 355.

[15] W. XI. 131.

[16] W. XI. 127.

[17] W. XI. 128.

[18] Longe, p. 215.

[19] W. XII. 94.

[20] Orrery, p. 16.

CHAPTER II

[1] P. I. 7.

[2] P. I. 8.

[3] P. I. 10.

[4] Corr. I. 366.

[5] P. I. 49.

[6] Corr. I. 366.

[7] Corr. I. 10.

[8] W. XI. 378.

[9] P. I. 37.

[10] Ibid.

[11] P. I. 38.

[12] P. I. 42.

[13] P. I. 27.
[14] P. I. 28.
[15] P. I. 29.
[16] P. I. 32.
[17] *Ibid.*
[18] P. I. 33.

[19] Corr. I. 363.
[20] Corr. I. 365.
[21] P. I. 17.
[22] P. I. 21.
[23] P. I. 25.
[24] P. I. 19.

CHAPTER III

[1] P. I. 47.
[2] P. I. 48.
[3] P. I. 49.
[4] P. I. 50.
[5] The text we have given is a modernized and slightly emended version of the literal transcript given by Moore Smith.
[6] P. I. 52.
[7] *Ibid.*

[8] P. I. 53.
[9] *Ibid.*
[10] *Ibid.*
[11] P. I. 54.
[12] *Ibid.*
[13] P. I. 55.
[14] *Ibid.*
[15] Corr. I. 363.
[16] W. I. 119.

CHAPTER IV

[1] Moore Smith, p. 31.
[2] Corr. I. 32*n.*
[3] Courtenay, *Life of Sir William Temple* II. 21; Corr. I. 59*n.*
[4] Longe, p. 216.

[5] W. XI. 127.
[6] Longe, p. 227.
[7] W. I. xcii.
[8] W. XI. 380.
[9] Corr. I. 33*n.*

CHAPTER V

[1] W. I. 187.
[2] Temple, I. 151.
[3] Temple, I. 238.
[4] W. I. 192.
[5] *Ibid.*
[6] W. I. 199.
[7] W. I. 200.
[8] W. I. 208.
[9] Temple, I. 234.
[10] Marvell, ed. Grosart, III. 313. Celia Fiennes describes an Eskimo kayak which was kept in Trinity House, Hull, with an effigy of the Eskimo who was captured in it. He would not speak or eat 'and so in a few days died'.

[11] *Op. cit.* III. 425.
[12] W. I. 210.
[13] W. I. 13.
[14] It contains references to Sir Humphrey Edwin's mayoralty of London, which was in 1697; and to Bernier's account of India, which Swift was reading in that year.
[15] The Licensing Act of the Restoration ran out in 1695, and was not renewed.
[16] W. I. 142, 144.

CHAPTER VI

[1] W. I. 122.
[2] W. I. 124.
[3] W. I. 114.
[4] Moore Smith, p. 69.
[5] W. I. 115.
[6] W. I. 116.
[7] W. I. 117.
[8] W. I. 118.
[9] *Ibid.*
[10] W. I. 124.
[11] W. I. 119.
[12] *Ibid.*
[13] W. I. 120.

[14] *Ibid.*
[15] W. I. 121.
[16] W. I. 62.
[17] W. I. 60.
[18] W. I. 12.
[19] Moore Smith, p. 147.
[20] W. I. 54.
[21] W. I. 103.
[22] W. I. 128.
[23] W. I. 110.
[24] P. I. 49.
[25] W. I. 125.
[26] W. I. 143.

CHAPTER VII

[1] P. I. 68.
[2] P. I. 70.
[3] Temple, I. 295.
[4] W. I. 269.
[5] W. X. 126.
[6] W. V. 380.
[7] In *The Tatler* no. 66 (W. IX. 21) which may have been written by Swift, the average parson is severely criticized for his neglect of gesture and his poor elocution. It concludes: 'I do not doubt that if our preachers would learn to speak, and our readers to read, within six months' time we should not have a dissenter within a mile of a church in Great Britain.'
[8] W. V. 380.
[9] *Ibid.*

[10] P. I. 74.
[11] *Ibid.*
[12] P. I. 77.
[13] W. I. 333.
[14] P. I. 118.
[15] Corr. I. 71.
[16] W. III. 27.
[17] P. I. 80.
[18] Wickham Legg: *Life of Prior*, p. 127.
[19] Sheridan, p. 40. He says it happened at Button's but, as Craik pointed out, Button's was not established until 1712.
[20] *The Earlier Life & Works of Daniel Defoe*, ed. Henry Morley (1889), p. 295.

CHAPTER VIII

[1] P. I. 84.
[2] Aitken, *Life of Steele*, I. 134-6.
[3] P. I. 90.
[4] P. I. 95.
[5] W. III. 267.
[6] P. I. 96.

[7] Corr. I. 54.
[8] Journal, February 21, 1711.
[9] Journal, October 25, 1710.
[10] Corr. I. 62.
[11] Corr. I. 70.

CHAPTER IX

¹ W. XII. 120.
² W. IV. 16.
³ W. IV. 21.
⁴ W. IV. 18.
⁵ W. IV. 10.
⁶ Corr. I. 107.
⁷ W. III. 66.
⁸ W. III. 62.
⁹ W. III. 54.
¹⁰ W. III. 75.
¹¹ W. III. 65.
¹² W. III. 64.
¹³ W. III. 75.
¹⁴ Ibid.
¹⁵ W. III. 51.
¹⁶ W. III. 12.
¹⁷ W. III. 17.

¹⁸ W. III. 6.
¹⁹ W. III. 16.
²⁰ W. III. 29.
²¹ W. III. 30.
²² W. III. 40.
²³ W. III. 307.
²⁴ W. III. 41.
²⁵ W. III. 46.
²⁶ W. III. 308.
²⁷ Corr. II. 11.
²⁸ W. V. 381. The date is fixed by Swift's account book.
²⁹ Corr. I. 157.
³⁰ Temple, I. 478.
³¹ Corr. I. 166.
³² P. I. 124.

CHAPTER X

¹ W. I. 14.
² W. I. 17.
³ W. III. 89.
⁴ W. III. 95.
⁵ W. III. 96.
⁶ Temple, I. 350.
⁷ Corr. I. 173.
⁸ W. V. 216.
⁹ Dartmouth's note to Burnet (ed.

1823) VI. 31.
¹⁰ Wentworth Papers: January 1, 1712.
¹¹ Longe, p. 339.
¹² Longe, p. 248.
¹³ Journal, May 4, 1711.
¹⁴ W. XI. 387.
¹⁵ W. XI. 382.
¹⁶ H.M.C. Portland V.

CHAPTER XI

¹ Corr. I. 194.
² Journal, September 9, 1710.
³ Journal, September 30, 1710.
⁴ Journal, October 7, 1710.
⁵ W. V. 283.
⁶ Journal, March 28, 1711.
⁷ Corr. I. 280.
⁸ W. V. 431.
⁹ Corr. I. 280.

¹⁰ Journal, October 13, 1710.
¹¹ Journal, December 26, 1711.
¹² P. I. 137.
¹³ W. IX. 60. Harrison's Tatler followed Steele's.
¹⁴ Journal, April 12, 1713.
¹⁵ Corr. IV. 78.
¹⁶ Journal, April 5, 1711.

CHAPTER XII

¹ W. IX. 71.
² W. IX. 77.
³ W. IX. 179.
⁴ W. IX. 229.

⁵ W. IX. 261.
⁶ W. IX. 113.
⁷ W. IX. 234.
⁸ W. IX. 257.

[9] W. IX. 244.
[10] W. IX. 187.
[11] W. IX. 165.
[12] W. IX. 182.
[13] W. IX. 144.
[14] W. IX. 157.
[15] Trevelyan: *The Reign of Queen Anne*, I. 198n.
[16] W. V. 7.
[17] W. V. 8.
[18] *Ibid.*

[19] P. I. 139.
[20] Journal, October 12, 1710.
[21] W. IX. 115.
[22] Aitken, *Life of Steele*, I. 294.
[23] Corr. III. 118.
[24] W. V. 33.
[25] W. V. 52.
[26] W. V. 72.
[27] W. V. 99.
[28] *Ibid.*

CHAPTER XIII

[1] W. V. 215.
[2] W. V. 216.
[3] *Ibid.*
[4] H.M.C. Portland V. 120.
[5] *Ibid.*
[6] Wentworth Papers, December 11, 1711.
[7] W. V. 443.

[8] W. V. 451.
[9] Note to Burnet (ed. 1823) VI. 31.
[10] P. I. 147.
[11] Corr. I. 307.
[12] Journal, December 25, 1711.
[13] P. I. 192.
[14] Corr. II. 212.

CHAPTER XIV

[1] Journal, April 26 and 27, 1712.
[2] W. V. 245.
[3] W. V. 223.
[4] P. I. 160.
[5] W. V. 245.
[6] P. I. 163.

[7] W. V. 265.
[8] W. V. 266.
[9] W. XI. 20.
[10] W. X. 28.
[11] W. III. 182.
[12] W. XI. 74.

CHAPTER XV

[1] Letter of October 5, 1709 (Dublin: National Library 32111/0).
[2] Vanessa and her Correspondence with Jonathan Swift. Ed. Freeman (1921).
[3] Corr. I. 307.
[4] Corr. III. 62.
[5] P. II. 712.
[6] P. II. 697.
[7] P. II. 687.
[8] P. II. 691.
[9] *Ibid.*
[10] P. II. 692.
[11] P. II. 693.
[12] P. II. 696.
[13] P. II. 697.

[14] P. II. 699.
[15] P. II. 701.
[16] P. II. 702.
[17] *Ibid.*
[18] P. II. 704.
[19] P. II. 706.
[20] *Ibid.*
[21] P. II. 707.
[22] P. II. 709.
[23] P. II. 710.
[24] P. II. 711.
[25] P. II. 712.
[26] P. II. 703.
[27] Corr. II. 53.
[28] Corr. II. 61.

CHAPTER XVI

[1] P. I. 170.
[2] P. I. 171.
[3] P. I. 173.
[4] *Ibid.*
[5] Corr. II. 34.
[6] W. V. 286.
[7] W. V. 296.
[8] *Ibid.*

[9] W. V. 299.
[10] P. I. 180.
[11] P. I. 183.
[12] W. V. 317.
[13] *Ibid.*
[14] W. V. 331.
[15] W. V. 352.
[16] W. V. 337.

CHAPTER XVII

[1] H.M.C. Portland V. 464-8.
[2] *Ibid.*
[3] H.M.C. Portland V. 661-2.
[4] H.M.C. Portland V. 464.
[5] Bolingbroke to Oxford, December 31, 1713; H.M.C. Portland V.
[6] P. I. 201.
[7] Corr. II. 416.
[8] Corr. II. 417.
[9] Corr. II. 414.

[10] W. V. 449.
[11] *Ibid.*
[12] W. V. 407.
[13] W. V. 403.
[14] P. I. 189.
[15] Corr. II. 214.
[16] Corr. II. 211.
[17] P. I. 202.
[18] Corr. II. 236.

CHAPTER XVIII

[1] Ford: end of August 1714.
[2] P. I. 203.
[3] Corr. II. 276.
[4] W. XII. 95.
[5] Sheridan, p. 277.
[6] Corr. III. 443.
[7] *Ibid.*
[8] Corr. II. 403.

[9] Corr. III. 34n.
[10] Letter of July 7, 1719 (Dublin: National Library 3211/11).
[11] Orrery, p. 70.
[12] Corr. III. 441.
[13] Corr. III. 442.
[14] Ford, November 22, 1708.

CHAPTER XIX

[1] P. II. 722.
[2] P. II. 723.
[3] P. II. 726.
[4] P. II. 727.
[5] P. II. 728.
[6] P. II. 730.
[7] *Ibid.*
[8] P. II. 731.
[9] Corr. III. 444.

[10] *Ibid.*
[11] Corr. III. 445.
[12] P. II. 734.
[13] P. II. 737.
[14] P. II. 738.
[15] Corr. III. 463.
[16] W. XII. 95.
[17] Sheridan, p. 290.
[18] W. XII. 95.

CHAPTER XX

[1] W. V. 363.
[2] W. V. 448.
[3] W. V. 445.
[4] Photostat (Dublin: National Library 3211/2).
[5] Corr. III. 148.
[6] W. VII. 171.
[7] P. I. 211.
[8] P. I. 215.
[9] W. XI. 153.
[10] Delany, p. 63.
[11] W. VII. 19.
[12] Cp. Chief Justice Cox to Southwell, January 5, 1714. 'But the profit of feeding cattle, which pay no tithe, has turned the arable to pasture.' He is speaking of the drop in the income of his son's living of Callan. (B.M. Add. MSS. 38157.)
[13] W. VII. 18.
[14] W. VII. 22.
[15] W. VII. 25.
[16] P. I. 236.
[17] W. III. 202.
[18] W. III. 204.
[19] W. III. 212.
[20] W. XI. 119.
[21] P. I. 225.
[22] P. I. 295.
[23] P. I. 322.

CHAPTER XXI

[1] Corr. II. 228.
[2] W. VIII. 200.
[3] W. VIII. 205.
[4] W. VIII. 217.
[5] W. III. 309.
[6] W. VIII. 286.
[7] W. VIII. 139.
[8] W. VIII. 136.
[9] W. VIII. 303.
[10] W. VIII. 142.
[11] W. VIII. 140.
[12] W. VIII. 143.
[13] W. VIII. 135.
[14] W. VIII. 256.
[15] W. VIII. 278.
[16] W. VIII. 307.
[17] W. VIII. 269.

CHAPTER XXII

[1] Corr. II. 92.
[2] W. VIII. 279.
[3] W. VIII. 61.
[4] W. XI. 375.
[5] W. VIII. 232.
[6] W. VIII. 277.
[7] W. VIII. 301.
[8] W. III. 309.

CHAPTER XXIII

[1] W. VI. 13.
[2] W. VI. 24.
[3] W. VI. 25.
[4] The Drapier's Letters, Ed. Davis, p. xxvi.
[5] W. VI. 39.
[6] W. VI. 42.
[7] W. VI. 51.
[8] W. VI. 60.
[9] W. VI. 65.
[10] W. VI. 67.
[11] W. VI. 71.
[12] W. VI. 90.
[13] Davis, *op. cit.* p. xxxix.
[14] W. VI. 103.
[15] W. VI. 104.
[16] W. VI. 111.
[17] W. VI. 113.
[18] W. VI. 114.
[19] W. VI. 115.
[20] *Ibid.*
[21] W. VI. 119.

CHAPTER XXIV

[1] Davis, *op. cit.* p. 270.
[2] Davis, *op. cit.* p. xlvii.
[3] W. VI. 136.
[4] W. VI. 138.
[5] W. VI. 140.
[6] W. VI. 144.
[7] W. VI. 151.
[8] W. VI. 152.
[9] W. VI. 127.
[10] W. VI. 129.

[11] Ford, November 27, 1724.
[12] W. VI. 163.
[13] W. VI. 165.
[14] W. VI. 168.
[15] W. VI. 175.
[16] P. II. 380.
[17] W. VI. 190.
[18] W. VI. 194.
[19] W. VI. 202.
[20] W. VII. 129.

CHAPTER XXV

[1] Delany, p. 56.
[2] P. II. 751.
[3] P. II. 747.
[4] *Ibid.*
[5] P. II. 754.
[6] *Ibid.*
[7] P. II. 759.
[8] W. VII. 77.
[9] It is only fair to Tighe, whom Swift so violently lampooned, to say that Farquhar, in dedicating *The Inconstant* to him in 1702, paid him a high compliment when he was twenty years younger. 'From the part of Mirabel in this play, and another character in one of my former, people are willing to compliment my performance in drawing a gay, splendid, generous, easy, fine young gentleman. My genius, I confess, has a bent to that kind of description; and my veneration for you, Sir, may pass as unquestionable, since in all these happy accomplishments you come so near to my darling character, abating his inconstancy.' Tighe and Farquhar were at Trinity together. The other character to which Farquhar compares him is Sir Harry Wildair. Swift had had some personal quarrel with Tighe immediately before coming to London in September 1710 (Journal, October 26, 1710).
[10] Letter to Thomas Staunton, February 10, 1711 (Freeman, *op. cit.*).
[11] W. XI. 398.
[12] W. XI. 393.
[13] W. III. 314.
[14] Sheridan, p. 316.
[15] W. XI. 130.
[16] W. XI. 142-3.
[17] P. II. 730.
[18] P. II. 738.
[19] Delany, p. 144.

CHAPTER XXVI

[1] It appears as the frontispiece to *Letters to & from Henrietta, Countess of Suffolk* (1824).
[2] *Op. cit.* I. 137.
[3] *Op. cit.* I. 148.
[4] Mary Bellenden wrote to her, on April 9, 1722: 'I really do believe you have as many people that love and value you, as ever came to one woman's share — I put myself foremost in the list.' *Op. cit.*
[5] W. XI. 147.
[6] W. XI. 148.
[7] The relations between the Duchess of Queensberry, Mrs. Howard and Gay are well conveyed in a letter of Mrs. Howard to Gay, concerning the first performance of *The Beggars' Opera*.

'So much for her Grace: now for yourself, John. I desire you will mind the main chance, and be in town time enough to let the opera have play enough for its life, and for your pockets. Your head is your best friend; it would clothe, wash, and lodge you; but you neglect it and follow that false friend, your heart, which is such a foolish, tender thing, that it makes others despise your head that have not half so good a one upon their shoulders. In short, John, you may be a snail, or a silkworm, but by my consent you shall never be a *hare* again.

'We go to town next week: try your interest and bring the Duchess up by the birthday. I did not think to have named her any more in this letter; I find I am a little foolish about her: don't you be a great deal so: for if *she* will not come, do you come without her.' October 1727. *Op. cit.* I. 282.

The reference to the hare is to Gay's Fable (No. 50) concerning

A hare, who in a civil way
Complied with everything, like Gay.

[8] Letter of September 28, 1734. *Op. cit.* II. 109.

CHAPTER XXVII

[1] P. II. 421.
[2] *Ibid.*
[3] P. II. 422.
[4] W. VII. 88.
[5] W. XI. 132.
[6] W. VII. 124.
[7] W. VII. 140.
[8] W. VII. 188.
[9] W. VII. 148.
[10] W. VII. 132.
[11] W. VII. 134.

[12] W. IV. 203.
[13] W. IV. 213.
[14] W. VII. 215.
[15] W. VII. 214.
[16] W. VII. 216.
[17] W. VII. 213.
[18] W. VII. 214.
[19] W. VII. 210.
[20] W. VII. 220.
[21] W. VII. 222.
[22] W. VII. 223.

CHAPTER XXVIII

[1] Annotated copy of *Remarks* in Harvard College Library quoted in P. III. 902; Orrery, p. 83.
[2] Corr. IV. 43.
[3] P. II. 747.
[4] P. III. 908.
[5] P. III. 900.
[6] Quoted in P. III. 902.
[7] P. II. 631.
[8] Corr. V. 219.
[9] P. III. 852.
[10] Delany, p. 75.

[11] W. XI. 142.
[12] Petrie, *Bolingbroke*, p. 32.
[13] W. VII. 270.
[14] P. II. 591.
[15] P. II. 529.
[16] *Ibid.*
[17] Lyon's notes in Hawkesworth (Forster 579).
[18] W. III. 309.
[19] W. I. 286.
[20] W. I. 276.
[21] P. II. 578.

CHAPTER XXIX

1 Corr. IV. 136.
2 Corr. IV. 135.
3 Corr. IV. 167.
4 P. II. 474.
5 P. II. 478.
6 P. II. 485.
7 *Ibid.*
8 P. II. 486.
9 P. II. 492.
10 P. II. 493.
11 P. II. 494.
12 *Ibid.*
13 Coghill to Southwell, February 21, 1729 (B.M. Add. MSS. 21122).
14 P. II. 495.
15 *Ibid.*
16 P. II. 496.
17 *Ibid.*
18 P. II. 497.
19 P. II. 498.
20 P. II. 554.
21 P. II. 555.
22 P. II. 556.
23 P. II. 558.
24 P. II. 561.
25 P. II. 562.
26 P. II. 565.
27 P. II. 566.
28 P. II. 567.
29 P. II. 570.
30 P. II. 571.
31 *Ibid.*
32 *Ibid.*
33 Corr. VI. 115.
34 P. II. 571.
35 *Ibid.*
36 P. II. 548.
37 P. II. 549.
38 P. II. 641.
39 P. II. 635.
40 P. II. 637.

CHAPTER XXX

1 *Memoirs* (1748), I. 58.
2 *Ibid.* I. 91.
3 P. III. 861.
4 Corr. IV. 433.
5 W. XI. 217.
6 Corr. IV. 309.
7 W. XI. 313.
8 W. XI. 314.
9 Corr. III. 127-8.
10 P. III. 805.
11 *Ireland in the 18th Century*, II. 14.
12 P. III. 829.
13 P. III. 830.
14 P. III. 831.
15 *Ibid.*
16 P. III. 833.
17 P. III. 837.
18 P. III. 839.
19 W. VIII. 307.
20 P. III. 1040.
21 Corr. IV. 328.
22 Corr. V. 387.
23 P. III. 843.
24 P. III. 840.
25 Sheridan, p. 342.
26 P. I. 199. The addition was made between October 5 and 8, 1737.
27 Corr. VI. 92.
28 Corr. VI. 220. It is appropriately ironic that Swift's perfidious vicars-choral were, almost certainly, practising for the first performance of Handel's *Messiah*, by the combined choirs of St. Patrick's and Christ Church, which was given on April 13, 1742. *The Messiah* was commissioned, at this time, by the Dublin Charitable Music Society, which met at the Bull's Head Tavern in Fishamble Street. (See R. Wyse-Jackson, *Jonathan Swift: Dean and Pastor*, 1939.) No doubt, Swift *had* given them permission.
29 Sheridan, p. 247.

APPENDICES
AND INDEX

APPENDIX I

In an attempt to find a reason for Swift's mysterious relation to Stella, Mr. Denis Johnston, in an essay in *The Dublin Historical Record* (June 1941) put forward a new version of an old legend: that Swift and Stella were consanguineous. In the form that they were both natural children of Sir William Temple's this theory had some currency in the eighteenth century (see *Orrery*, p. 16). But though it is possible that Stella was his daughter, it is impossible that Swift was his son. Sir William Temple was serving abroad at the time required.

Mr. Johnston, accepting the not unreasonable theory that Stella was Sir William Temple's daughter, argues that Swift was the natural son of Temple's father, Sir John Temple, who was in Ireland as Master of the Rolls at the time required. We need not enter into the details of the very ingenious argument, for it depends, very largely, on the assumption that the connection between Jonathan Swift and Sir William Temple was peculiar to himself and otherwise inexplicable. But, in fact, there was a connection between the *families*. Swift's cousin, Thomas, was also protected by Sir William Temple: he served as chaplain-secretary at Moor Park during Jonathan's absence, and by Sir William's influence was presented to the near-by rectory of Puttenham. Plainly, therefore, there was nothing peculiar to Jonathan in the Temple connection. Once this is admitted, Mr. Johnston's theory falls to the ground.

APPENDIX II

Swift's disease has been convincingly identified with what is now called Menière's symptom-complex. A lesion of the labyrinth gives rise to deafness in one ear (in Swift's case the left), giddiness and vomiting, generally accompanied by nystagmus (an oscillation of the eyeball) and tinnitus (a roaring in the ear) and sometimes by a loss of consciousness. The cause is obscure. But in Porter's *Diseases of the Throat, Nose and Ear*, from which these details are taken, it is said that the condition may be due — among other possible causes — to 'gastro-intestinal disturbances in people whose auditory and vestibular apparatus is specially sensitive'. So that it is possible that Swift's belief as to the origin of the disease in his own case is not altogether illusory. On the other hand, it may equally well be that the condition of the stomach was an effect and not a cause of the disturbance of the labyrinth.

In Swift's case the lesion of the labyrinth was evidently progressive, though the effects were intermittent. At their worst they are described by Porter as 'unbearable tinnitus or intense giddiness, which so prostrates the patient that he is unable to work, and may even contemplate suicide'. But there appears to be no medical justification for the theory that the disease of the labyrinth had some causal connection with Swift's final partial paralysis of the brain, which culminated in virtual idiocy. That appears to have been the ordinary cerebral thrombosis of senility. But, subjectively, Swift's condition must frequently have been one which made him fear eventual madness; and it must have undermined all sense of security in life.

APPENDICES

APPENDIX III

According to Courtenay's *Life of Temple* (Vol. II, pp. 195 *sq.*) one De Cros, a minor diplomat in the service of the Duke of Holstein, who was rather contemptuously dismissed in Temple's *Memoirs* of 1691, published an attack on Temple's diplomacy and character in the form of *A Letter from M. de Cros*. This appeared in 1693. It contains the following passage:

> I shall enlarge no further, that I may not engage myself to publish the misfortunes of Sir William's family, which I suppose would not be like a gentleman. I have no reason that I know of to complain, neither of his lady, nor of his son, *nor of his daughters*.

The italic is apparently in the original pamphlet, which we have not seen; and it certainly appears to be an insinuation that Temple had a natural daughter: since he had only the one legitimate daughter, Diana, who died in 1684.

This reference, which we had not noticed when the text was written, may be held to favour M. Pons' conclusion. Certainly it points to the currency of a rumour that Stella was Temple's daughter as early as 1693. But it is the insinuation of an avowed enemy of Temple; and in view of Stella's position, such a rumour was to be expected. The question remains whether it was true.

APPENDIX IV

A DESCRIPTION OF MOTHER LUDWELL'S CAVE

This poem was originally printed and ascribed to Swift by Julia Longe in her memoir of Martha, Lady Giffard (1911), not very accurately. It was reprinted with great care in G. C. Moore Smith's *The Early Essays & Romances of William Temple* (1930). Miss Longe suggested that the MS. was in the handwriting of Stella. This, though probable, cannot of course be proved. There is, however, strong internal evidence that Stella was the copyist.

Moore Smith followed Miss Longe in ascribing the authorship of the poem to Swift. Harold Williams, however, rejected it from his edition of Swift's poems (1937). Nevertheless, we are convinced it is Swift's. Moore Smith (p. 206) pointed out the striking parallel between the reference to Camilla in l. 13 of the *Description* and the reference to her in Swift's poem on *Sir William Temple's late illness and Recovery*. It is hard to believe that there were two poets at Moor Park in 1693, similarly enthusiastic about Mother Ludwell's Cave, and whose thoughts were running on Camilla. But Moore Smith missed an even more cogent parallel: the reading of the motto from Horace's *Epistles*, I. xvi. 15 which is prefixed to the poem. This should be:

> Hae latebrae dulces, etiam, si credis, amœnae.

It is slightly misquoted in the MS. of the *Description*, as

> Hae latebrae dulces, et si mihi credis, amœnae.

In a letter of Swift to Atterbury (August 3, 1713) the same quotation occurs: 'I am here in a way sinking into utter oblivion, for *hae latebrae nec dulces, nec, si mihi credis, amœnae . . .*' It is hardly conceivable that there should have been another poet of Mother Ludwell's Cave writing at Moor Park who made precisely the same slight misquotation of the line from Horace as Swift did. The misquoted line is as good as a signature.

Though the actual MS. of the *Description* cannot be proved to be in Stella's handwriting, the internal evidence points that way. The last four lines of the poem appear to be an afterthought; and if they are considered as an integral part of the poem, are flat, and rather silly. But if the copyist was a little girl, and they were added for her edification, they become entirely charming.

In l. 4, 'that hackney fry' recalls 'the ignorant fry' (*Ode to Sir William Temple*); l. 6. Compare 'Their Phoebus I, my spring their Hippocrene' (*Verses on St. Patrick's Well*); l. 10. 'And Crooksbury supplies the cloven hill.' Crooksbury is a hill near Moor Park; the cloven hill is Parnassus with its twin peaks, as notably in *The Battle of the Books*; l. 40. The 'capacious iron bowl' is clearly shown in the engraving of the Cave by Sparrow (1785), reproduced by Moore Smith; l. 46. The virgin footsteps are probably little Stella's, who comes as lightly as Camilla. Her quiet movements 'seem to fly a dance'; l. 52. Possibly 'such as' has crept in from l. 51 in the place of some such word as 'offer', which we have suggested in the text. The seats themselves are conspicuous in the print of 1785; l. 61. 'Nay, he a rich and gaudy silence leaves.' This is the estate at Sheen which also Temple has abandoned for Moor Park; ll. 71-2. Compare 'It is a peculiar part of nature which art debauches, but cannot improve.' (To Varina, April 29, 1696.)

APPENDIX V

SWIFT AND THE GUISCARD AFFAIR

Rightly or wrongly, Swift was very positive that the feud between Oxford and Bolingbroke began over the Guiscard affair.

I have some very good reasons to know, that the first misunderstanding between Mr. Harley and Mr. St. John . . . took its rise during the time that the former lay ill of his wounds, and his recovery doubtful. Mr. St. John affected to say in several companies, that Guiscard intended the blow against him; which, if it were true, the consequence must be, that Mr. St. John had all the merit, while Mr. Harley remained with nothing but the danger and the pain. But, I am apt to think, Mr. St. John was either mistaken or misinformed. However, the matter was thus represented in the weekly paper called the *Examiner*; which Mr. St. John perused before it was printed, but made no alteration in that passage. This management was looked upon, at least, as a piece of youthful indiscretion in Mr. St. John; and, perhaps, was represented in a worse view to Mr. Harley. (*Memoirs:* October 1714; V. 389).

In June 1715, in the *Enquiry*, Part I, Swift put it rather differently:

When Mr. Harley was stabbed by Guiscard, the writer of a weekly paper, called the *Examiner*, taking occasion to reflect upon that accident, happened to let fall an idle circumstance, I know not upon what grounds, that the French assassin confessed he, at first, intended to have murdered Mr. Secretary St. John; who sitting at too great a distance, he was forced to vent his rage on the other. Whether the secretary had been thus informed, or was content that others should believe it, I never yet could learn; but nothing could be more unfortunate than the tendency of such a report, which, by a very unfair division, derived the whole merit of that accident to Mr. St. John, and left Mr. Harley nothing but the danger and the pain ... This report was not unresented by Mr. Harley's friends; and the rather because the fact was directly otherwise, as it soon appeared by Guiscard's confession. (V. 440)

What Swift actually wrote in *The Examiner* (No. 33, March 15, 1711) was this:

I shall take occasion to hint at some particularities in this surprising fact, for the sake of those at a distance, or who may not be thoroughly informed. The murderer confessed in Newgate, that his chief design was against Mr. Secretary St. John, who happened to change seats with Mr. Harley, for more convenience of examining the criminal: and being asked what provoked him to stab the chancellor? he said, that not being able to come at the secretary, as he intended, it was some satisfaction to murder the person whom he thought Mr. St. John loved best. (IX. 211)

The stabbing took place on March 8, 1711; on the next day Swift was with St. John early 'and he told me several particularities of this accident, too long to relate now' (*Journal*, March 9). On March 11, he was with St. John again, visiting Harley, and wrote to Stella, 'I have a mind to write and publish an account of all the particularities of this fact: it will be very curious, and I would do it when Mr. Harley is past danger.' Presumably, he set to work immediately, for his account was published on March 15, and a proof had been shown to St. John, probably early on the 15th, when Swift was with him. On the next day, March 16, he wrote to Stella: 'I have made but little progress in this letter for so many days, thanks to Guiscard and Mr. Harley; and it would be endless to tell you all the particulars of that odious fact.' On the 17th he dined with Erasmus Lewis, who was probably the first of Harley's friends to resent the account in *The Examiner*.

It is clear from this that St. John was the source of Swift's information, as Swift implied in the *Memoirs*, and that the subsequent exculpation of St. John in the *Enquiry* ('I know not upon what grounds') was fictitious. Swift was acutely aware that he had put his foot in it. He had begun a sixpenny pamphlet on the affair before he realised this, but when he did he promptly handed over his materials to Mrs. Manley. 'She has cooked it into a sixpenny pamphlet, in her own style', he told Stella on April 16, 'only the first page is left as I was beginning it. But I was afraid of disobliging Mr. Harley or Mr. St. John in one critical point about it, and so would not do it myself. It is worth your reading, for the circumstances are all true.' He must have reflected wryly on the unconscious irony of his statement in the *Examiner* that Guiscard had said that 'not being able to come at the secretary, as he intended, it was some satisfaction to murder the person whom he thought Mr. St. John loved best.'

In fact, it seems to have been true that Guiscard did intend to kill St. John, but not in the least on political grounds, but on the very personal one, that he had been St. John's boon companion in his disreputable pleasures, and wanted to revenge himself upon him for having deserted him and connived at the reduction of his pension by Harley. Considering these circumstances, St. John's suggestion to Swift that he was the hero of the piece was a remarkable piece of effrontery.

APPENDICES

APPENDIX VI

The late C. H. Firth, in a famous article on 'Harley & Swift's Preferment' (*Review of English Studies* II, 1926, pp. 1-17), collected all the historical evidence concerning Oxford's disposal of the English preferments which Swift coveted. Rather rashly — for none of his evidence warranted the statement — he remarked that 'Oxford's jobbery . . . was one of the obstacles to Swift's promotion'. He contradicted this *obiter dictum* by his own conclusion, that 'the compromise by which Bolingbroke was made a Viscount, like the compromise by which Swift was made an Irish Dean, was her [the Queen's] doing, and the phrase "The Queen will determine" was not a mere figure of speech.' Firth's unjustified and unjustifiable remark has been magnified by Ricardo Quintana, in his valuable book *The Mind and Art of Jonathan Swift*, into the statement that 'Oxford consistently sacrificed Swift in the interests of mean jobbery'. There is no justification for it. The only evidence Quintana adduces is Firth's own article, which contains none.

APPENDIX VII

The Tory party in 1712 was a new party, formed by the coalescence during William III's reign of Whigs and Tories. Matthew Prior explained the development to Portland, in a letter of March 18, 1699:

> The Whigs have given him (the King) good words, and seem to do the best in Parliament for his interest; but if they do their best or no, or only seem to do it is the question, since it is evident that most of those members who have not been in former parliaments and do in this compose that body which they call the country party, are those who have obstructed the King's business, and yet most of them are and have been always Whigs; on t'other side the Tories in these last affairs have voted against their principle, because the chief of their party are peevish, and the multitude of them follow their example, whilst these leading men are against the Court, right or wrong, because they are not of it. (*H.M.C. Bath III.* 324)

For the details of this important change whereby the party of 'new Tories', of whom Harley was the leader, was formed, see Feiling's *History of the Tory Party*, in which he shows that the nucleus was 'formed of two wings — one by origin Tory (Clarges, Musgrave, Granville), the other by origin Whig (Harley, Harcourt, Foley and Howe); and that this nucleus usually hung together, distinct alike from old high-prerogative Tories and ministerial Whigs.'

APPENDIX VIII

On August 12, 1720, Swift, looking back on the past, wrote to Vanessa: 'What would you give to have the history of Cad—— & —— exactly written, through all its steps from the beginning to this time? . . . It ought to be an exact chronicle of twelve years, from the time of spilling the coffee to drinking of coffee, from Dunstable to Dublin, with every single passage since.' This was an occasion on which Swift's dates would be accurate. He was taking pleasure in the memory, and he was trying to give pleasure to Vanessa. A mistake would have hurt her. Twelve years takes the beginning of their friendship back to 1708.

The first event in this retrospect is 'the spilling of coffee', which apparently happened at Dunstable. It undoubtedly did, for Swift referred to the incident in a letter he wrote to Mrs. Vanhomrigh on June 6, 1713, after passing through Dunstable on his way to Dublin to be installed as Dean of St. Patrick's: 'I could not see any marks in the chimney at Dunstable of the coffee Hessy spilt there.' From the two references it is evident that Mrs. Vanhomrigh, as well as Vanessa and Swift, were present when it happened. The only occasion when the three of them could have been together in a Dunstable inn round about 1708 was during Swift's journey to London in December 1707.

We know that Mrs. Vanhomrigh and her family were travelling to London from Chester towards the end of that month. A letter to Joshua Dawson of January 3, 1708, announces the arrival of the family in London a day or two before. (*Corr.* I. 389). So that the Vanhomrighs were at Dunstable in the last days of December 1707. On the other hand we know that Swift, who arrived with Pembroke at Parkgate on November 30, left him there and went to visit his mother at Leicester. He intended to stay there until Sir Andrew Fountaine gave him notice that Pembroke had arrived in London. Pembroke could not leave Chester until December 3, and he was to stay at Wilton for a week, so that he could hardly have reached London before December 20. (*Corr.* I. 61) Swift therefore could not have set out from Leicester before December 23. Thus his journey and the Vanhomrighs' must practically have coincided. Apparently by pure accident, they met at the inn at Dunstable, which was the regular last stopping place on the road to London from both Chester and Leicester. This seems to have been Swift's first meeting with Vanessa. In *Cadenus & Vanessa* he says he first

> Had met her in a public place,
> Without distinguishing her face.

APPENDIX IX

THE SOCIAL STATUS OF STELLA

The question of Stella's social status is difficult and obscure. Swift's account of her is embarrassed and contradictory. His remark that she was 'looked upon as one of the most beautiful, graceful, and agreeable young women in London' (XI. 127), implies that in the years before Sir William Temple's death she mixed in good society; but, as Mr. Ball pointed out (*Corr.* IV. 451), there is nothing to bear this out in the *Journal.* There she appears to have no acquaintance at all among the London *monde.* The one exceptional reference — 'The Secretary and I dined at Sir William Wyndham's, who married Lady Catherine Seymour, your acquaintance, I suppose.' (June 21, 1711) — may be ironical: for this was the daughter of the proud and inaccessible Duke of Somerset. On the other hand, the Somersets were friends of Temple and Lady Giffard, and Lady Catherine and Stella may have met as girls.

But the main impression given by Swift's account of her is that Stella's social status was very modest. His words: 'Her father was a younger brother of a good family in Nottinghamshire, her mother of a lower degree; and indeed she had little to boast of her birth' (XI. 127), taken in their natural sense, mean that Stella 'had little to boast of her birth', though they are often interpreted as applying to her mother. And the natural sense is confirmed by Swift's subsequent statement: 'There seemed to be a combination among all that knew her, to treat her with a dignity much beyond her rank.' (XI. 129)

The implication of the whole narrative is that relatively few people did know her, and those who did were virtually confined to Swift's Dublin set of old Trinity men. Addison's acquaintance with her is mentioned as something quite exceptional. Another exception was Charles Ford who, though Irish-born, was educated in England and was, as much as his income would allow, a cultivated London clubman. It is clear that Stella had no acquaintance with the Duke of Ormond's daughters (*Journal*, June 4, 1711).

It is noticeable that Swift's Irish set, to whom Stella was *persona grata*, had, so far as the evidence goes, no relations with the Vanhomrighs. When any of them were in London, during the period of the *Journal*, as the Bishop of Clogher, Dilly Ashe, Provost Pratt, Sam Dopping, Raymond and Jemmy Leigh were, though Swift records their doings as of interest to Stella, he never mentions them as visiting the Vanhomrighs. The natural inference is that Mrs. Van thought herself a cut above the Irish set, and they kept clear of her; perhaps regarded her as a social climber. Her friends were exclusively Dublin Castle society. The only persons who frequented the Vans and who seem to have been known to Stella were Charles Ford and Sir Andrew Fountaine. Of these two, it is doubtful whether Stella knew Sir Andrew otherwise than by name.

If this account is correct, it was very natural that Stella should be a little catty about the Vans. She wrote to Swift that they were 'persons of no consequence' (February 26, 1711), and Swift replied that they 'kept as good female society as I do male; I see all the drabs of quality at this end of the town with them': which was true, but not likely to be welcome to Stella. We suspect that Swift subsequently adopted this phrase, partly to tease Stella, and spoke of the Vans familiarly as 'my acquaintances of no consequence'. It would help to explain Chetwode's apparent reference to Vanessa's visit to Letcombe: 'I know you would have your frisk like the Berkshire acquaintance without consequence.' (*Corr.* II. 276)

We may disregard Orrery's statement that the reason why Swift did not openly marry Stella was his shrinking from 'a low alliance' (*Remarks*, p. 16); but we can hardly ignore his categorical assertion that Stella's social status was definitely inferior to Swift's, for Delany did not controvert it. Moreover, Orrery's belief that if Stella had really been Temple's natural daughter, Swift would have married her openly, though worthless as evidence of Swift's motives, is valuable as an indication of contemporary opinion about them both.

The conclusion is that Stella's social status, in the eyes of the world, was definitely inferior to Vanessa's; and that they moved in social circles which scarcely intersected at all. Swift himself and Ford were the only points of intersection. Stella was esteemed by Swift's Anglo-Irish friends: to his English ones she was unknown. And Stella's influence was always at work, however gently, to pull Swift away from England and back to Ireland. She had very good reasons for regarding the prospect of Swift in an English Deanery with aversion. In the Anglo-Irish circle she was at home and was his equal; in England she was something of an outcast and his inferior. Conversely, Vanessa was something of an outcast in Ireland.

APPENDIX X

Since the text was written, the pamphlet, *Some Free Thoughts on the Present State of Affairs*, has been published in its original form in The Shakespeare Head edition of Swift's Prose Works, edited by Herbert Davis and Irwin Ehrenpreis (Vol. VIII, pp. 75-98). It shows that various passages in which Swift criticized the personal conduct of Bolingbroke more severely than that of Oxford were omitted from the version published by Faulkner in 1741, when the text was first printed. Thus Swift originally wrote:

> While on one side too great a reserve, and certainly too great a resentment on the other . . . have enflamed animosities to such a height as to make all reconcilement impracticable.

This was modified to 'very great' in both cases.
Again the following passage was entirely deleted:

> Whether some have not insisted upon too implicit a resignation to their wisdom, abilities and good intentions, as well as to the merit of having been sole movers in that great change at Court about four years ago; whether others have not contended for a greater part in the direction of affairs than might possibly belong to them, and upon refusal have not carried their resentments further than private friendship, gratitude, or, the safety of the public would admit . . .

'Gratitude', we know, Swift himself told Ford to delete. But the whole passage was taken out.

The effect of these deletions, which must have been due to Bolingbroke, is to shift the balance of Swift's censure. He had originally borne more hardly on Bolingbroke's lack of loyalty than on Oxford's secretiveness and moderation. And that explains why he wrote to Ford: 'Upon second thoughts how comical a thing it was to shew that pamphlet to Lord Bol— of all men living. Just as if *The Public Spirit* had been sent to Argyll for his approbation.' (July 18, 1714)

APPENDIX XI

The evidence for Swift's marriage is fully set out by the late Archbishop Bernard in his essay 'The Relations between Swift & Stella' (W. XII. 95). Over and above the testimony for the marriage mentioned in our text (of Bishop Evans, Orrery, Delany, Deane Swift, and Sheridan) there is Dr. Johnson's statement that he was told by Dr. Madden that it took place in the garden of the deanery of Clogher, and Monck Berkeley's statement in 1789 that 'in 1716 they were married by the Bishop of Clogher, who himself related the story to Bishop Berkeley, by whose relict the story was communicated to me'. Since the latter story goes back to the direct statement of the Bishop of Clogher himself its corroboration is of some importance. It has been dismissed on the ground that Berkeley was travelling on the Continent at the time, though admittedly as tutor to Bishop Ashe's son, and that since Bishop Ashe died on February 27, 1718, there was no opportunity for him to relate the story himself to Berkeley except by letter, which was unlikely. This objection is disposed of by Mr. J. M. Hone's discovery that the *London Gazette* of April 7, 1716 reported that Berkeley attended Provost Pratt from Ireland on a visit of ceremony in London. Evidenly Berkeley *was* in a position to be informed verbally by Bishop Ashe. (*Bishop Berkeley*, Hone and Rossi, p. 124).

There is, of course, no decisive proof of the marriage; but it seems to us that the weight of the evidence makes it overwhelmingly probable.

POSTSCRIPT

Too late for reference in the text (p. 30) I received from Mr. Maurice Johnson a copy of his paper (*PMLA*, Dec. 1952) in which he examines the authenticity of the remark attributed to Dryden by Dr. Johnson: 'Cousin Swift, you will never be a poet.' Mr. Johnson shows that the terseness of the remark is probably Dr. Johnson's own. Anyhow, the words, as they first appeared in Cibber's *Lives of the Poets*, are much less crushing: 'Cousin Swift, turn your thoughts another way, for nature has never formed you for a Pindaric poet.' Whether Dr. Johnson had any independent source of information cannot be positively determined; but it seems unlikely.

INDEX

TO THE WRITINGS OF SWIFT DISCUSSED OR MENTIONED IN THE TEXT

INDEX